THE BROWNINGS:
Letters and Poetry

THE
BROWNINGS:

Letters and Poetry

—◦❂◦❋◦❂◦—

*Selected and
with an Introduction by*

CHRISTOPHER RICKS

*Illustrations by
Barnett I. Plotkin*

DOUBLEDAY & COMPANY, Inc.
Garden City, New York

CONTENTS

CONTENTS

Robert Browning
1812–1889

CONTENTS

ix

CONTENTS

THE BROWNINGS:
Letters and Poetry

INTRODUCTION

GENIUS AND TALENT. Robert Browning and Elizabeth Barrett Browning. And is it simply the nature of human beings that genius should be strange, secretive, and even frightening, whereas talent is lucid, accessible and likeable? The face of Robert Browning gives nothing away — handsome and polished, it offers no hold to those who would pry into the soul behind. Its metallic mirror gives us back ourselves. But the face of Elizabeth Barrett Browning speaks openly of her sufferings — of ill-health, of an iron father, of miscarriages — yet speaking in the accents of courage and good sense. Any woman of sensitivity and talent can imagine herself as Elizabeth, in the hope that she might get as much as did Elizabeth out of a life which sometimes seemed to offer so little. No man can imagine himself as Robert. And if that is because genius is a mystery, it is even more because Robert Browning is a mystery. 'The longer I know Browning', wrote William Allingham, that shrewd observer of the Victorian scene, 'the less do I know how much weight to give to his utterances'. That was in 1875. In 1889 Browning was buried in Westminster Abbey. Henry James commemorated the occasion with a puzzled admiration: 'A good many oddities and a good many great writers have been entombed in the Abbey; but none of the odd ones have been so great and none of the great ones so odd'.

ROBERT BROWNING was born on May 7, 1812, in Camberwell, a suburb of London. Of his mother, hardly anything is known except that apparently she loved Robert very much and he loved her very much — a fact which can be either reassuring or sinister according to one's psychological predilections. Robert's father was more distinctive: after returning from his mother's sugar plantation in the West Indies with a fixed 'hatred of the

1

slave system', he became a clerk in the Bank of England (he did not retire till 1852). Neither rich nor poor, he was a scholar and a book collector, with a talent for grotesque drawing and comic doggerel (like his son, he was to write a poem on the Pied Piper of Hamelin). Young Robert Browning enjoyed the free run of a remarkable library and the gentle indulgence of kind parents. 'Spoiled'? Not much more than any gifted child is likely to be. He was not happy at boarding school, so he returned home. Already his poetic gifts were evident (though he was to destroy his earliest poems), and his reading of Shelley in 1826 made the profoundest impression on him. His vegetarianism may not amount to a profound imitation of Shelley, but his temporary atheism is a different matter — to have been, however briefly, an atheist is to have seen the world with different eyes. Yet the crucial influence of Shelley was simply a dedication to poetry as a way of life. Unfortunately a way of life is not necessarily a way of earning a living. Perhaps the University would help? Robert enrolled in 1828 in the University of London to study Greek, Latin, and German, but before the year was over he had dropped out. Then what about the law as a profession? But this poet who was later to create such vivid studies in willpower was himself strong-willed, and his parents let him have his way. Robert Browning was to be a poet or nothing.

For a while it must have seemed that he would be nothing. Then in March 1833, two months before his coming of age, there was published anonymously his first venture: *Pauline*. The costs of publication, £30, had been generously found by his aunt. But this autobiographical poem about the victory of young love over doubt and egotism was not itself victorious — according to the poet, not one single copy was sold. And to the shock of failure was added the shock of nakedness, for *Pauline* was seen as not just autobiographical but morbidly confessional. The literary opinions of John Stuart Mill, after all, were not those of a nobody, and Mill's marginal jottings on the poem began with the words: 'With considerable poetic powers, the writer seems to me possessed with a more intense and morbid self-consciousness than I ever knew in any sane human being'. Browning was hardly likely to have become *less* morbidly self-conscious when Mill's words were reported to him. We shall never know (that too is part of the secretiveness) how much of Browning's later secretiveness is due to the lacerating *débâcle* of *Pauline*.

Yet if Browning owed some of his suffering to Mill, he owed, too, much of his achievement. For if poetry is not to be autobiographical, a giveaway, it must be dramatic. From now on, Browning vowed that his poems would be 'dramatic in principle, and so many utterances of so many imaginary persons, not mine'. It was to be nearly ten years before his genius arrived at its proper form: the dramatic monologue. For the moment he was to throw himself, with passionate mistakenness, into writing plays.

As Elizabeth Barrett was to point out, 'A great dramatic power may develop itself otherwise than in the formal drama'. 'Action in Character, rather than Character in Action' — Browning's own words about his play *Strafford* are a good recipe for a poor play, but an even better recipe for a good dramatic monologue. Browning was fascinated by characters whose willpower is so intense as virtually to exclude the possibility of their changing, and it would be hard to think of a better summing-up of his great dramatic monologues than Elizabeth's words: 'When a man spins evermore on his own axis, like a child's toy I saw the other day, . . what is the use of him but to make a noise? No greater tormentor is there, than self-love, . . even to self'.

Browning had thought of becoming an actor, and it was on the very day that he saw the great actor Edmund Kean in *Richard III* that he had begun *Pauline*. In 1835, shortly after the publication of his second poem, *Paracelsus*, Browning met the most famous actor of the day: William Macready. The year after, Macready suggested that Browning should write a tragedy for him. So it is to Macready that we owe (if owe is the right word for a bad debt) the dispiriting sequence of Browning's plays: *Strafford* (1837), *King Victor and King Charles* (1842), *The Return of the Druses* (1843), *A Blot in the 'Scutcheon* (1843), *Colombe's Birthday* (1844), *Luria* and *A Soul's Tragedy* (1846). Browning learned much in the writing of these plays, of course, just as Henry James learned much during his own misguided attempts at theatrical glory. And there is much that we can learn from the plays, about Browning's development, his persistent concerns, his psychology. What we cannot learn from the plays is simply the most important thing of all: that Browning had poetic genius.

Fortunately, genius is a resilient thing, and Browning learned the true nature of his powers by misusing them. A defence of the plays would have to echo Keats's defence of *Endymion*: 'In *Endymion*, I leaped headlong into the sea, and thereby became better acquainted with the soundings, the quicksands, and the rocks, than if I had stayed upon the green shore, and piped a silly pipe, and took tea and comfortable advice'.

Moreover, Browning learned as he went along; his development of the dramatic monologue was to proceed while he attempted the plays, and *Pippa Passes* (1841) represents an important half-way-stage between drama and the dramatic monologue.

Ever since the publication of *Pauline*, Browning had been working too on a long poem: *Sordello*, a historical narrative set in 12th-century Italy. In 1838, Browning visited Italy 'to finish my poem among the scenes it describes'. But the reception of *Sordello* in 1840 was in some ways even more disastrous than that of *Pauline*. It was held to be utterly incomprehensible, and it attracted more quips than any other 19th-century poem. Mrs. Carlyle said that she had read it without ever finding out whether Sordello was a man, a city, or a book. Harriet Martineau was so baffled by it that she thought she must be ill. And until the end of his days Robert Browning was to be dogged by the accusation that his poems were so obscure as to be incomprehensible. Browning was to rebut the accusation in a very vigorous letter to John Ruskin (December 10, 1855): 'For your bewilderment more especially noted — how shall I help *that?* We don't read poetry the same way, by the same law; it is too clear. I cannot begin writing poetry till my imaginary reader has conceded licences to me which you demur at altogether. I *know* that I don't make out my conception by my language; all poetry being a putting the infinite within the finite. You would have me paint it all plain out, which can't be; but by various artifices I try to make shift with touches and bits of outlines which *succeed* if they bear the conception from me to you. You ought, I think, to keep pace with the thought tripping from ledge to ledge of my "glaciers", as you call them; not stand poking your alpenstock into the holes, and demonstrating that no foot could have stood there; — suppose it sprang over there? In *prose* you may criticise so — because that is the absolute representation of portions of truth, what chronicling is to history — but in asking for more *ultimates* you must accept less *mediates*, nor expect that a Druid stone-circle will be traced for you with as few breaks to the eye as the North Crescent and South Crescent that go together so cleverly in many a suburb . . .'. For the last years of his life Browning was to be honoured by the Browning Society (founded in 1881), and yet that honour was itself a two-edged compliment. The admirers of the Poet Laureate did not need a Tennyson Society in order to puzzle over and solve the riddles of Tennyson's verse.

Sordello, then, for all its descriptive beauty and its psychological subtlety, was a failure. But the next year Browning began publication of

the eight pamphlets which he called *Bells and Pomegranates*. The first
was *Pippa Passes* (1841), price sixpence. The pamphlets included, too,
the dead weight of six of his plays. But that dead weight ultimately
weighs nothing against the two pamphlets which manifested the arrival
of a great poet: *Dramatic Lyrics* (1842) and *Dramatic Romances and
Lyrics* (1845). Each of the eight pamphlets cost Browning's father about
£16 to publish, but here at least he was not throwing good money after
bad. For here were 'My Last Duchess' and 'Soliloquy of the Spanish
Cloister', 'Porphyria's Lover' and 'The Pied Piper of Hamelin'. Here
were 'Home-Thoughts, from Abroad' and 'The Bishop Orders his Tomb
at St. Praxed's Church', 'The Flight of the Duchess' and 'Meeting at
Night'. Browning in his thirties was triumphantly vindicating the hopes
of the boy who had seen in Shelley the high destinies of poetry.

Hindsight shows this achievement clearly enough. At the time, reviewers were reviewers. John Forster praised *Dramatic Lyrics*, justly but
mildly. *Dramatic Romances and Lyrics* was accorded faint praises. The
literary scene was unruffled.

One reader, though, was to prove more important than any reviewer.
She was a reader who was also a writer, and in her poem 'Lady Geraldine's
Courtship' (in *Poems*, 1844) she paid passionate tribute to a fellow-poet:

'Or from Browning some pomegranate which, if cut deep
down the middle,
Shows a heart within blood-tinctured of a veined humanity.'

A compliment to *Bells and Pomegranates* at once graceful and vivid. A
compliment which would romantically become fact when Browning wrote
to thank her for her kind words. Each would show the other 'a heart
within', and Browning's *Dramatic Romances* would usher in one of the
most dramatic romances in 19th-century life.

Elizabeth Barrett Barrett was born on March 6, 1806. She was to be all
too conscious that she was six years older than the man who fell in love
with her. ('Probably, or certainly rather, I have one advantage over
you, . . one, of which women are not fond of boasting — that of *being
older by years*'.) But to Robert this very obstacle (as some would call it)
was another of the challenges which spurred him into winning Elizabeth.
The eldest of twelve children, she was already a young woman when her
mother died in 1828. The family was one of rigid propriety, a propriety
enforced the more severely, perhaps, because of the financial mishaps

which had fallen on them. Like Robert, Elizabeth had early manifested poetic ambitions and talents, and her recognition as a poet preceded his. Her first success was *The Seraphim and other Poems* (1838), and she herself was to seem an angel to Browning:

> O lyric Love, half angel and half bird
> And all a wonder and a wild desire, —
> Boldest of hearts that ever braved the sun,
> Took sanctuary within the holier blue,
> And sang a kindred soul out to his face, —
> Yet human at the red-ripe of the heart.

When Robert paid that tribute to Elizabeth after her death, as the climax of the first Book of *The Ring and the Book*, he knew that he was returning her compliment, the words which first brought them together.

But angels do not suffer pain, whereas Elizabeth lived in the element of pain. As a child she had once been gravely ill, and then in 1837 her health altogether broke down. It seems that her lungs were affected, and she moved to Torquay. It was there that she suffered the worst blow of her life: the death by drowning of her elder brother Edward, a death for which she could not help feeling herself partly responsible since it had been at her entreaty that Edward had stayed on at Torquay. Was it perhaps the death of his son, his namesake, that hardened still further the personality of Edward Moulton-Barrett, Elizabeth's austere father?

It is hardly surprising that Elizabeth often thought of death as preferable to life, or that nothing mattered more to her than the poetic world which she created by her pen as a poet and the literary world which she entered with her pen as a correspondent. The two worlds were to come together when she penned the fateful words 'Or from Browning some pomegranate . . .'. The confirmed invalid met the confirmed bachelor, and sixteen months later he was no longer a bachelor and she was virtually no longer an invalid.

'I love your verses with all my heart, dear Miss Barrett', wrote Robert Browning on January 10, 1845: 'I do, as I say, love these books with all my heart — and I love you too'. Innocent and prophetic, Browning's first letter inaugurated one of the most remarkable correspondences that we know, and certainly the most remarkable of its kind. For the fact that they had to write down so much of what they would otherwise have had to speak led at once to the right kind of caution and the right kind of audacity. On May 20, 1845, Browning was allowed to visit Elizabeth, a fragile recluse who permitted herself hardly any visitors. Browning was all the while conscious that he must never tax Elizabeth's strength, and he soon became conscious of a more intimidating strength than hers: that of her father, Edward Moulton-Barrett, a man in the grip of a monomania which forbad any of his children to marry. So Browning's visits were of necessity secret, even furtive. All the more open were his letters, and Elizabeth replied with equal candour. The caution possible in a letter made it easy for their relationship to modify anything that proved to have been rash or to circumvent anything that was perilous. For neither the woman of thirty-nine nor the man of thirty-three had the confident experience which would have allowed an audacious wooing. Yet the letters allowed their own kind of audacity. Paper does not blush.

The selection from the letters which follows later in this volume tells its own story. ('I, for my part', wrote Elizabeth in these very letters, 'value letters as the most vital part of biography'.) It is the story of a woman brought back to the land of the living, and of the rewards and strains which this feat brought upon the man who brought her back. Certainly the feat had its oddities and even its absurdities – the best biography of Browning, that by Betty Miller, is the best precisely because it was willing to gaze with the eyes of unsentimental common sense at this romance, not in order to cut it down to size or to demean it, but because Robert Browning and Elizabeth Barrett were not fairy-tale lovers but perplexed and altogether human. Perhaps the most important feature of the romance, and one which Mrs. Miller rightly emphasised, is the amatory Dutch Auction in which both Robert and Elizabeth engaged. From the start each insisted that the other was altogether the superior. At times they sound like two endlessly deferential people waiting to get out of a door: After you – No, after you. Elizabeth was to speak rather firmly against 'that praeternatural submissiveness of yours', but a few days later Robert was still insisting: 'I solemnly assure you I cannot imagine any point of view wherein I ought to appear to any rational creature the benefitting party and you the benefitted'. 'There is no love but from beneath', he protested, 'far beneath, – that is the law of its nature'. But Elizabeth, with that attractively dry manner which is so different from the lank limp poetess of her legend, saw that their Dutch Auction didn't make sense: 'I have just so much logic as to be able to see (though I am a woman) that for me to be too good for you, and for you

7

to be too good for *me*, cannot be true at once, both ways'. Still, a lovers' Dutch Auction may be against reason, but *Le coeur a ses raisons que la raison ne connaît point*. Robert and Elizabeth may have carried to extraordinary lengths their conviction that each of them was unworthy of the other, but what they were carrying was a conviction common to lovers.

Lovers, not echoes. For Elizabeth was quite willing to offer specific adverse criticism of Robert's poems, and Robert was quite willing to argue passionately in defence of duelling or against paying the ransom demanded when Elizabeth's loved dog, Flush, was kidnapped. They may often have deferred to each other, but neither was servile. During their married life they were to disagree about some of the matters which were of the greatest importance to them both: the upbringing of their son Robert Wiedemann Browning (nicknamed Penini or Pen): the political honesty or perfidy of Louis Napoleon, subsequently Napoleon III (Elizabeth for, Robert against): whether mesmerism and spiritualism were revelations or impostures (Elizabeth for, Robert against). These disputes were real and important, and they remind us that Robert and Elizabeth engaged upon something harder than elopement: married life. Elizabeth's tact and solicitude towards Robert and Robert's inexhaustible tenderness whenever she was ill may have been saintly, but did not emanate from plaster saints.

'We two, one another's best': the words of John Donne are to the point, for Robert Browning and Elizabeth Barrett were among the most enthusiastic devotees of Donne's poetry in the 19th century. Again and again in their correspondence they found that their love brought to mind the great love-poet, and if Robert was obliged to say farewell all too often during their courtship, he was able to refer to Donne's 'Valediction: forbidding Mourning'.

> Our two souls therefore, which are one,
>   Though I must go, endure not yet
> A breach but an expansion,
>   Like gold to airy thinness beat.
>
> If they be two, they are two so
>   As stiff twin compasses are two;
> Thy soul, the fixed foot, makes no show
>   To move, but doth if the other do.

8

And though it in the centre sit,
  Yet when the other far doth roam,
It leans, and hearkens after it,
  And grows erect, as it comes home.

Such wilt thou be to me, who must
  Like the other foot, obliquely run;
Thy firmness makes my circle just,
  And makes me end, where I begun.

So that when Robert exclaims 'I seem to have foretold, *foreknown* you in other likings of mine', we may hear behind his words the timeless wonder of his great predecessor:

Twice or thrice had I loved thee,
  Before I knew thy face or name:
So in a voice, so in a shapeless flame,
  Angels affect us oft, and worshipped be . . .

Confined to her room, Elizabeth was living more and more in the world of literature, and so it is natural that she should have looked upon her predicament in the light of those similar predicaments crystallized by the poets. Early in their correspondence she was to visualise herself as the desolate heroine of Tennyson's 'Mariana' —

She only said, 'My life is dreary,
  He cometh not,' she said;
She said, 'I am aweary, aweary,
  I would that I were dead!'

What did it all come to, her present letter to Robert? 'It is a multitude of words about nothing at all, . . this — but I am like Mariana in the moated grange and sit listening too often to the mouse in the wainscot'.

All day within the dreamy house,
  The doors upon their hinges creaked;
The blue fly sung in the pane; the mouse
  Behind the mouldering wainscot shrieked,
Or from the crevice peered about. . . .

'Do *you* conjecture sometimes', she asked wistfully, 'that I live all alone here like Mariana in the moated Grange? It is not quite so — '. Yet the words of Tennyson, the predicament of Mariana, ran ever in her mind, to be glimpsed by us when she refers to 'the black fly buzzing in the pane', or when she exclaims: 'My aunt's presence here has seemed to throw me back suddenly and painfully into real life out of my dream-life with you — into the old dreary flats of real life'. For it was Mariana who

> drew her casement-curtain by,
> And glanced athwart the glooming flats.
> She only said, 'The night is dreary . . .'

But Mariana's lover was never to come, whereas sometimes Elizabeth was able to see her predicament less sombrely, with some sense of a possible happy ending. 'Poor Cinderella *** sitting in her old place among the ashes, just as she had touched the hand of the king's son'. For the king's son is a prince, and Robert invoked a happy legend of a prince when he looked back at the chain of their destinies: 'For first you had to be created, only that; and then, in my time; and then, not in Timbuctoo but Wimpole Street, and then . . the strange hedge round the sleeping Palace keeping the world off — and then . . .'

Often, though, it seemed that Elizabeth was guarded by more than just a fairy hedge. ('I should like not to be able to see out of any one of my three windows for the thickness of the ivy', she once wrote.) Guarded too by a dragon, the dragon of those gardens of the Hesperides to which both Robert and Elizabeth referred. For Edward Moulton-Barrett is the silent menacing off-stage presence who haunts the courtship. Very early in their correspondence, Elizabeth had likened her letters to those of an 18th-century epistolary novel — 'do not take me for a born heroine of Richardson, or think that I sin always to this length'. In the novels of Richardson, both Pamela and Clarissa find themselves guarded as prisoners, and it is hard to think of a real-life correspondence which more suggests the scribbled breathlessness and anxiety of the Richardsonian novel than does the correspondence of Robert and Elizabeth.

> RB   Here is my Uncle's foot on the stair . . his knock hurried the last sentence — here he is by me!
>
> EBB   Dearest, since the last word was written, Mrs. Hedley came back leading Mr. Bevan, and Papa who had just entered the room found the door shut upon him . . I

was nervous . . oh, so nervous! and the six feet, and
something more, of Mr. Bevan seemed to me as if
they never would end, so tall the man is.

EBB   How Papa has startled me. He came in while I was
writing . . (I shut the writing-case as he walked over
the floor—) and then, after the usual talk of the
weather, and how the nights 'were growing cold,' . .
he said suddenly . . looking to the table . . 'What
a beautiful colour those little blue flowers have — '
Calling them just *so*, . . 'little blue flowers.' I could
scarcely answer I was so frightened — but he observed
nothing and turned and left the room . . .

Even at this distance in time, Edward Moulton-Barrett is a daunting
figure. Nothing can better bring out his desolate and desolating harshness
than a bare sequence from the letters of the daughter who loved him but
who found herself loving someone else more:

August 25, 1845: It has happened throughout my life by an
accident (as far as anything is accident) that my own sense of
right and happiness on any important point of overt action,
has never run contrariwise to the way of obedience required
of me . . while in things not exactly *overt*, I and all of us
are apt to act sometimes up to the limit of our means of
acting, with shut doors and windows, and no waiting for
cognisance or permission. Ah — and that last is the worst of
it all perhaps! to be forced into concealments from the heart
naturally nearest to us; and forced away from the natural
source of counsel and strength! — and then, the disingenuousness — the cowardice — the 'vices of slaves'! — and everyone
you see . . all my brothers, . . constrained *bodily* into
submission . . apparent submission at least . . by that
worst and most dishonouring of necessities, the necessity of
living, everyone of them all, except myself, being dependent
in money-matters on the inflexible will . . do you see? But
what you do *not* see, what you *cannot* see, is the deep tender
affection behind and below all those patriarchal ideas of governing grown up children 'in the way they *must* go!' and
there never was (under the strata) a truer affection in a
father's heart . . no, nor a worthier heart in itself . . a heart
loyaller and purer, and more compelling to gratitude and

reverence, than his, as I see it! The evil is in the system — and he simply takes it to be his duty to rule, and to make happy according to his own views of the propriety of happiness — he takes it to be his duty to rule like the Kings of Christendom, by divine right. But he loves us through and through it — and I, for one, love *him!*

September 16, 1845: I might certainly tell you that my own father, if he knew that you had written to me *so,* and that I had answered you — *so,* even, would not forgive me at the end of ten years — and this, from none of the causes mentioned by me here and in no disrespect to your name and your position . . though he does not over-value poetry even in his daughter, and is apt to take the world's measures of the means of life . . but for the singular reason that he never *does* tolerate in his family (sons or daughters) the development of one class of feelings.

September 25, 1845: [Elizabeth was hoping to go on a trip to Pisa] I have spoken again, and the result is that we are in precisely the same position; only with bitterer feelings on one side. If I go or stay they *must* be bitter: words have been said that I cannot easily forget, nor remember without pain; and yet I really do almost smile in the midst of it all, to think how I was treated this morning as an undutiful daughter because I tried to put on my gloves . . for there was no worse provocation. At least he complained of the undutifulness and rebellion (!!!) of everyone in the house — and when I asked if he meant that reproach for *me,* the answer was that he meant it for all of us, one with another. And I could not get an answer. He would not even grant me the consolation of thinking that I sacrificed what I supposed to be good, to *him.* I told him that my prospects of health seemed to me to depend on taking this step, but that through my affection for him, I was ready to sacrifice those to his pleasure if he exacted it — only that it was necessary to my self-satisfaction in future years, to understand definitely that the sacrifice *was* exacted by him and *was* made to him, . . and not thrown away blindly and by a misapprehension. And he would not answer *that.* I might do my own way, he said — *he* would not speak — *he* would not say that he was not displeased with me, nor the contrary: — I had better do what I liked: — for his part he washed his hands of me altogether.

INTRODUCTION

October 11, 1845: [Elizabeth, who had said 'I have no spell for charming the dragons', realised that her father would thwart her visit to Pisa] — and now that the hour approaches, I do feel as if the house stood upon gunpowder, and as if I held Guy Fawkes's lantern in my right hand. And no: I shall not go. The obstacles will not be those of Mr. Kenyon's finding — and what their precise character will be I do not see distinctly. Only that they will be sufficient, and thrown by one hand just where the wheel should turn, . . *that*, I see — and you will, in a few days.

October 14, 1845: The bitterest 'fact' of all is, that I had believed Papa to have loved me more than he obviously does: but I never regret knowledge . . I mean I never would *un*know anything . . even were it the taste of the apples by the Dead sea — and this must be accepted like the rest.

December 13, 1845: For 'conditions' — now I will tell you what I said once in a jest . . 'If a prince of Eldorado should come, with a pedigree of lineal descent from some signory in the moon in one hand, and a ticket of good-behaviour from the nearest Independent chapel, in the other' — ?

'Why even *then*,' said my sister Arabel, 'it would not *do*.' And she was right, and we all agreed that she was right. It is an obliquity of the will — and one laughs at it till the turn comes for crying.

January 22, 1846: Do *you*, on the other hand, endeavour to comprehend how there may be an eccentricity and obliquity in certain relations and on certain subjects, while the general character stands up worthily of esteem and regard — even of yours. Mr. Kenyon says broadly that it is monomania — neither more nor less. Then the principle of passive filial obedience is held — drawn (and quartered) from Scripture. He *sees* the law and the gospel on his side. Only the other day, there was a setting forth of the whole doctrine, I hear, down-stairs — 'passive obedience, and particularly in respect to marriage.'

January 27, 1846: For *him* . . he would rather see me dead at his foot than yield the point: and he will say so, and mean it, and persist in the meaning. *** We can alter nothing by ever so many words. After all, he is the victim. He isolates himself — and now and then he feels it . . the cold dead

13

silence all round, which is the effect of an incredible system. If he were not stronger than most men, he could not bear it as he does.

March 2, 1846: Dearest, it was plain to see yesterday evening when he came into this room for a moment at seven o'clock, before going to his own to dress for dinner . . plain to see, that he was not altogether pleased at finding you here in the morning. There was no pretext for objecting gravely — but it was plain that he was not pleased. Do not let this make you uncomfortable, he will forget all about it, and I was not *scolded*, do you understand. It was more manner, but my sisters thought as I did of the significance: — and it was enough to prove to me (if I had not known) what a desperate game we should be playing if we depended on a yielding nerve *there*.

April 3, 1846: Do you know, I am glad — I could almost thank God — that Papa keeps so far from me . . that he has given up coming in the evening . . I could almost thank God. If he were affectionate, and made me, or *let* me, feel myself necessary to him, . . how should I bear (even with my reason on my side) to prepare to give him pain?

May 15, 1846: Papa brought me some flowers yesterday when he came home . . and they went a little to my heart as I took them.

June 13, 1846: Tyranny? Perhaps. Yet in that strange, stern nature, there is a capacity to love — and I love him — and I shall suffer, in causing him to suffer.

July 17, 1846: The difficulty (almost the despair!) has been with me, to make you understand the two ends of truth . . both that he is *not* stone . . and that he *is* immovable *as* stone. Perhaps only a very peculiar nature could have held so long the position he holds in his family. His hand would not lie so heavily, without a pulse in it. Then he is upright — faithful to his conscience. You would respect him, . . and love him perhaps in the end. For me, he might have been king and father over me *to* the end, if he had thought it worth while to love me openly enough — yet, even *so*, he should not have let you come too near.

August 3, 1846: Dearest, he came into the room at about

seven, before he went to dinner—I was lying on the sofa and had on a white dressing gown, to get rid of the strings . . so oppressive the air was, for all the purifications of lightning. He looked a little as if the thunder had passed into him, and said, 'Has this been your costume since the morning, pray?'

'Oh no'—I answered—'Only just now, because of the heat.'

'Well,' he resumed, with a still graver aspect . . (so displeased he looked, dearest!) 'it appears, Ba, that *that man* has spent the whole day with you.' To which I replied as quietly as I could, that you had several times meant to go away, but that the rain would not let you,—and there the colloquy ended. Brief enough—but it took my breath away . . or what was left by the previous fear.

August 27, 1846: May your father indeed be able to love me a little, for *my* father will never love me again.

Such glimpses show us a Mr. Barrett who is as tragically armoured and yet pitifully vulnerable a figure as Dickens's Mr. Dombey. But if Scripture supported Mr. Barrett on the duty of filial obedience, Scripture supported the young too: 'Therefore shall a man leave his father and his mother, and shall cleave unto his wife: and they shall be one flesh'. Mr. Barrett seemed rather to be 'immovable marble' than flesh, and Browning realised that the marble would never miraculously soften. 'If the cold plunge *must* be taken, all this shivering delay on the bank is hurtful as well as fruitless'.

The last push was inadvertently provided by Mr. Barrett himself, who announced that the Barretts must move out of Wimpole Street for a month so that the house could be cleaned. Gripped by the conviction that it was now or never, Robert Browning and Elizabeth Barrett were secretly married at St. Marylebone Church on September 12, 1846. Seven days later, they secretly left the country: Paris, Marseilles, Pisa. Tennyson's Mariana had become Keats's Madeline:

> And they are gone: ay, ages long ago
> These lovers fled away into the storm.

But they fled into calm as well as into storm, and their flight was not only an end but also a beginning. Fifteen tender years of marriage were to be granted them before Mrs. Browning died in Florence in 1861. It is natural to wonder what effect those twenty months of fiercely secret courtship must have had upon the work of these two very different poets. In the simplest sense, we should never otherwise have had Elizabeth's *Sonnets from the Portuguese*. Yet the discreet imposture practised in that title (these love-poems to Robert are not 'from the Portuguese' at all) is a reminder of how very important imposture is to Browning's own poems. He was to return again and again to the theme of the necessity to grasp love at the right moment, and the terrible penalty paid for any failure of nerve here, with a tragic sense of that about which he had once made a heartfelt jest: 'and did not the prophet write that "there was a tide in the affairs of men, which taken at the E.B.B." led on to the fortune of Your R.B.' As the other side of the coin, he was to explore with obsessional pertinacity the nature of impostors, their self-justifications and their desperate fight for survival. His courtship of Elizabeth taught him not only that a mask was sometimes necessary, but also how bitter the conflict could be between completely different systems of value. 'He *sees* the law and the gospel on his side', Elizabeth had written of her father, and Browning — who had all along had a special interest in the way in which strong will and impassioned conviction can become monomania — must have had brought home to him in the most vital way the nature of such conflicts. In Mr. Barrett — a man whom he was never to meet — Browning will have been aware of all that willpower could achieve and of all that it could not achieve. And the necessity of his own predicament, the honest man forced into disguise, has its bearing on his poems. 'The sense of mask-wearing for another year would be suffocating', wrote Elizabeth, and Robert knew just what she meant: ' — and after, when Mrs. J. obligingly turned and said "How I should like to introduce *you* to Miss Barrett . . did you ever see her?" . . to which I answered in the old way, "that nobody, as she knew, saw you." At all these times did not I feel the "mask" you speak of!' Or he would cry out, in the words of Othello, 'Oh, hardness to dissemble!' But Browning's was the poetry of experience, and this experience proved grist to his mill. As Elizabeth said, 'By the time all this is over we shall be fit to take a degree in some Jesuits' college — we shall have mastered all the points of casuistry'. This, to a poet whose best work is fascinated by — and superbly analytical of — casuistry.

The fifteen years of marriage had great rewards and much suffering.

Elizabeth was to have two miscarriages before, at the age of forty-three, she gave birth to her son Robert Wiedemann Browning ('Pen'). Her health was to improve remarkably and yet always to be a cause for anxiety. Her greatest suffering was the unyielding silence of her father — her prophecies proved grimly true, so that five years after the marriage, when the Brownings visited England and Elizabeth attempted once again a reconciliation with her father, she met what could truly be called a stony silence. She wrote to her sister:

> I could never tell you, if I tried, what I felt when those letters came back to me, nine or ten of them, all with their unbroken seals testifying to the sealed up heart which refused to be opened by me. Oh, if my child were cast out of society for the most hideous of possible crimes, could I keep my heart so sealed up towards *him?* Not while a pulse of life stirred in it. If God and man cried aloud to me not to open, I should yet open — I could not help it. Think of the black unbroken seals, Henrietta, and the black-edged paper. How did he know that I might not have been widowed and calling out to him in my desolation? — But he let the letters lie on there, whatever they were. He fulfilled what he considered (he said, writing to Robert) 'his duty to himself, his family and society'.

Robert, too, had had his parental sadnesses. His mother had died in 1849, and he felt her death keenly. And then hard on her death came a ludicrous tragi-comic episode in which Browning's aged father was sued for breach of promise by a middle-aged matron. Browning was embarrassed to the point of laceration by his father's prompt unfaithfulness to his dear departed. Nearly twenty years later, and eight years after the death of Elizabeth, Robert apparently blundered into a tragi-comic imitation of his father, and proposed to Lady Ashburton — a proposal so ineptly worded by this master of language as to leave Lady Ashburton no choice but indignantly to spurn it. She indeed could spurn it, but Browning himself in a deeper sense could not — he was never to forgive himself for this breach of faith with the dead Elizabeth. It was not until his very last volume, *Asolando* (published on the day of his death in 1889) that he created once more a poetry of calm assurance, free from the self-disgust which came upon him after the Lady Ashburton fiasco.

But his first proposal of marriage had been a true one. During those fifteen years, ensconced in their home Casa Guidi in Florence, from which they made only occasional trips, he and Elizabeth explored their creativity. He, most notably with *Men and Women* in 1855, two volumes which brought together the best poems of his greatest decade: among them, 'Fra Lippo Lippi', 'A Toccata of Galuppi's', 'By the Fire-Side', ' "Childe Roland to the Dark Tower Came" ', 'Andrea del Sarto', 'Two in the Campagna', 'A Grammarian's Funeral' — but to name the glories of *Men and Women* is virtually to transcribe the contents-list, since as Elizabeth had said of his poems ten years before (after listing 'and . . . and . . . and') 'and the short lyrics . . for one comes to *"select"* every-thing at last'.

These were her most creative years, too — the years of *Sonnets from the Portuguese* (1850), and of *Aurora Leigh* (1857) — even though from our perspective her creativity must be seen as a far smaller thing than his. Nobody would now agree with John Ruskin that *Aurora Leigh* is 'the greatest *poem* in the English language', and it is hard to see why a poem so lacking in structure and sometimes so verbose should have been so astounding a success. But the curious thing about *Aurora Leigh* is that for all its faults it is not at all pretentious. Ambitious, yes, and too much so for Mrs. Browning's talents — but not bogus or pretentious. 'My chief *intention* just now', she had written to Robert early in their correspond-ence, 'is the writing of a sort of novel-poem — a poem as completely modern as "Geraldine's Courtship", running into the midst of our con-ventions, and rushing into drawing-rooms and the like, "where angels fear to tread"; and so, meeting face to face and without mask the Humanity of the age and speaking the truth as I conceive of it out plainly. That is my intention. It is not mature enough yet to be called a plan'. She may have failed in her large intention, but she succeeded nevertheless during the course of *Aurora Leigh* in fashioning much social satire, much delicate pathos, and much descriptive beauty.

On June 29, 1861, Elizabeth Barrett Browning died in Florence. She was fifty-five. Browning's poignant letter to his sister asks to be quoted in full.

> Dearest, I know I have shocked you deeply, and perhaps more than was need, but you must forgive me and consider the need of doing something at once, as the news might

have reached you even more abruptly, — and my own stupid state of mind yesterday. I can't even yet say of myself whether I was surprised or not, by this calamity; there is such a balance of reasons for fear (reasons for reassurance as they seemed then) that I don't know what I feel nor felt. She had been gravely affected by a series of misfortunes moral and physical — or united, as they always were. The Villafranca Peace and the illness with it thro' the summer at Siena the year before last, last year's still worse trial for six months together, the daily waiting for news from Henrietta and the end (stopping as it did all chance of good and reparation from the summer) rendered her weaker — weaker — she did *nothing* at Rome, took some three or four little drives, never walked two paces out of the room, so could not but be in a worse state to meet an illness: yet, on the other hand, her cheerfulness, and the quick succeeding of good and quiet looks to the suffering, and the quiet of the last six months, made everyone say 'how wonderfully she recovers, — she will soon be strong again, another *quiet* summer and *then*,' &c. &c. Also her own impressions were in furtherance of this hope, and when I determined to forego the journey to Paris, in opposition to her expressed wishes, I not only knew but got her to confess candidly that for *herself* the reprieve from going and the trials it would entail on her would be an incstimable advantage — only, 'still,' 'for my sake,' &c., she would run the risk. *I* would not, however. We travelled, as I have told you, easily and with as little fatigue as possible, and on reaching here I let her repose at will, not asking her to go out, but take the air and exercise of the large rooms to begin with. She saw no one, two or three friends at most, had no one to tea (except when intimates looked in once or twice) and began to look well, everybody said. But the weather was suffocatingly hot, and she said to me 'My cough has got well at once, as is always the way in such weather, but, curiously, it begins to affect me, as usual.' I said 'Let us *go* at once.' We talked of places, the choice being with respect to her different requirements — when last Thursday week it seems that, while I was away at the newsroom, Miss Blagden came, say at six or seven in the evening: the windows which had been closely shut all day (as the only way of excluding the burning external air) were opened to the ground to admit the breeze which usually springs up after such days, and she placed her chair, I am

told, in the doorway, between cross draughts of many windows
— all the rooms opening into each other, — whereupon Isa B.
remonstrated, but Ba said 'Oh, the cushion at the back of
the chair prevents my suffering.' It was her constant way,
besides. I came in and we had tea, and then she remarked 'I
think I have a sore throat.'

Next day was past just as usual, only she told me she had
a cold: at night she coughed much and sate up, restlessly, a
good deal, and next morning took two Cooper's pills, I afterwards heard, with a view to staving off the attack she felt imminent: still, nothing happened unusual in the day, but toward night she felt so oppressed that she said, 'I think you
shall go and get me a blister and a little Ipecacuanha wine,
to relieve the oppression: I find the medicine has acted
inordinately,' — she rarely had recourse to it, but had taken
this dose before with benefit — this time, the effects were
beyond her expectation. I ran (at 10 p.m.) to the chemist's,
got and applied the blister, and administered the wine but
she seemed little relieved till at 1 o'clock about or later she
began to suffer distressingly from the accumulation of phlegm,
which she had no power to cough up. I left her with Annunziata, dressed and knocked up (with difficulty) Dr. Wilson,
a physician of great repute here, and specially conversant in
maladies of the chest: he followed with me, and we found
her worse, laboring most distressingly and ineffectually: Wilson prescribed promptly — got two prescriptions made up by
two chymists (our porter and I got them), put on sinapisms
to breast and back, and hot water with mustard to the feet.
For a long while she continued unrelieved — he remained
till nearly five. At last she recovered and we hoped all was
over, but this was the second night she had passed in violent exertion without a minute's sleep. From this time
things went on thus, — the symptoms were said to be always
'a little better'; but Wilson examined carefully and reported,
with a very serious face, that one lung was condensed (the
right) and that he suspected an abscess in it; but he was
aware of her long previous experience of the possibility of
making shift with damaged lungs, and could not say how
it might be — 'it would require a long time to get well.'
I told part of this to Ba who repeatedly answered 'It is the
old story — they don't know my case — I have been tapped
and sounded so, and condemned so, repeatedly: this time
it is said the right is the affected lung while the left is free

20

— Dr. Chambers said just the contrary. This is only one of my old attacks. I know all about it and I shall get better' — 'It was not so bad an attack as that of two years ago,' and so she continued: every day I carried her into the drawing-room where she sate only in her nightgown in her own chair, for the airiness of the room. She read newspapers, a little — saw nobody of course — going to bed about seven; I sate up most nights, — lay down by her only once, I think, or twice at most, when I was up so often that I discontinued it, which she seemed not to notice; for we brought a small bed into the drawingroom and placed her in it, and she began to doze very much, restlessly, and seemed unaware I was not in bed on a sopha behind: from the first the prescription was 'nourishment, even wine, a little, often if in small quantities.' But Ba never could or would try to take solid nourishment: she had strong brodo (clear soup) but would take nothing else.

So we went on, 'rather better, but still with the unfavourable symptoms' — was I told twice a day. She was cheerful as ever, with voice all but extinct — still, 'it would be nothing' she repeated. On Thursday night we tried asses' milk, with success — 'had a better night decidedly' — always much expectoration however, and her feet swelled a little. I let Isa Blagden come and kiss her: she whispered 'I am decidedly better,' and gave that impression to Isa. On Friday she had asses' milk, broth twice, some bread and butter: we talked about our plans — about the house, Casa Guidi, which had suddenly grown distasteful to both of us, noisy, hot, close — poor place we have liked so for fourteen years! I said 'it would be best to take a Villa — you decide on Rome for the winter, and properly, — what good of coming in the summer to a town house you cannot stay in?' She said 'Ah, but I can't leave Florence, I like Florence, — you would like to establish ourselves in Rome.' I said 'no, there's Villa Niccolini, for instance — that would just suit.' She said 'that would suit — try, inquire' — and after seemed so interested about it that I said 'There's no hurry, — we can get in there at once if you like, and it will be just as cool as Siena, with the convenience of being near the city.' 'Oh,' she said, 'that's not it — we must change the air now, that is my one chance. I meant, that if you take it for three years you can send up our furniture and we can enter at once in it when we return next spring.' I observed a tendency to light headedness in all this — as she did — complaining of it to the doctor, and telling me how she had strange thoughts, about the windows, which 'seemed to be hung in the Hungarian colours.' And she smiled to Isa Blagden, at eight on Friday, as she took the glass, 'Oh, I not only have asses' milk but asses' thoughts — I am so troubled with silly politics and nonsense.' Isa told her something she had heard about the politics of Ricasoli which interested her so much that I interposed — 'No talking, come, go Isa' — and I pushed her out; but Isa says that while my back was turned for a moment to pour out some medicine she whispered 'Did you say Ricasoli said his politics were identical with those of Cavour, only they took different views of the best way of carrying them out?' — Yes — 'Ah, so I thought.' Isa left convinced she was better, the doctor came — 'perhaps a little better.' We talked over her aversion to food. I caused to be made a very strong fowl-jelly, placed in ice in readiness, and then asked if she would not try it during the night — 'no'. I did not know how little good it would do — the weakness came from other causes, and *these* were important, the other could be easily got rid of. I sat by her at night. She coughed little, took the emulgent duly, and another medicine, but dozed constantly: if I spoke she looked, knew me, smiled, said she was better, and relapsed. I continued this till past three in the morning, when the dozing made me very uneasy. She said 'You did right not to wait — what a fine steamer — how comfortable!' I called Annunziata, bade her get hot water, as the Doctor had done, and send the porter for himself. I bade her sit up for the water. She did with little help — smiling, letting us act, and repeating 'Well, you do make an exaggerated case of it!' 'My hands too' she said and put them in another basin. I said you know me? 'My Robert — my heavens, my beloved' — kissing me (but I can't tell you) she said 'Our lives are held by God.' I asked, 'will you take jelly for my sake?' 'Yes.' I brought a saucerful and fed it by spoonfuls into her mouth. I then brought a second, and poured some into a glass — she took all. She put her arms round me — 'God bless you' repeatedly — kissing me with such vehemence that when I laid her down she continued to kiss the air with her lips, and several times raised her own hands and kissed them; I said 'Are you comfortable?' 'Beautiful.' I only put in a thing or two out of the many in my heart of hearts. Then she motioned to have her hands *sponged* — some of the jelly annoying her: this was done, and she began to sleep again – the *last*, I saw. I felt she must be raised, took her in my arms, I felt the struggle to cough begin, and end unavailingly – no pain, no sigh, – only a quiet *sight*. Her head fell on me. I thought she might have fainted, but presently there was the least knitting of the brows, and A. cried 'Quest' anima benedetta è passata!'

It was so. She is with God, who takes from me the life of my life in one sense, – not so, in the truest. My life is fixed and sure now. I shall live out the remainder in her direct influence, endeavouring to complete mine, miserably imperfect now, but so as to take the good she was meant to give me. I go away from Italy at once, having no longer any business there: I have our child about whom I shall exclusively employ myself, doing her part by him. I shall live in the presence of her, in every sense, I hope and believe – so that so far my loss is not *irreparable* – but the future is nothing to me now, except inasmuch as it confirms and realizes the past. I cannot plan now, or at least talk about plans, but I shall leave Italy at once, only staying to take away the necessity of a return, for years at least. Pen has been perfect to me: he sate all yesterday with his arms round me; said things like her to me. I shall try and work hard, educate him, and live worthy of my past fifteen years' happiness. I do not feel paroxysms of grief, but as if the very blessing, she died giving me, insensible to all beside, had begun to work already. She will be buried tomorrow. Several times in writing this I have for a moment referred in my mind to her – 'I will ask Ba about that.' The grief of everybody is sincere, I am told. Everybody is kind in offers of help – all is done for me that can be; and it is not a little just now. Isa came at the early morning and stayed till night, taking away Pen. I shall now go in and sit with herself – my Ba, for ever. The service will be that of the Ch. of En., that I may hear those only words at the beginning. Bless you both, dearest papa and sis. I will write after tomorrow. Don't be in any concern for me, I have some of her strength, really, added to mine. Love to dear Milsand. Ever your own.

R. BROWNING.

How she looks now – how perfectly beautiful!

The literary world mourned – to *The Athenaeum* she was 'the greatest English poetess that has ever lived'. (A warm but dangerous kind of praise, suggesting that poetesses exist in a different league from poets, and calling up Dr. Johnson's remark about a woman preacher: 'Sir, a woman's preaching is like a dog's walking on his hinder legs. It is not done well: but you are surprized to find it done at all.')

Robert Browning mourned too. Yet just as conspicuously sincere as his grief was his energetic resolve. He returned to England for the rest of his life, and there he set about living up to the admonition of Thomas Carlyle: 'I expect *a new epoch for him* in regard to his work in this world, now that he is coming back to England at last'.

The new epoch began with *The Ring and the Book*, which Browning worked on from 1862 to 1868. A year before Elizabeth died, he had picked up a vellum-covered volume on a bookstall in Florence. It told of a brutal murder, of violence, intrigue, and squalor, and Elizabeth had viewed it with distaste. But here was a subject which offered not only the most inviting opportunities for psychological analysis but also for Browning's extraordinary ability to put himself into other people's shoes. 'The same transaction seen from a number of differing points of view, or glimpses in a mirror' — his words sum up the method of this remarkable poem, a poem which gives us in turn the murder as seen by the different factions in Rome, by the lawyers, by the murderer Guido, by the rescuer Caponsacchi, by the dying victim Pompilia, and by the Pope who broods upon Guido's appeal for mercy. Not all of the dramatic monologues which make up this unique poem burn with the same vitality. But in the force of its finest monologues and in the power of its conception *The Ring and the Book* stands as an astonishing achievement. 'A Relativist Poem': that is what Robert Langbaum calls it in *The Poetry of Experience*, the best study of Browning's poetry that there is. With that strange imagination which went even beyond impersonation (in Elizabeth's words, 'dramatic impersonations, gruff with nature') — beyond into embodiment, Browning gave expression as few other poets have done to the conviction that truth is relative and yet not non-existent, the conviction that there are truths as well as truth. Elizabeth had invoked 'the two ends of truth' to explain her inexplicable father. And Browning had once compared himself to Elizabeth as a poet, to his own disadvantage: 'You speak out, *you* — I only make men and women speak — give you truth broken into prismatic hues, and fear the pure white light, even if it is in me'. *Only?* The word *empathy* did not exist in Browning's day, but there are few poets who more vividly manifest 'the power of entering into the experience of or understanding objects or

24

emotions outside ourselves' (1912). Browning's comment on his late monologue 'Prince Hohenstiel-Schwangau' could be applied to all his best monologues: 'it is just what I imagine the man might, if he pleased, say for himself'.

The Ring and the Book, because of its longueurs, is not the most assuredly successful of Browning's poems, but it is the one which makes clearest the persistent aspiration of a poet who once said 'Moral character and action depend so much on circumstances that it is almost impossible for men to judge each other fairly'. Almost impossible — and yet the vital tension of Browning's best work comes from the recognition that at the same time it is altogether impossible for men to abandon the attempt to judge each other fairly.

It was The Ring and the Book which established Browning's fame. The last twenty years of his life were years of social and literary success, of meeting Queen Victoria, of dinner jackets and reprintings, and of the Browning Society. They were, as well, the years of the misguided proposal to Lady Ashburton and of the raffish delinquencies of Browning's son Pen. But Browning ripened and smiled and even — some thought — grew handsomer year by year. His long tortuous poems of the 1870's and 1880's have their technical and biographical interest, and occasionally they offer something more than that: poetic mastery. But by and large this poet who had once described himself as a volcano was gradually becoming extinct — though still capable of hurling up fierily scorching verses. He was still, as Elizabeth had said, 'a master in clenched passion'. On July 8, 1889 — only six months before his death — he glanced into a newly published volume of Edward FitzGerald's letters, collected now that FitzGerald was dead. But FitzGerald had outlived Mrs. Browning, and the letter on which Browning's eye happened to fall was dated July 15, 1861:

> Mrs. Browning's Death is rather a relief to me, I must say: no more Aurora Leighs, thank God! A woman of real Genius, I know: but what is the upshot of it all? She and her Sex had better mind the Kitchen and their Children; and perhaps the Poor: except in such things as little Novels, they only devote themselves to what Men do much better, leaving that which Men do worse or not at all.

Browning was stung at once into warring with the dead. Could it be that the fervour of his verses against FitzGerald owed something to Browning's faint uneasiness that he had once momentarily broken faith with the dead Elizabeth?

> I chanced upon a new book yesterday:
> I opened it, and where my finger lay
> 'Twixt page and uncut page these words I read
> — Some six or seven at most — and learned thereby
> That you, FitzGerald, whom by ear and eye
> She never knew, 'thanked God my wife was dead.'
>
> Ay, dead! and were yourself alive, good Fitz,
> How to return you thanks would task my wits:
> Kicking you seems the common lot of curs —
> While more appropriate greeting lends you grace:
> Surely to spit there glorifies your face —
> Spitting — from lips once sanctified by Hers.

Six months later, a very different new book was published: Browning's *Asolando*. News of its successful reception on the day of publication, December 12, 1889, was brought to the dying Browning in Venice — news which elicited (according to Pen) his last intelligible words: 'How gratifying'.

How gratifying. And how proper, how reserved, those last words of Browning were. To the end he retained a profound reserve, to the end he remained a baffling figure. Baffling partly because of the contradictions of his work. 'The longer I live', said Thomas Hardy, 'the more does Browning's character seem *the* literary puzzle of the 19th Century. How could smug Christian optimism worthy of a dissenting grocer find a place inside a man who was so vast a seer and feeler when on neutral ground?'

Browning's character: did Browning really have a character? What lay behind — in the words of one of his contemporaries — 'that false courtesy — which is, perhaps, his solitary blemish'? William Bell Scott gave up: 'The connection between Browning's face and his work seems to me as little understandable as well can be'. Much of his poetry is directly concerned with identity, and this poet who was so fascinated by acting and who had wanted to be an actor seems an embodiment of a paradox about the actor: that his real life is somehow less substantial, less real, than his hours on the stage. Henry James could not stop wondering about Browning, that 'loud, sound, normal, hearty presence, all so assertive and so whole' somehow emanating from a man who did not seem simply normal or hearty. James decided that there were two Brownings, existing in 'independent compartments', 'two distinct and alternate presences, the assertion of either of which on any occasion directly involved the entire extinction of the other'. As James saw it, in Browning 'the poet and the "member of society" were, in a word, dissociated in him as they can rarely elsewhere have been', and James transformed his insight into the story 'The Private Life'. The story is notoriously about Browning insofar as it is about an artist who is a public bore and a private genius. But Browning is relevant, too, to that other 'private life' which figures in James's eerie story, even though the character Lord Mellifont is admittedly based on Lord Leighton. For Lord Mellifont simply ceases to exist when he is on his own. 'He couldn't have been, in the time, anywhere but where I had left him. Yet the place was utterly empty — as empty as this stretch of valley before us. He had vanished — he had ceased to be'. For to have two identities is perhaps to have no identity, as James must have realised when he mentioned 'the entire extinction of the other'. What's become of Browning since he gave us all the slip? Even Elizabeth had looked back during their correspondence to 'the curious double feeling I had about you — you personally, and you as the writer of these letters, and the crisis of the feeling, when I was positively vexed and jealous of myself for not succeeding better in making a unity of the two'. But was the failure simply Elizabeth's?

Ever since the Victorian critic Richard Holt Hutton, we have known that Browning was a poetic ventriloquist. The ventriloquist has many identities and no identity, and there are possibilities of madness in his many voices and his transmigrations of soul. The metempsychotic Browning, able likewise to shift his soul into other bodies, knew about the psychotic. And his fascinated loathing of mesmerism and spiritualism may be not just a fear of having his self discovered, but of having his lack of a self discovered. 'Love in a Life' is certainly a superb poem about not ever being able to catch up with one's true love, but that need not preclude its also being about the tantalizing fugitiveness of one's true self:

> Room after room,
> I hunt the house through
> We inhabit together . . .
> Yet the day wears,

And door succeeds door;
I try the fresh fortune —
Range the wide house from the wings to the centre.
Still the same chance! she goes out as I enter.
Spend my whole day in the quest, — who cares?
But 'tis twilight, you see, — with such suites to explore,
Such closets to search, such alcoves to importune!

It was John Stuart Mill who spoke of Browning's 'self-seeking and self-worshipping state' — and by self-seeking he did not mean careerist. The 'morbid self-consciousness' of which Mill spoke, the 'curious idealization of self-worship' — these are morbid and curious because what they most seek is the assurance that a self is really there. Browning shared the Victorian nightmare: of gazing into an empty mirror.

What was *Sordello* about? 'My stress lay on the incidents in the development of a soul: little else is worth study'. But Browning's word *development* is an equivocal one. 'God is the perfect poet', he could insist — but would the perfect poet, then, possess an identity and a self only in the very puzzling sense in which God might be said to possess them? Elizabeth said she was confident that Robert possessed 'the superabundant mental life and individuality which admits of shifting a personality and speaking the truth still'. Yet even she felt some uneasiness about that individuality, and she went on to urge him: 'I do not think that, with all that music in you, only your own personality should be dumb, nor that having thought so much and deeply on life and its ends, you should not teach what you have learnt, in the directest and most impressive way, the mask thrown off however moist with the breath'.

The masking or dumbness or suppression of the self by which Browning achieved his unparalleled transmigrations of soul into 'Men and Women' is like those self-extinguishings which are central to both mesmerism and spiritualism — and to acting. 'Did you ever feel afraid of your own soul, as I have done?', Elizabeth asked him — and described to him the plan of a play:

My plan was of a man haunted by his own soul, . . (making her a separate personal Psyche, a dreadful, beautiful Psyche) — the man being haunted and terrified through all the turns of life by her.

INTRODUCTION

'The subject of your play is tempting indeed', Browning had replied, and he will have understood the depth of feeling with which she told of the prayer which had meant so much to her when she was a child, 'a supplication which I found in "King's Memoirs" and which took my fancy and met my general views exactly . . "O God, if there be a God, save my soul if I have a soul" '.

Browning — How to Know Him: that was the wishful title of W. L. Phelps's book in 1915. If anybody knew the soul of Robert Browning, it was Elizabeth Barrett. Neither of them will ever cease to attract biographers. Yet each of them left not solely biographies to be written but poems to be read. The poems of Elizabeth Barrett Browning possess the interest which attaches to her talent, her discrimination, her political commitment to the cause of Italian unity and liberty, and her compassion. The poems of Robert Browning are such that no single claim can encompass all his varied gifts. And yet two claims predominate: he is the only great 19th-century English poet who knows about evil, and he is the only great Victorian poet who can compact the serious and the comic into a tragic grotesquerie. Browning knew that we always covet a biography of a good poet, but that we do not always *need* a biography. As he said of the 'objective poet':

> The man passes, the work remains. The work speaks for it-self, as we say: and the biography of the worker is no more necessary to an understanding or enjoyment of it, than is a model or anatomy of some tropical tree, to the right tasting of the fruit we are familiar with on the market-stall, — or a geologist's map and stratification, to the prompt recognition of the hill-top, our land-mark of every day.

Browning's poems remain, in the fullest sense, a land-mark.

Christopher Ricks

Selected Letters of
ROBERT BROWNING
AND
ELIZABETH BARRETT BARRETT

Ellipses (. . and . . .) were used by both Robert Browning and Elizabeth Barrett Barrett as a form of punctuation within their letters and do not indicate omission. In this edition, asterisks within the correspondence and between their letters (* * *) have been used to show that material has been excluded. THE EDITORS.

R. B. to E. B. B.

New Cross, Hatcham, Surrey.
[January 10, 1845.]

I LOVE your verses with all my heart, dear Miss Barrett, — and this is no off-hand complimentary letter that I shall write, — whatever else, no prompt matter-of-course recognition of your genius, and there a graceful and natural end of the thing. Since the day last week when I first read your poems, I quite laugh to remember how I have been turning and turning again in my mind what I should be able to tell you of their effect upon me, for in the first flush of delight I thought I would this once get out of my habit of purely passive enjoyment, when I do really enjoy, and thoroughly justify my admiration — perhaps even, as a loyal fellow-craftsman should, try and find fault and do you some little good to be proud of hereafter! — but nothing comes of it all — so into me has it gone, and part of me has it become, this great living poetry of yours, not a flower of which but took root and grew — Oh, how different that is from lying to be dried and pressed flat, and prized highly, and put in a book with a proper account at top and bottom, and shut up and put away . . . and the book called a 'Flora,' besides! After all, I need not give up the thought of doing that, too, in time; because even now, talking with whoever is worthy, I can give a reason for my faith in one and another excellence, the fresh strange music, the affluent language, the exquisite pathos and true new brave thought; but in this addressing myself to you — your own self, and for the first time, my feeling rises altogether. I do, as I say, love these books with all my heart — and I love you too. Do you know I was once not very far from seeing — really seeing you? Mr. Kenyon said to me one morning 'Would you like to see Miss Barrett?' then he went to announce me, — then he returned . . you were too unwell, and now it is years ago, and I feel as at some untoward passage in my travels, as if I had been close, so close, to some world's-wonder in chapel or crypt, only a screen to push and I might have entered, but there was some slight, so it now seems, slight and just sufficient bar to admission, and the half-opened door shut, and I went home my thousands of miles, and the sight was never to be?

Well, these Poems were to be, and this true thankful joy and pride with which I feel myself,

Yours ever faithfully,
ROBERT BROWNING.

Miss Barrett
50 Wimpole Street.

R. Browning.

E.B.B. to R.B.

50 Wimpole Street: Jan. 11, 1845.

I thank you, dear Mr. Browning, from the bottom of my heart. You meant to give me pleasure by your letter — and even if the object had not been answered, I ought still to thank you. But it is thoroughly answered. Such a letter from such a hand! Sympathy is dear — very dear to me: but the sympathy of a poet, and of such a poet, is the quintessence of sympathy to me! Will you take back my gratitude for it? — agreeing, too, that of all the commerce done in the world, from Tyre to Carthage, the exchange of sympathy for gratitude is the most princely thing!

For the rest you draw me on with your kindness. It is difficult to get rid of people when you once have given them too much pleasure — *that* is a fact, and we will not stop for the moral of it. What I was going to say — after a little natural hesitation — is, that if ever you emerge without inconvenient effort from your 'passive state,' and will *tell* me of such faults as rise to the surface and strike you as important in my poems,

34

(for of course, I do not think of troubling you with criticism in detail) you will confer a lasting obligation on me, and one which I shall value so much, that I covet it at a distance. I do not pretend to any extraordinary meekness under criticism and it is possible enough that I might not be altogether obedient to yours. But with my high respect for your power in your Art and for your experience as an artist, it would be quite impossible for me to hear a general observation of yours on what appear to you my master-faults, without being the better for it hereafter in some way. I ask for only a sentence or two of general observation – and I do not ask even for *that*, so as to tease you – but in the humble, low voice, which is so excellent a thing in women – particularly when they go a-begging! The most frequent general criticism I receive, is, I think, upon the style, – 'if I *would* but change my style'! But *that* is an objection (isn't it?) to the writer bodily? Buffon says, and every sincere writer must feel, that '*Le style c'est l'homme*'; a fact, however, scarcely calculated to lessen the objection with certain critics.

Is it indeed true that I was so near to the pleasure and honour of making your acquaintance? and can it be true that you look back upon the lost opportunity with any regret? But – you know – if you had entered the 'crypt,' you might have caught cold, or been tired to death, and *wished* yourself 'a thousand miles off;' which would have been worse than travelling them. It is not my interest, however, to put such thoughts in your head about its being 'all for the best'; and I would rather hope (as I do) that what I lost by one chance I may recover by some future one. Winters shut me up as they do dormouse's eyes; in the spring, *we shall see:* and I am so much better that I seem turning round to the outward world again. And in the meantime I have learnt to know your voice, not merely from the poetry but from the kindness in it. Mr. Kenyon often speaks of you – dear Mr. Kenyon! – who most unspeakably, or only speakably with tears in my eyes, – has been my friend and helper, and my book's friend and helper! critic and sympathiser, true friend of all hours! You know him well enough, I think, to understand that I must be grateful to him.

I am writing too much, – and notwithstanding that I am writing too much, I will write of one thing more. I will say that I am your debtor, not only for this cordial letter and for all the pleasure which came with it, but in other ways, and those the highest: and I will say that while I live to follow this divine art of poetry, in proportion to my love for it and my devotion to it, I must be a devout admirer and student of your works. This is in my heart to say to you – and I say it.

And, for the rest, I am proud to remain

Your obliged and faithful
ELIZABETH B. BARRETT.

Robert Browning, Esq.,
New Cross, Hatcham, Surrey.

R. B. to E. B. B.

New Cross, Hatcham, Surrey
[*Jan. 13, 1845.*]

Dear Miss Barrett, – I just shall say, in as few words as I can, that you make me very happy, and that, now the beginning is over, I dare say I shall do better, because my poor praise, number one, was nearly as felicitously brought out, as a certain tribute to no less a personage than Tasso, which I was amused with at Rome some weeks ago, in a neat pencilling on the plaister-wall by his tomb at Sant' Onofrio – 'Alla cara memoria – di – (please fancy solemn interspaces and grave capital letters at the new lines) di – Torquato Tasso – il Dottore Bernardini – offriva – il seguente Carme – O *tu*' – and no more, – the good man, it should seem, breaking down with the overload of love here! But my 'O tu' – was breathed out most sincerely, and now you have taken it in gracious part, the rest will come after. Only, – and which is why I write now – it looks as if I have introduced some phrase or other about 'your faults' so cleverly as to give exactly the opposite meaning to what I meant, which was, that in my first ardour I had thought to tell you of *everything* which impressed me in your verses, down, even, to whatever 'faults' I could find, – a good earnest, when I had got to *them*, that I had left out not much between – as if some Mr. Fellows were to say, in the overflow of his first enthusiasm of rewarded adventure: 'I will describe you all the outer life and ways of these Lycians, down to their very sandal-thongs,' whereto the be-corresponded one rejoins – 'Shall I get next week, then,

36

your dissertation on sandal-thongs'? Yes, and a little about the 'Olympian Horses,' and God-charioteers as well! What 'struck me as faults,' were not matters on the removal of which, one was to have—poetry, or high poetry,—but the very highest poetry, so I thought, and that, to universal recognition. For myself, or any artist, in many of the cases there would be a positive loss of time, peculiar artist's pleasure—for an instructed eye loves to see where the brush has dipped twice in a lustrous colour, has lain insistingly along a favourite outline, dwelt lovingly in a grand shadow; for these 'too muches' for the everybody's picture are so many helps to the making out the real painter's picture as he had it in his brain. And all of the Titian's Naples Magdalen must have once been golden in its degree to justify that heap of hair in her hands—the *only* gold effected now!

But about this soon—for night is drawing on and I go out, yet cannot, quiet at conscience, till I report (to *myself*, for I never said it to you, I think) that your poetry must be, cannot but be, infinitely more to me than mine to you—for you *do* what I always wanted, hoped to do, and only seem now likely to do for the first time. You speak out, *you*,—I only make men and women speak—give you truth broken into prismatic hues, and fear the pure white light, even if it is in me, but I am going to try; so it will be no small comfort to have your company just now, seeing that when you have your men and women aforesaid, you are busied with them, whereas it seems bleak, melancholy work, this talking to the wind (for I have begun)—yet I don't think I shall let *you* hear, after all, the savage things about Popes and imaginative religions that I must say.

See how I go on and on to you, I who, whenever now and then pulled, by the head and hair, into letter-writing, get sorrowfully on for a line or two, as the cognate creature urged on by stick and string, and then come down 'flop' upon the sweet haven of page one, line last, as serene as the sleep of the virtuous! You will never more, I hope, talk of 'the honour of my acquaintance,' but I will joyfully wait for the delight of your friendship, and the spring, and my Chapel-sight after all!

Ever your most faithfully,
R. BROWNING.

For Mr. Kenyon—I have a convenient theory about *him*, and his otherwise quite unaccountable kindness to me; but 'tis quite night now, and they call me.

E.B.B. to R.B.

50 Wimpole Street: Jan. 15, 1845.

Dear Mr. Browning, — The fault was clearly with me and not with you.

When I had an Italian master, years ago, he told me that there was an unpronounceable English word which absolutely expressed me, and which he would say in his own tongue, as he could not in mine — '*testa lunga.*' Of course, the signor meant *headlong!* — and now I have had enough to tame me, and might be expected to stand still in my stall. But you see I do not. Headlong I was at first, and headlong I continue — precipitously rushing forward through all manner of nettles and briars instead of keeping the path; guessing at the meaning of unknown words instead of looking into the dictionary — tearing open letters, and never untying a string, — and expecting everything to be done in a minute, and the thunder to be as quick as the lightning. And so, at your half word I flew at the whole one, with all its possible consequences, and wrote what you read. Our common friend, as I think he is, Mr. Horne, is often forced to entreat me into patience and coolness of purpose, though his only intercourse with me has been by letter. And, by the way, you will be sorry to hear that during his stay in Germany *he* has been 'headlong' (out of a metaphor) twice; once, in falling from the Drachenfels, when he only just saved himself by catching at a vine; and once quite lately, at Christmas, in a fall on the ice of the Elbe in skating, when he dislocated his left shoulder in a very painful manner. He is doing quite well, I believe, but it was sad to have such a shadow from the German Christmas tree, and he a stranger.

In art, however, I understand that it does not do to be headlong, but patient and laborious — and there is a love strong enough, even in me, to overcome nature. I apprehend what you mean in the criticism you just intimate, and shall turn it over and over in my mind until I get practical good from it. What no mere critic sees, but what you, an artist, know, is the difference between the thing desired and the thing attained, between the idea in the writer's mind and the εἴδωλον cast off in his work. All the effort — the quick'ning of the breath and beating of the heart in pursuit, which is ruffling and injurious to the general effect of a composition; all which you call 'insistency,' and which many would call superfluity, and which *is* superfluous in a sense — *you* can pardon, because you understand. The great chasm between the thing I say, and the thing I would say, would be quite dispiriting to me, in spite even of such kindnesses as yours, if the desire did not master the despondency. 'Oh for a horse with wings!' It is wrong of me to write so of myself — only you put your finger on the root of a fault, which has, to my fancy, been a little misapprehended. I do not *say everything I think* (as has been said of me by master-critics) but I *take every means to say what I think*, which is different! — or I fancy so!

In one thing, however, you are wrong. Why should you deny the full measure of my delight and benefit from your writings? I could tell you why you should not. You have in your vision two worlds, or to use the language of the schools of the day, you are both subjective and objective in the habits of your mind. You can deal both with abstract thought and with human passion in the most passionate sense. Thus, you have an immense grasp in Art; and no one at all accustomed to consider the usual forms of it, could help regarding with reverence and gladness the gradual expansion of your powers. Then you are 'masculine' to the height — and I, as a woman, have studied some of your gestures of language and intonation wistfully, as a thing beyond me far! and the more admirable for being beyond.

Of your new work I hear with delight. How good of you to tell me. And it is not dramatic in the strict sense, I am to understand — (am I right in understanding so?) and you speak, in your own person 'to the winds'? no — but to the thousand living sympathies which will awake to hear you. A great dramatic power may develop itself otherwise than in the formal drama; and I have been guilty of wishing, before this hour (for reasons which I will not thrust upon you after all my tedious writing), that you would give the public a poem unassociated directly or indirectly with the stage, for a trial on the popular heart. I reverence the drama, but —

But I break in on myself out of consideration for you. I might have done it, you will think, before. I vex your 'serene sleep of the virtuous' like a nightmare. Do not say 'No.' I am *sure* I do! As to the vain parlance of the world, I did not talk of the 'honour of your acquaintance' without a true sense of honour, indeed; but I shall willingly exchange it all (and *now*, if you please, at this moment, for fear of worldly mutabilities) for the 'delight of your friendship.'

> Believe me, therefore, dear Mr. Browning;
>
> Faithfully yours, and gratefully,
> ELIZABETH B. BARRETT.

For Mr. Kenyon's kindness, as *I* see it, no theory will account. I class it with mesmerism for that reason.

R. B. to E. B. B.

New Cross, Hatcham, Monday Night.
[postmark *January 28, 1845.*]

Dear Miss Barrett, — Your books lie on my table here, at arm's length from me, in this old room where I sit all day: and when my head aches or wanders or strikes work, as it now or then will, I take my chance for either green-covered volume, as if it were so much fresh trefoil to feel in one's hands this winter-time, — and round I turn, and, putting a decisive elbow on three or four half-done-with 'Bells' of mine, read, read, read, and just as I have shut up the book and walked to the window, I recollect that you wanted me to find faults there, and that, in an unwise hour, I engaged to do so. Meantime, the days go by (the white-throat is come and sings now) and as I would not have you 'look down on me from your white heights' as promise breaker, evader, or forgetter, if I could help: and as, if I am very candid and contrite, you may find it in your heart to write to me again — who knows? — I shall say at once that the said faults cannot be lost, must be *somewhere*, and shall be faithfully brought you back whenever they turn up, — as people tell one of missing matters. I am rather exacting, myself, with my own gentle audience, and get to say spiteful things about them when they are backward in their dues of appreciation — but really, *really* — could I be quite sure that anybody as good as — I must go on, I suppose, and say — as myself, even, were honestly to feel towards me as I do, towards the writer of 'Bertha,' and the 'Drama,' and the 'Duchess,' and the 'Page' and — the whole two volumes, I should be paid after a fashion, I know.

One thing I can do — pencil, if you like, and annotate, and dissertate upon that I love most and least — I think I can do it, that is.

Here an odd memory comes — of a friend who, — volunteering such a service to a sonnet-writing somebody, gave him a taste of his quality in a side-column of short criticisms on sonnet the First, and starting off the beginning three lines with, of course, 'bad, worse, worst' — made by a generous mintage of words to meet the sudden run of his epithets, 'worser, worserer, worserest' pay off the second terzet in full — no 'badder, badderer, badderest' fell to the *Second's* allowance, and 'worser' &c. answered the demands of the Third; 'worster, worsterer, worsterest' supplied the emergency of the Fourth; and, bestowing his last 'worserestest and worstestest' on lines 13 and 14, my friend (slapping his forehead like an emptied strong-box) frankly declared himself bankrupt, and honourably incompetent, to satisfy the reasonable expectations of the rest of the series!

What an illustration of the law by which opposite ideas suggest opposite, and contrary images come together!

See now, how, of that 'Friendship' you offer me (and here Juliet's word rises to my lips) — I feel sure once and for ever. I have got already, I see, into this little pet-handwriting of mine (not anyone else's) which scratches on as if theatrical copyists (ah me!) and BRADBURY AND EVANS' READER were not! But you shall get something better than this nonsense one day, if you will have patience with me — hardly better, though, because this does me real good, gives real relief, to write. After all, you know nothing, next to nothing of me, and that stops me. Spring is to come, however!

If you hate writing to me as I hate writing to nearly everybody, I pray you never write — if you do, as you say, care for anything I have done. I will simply assure you, that meaning to begin work in deep earnest, *begin* without affectation, God knows, — I do not know what will help me more than hearing from you, — and therefore, if you do not so very much hate it, I know I *shall* hear from you — and very little more about your 'tiring me.'

Ever yours faithfully,
ROBERT BROWNING.

41

THE BROWNINGS

E.B.B. to R.B.

50 [Wimpole] Street: Feb. 3, 1845.

Why how could I hate to write to you, dear Mr. Browning? Could you believe in such a thing? If nobody likes writing to everybody (except such professional letter writers as you and I are *not*), yet everybody likes writing to somebody, and it would be strange and contradictory if I were not always delighted both to hear from *you* and to write to *you*, this talking upon paper being as good a social pleasure as another, when our means are somewhat straitened. As for me, I have done most of my talking by post of late years – as people shut up in dungeons take up with scrawling mottoes on the walls. Not that I write to many in the way of regular correspondence, as our friend Mr. Horne predicates of me in his romances (which is mere romancing!), but that there are a few who will write and be written to by me without a sense of injury. Dear Miss Mitford, for instance. You do not know her, I think, personally, although she was the first to tell me (when I was very ill and insensible to all the glories of the world except poetry), of the grand scene in 'Pippa Passes.' *She* has filled a large drawer in this room with delightful letters, heart-warm and soul-warm, . . driftings of nature (if sunshine could drift like snow), and which, if they should ever fall the way of all writing, into print, would assume the folio shape as a matter of course, and take rank on the lowest shelf of libraries, with Benedictine editions of the Fathers, κ.τ.λ. I write this to you to show how I can have pleasure in letters, and never think them too long, nor too frequent, nor too illegible from being written in little 'pet hands.' I can read any MS. except the writing on the pyramids. And if you will only promise to treat me *en bon camarade*, without reference to the conventionalities of 'ladies and gentlemen,' taking no thought for your sentences (nor for mine), nor for your blots (nor for mine), nor for your blunt speaking (nor for mine), nor for your badd speling (nor for mine), and if you agree to send me a blotted thought whenever you are in the mind for it, and with as little ceremony and less legibility than you would think it necessary to employ towards your printer – why, *then*, I am ready to

42

sign and seal the contract, and to rejoice in being 'articled' as your correspondent. Only *don't* let us have any constraint, any ceremony! *Don't* be civil to me when you feel rude, — nor loquacious when you incline to silence, — nor yielding in the manners when you are perverse in the mind. See how out of the world I am! Suffer me to profit by it in almost the only profitable circumstance, and let us rest from the bowing and the courtesying, you and I, on each side. You will find me an honest man on the whole, if rather hasty and prejudging, which is a different thing from prejudice at the worst. And we have great sympathies in common, and I am inclined to look up to you in many things, and to learn as much of everything as you will teach me. On the other hand you must prepare yourself to forbear and to forgive — will you? While I throw off the ceremony, I hold the faster to the kindness.

Is it true, as you say, that I 'know so "little"' of you? And is it true, as others say, that the productions of an artist do not partake of his real nature, . . that in the minor sense, man is not made in the image of God? It is *not* true, to my mind — and therefore it is not true that I know little of you, except in as far as it is true (which I believe) that your greatest works are to come. Need I assure you that I shall always hear with the deepest interest every word you will say to me of what you are doing or about to do? I hear of the 'old room' and the ' "Bells" lying about,' with an interest which you may guess at, perhaps. And when you tell me besides, of *my poems being there*, and of your caring for them so much beyond the tidemark of my hopes, the pleasure rounds itself into a charm, and prevents its own expression. Overjoyed I am with this cordial sympathy — but it is better, I feel, to try to justify it by future work than to thank you for it now. I think — if I may dare to name myself with you in the poetic relation — that we both have high views of the Art we follow, and stedfast purpose in the pursuit of it, and that we should not, either of *us*, be likely to be thrown from the course, by the casting of any Atalanta-ball of speedy popularity. But I do not know, I cannot guess, whether you are liable to be pained deeply by hard criticism and cold neglect, such as original writers like yourself are too often exposed to — or whether the love of Art is enough for you, and the exercise of Art the filling joy of your life. Not that praise must not always, of necessity, be delightful to the artist, but that it may be redundant to his content. Do you think so? or not? It appears to me that poets who, like Keats, are highly susceptible to criticism, must be jealous, in their own persons, of the future honour of their works. Because, if a work is worthy, honour must follow it though the worker should not live to see that following overtaking. Now, is it not enough that the work be honoured — enough I mean, for the worker? And is it not enough to keep down a poet's ordinary wearing anxieties, to think, that if his work be worthy it will have honour, and, if not, that 'Sparta must have nobler sons than he'? I am writing nothing applicable, I see, to anything in question, but when one falls into a favourite train of thought, one indulges oneself in thinking on. I began in thinking and wondering what sort of artistic constitution you had, being determined, as you may observe (with a sarcastic smile at the impertinence), to set about knowing as much as possible of you immediately. Then you spoke of your 'gentle audience' (*you began*), and I, who know that you have not one but many enthusiastic admirers — the 'fit and few' in the intense meaning — yet not the *diffused* fame which will come to you presently, wrote on, down the margin of the subject, till I parted from it altogether. But, after all, we are on the proper matter of sympathy. And after all, and after all that has been said and mused upon the 'natural ills', the anxiety, and wearing out experienced by the true artist, — is not the *good* immeasurably greater than the *evil?* Is it not great good, and great joy? For my part, I wonder sometimes — I surprise myself wondering — how without such an object and purpose of life, people find it worth while to live at all. And, for happiness — why, my only idea of happiness, as far as my personal enjoyment is concerned, (but I have been straightened in some respects and in comparison with the majority of livers!) lies deep in poetry and its associations. And then, the escape from pangs of heart and bodily weakness — when you throw off *yourself* — what you feel to be *yourself* — into another atmosphere and into other relations, where your life may spread its wings out new, and gather on every separate plume a brightness from the sun of the sun! Is it possible that imaginative writers should be so fond of depreciating and lamenting over their own destiny? Possible, certainly — but reasonable, not at all — and grateful, less than anything!

My faults, my faults — Shall I help you? Ah — you see them too well, I fear. And do you know that *I* also have something of your feeling about 'being about to *begin*,' or I should dare to praise you for having it. But in you, it is different — it is, in you, a virtue. When Prometheus had recounted a long list of sorrows to be endured by Io, and declared at last that he was μηδέπω ἐν προοιμίοις, poor Io burst out crying. And when the author of 'Paracelsus' and the 'Bells and Pomegranates' says that he is only 'going to begin' we may well (to take 'the opposite idea,' as you write) rejoice and clap our hands. Yet I believe that, whatever you may have done, you *will* do what is greater. It is my faith for you.

And how I should like to know what poets have been your sponsors, 'to promise and vow' for you, — and whether you have held true to early tastes, or leapt violently from them, and what books you read, and what hours you write in. How curious I could prove myself! — (if it isn't proved already).

But this is too much indeed, past all bearing, I suspect. Well, but if I ever write to you again — I mean, if you wish it — it may be in the other extreme of shortness. So do not take me for a born heroine of Richardson, or think that I sin always to this length, else, — you might indeed repent your quotation from Juliet — which I guessed at once — and of course —

> I have no joy in this contract to-day!
> It is too unadvised, too rash and sudden.

Ever faithfully yours,
ELIZABETH B. BARRETT

R.B. to E.B.B.

Hatcham, [postmark *February 11, 1845.*]

Dear Miss Barrett, — People would hardly ever tell falsehoods about a matter, if they had been let tell truth in the beginning, for it is hard to prophane one's very self, and nobody who has, for instance, used certain words and ways to a mother or a father *could,* even if by the devil's help he *would,* reproduce or mimic them with any effect to anybody else that was to be won over — and so, if 'I love you' were always outspoken when it might be, there would, I suppose, be no fear of its desecration at any after time. But lo! only last night, I had to write, on the part of Mr. Carlyle, to a certain ungainly, foolish gentleman who keeps back from him, with all the fussy impotence of stupidity (not bad feeling, alas! for *that* we could deal with) a certain MS. letter of Cromwell's which completes the collection now going to press; and this long-ears had to be 'dear Sir'd and obedient servanted' till I *said* (to use a mild word) 'commend me to the sincerities of this kind of thing.'! When I spoke of you knowing little of me, one of the senses in which I meant so was this — that I would not well vowel-point my common-place letters and syllables with a masoretic *other* sound and sense, make my 'dear' something intenser than 'dears' in ordinary, and 'yours ever' a thought more significant than the run of its like. And all this came of your talking of 'tiring me,' 'being too envious,' &c.&c., which I should never have heard of had the plain truth looked out of my letter with its unmistakable eyes. *Now*, what you say of the 'bowing,' and convention that is to be, and *tant de façons* that are not to be, helps me once and for ever — for have I not a right to say simply that, for reasons I know, for other reasons I don't exactly know, but might if I chose to think a little, and for still other reasons which, most likely all the choosing and thinking in the world would not make me know, I had rather hear from you than see anybody else. Never you care, dear noble Carlyle, nor you, my own friend Alfred over the sea, nor a troop of true lovers! — Are not their fates written? there! Don't you answer this, please, but, mind it is on record, and now then, with a lighter conscience I shall begin replying to your questions. But then — what I have printed gives *no* knowledge of me — it evidences abilities of various kinds, if you will — and a dramatic sympathy with certain modifications of passion . . . *that* I think — But I never have begun, even, what I hope I was born to begin and end — 'R.B. a poem' — and next, if I speak (and, God knows, feel), as if what you have read were sadly imperfect demonstrations of even mere ability, it is from no absurd vanity, though it might seem so — these scenes and song-scraps *are* such mere and very escapes of my inner power, which lives in me like the light in those crazy Mediterranean phares I have watched at sea, wherein the light is ever revolving in a dark gallery, bright and alive, and only after a weary interval leaps out, for a moment, from the one narrow chink, and then goes on with the blind wall between it and you; and, no doubt, *then*, precisely, does the poor drudge that carries the cresset set himself most busily to trim the wick — for don't think I want to say I have not worked hard — (this head of mine knows better) — but the work has been *inside*, and not when at stated times I held up my light to you — and, that there is no self-delusion here, I would prove to you (and nobody else), even by opening this desk I write on, and showing what stuff, in the way of wood, I *could* make a great bonfire with, if I might only knock the whole clumsy top off my tower! Of course, every writing body says the same, so I gain nothing by the avowal; but when I remember how I have done what was published, and half done what may never be, I say with some right, you can know but little of me. Still, I *hope* sometimes, though phrenologists will have it that I *cannot*, and am doing better with this darling 'Luria' — so safe in my head, and a tiny slip of paper I cover with my thumb!

Then you inquire about my 'sensitiveness to criticism,' and I shall be glad to tell you exactly, because I have, more than once, taken a course you might else not understand. I shall live always — that is for me — I am living here this 1845, that is for London. I write from a thorough conviction that it is the duty of me, and with the belief that, after every drawback and shortcoming, I do my best, all things considered — that is for *me*, and, so being, the not being listened to by one human creature would, I hope, in nowise affect me. But of course I must, if for merely scientific purposes, know all about this 1845, its ways and doings, and something I do know, as that for a dozen cabbages, if I pleased to grow them in the garden here, I might demand, say, a dozen pence at Covent Garden Market, — and that for a dozen scenes, of the average goodness, I may challenge as many plaudits at the theatre close by; and a dozen pages of verse, brought to the Rialto where verse-merchants most do congregate, ought to bring me a fair proportion of the Reviewers' gold currency, seeing the other traders pouch their winnings, as I do see. Well, when they won't pay me for my cabbages, nor praise me for my poems, I may, if I please, say 'more's the shame,' and bid both parties 'decamp to the crows,' in Greek phrase, and *yet* go very lighthearted back to a garden-full of rose-trees, and a soul-full of comforts. If they had bought my greens I should have been able to buy the last number of *Punch*, and go through the toll-gate of Waterloo Bridge, and give the blind clarionet-player a trifle, and all without changing my gold. If they had taken to my books, my father and mother would have been proud of this and the other 'favourable critique,' and — at least so folks hold — I should have to pay Mr. Moxon less by a few pounds, whereas — but you see! Indeed I force myself to say ever and anon, in the interest of the market-gardeners regular, and Keatses proper, 'It's nothing to *you*, critics, hucksters, all of you, if I *have* this garden and this conscience — I might go die at Rome, or take to gin and the newspaper, for what *you* would care!' So I don't quite lay open my resources to everybody. But it does so happen, that I have met with much more than I could have expected in this matter of kindly and prompt recognition. I never wanted a real set of good hearty praisers — and no bad reviewers — I am quite content with my share. No — what I laughed at in my 'gentle audience' is a sad trick the real admirers have of admiring at the wrong place — enough to make an apostle swear. *That* does make me savage — *never* the other kind of people; why, think now — take your own 'Drama of Exile' and let *me* send it to the first twenty men and women that shall knock at your door to-day and after — of whom the first five are the Postman, the seller of cheap sealing-wax, Mr. Hawkins Junr, the Butcher for orders, and the Tax-gatherer — will you let me, by Cornelius Agrippa's assistance, force these five and these fellows to read, and report on, this 'Drama' — and, when I have put these faithful reports into fair English, do you believe they would be better than, if as good, as, the general run of Periodical criticisms? Not they, I will venture to affirm. But then — once again, I get these people together and give them your book, and persuade them, moreover, that by praising it, the Postman will be helping its author to divide Long Acre into two beats, one of which she will take with half the salary and all the red collar, — that a sealing-wax vendor will see red wafers brought into vogue, and so on with the rest — and won't you just wish for your *Spectators* and *Observers* and Newcastle-upon-Tyne-Hebdomadal *Mercuries* back again! You see the inference — I do sincerely esteem it a perfectly providential and miraculous thing that they are so well-behaved in ordinary, these critics; and for Keats and Tennyson to 'go softly all their days' for a gruff word or two is quite inexplicable to me, and always has been. Tennyson reads the *Quarterly* and does as they bid him, with the most solemn face in the world — out goes this, in goes that, all is changed and ranged. Oh me!

Out comes the sun, in comes the *Times* and eleven strikes (it *does*) already, and I have to go to Town, and I have no alternative but that this story of the Critic and Poet, 'the Bear and the Fiddle,' should 'begin but break off in the middle'; yet I doubt — nor will you henceforth, I know, say, 'I vex you, I am sure, by this lengthy writing.' Mind that spring is coming, for all this snow; and know me for yours ever faithfully,

R. BROWNING.

I don't dare — yet I will — ask *can* you read this? Because I *could* write a little better, but not so fast. Do you keep writing just as you do now!

* * *

E.B.B. to R.B.

50 Wimpole Street: March 20, 1845.

Whenever I delay to write to you, dear Mr. Browning, it is not, be sure, that I take my 'own good time,' but submit to my own bad time. It was kind of you to wish to know how I was, and not unkind of me to suspend my answer to your question — for indeed I have not been very well, nor have had much heart for saying so. This implacable weather! this east wind that seems to blow through the sun and moon! who can be well in such a wind? Yet for me, I should not grumble. There has been nothing very bad the matter with me, as there used to be — I only grow weaker than usual, and learn my lesson of being mortal, in a corner — and then all this must end! April is coming. There will be both a May and a June if we live to see such things, and perhaps, after all, we may. And as to seeing *you* besides, I observe that you distrust me, and that perhaps you penetrate my morbidity and guess how when the moment comes to see a living human face to which I am not accustomed, I shrink and grow pale in the spirit. Do you? You are learned in human nature, and you know the consequences of leading such a secluded life as mine — notwithstanding all my fine philosophy about social duties and the like — well — if you have such knowledge or if you have it not, I cannot say, but I do say that I will indeed see you when the warm weather has revived me a little, and put the earth 'to rights' again so as to make pleasures of the sort possible. For if you think that I shall not *like* to see you, you are wrong, for all your learning. But I shall be afraid of you at first — though I am not, in writing thus. You are Paracelsus, and I am a recluse, with nerves that have been all broken on the rack, and now hang loosely — quivering at a step and breath.

And what you say of society draws me on to many comparative thoughts of your life and mine. You seem to have drunken of the cup of life full, with the sun shining on it. I have lived only inwardly; or with *sorrow,* for a strong emotion. Before this seclusion of my illness, I was secluded still, and there are few of the youngest women in the world who have not seen more, heard more, known more, of society, than I, who am scarcely to be called young now. I grew up in the country — had no social opportunities, had my heart in books and poetry, and my experience in reveries. My sympathies drooped towards the ground like an untrained honeysuckle — and but for *one*, in my own house — but of this I cannot speak. It was a lonely life, growing green like the grass around it. Books and dreams were what I lived in — and domestic life only seemed to buzz gently around, like the bees about the grass. And so time passed, and passed — and afterwards, when my illness came and I seemed to stand at the edge of the world with all done, and no prospect (as appeared at one time) of ever passing the threshold of one room again; why then, I turned to thinking with some bitterness (after the greatest sorrow of my life had given me room and time to breathe) that I had stood blind in this temple I was about to leave — that I had seen no Human nature, that my brothers and sisters of the earth were *names* to me, that I had beheld no great mountain or river, nothing in fact. I was as a man dying who had not read Shakespeare, and it was too late! do you understand? And do you also know what a disadvantage this ignorance is to my art? Why if I live on and yet do not escape from this seclusion, do you not perceive that I labour under signal disadvantages — that I am, in a manner, as a *blind poet?* Certainly, there is a compensation to a degree. I have had much of the inner life, and from the habit of self-consciousness and self-analysis, I make great guesses at Human nature in the main. But how willingly I would as a poet exchange some of this lumbering, ponderous, helpless knowledge of books, for some experience of life and man, for some . . .

But all grumbling is a vile thing. We should all thank God for our measures of life, and think them enough for each of us. I write so, that you may not mistake what I wrote before in relation to society, although you do not see from my point of view; and that you may understand what I mean fully when I say, that I have lived all my chief *joys*, and indeed nearly all emotions that go warmly by that name and relate to myself personally, in poetry and in poetry alone. Like to write? Of course, of course I do. I seem to live while I write — it is life, for me. Why, what is to live? Not to eat and drink and breathe, — but to feel the life in you down all the fibres of being, passionately and joyfully. And thus, one lives in composition surely — not always — but when the wheel goes round and the procession is uninterrupted. Is it not so with you? oh — it must be so. For the rest, there will be necessarily a reaction; and, in my own particular case, whenever I see a poem of mine in print, or even smoothly transcribed, the reaction is most painful. The pleasure, the sense of power, without which I could not write a line, is gone in a moment; and nothing remains but disappointment and humiliation. I never wrote a poem which you could not persuade me to tear to pieces if you took me at the right moment! I have a *seasonable* humility, I do assure you.

How delightful to talk about oneself; but as you 'tempted me and I did eat,' I entreat your longsuffering of my sin, and ah! if you would but sin back so in turn! You and I seem to meet in a mild contrarious harmony . . as in the 'si no, si no' of an Italian duet. I want to see more of men, and you have seen too much, you say. I am in ignorance, and you, in satiety. 'You don't even care about reading now.' Is it possible? And I am as 'fresh' about reading, as ever I was — as long as I keep out of the shadow of the dictionaries and of theological controversies, and the like. Shall I whisper it to you under the memory of the last rose of last summer? *I am very fond of romances*; yes! and I read them not only as some wise people are known to do, for the sake of the eloquence here and the sentiment there, and the graphic intermixtures here and there, but for the story! just as little children would, sitting on their papa's knee. My childish love of a story never wore out with my love of plum cake, and now there is not a hole in it. I make it a rule, for the most part, to read all the romances that other people are kind enough to write — and woe to the miserable wight who tells me how the third volume endeth. Have you in you any surviving innocence of this sort? or do you call it idiocy? If you do, I will forgive you, only smiling to myself — I give you notice, — with a smile of superior pleasure! Mr. Chorley made me quite laugh the other day by recommending Mary Howitt's 'Improvisatore,' with a sort of deprecating reference to the *descriptions* in the book, just as if I never read a novel — I! I wrote a confession back to him which made him shake his head perhaps, and now I confess to *you*, unprovoked. I am one who could have forgotten the plague, listening to Boccaccio's stories; and I am not ashamed of it. I do not even 'see the better part,' I am so silly.

Ah! you tempt me with a grand vision of Prometheus! I, who have just escaped with my life, after treading Milton's ground, you would send me to Æschylus's. No, *I do not dare*. And besides . . . I am inclined to think that we want new *forms*, as well as thoughts. The old gods are dethroned. Why should we go back to the antique moulds, classical moulds, as they are so improperly called? If it is a necessity of Art to do so, why then those critics are right who hold that Art is exhausted and the world too worn out for poetry. I do not, for my part, believe this: and I believe the so-called necessity of Art to be the mere feebleness of the artist. Let us all aspire rather to *Life*, and let the dead bury their dead. If we have but courage to face these conventions, to touch this low ground, we shall take strength from it instead of losing it; and of that, I am intimately persuaded. For there is poetry *everywhere*; the 'treasure' (see the old fable) lies all over the field. And then Christianity is a worthy *myth*, and poetically acceptable.

I had much to say to you, or at least something, of the 'blind hopes' &c., but am ashamed to take a step into a new sheet. If you mean 'to travel,' why, I shall have to miss you. Do you really mean it? How is the play going on? and the poem?

May God bless you!

Ever and truly yours,

E.B.B.

* * *

R. B. to E. B. B.

Tuesday Evening.
[postmark *May 21, 1845*.]

I trust to you for a true account of how you are — if tired, if not tired, if I did wrong in any thing, — or, if you please, *right* in any thing — (only, not one more word about my 'kindness,' which, to get done with, I will grant is exceptive) — but, let us so arrange matters if possible, — and why should it not be — that my great happiness, such as it will be if I see you, as this morning, from time to time, may be obtained at the cost of as little inconvenience to you as we can contrive. For an instance — just what strikes me — they all say here I speak very loud — (a trick caught from having often to talk with a deaf relative of mine). And did I stay too long?

I will tell *you* unhesitatingly of such 'corrigenda' — nay, I will again say, do not humiliate me — *do not* again, — by calling me 'kind' in that way.

I am proud and happy in your friendship — now and ever. May God bless you!

R.B.

E. B. B. to R. B.

Wednesday Morning.
[postmark *May 22, 1845.*]

Indeed there was nothing wrong — how could there be? And there was everything right — as how should there not be? And as for the 'loud speaking,' I did not hear any — and, instead of being worse, I ought to be better for what was certainly (to speak it, or be silent of it), happiness and honour to me yesterday.

Which reminds me to observe that you are so restricting our vocabulary, as to be ominous of silence in a full sense, presently. First, one word is not to be spoken — and then, another is not. And why? Why deny me the use of such words as have natural feelings belonging to them — and how can the use of such be 'humiliating' to *you?* If my heart were open to you, you could see nothing offensive to you in any thought there or trace of thought that has been there — but it is hard for you to understand, with all your psychology (and to be reminded of it I have just been looking at the preface of some poems by some Mr. Gurney where he speaks of 'the reflective wisdom of a Wordsworth and the profound psychological utterances of a Browning') it is hard for you to understand what my mental position is after the peculiar experience I have suffered, and what τι εμοι και σοι a sort of feeling is irrepressible from me to you, when, from the height of your brilliant happy sphere, you ask, as you did ask, for personal intercourse with me. What words but 'kindness' . . but 'gratitude' — but I will not in any case be *unkind* and *un-*

53

grateful, and do what is displeasing to you. And let us both leave the subject with the words — because we perceive in it from different points of view; we stand on the black and white sides of the shield; and there is no coming to a conclusion.

But you will come really on Tuesday — and again, when you like and can together — and it will not be more 'inconvenient' to me to be pleased, I suppose, than it is to people in general — will it, do you think? Ah — how you misjudge! Why it must obviously and naturally be delightful to me to receive you here when you like to come, and it cannot be necessary for me to say so in set words — believe it of

Your friend,
E.B.B.

[Robert Browning's letter, to which Elizabeth Barrett Barrett's letter of May 24 is an answer, was destroyed.]

E.B.B. to R.B.

Friday Evening.
[postmark *May 24, 1845.*]

I intended to write to you last night and this morning, and could not — you do not know what pain you give me in speaking so wildly. And if I disobey you, my dear friend, in speaking, (I for my part) of your wild speaking, I do it, not to displease you, but to be in my own eyes, and before God, a little more worthy, or less unworthy, of a generosity from which I recoil by instinct and at the first glance, yet conclusively; and because my silence would be the most disloyal of all means of expression, in reference to it. Listen to me then in this. You have said some intemperate things . . . fancies, — which you will not say over again, nor unsay, but *forget at once*, and *for ever*, *having said at all*; and which (so) will die out between *you and me alone*, like a misprint between you and the printer. And this you will do *for my sake* who am your friend (and you have none truer) — and this I ask, because it is a condition necessary to our future liberty of intercourse. You remember — surely you do — that I am in the most exceptional of positions; and that, just *because of it*, I am able to receive you as I did on Tuesday; and that, for me to listen to 'unconscious exaggerations,' is as unbecoming to the humilities of my position, as unpropitious (which is of more consequence) to the prosperities of yours. Now, if there should be one word of answer attempted to this; or of reference; *I must not* . . I *will not see you again* — and you will justify me later in your heart. So for my sake you will not say it — I think you will not — and spare me the sadness of having to break through an intercourse just as it is promising pleasure to me; to me who have so many sadnesses and so few pleasures. You will! — and I need not be uneasy — and I shall owe you that tranquillity, as one gift of many. For, that I have much to receive from you in all the free gifts of thinking, teaching, master-spirits, . . *that*, I know! — it is my own praise that I appreciate you, as none can more. Your influence and help in poetry will be full of good and gladness to me — for with many to love me in this house, there is no one to judge me . . *now*. Your friendship and sympathy will be dear and precious to me all my life, if you indeed leave them with me so long or so little. Your mistakes in me . . which *I* cannot mistake (— and which have humbled me by too much honouring —) I put away gently, and with grateful tears in my eyes; because *all that hail* will beat down and spoil crowns, as well as 'blossoms.'

If I put off next Tuesday to the week after — I mean your visit, — shall you care much? For the relations I named to you, are to be in London next week; and I am to see one of my aunts whom I love, and have not met since my great affliction — and it will all seem to come over again, and I shall be out of spirits and nerves. On Tuesday week you can bring a tomahawk and do the criticism, and I shall try to have my courage ready for it — Oh, you will do me so much good — and Mr. Kenyon calls me 'docile' sometimes I assure you; when he wants to flatter me out of being obstinate — and in good earnest, I believe I shall do everything you tell me. The 'Prometheus' is done — but the monodrama is where it was — and the novel, not at all. But I think of some half promises half given, about something I read for 'Saul' — and the 'Flight of the Duchess' — where is she?

You are not displeased with me? *no, that* would be hail and lightning together — I do not write as I might, of some words of yours — but you know that I am not a stone, even if silent like one. And if in the *un*-silence, I have said one word to vex you, pity me for having had to say it — and for the rest, may God bless you far beyond the reach of vexation from my words or my deeds!

Your friend in grateful regard,

E.B.B.

R. B. to E. B. B.

Saturday Morning.
[postmark *May 24, 1845.*]

Don't you remember I told you, once on a time, that you 'knew nothing of me'? whereat you demurred — but I meant what I said, and knew it was so. To be grand in a simile, for every poor speck of a Vesuvius or a Stromboli in my microcosm there are huge layers of ice and pits of black cold water — and I make the most of my two of three fire-eyes, because I know by experience, alas, how these tend to extinction — and the ice grows and grows — still this last is true part of me, most characteristic part, *best* part perhaps, and I disown nothing — only, — when you talked of '*knowing* me'! Still, I am utterly unused, of these late years particularly, to dream of communicating anything about *that* to another person (all my writings are purely dramatic as I am always anxious to say) that when I make never so little an attempt, no wonder if I *bungle* notably — 'language,' too, is an organ that never studded this heavy heavy head of mine. Will you not think me very brutal if I tell you I could almost smile at your misapprehension of what I meant to write? — Yet I *will* tell you, because it will undo the bad effect of my thoughtlessness, and at the same time exemplify the point I have all along been honestly earnest to set you right upon . . my real inferiority to you; just that and no more. I wrote to you, in an unwise moment, on the spur of being again 'thanked,' and, unwisely writing just as if thinking to myself, said what must have looked absurd enough as seen apart from the horrible counterbalancing never-to-be-written *rest of me* — by

56

the side of which, could it be written and put before you, my note would sink to its proper and relative place, and become a mere 'thank you' for your good opinion — which I assure you is far too generous — for I really believe you to be my superior in many respects, and feel uncomfortable till *you* see that, too — since I hope for your sympathy and assistance, and frankness is everything in such a case. I do assure you, that had you read my note, *only* having '*known*' so much of me as is implied in having inspected, for instance, the contents, merely, of that fatal and often-referred-to 'portfolio' there (*Dii meliora piis!*), you would see in it, (the note not the portfolio) the blandest utterance ever mild gentleman gave birth to. But I forgot that one may make too much noise in a silent place by playing the few notes on the 'ear-piercing fife' which in Othello's regimental band might have been thumped into decent subordination by his 'spirit-stirring drum' — to say nothing of gong and ophicleide. Will you forgive me, on promise to remember for the future, and be more considerate? Not that you must too much despise me, neither; nor, of all things, apprehend I am attitudinizing à la Byron, and giving you to understand unutterable somethings, longings for Lethe and all that — far from it! I never committed murders, and sleep the soundest of sleeps — but 'the heart is desperately wicked,' that is true, and though I dare not say 'I know' mine, yet I have had signal opportunities, I who began life from the beginning, and can forget nothing (but names, and the date of the battle of Waterloo), and have known good and wicked men and women, gentle and simple, shaking hands with Edmund Kean and Father Mathew, you and — Ottima! Then, I had a certain faculty of self-consciousness, years and years ago, at which John Mill wondered, and which ought to be improved by this time, if constant use helps at all — and, meaning, on the whole, to be a Poet, if not *the* Poet . . for I am vain and ambitious some nights, — I do myself justice, and dare call things by their names to myself, and say boldly, this I love, this I hate, this I would do, this I would not do, under all kinds of circumstances, — and talking (thinking) in this style *to myself*, and beginning, however tremblingly, in spite of conviction, to write in this style *for myself* — on the top of the desk which contains my 'Songs of the Poets — NO.1 M.P.', I wrote, — what you now forgive, I know! Because I am, from my heart, sorry that by a foolish fit of inconsideration I should have given pain for a minute to you, towards whom, on every account, I would rather soften and 'sleeken every word as to a bird' . . (and, not such a bird as my black self that go screeching about the world for 'dead horse' — corvus (picus) — mirandola!) I, too, who have been at such pains to acquire the reputation I enjoy in the world, — (ask Mr. Kenyon,) and who dine, and wine, and dance and enhance the company's pleasure till they make me ill and I keep house, as of late: Mr. Kenyon, (for I only quote where you may verify if you please) *he* says my common sense strikes him, and its contrast with my muddy metaphysical poetry! And so it shall strike you — for though I am glad that, since you *did* misunderstand me, you said so, and have given me an opportunity of doing by another way what I wished to do in *that*, — yet, if you had *not* alluded to my writing, as I meant you should not, you would have certainly understood *something* of its drift when you found me next Tuesday precisely the same quiet (no, for I feel I speak too loudly, in spite of your kind disclaimer, but —) the same mild man-about-town you were gracious to, the other morning — for, indeed, my own way of worldly life is marked out long ago, as precisely as yours can be, and I am set going with a hand, winker-wise, on each side of my head, and a directing finger before my eyes, to say nothing of an instinctive dread I have that a certain whip-lash is vibrating somewhere in the neighbourhood in playful readiness! So 'I hope here be proofs,' Dogberry's satisfaction that, first, I am but a very poor creature compared to you and entitled by my wants to look up to you, — all I meant to say from the first of the first — and that, next, I shall be too much punished if, for this piece of mere inconsideration, you deprive me, more or less, or sooner or later, of the pleasure of seeing you, — a little over boisterous gratitude for which, perhaps, caused all the mischief! The reasons you give for deferring my visits next week are too cogent for me to dispute — that is too true — and, being now and henceforward 'on my good behaviour,' I will at once cheerfully submit to them, if needs must — but should your mere kindness and forethought, as I half suspect, have induced you to take such a step, you will now smile with me, at this new and very unnecessary addition to the 'fears of me' I have got so triumphantly over in your case! Wise man, was I not, to clench my first favourable impression so adroitly . . like a recent Cambridge worthy, my sister heard of; who, being on his theological (or rather, scripture-historical) examination, was asked by the Tutor, who wished to let him off easily, 'who was the first King of Israel?' — 'Saul' answered the trembling youth. 'Good!' nodded approvingly the Tutor. 'Otherwise called *Paul*,' subjoined the youth in his elation! Now I have begged pardon, and blushingly assured you *that* was only a slip of the tongue, and that I did really *mean* all the while, (Paul or no Paul), the veritable son of Kish, he that owned the asses, and found listening to the harp the best of all things for an evil spirit! Pray write me a line to say, 'Oh . . if *that's* all!' and remember me for good (which is very compatible with a moment's stupidity) and let me not for one fault, (and that the only one that shall be), lose *any pleasure* . . for your friendship I am sure I have not lost — God bless you, my dear friend!

R. BROWNING.

And by the way, will it not be better, as co-operating with you more effectually in your kind promise to forget the 'printer's error' in my blotted proof, to send me back that same 'proof,' if you have not inflicted proper and summary justice on it? When Mephistopheles last came to see us in this world outside here, he counselled sundry of us 'never to write a letter, — and never to burn one' — do you know that? But I never mind what I am told! Seriously, I am ashamed . . I shall next ask a servant for my paste in the 'high fantastical' style of my own 'Luria.'

E.B.B. to R.B.

Sunday.
[May 25, 1845.]

I owe you the most humble of apologies dear Mr. Browning, for having spent so much solemnity on so simple a matter, and I hasten to pay it; confessing at the same time (as why should I not?) that I am quite as much ashamed of myself as I ought to be, which is not a little. You will find it difficult to believe me perhaps when I assure you that I never made such a mistake (I mean of over-seriousness to indefinite compliments), no, never in my life before — indeed my sisters have often jested with me (in matters of which they were cognizant) on my supernatural indifference to the superlative degree in general, as if it meant nothing in grammar. I usually know well that 'boots' may be called for in this world of ours, just as you called for yours; and that to bring 'Bootes,' were the vilest of mal-à-pro-pos-ities. Also, I should have understood 'boots' where you wrote it, in the letter in question; if it had not been for *the relation of two things* in it—and now I perfectly seem to see *how* I mistook that relation; (*'seem to see'*; because I have not looked into the letter again since your last night's commentary, and will not—) inasmuch as I have observed before in my own mind, that a good deal of what is called obscurity in you, arises from a habit of very subtle association; so subtle, that you are probably unconscious of it, . . and the effect of which is to throw together on the same level and in the same light, things of likeness and unlikeness—till the reader grows confused as I did, and takes one for another. I may say however, in a poor justice to myself, that I wrote what I wrote so unfortunately, *through reverence for you*, and not at all from vanity on my own account . . although I do feel palpably while I write these words here and now, that I might as well leave them unwritten; for that no man of the world who ever lived in the world (not even *you*) could be expected to believe them, though said, sung, and sworn.

For the rest, it is scarcely an apposite moment for you to talk, even 'dramatically,' of my 'superiority' to you, . . unless you mean, which perhaps you do mean, my superiority in *simplicity*—and, verily, to some of the 'adorable ingenuousness,' sacred to the shade of Simpson, I may put in a modest claim, . . 'and have my claim allowed.' 'Pray do not mock me' I quote again from your Shakespeare to you who are a dramatic poet; and I will admit anything that you like, (being humble just now)—even that I *did not know you*. I was certainly innocent of the knowledge of the 'ice and cold water' you introduce me to, and am only just shaking my head, as Flush would, after a first wholesome plunge. Well—if I do not know you, I shall learn, I suppose, in time. I am ready to try humbly to learn—and I may perhaps—if you are not done in Sanscrit, which is too hard for me, . . notwithstanding that I had the pleasure yesterday to hear, from America, of my profound skill in 'various languages less known than Hebrew'!—a liberal paraphrase on Mr. Horne's large fancies on the like subject, and a satisfactory reputation in itself—as long as it is not necessary to deserve it. So I here enclose to you your letter back again, as you wisely desire; although you never could doubt, I hope, for a moment, of its safety with me in the completest of senses: and then, from the heights of my superior . . stultity, and other qualities of the like order, . . I venture to advise you . . however (to speak of the letter critically, and as the dramatic composition it is) it is to be admitted to be very beautiful, and well worthy of the rest of its kin in the portfolio, . . 'Lays of the Poets,' or otherwise, . . . I venture to advise you to burn it at once. And then, my dear friend, I ask you (having some claim) to burn at the same time the letter I was fortunate enough to write to you on Friday, and this present one — don't send them back to me; I hate to have letters sent back — but burn them for me and never mind Mephistopheles. After which friendly turn, you will do me the one last kindness of forgetting all this exquisite nonsense, and of refraining from mentioning it, by breath or pen, *to me or another*. Now I trust you so far: — you will put it with the date of the battle of Waterloo — and I, with every date in chronology; seeing that I can remember none of them. And we will shuffle the cards and take patience, and begin the game again, if you please — and I shall bear in mind that you are a dramatic poet, which is not the same thing, by any means, with *us* of the primitive simplicities, who don't tread on cothurns nor shift the mask in the scene. And I will reverence you both as 'a poet' and as '*the* poet'; because it is no false 'ambition,' but a right you have — and one which those who live longest, will see justified to the uttermost. In the meantime I need not ask Mr. Kenyon if you have any sense, because I have no doubt that you have quite sense enough — and even if I had a doubt, I shall prefer judging for myself without interposition; which I can do, you know, as long as you like to come and see me. And you can come this week if you do like it — because our relations don't come till the end of it, it appears — not that I made a pretence 'out of kindness' — pray don't judge me so outrageously — but if you like to come . . not on Tuesday . . but on Wednesday at three o'clock, I shall be very glad to see you; and I, for one, shall have forgotten everything by that time; being quick at forgetting my own faults usually. If Wednesday does not suit you, I am not sure that I *can* see you this week — but it depends on circumstances. Only don't think yourself *obliged* to come on Wednesday. You know I *began* by entreating you to be open and sincere with me — and no more — I *require* no 'sleekening of every word.' I love the truth and can bear it — whether in word or deed — and those who have known me longest would tell you so fullest. Well! — May God bless you. We shall know each other some day perhaps — and I am

Always and faithfully your friend,

E.B.B.

R.B. to E.B.B.

[postmark *May 26, 1845.*]

Nay — I *must* have last word — as all people in the wrong desire to have — and then, no more of the subject. You said I had given you *great pain* — so long as I stop *that*, think anything of me you choose or can! But *before* your former letter came, I saw the pre-ordained uselessness of mine. Speaking is to some *end*, (apart from foolish self-relief, which, after all, I can do without) — and where there is *no* end — you see! or, to finish characteristically — since the offering to cut off one's right hand to save anybody a headache, is in vile taste, even for our melodramas, seeing that it was never yet believed in on the stage or off it, — how much worse to really make the ugly chop, and afterwards come sheepishly in, one's arm in a black sling, and find that the delectable gift had changed aching to nausea! There! And now, 'exit, prompt-side, nearest door, Luria' — and enter R.B. — next Wednesday, — as boldly as he suspects most people do just after they have been soundly frightened!

I shall be most happy to see you on the day and at the hour you mention.

God bless you, my dear friend,
R.B.

E.B.B. to R.B.

Monday Morning.
[postmark *May 27, 1845.*]

You will think me the most changeable of all the changeable; but indeed it is *not* my fault that I cannot, as I wished, receive you on

Wednesday. There was a letter this morning; and our friends not only come to London but come to this house on Tuesday (to-morrow) to pass two or three days, until they settle in an hotel for the rest of the season. Therefore you see, it is doubtful whether the two days may not be three, and the three days four; but if they go away in time, and if Saturday should suit you, I will let you know by a word; and you can answer by a yea or nay. While they are in the house, I must give them what time I can – and indeed, it is something to dread altogether.

Tuesday.

I send you the note I had begun before receiving yours of last night, and also a fragment from Mrs. Hedley's herein enclosed, a full and complete certificate, . . that you may know . . quite *know*, . . what the real and only reason of the obstacle to Wednesday is. On Saturday perhaps, or on Monday more certainly, there is likely to be no opposition, . . at least not on the 'côté gauche' (*my* side!) to our meeting – but I will let you know more.

For the rest, we have both been a little unlucky, there's no denying, in overcoming the embarrassments of a first acquaintance – but suffer me to say as one other last word, (and *quite, quite the last this time!*) in case there should have been anything approaching, however remotely, to a distrustful or unkind tone in what I wrote on Sunday, (and I have a sort of consciousness that in the process of my self-scorning I was not in the most sabbatical of moods perhaps –) that I do recall and abjure it, and from my heart entreat your pardon for it, and profess, notwithstanding it, neither to 'choose' nor 'to be able' to think otherwise of you than I have done, . . as of one *most* generous and *most* loyal; for that if I chose, I could not; and that if I could, I should not choose.

Ever and gratefully your friend,
E.B.B.

– And now we shall hear of 'Luria,' shall we not? and much besides. And Miss Mitford has sent me the most high comical of letters to read, addressed to her by 'R.B. Haydon historical painter' which has made me quite laugh; and would make *you*; expressing his righteous indignation at the 'great fact' and gross impropriety of any man who has 'thoughts too deep for tears' agreeing to wear a 'bag-wig' . . the case of poor Wordsworth's going to court, you know. — Mr. Haydon being infinitely serious all the time, and yet holding the doctrine of the divine right of princes in his left hand.

How is your head? may I be hoping the best for it? May God bless you.

R. B. to E. B. B.

[postmark *May 28, 1845.*]

Saturday, Monday, as you shall appoint — no need to say that, or my thanks — but this note troubles you, out of my bounden duty to help you, or Miss Mitford, to make the Painter run violently down a steep place into the sea, if that will amuse you, by further informing him, what I know on the best authority, that Wordsworth's 'bag-wig,' or at least, the more important of his court-habiliments, were considerably furnished for the nonce by *Mr. Rogers* from his own wardrobe, to the manifest advantage of the Laureate's pocket, but more problematic improvement of his person, when one thinks on the astounding difference of 'build' in the two Poets: — the fact should be put on record, if only as serving to render less chimerical a promise sometimes figuring in the columns of provincial newspapers — that the two apprentices, some grocer or other advertises for, will be 'boarded and *clothed* like *one* of the family.' May not your unfinished (really good) head of the great man have been happily kept waiting for the body which can now be added on, with all this picturesqueness of circumstances. Precept on precept . . but then, *line upon line*, is allowed by as good authority, and may I not draw *my* confirming black line after yours, yet not break pledge? I am most grateful to you for doing me justice — doing yourself, your own judgment, justice, since even the play-wright of Theseus and the Amazon found it one of his hardest devices to 'write me a speech, lest the lady be frightened, wherein it shall be said that I, Pyramus, am not Pyramus, but &c. &c.' God bless you — one thing more, but one — you *could never have* misunderstood the *asking for the letter again,* I feared you might refer to it 'pour constater le fait' —

And now I am yours —
R.B.

My head is all but well now; thank you.

E.B.B. to R.B.

Friday Morning.
[postmark *May 30, 1845.*]

Just one word to say that if Saturday, to-morrow, should be fine — because in the case of its raining I *shall not expect you;* you will find me at three o'clock.

Yes — the circumstance of the costume were mentioned in the letter; Mr. Rogers' bag-wig and the rest, and David Wilkie's sword — and also that the Laureate, so equipped, fell down upon both knees in the superfluity of etiquette, and had to be picked up by two lords-in-waiting. It is a large exaggeration I do not doubt — and then I never sympathised with the sighing kept up by people about that acceptance of the Laureateship which drew the bag-wig as a corollary after it. Not that the Laureateship honoured *him,* but that he honoured it; and that, so honouring it, he preserves a symbol instructive to the masses, who are children and to be taught by symbols now as formerly. Isn't it true? or at least may it not be true? And won't the court laurel (such as it is) be all the worthier of *you* for Wordsworth's having worn it first?

And in the meantime I shall see you to-morrow perhaps? or if it should rain, on Monday at the same hour.

Ever yours, my dear friend,
E.B.B.

* * *

E.B.B. to R.B.

[postmark *July 28, 1845.*]

*** *Sunday.* — I wrote so much yesterday and then went out, not knowing very well how to speak or how to be silent (is it better to-day?) of some expressions of yours . . and of your interest in me — which are deeply affecting to my feelings — whatever else remains to be said of them. And you know that you make great mistakes, . . of fennel for hemlock, of four o'clocks for five o'clocks, and of other things of more consequence, one for another; and may not be quite right besides as to my getting well *'if I please!'* . . which reminds me a little of what Papa says sometimes when he comes into this room unexpectedly and convicts me of having dry toast for dinner, and declares angrily that obstinacy and dry toast have brought me to my present condition, and that if I *pleased* to have porter and beefsteaks instead, I should be as well as ever I was, in a month! . . But where is the need of talking of it. What I wished to say was this — that if I get better or worse . . as long as I live and to the last moment of life, I shall remember with an emotion which cannot change its character, all the generous interest and feeling you have spent on me — *wasted* on me I was going to write — but I would not provoke any answering — and in one obvious sense, it need not be so. I never shall forget these things, my dearest friend; nor remember them more coldly. God's goodness! — I believe in it, as in His sunshine here — which makes my head ache a little, while it comes in at the window, and makes most other people gayer — it does *me* good too in a different way. And so, may God bless you! and me in this . . just this, . . that I may never have the sense, . . intolerable in the remotest apprehension of it . . of being, in any way, directly or indirectly, the means of ruffling your smooth path by so much as one of my flint-stones! In the meantime you do not tire me indeed even when you go later for sooner . . and I do not tire myself even when I write longer and duller letters to you (if the last is possible) than the one I am ending now . . as the most grateful (leave me that word) of your friends.

E.B.B.

* * *

E.B.B. to R.B.

Wednesday.
[postmark *August 25, 1845.*]

But what have *I* done that you should ask what have *you* done? I have not brought any accusation, have I . . no, nor *thought* any, I am sure — and it was only the 'kindness and considerateness' — argument that was irresistible as a thing to be retorted, when your thanks came so naturally and just at the corner of an application. And then, you know, it is gravely true, seriously true, sadly true, that I am always expecting to hear or to see how tired you are at last of me! — sooner or later, you know! — But I did not mean any seriousness in that letter. No, nor did I mean . . (to pass to another question . .) to provoke you to the
　　　　　　　Mister Hayley . . so are *you* . .
reply complimentary. All I observed concerning yourself, was the *combination* — which not an idiom in chivalry could treat grammatically as a thing common to *me* and you, inasmuch as everyone who has known me for half a day, may know that, if there is anything peculiar in me, it lies for the most part in the extraordinary deficiency in this and this and this, . . there is no need to describe what. Only nuns of the strictest sect of the nunneries are rather wiser in some points, and have led less restricted lives than I have in others. And if it had not been for my 'carpet-work' ——

Well — and do you know that I have, for the last few years, taken quite to despise book-knowledge and its effect on the mind — I mean when people *live by it* as most readers by profession do, . . cloistering their souls under these roofs made with heads, when they might be under

67

the sky. Such people grow dark and narrow and low, with all their pains.

Friday. — I was writing you see before you came—and now I go on in haste to speak 'off my mind' some things which are on it. First . . of yourself; how can it be that you are unwell again, . . and that you should talk (now did you not? — did I not hear you say so?) of being 'weary in your soul' . . *you?* What should make *you,* dearest friend, weary in your soul; or out of spirits in any way? — Do . . tell me . . I was going to write without a pause — and almost I might, perhaps, . . even as one of the two hundred of your friends, . . almost I might say out that 'Do tell me.' Or is it (which I am inclined to think most probable) that you are tired of a same life and want change? It may happen to anyone some-times, and is independent of your will and choice, you know — and I know, and the whole world knows: and would it not therefore be wise of you, in that case, to fold your life new again and go abroad at once? What can make you weary in your soul, is a problem to me. You are the last from whom I should have expected such a word. And you did say so, I *think.* I *think* that it was not a mistake of mine. And *you,* . . with a full liberty, and the world in your hand for every purpose and pleasure of it! — Or is it that, being unwell, your spirits are affected by *that?* But then you might be more unwell than you like to admit —. And I am teasing you with talking of it . . am I not? — and being disagreeable is only one third of the way towards being useful, it is good to remember in time.

And then the next thing to write off my mind is . . that you must not, you must not, make an unjust opinion out of what I said to-day. I have been uncomfortable since, lest you should — and perhaps it would have been better if I had not said it apart from all context in that way; only that you could not long be a friend of mine without knowing and seeing what so lies on the surface. But then, . . as far as I am con-cerned, . . no one cares less for a 'will' than I do (and this though I never had one, . . in clear opposition to your theory which holds gen-erally nevertheless) for a will in the common things of life. Every now and then there must of course be a crossing and vexation — but in one's mere pleasures and fantasies, one would rather be crossed and vexed a little than vex a person one loves . . and it is possible to get used to the harness and run easily in it at last; and there is a side-world to hide one's thoughts in, and 'carpet-work' to be immoral on in spite of Mrs. Jameson, . . and the word 'literature' has, with me, covered a good deal of liberty as you must see . . real liberty which is never enquired into

—and it has happened throughout my life by an accident (as far as anything is accident) that my own sense of right and happiness on any important point of overt action, has never run contrariwise to the way of obedience required of me . . while in things not exactly *overt*, I and all of us are apt to act sometimes up to the limit of our means of acting, with shut doors and windows, and no waiting for cognisance or permission. Ah — and that last is the worst of it all perhaps! to be forced into concealments from the heart naturally nearest to us; and forced away from the natural source of counsel and strength! — and then, the disingenuousness — the cowardice — the 'vices of slaves'! — and everyone you see . . all my brothers, . . constrained *bodily* into submission . . apparent submission at least . . by that worst and most dishonouring of necessities, the necessity of *living*, everyone of them all, except myself, being dependent in money-matters on the inflexible will . . do you see? But what you do *not* see, what you *cannot* see, is the deep tender affection behind and below all those patriarchal ideas of governing grown up children 'in the way they *must* go!' and there never was (under the strata) a truer affection in a father's heart . . no, nor a worthier heart in itself . . a heart loyaller and purer, and more compelling to gratitude and reverence, than his, as I see it! The evil is in the system — and he simply takes it to be his duty to rule, and to make happy according to his own views of the propriety of happiness — he takes it to be his duty to rule like the Kings of Christendom, by divine right. But he loves us through and through it — and *I*, for one, love *him!* and when, five years ago, I lost what I loved best in the world beyond comparison and rivalship . . far better than himself as he knew . . for everyone who knew *me* could not choose but know what was my first and chiefest affection . . when I lost *that*, . . I felt that he stood the nearest to me on the closed grave . . or by the unclosing sea . . I do not know which nor could ask. And I will tell you that not only he has been kind and patient and forbearing to me through the tedious trial of this illness (far more trying to standers by than you have an idea of perhaps) but that he was generous and forbearing in that hour of bitter trial, and never reproached me as he might have done and as my own soul has not spared — never once said to me then or since, that if it had not been for *me*, the crown of his house would not have fallen. He *never did* . . and he might have said it, and more — and I could have answered nothing. Nothing, except that I had paid my own price — and that the price I paid was greater than his *loss* . . his!! For see how it was; and how,

69

'not with my hand but heart,' I was the cause or occasion of that misery — and though not with the intention of my heart but with its weakness, yet the *occasion,* any way!

They sent me down you know to Torquay — Dr. Chambers saying that I could not live a winter in London. The worst — what people call the worst — was apprehended for me at that time. So I was sent down with my sister to my aunt there — and he, my brother whom I loved so, was sent too, to take us there and return. And when the time came for him to leave me, I, to whom he was the dearest of friends and brothers in one . . the only one of my family who . . well, but I cannot write of these things; and it is enough to tell you that he was above us all, better than us all, and kindest and noblest and dearest to *me,* beyond comparison, any comparison, as I said — and when the time came for him to leave me I, weakened by illness, could not master my spirits or drive back my tears — and my aunt kissed them away instead of reproving me as she should have done; and said that *she* would take care that I should not be grieved . . she! . . and so she sate down and wrote a letter to Papa to tell him that he would 'break my heart' if he persisted in calling away my brother — As if hearts were broken so! I have thought bitterly since that my heart did not break for a good deal more than *that!* And Papa's answer was — burnt into me, as with fire, it is — that 'under such circumstances he did not refuse to suspend his purpose, but that he considered it to be *very wrong in me to exact such a thing'.* So there was no separation *then:* and month after month passed — and sometimes I was better and sometimes worse — and the medical men continued to say that they would not answer for my life . . they! if I were agitated — and so there was no more talk of a separation. And once *he* held my hand, . . how I remember! and said that he 'loved me better than them all and that he *would not* leave me . . till I was well,' he said! how I remember *that!* And ten days from that day the boat had left the shore which never returned; never — and he *had* left me! gone! For three days we waited — and I hoped while I could — oh — that awful agony of three days! And the sun shone as it shines to-day, and there was no more wind than now; and the sea under the windows was like this paper for smoothness — and my sisters drew the curtains back that I might see for myself how smooth the sea was, and how it could hurt nobody — and other boats came back one by one.

Remember how you wrote in your 'Gismond'

> What says the body when they spring
> Some monstrous torture-engine's whole
> Strength on it? No more says the soul,

and you never wrote anything which *lived* with me more than *that*. It is such a dreadful truth. But you knew it for truth, I hope, by your genius, and not by such proof as mine — I, who could not speak or shed a tear, but lay for weeks and months half conscious, half unconscious, with a wandering mind, and too near to God under the crushing of His hand, to pray at all. I expiated all my weak tears before, by not being able to shed then one tear — and yet they were forbearing — and no voice said 'You have done this.'

Do not notice what I have written to you, my dearest friend. I have never said so much to a living being — I never *could* speak or write of it. I asked no question from the moment when my last hope went: and since then, it has been impossible for me to speak what was in me. I have borne to do it to-day and to you, but perhaps if you were to write — so do not let this be noticed between us again — *do not!* And besides there is no need! I do not reproach myself with such acrid thoughts as I had once — I *know* that I would have died ten times over for *him*, and that therefore though it was wrong of me to be weak, and I have suffered for it and shall learn by it I hope; *remorse* is not precisely the word for me — not at least in its full sense. Still you will comprehend from what I have told you how the spring of life must have seemed to break within me *then*; and how natural it has been for me to loathe the living on — and to lose faith (even without the loathing), to lose faith in myself . . which I have done on some points utterly. It is not from the cause of illness — no. And you will comprehend too that I have strong reasons for being grateful to the forbearance. . . It would have been *cruel*, you think, to reproach me. Perhaps so! yet the kindness and patience of the desisting from reproach, are positive things all the same.

Shall I be too late for the post, I wonder? Wilson tells me that you were followed up-stairs yesterday (I write on Saturday this latter part) by somebody whom you probably took for my father. Which is Wilson's idea — and I hope not yours. No — it was neither father nor other relative of mine, but an old friend in rather an ill temper.

And so good-bye until Tuesday. Perhaps I shall . . not . . hear from you to-night. Don't let the tragedy or aught else do you harm — will you?

and try not to be 'weary in your soul' any more — and forgive me this gloomy letter I half shrink from sending you, yet will send.

May God bless you.

E.B.B.

* * *

E.B.B. to R.B.

[postmark *September 16, 1845.*]

I scarcely know how to write what is to be written nor indeed why it is to be written and to what end. I have tried in vain — and you are waiting to hear from me. I am unhappy enough even where I am happy — but ungrateful nowhere — and I thank you from my heart — profoundly from the depths of my heart . . which is nearly all I can do.

One letter I began to write and asked in it how it could become me to speak at all if *'from the beginning and at this moment you never dreamed of'* . . and there, I stopped and tore the paper; because I felt that you were too loyal and generous, for me to bear to take a moment's advantage of the same, and bend down the very flowering branch of your generosity (as it might be) to thicken a little the fence of a woman's caution and reserve. You will not say that you have not acted as if you 'dreamed' — and I will answer therefore to the general sense of your letter and former letters, and admit at once that I *did* state to you the difficulties most difficult to myself . . though not all . . and that if I had been worthier of you I should have been proportionally less in haste to 'bid you leave that subject.' I do not understand how you can seem at the same moment to have faith in my integrity and to have doubt whether all this time I may not have felt a preference for another . . which you are ready 'to serve,' you say. Which is generous in you — but in *me*, where were the integrity? Could you really hold me to be blameless, and do you think that true-hearted women act usually so? Can it be necessary for me to tell you that I could not have acted so, and did

72

not? And shall I shrink from telling you besides . . you, who have been generous to me and have a right to hear it . . and have spoken to me in the name of an affection and memory most precious and holy to me, in this same letter . . that neither now nor formerly has any man been to my feelings what you are . . and that if I were different in some respects and free in others by the providence of God, I would accept the great trust of your happiness, gladly, proudly, and gratefully; and give away my own life and soul to that end. I *would* do it . . *not, I do* . . observe! it is a truth without a consequence; only meaning that I am not all stone — only proving that I am not likely to consent to help you in wrong against yourself. You see in me what is not: — *that*, I know: and you overlook in me what is unsuitable to you . . *that* I know, and have sometimes told you. Still, because a strong feeling from some sources is self-vindicating and ennobling to the object of it, I will not say that, if it were proved to me that you felt this for me, I would persist in putting the sense of my own unworthiness between you and me — not being heroic, you know, nor pretending to be so. But something worse than even a sense of unworthiness, *God* has put between us! and judge yourself if to beat your thoughts against the immovable marble of it, can be anything but pain and vexation of spirit, waste and wear of spirit to you . . judge! The present is here to be seen . . speaking for itself! and the best future you can imagine for me, what a precarious thing it must be . . a thing for making burdens out of . . only not for your carrying, as I have vowed to my own soul As dear Mr. Kenyon said to me to-day in his smiling kindness . . 'In ten years you may be strong perhaps' — or 'almost strong'! that being the encouragement of my best friends! What would he say, do you think, if he could know or guess . . ! what *could* he say but that you were . . a poet! — and I . . still worse! *Never* let him know or guess!

And so if you are wise and would be happy (and you have excellent practical sense after all and should exercise it) you must leave me — these thoughts of me, I mean . . for if we might not be true friends for ever, I should have less courage to say the other truth. But we may be friends always . . and cannot be so separated, that your happiness, in the knowledge of it, will not increase mine. And if you will be persuaded by me, as you say, you will be persuaded *thus* . . and consent to take a resolution and force your mind at once into another channel. Perhaps I might bring you reasons of the class which you tell me 'would silence you for ever.' I might certainly tell you that my own father, if he knew that you had written to me *so*, and that I had answered you — *so*, even, would not forgive me at the end of ten years — and this, from none of the causes mentioned by me here and in no disrespect to your name and your position . . though he does not over-value poetry even in his daughter, and is apt to take the world's measures of the means of life . . but for the singular reason that he never *does* tolerate in his family (sons or daughters) the development of one class of feelings. Such an objection I could not bring to you of my own will — it rang hollow in my ears — perhaps I thought even too little of it: — and I brought to you what I thought much of, and cannot cease to think much of equally. Worldly thoughts, these are not at all, nor have been: there need be no soiling of the heart with any such: — and I will say, in reply to some words of yours, that you cannot despise the gold and gauds of the world more than I do, and should do even if I found a use for them. And if I *wished* to be very poor, in the world's sense of poverty, I *could not*, with three or four hundred a year of which no living will can dispossess me. And is it not the chief good of money, the being free from the need of thinking of it? It seems so to me.

The obstacles then are of another character, and the stronger for being so. Believe that I am grateful to you — *how* grateful, cannot be shown in words nor even in tears . . grateful enough to be truthful in all ways. You know I might have hidden myself from you — but I would not: and by the truth told of myself, you may believe in the earnestness with which I tell the other truths — of you . . and of this subject. The subject will not bear consideration — it breaks in our hands. But that God is stronger than we, cannot be a bitter thought to you but a holy thought . . while He lets me, as much as I can be anyone's, be only yours.

E.B.B.

R.B. to E.B.B.

[postmark *September 17, 1845.*]

I do not know whether you imagine the precise effect of your letter on me — very likely you do, and write it just for that — for I conceive *all* from your goodness. But before I tell you what is that effect, let me say in as few words as possible what shall stop any fear — though only for a moment and on the outset — that you have been misunderstood, that the goodness *outside*, and round and over all, hides all or anything. I understand you to signify to me that you see, at this present, insurmountable obstacles to that — can I speak it — entire gift, which I shall own, was, while I dared ask it, above my hopes — and wishes, even, so it seems to me . . and yet could not but be asked, so plainly was it dictated to me, by something quite out of those hopes and wishes. Will it help me to say that once in this Aladdin-cavern I knew I ought to stop for no heaps of jewel-fruit on the trees from the very beginning, but go on to the lamp, *the* prize, the last and best of all? Well, I understand you to pronounce that at present you believe this gift impossible — and I acquiesce entirely — I submit wholly to you; repose on you in all the faith of which I am capable. Those obstacles are solely for *you* to see and to declare . . had *I* seen them, be sure I should never have mocked you or myself by affecting to pass them over . . what *were* obstacles, I mean: but you *do* see them, I must think, — and perhaps they strike me the more from my true, honest unfeigned inability to imagine what they are, — not that I shall endeavour. After what you *also* apprise me of, I know and am joyfully confident that if ever they cease to be what you now consider them, you who see now *for me*, whom I implicitly trust in to see for me; you will *then*, too, see and remember me, and how I trust, and shall then be still trusting. And until you so see, and so inform me, I shall never utter a word — for that would involve the vilest of implications. I thank God — I *do* thank him, that in this whole matter I have been, to the utmost of my power, not unworthy of his introducing you to me, in this respect that, being no longer in the first freshness of life, and having for many years now made up my mind to the impossibility of loving any woman . . having wondered at this in the beginning, and fought not a little against it, having acquiesced in it at last, and accounted for it all to myself, and become, if anything, rather proud of it than sorry . . I say, when real love, making itself at once recognized as such, *did* reveal itself to me at last, I *did* open my heart to it with a cry — nor care for its overturning all my theory — nor mistrust its effect upon a mind set in ultimate order, so I fancied, for the few years more — nor apprehend in the least that the new element would harm what was already organized without its help. Nor have I, either, been guilty of the more pardonable folly, of treating the new feeling after the pedantic fashions and instances of the world. I have not spoken when *it* did not speak, because 'one' might speak, or has spoken, or *should* speak, and 'plead' and all that miserable work which, after all, I may well continue proud that I am not called to attempt. *Here* for instance, *now* . . 'one' should despair; but 'try again' first, and work blindly at removing those obstacles (– if I saw them, I should be silent, and only speak when a month hence, ten years hence, I could bid you look where they *were*) – and 'one' would do all this, not for the *play-acting's* sake, or to 'look the character' . . (*that* would be something quite different from folly . .) but from a not unreasonable anxiety lest by too sudden a silence, too complete an acceptance of your will; the earnestness and endurance and unabatedness . . the *truth*, in fact, of what had already been professed, should get to be questioned – But I believe that you believe me – And now that all is clear between us I will say, what you will hear, without fearing for me or yourself, that I am utterly contented . . ('grateful' I have done with . . it must go –) I accept what you give me, what those words deliver to me, as – not all I asked for . . as I said . . but as more than I ever hoped for, – *all*, in the best sense, that I deserve. That phrase in my letter which you objected to, and the other – may stand, too – I never attempted to declare, describe my feeling for you – one word of course stood for it all . . but having to put down some one *point*, so to speak, of it – you could not wonder if I took any extreme one *first* . . never minding all the untold portion that led up to it, made it possible and natural – it is true, 'I could not dream of *that*' – that I was eager to get the horrible notion away from never so flitting a visit to you, that you were thus and thus to me *on condition* of my proving just the same to you – just as if we had waited to acknowledge that the moon lighted us till we ascertained within these two or three hundred years that the earth happens to light the moon as well! But I felt that, and so said it: – now you have declared what I should never have presumed to hope – and I repeat to you that I, with all to be thankful for to God, am most of all thankful for this the last of his providences . . which is no doubt, the natural and inevitable feeling, could one always see clearly. Your regard for me is *all* success – let the rest come, or not come. In my heart's thankfulness I would . . I am sure I would promise anything that would gratify you . . but it would *not* do that, to agree, in words, to change my affections, put them elsewhere &c. &c. That would be pure foolish talking, and quite foreign to the practical results which you will attain in a better way from a higher motive. I will cheerfully promise you, however, to be 'bound by no words,' blind to no miracle; in sober earnest, it is not because I renounced once for all oxen and the owning and having to do with them, that I will obstinately turn away from any unicorn when such an apparition blesses me . . but meantime I shall walk at peace on our hills here nor go looking in all corners for the bright curved horn! And as for you . . if I did not dare 'to dream of that' —, now it is mine, my pride and joy prevent in no manner my taking the whole consolation of it at once, *now* — I will be confident that, if I obey you, I shall get no wrong for it — if, endeavouring to spare you fruitless pain, I do not eternally revert to the subject; do indeed 'quit' it just now, when no good can come of dwelling on it to you; you will never say to yourself — so I said — 'the "generous impulse" *has* worn itself out . . time is doing his usual work — this was to be expected' &c &c. You will be the first to say to me 'such an obstacle has ceased to exist . . or is now become one palpable to *you*, one *you* may try and overcome' — and I shall be there, and ready — ten years hence as now — if alive.

One final word on the other matters — the 'worldly matters' — I shall own I alluded to them rather ostentatiously, because — because *that would be* the *one* poor sacrifice I could make you — one I would cheerfully make, but a sacrifice, and the only one: this careless 'sweet habitude of living' — this absolute independence of mine, which, if I had it not, my heart would starve and die for, I feel, and which I have fought so many good battles to preserve — for that has happened, too — this light rational life I lead, and know so well that I lead; this I could give up for nothing less than — what you know — but I *would* give it up, not for you merely, but for those whose disappointment might re-act on you — and I should break no promise to myself — the money getting would not be for the sake of *it*; 'the labour not for that which is nought' — indeed the necessity of doing this, if at all, *now*, was one of the reasons which make me go on to that *last request of all* — at once; one must not be too old, they say, to begin their ways. But, in spite of all the babble, I feel sure that whenever I make up my mind to that, I can be rich enough and to spare — because along with what you have thought *genius* in me, is certainly talent, what the world recognizes as such; and I have tried it in various ways, just to be sure that I *was* a little magnanimous in never intending to use it. Thus, in more than one of the reviews and newspapers that laughed my 'Paracelsus' to scorn ten years ago — in the same column, often, of these reviews, would follow a most laudatory notice of an Elementary French book, on a new plan, which I '*did*' for my old

French master, and he published — '*that* was really an useful work'! — So that when the only obstacle is only that there is so much *per annum* to be producible, you will tell me. After all it would be unfair in me not to confess that this was always intended to be *my* own single stipulation — 'an objection' which I could see, certainly, — but meant to treat myself to the little luxury of removing.

So, now, dearest — let me once think of that, and of you as my own, my dearest — this once — dearest, I have done with words for the present. I will wait. God bless you and reward you — I kiss your hands *now*. This is my comfort, that if you accept my feeling as all but *un*expressed now, more and more will become spoken — or understood, that is — we both live on — you will know better *what* it was, how much and manifold, what one little word had to give out.

God bless you —
Your R.B.

* * *

E. B. B. to R. B.

[postmark *September 25, 1845.*]

I have spoken again, and the result is that we are in precisely the same position; only with bitterer feelings on one side. If I go or stay they *must* be bitter: words have been said that I cannot easily forget, nor remember without pain; and yet I really do almost smile in the midst of it all, to think how I was treated this morning as an undutiful daughter because I tried to put on my gloves . . for there was no worse provocation. At least he complained of the undutifulness and rebellion (! ! !) of everyone in the house — and when I asked if he meant that reproach for *me*, the answer was that he meant it for all of us, one with another. And I could not get an answer. He would not even grant me the consolation of thinking that I sacrificed what I supposed to be good, to *him*. I told him that my prospects of health seemed to me to depend on taking this step, but that through my affection for him, I was ready to sacrifice those to his pleasure if he exacted it — only it was necessary to my self-satisfaction in future years, to understand definitely that the sacrifice *was* exacted by him and *was* made to him, . . and not thrown away blindly and by a misapprehension. And he would not answer *that*. I might do my own way, he said — *he* would not speak — *he* would not say that he was not displeased with me, nor the contrary: — I had better do what I liked: — for his part, he washed his hands of me altogether.

And so I have been very wise — witness how my eyes are swelled with annotations and reflections on all this! The best of it is that now George himself admits I can do no more in the way of speaking, . . I have no spell for charming the dragons, . . and allows me to be passive and enjoins me to be tranquil, and not 'make up my mind' to any dreadful exertion for the future. Moreover he advises me to go on with the preparations for the voyage, and promises to state the case himself at the last hour to the 'highest authority'; and judge finally whether it be possible for me to go with the necessary companionship. And it seems best to go to Malta on the 3rd of October — if at all . . from steam-packet reasons . . without excluding Pisa . . remember . . by any means.

Well! — and what do you think? Might it be desirable for me to give up the whole? Tell me. I feel aggrieved of course and wounded — and whether I go or stay that feeling must last — I cannot help it. But my spirits sink altogether at the thought of leaving England *so* — and then I doubt about Arabel and Stormie . . and it seems to me that I *ought not* to mix them up in a business of this kind where the advantage is merely personal to myself. On the other side, George holds that if I give up and stay even, there will be displeasure just the same, . . and that, when once gone, the irritation will exhaust and smooth itself away — which however does not touch my chief objection. Would it be better . . more *right* . . to give it up? Think for me. Even if I hold on to the last, at the last I shall be thrown off — *that* is my conviction. But . . shall I give up *at once?* Do think for me.

And I have thought that if you like to come on Friday instead of Saturday . . as there is the uncertainty about next week, . . it would divide the time more equally: but let it be as you like and according to circumstances as you see them. Perhaps you have decided to go

79

at once with your friends — who knows? I wish I could know that you were better today. May God bless you.

Ever yours,
E.B.B.

R. B. to E. B. B.

[postmark *September 25, 1845.*]

You have said to me more than once that you wished I might never know certain feelings *you* had been forced to endure. I suppose all of us have the proper place where a blow should fall to be felt most — and I truly wish *you* may never feel what I have to bear in looking on, quite powerless, and silent, while you are subjected to this treatment, which I refuse to characterize — so blind is it *for* blindness. I think I ought to understand what a father may exact, and a child should comply with; and I respect the most ambiguous of love's caprices if they give never so slight a clue to their all-justifying source. Did I, when you signified to me the probable objections — you remember what — to myself, my own happiness, — did I once allude to, much less argue against, or refuse to acknowledge those objections? For I wholly sympathize, however it go against me, with the highest, wariest, pride and love for you, and the proper jealousy and vigilance they entail — but now, and here, the jewel is not being over guarded, but ruined, cast away. And whoever is privileged to interfere should do so in the possessor's own interest — all common sense interferes — all rationality against absolute no-reason at all. And you ask whether you ought to obey this no-reason? I will tell you: all passive obedience and implicit submission of will and intellect is by far too easy, if well considered, to be the course prescribed by God to Man in this life of probation — for they *evade* probation altogether, though foolish people think otherwise. Chop off your legs, you will never go astray; stifle your reason altogether and you will find it is difficult to reason ill. 'It is hard to make these sacrifices!' — not so hard as to lose the reward or incur the penalty of an Eternity to come; 'hard to effect them, then, and go through with them' — *not* hard, when the leg is to be *cut off* — that it is rather harder to keep it quiet on a stool, I know very well. The partial indulgence, the proper exercise of one's faculties, there is the difficulty and problem for solution, set by that Providence which might have made the laws of Religion as indubitable as those of vitality, and revealed the articles of belief as certainly as that condition, for instance, by which we breathe so many times in a minute to support life. But there is no reward proposed for the feat of breathing, and a great one for that of believing — consequently there must go a great deal more of voluntary effort to this latter than is implied in the getting absolutely rid of it at once, by adopting the direction of an infallible church, or private judgment of another — for all our life is some form of religion, and all our action some belief, and there is but one law, however modified, for the greater and the less. In your case I do think you are called upon to do your duty to yourself; that is, to God in the end. Your own reason should examine the whole matter in dispute by every light which can be put in requisition; and every interest that appears to be affected by your conduct should have its utmost claims considered — your father's in the first place; and that interest, not in the miserable limits of a few days' pique or whim in which it would seem to express itself; but in its whole extent . . the *hereafter* which all momentary passion prevents him seeing . . indeed, the *present* on either side which everyone else must see. And this examination made, with whatever earnestness you will, I do think and am sure that on its conclusion you should act, in confidence that a duty has been performed . . *difficult*, or how were it a duty? Will it *not* be infinitely harder to act so than to blindly adopt his pleasure, and die under it? Who can *not* do that?

I fling these hasty rough words over the paper, fast as they will fall — knowing to whom I cast them, and that any sense they may contain or point to, will be caught and understood, and presented in a better light. The hard thing . . this is all I want to say . . is to act on one's own best conviction — not to abjure it and accept another will, and say 'there is my plain duty' — easy it is, whether plain or no!

How 'all changes!' When I first knew you — you know what followed. I supposed you to labour under an incurable complaint — and, of course, to be completely dependent on your father for its commonest alleviations; the moment after that inconsiderate letter, I reproached myself bitterly with the selfishness apparently involved in any proposition I might then have made — for though I have never been at all frightened of the world, nor mistrustful of my power to deal with it, and get my purpose out of it if once I thought it worth while, yet I could not but feel the consideration, of *what* failure would *now* be, paralyse all effort even in fancy. When you told me lately that 'you could never be poor' — all my solicitude was at an end — I had but myself to care about, and I told you, what I believed and believe, that I can at any time amply provide for that, and that I could cheerfully and confidently undertake the removing *that* obstacle. Now again the circumstances shift — and you are in what I should wonder at as the veriest slavery — and I who *could* free you from it, I am here scarcely daring to write . . though I know you must feel for me and forgive what forces itself from me . . what retires so mutely into my heart at your least word . . what *shall not* be again written or spoken, if you so will . . that I should be made happy beyond all hope of expression by. Now while I *dream*, let me once dream! I would marry you now and thus — I would come when you let me, and go when you bade me — I would be no more than one of your brothers — '*no more*' — that is, instead of getting tomorrow for Saturday, I should get Saturday as well — two hours for one — when your head ached I should be *here*. I deliberately choose the realization of that dream (— of sitting simply by you for an hour every day) rather than any other, excluding you, I am able to form for this world, or any world I know — And it will continue but a dream.

God bless my dearest E.B.B.
R.B.

You understand that I see you to-morrow, Friday, as you propose. I am better — thank you — and will go out to-day. You know what I am, what I would speak, and all I would do.

* * *

E.B.B. to R.B.

Two letters in one — Wednesday.
[postmark *November 15, 1845.*]

I shall see you to-morrow and yet am writing what you will have to read perhaps. When you spoke of 'stars' and 'geniuses' in that letter, I did not seem to hear; I was listening to those words of the letter which were of a better silver in the sound than even your praise could be: and now that at last I come to hear them in their extravagance (oh such pure extravagance about 'glorious geniuses' —) I can't help telling you they were heard last, and deserved it.

Shall I tell you besides? — The first moment in which I seemed to admit to myself in a flash of lightning the *possibility* of your affection for me being more than dream-work . . the first moment was *that* when you intimated (as you have done since repeatedly) that you cared for me not for a reason, but because you cared for me. Now such a 'parceque' which reasonable people would take to be irrational, was just the only one fitted to the uses of my understanding on the particular question we were upon . . just the 'woman's reason' suitable to the woman . . : for I could understand that it might be as you said, and, if so, that it was altogether unanswerable . . do you see? If a fact includes its own cause . . why there it stands for ever — one of 'earth's immortalities' — *as long as it includes it.*

And when unreasonableness stands for a reason, it is a promising state of things, we may both admit, and proves what it would be as well not too curiously to enquire into. But then . . to look at it in a brighter aspect, . . I do remember how, years ago, when talking the foolishnesses which women will talk when they are by themselves, and not forced to be sensible, . . one of my friends thought it 'safest to begin with a little aversion,' and another, wisest to begin with a great deal of esteem, and how the best attachments were produced so and so, . . I took it into my head to say that the best was where there was no cause at all for it, and the more wholly unreasonable, the better still; that the motive should

83

lie in the feeling itself and not in the object of it—and that the affection which could (if it could) throw itself out on an idiot with a goître would be more admirable than Abelard's. Whereupon everybody laughed, and someone thought it affected of me and no true opinion, and others said plainly that it was immoral, and somebody else hoped, in a sarcasm, that I meant to act out my theory for the advantage of the world. To which I replied quite gravely that I had not virtue enough —and so, people laughed as it is fair to laugh when other people are esteemed to talk nonsense. And all this came back to me in the south wind of your 'parceque,' and I tell it as it came . . now.

Which proves, if it proves anything, . . while I have every sort of natural pleasure in your praises and like you to like my poetry just as I should, and perhaps more than I should; yet *why* it is all behind . . and in its place—and *why* I have a tendency moreover to sift and measure any praise of yours and to separate it from the superfluities, far more than with any other person's praise in the world. ***

* * *

R. B. to E. B. B.

Sunday Evening
[postmark *January 19, 1846.*]

You may have seen, I put off all the weighty business part of the letter—but I shall do very little with it now. To be sure, a few words will serve, because you understand me, and believe in *enough* of me. First, then, I am wholly satisfied, thoroughly made happy in your assurance. I would build up an infinity of lives, if I could plan them, one on the other, and all resting on you, on your word—I fully believe in it,—of my feeling, the gratitude, let there be no attempt to speak. And for 'waiting'; 'not hurrying,'—I leave all with you henceforth—all you say is most wise, most convincing.

On the saddest part of all,—silence. You understand, and I can understand through you. Do you know, that I never *used* to dream unless indisposed, and rarely then—(of late I dream of you, but quite of late) — and *those* nightmare dreams have invariably been of *one* sort. I stand by (powerless to interpose by a word even) and see the infliction of tyranny on the unresisting man or beast (generally the last) — and I wake just in time not to die: let no one try this kind of experiment on me or mine! Though I have observed that by a felicitous arrangement, the man with the whip puts it into use with an old horse commonly. I once knew a fine specimen of the boilingly passionate, desperately respectable on the Eastern principle that reverences a madman — and this fellow, whom it was to be death to oppose, (some bloodvessel was to break) — he, once at a dinner party at which I was present, insulted his wife (a young pretty simple believer in his awful immunities from the ordinary terms that keep men in order) — brought the tears into her eyes and sent her from the room . . purely to 'show off' in the eyes of his guests . . (all males, law-friends &c., he being a lawyer.) This feat accomplished, he, too, left us with an affectation of compensating relentment, to 'just say a word and return' — and no sooner was his back to the door than the biggest, stupidest of the company began to remark 'what a fortunate thing it was that Mr. So-and-so had such a submissive wife — not one of the women who would resist — that is, attempt to resist — and so exasperate our gentleman into . . Heaven only knew what!' I said it *was*, in one sense, a fortunate thing; because one of these women, without necessarily being the lion-tressed Bellona, would richly give him his desert, I thought — 'Oh, indeed?' No — *this* man was not to be opposed — wait, you might, till the fit was over, and then try what kind argument would do — and so forth to unspeakable nausea. Presently we went up-stairs — there sate the wife with dried eyes, and a smile at the tea-table — and by her, in all the pride of conquest, with her hand in his, our friend — disposed to be very good-natured of course. I listened *arrectis auribus*, and in a minute he said he did not know somebody I mentioned. I told him, *that* I easily conceived — such a person would never condescend to know *him*, &c, and treated him to every consequence ingenuity could draw from that text — and at the end marched out of the room; and the valorous man, who had sate like a post, got up, took a candle, followed me to the door, and only said in unfeigned wonder, 'What *can* have possessed you, my *dear* B?' — All which I as much expected beforehand, as that the above mentioned man of the whip keeps quiet in the presence of an ordinary-couraged dog. All this is quite irrelevant to *the* case — indeed, I write to get rid of the thought altogether. But I do hold it the most stringent duty of all who can, to stop a condition, a relation of one human being to another which God never allowed to exist between Him and ourselves. *Trees* live and die, if you please, and accept will for a law — but with us, all commands surely refer to a previously-implanted conviction in ourselves of their rationality and justice. Or why declare that 'the Lord *is* holy, just and good' unless there is recognised and independent conception of holiness and goodness, to which the subsequent assertion is referable? 'You know what *holiness* is, what it is to be good? Then, He *is* that' — not, '*that* is so — because *he* is that'; though, of course, when once the converse is demonstrated, this, too, follows, and may be urged for practical purposes. All God's urgency, so to speak, is on the *justice* of his judgments, *rightness* of his rule: yet why? one might ask — if one does believe that the rule *is* his; why ask further? — Because, his is a 'reasonable service,' once for all.

Understand why I turn my thoughts in this direction. If it is indeed as you fear, and no endeavour, concession, on my part will avail, under any circumstances — (and by endeavour, I mean all heart and soul could bring the flesh to perform) — in that case, you will not come to me with a shadow past hope of chasing.

The likelihood is, I over frighten myself for you, by the involuntary contrast with those here — you allude to them — if I went with this letter downstairs and said simply 'I want this taken to the direction to-night, and am unwell and unable to go, will you take it now?' my father would not say a word, or rather would say a dozen cheerful absurdities about his 'wanting a walk,' 'just having been wishing to go out' &c. At night he sits studying my works — illustrating them (I will bring you drawings to make you laugh) — and *yesterday* I picked up a crumpled bit of paper . . 'his notion of what a criticism on this last number ought to be, — none, that have appeared, satisfying him!' — So judge of what he will say! And my mother loves me just as much more as must of necessity be.

Once more, understand all this . . for the clock scares me of a sudden — I meant to say more — far more.

But may God bless you ever — my own dearest, my Ba —

I am wholly your R.

[*Tuesday*]

* * *

86

SELECTED LETTERS

E. B. B. to R. B.

Monday
[postmark January 27, 1846.]

You have had my letter and heard about the penholder. Your fancy of 'not seeming grateful enough,' is not wise enough for *you*, dearest; when you know that *I* know your common fault to be the undue magnifying of everything that comes from me, and I am always complaining of it outwardly and inwardly. That suddenly I should set about desiring you to be more grateful, — even for so great a boon as an old penholder, — would be a more astounding change than any to be sought or seen in a prime minister.

Another mistake you made concerning Henrietta and her opinion — and there's no use nor comfort in leaving you in it. Henrietta says that the 'anger would not be so formidable after all'! Poor dearest Henrietta, who trembles at the least bending of the brows . . who has less courage than I, and the same views of the future! What she referred to, was simply the infrequency of the visits. 'Why was I afraid,' she said — 'where was the danger? who would be the *informer?*' — Well! I will not say any more. It is just natural that you, in your circumstances and associations, should be unable to see what I have seen from the beginning — only you will not hereafter reproach me, in the most secret of your thoughts, for not having told you plainly. If I could have told you with greater plainness I should blame myself (and I do not) because it is not an opinion I have, but a perception. I see, I know. The result . . the end of all . . perhaps now and then I see *that* too . . in the 'lucid moments' which are not the happiest for anybody. Remember, in all cases, that I shall not repent of any part of our past intercourse; and that, therefore, when the time for decision comes, you will be free to look at the question as if you saw it then for the first moment, without being hampered by considerations about 'all those yesterdays.'

For *him* . . he would rather see me dead at his foot than yield the point: and he will say so, and mean it, and persist in the meaning.

Do you ever wonder at me . . that I should write such things, and have written others so different? *I have thought that in myself very often.* Insincerity and injustice may seem the two ends, while I occupy the straight betwixt two — and I should not like you to doubt how this may be! Sometimes I have begun to show you the truth, and torn the paper; I *could* not. Yet now again I am borne on to tell you, . . to save you from some thoughts which you cannot help perhaps.

There has been no insincerity — nor is there injustice. I believe, I am certain, I have loved him better than the rest of his children. I have heard the fountain within the rock, and my heart has struggled in towards him through the stones of the rock . . thrust off . . dropping off . . turning in again and clinging! Knowing what is excellent in him well, loving him as my only parent left, and for himself dearly, notwithstanding that hardness and the miserable 'system' which made him appear harder still, I have loved him and been proud of him for his high qualities, for his courage and fortitude when he bore up so bravely years ago under the worldly reverses which he yet felt acutely — more than you and I could feel them — but the fortitude was admirable. Then came the trials of love — then, I was repulsed too often, . . made to suffer in the suffering of those by my side . . depressed by petty daily sadnesses and terrors, from which it is possible however for an elastic affection to rise again as past. Yet my friends used to say 'You look broken-spirited' — and it was true. In the midst, came my illness, — and when I was ill he grew gentler and let me draw nearer than ever I had done: and after that great stroke . . you *know* . . though *that* fell in the middle of a storm of emotion and sympathy on my part, which drove clearly against him, God seemed to strike our hearts together by the shock; and I was grateful to him for not saying aloud what I said to myself in my agony, '*If it had not been for you*' . . ! And comparing my self-reproach to what I imagined his self-reproach must certainly be (for if *I* had loved selfishly, *he* had not been kind), I felt as if I could love and forgive him for two . . (I knowing that serene generous departed spirit, and seeming left to represent it) . . and I did love him better than all those left to *me* to love in the world here. I proved a little my affection for him, by coming to London at the risk of my life rather than diminish the comfort of his home by keeping a part of my family away from him. And afterwards for long and long he spoke to me kindly and gently, and of me affectionately and with too much praise; and God knows that I had as much joy as I imagined myself capable of again, in the sound of his footstep on the stairs, and of his voice when he prayed in this room; my best hope, as I have told him since, being, to die beneath his eyes. Love is so much to me naturally — it is, to all women! and it was so much to *me* to feel sure at last that *he* loved me — to forget all blame — to pull the weeds up from that last illusion of life: — and this, till the Pisa-business, which threw me off, far as ever, again — farther than ever — when George said 'he could not flatter me' and I dared not flatter myself. But do *you* believe that I never wrote what I did not feel: I never did. And I ask one kindness more . . do not notice what I have written here. Let it pass. We can alter nothing by ever so many words. After all, he is the victim. He isolates himself — and now and then he feels it . . the cold dead silence all round, which is the effect of an incredible system. If he were not stronger than most men, he could not bear it as he does. With such high qualities too! — so upright and honourable — you would esteem him, you would like him, I think. And so . . dearest . . let *that* be the last word.

I dare say you have asked yourself sometimes, why it was that I never managed to draw you into the house here, so that you might make your own way. Now *that* is one of the things impossible to me. I have not influence enough for *that*. George can never invite a friend of his even. Do you see? The people who do come here, come by particular license and association . . Capt. Surtees Cook being one of them. Once . . when I was in high favour too . . I asked for Mr. Kenyon to be invited to dinner — he an old college friend, and living close by and so affectionate to me always — I felt that he must be hurt by the neglect, and asked. *It was in vain*. Now, you see —

May God bless you always! I wrote all my spirits away in this letter yesterday, and kept it to finish to-day . . being yours every day, glad or sad, ever beloved! —

Your BA.

* * *

R. B. to E. B. B.

Wednesday.
[postmark *January 28, 1846.*]

Ever dearest—I will say, as you desire, nothing on that subject—but this strictly for myself: you engaged me to consult my own good in the keeping or breaking our engagement; not *your* good as it might even seem to me; much less seem to another. My only good in this world—that against which all the world goes for nothing—is to spend my life with you, and be yours. You know that when I *claim* anything, it is really yourself in me—you *give* me a right and bid me use it, and I, in fact, am most obeying you when I appear most exacting on my own account—so, in that feeling, I dare claim, once for all, and in all possible cases (except that dreadful one of your becoming worse again . . in which case I wait till life ends with both of us), I claim your promise's fulfilment—say, at the summer's end: it cannot be for your good that this state of things should continue. We can go to Italy for a year or two and be happy as day and night are long. For me, I adore you. This is all unnecessary, I feel as I write: but you will think of the main fact as *ordained*, granted by God, will you not, dearest?—so, not to be put in doubt *ever again*—then, we can go quietly thinking of after matters. Till to-morrow, and ever after, God bless my heart's own, own Ba. All my soul follows you, love—encircles you—and I live in being yours.

E. B. B. to R. B.

Friday Morning.
[postmark *January 31, 1846.*]

Let it be this way, ever dearest. If in the time of fine weather, I am not ill, . . *then* . . *not now* . . you shall decide, and your decision shall be duty and desire to me, both—I will make no difficulties. Remember, in the meanwhile, that I *have* decided to let it be as you shall choose . . *shall* choose. That I love you enough to give you up 'for your good,' is proof (to myself at least) that I love you enough for any other end: — but you thought *too much of me in the last letter*. Do not mistake me. I believe and trust in all your words — only you are generous unawares, as other men are selfish.

More, I meant to say of this; but you moved me as usual yesterday into the sunshine, and then I am dazzled and cannot see clearly. Still I see that you love me and that I am bound to you! — and 'what more need I see,' you may ask; while I cannot help looking out to the future, to the blue ridges of the hills, to the *chances* of your being happy with me. Well! I am yours as *you* see . . and not yours to teaze you. You shall decide everything when the time comes for doing anything . . and from this to then, I do not, dearest, expect you to use 'the liberty of leaping out of the window,' unless you are sure of the house being on fire! Nobody shall push you out of the window — least of all, *I*.

For Italy . . you are right. We should be nearer the sun, as you say, and further from the world, as I think — out of hearing of the great storm of gossiping, when 'scirocco is loose.' Even if you liked to live altogether abroad, coming to England at intervals, it would be no sacrifice for me — and whether in Italy or England, we should have sufficient or more than sufficient means of living, without modifying by a line that 'good free life' of yours which you reasonably praise — which, if it had been necessary to modify, *we must have parted*, . . because I could not have borne to see you do it; though, that you once offered it for my sake, I never shall forget. ＊＊＊

＊＊＊

E. B. B. to R. B.

Tuesday Evening
[postmark *March 4, 1846.*]

＊＊＊ You do not see aright what I meant to tell you on another subject. If he was displeased, (and it was expressed by a shadow a mere negation of pleasure) it was not with you as a visitor and my friend. You must not fancy such a thing. It was a sort of instinctive indisposition towards seeing you here — unexplained to himself, I have no doubt — of course unexplained, or he would have desired me to receive you never again, *that* would have been done at once and unscrupulously. But without defining his own feeling, he rather disliked seeing you here — it just touched one of his vibratory wires, brushed by and touched it — oh, we understand in this house. He is not a nice observer, but, at intervals very wide, he is subject to lightnings — call them fancies, sometimes right, sometimes wrong. Certainly it was not in the character of a 'sympathising friend' that you made him a very little cross on Monday. And yet you never were nor will be in danger of being *thanked*, he would not think of it. For the reserve, the apprehension — dreadful those things are, and desecrating to one's own nature — but we did not make this position, we only endure it. The root of the evil is the miserable misconception of the limits and character of parental rights — it is a mistake of the intellect rather than of the heart. Then, after using one's children as one's chattels for a time, the children drop lower and lower toward the level of the chattels, and the duties of human sympathy to them become difficult in proportion. And (it seems strange to say it, yet it is true) *love*, he does not conceive of at all. He has feeling, he can be moved deeply, he is capable of affection in a peculiar way, but *that*, he does not understand, any more than he understands Chaldee, respecting it less of course.

And you fancy that I could propose Italy again? after saying too that I never would? Oh no, no — yet there is time to think of this, a superfluity of time, . . 'time, times and half a time' and to make one's head swim with leaning over a precipice is not wise. The roar of the world comes up too, as you hear and as I heard from the beginning. There will be no lack of 'lying,' be sure — 'pure lying' too — and nothing you can do, dearest dearest, shall hinder my being torn to pieces by most of the particularly affectionate friends I have in the world. Which I do not think of much, any more than of Italy. You will be mad, and I shall be bad . . and *that* will be the effect of being poets! 'Till when, where are you?' — why in the very deepest of my soul — wherever in it is the fountain head of loving! beloved, *there* you are!

Some day I shall ask you 'in form,' — as I care so much for forms, it seems, — what your 'faults' are, these immense multitudinous faults of yours, which I hear such talk of, and never, never can get to see. Will you give me a catalogue raisonnée of your faults? I should like it, I think. In the meantime they seem to be faults of obscurity, that is, invisible faults, like those in the poetry which do not keep it from selling as I am *so, so* glad to understand. I am glad too that Mr. Milnes knows you a little.

Now I must end, there is no more time to-night. God bless you, very dearest! Keep better . . try to be well — as *I* do for you since you ask me. Did I ever think that *you* would think it worth while to ask me *that?* What a dream! reaching out into the morning! To-day however I did not go down-stairs, because it was colder and the wind blew its way into the passages: if I can to-morrow without risk, I will, . . be sure . . be sure. Till Thursday then! — till eternity!

'Till when, where am I,' but with you? and what, but yours

Your
BA.

* * *

E. B. B. to R. B.

Monday Morning.
[postmark *May 26, 1846.*]

My beloved I scarcely know what to say about the poem. It is almost profane and a sin to keep you from writing it when your mind goes that way, — yet I am afraid that you cannot begin without doing too much and without suffering as a consequence in your head. Now if you make yourself ill, what will be the end? So you see my fears! Let it be however as it must be! Only you will promise to keep from all excesses, and to write very very gently. Ah — can you keep such a promise, if it is made ever so? There are the fears again.

You are very strange in what you say about my reading your poetry — as if it were not my peculiar gladness and glory! — my own, which no

93

THE BROWNINGS

man can take from me. And not *you*, indeed! Yet I am not likely to mistake your poetry for the flower of your nature, knowing what that flower is, knowing something of what that flower is without a name, and feeling something of the mystical perfume of it. When I said, or when others said for me, that my poetry was the flower of me, was it praise, did you think, or blame? might it not stand for a sarcasm? It might, — if it were not true, miserably true after a fashion.

Yet something of the sort is true, of course, with all poets who write directly from their personal experience and emotions — their ideal rises to the surface and floats like the bell of the waterlily. The roots and the muddy water are *sub-audita*, you know — as surely there, as the flower.

But *you* . . you have the superabundant mental life and individuality which admits of shifting a personality and speaking the truth still. *That* is the highest faculty, the strongest and rarest, which exercises itself in Art, — we are all agreed there is none so great faculty as the dramatic. Several times you have hinted to me that I made you careless for the drama, and it has puzzled me to fancy how it could be, when I understand myself so clearly both the difficulty and the glory of dramatic art. Yet I am conscious of wishing you to take the other crown besides — and after having made your own creatures speak in clear human voices, to speak yourself out of that personality which God made, and with the voice which He tuned into such power and sweetness of speech. I do not think that, with all that music in you, only your own personality should be dumb, nor that having thought so much and deeply on life and its ends, you should not teach what you have learnt, in the directest and most impressive way, the mask thrown off however moist with the breath. And it is not, I believe, by the dramatic medium, that poets teach most impressively — I have seemed to observe *that!* . . it is too difficult for the common reader to analyse, and to discern between the vivid and the earnest. Also he is apt to understand better always, when he sees the lips move. Now, here is yourself, with your wonderful faculty! — it is wondered at and recognised on all sides where there are eyes to see — it is called wonderful and admirable! Yet, with an inferior power, you might have taken yourself closer to the hearts and lives of men, and made yourself dearer, though being less great. Therefore I do want you to do this with your surpassing power — it will be so easy to you to speak, and so noble, when spoken.

Not that I usen't to fancy I could see you and know you, in a reflex image, in your creations! I used, you remember. How these broken

94

lights and forms look strange and unlike now to me, when I stand by the complete idea. Yes, *now* I feel that no one can know you worthily by those poems. Only . . I guessed a little. Now let us have your own voice speaking of yourself — if the voice may not hurt the speaker — which is my fear. ***

***

R.B. to E.B.B.

Friday.
[postmark *June 12, 1846.*]

When I am close to you, in your very room, I see through your eyes and feel what you feel — but after, the sight widens with the circle of outside things — I cannot fear for a moment what seemed redoubtable enough yesterday — nor do I believe that there will be two opinions anywhere in the world as to your perfect right to do as you please under the present circumstances. People are not quite so tolerant to other people's preposterousness, and that which yourself tell me exceeds anything I ever heard of or imagined — but, dearest, on twice thinking, one surely ought not to countenance it as you propose — why should not my father and mother know? What possible harm can follow from their knowing? Why should I wound them to the very soul and for ever, by as gratuitous a piece of unkindness as if, — no, — there is no comparison will do! Because, since I was a child I never looked for the least or greatest thing within the compass of their means to give, but given it was, — nor for liberty but it was conceded, nor confidence but it was bestowed. I dare say they would break their hearts at such an end of all. For in any case they will take my feeling for their own with implicit trust — and if I brought them a beggar, or a famous actress even, they would believe in her because of me, — if a Duchess or Miss Hudson, or Lady Selina Huntingdon rediviva . . they would do just the same, sorrow to say! As to any harm or blame that can attach itself to *them,*

95

— it is too absurd to think of! What earthly control can they have over me? They live here, — I go my own way, being of age and capability. How can they interfere?

And then, blame for *what*, in either God's or the devil's name? I believe you to be the one woman in the world I am able to marry because able to love. I wish, on some accounts, I had foreseen the contingency of such an one's crossing my path in this life — but I did not, and on all ordinary grounds preferred being free and poor, accordingly. All is altered now. Does anybody doubt that I can by application in proper quarters obtain quite enough to support us both in return for no extraordinary expenditure of such faculties as I have? If it *is* to be doubted, I have been greatly misinformed, that is all. Or, setting all friends and their proposals and the rest of the hatefulness aside — I should say that so simple a procedure as writing to anybody . . Lord Monteagle, for instance, who reads and likes my works, as he said at Moxon's two days ago on calling there for a copy to give away . . surely to write to him, 'When you are minister next month, as is expected, will you give me for my utmost services about as much as you give Tennyson for nothing?' — *this* would be rational and *as* easy as all rationality. *Let me do so, and at once, my own Ba!* And do you, like the unutterably noble creature I know you, transfer your own advantages to your brothers or sisters . . making if you please a proper reservation in the case of my own exertions failing, as failure comes everywhere. So shall the one possible occasion of calumny be removed and all other charges go for the simple absurdities they will be. I am entirely in earnest about this, and indeed had thought for a moment of putting my own share of the project into immediate execution — but on consideration, — no! So I will live and so die with you. I will not be poorly endeavouring to startle you with unforeseen generosities, catch you in pretty pitfalls of magnanimities, be always surprising you, or trying to do it. No, I resolve to do my best, *through* you — by your counsel, with your help, under your eye . . the most strenuous endeavour will only approximate to an achievement of *that*, — and to suppose a superfluousness of devotion to you (as all these surprises do) would be miserably foolish. So, dear, dear Ba, understand and advise me. I took up the paper with ordinary feelings . . but the absurdity and tyranny suddenly flashed upon me . . it must not be borne — indeed its only safety in this instance is in its impotency. I am not without fear of some things in this world — but the 'wrath of men,' all the men living put together, I fear as I fear the fly I have just put out of the window; but I fear God—and am ready, he knows, to die this moment in taking his part against any piece of injustice and oppression, so I aspire to die!

See this long letter, and all about a tiny one, a plain palpable commonplace matter about which you agree with me, you the dear quiet Ba of my heart, with me that make all this unnecessary fuss! See what is behind all the 'bated breath and whispered humbleness?' — but it is *right*, after all, to revolt against such monstrous tyranny. And I ought not, I feel, to have forgotten the feelings of my father and mother as I did — because I know as certainly as I know anything that if I could bring myself to ask them to give up everything in the world; they would do it and cheerfully.

So see, and forgive your own

R.

* * *

E.B.B. to R.B.

Thursday.
[postmark *July 17, 1846*.]

Dearest, if *you* feel *that*, must I not feel it more deeply? Twice or three times lately he has said to me 'my love' and even 'my puss,' his old words before he was angry last year, . . and I quite quailed before them as if they were so many knife-strokes. Anything but his *kindness*, I can bear now.

Yet I am glad that you feel *that* . . The difficulty, (almost the despair!) has been with me, to make you understand the two ends of truth . . both that he is *not* stone . . and that he *is* immovable *as* stone. Perhaps only a very peculiar nature could have held so long the position he holds in his family. His hand would not lie so heavily, without a pulse in it. Then he is upright — faithful to his conscience. You

97

would respect him, . . and love him perhaps in the end. For me, he might have been king and father over to me *to* the end, if he had thought it worthwhile to love me openly enough — yet, even *so*, he should not have let you come too near. And you could not (so) have come too near — for he would have had my confidence from the beginning, and no opportunity would have been permitted to you of proving your affection for me, and I should have thought always what I thought at first. So the nightshade and the eglantine are twisted, twined, one in the other, . . and the little pink roses lean up against the pale poison of the berries — we cannot tear this from that, let us think of it ever so much!

We must be humble and beseeching *afterwards* at least, and try to get forgiven — Poor Papa! I have turned it over and over in my mind, whether it would be less offensive, less *shocking* to him, if an application were made first. If I were strong, I think I should incline to it at all risks — but as it is, . . it might . . would, probably, . . take away the power of action from me altogether. We should be separated, you see, from *that moment*, . . hindered from writing . . hindered from meeting . . and I could evade nothing, as I am — not to say that I should have fainting fits at every lifting of his voice, through that inconvenient nervous temperament of mine which has so often made me ashamed of myself. Then . . the positive disobedience might be a greater offence than the unauthorised act. I shut my eyes in terror sometimes. May God direct us to the best.

Oh — do not write about this, dearest, dearest? — I throw myself out of it into the pure, sweet, deep thought of you . . which is the love of you always. I am yours . . your own. I never doubt of being yours. I feel too much yours. It is might and right together. You are more to me, beside, than the whole world.

Write nothing of this, dearest of all! — it is of no use. Today . . this morning . . I went out in the carriage, and we drove round the Park; and Mrs. Jameson did not come afterward. Will she put it off till Saturday? I have heard nothing against Saturday, by the way, worse than that conjecture of mine.

And I have written you, perhaps, a teazing, painful letter . . I, who love you today 'as much as ever'. It is my destiny, I sometimes think, to torment you. And let me say what I will, remember how nothing that I say can mean a *doubt* — you never shall have reason to reproach me for the falseness of cowardice — that double falseness . . both to me and

to you. Only I wish this were Christmas Day, and we . . even at Salerno
. . in the 'bad air'! There's no harm in such a wish — now *is* there?

Ever and ever I am your own

BA.

* * *

R. B. to E. B. B.

Wednesday Morning.
[postmark *July 29, 1846.*]

*** And — now! now, Ba, to the subject-matter: whatever you decide on
writing to Mrs. Jameson will be rightly written — it seems to me *nearly*
immaterial; (putting out of the question the confiding the whole secret,
which, from its responsibility, as you feel, must not be done) whether
you decline her kindness for untold reasons which two months (Ba?) will
make abundantly plain, — or whether you farther inform her that there *is*
a special secret — of which she must bear the burthen, even in that miti-
gated form, for the same two months, — as I say, it seems immaterial —
but it is most material that you should see how the ground is crumbling
from beneath our feet, with its chances and opportunities — do not talk
about 'four months,' — till December, that is — unless you mean what
must follow as a consequence. The next thing will be Mr. Kenyon's application to me — *he certainly knows everything* . . how else, after such a
speech from your sister? But his wisdom as well as his habits incline him
to use the force that is in kindness, patience, gentleness: your father
might have entered the room suddenly yesterday and given vent to all
the passionate indignation in the world. I dare say we should have been
married to-day: but I shall have the quietest, most considerate of ex-
positions made me (with one arm on my shoulder), of how I am sure to
be about to kill you, to ruin you, your social reputation, your public estimation, destroy the peace of this member of your family, the prospects
of that other, — and the end will be?

99

THE BROWNINGS

Because I *can* not only die for you but live without you *for you* — once sure it IS for you: I know what you once bade me promise — but I do not know what assurances on assurance, all on the ground of a presumed knowledge of your good above your own possible knowledge, — might not effect! *I do not know!*

This is through you! You *ought* to know now that 'it would *not* be better for me to leave you'! That after this devotion of myself to you I cannot undo it all, and devote myself to objects so utterly insignificant that you yourself do not venture to specify them — 'it would be better — people will say such things' . . I will never *force* you to know this, how-ever — if your admirable senses do not instruct you, I shall never seem to, as it were, threaten you, by prophecies of what my life would prob-ably be, disengaged from you — it should certainly not be passed where the 'people' are, nor where their 'sayings' influenced me any more — but I ask you to look into my heart, and into your own belief in what is worthy and durable and *the better* — and then *decide:* for instance, to speak of waiting for four months will be a decision.

See, dearest — I began lightly, — I cannot end so. I know, after all, the words were divine, self-forgetting words — after all, that you *are* mine, by the one tenure, of your own free gift, — that all the *other* words have not been mere breath, nor the love, a playful show, an acting, an error you will correct. I believe in you, or what shall I believe in? I wish I could take my life, my affections, my ambitions, all my very self, and fold over them your little hand, and leave them there — then you would see what belief is mine! But if you had *not* seen it, would you have ut-tered one word, written one line, given one kiss to me? May God bless you, Ba —

R.B.

* * *

E.B.B. to R.B.

Sunday Morning and Evening.
[postmark *August 3, 1846.*]

Ever dearest, you were wet surely? The rain came before you reached
the front door; and for a moment (before I heard it shut) I hoped you
might return. Dearest, how I blame myself for letting you go — for not
sending you a cab in despite of you! I was frightened out of all wisdom
by the idea of who was down-stairs and listening perhaps, and watching
— as if the cab would have made you appear more emphatically *you!*
And then you said 'the rain was over' — and I believed you as usual. If
this isn't a precedent of the evils of too much belief . . . ! !

Altogether, yesterday may pass among the 'unsatisfactory days', I think
— for if I was not frightened of the storm, and *indeed* I was not, much —
of the state of affairs down in the provinces, I was most sorely frightened
— uneasy the whole time. I seem to be with you, Robert, at this moment,
more than yesterday I was . . though if I look up now, I do not see you
sitting there! — but when you sate there yesterday, I was looking at Papa's
face as I saw it through the floor, and now I see only yours.

Dearest, he came into the room at about seven, before he went to
dinner — I was lying on the sofa and had on a white dressing gown, to
get rid of the strings . . so oppressive the air was, for all the purifications
of lightning. He looked a little as if the thunder had passed into him, and
said, 'Has this been your costume since the morning, pray?'

'Oh no' — I answered — 'Only just now, because of the heat.'

'Well,' he resumed, with a still graver aspect . . (so displeased he
looked, dearest!) 'it appears, Ba, that *that man* has spent the whole day
with you.' To which I replied as quietly as I could, that you had several
times meant to go away, but that the rain would not let you, — and there
the colloquy ended. Brief enough — but it took my breath away . . or
what was left by the previous fear. And think how it must have been
a terrible day, when the lightning of it made the least terror.

I was right too about the message — he took up the fancy that I might be ill perhaps with fear . . 'and only Mr. Browning in the room'! ! which was not to be permitted. He was *peremptory* with Arabel, she told me.

Well — we need not talk any more of it — it has made one of us uncomfortable long enough. Shall you dare come on Tuesday after all? He will be out. If he is not — if my aunt should not be . . if a new obstacle should occur . . why you shall hear on Tuesday. At any rate I shall write, I think. He did not see you go yesterday — he had himself preceded you by an hour . . at five o'clock . . which if it had been known, would have relieved me infinitely. Yet it did not prevent . . you see . . the appalling commentary at seven' — No.

With all the rest I am afraid besides of Mr. Chorley and his idea about your 'mysteriousness'. Let Mr. Kenyon hold that thread in one hand, and in the other the thread Henrietta gave him so carelessly, why he need not ask you for information — which reminds me of the case you put to me, Robert — and certainly you could not help a confession, in such possible circumstances. Only, even granting the circumstances, you need not confess more than is wrung from you — need you? Because Mr. Kenyon would undo us.

Before yesterday's triple storms, I had a presentiment which oppressed me during two days . . a presentiment that it would all end *ill*, through some sudden accident or misery of some kind. What is the use of telling you this? I do not know. I will tell you besides, that it cannot . . . shall not . . . be, by my fault or failing. I may be broken indeed, but never bent.

If things should go smoothly, however, I want to say one word, once for all, in relation to them. Once or twice you have talked as if a change were to take place in your life through marrying — whereas I do beg you to keep in mind that not a pebble in the path changes, nor is pushed aside because of me. If you should make me feel myself in the way, should I like it, do you think? And how could I disturb a single habit or manner of yours . . as an unmarried man . . though being within call — I? The best of me is, that I am really very quiet and not difficult to content — having not been spoilt by an excess of prosperity even in little things. It will be prosperity in the greatest, if you seem to be happy — believe that, and leave all the rest. You will go out just as you do now . . when you choose, and as a matter of course, and without need of a word — you will be precisely as you are now in everything, — lord of the house-door-key, and of your own ways — so that when I shall go to Greece, you shall not feel yourself much better off than before I went. That shall be a reserved vengeance, Robert.

While I write, comes Mr. Kenyon, — and through a special interposition of guardian-angels, he has broken his spectacles and carries them in his hand. On which I caught at the opportunity and told him that they were the most unbecoming things in the world, and that fervently (and sincerely) I hoped never to see them mended. The next word was . . 'Did you see Browning yesterday?' 'Yes'. 'I thought so, I intended to come myself, but I thought it probable that he would be here, and so I stayed away —'

Now — I confess to you that that thought carries me a good way over to your impression. It is at least 'suspicious,' that he who knew you were with me on Saturday and Tuesday should expect to find you again on the next Saturday. 'Oh — how uncomfortable' — the miracle of the broken spectacles not saving one from the discomfort of the position open to the bare eyes! —

He talked of you a little — asked what you were doing — praised you as usual . . for inexhaustible knowledge and general reasonableness, this time. Did I not think so? Yes — of course I thought so.

Presently he made me look aghast by just this question — 'Is there an attachment between your sister Henrietta and Capt. Cook?' — (put as abruptly as I put it here).

My heart leapt up — as Wordsworth's to the rainbow in the sky — but there was a recoil in my leap. 'Why, Mr. Kenyon?' — I said . . 'what extraordinary questions, opening into unspeakable secrets, you do ask.'

'But I did not know that it was a secret. How was I to know? I have seen him here very often, and it is a natural enquiry which I might have put to anybody in the house touching a matter open to general observation. I thought the affair might be an arranged one by anybody's consent.'

'But you ought to know,' I answered, 'that such things are never permitted in this house. So much for the consent. As for the matter itself you are right in your supposition — but it is a great secret, — and I entreat you not to put questions about it to anybody in or out of the house.' Something to that effect I believe I said — I was frightened . . frightened . . and not exactly for Henrietta. What did he mean? — Had *he* too in his mind . . .

He touched on Mrs. Jameson . . just *touched* . . He had desired my sisters to tell me. He thought I had better write a note to thank her for her kindness. He had told her that if I had any thoughts of Italy they could be accomplished only by a sea-voyage, which was impossible to her. I briefly expressed a sense of the kindness and said that I meant to write. On which the subject was changed in mutual haste, as seemed to me.

Is not this the book of the chronicles? . . And you shall hear again on Tuesday, if the post should be faithful to me that morning. I might be inclined to put off our Tuesday's meeting, but Mrs. Hedley remains in London for a few days after her daughter's marriage, and 'means to see a great deal' of me — therefore Wednesday, Thursday, Friday, . . where should we look, from Tuesday? but I must consider and will write. May God bless you! Do say how you are after that rain. The storm is calm,

and ever and ever I am your own BA.

* * *

R. B. to E. B. B.

Sunday Morning.
[postmark *August 31, 1846.*]

I wonder what I shall write to you, Ba — I could suppress my feelings here, as I do on other points, and say nothing of the hatefulness of this state of things which is prolonged so uselessly. There is the point — show me one good reason, or show of reason, why we gain anything by deferring our departure till next week instead of to-morrow, and I will bear to perform yesterday's part for the amusement of Mr. Kenyon a dozen times over without complaint. But if the cold plunge *must* be taken, all this shivering delay on the bank is hurtful as well as fruitless. I *do* understand your anxieties, dearest — I take your fears and make them mine, while I put my own natural feeling of quite another kind away from us both, succeeding in *that* beyond all expectation. There is no amount of patience or suffering I would not undergo to relieve you from these apprehensions. But if, on the whole, you really determine to act as we propose in spite of them, — why, a new leaf is turned over in our journal, an old part of our adventure done with, and a new one entered upon, altogether distinct from the other. Having once decided to go to Italy with me, the next thing to decide is on the best means of going — or rather, there is just this connection between the two measures, that by the success or failure of the last, the first will have to be justified or condemned. You tell me you have decided to go — then, dearest, you will be prepared to go earlier than you promised yesterday — by the end of September at very latest. In proportion to the too probable excitement and painful circumstances of the departure, the greater amount of advantages should be secured for the departure itself. How can I take you away in even the beginning of October? We shall be a fortnight on the journey — with the year, as everybody sees and says, a full month in advance . . cold mornings and dark evenings already. Everybody would cry out on such folly when it was found that we let the favourable weather escape, in full assurance that the Autumn would come to us unattended by any one beneficial circumstance.

My own dearest, I am wholly your own, for ever, and under every determination of yours. If you find yourself unable, or unwilling to make this effort, tell me so and plainly and at once — I will not offer a word in objection, — I will continue our present life, if you please, so far as may be desirable, and wait till next autumn, and the next and the next, till providence end our waiting. It is clearly not for me to pretend to instruct you in your duties to God and yourself; . . enough, that I have long ago chosen to accept your decision. If, on the other hand, you make up your mind to leave England now, you will be prepared by the end of September.

I should think myself the most unworthy of human beings if I could employ any arguments with the remotest show of a tendency to *frighten* you into a compliance with any scheme of mine. Those methods are for people in another relation to you. But you love me, and, at lowest, shall I say, wish me well — and the fact is too obvious for me to commit any indelicacy in reminding you, that in any dreadful event to our journey of which I could accuse myself as the cause, — as of this undertaking to travel with you in the worst time of year when I could have taken the best, — in the case of your health being irretrievably shaken, for instance . . the happiest fate I should pray for would be to live and die in some corner where I might never hear a word of the English language, much less a comment in it on my own wretched imbecility, — to disappear and be forgotten.

So that must not be, for all our sakes. My family will give me to you that we may be both of us happy . . but for such an end — no!

Dearest, do you think all this earnestness foolish and uncalled for? — that I might know you spoke yesterday in mere jest, — as yourself said, 'only to hear what I would say'? Ah but consider, my own Ba, the way of our life, as it is, and is to be — a word, a simple word from you, is not as a word is counted in the world — the word between us is different — I am guided by your will, which a word shall signify to me. Consider that just such a word, so spoken, even with that lightness, would make me lay my life at your feet at any minute. Should we gain anything by my trying, if I could, to deaden the sense of hearing, dull the medium of communication between us; and procuring that, instead of this prompt rising of my will at the first intimation from yours, the same effect should only follow after fifty speeches, and as many protestations of complete serious desire for their success on your part, accompanied by all kinds of acts and deeds and other evidences of the same?

At all events, God knows I have said this in the deepest, truest love of you. I will say no more, praying you to forgive whatever you shall judge to need forgiveness here, — dearest Ba! I will also say, if that may help me, — and what otherwise I might not have said, — that I am not too well this morning, and write with an aching head. My mother's suffering continues too. ✽✽✽

✽ ✽ ✽

R. B. to E. B. B.

Thursday.
[postmark *September 3, 1846.*]

I am rejoiced that poor Flush is found again, dearest — altogether rejoiced.

And now that you probably have him by your side, I will tell you what I should have done in such a case, because it explains our two ways of seeing and meeting oppression lesser or greater. I would not have given five shillings on that fellow's application. I would have said, — and in entire earnestness 'You are responsible for the proceedings of your gang, and you I mark — don't talk nonsense to me about cutting off heads or paws. Be as sure as that I stand here and tell you, I will spend my whole life in putting you down, the nuisance you declare yourself — and by every imaginable means I will be the death of you and as many of your accomplices as I can discover — but you I have discovered and will never lose sight of — now try my sincerity, by delaying to produce the dog by to-morrow. And for the ten pounds — see!' Whereupon I would give them to the first beggar in the street. You think I should receive Flush's head? Perhaps — so God allows matters to happen! on purpose, it may be, that I should vindicate him by the punishment I would exact.

Observe, Ba, this course ought not to be yours, because it *could* not be — it would not suit your other qualities. But all religion, right and justice, with me, seem implied in such a resistance to wickedness and refusal to multiply it a hundredfold — for from this prompt payment of ten pounds for a few minutes' act of the easiest villainy, there will be encouragement to — how many similar acts in the course of next month? And how will the poor owners fare who have not money enough for their dogs' redemption? I suppose the gentleman, properly disgusted with such obstinacy, will threaten roasting at a slow fire to test the sincerity of attachment! No — the world would grow too detestable a den of thieves and oppressors that way! And this is too great a piece of indignation to be expressed when one has the sick vile headache that oppresses me this morning. Dearest, I am not inclined to be even as tolerant as usual. Will you be tolerant, my Ba, and forgive me — till tomorrow at least — when, what with physic, what with impatience, I shall be better one way or another?

Ever your own R.

* * *

E.B.B. to R.B.

Sunday.
[postmark September 7, 1846.]

Not well—not well! But I shall see you with my own eyes soon
after you read what I write to-day; so I shall not write much. Only a few
words to tell you that Flush is found, and lying on the sofa, with one
paw and both ears hanging over the edge of it. Still my visit to Taylor was
not the successful one. My hero was not at home.

I went, you know, . . did I tell you? . . with Wilson in the cab.
We got into obscure streets; and our cabman stopped at a public house to
ask his way. Out came two or three men, . . 'Oh, you want to find Mr.
Taylor, I dare say!' (mark that no name had been mentioned!) and
instantly an unsolicited philanthropist ran before us to the house, and
out again to tell me that the great man 'wasn't at home! but wouldn't I
get out?' Wilson, in an aside of terror, entreated me not to think of such
a thing—she believed devoutly in the robbing and murdering, and was
not reassured by the gang of benevolent men and boys who 'lived but to
oblige us' all round the cab. 'Then wouldn't I see Mrs. Taylor,' suggested
the philanthropist,—and notwithstanding my negatives, he had run
back again and brought an immense feminine bandit, . . fat enough to
have had an easy conscience all her life, . . who informed me that 'her
husband might be in in a few minutes, or in so many hours—wouldn't
I like to get out and wait' (Wilson pulling at my gown, the philanthropist
echoing the invitation of the feminine Taylor.) — 'No, I thanked them all
—it was not necessary that I should get out, but it was, that Mr. Taylor
should keep his promise about the restoration of a dog which he had
agreed to restore—and I begged her to induce him to go to Wimpole
Street in the course of the day, and not defer it any longer.' To which,
replied the lady, with the most gracious of smiles—'Oh yes certainly'
—and indeed she did believe that Taylor had left home precisely on that
business—poising her head to the right and left with the most easy grace
—'She was sure that Taylor would give his very best attention.' . . .

So, in the midst of the politeness, we drove away, and Wilson seemed to be of opinion that we had escaped with our lives barely. Plain enough it was, that the gang was strong there. The society . . the 'Fancy' . . had their roots in the ground. The faces of those men! —
I had not been at home long, when Mr. Taylor did actually come — desiring to have six guineas confided to his honour!! . . and promising to bring back the dog. I sent down the money, and told them to trust the gentleman's honour, as there seemed no other way for it — and while the business was being concluded, in came Alfred, and straightway called our 'honourable friend' (meeting him in the passage) a swindler and a liar and a thief. Which no gentleman could bear, of course. Therefore with reiterated oaths he swore, 'as he hoped to be saved, we should never see our dog again' — and rushed out of the house. Followed a great storm. I was very angry with Alfred, who had no business to risk Flush's life for the sake of the satisfaction of trying on names which fitted. Angry I was with Alfred, and terrified for Flush, — seeing at a glance the probability of his head being cut off as the proper vengeance! and down-stairs I went with the resolution of going again myself to Mr. Taylor's in Manning Street, or Shoreditch (or) wherever it was, and saving the victim at any price. It was the evening, getting dusk — and everybody was crying out against me for being 'quite mad' and obstinate, and wilful — I was called as many names as Mr. Taylor. At last, Sette said that *he* would do it, promised to be as civil as I could wish, and got me to be 'in a good humour and go up to my room again.' And he went instead of me, and took the money and fair words, and induced the 'man of honour' to forfeit his vengeance and go and fetch the dog. Flush arrived here at eight o'clock (at the very moment with your letter, dearest!), and the first thing he did was to dash up to this door, and then to drink his purple cup full of water, filled three times over. He was not so enthusiastic about seeing me, as I expected — he seemed bewildered and frightened — and whenever anyone said to him 'Poor Flush, did the naughty men take you away?' he put up his head and moaned and yelled. He has been very unhappy certainly. Dirty he is, and much thinner, and continually he is drinking. Six guineas, was his ransom — and now I have paid twenty for him to the dog-stealers.

Arabel says that I wanted *you* yesterday, she thought, to manage me a little. She thought I was suddenly seized with madness, to prepare to walk out of the house in that state of excitement and that hour of the evening. But now — *was* I to let them cut off Flush's head? —

There! I have told you the whole history of yesterday's adventures — and tomorrow I shall see you, my own dear, dear! — Only remember for my sake, *not* to come if you are not fit to come. Dearest, remember not to run any hazards! — That dinner! which I *will* blame, because it deserves it! Mind not to make me be as bad as that dinner, in being the means of working you harm! So I expect you tomorrow *conditionally* . . if you are well enough! — and I thank you for the kind dear letter, welcome next to you, . . being ever and ever your own

BA.

I have been to the *vestry* again to-day.

* * *

R. B. to E. B. B.

Thursday Morning.
[postmark *September 10, 1846.*]

What do you expect this letter will be about, my own dearest? Those which I write on the mornings after our days seem naturally to *answer* any strong point brought out in the previous discourse, and not then completely disposed of . . so they generally run in the vile fashion of a disputatious 'last word'; 'one word yet' — do not they? Ah, but you should remember that never does it feel so intolerable, — the barest fancy of a possibility of losing you — as when I have just seen you and heard you and, alas — left you for a time; on these occasions, it seems so horrible — that if the least recollection of a fear of yours, or a doubt . . . anything which might be nursed, or let grow quietly into a serious obstacle to what we desire — if *that* rises up threateningly, — do you wonder that I begin by attacking *it*? There are always a hundred deepest reasons for gratitude and love which I could write about, but which my after life shall prove I never have forgotten . . still, that very after-life depends perhaps on the letter of the morning reasoning with you, teazing, contradicting. Dearest Ba, I do not tell you that I am justified in plaguing you thus, at any time . . only to get your pardon, if I can, on the grounds — the true grounds.

And this pardon, if you grant it, shall be for the past offences, not for any fresh one I mean to commit now. I will not add one word to those spoken yesterday about the extreme perilousness of delay. You *give* me yourself. Hitherto, from the very first till this moment, the giving hand has been advancing steadily — it is not for me to grasp it lest it stop within an inch or two of my forehead with its crown.

I am going to Town this morning, and will leave off now.

What a glorious dream; through nearly two years — without a single interval of blankness, — much less, bitter waking!

I may say *that*, I suppose, safely through whatever befalls!

Also I will ever say, God bless you, my dearest dearest, — my perfect angel you have been! While I am only your R.

My mother is deeply gratified at your present.

12 o'clock On returning I find your note,

'I will do as you wish — understand' — then I understand you are in earnest. If you *do* go on Monday, our marriage will be impossible for another year — the misery! You see what we have gained by waiting. We must be *married directly* and go to Italy. I will go for a licence to-day and we can be married on Saturday. I will call to-morrow at 3 and arrange everything with you. We can leave from Dover &c., *after* that, — but otherwise, impossible! Inclose the ring, or a substitute — I have not a minute to spare for the post.

Ever your own R.

R.B. to E.B.B.

4 p.m. Thursday.
[postmark *September 10, 1846.*]

I broke open your sealed letter and added the postscript just now. The post being thus saved, I can say a few words more leisurely.

111

I will go to-morrow, I think, and not to-day for the licence—there are fixed hours I fancy at the office—and I might be too late. I will also make the arrangement with my friend for Saturday, if we should want him,—as we shall, in all probability—it would look suspiciously to be unaccompanied. We can arrange to-morrow.

Your words, first and last, have been that you 'would not fail me'—you will not.

And the marriage over, you can take advantage of circumstances and go early or late in the week, as may be practicable. There will be facilities in the general packing &c.,—your own measures may be taken unobserved. Write short notes to the proper persons,—promising longer ones, if necessary.

See the *tone* I take, the way I write to *you* . . but it is all through you, in the little brief authority you give me,—and in the perfect belief of your truth and firmness—indeed, I do not consider this an extraordinary occasion for proving those qualities—this conduct of your father's is quite characteristic.

Otherwise, too, the departure with its bustle is not unfavourable. If you hesitated, it would be before a little hurried shopping and letter-writing! I expected it, and therefore spoke as you heard yesterday. *Now your* part must begin. It may as well begin and end, both, *now* as at any other time. I will bring you every information possible to-morrow.

It seems as if I should insult you if I spoke a word to confirm you, to beseech you, to relieve you from your promise, if you claim it.

God bless you, prays your own R.

E.B.B. to R.B.

Thursday.
[postmark *September 11, 1846.*]

Dearest, I write one word, and have one will which is yours. At the same time, do not be precipitate—we shall not be taken away on Monday, no, nor for several days afterward. George has simply gone to look for houses — going to Reigate first.

Oh yes — come to-morrow. And then, you shall have the ring . . soon enough and safer.

Not a word of how you are! — *you* so good as to write me that letter beyond compact, yet not good enough, to say how you are! Dear, dearest . . take care, and keep yourself unhurt and calm. I shall not fail to you — I do not, I will not. I will act by your decision, and I wish you to decide. I was yours long ago, and though you give me back my promise at this eleventh hour, . . you generous, dear unkind! . . . you know very well that you can do as well without it. So take it again for my sake and not your own.

I cannot write, I am so tired, having been long out. Will not this dream break on a sudden? Now is the moment for the breaking of it, surely.

But come to-morrow, come. Almost everybody is to be away at Richmond, at a picnic, and we shall be free on all sides.

Ever and ever your BA.

[On the morning of September 12, R.B. and E.B.B. were married.]

R. B. to E. B. B.

1 p.m. Saturday.
[postmark *September 12, 1846.*]

You will only expect a few words — what will those be? When the heart is full it may run over, but the real fulness stays within.

You asked me yesterday 'if I should repent?' Yes — my own Ba, — I could wish all the past were to do over again, that in it I might somewhat more, — never so little more, conform in the outward homage to the inward feeling. What I have professed . . (for I have performed nothing) seems to fall short of what my first love required even — and when I think of *this* moment's love . . I could repent, as I say.

113

Words can never tell you, however, — form them, transform them anyway, — how perfectly dear you are to me — perfectly dear to my heart and soul.

I look back, and in every one point, every word and gesture, every letter, every *silence* — you have been entirely perfect to me — I would not change one word, one look.

My hope and aim are to preserve this love, not to fall from it — for which I trust to God who procured it for me, and doubtlessly can preserve it.

Enough now, my dearest, dearest, own Ba! You have given me the highest, completest proof of love that ever one human being gave another. I am all gratitude — and all pride (under the proper feeling which ascribes pride to the right source) all pride that my life has been so crowned by you.

God bless you prays your very own R.

I will write to-morrow of course. Take every care of *my life* which is in that dearest little hand; try and be composed, my beloved.

Remember to thank Wilson for me.

* * *

E. B. B. to R. B.

Monday Evening.
[postmark *September 15, 1846.*]

First, God is to be thanked for this great joy of hearing that you are better, my ever dearest — it is a joy that floats over all the other emotions. Dearest, I am so glad! I had feared that excitement's telling on you quite in another way. When the whole is done, and we have left England and the talkers thereof behind our backs, you will be well, steadfastly and satisfactorily, I do trust. In the meantime, there seems so much to do, that I am frightened to look towards the heaps of it. As to accoutrements, everything has been arranged as simply as possible that way — but still there are necessities — and the letters, the letters! I am paralysed when I think of having to write such words as 'Papa, I am married; I hope you will not be too displeased.' Ah, poor Papa! You are too sanguine if you expect any such calm from him as an assumption of indifference would imply. To the utmost, he will be angry, — and he will cast me off as far from him. Well — there is no comfort in such thoughts. How I felt to-night when I saw him at seven o'clock, for the first time since Friday, and the event of Saturday! He spoke kindly too, and asked me how I was. Once I heard of his saying of me that I was 'the purest woman he ever knew,' — which made me smile at the moment, or laugh I believe, outright, because I understood perfectly what he meant by *that* — viz — that I had not troubled him with the iniquity of love affairs, or any impropriety of seeming to think about being married. But now the whole sex will go down with me to the perdition of faith in any of us. See the effect of my wickedness! — 'Those women!'

But we will submit, dearest. I will put myself under his feet, to be forgiven a little, . . enough to be taken up again into his arms. I love him — he is my father — he has good and high qualities after all: he is my father *above* all. And *you*, because you are so generous and tender to me, will let me, you say, and help me to try to win back the alienated affection — for which, I thank you and bless you, — I did not thank you enough this morning. Surely I may say to him, too, . . 'With the exception of this act, I have submitted to the least of your wishes all my life long. Set the life against the act, and forgive me, for the sake of the daughter you once loved.' Surely I may say *that*, — and then remind him of the long suffering I have suffered, — and entreat him to pardon the happiness which has come at last.

And *he* will wish in return, that I had died years ago! For the storm will come and endure. And at last, perhaps, he will forgive us — it is my hope.

I accede to all you say of Mr. Kenyon. I will ask him for his address in the country, and we will send, when the moment comes, our letters together.

From Mrs. Jameson I had the letter I enclose, this morning, (full of kindness — is it not?) and another really as kind from Miss Bayley, who begs me, if I cannot go to Italy, to go to Hastings and visit her. To both I must write at some length. Will *you* write to Mrs. Jameson, besides what I shall write? And what are we to say as to travelling? As she is in Paris, perhaps we may let her have the solution of our problem sooner than the near people. May we? shall we? Yet we dare not, I suppose, talk too historically of what happened last Saturday. It is like the dates in the newspaper — advertisements, which we must eschew, as you observe.

Other things, too, you observe, my beloved, which are altogether out of date. In your ways towards me, you have acted throughout too much 'the woman's part,' as that is considered. You loved me because I was lower than others, that you might be generous and raise me up: — very characteristic for a woman (in her ideal standard) but quite wrong for a man, as again and again I used to signify to you, Robert — but you went on and did it all the same. And now, you still go on — you persist — you will be the woman of the play, to the last; let the prompter prompt ever so against you. You are to do everything I like, instead of my doing what *you* like, . . and to 'honour and obey' *me*, in spite of what was in the vows last Saturday, — is *that* the way of it and of you? and are vows to be kept *so*, pray? after that fashion? Then, *don't* put 'at home' at the corner of the cards, dearest! It is my command!

And forgive the inveterate jesting, which jests with eyes full of tears. I love you — I bless God for you. You are too good for me, as always I knew. I look up to you continually.

It is best, I continue to think, that you should not come here — best for *you*, because the position, if you were to try it, would be less tolerable than ever — and best for both of us, that in case the whole truth were ever discovered (I mean, of the previous marriage) we might be able to call it simply an act in order to security. I don't know how to put my feeling into words, but I do seem to feel that it would be better, and less offensive to those whom we offend at any rate, to avoid all possible remark on this point. It seems better to a sort of instinct I have.

Then, if I see you — farewell, the letter-writing. Oh no — there will be time enough when we are on the railway! — We shall talk then.

Ah — you say such things to me! Dearest, dearest*est!* — And you do not start at that word, 'Irrevocable,' as I have had fancies that you might, when the time came!' But you may recover, by putting out your hand, all you have given me, . . nearly all. I never, never, being myself, could willingly vex you, torment you. If I approach to it, you will tell me. I will confide in you, to that end also. Dearest.

And your father's goodness, and the affectionateness of them all. When they shall have learnt most that I am not worthy of you, they will have learnt besides that I can be grateful to *them* and you. Certainly I am capable, I hope, of loving them all, well and with appreciation. And then . . imagine the comfort I take to the deepest of my heart from these hands held out to me! For your sake! Yes, for your sake entirely! — and, so, the more dearly comforting to

Your very own BA.

There is still difficulty about the house. They think of Tunbridge Wells.

* * *

E. B. B. to R. B.

[postmark *September 17, 1846.*]

Dearest, the general departure from this house takes place on Monday — and the house at Little Bookham is six miles from the nearest railroad, and a mile and a half from Leatherhead where a coach runs. Now you are to judge. Certainly if I go with you on Saturday I shall not have half the letters written — you, who talk so largely of epic poems, have not the least imagination of my state of mind and spirits. I began to write a letter to Papa this morning, and could do nothing but cry, and looked so pale thereupon, that everybody wondered what could be the matter. Oh — quite well I am now, and I only speak of myself in that way to show you how the inspiration is by no means sufficient for epic poems. Still, I may certainly write the necessary letters, . . and do the others on the road . . could I, do you think? I would rather have waited — indeed rather — only it may be difficult to leave Bookham . . yet *possible* — so tell me what you would have me do.

Wilson and I have a light box and a carpet bag between us — and I will be docile about the books, dearest. Do you take a desk? Had I better not, I wonder?

Then for box and carpet bag . . Remember that we cannot take them out of the house with us. We must send them the evening before — Friday evening, if we went on Saturday . . and where? Have you a friend anywhere, to whose house they might be sent, or could they go direct to the railroad office — and what office? In that case they should have your name on them, should they not?

Now think for me, ever dearest — and tell me what you do not tell me . . that you continue better. Ah no — you are ill again — or you would not wait to be told to tell me. And the dear, dear little *bud!* — I shall keep it to the end of my life, if you love me so long, . . or *not, sir!* I thank you, dearest.

Your mother! — I am very, very sorry. Would it be better and kinder to wait on *her* account? — tell me that too.

Yes, they are perfectly kind. We must love them well: — and *I* shall, I am sure.

Mr. Kenyon sends the 'Fawn,' *which is Landor's Fawn,* and desires me to send it to you when I have done with it. As if I could read a word! He directs me to write to him to Taunton, Somersetshire. May God bless you, beloved.

No more to-night from your very own

BA.

Are not passengers allowed to carry a specific proportion of luggage? What do you mean then, by paying for every ounce? As to Dieppe, the diligence would be more fatiguing than the river, and, without strong reasons, one would prefer of course the Havre plan. Still I am not afraid of either. Think.

You might put in the newspaper . . of Wimpole Street and Jamaica, or . . and Cinnamon Hill, Jamaica. That is right and I thought of it at first — only stopped . . seeming to wish to have as little about poor Papa as possible. Do as you think best now.

R.B. to E.B.B.

[postmark *September 17, 1846.*]

My only sweetest, I will write just a word to catch the earlier post, — time pressing. Bless you for all you suffer . . I *know* it though it would be very needless to call your attention to the difficulties. I know much, if not all, and can only love and admire you, — not help, alas!

Surely these difficulties will multiply, if you go to Bookham — the way will be to leave at once. The letters may easily be written during the journey . . at Orléans, for example. But now, — you propose *Saturday* . . nothing leaves Southampton according to *to-day's* advertisement, till *Tuesday* . . the days seemed changed to *Tuesdays* and *Fridays*. Tomorrow at 8¼ p.m. and Friday the 22, 10¼. Provoking! I will go to town directly to the railway office and enquire particularly — getting the timetable also. Under these circumstances, we have only the choice of Dieppe (as needing the shortest diligence-journey) — or the Sunday morning Havre-packet, at 9 a.m. — which you do not consider practicable: though it would, I think, take us the quickliest out of all the trouble. I will let you know all particulars in a note to-night . . it shall reach you tonight.

If we went from London only, the luggage could be sent here or in any case, perhaps . . as one fly will carry them with me and mine, and save possibility of delay.

I am *very* well, dearest dearest — my mother no worse, better, perhaps — she is out now. Our staying and getting into trouble would increase her malady.

As you leave it to me, — the name, and 'Wimpole St.' will do. Jamaica sounds in the wrong direction, does it not? and the other place is distinctive enough.

Take no desk . . I will take a large one — take nothing you can leave — but secure letters &c. I will take out a passport. Did you not tell me roughly at how much you estimated our expenses for the journey? Because I will take about *that* much, and get Rothschild's letter of credit for Leghorn. One should avoid carrying money about with one.

All this in such haste! Bless you, my dearest dearest Ba.

Your R.

All was right in the licence, and Certificate and Register — the whole name is there, E.B.M.B. The clergyman made the mistake in not having the *two* names, but all runs right to *read* . . the essential thing.

R.B. to E.B.B.

5 o'clock.
[postmark *September 17, 1846.*]

My own Ba, I believe, or am sure the mistake has been mine — in the flurry I noted down the departures from *Havre* — instead of *Southampton*. You must either be at the Vauxhall Station by *four* o'clock — so as to arrive in 3 hours and a half at Southampton and leave by 8¼ p.m. — or must go by the Sunday Boat, — or *wait* till Tuesday. Dieppe is impossible, being too early. You must decide — and let me know directly. To-morrow *is* too early — yet one . . that is, *I* — could manage.

Ever your own, in all haste
R.B.

R.B. to E.B.B.

7½ — Thursday
[postmark *September 18, 1846.*]

My own Ba — forgive my mistaking! I had not enough confidence in my own correctness. The advertisement of the Tuesday and Friday Boats is of the South of England Steam Company. The Wednesday and Saturday is that of the *South Western*. There must be then *two* companies, because on the Southampton Railway Bill it is expressly stated that there are departures for Havre on all four days. Perhaps you have seen my blunder. In that case you can leave by 1–/2½ as you may appoint –

Your R.

E. B. B. to R. B.

[postmark *September 18, 1846*.]

Dearest take this word, as if it were many. I am so tired – and then it shall be the right word.

Sunday and Friday are impossible. On Saturday I will go to you, if you like – with half done, . . nothing done . . scarcely. Will you come for me to Hodgson's? or shall I meet you at the station? At what o'clock should I set out, to be there at the hour you mention?

Also, for the boxes . . we cannot carry them out of the house, you know, Wilson and I. They must be sent on Friday evening to the Vauxhall station, 'to be taken care of.' Will the people keep them carefully? Ought someone to be spoken to beforehand? If we sent them to New Cross, they would not reach you in time.

Hold me my beloved – with your love. It is very hard – But Saturday seems the only day for us. Tell me if you think so indeed.

Your very own BA.

The boxes must have your name on them of course. Let there be no great haste about sending out the cards. *Saturday* might be mentioned in the advertisement, *without* the date – might it not?

E. B. B. to R. B.

[postmark *September 18, 1846*.]

Dearest, here is the paper of addresses. I cannot remember, I am so confused, half of them.

Surely you say wrong in the hour for to-morrow. Also there is the express train. Would it not be better?

Your BA.

R. B. to E. B. B.

11½ *Friday*.
[postmark *September 18, 1846*.]

My own best Ba. How thankful I am you have seen my blunder — I took the other company's days for the South Western's changed. What I shall write now is with the tables before me (of the Railway) and a transcript from *to-day's* advertisement in the *Times*.

The packet will leave to-morrow evening, from the Royal Pier, Southampton at *nine*. We leave Nine Elms, Vauxhall, at *five* — to arrive at *eight*. Doors close *five* minutes before. I will be at Hodgson's *from* half-past three to *four precisely* when I shall hope you can be ready. I shall go to Vauxhall, apprise them that luggage is coming (yours) and send *mine* there — so that we both shall be unencumbered and we can take a cab or coach from H's.

Never mind your scanty preparations . . we can get everything at Leghorn, — and the new boats carry parcels to Leghorn on the 15th of every month, remember — so can bring what you may wish to send for.

I enclose a letter to go with yours. The cards as you choose — they are here — we can write about them from Paris or elsewhere. The advertisement, as you advise. All shall be cared for.

God bless and strengthen you, my ever dearest dearest — I will not trust myself to speak of my feelings for you — worship well belongs to such fortitude. One struggle more — if all the kindness on your part brought a strangely insufficient return, is it not possible that this step may produce all you can hope? Write to me one word more. Depend on me. I go to Town about business.

Your own, own R.

E. B. B. to R. B.

Friday Night.
[postmark *September 19, 1846.*]

At from half-past three to four, then — four will not, I suppose, be too late. I will not write more — *I cannot.* By to-morrow at this time, I shall have *you* only, to love me — my beloved!

You *only!* As if one said *God only.* And we shall have *Him* beside, I pray of Him.

I shall send to your address at New Cross your Hanmer's poems — and the two dear books you gave me, which I do not like to leave here and am afraid of hurting by taking them with me. Will you ask *our* Sister to put the parcel into a drawer, so as to keep it for us?

Your letters to me I take with me, let the 'ounces' cry out aloud, ever so. I *tried* to leave them, and I could not. That is, they would not be left: it was not my fault — I will not be scolded.

Is this my last letter to you, ever dearest? Oh — if I loved you less — a little, little less.

Why I should tell you that our marriage was invalid, or ought to be; and that you should by no means come for me to-morrow. It is dreadful . . dreadful . . to have to give pain here by a voluntary act — for the first time in my life.

Remind your mother and father of me affectionately and gratefully

—and your Sister too! Would she think it too bold of me to say *our* Sister, if she had heard it on the last page?

Do you pray for me to-night, Robert? Pray for me, and love me, that I may have courage, feeling both —

Your own
BA.

The boxes are *safely sent*. Wilson has been perfect to me. And *I* . . calling her 'timid,' and afraid of her timidity! I begin to think that none are so bold as the timid, when they are fairly roused.

ELIZABETH BARRETT BROWNING
1806–1861

AN ISLAND

'All goeth but Goddis will.' — *Old Poet.*

I.

My dream is of an island-place
    Which distant seas keep lonely,
A little island on whose face
    The stars are watchers only:
Those bright still stars! they need not seem
Brighter or stiller in my dream.

II.

An island full of hills and dells,
    All rumpled and uneven
With green recesses, sudden swells,
    And odorous valleys driven
So deep and straight that always there
The wind is cradled to soft air.

III.

Hills running up to heaven for light
    Through woods that half-way ran,
As if the wild earth mimicked right
    The wilder heart of man:
Only it shall be greener far
And gladder than hearts ever are.

127

IV.

More like, perhaps, that mountain piece
    Of Dante's paradise,
Disrupt to an hundred hills like these,
    In falling from the skies;
Bringing within it, all the roots
Of heavenly trees and flowers and fruits:

V.

For — saving where the gray rocks strike
    Their javelins up the azure,
Or where deep fissures miser-like
    Hoard up some fountain treasure,
(And e'en in them, stoop down and hear,
Leaf sounds with water in your ear,) —

VI.

The place is all awave with trees,
    Limes, myrtles purple-beaded,
Acacias having drunk the lees
    Of the night-dew, faint-headed,
And wan gray olive-woods which seem
The fittest foliage for a dream.

VII.

Trees, trees on all sides! they combine
    Their plumy shades to throw,
Through whose clear fruit and blossom fine
    Whene'er the sun may go,
The ground beneath he deeply stains,
As passing through cathedral panes.

VIII.

But little needs this earth of ours
  That shining from above her,
When many Pleiades of flowers
  (Not one lost) star her over,
The rays of their unnumbered hues
Being all refracted by the dews.

IX.

Wide-petalled plants that boldly drink
  The Amreeta of the sky,
Shut bells that dull with rapture sink,
  And lolling buds, half shy;
I cannot count them, but between
Is room for grass and mosses green,

X.

And brooks, that glass in different strengths
  All colors in disorder,
Or, gathering up their silver lengths
  Beside their winding border,
Sleep, haunted through the slumber hidden,
By lilies white as dreams in Eden.

XI.

Nor think each archèd tree with each
  Too closely interlaces
To admit of vistas out of reach,
  And broad moon-lighted places
Upon whose sward the antlered deer
May view their double image clear.

XII.

For all this island's creature-full,
  (Kept happy not by halves)
Mild cows, that at the vine-wreaths pull,
  Then low back at their calves
With tender lowings, to approve
The warm mouths milking them for love.

XIII.

Free gamesome horses, antelopes,
  And harmless leaping leopards,
And buffaloes upon the slopes,
  And sheep unruled by shepherds:
Hares, lizards, hedgehogs, badgers, mice,
Snakes, squirrels, frogs, and butterflies.

XIV.

And birds that live there in a crowd,
  Horned owls, rapt nightingales,
Larks bold with heaven, and peacocks proud,
  Self-sphered in those grand tails;
All creatures glad and safe, I deem.
No guns nor springes in my dream!

XV.

The island's edges are a-wing
  With trees that overbranch
The sea with song-birds welcoming
  The curlews to green change;
And doves from half-closed lids espy
The red and purple fish go by.

XVI.

One dove is answering in trust
    The water every minute,
Thinking so soft a murmur must
    Have her mate's cooing in it:
So softly doth earth's beauty round
Infuse itself in ocean's sound.

XVII.

My sanguine soul bounds forwarder
    To meet the bounding waves;
Beside them straightway I repair,
    To live within the caves:
And near me two or three may dwell
Whom dreams fantastic please as well.

XVIII.

Long winding caverns, glittering far
    Into a crystal distance!
Through clefts of which shall many a star
    Shine clear without resistance,
And carry down its rays the smell
Of flowers above invisible.

XIX.

I said that two or three might choose
    Their dwelling near mine own:
Those who would change man's voice and use,
    For Nature's way and tone—
Man's veering heart and careless eyes,
For Nature's steadfast sympathies.

XX.

Ourselves, to meet her faithfulness,
  Shall play a faithful part;
Her beautiful shall ne'er address
  The monstrous at our heart:
Her musical shall ever touch
Something within us also such.

XXI.

Yet shall she not our mistress live,
  As doth the moon of ocean,
Though gently as the moon she give
  Our thoughts a light and motion:
More like a harp of many lays,
Moving its master while he plays.

XXII.

No sod in all that island doth
  Yawn open for the dead;
No wind hath borne a traitor's oath;
  No earth, a mourner's tread;
We cannot say by stream or shade,
'I suffered *here*, — was *here* betrayed.'

XXIII.

Our only 'farewell' we shall laugh
  To shifting cloud or hour,
And use our only epitaph
  To some bud turned a flower:
Our only tears shall serve to prove
Excess in pleasure or in love.

XXIV.

Our fancies shall their plumage catch
  From fairest island-birds,
Whose eggs let young ones out at hatch,
  Born singing! then our words
Unconsciously shall take the dyes
Of those prodigious fantasies.

XXV.

Yea, soon, no consonant unsmooth
  Out smile-tuned lips shall reach;
Sounds sweet as Hellas spake in youth
  Shall glide into our speech:
(What music, certes, can you find
As soft as voices which are kind?)

XXVI.

And often, by the joy without
  And in us, overcome,
We, through our musing, shall let float
  Such poems, — sitting dumb, —
As Pindar might have writ if he
Had tended sheep in Arcady;

XXVII.

Or Æschylus — the pleasant fields
  He died in, longer knowing;
Or Homer, had men's sins and shields
  Been lost in Meles flowing;
Or Poet Plato, had the undim
Unsetting Godlight broke on him.

XXVIII.

Choose me the cave most worthy choice,
　　To make a place for prayer,
And I will choose a praying voice
　　To pour our spirits there:
How silverly the echoes run!
Thy will be done, — thy will be done.

XXIX.

Gently yet strangely uttered words!
　　They lift me from my dream;
The island fadeth with its swards
　　That did no more than seem:
The streams are dry, no sun could find —
The fruits are fallen, without wind.

XXX.

So oft the doing of God's will
　　Our foolish wills undoeth!
And yet what idle dream breaks ill,
　　Which morning-light subdueth?
And who would murmur and misdoubt,
When God's great sunrise finds him out?

A SEA-SIDE WALK

I.

We walked beside the sea
After a day which perished silently
Of its own glory — like the princess weird
Who, combating the Genius, scorched and seared,

Uttered with burning breath, 'Ho! victory!'
And sank adown, a heap of ashes pale:
    So runs the Arab tale.

II.

The sky above us showed
A universal and unmoving cloud
On which the cliffs permitted us to see
Only the outline of their majesty,
As master-minds when gazed at by the crowd:
And shining with a gloom, the water gray
    Swang in its moon-taught way.

III.

Nor moon, nor stars were out;
They did not dare to tread so soon about,
Though trembling, in the footsteps of the sun:
The light was neither night's nor day's, but one
Which, life-like, had a beauty in its doubt.
And silence's impassioned breathings round
    Seemed wandering into sound.

IV.

O solemn-beating heart
Of nature! I have knowledge that thou art
Bound unto man's by cords he cannot sever;
And, what time they are slackened by him ever,
So to attest his own supernal part,
Still runneth thy vibration fast and strong
    The slackened cord along:

V.

For though we never spoke
Of the gray water and the shaded rock,
Dark wave and stone unconsciously were fused

Into the plaintive speaking that we used
Of absent friends and memories unforsook;
And, had we seen each other's face, we had
    Seen haply each was sad.

THE MEASURE

HYMN IV

'He comprehended the dust of the earth in a measure'
(שליש) . — *Isaiah* xl.
'Thou givest them tears to drink in a measure'
(שליש) [1]. — *Psalm* lxxx.

I.

God the Creator, with a pulseless hand
Of unoriginated power, hath weighed
The dust of earth and tears of man in one
    Measure, and by one weight:
    So saith his holy book.

II.

Shall we, then, who have issued from the dust
And there return, — shall we, who toil for dust,
And wrap our winnings in this dusty life,
    Say 'No more tears, Lord God!
    The measure runneth o'er'?

III.

Oh, Holder of the balance, laughest Thou?
Nay, Lord! be gentler to our foolishness,
For his sake who assumed our dust and turns

---

[1] I believe that the word occurs in no other part of the Hebrew Scriptures.

On Thee pathetic eyes
Still moistened with our tears.

IV.

And teach us, O our Father, while we weep,
To look in patience upon earth and learn —
Waiting, in that meek gesture, till at last
These tearful eyes be filled
With the dry dust of death.

GRIEF

I tell you, hopeless grief is passionless;
That only men incredulous of despair,
Half-taught in anguish, through the midnight air
Beat upward to God's throne in loud access
Of shrieking and reproach. Full desertness,
In souls as countries, lieth, silent-bare
Under the blanching, vertical eye-glare
Of the absolute Heavens. Deep-hearted man, express
Grief for thy Dead in silence like to death —
Most like a monumental statue set
In everlasting watch and moveless woe
Till itself crumble to the dust beneath.
Touch it; the marble eyelids are not wet:
If it could weep, it could arise and go.

DISCONTENT

Light human nature is too lightly tost
And ruffled without cause, complaining on —
Restless with rest, until, being overthrown,

It learneth to lie quiet. Let a frost
Or a small wasp have crept to the innermost
Of our ripe peach, or let the wilful sun
Shine westward of our window, — straight we run
A furlong's sigh as if the world were lost.
But what time through the heart and through the brain
God hath transfixed us, — we, so moved before,
Attain to a calm. Ay, shouldering weights of pain,
We anchor in deep waters, safe from shore,
And hear submissive o'er the stormy main
God's chartered judgments walk for evermore.

PATIENCE TAUGHT BY NATURE

'O dreary life,' we cry, 'O dreary life!'
And still the generations of the birds
Sing through our sighing, and the flocks and herds
Serenely live while we are keeping strife
With Heaven's true purpose in us, as a knife
Against which we may struggle! Ocean girds
Unslackened the dry land, savannah-swards
Unweary sweep, hills watch unworn, and rife
Meek leaves drop yearly from the forest-trees
To show, above, the unwasted stars that pass
In their old glory: O thou God of old,
Grant me some smaller grace than comes to these! —
But so much patience as a blade of grass
Grows by, contented through the heat and cold.

from A VISION OF POETS

[A poet has met a visionary lady who says that she will show him the truth of poets and of poetry.]

*　　*　　*　　*　　*

She ceased: her palfrey's paces sent
No separate noises as she went;
'Twas a bee's hum, a little spent.

And while the poet seemed to tread
Along the drowsy noise so made,
The forest heaved up overhead

Its billowy foliage through the air,
And the calm stars did far and spare
O'erswim the masses everywhere;

Save when the overtopping pines
Did bar their tremulous light with lines
All fixed and black. Now the moon shines

A broader glory. You may see
The trees grow rarer presently;
The air blows up more fresh and free:

Until they come from dark to light,
And from the forest to the sight
Of the large heaven-heart, bare with night,

A fiery throb in every star,
Those burning arteries that are
The conduits of God's life afar, —

A wild brown moorland underneath,
And four pools breaking up the heath
With white low gleamings, blank as death.

Beside the first pool, near the wood,
A dead tree in set horror stood,
Peeled and disjointed, stark as rood;

Since thunder-stricken, years ago,
Fixed in the spectral strain and throe
Wherewith it struggled from the blow:

A monumental tree, alone,
That will not bend in storms, nor groan,
But break off sudden like a stone.

Its lifeless shadow lies oblique
Upon the pool where, javelin-like,
The star-rays quiver while they strike.

'Drink,' said the lady, very still —
'Be holy and cold.' He did her will
And drank the starry water chill.

The next pool they came near unto
Was bare of trees; there, only grew
Straight flags, and lilies just a few

Which sullen on the water sate
And leant their faces on the flat,
As weary of the starlight-state.

'Drink,' said the lady, grave and slow —
'World's use behoveth thee to know.'
He drank the bitter wave below.

The third pool, girt with thorny bushes
And flaunting weeds and reeds and rushes
That winds sang through in mournful gushes,

Was whitely smeared in many a round
By a slow slime; the starlight swound
Over the ghastly light it found.

'Drink,' said the lady, sad and slow —
'*World's love* behoveth thee to know.'
He looked to her commanding so;

Her brow was troubled, but her eye
Struck clear to his soul. For all reply
He drank the water suddenly, —

Then, with a deathly sickness, passed
Beside the fourth pool and the last,
Where weights of shadow were downcast

From yew and alder and rank trails
Of nightshade clasping the trunk-scales
And flung across the intervals

From yew to yew: who dares to stoop
Where those dank branches overdroop,
Into his heart the chill strikes up;

He hears a silent gliding coil,
The snakes strain hard against the soil,
His foot slips in their slimy oil,

And toads seem crawling on his hand,
And clinging bats but dimly scanned
Full in his face their wings expand.

A paleness took the poet's cheek:
'Must I drink *here?*' he seemed to seek
The lady's will with utterance meek:

'Ay, ay,' she said, 'it so must be;'
(And this time she spake cheerfully),
'Behoves thee know *World's cruelty.*'

He bowed his forehead till his mouth
Curved in the wave, and drank unloth
As if from rivers of the south;

His lips sobbed through the water rank,
His heart paused in him while he drank,
His brain beat heart-like, rose and sank,

And he swooned backward to a dream
Wherein he lay 'twixt gloom and gleam,
With Death and Life at each extreme:

* * * * *

[But *after the great poets of the past, there appears a company of
poetic impostors.*]

* * * * *

'What living man will bring a gift
Of his own heart and help to lift
The tune? — The race is to the swift.'

So asked the angel. Straight the while,
A company came up the aisle
With measured step and sorted smile;

Cleaving the incense-clouds that rise,
With winking unaccustomed eyes
And love-locks smelling sweet of spice.

One bore his head above the rest
As if the world were dispossessed,
And one did pillow chin on breast,

Right languid, an as he should faint,
One shook his curls across his paint
And moralized on worldly taint;

One, slanting up his face, did wink
The salt rheum to the eyelid's brink,
To think — O gods! or — not to think.

Some trod out stealthily and slow,
As if the sun would fall in snow
If they walked to instead of fro;

And some, with conscious ambling free,
Did shake their bells right daintily
On hand and foot, for harmony;

And some, composing sudden sighs
In attitudes of point-device,
Rehearsed impromptu agonies.

And when this company drew near
The spirits crowned, it might appear
Submitted to a ghastly fear;

As a sane eye in master-passion
Constrains a maniac to the fashion
Of hideous maniac imitation

In the least geste — the dropping low
O' the lid, the wrinkling of the brow,
Exaggerate with mock and mow, —

So mastered was that company
By the crowned vision utterly,
Swayed to a maniac mockery.

One dulled his eyeballs, as they ached
With Homer's forehead, though he lacked
An inch of any; and one racked

His lower lip with restless tooth,
As Pindar's rushing words forsooth
Were pent behind it; one his smooth

Pink cheeks did rumple passionate
Like Æschylus, and tried to prate
On trolling tongue of fate and fate;

One set her eyes like Sappho's — or
Any light woman's; one forbore
Like Dante, or any man as poor

In mirth, to let a smile undo
His hard-shut lips; and one that drew
Sour humors from his mother, blew

His sunken cheeks out to the size
Of most unnatural jollities,
Because Anacreon looked jest-wise;

So with the rest: it was a sight
A great world-laughter would requite,
Or great world-wrath, with equal right.

Out came a speaker from that crowd
To speak for all, in sleek and proud
Exordial periods, while he bowed

His knee before the angel — 'Thus,
O angel who hast called for us,
We bring thee service emulous,

'Fit service from sufficient soul,
Hand-service to receive world's dole,
Lip-service in world's ear to roll

'Adjusted concords — soft enow
To hear the wine-cups passing, through,
And not too grave to spoil the show:

'Thou, certes, when thou askest more,
O sapient angel, leanest o'er
The window-sill of metaphor.

'To give our hearts up? fie! that rage
Barbaric antedates the age;
It is not done on any stage.

'Because your scald or gleeman went
With seven or nine-stringed instrument
Upon his back, — must ours be bent?

'We are not pilgrims, by your leave;
No, nor yet martyrs; if we grieve,
It is to rhyme to — summer eve:

'And if we labor, it shall be
As suiteth best with our degree,
In after-dinner reverie.'

More yet that speaker would have said,
Poising between his smiles fair-fed
Each separate phrase till finishèd;

But all the foreheads of those born
And dead true poets flashed with scorn
Betwixt the bay leaves round them worn,

Ay, jetted such brave fire that they,
The new-come, shrank and paled away
Like leaden ashes when the day

Strikes on the hearth. A spirit-blast,
A presence known by power, at last
Took them up mutely: they had passed.

*　　*　　*　　*　　*

TO FLUSH, MY DOG

I.

Loving friend, the gift of one
Who her own true faith has run
 Through thy lower nature,
Be my benediction said
With my hand upon thy head,
 Gentle fellow-creature!

II.

Like a lady's ringlets brown,
Flow thy silken ears adown
 Either side demurely
Of thy silver-suited breast
Shining out from all the rest
 Of thy body purely.

III.

Darkly brown thy body is,
Till the sunshine striking this
 Alchemize its dulness,
When the sleek curls manifold
Flash all over into gold
 With a burnished fulness.

IV.

Underneath my stroking hand,
Startled eyes of hazel bland
 Kindling, growing larger,
Up thou leapest with a spring,

146

Full of prank and curveting,
Leaping like a charger.

V.

Leap! thy broad tail waves a light,
Leap! thy slender feet are bright,
  Canopied in fringes;
Leap! those tasselled ears of thine
Flicker strangely, fair and fine
  Down their golden inches.

VI.

Yet, my pretty, sportive friend,
Little is't to such an end
  That I praise thy rareness;
Other dogs may be thy peers
Haply in these drooping ears
  And this glossy fairness.

VII.

But of *thee* it shall be said,
This dog watched beside a bed
  Day and night unweary,
Watched within a curtained room
Where no sunbeam brake the gloom
  Round the sick and dreary.

VIII.

Roses, gathered for a vase,
In that chamber died apace,
  Beam and breeze resigning;
This dog only, waited on,
Knowing that when light is gone
  Love remains for shining.

IX.

Other dogs in thymy dew
Tracked the hares and followed through
  Sunny moor or meadow;
This dog only, crept and crept
Next a languid cheek that slept,
  Sharing in the shadow.

X.

Other dogs of loyal cheer
Bounded at the whistle clear,
  Up the woodside hieing;
This dog only, watched in reach
Of a faintly uttered speech
  Or a louder sighing.

XI.

And if one or two quick tears
Dropped upon his glossy ears
  Or a sigh came double,
Up he sprang in eager haste,
Fawning, fondling, breathing fast,
  In a tender trouble.

XII.

And this dog was satisfied
If a pale thin hand would glide
  Down his dewlaps sloping, —
Which he pushed his nose within,
After, — platforming his chin
  On the palm left open.

XIII.

This dog, if a friendly voice
Call him now to blither choice
   Than such chamber-keeping,
'Come out!' praying from the door, —
Presseth backward as before,
   Up against me leaping.

XIV.

Therefore to this dog will I,
Tenderly not scornfully,
   Render praise and favor:
With my hand upon his head,
Is my benediction said
   Therefore and for ever.

XV.

And because he loves me so,
Better than his kind will do
   Often man or woman,
Give I back more love again
Than dogs often take of men,
   Leaning from my Human.

XVI.

Blessings on thee, dog of mine,
Pretty collars make thee fine,
   Sugared milk make fat thee!
Pleasures wag on in thy tail,
Hands of gentle motion fail
   Nevermore, to pat thee!

XVII.

Downy pillow take thy head,
Silken coverlid bestead,
  Sunshine help thy sleeping!
No fly's buzzing wake thee up,
No man break thy purple cup
  Set for drinking deep in.

XVIII.

Whiskered cats arointed flee,
Sturdy stoppers keep from thee
  Cologne distillations;
Nuts lie in thy path for stones,
And thy feast-day macaroons
  Turn to daily rations!

XIX.

Mock I thee, in wishing weal? —
Tears are in my eyes to feel
  Thou art made so straitly,
Blessing needs must straiten too, —
Little canst thou joy or do,
  Thou who lovest *greatly*.

XX.

Yet be blessèd to the height
Of all good and all delight
  Pervious to thy nature;
Only *loved* beyond that line,
With a love that answers thine,
  Loving fellow-creature!

WINE OF CYPRUS

Given to me by H. S. Boyd, author of
'Select Passages from the Greek Fathers,' etc.

TO WHOM THESE STANZAS ARE ADDRESSED

I.

If old Bacchus were the speaker,
    He would tell you with a sigh
Of the Cyprus in this beaker
    I am sipping like a fly, —
Like a fly or gnat on Ida
    At the hour of goblet-pledge,
By queen Juno brushed aside, a
    Full white arm-sweep, from the edge.

II.

Sooth, the drinking should be ampler
    When the drink is so divine,
And some deep-mouthed Greek exemplar
    Would become your Cyprus wine:
Cyclops' mouth might plunge aright in,
    While his one eye overleered,
Nor too large were mouth of Titan
    Drinking rivers down his beard.

III.

Pan might dip his head so deep in,
    That his ears alone pricked out,

151

Fauns around him pressing, leaping,
  Each one pointing to his throat:
While the Naiads, like Bacchantes,
  Wild, with urns thrown out to waste,
Cry, 'O earth, that thou wouldst grant us
  Springs to keep, of such a taste!'

IV.

But for me, I am not worthy
  After gods and Greeks to drink,
And my lips are pale and earthy
  To go bathing from this brink:
Since you heard them speak the last time,
  They have faded from their blooms,
And the laughter of my pastime
  Has learnt silence at the tombs.

V.

Ah, my friend! the antique drinkers
  Crowned the cup and crowned the brow.
Can I answer the old thinkers
  In the forms they thought of, now?
Who will fetch from garden-closes
  Some new garlands while I speak,
That the forehead, crowned with roses,
  May strike scarlet down the cheek?

VI.

Do not mock me! with my mortal
  Suits no wreath again, indeed;
I am sad-voiced as the turtle
  Which Anacreon used to feed:
Yet as that same bird demurely
  Wet her beak in cup of his,
So, without a garland, surely
  I may touch the brim of this.

VII.

Go, — let others praise the Chian!
   This is soft as Muses' string,
This is tawny as Rhea's lion,
   This is rapid as his spring,
Bright as Paphia's eyes e'er met us,
   Light as ever trod her feet;
And the brown bees of Hymettus
   Make their honey not so sweet.

VIII.

Very copious are my praises,
   Though I sip it like a fly!
Ah — but, sipping, — times and places
   Change before me suddenly:
As Ulysses' old libation
   Drew the ghosts from every part,
So your Cyprus wine, dear Grecian,
   Stirs the Hades of my heart.

IX.

And I think of those long mornings
   Which my thought goes far to seek,
When, betwixt the folio's turnings,
   Solemn flowed the rhythmic Greek:
Past the pane the mountain spreading,
   Swept the sheep's-bell's tinkling noise,
While a girlish voice was reading,
   Somewhat low for $\alpha\iota$'s and $o\iota$'s.

X.

Then, what golden hours were for us!
   While we sat together there,
How the white vests of the chorus

Seemed to wave up a live air!
How the cothurns trod majestic
Down the deep iambic lines,
And the rolling anapæstic
Curled like vapor over shrines!

XI.

Oh, our Æschylus, the thunderous,
How he drove the bolted breath
Through the cloud, to wedge it ponderous
In the gnarlèd oak beneath!
Oh, our Sophocles, the royal,
Who was born to monarch's place,
And who made the whole world loyal
Less by kingly power than grace!

XII.

Our Euripides, the human,
With his droppings of warm tears,
And his touches of things common
Till they rose to touch the spheres!
Our Theocritus, our Bion,
And our Pindar's shining goals! —
These were cup-bearers undying
Of the wine that's meant for souls.

XIII.

And my Plato, the divine one,
If men know the gods aright
By their motions as they shine on
With a glorious trail of light!
And your noble Christian bishops,
Who mouthed grandly the last Greek!
Though the sponges on their hyssops
Were distent with wine — too weak.

XIV.

Yet, your Chrysostom, you praised him
  As a liberal mouth of gold;
And your Basil, you upraised him
  To the height of speakers old:
And we both praised Heliodorus
  For his secret of pure lies, —
Who forged first his linkèd stories
  In the heat of ladies' eyes.

XV.

And we both praised your Synesius
  For the fire shot up his odes,
Though the Church was scarce propitious
  As he whistled dogs and gods.
And we both praised Nazianzen
  For the fervid heart and speech:
Only I eschewed his glancing
  At the lyre hung out of reach.

XVI.

Do you mind that deed of Atè
  Which you bound me to so fast, —
Reading 'De Virginitate,'
  From the first line to the last?
How I said at ending, solemn
  As I turned and looked at you,
That Saint Simeon on the column
  Had had somewhat less to do?

XVII.

For we sometimes gently wrangled,
  Very gently, be it said,
Since our thoughts were disentangled

155

By no breaking of the thread!
And I charged you with extortions
On the nobler fames of old —
Ay, and sometimes thought your Porsons
Stained the purple they would fold.

XVIII.

For the rest — a mystic moaning
  Kept Cassandra at the gate,
With wild eyes the vision shone in,
  And wide nostrils scenting fate.
And Prometheus, bound in passion
  By brute Force to the blind stone,
Showed us looks of invocation
  Turned to ocean and the sun.

XIX.

And Medea we saw burning
  At her nature's planted stake:
And proud Œdipus fate-scorning
  While the cloud came on to break —
While the cloud came on slow, slower,
  Till he stood discrowned, resigned! —
But the reader's voice dropped lower
  When the poet called him BLIND.

XX.

Ah, my gossip! you were older,
  And more learnèd, and a man!
Yet that shadow, the enfolder
  Of your quiet eyelids, ran
Both our spirits to one level;
  And I turned from hill and lea
And the summer-sun's green revel,
  To your eyes that could not see.

XXI.

Now Christ bless you with the one light
    Which goes shining night and day!
May the flowers which grow in sunlight
    Shed their fragrance in your way!
Is it not right to remember
    All your kindness, friend of mine,
When we two sat in the chamber,
    And the poets poured us wine?

XXII.

So, to come back to the drinking
    Of this Cyprus, — it is well,
But those memories, to my thinking,
    Make a better œnomel;
And whoever be the speaker,
    None can murmur with a sigh
That, in drinking from *that* beaker,
    I am sipping like a fly.

HECTOR IN THE GARDEN

I.

Nine years old! The first of any
    Seem the happiest years that come:
    Yet when *I* was nine, I said
    No such word! I thought instead
That the Greeks had used as many
    In besieging Ilium.

157

II.

Nine green years had scarcely brought me
  To my childhood's haunted spring;
  I had life, like flowers and bees.
  In betwixt the country trees,
And the sun the pleasure taught me
  Which he teacheth every thing.

III.

If the rain fell, there was sorrow:
  Little head leant on the pane,
  Little finger drawing down it
  The long trailing drops upon it,
And the 'Rain, rain, come to-morrow,'
  Said for charm against the rain.

IV.

Such a charm was right Canidian,
  Thought you meet it with a jeer!
  If I said it long enough,
  Then the rain hummed dimly off,
And the thrush with his pure Lydian
  Was left only to the ear;

V.

And the sun and I together
  Went a-rushing out of doors:
  We our tender spirits drew
  Over hill and dale in view,
Glimmering hither, glimmering thither
  In the footsteps of the showers.

VI.

Underneath the chestnuts dripping,
  Through the grasses wet and fair,
  Straight I sought my garden-ground
  With the laurel on the mound,
And the pear-tree oversweeping
  A side-shadow of green air.

VII.

In the garden lay supinely
  A huge giant wrought of spade!
  Arms and legs were stretched at length
  In a passive giant strength, —
The fine meadow turf, cut finely,
  Round them laid and interlaid.

VIII.

Call him Hector, son of Priam!
  Such his title and degree.
  With my rake I smoothed his brow,
  Both his cheeks I weeded through,
But a rhymer such as I am,
  Scarce can sing his dignity.

IX.

Eyes of gentianellas azure,
  Staring, winking at the skies:
  Nose of gillyflowers and box;
  Scented grasses put for locks,
Which a little breeze at pleasure
  Set a-waving round his eyes:

X.

Brazen helm of daffodillies,
  With a glitter toward the light;
  Purple violets for the mouth,
  Breathing perfumes west and south;
And a sword of flashing lilies,
  Holden ready for the fight:

XI.

And a breastplate made of daisies,
  Closely fitting, leaf on leaf;
  Periwinkles interlaced
  Drawn for belt about the waist;
While the brown bees, humming praises,
  Shot their arrows round the chief.

XII.

And who knows (I sometimes wondered)
  If the disembodied soul
  Of old Hector, once of Troy,
  Might not take a dreary joy
Here to enter — if it thundered,
  Rolling up the thunder-roll?

XIII.

Rolling this way from Troy-ruin,
  In this body rude and rife
  Just to enter, and take rest
  'Neath the daisies of the breast —
They, with tender roots, renewing
  His heroic heart to life?

XIV.

Who could know? I sometimes started
  At a motion or a sound!
  Did his mouth speak — naming Troy
  With an ὀτοτοτοτοῖ?
Did the pulse of the Strong-hearted
  Make the daisies tremble round?

XV.

It was hard to answer, often:
  But the birds sang in the tree,
  But the little birds sang bold
  In the pear-tree green and old,
And my terror seemed to soften
  Through the courage of their glee.

XVI.

Oh, the birds, the tree, the ruddy
  And white blossoms sleek with rain!
  Oh, my garden rich with pansies!
  Oh, my childhood's bright romances!
All revive, like Hector's body,
  And I see them stir again.

XVII.

And despite life's changes, chances,
  And despite the deathbell's toll,
  They press on me in full seeming.
  Help, some angel! stay this dreaming!
As the birds sang in the branches,
  Sing God's patience through my soul!

XVIII.

That no dreamer, no neglecter
    Of the present's work unsped,
I may wake up and be doing,
Life's heroic ends pursuing,
Though my past is dead as Hector,
    And though Hector is twice dead.

THE MASK

I.

I have a smiling face, she said,
    I have a jest for all I meet,
I have a garland for my head
    And all its flowers are sweet, —
And so you call me gay, she said.

II.

Grief taught to me this smile, she said,
    And Wrong did teach this jesting bold;
These flowers were plucked from garden-bed
    While a death-chime was tolled:
And what now will you say? — she said.

III.

Behind no prison-grate, she said,
    Which slurs the sunshine half a mile,
Live captives so uncomforted
    As souls behind a smile.
God's pity let us pray, she said.

IV.

I know my face is bright, she said, —
  Such brightness dying suns diffuse:
I bear upon my forehead shed
  The sign of what I lose,
The ending of my day, she said.

V.

If I dared leave this smile, she said,
  And take a moan upon my mouth,
And tie a cypress round my head,
  And let my tears run smooth,
It were the happier way, she said.

VI.

And since that must not be, she said,
  I fain your bitter world would leave.
How calmly, calmly smile the Dead,
  Who do not, therefore, grieve!
The yea of Heaven is yea, she said.

VII.

But in your bitter world, she said,
  Face-joy's a costly mask to wear;
'T is bought with pangs long nourishèd,
  And rounded to despair:
Grief's earnest makes life's play, she said.

VIII.

Ye weep for those who weep? she said —
  Ah fools! I bid you pass them by.
Go, weep for those whose hearts have bled
  What time their eyes were dry.
Whom sadder can I say? she said.

HUMAN LIFE'S MYSTERY

I.

We sow the glebe, we reap the corn,
  We build the house where we may rest,
And then, at moments, suddenly
We look up to the great wide sky,
Inquiring wherefore we were born,
  For earnest or for jest?

II.

The senses folding thick and dark
  About the stifled soul within,
We guess diviner things beyond,
And yearn to them with yearning fond;
We strike out blindly to a mark
  Believed in, but not seen.

III.

We vibrate to the pant and thrill
  Wherewith Eternity has curled
In serpent-twine about God's seat:
While, freshening upward to his feet,
In gradual growth his full-leaved will
  Expands from world to world.

IV.

And, in the tumult and excess
  Of act and passion under sun,
We sometimes hear — oh, soft and far,
As silver star did touch with star,

The kiss of Peace and Righteousness
  Through all things that are done.

V.

God keeps his holy mysteries
  Just on the outside of man's dream;
In diapason slow, we think
To hear their pinions rise and sink,
While they float pure beneath his eyes,
  Like swans adown a stream.

VI.

Abstractions, are they, from the forms
  Of his great beauty? — exaltations
From his great glory? — strong previsions
Of what we shall be? — intuitions
Of what we are — in calms and storms
  Beyond our peace and passions?

VII.

Things nameless! which, in passing so,
  Do stroke us with a subtle grace;
We say, 'Who passes?' — they are dumb;
We cannot see them go or come,
Their touches fall soft, cold, as snow
  Upon a blind man's face.

VIII.

Yet, touching so, they draw above
  Our common thoughts to Heaven's unknown;
Our daily joy and pain advance
To a divine significance
Our human love — O mortal love,
  That light is not its own!

IX.

And sometimes horror chills our blood
  To be so near such mystic Things,
And we wrap round us for defence
Our purple manners, moods of sense —
As angels from the face of God
  Stand hidden in their wings.

X.

And sometimes through life's heavy swound
  We grope for them, with strangled breath
We stretch our hands abroad and try
To reach them in our agony;
And widen, so, the broad life-wound
  Soon large enough for death.

A CHILD'S THOUGHT OF GOD

I.

They say that God lives very high;
  But if you look above the pines
You cannot see our God; and why?

II.

And if you dig down in the mines
  You never see Him in the gold;
Though from Him all that's glory shines.

III.

God is so good, He wears a fold
　　Of heaven and earth across his face —
Like secrets kept, for love, untold.

IV.

But still I feel that his embrace
　　Slides down by thrills, through all things made,
Through sight and sound of every place:

V.

As if my tender mother laid
　　On my shut lips her kisses' pressure,
Half-waking me at night, and said
　　'Who kissed you through the dark, dear guesser?'

A DEAD ROSE

I.

　　O Rose, who dares to name thee?
No longer roseate now, nor soft nor sweet,
But pale and hard and dry as stubble wheat, —
　　Kept seven years in a drawer, thy titles shame thee.

II.

　　The breeze that used to blow thee
Between the hedgerow thorns, and take away
An odor up the lane to last all day, —
　　If breathing now, unsweetened would forgo thee.

167

III.

The sun that used to smite thee,
And mix his glory in thy gorgeous urn
Till beam appeared to bloom, and flower to burn, —
If shining now, with not a hue would light thee.

IV.

The dew that used to wet thee,
And, white first, grow incarnadined because
It lay upon thee where the crimson was, —
If dropping now, would darken where it met thee.

V.

The fly that 'lit upon thee
To stretch the tendrils of its tiny feet
Along thy leaf's pure edges after heat, —
If 'lighting now, would coldly overrun thee.

VI.

The bee that once did suck thee,
And build thy perfumed ambers up his hive,
And swoon in thee for joy, till scarce alive, —
If passing now, would blindly overlook thee.

VII.

The heart doth recognize thee,
Alone, alone! the heart doth smell thee sweet,
Doth view thee fair, doth judge thee most complete,
Perceiving all those changes that disguise thee.

VIII.

Yes, and the heart doth owe thee
More love, dead rose, than to any roses bold
Which Julia wears at dances, smiling cold: —
Lie still upon this heart which breaks below thee!

A WOMAN'S SHORTCOMINGS

I.

She has laughed as softly as if she sighed,
　　She has counted six, and over,
Of a purse well filled and a heart well tried —
　　Oh, each a worthy lover!
They 'give her time;' for her soul must slip
　　Where the world has set the grooving;
She will lie to none with her fair red lip:
　　But love seeks truer loving.

II.

She trembles her fan in a sweetness dumb,
　　As her thoughts were beyond recalling,
With a glance for *one*, and a glance for *some*,
　　From her eyelids rising and falling;
Speaks common words with a blushful air,
　　Hears bold words, unreproving;
But her silence says — what she never will swear —
　　And love seeks better loving.

III.

Go, lady, lean to the night-guitar
　　And drop a smile to the bringer;

Then smile as sweetly, when he is far,
   At the voice of an in-door singer.
Bask tenderly beneath tender eyes;
   Glance lightly, on their removing;
And join new vows to old perjuries —
   But dare not call it loving.

IV.

Unless you can think, when the song is done,
   No other is soft in the rhythm;
Unless you can feel, when left by One,
   That all men else go with him;
Unless you can know, when unpraised by his breath,
   That your beauty itself wants proving;
Unless you can swear 'For life, for death!' —
   Oh, fear to call it loving!

V.

Unless you can muse in a crowd all day
   On the absent face that fixed you;
Unless you can love, as the angels may,
   With the breadth of heaven betwixt you;
Unless you can dream that his faith is fast,
   Through behoving and unbehoving;
Unless you can *die* when the dream is past —
   Oh, never call it loving!

A MAN'S REQUIREMENTS

I.

Love me, Sweet, with all thou art,
   Feeling, thinking, seeing;
Love me in the lightest part,
   Love me in full being.

II.

Love me with thine open youth
 In its frank surrender;
With the vowing of thy mouth,
 With its silence tender.

III.

Love me with thine azure eyes,
 Made for earnest granting;
Taking color from the skies,
 Can Heaven's truth be wanting?

IV.

Love me with their lids, that fall
 Snow-like at first meeting;
Love me with thine heart, that all
 Neighbors then see beating.

V.

Love me with thine hand stretched out
 Freely — open-minded;
Love me with thy loitering foot, —
 Hearing one behind it.

VI.

Love me with thy voice, that turns
 Sudden faint above me;
Love me with thy blush that burns
 When I murmur *Love me!*

VII.

Love me with thy thinking soul,
   Break it to love-sighing;
Love me with thy thoughts that roll
   On through living — dying.

VIII.

Love me in thy gorgeous airs,
   When the world has crowned thee;
Love me, kneeling at thy prayers,
   With the angels round thee.

IX.

Love me pure, as musers do,
   Up the woodlands shady:
Love me gaily, fast and true,
   As a winsome lady.

X.

Through all hopes that keep us brave,
   Farther off or nigher,
Love me for the house and grave,
   And for something higher.

XI.

Thus, if thou wilt prove me, Dear,
   Woman's love no fable,
I will love *thee* — half a year —
   As a man is able.

A DENIAL

I.

We have met late — it is too late to meet,
  O friend, not more than friend!
Death's forecome shroud is tangled round my feet,
And if I step or stir, I touch the end.
    In this last jeopardy
Can I approach thee, I, who cannot move?
How shall I answer thy request for love?
    Look in my face and see.

II.

I love thee not, I dare not love thee! go
  In silence; drop my hand.
If thou seek roses, seek them where they blow
In garden-alleys, not in desert-sand.
    Can life and death agree,
That thou shouldst stoop thy song to my complaint?
I cannot love thee. If the word is faint,
    Look in my face and see.

III.

I might have loved thee in some former days.
  Oh, then, my spirits had leapt
As now they sink, at hearing thy love-praise!
Before these faded cheeks were overwept,
    Had this been asked of me,
To love thee with my whole strong heart and head, —
I should have said still . . . yes, but *smiled* and said,
    'Look in my face and see!'

IV.

But now . . . God sees me, God, who took my heart
  And drowned it in life's surge.
In all your wide warm earth I have no part —
A light song overcomes me like a dirge.
    Could Love's great harmony
The saints keep step to when their bonds are loose,
Not weigh me down? am I a wife to choose?
    Look in my face and see —

V.

While I behold, as plain as one who dreams,
  Some woman of full worth,
Whose voice, as cadenced as a silver stream's,
Shall prove the fountain-soul which sends it forth;
    One younger, more thought-free
And fair and gay, than I, thou must forget,
With brighter eyes than these . . . which are not wet . . .
    Look in my face and see!

VI.

So farewell thou, whom I have known too late
  To let thee come so near.
Be counted happy while men call thee great,
And one belovèd woman feels thee dear! —
    Not I! — that cannot be.
I am lost, I am changed, — I must go farther, where
The change shall take me worse, and no one dare
    Look in my face and see.

VII.

Meantime I bless thee. By these thoughts of mine
  I bless thee from all such!
I bless thy lamp to oil, thy cup to wine,

Thy hearth to joy, thy hand to an equal touch
   Of loyal troth. For me,
I love thee not, I love thee not! — away!
Here's no more courage in my soul to say
   'Look in my face and see.'

QUESTION AND ANSWER

I.

Love you seek for, presupposes
   Summer heat and sunny glow.
Tell me, do you find moss-roses
   Budding, blooming in the snow?
Snow might kill the rose-tree's root —
Shake it quickly from your foot,
   Lest it harm you as you go.

II.

From the ivy where it dapples
   A gray ruin, stone by stone,
Do you look for grapes or apples,
   Or for sad green leaves alone?
Pluck the leaves off, two or three —
Keep them for morality
   When you shall be safe and gone.

SONNETS FROM THE PORTUGUESE

I.

I thought once how Theocritus had sung
Of the sweet years, the dear and wished-for years,

Who each one in a gracious hand appears
To bear a gift for mortals, old or young:
And, as I mused it in his antique tongue,
I saw, in gradual vision through my tears,
The sweet, sad years, the melancholy years,
Those of my own life, who by turns had flung
A shadow across me. Straightway I was 'ware,
So weeping, how a mystic Shape did move
Behind me, and drew me backward by the hair:
And a voice said in mastery, while I strove, —
'Guess now who holds thee?' — 'Death,' I said. But, there,
The silver answer rang, — 'Not Death, but Love.'

II.

But only three in all God's universe
Have heard this word thou hast said, — Himself, beside
Thee speaking, and me listening! and replied
One of us . . . *that* was God, . . . and laid the curse
So darkly on my eyelids, as to amerce
My sight from seeing thee, — that if I had died,
The deathweights, placed there, would have signified
Less absolute exclusion. 'Nay' is worse
From God than from all others, O my friend!
Men could not part us with their worldly jars,
Nor the seas change us, nor the tempests bend;
Our hands would touch for all the mountain-bars:
And, heaven being rolled between us at the end,
We should but vow the faster for the stars.

III.

Unlike are we, unlike, O princely Heart!
Unlike our uses and our destinies.
Our ministering two angels look surprise
On one another, as they strike athwart
Their wings in passing. Thou, bethink thee, art
A guest for queens to social pageantries,
With gages from a hundred brighter eyes
Than tears even can make mine, to play thy part

Of chief musician. What hast *thou* to do
With looking from the lattice-lights at me,
A poor, tired, wandering singer, singing through
The dark, and leaning up a cypress tree?
The chrism is on thine head, — on mine, the dew, —
And Death must dig the level where these agree.

IV.

Thou hast thy calling to some palace-floor,
Most gracious singer of high poems! where
The dancers will break footing, from the care
Of watching up thy pregnant lips for more.
And dost thou lift this house's latch too poor
For hand of thine? and canst thou think and bear
To let thy music drop here unaware
In folds of golden fulness at my door?
Look up and see the casement broken in,
The bats and owlets builders in the roof!
My cricket chirps against thy mandolin.
Hush, call no echo up in further proof
Of desolation! there's a voice within
That weeps . . . as thou must sing . . . alone, aloof.

V.

I lift my heavy heart up solemnly,
As once Electra her sepulchral urn,
And, looking in thine eyes, I overturn
The ashes at thy feet. Behold and see
What a great heap of grief lay hid in me,
And how the red wild sparkles dimly burn
Through the ashen grayness. If thy foot in scorn
Could tread them out to darkness utterly,
It might be well perhaps. But if instead
Thou wait beside me for the wind to blow
The gray dust up, . . . those laurels on thine head,
O my Belovèd, will not shield thee so,
That none of all the fires shall scorch and shred
The hair beneath. Stand farther off then! go.

177

VI.

Go from me. Yet I feel that I shall stand
Henceforward in thy shadow. Nevermore
Alone upon the threshold of my door
Of individual life, I shall command
The uses of my soul, nor lift my hand
Serenely in the sunshine as before,
Without the sense of that which I forbore —
Thy touch upon the palm. The widest land
Doom takes to part us, leaves thy heart in mine
With pulses that beat double. What I do
And what I dream include thee, as the wine
Must taste of its own grapes. And when I sue
God for myself, He hears that name of thine,
And sees within my eyes the tears of two.

VII.

The face of all the world is changed, I think,
Since first I heard the footsteps of thy soul
Move still, oh, still, beside me, as they stole
Betwixt me and the dreadful outer brink
Of obvious death, where I, who thought to sink,
Was caught up into love, and taught the whole
Of life in a new rhythm. The cup of dole
God gave for baptism, I am fain to drink,
And praise its sweetness, Sweet, with thee anear.
The names of country, heaven, are changed away
For where thou art or shalt be, there or here;
And this . . . this lute and song . . . loved yesterday,
(The singing angels know) are only dear
Because thy name moves right in what they say.

VIII.

What can I give thee back, O liberal
And princely giver, who hast brought the gold
And purple of thine heart, unstained, untold,

178

And laid them on the outside of the wall
For such as I to take or leave withal,
In unexpected largesse? am I cold,
Ungrateful, that for these most manifold
High gifts, I render nothing back at all?
Not so; not cold, — but very poor instead.
Ask God who knows. For frequent tears have run
The colors from my life, and left so dead
And pale a stuff, it were not fitly done
To give the same as pillow to thy head.
Go farther! let it serve to trample on.

IX.

Can it be right to give what I can give?
To let thee sit beneath the fall of tears
As salt as mine, and hear the sighing years
Re-sighing on my lips renunciative
Through those infrequent smiles which fail to live
For all thy adjurations? O my fears,
That this can scarce be right! We are not peers,
So to be lovers; and I own, and grieve,
That givers of such gifts as mine are, must
Be counted with the ungenerous. Out, alas!
I will not soil thy purple with my dust,
Nor breathe my poison on thy Venice-glass,
Nor give thee any love — which were unjust.
Beloved, I only love thee! let it pass.

X.

Yet, love, mere love, is beautiful indeed
And worthy of acceptation. Fire is bright,
Let temple burn, or flax; an equal light
Leaps in the flame from cedar-plank or weed:
And love is fire. And when I say at need
I love thee . . . mark! . . . I love thee — in thy sight
I stand transfigured, glorified aright,
With conscience of the new rays that proceed

Out of my face toward thine. There's nothing low
In love, when love the lowest: meanest creatures
Who love God, God accepts while loving so.
And what I *feel*, across the inferior features
Of what I *am*, doth flash itself, and show
How that great work of Love enhances Nature's.

XI.

And therefore if to love can be desert,
I am not all unworthy. Cheeks as pale
As these you see, and trembling knees that fail
To bear the burden of a heavy heart, —
This weary minstrel-life that once was girt
To climb Aornus, and can scarce avail
To pipe now 'gainst the valley nightingale
A melancholy music, — why advert
To these things? O Belovèd, it is plain
I am not of thy worth nor for thy place!
And yet, because I love thee, I obtain
From that same love this vindicating grace,
To live on still in love, and yet in vain, —
To bless thee, yet renounce thee to thy face.

XII.

Indeed this very love which is my boast,
And which, when rising up from breast to brow,
Doth crown me with a ruby large enow
To draw men's eyes and prove the inner cost, —
This love even, all my worth, to the uttermost,
I should not love withal, unless that thou
Hadst set me an example, shown me how,
When first thine earnest eyes with mine were crossed,
And love called love. And thus, I cannot speak
Of love even, as a good thing of my own:
Thy soul hath snatched up mine all faint and weak,
And placed it by thee on a golden throne, —
And that I love (O soul, we must be meek!)
Is by thee only, whom I love alone.

XIII.

And wilt thou have me fashion into speech
The love I bear thee, finding words enough,
And hold the torch out, while the winds are rough,
Between our faces, to cast light on each? —
I drop it at thy feet. I cannot teach
My hand to hold my spirit so far off
From myself — me — that I should bring thee proof
In words, of love hid in me out of reach.
Nay, let the silence of my womanhood
Commend my woman-love to thy belief, —
Seeing that I stand unwon, however wooed,
And rend the garment of my life, in brief,
By a most dauntless, voiceless fortitude,
Lest one touch of this heart convey its grief.

XIV.

If thou must love me, let it be for nought
Except for love's sake only. Do not say
'I love her for her smile — her look — her way
Of speaking gently, — for a trick of thought
That falls in well with mine, and certes brought
A sense of pleasant ease on such a day' —
For these things in themselves, Belovèd, may
Be changed, or change for thee, — and love, so wrought,
May be unwrought so. Neither love me for
Thine own dear pity's wiping my cheeks dry, —
A creature might forget to weep, who bore
Thy comfort long, and lose thy love thereby!
But love me for love's sake, that evermore
Thou mayst love on, through love's eternity.

XV.

Accuse me not, beseech thee, that I wear
Too calm and sad a face in front of thine;

For we two look two ways, and cannot shine
With the same sunlight on our brow and hair.
On me thou lookest with no doubting care,
As on a bee shut in a crystalline;
Since sorrow hath shut me safe in love's divine,
And to spread wing and fly in the outer air
Were most impossible failure, if I strove
To fail so. But I look on thee — on thee —
Beholding, besides love, the end of love,
Hearing oblivion beyond memory;
As one who sits and gazes from above,
Over the rivers to the bitter sea.

XVI.

And yet, because thou overcomest so,
Because thou art more noble and like a king,
Thou canst prevail against my fears and fling
Thy purple round me, till my heart shall grow
Too close against thine heart henceforth to know
How it shook when alone. Why, conquering
May prove as lordly and complete a thing
In lifting upward, as in crushing low!
And as a vanquished soldier yields his sword
To one who lifts him from the bloody earth,
Even so, Belovèd, I at last record,
Here ends my strife. If *thou* invite me forth,
I rise above abasement at the word.
Make thy love larger to enlarge my worth.

XVII.

My poet, thou canst touch on all the notes
God set between his After and Before,
And strike up and strike off the general roar
Of the rushing worlds a melody that floats
In a serene air purely. Antidotes
Of medicated music, answering for
Mankind's forlornest uses, thou canst pour

From thence into their ears. God's will devotes
Thine to such ends, and mine to wait on thine.
How, Dearest, wilt thou have me for most use?
A hope, to sing by gladly? or a fine
Sad memory, with thy songs to interfuse?
A shade, in which to sing — of palm or pine?
A grave, on which to rest from singing? Choose.

XVIII.

I never gave a lock of hair away
To a man, Dearest, except this to thee,
Which now upon my fingers thoughtfully,
I ring out to the full brown length and say
'Take it.' My day of youth went yesterday;
My hair no longer bounds to my foot's glee,
Nor plant I it from rose or myrtle-tree,
As girls do, any more: it only may
Now shade on two pale cheeks the mark of tears,
Taught drooping from the head that hangs aside
Through sorrow's trick. I thought the funeral-shears
Would take this first, but Love is justified, —
Take it thou, — finding pure, from all those years,
The kiss my mother left here when she died.

XIX.

The soul's Rialto hath its merchandise;
I barter curl for curl upon that mart,
And from my poet's forehead to my heart
Receive this lock which outweighs argosies, —
As purply black, as erst to Pindar's eyes
The dim purpureal tresses gloomed athwart
The nine white Muse-brows. For this counterpart, . . .
The bay-crown's shade, Belovèd, I surmise,
Still lingers on thy curl, it is so black!
Thus, with a fillet of smooth-kissing breath,
I tie the shadows safe from gliding back,
And lay the gift where nothing hindereth;

Here on my heart, as on thy brow, to lack
No natural heat till mine grows cold in death.

XX.

Belovèd, my Belovèd, when I think
That thou wast in the world a year ago,
What time I sat alone here in the snow
And saw no footprint, heard the silence sink
No moment at thy voice, but, link by link,
Went counting all my chains as if that so
They never could fall off at any blow
Struck by thy possible hand, — why, thus I drink
Of life's great cup of wonder! Wonderful,
Never to feel thee thrill the day or night
With personal act or speech, — nor ever cull
Some prescience of thee with the blossoms white
Thou sawest growing! Atheists are as dull,
Who cannot guess God's presence out of sight.

XXI.

Say over again, and yet once over again,
That thou dost love me. Though the word repeated
Should seem 'a cuckoo-song,' as thou dost treat it,
Remember, never to the hill or plain,
Valley and wood, without her cuckoo-strain
Comes the fresh Spring in all her green completed.
Belovèd, I, amid the darkness greeted
By a doubtful spirit-voice, in that doubt's pain
Cry, 'Speak once more — thou lovest!' Who can fear
Too many stars, though each in heaven shall roll,
Too many flowers, though each shall crown the year?
Say thou dost love me, love me, love me — toll
The silver iterance! — only minding, Dear,
To love me also in silence with thy soul.

XXII.

When our two souls stand up erect and strong,
Face to face, silent, drawing nigh and nigher,
Until the lengthening wings break into fire
At either curvèd point, — what bitter wrong
Can the earth do to us, that we should not long
Be here contented? Think. In mounting higher,
The angels would press on us and aspire
To drop some golden orb of perfect song
Into our deep, dear silence. Let us stay
Rather on earth, Belovèd, — where the unfit
Contrarious moods of men recoil away
And isolate pure spirits, and permit
A place to stand and love in for a day,
With darkness and the death-hour rounding it.

XXIII.

Is it indeed so? If I lay here dead,
Wouldst thou miss any life in losing mine?
And would the sun for thee more coldly shine
Because of grave-damps falling round my head?
I marvelled, my Belovèd, when I read
Thy thought so in the letter. I am thine —
But . . . so much to thee? Can I pour thy wine
While my hands tremble? Then my soul, instead
Of dreams of death, resumes life's lower range.
Then, love me, Love! look on me — breathe on me!
As brighter ladies do not count it strange,
For love, to give up acres and degree,
I yield the grave for thy sake, and exchange
My near sweet view of Heaven, for earth with thee!

XXIV.

Let the world's sharpness, like a clasping knife,
Shut in upon itself and do no harm

In this close hand of Love, now soft and warm,
And let us hear no sound of human strife
After the click of the shutting. Life to life —
I lean upon thee, Dear, without alarm,
And feel as safe as guarded by a charm
Against the stab of worldlings, who if rife
Are weak to injure. Very whitely still
The lilies of our lives may reassure
Their blossoms from their roots, accessible
Alone to heavenly dews that drop not fewer,
Growing straight, out of man's reach, on the hill.
God only, who made us rich, can make us poor.

XXV.

A heavy heart, Belovèd, have I borne
From year to year until I saw thy face,
And sorrow after sorrow took the place
Of all those natural joys as lightly worn
As the stringed pearls, each lifted in its turn
By a beating heart at dance-time. Hopes apace
Were changed to long despairs, till God's own grace
Could scarcely lift above the world forlorn
My heavy heart. Then *thou* didst bid me bring
And let it drop adown thy calmly great
Deep being! Fast it sinketh, as a thing
Which its own nature doth precipitate,
While thine doth close above it, mediating
Betwixt the stars and the unaccomplished fate.

XXVI.

I lived with visions for my company
Instead of men and women, years ago,
And found them gentle mates, nor thought to know
A sweeter music than they played to me.
But soon their trailing purple was not free
Of this world's dust, their lutes did silent grow,
And I myself grew faint and blind below

Their vanishing eyes. Then THOU didst come — to be,
Belovèd, what they seemed. Their shining fronts,
Their songs, their splendors (better, yet the same,
As river-water hallowed into fonts),
Met in thee, and from out thee overcame
My soul with satisfaction of all wants:
Because God's gifts put man's best dreams to shame.

XXVII.

My own Belovèd, who hast lifted me
From this drear flat of earth where I was thrown,
And, in betwixt the languid ringlets, blown
A life-breath, till the forehead hopefully
Shines out again, as all the angels see,
Before thy saving kiss! My own, my own,
Who camest to me when the world was gone,
And I who looked for only God, found *thee!*
I find thee; I am safe, and strong, and glad.
As one who stands in dewless asphodel
Looks backward on the tedious time he had
In the upper life, — so I, with bosom-swell,
Make witness, here, between the good and bad,
That Love, as strong as Death, retrieves as well.

XXVIII.

My letters! all dead paper, mute and white!
And yet they seem alive and quivering
Against my tremulous hands which loose the string
And let them drop down on my knee to-night.
This said, — he wished to have me in his sight
Once, as a friend: this fixed a day in spring
To come and touch my hand . . . a simple thing,
Yet I wept for it! — this, . . . the paper's light . . .
Said, *Dear, I love thee;* and I sank and quailed
As if God's future thundered on my past.
This said, *I am thine* — and so its ink has paled
With lying at my heart that beat too fast.

And this . . . O Love, thy words have ill availed
If, what this said, I dared repeat at last!

XXIX.

I think of thee! — my thoughts do twine and bud
About thee, as wild vines, about a tree,
Put out broad leaves, and soon there's nought to see
Except the straggling green which hides the wood.
Yet, O my palm-tree, be it understood
I will not have my thoughts instead of thee
Who art dearer, better! Rather, instantly
Renew thy presence; as a strong tree should,
Rustle thy boughs and set thy trunk all bare,
And let these bands of greenery which insphere thee
Drop heavily down, — burst, shattered, everywhere!
Because, in this deep joy to see and hear thee
And breathe within thy shadow a new air,
I do not think of thee — I am too near thee.

XXX.

I see thine image through my tears to-night
And yet to-day I saw thee smiling. How
Refer the cause? — Belovèd, is it thou
Or I, who makes me sad? The acolyte
Amid the chanted joy and thankful rite
May so fall flat, with pale insensate brow,
On the altar-stair. I hear thy voice and vow,
Perplexed, uncertain, since thou art out of sight,
As he, in his swooning ears, the choir's Amen.
Belovèd, dost thou love? or did I see all
The glory as I dreamed, and fainted when
Too vehement light dilated my ideal,
For my soul's eyes? Will that light come again,
As now these tears come — falling hot and real?

XXXI.

Thou comest! all is said without a word.
I sit beneath thy looks, as children do
In the noon-sun, with souls that tremble through
Their happy eyelids from an unaverred
Yet prodigal inward joy. Behold, I erred
In that last doubt! and yet I cannot rue
The sin most, but the occasion — that we two
Should for a moment stand unministered
By a mutual presence. Ah, keep near and close,
Thou dovelike help! and, when my fears would rise,
With thy broad heart serenely interpose:
Brood down with thy divine sufficiencies
These thoughts which tremble when bereft of those,
Like callow birds left desert to the skies.

XXXII.

The first time that the sun rose on thine oath
To love me, I looked forward to the moon
To slacken all those bonds which seemed too soon
And quickly tied to make a lasting troth.
Quick-loving hearts, I thought, may quickly loathe;
And, looking on myself, I seemed not one
For such man's love! — more like an out-of-tune
Worn viol, a good singer would be wroth
To spoil his song with, and which, snatched in haste,
Is laid down at the first ill-sounding note.
I did not wrong myself so, but I placed
A wrong on *thee*. For perfect strains may float
'Neath master-hands, from instruments defaced, —
And great souls, at one stroke, may do and doat.

XXXIII.

Yes, call me by my pet-name! let me hear
The name I used to run at, when a child,

From innocent play, and leave the cowslips piled,
To glance up in some face that proved me dear
With the look of its eyes. I miss the clear
Fond voices which, being drawn and reconciled
Into the music of Heaven's undefiled,
Call me no longer. Silence on the bier,
While I call God — call God! — So let thy mouth
Be heir to those who are now exanimate.
Gather the north flowers to complete the south,
And catch the early love up in the late.
Yes, call me by that name, — and I, in truth,
With the same heart, will answer and not wait.

XXXIV.

With the same heart, I said, I'll answer thee
As those, when thou shalt call me by my name —
Lo, the vain promise! is the same, the same,
Perplexed and ruffled by life's strategy?
When called before, I told how hastily
I dropped my flowers or brake off from a game,
To run and answer with the smile that came
At play last moment, and went on with me
Through my obedience. When I answer now,
I drop a grave thought, break from solitude;
Yet still my heart goes to thee — ponder how —
Not as to a single good, but all my good!
Lay thy hand on it, best one, and allow
That no child's foot could run fast as this blood.

XXXV.

If I leave all for thee, wilt thou exchange
And be all to me? Shall I never miss
Home-talk and blessing and the common kiss
That comes to each in turn, nor count it strange,
When I look up, to drop on a new range
Of walls and floors, another home than this?
Nay, wilt thou fill that place by me which is

Filled by dead eyes too tender to know change?
That's hardest. If to conquer love, has tried,
To conquer grief, tries more, as all things prove;
For grief indeed is love and grief beside.
Alas, I have grieved so I am hard to love.
Yet love me — wilt thou? Open thine heart wide,
And fold within the wet wings of thy dove.

XXXVI.

When we met first and loved, I did not build
Upon the event with marble. Could it mean
To last, a love set pendulous between
Sorrow and sorrow? Nay, I rather thrilled,
Distrusting every light that seemed to gild
The onward path, and feared to overlean
A finger even. And, though I have grown serene
And strong since then, I think that God has willed
A still renewable fear . . . O love, O troth . . .
Lest these enclaspèd hands should never hold,
This mutual kiss drop down between us both
As an unowned thing, once the lips being cold.
And Love, be false! if *he*, to keep one oath,
Must lose one joy, by his life's star foretold.

XXXVII.

Pardon, oh, pardon, that my soul should make,
Of all that strong divineness which I know
For thine and thee, an image only so
Formed of the sand, and fit to shift and break.
It is that distant years which did not take
Thy sovranty, recoiling with a blow,
Have forced my swimming brain to undergo
Their doubt and dread, and blindly to forsake
Thy purity of likeness and distort
Thy worthiest love to a worthless counterfeit:
As if a shipwrecked Pagan, safe in port,
His guardian sea-god to commemorate,

Should set a sculptured porpoise, gills a-snort
And vibrant tail, within the temple-gate.

XXXVIII.

First time he kissed me, he but only kissed
The fingers of this hand wherewith I write;
And ever since, it grew more clean and white,
Slow to world-greetings, quick with its 'Oh, list,'
When the angels speak. A ring of amethyst
I could not wear here, plainer to my sight,
Than that first kiss. The second passed in height
The first, and sought the forehead, and half missed,
Half falling on the hair. O beyond meed!
That was the chrism of love, which love's own crown,
With sanctifying sweetness, did precede.
The third upon my lips was folded down
In perfect, purple state; since when, indeed,
I have been proud and said, 'My love, my own.'

XXXIX.

Because thou hast the power and own'st the grace
To look through and behind this mask of me
(Against which years have beat thus blanchingly
With their rains), and behold my soul's true face,
The dim and weary witness of life's race, —
Because thou hast the faith and love to see,
Through that same soul's distracting lethargy,
The patient angel waiting for a place
In the new Heavens, — because nor sin nor woe,
Nor God's infliction, nor death's neighborhood,
Nor all which others viewing, turn to go,
Nor all which makes me tired of all, self-viewed, —
Nothing repels thee, . . . Dearest, teach me so
To pour out gratitude, as thou dost, good!

XL.

Oh, yes! they love through all this world of ours!
I will not gainsay love, called love forsooth.
I have heard love talked in my early youth,
And since, not so long back but that the flowers
Then gathered, smell still. Mussulmans and Giaours
Throw kerchiefs at a smile, and have no ruth
For any weeping. Polypheme's white tooth
Slips on the nut if, after frequent showers,
The shell is over-smooth, — and not so much
Will turn the thing called love, aside to hate
Or else to oblivion. But thou art not such
A lover, my Belovèd! thou canst wait
Through sorrow and sickness, to bring souls to touch,
And think it soon when others cry 'Too late.'

XLI.

I thank all who have loved me in their hearts,
With thanks and love from mine. Deep thanks to all
Who paused a little near the prison-wall
To hear my music in its louder parts
Ere they went onward, each one to the mart's
Or temple's occupation, beyond call.
But thou, who, in my voice's sink and fall
When the sob took it, thy divinest Art's
Own instrument didst drop down at thy foot
To hearken what I said between my tears, . . .
Instruct me how to thank thee! Oh, to shoot
My soul's full meaning into future years,
That *they* should lend it utterance, and salute
Love that endures, from Life that disappears!

XLII.

'My future will not copy fair my past' —
I wrote that once; and thinking at my side

My ministering life-angel justified
The word by his appealing look upcast
To the white throne of God, I turned at last,
And there, instead, saw thee, not unallied
To angels in thy soul! Then I, long tried
By natural ills, received the comfort fast,
While budding, at thy sight, my pilgrim's staff
Gave out green leaves with morning dews impearled.
I seek no copy now of life's first half:
Leave here the pages with long musing curled,
And write me new my future's epigraph,
New angel mine, unhoped for in the world!

XLIII.

How do I love thee? Let me count the ways.
I love thee to the depth and breadth and height
My soul can reach, when feeling out of sight
For the ends of Being and ideal Grace.
I love thee to the level of everyday's
Most quiet need, by sun and candle-light.
I love thee freely, as men strive for Right;
I love thee purely, as they turn from Praise.
I love thee with the passion put to use
In my old griefs, and with my childhood's faith.
I love thee with a love I seemed to lose
With my lost saints, — I love thee with the breath,
Smiles, tears, of all my life! — and, if God choose,
I shall but love thee better after death.

XLIV.

Belovèd, thou hast brought me many flowers
Plucked in the garden, all the summer through
And winter, and it seemed as if they grew
In this close room, nor missed the sun and showers.
So, in the like name of that love of ours,
Take back these thoughts which here unfolded too,
And which on warm and cold days I withdrew

From my heart's ground. Indeed, those beds and bowers
Be overgrown with bitter weeds and rue,
And wait thy weeding; yet here's eglantine,
Here's ivy! — take them, as I used to do
Thy flowers, and keep them where they shall not pine.
Instruct thine eyes to keep their colors true,
And tell thy soul their roots are left in mine.

CASA GUIDI WINDOWS

from PART II

[From their apartment in Casa Guidi, the Brownings looked
out at life in Florence. In Part I of Casa Guidi Windows,
Elizabeth had expressed her faith in the Grand Duke Leo-
pold of Tuscany, and her hope that Pope Pius IX would
continue to work for reform and for Italian independence
from Austria. But Part II tells the disillusioned story of the
events in Tuscany of 1848–9. The weak Grand Duke had
fled, and Guerazzi — from whom much was hoped — had
come to power. But, after a riot, Guerazzi was jailed; the
Austrians occupied Florence, and the Grand Duke returned,
protected by the Austrian soldiers.]

*   *   *   *   *

From Casa Guidi windows I looked out,
Again looked, and beheld a different sight.
The Duke had fled before the people's shout
'Long live the Duke!' A people, to speak right,
Must speak as soft as courtiers, lest a doubt
Should curdle brows of gracious sovereigns, white.
Moreover that same dangerous shouting meant
Some gratitude for future favors, which
Were only promised, the Constituent
Implied, the whole being subject to the hitch

In 'motu proprios,' very incident
To all these Czars, from Paul to Paulovitch.
Whereat the people rose up in the dust
Of the ruler's flying feet, and shouted still
And loudly; only, this time, as was just,
Not 'Live the Duke,' who had fled for good or ill,
But 'Live the People,' who remained and must,
The unrenounced and unrenounceable.
Long live the people! How they lived! and boiled
And bubbled in the cauldron of the street:
How the young blustered, nor the old recoiled,
And what a thunderous stir of tongues and feet
Trod flat the palpitating bells and foiled
The joy-guns of their echo, shattering it!
How down they pulled the Duke's arms everywhere!
How up they set new café-signs, to show
Where patriots might sip ices in pure air —
(The fresh paint smelling somewhat)! To and fro
How marched the civic guard, and stopped to stare
When boys broke windows in a civic glow!
How rebel songs were sung to loyal tunes,
And bishops cursed in ecclesiastic metres:
How all the Circoli grew large as moons,
And all the speakers, moonstruck, — thankful greeters
Of prospects which struck poor the ducal boons,
A mere free Press, and Chambers! — frank repeaters
Of great Guerazzi's praises — 'There's a man,
The father of the land, who, truly great,
Takes off that national disgrace and ban,
The farthing tax upon our Florence-gate,
And saves Italia as he only can!'
How all the nobles fled, and would not wait,
Because they were most noble, — which being so,
How Liberals vowed to burn their palaces,
Because free Tuscans were not free to go!
How grown men raged at Austria's wickedness,
And smoked, — while fifty striplings in a row
Marched straight to Piedmont for the wrong's redress!
You say we failed in duty, we who wore

196

Black velvet like Italian democrats,
    Who slashed our sleeves like patriots, nor forswore
The true republic in the form of hats?
    We chased the archbishop from the Duomo door,
We chalked the walls with bloody caveats
    Against all tyrants. If we did not fight
Exactly, we fired muskets up the air
    To show that victory was ours of right.
We met, had free discussion everywhere
    (Except perhaps i' the Chambers) day and night.
We proved the poor should be employed, . . . that's fair, —
    And yet the rich not worked for anywise, —
Pay certified, yet payers abrogated, —
    Full work secured, yet liabilities
To overwork excluded, — not one bated
    Of all our holidays, that still, at twice
Or thrice a week, are moderately rated.
    We proved that Austria was dislodged, or would
Or should be, and that Tuscany in arms
    Should, would dislodge her, ending the old feud;
And yet, to leave our piazzas, shops, and farms,
    For the simple sake of fighting, was not good —
We proved that also. 'Did we carry charms
    Against being killed ourselves, that we should rush
On killing others? what, desert herewith
    Our wives and mothers? — was that duty? tush!'
At which we shook the sword within the sheath
    Like heroes — only louder; and the flush
Ran up the cheek to meet the future wreath.
    Nay, what we proved, we shouted — how we shouted
(Especially the boys did), boldly planting
    That tree of liberty, whose fruit is doubted,
Because the roots are not of nature's granting!
    A tree of good and evil: none, without it,
Grow gods; alas and, with it, men are wanting!

*　　*　　*　　*　　*

    Alas, alas! it was not so this time.
Conviction was not, courage failed, and truth

Was something to be doubted of. The mime
Changed masks, because a mime. The tide as smooth
  In running in as out, no sense of crime
Because no sense of virtue, — sudden ruth
  Seized on the people: they would have again
Their good Grand-duke and leave Guerazzi, though
  He took that tax from Florence. 'Much in vain
He takes it from the market-carts, we trow,
  While urgent that no market-men remain,
But all march off and leave the spade and plough,
  To die among the Lombards. Was it thus
The dear paternal Duke did? Live the Duke!'
  At which the joy-bells multitudinous,
Swept by an opposite wind, as loudly shook
  Call back the mild archbishop to his house,
To bless the people with his frightened look, —
  He shall not yet be hanged, you comprehend!
Seize on Guerazzi; guard him in full view,
  Or else we stab him in the back, to end!
Rub out those chalked devices, set up new
  The Duke's arms, doff your Phrygian caps, and mend
The pavement of the piazzas broke into
  By barren poles of freedom: smooth the way
For the ducal carriage, lest his highness sigh
  'Here trees of liberty grew yesterday!'
'Long live the Duke!' — how roared the cannonry,
  How rocked the bell-towers, and through thickening spray
Of nosegays, wreaths, and kerchiefs tossed on high,
  How marched the civic guard, the people still
Being good at shouts, especially the boys!
  Alas, poor people, of an unfledged will
Most fitly expressed by such a callow voice!
  Alas, still poorer Duke, incapable
Of being worthy even of so much noise!

You think he came back instantly, with thanks
And tears in his faint eyes, and hands extended
  To stretch the franchise through their utmost ranks?
That having, like a father, apprehended,
  He came to pardon fatherly those pranks

Played out and now in filial service ended? —
  That some love-token, like a prince, he threw
To meet the people's love-call, in return?
  Well, how he came I will relate to you;
And if your hearts should burn, why, hearts *must* burn,
  To make the ashes which things old and new
Shall be washed clean in — as this Duke will learn.

From Casa Guidi windows gazing, then,
I saw and witness how the Duke came back.
  The regular tramp of horse and tread of men
Did smite the silence like an anvil black
  And sparkless. With her wide eyes at full strain,
Our Tuscan nurse exclaimed 'Alack, alack,
  Signora! these shall be the Austrians.' 'Nay,
Be still,' I answered, 'do not wake the child!'
  — For so, my two-months' baby sleeping lay
In milky dreams upon the bed and smiled,
  And I thought 'He shall sleep on, while he may,
Through the world's baseness: not being yet defiled,
  Why should he be disturbed by what is done?'
Then, gazing, I beheld the long-drawn street
  Live out, from end to end, full in the sun,
With Austria's thousand; sword and bayonet,
  Horse, foot, artillery, — cannons rolling on
Like blind slow storm-clouds gestant with the heat
  Of undeveloped lightnings, each bestrode
By a single man, dust-white from head to heel,
  Indifferent as the dreadful thing he rode,
Like a sculptured Fate serene and terrible.
  As some smooth river which has overflowed
Will slow and silent down its current wheel
  A loosened forest, all the pines erect,
So swept, in mute significance of storm,
  The marshalled thousands; not an eye deflect
To left or right, to catch a novel form
  Of Florence city adorned by architect
And carver, or of Beauties live and warm
  Scared at the casements, — all, straightforward eyes
And faces, held as steadfast as their swords,

And cognizant of acts, not imageries.
The key, O Tuscans, too well fits the wards!
Ye asked for mimes, — these bring you tragedies:
For purple, — these shall wear it as your lords.
Ye played like children, — die like innocents.
Ye mimicked lightnings with a torch, — the crack
Of the actual bolt, your pastime circumvents.
Ye called up ghosts, believing they were slack
To follow any voice from Gilboa's tents, . . .
Here's Samuel! — and, so, Grand-dukes come back!

*   *   *   *   *

from AURORA LEIGH

A POEM IN NINE BOOKS

DEDICATION TO JOHN KENYON, ESQ.

The words 'cousin' and 'friend' are constantly recurring in this poem, the last pages of which have been finished under the hospitality of your roof, my own dearest cousin and friend; — cousin and friend, in a sense of less equality and greater disinterestedness than 'Romney' 's.

Ending, therefore, and preparing once more to quit England, I venture to leave in your hands this book, the most mature of my works, and the one into which my highest convictions upon Life and Art have entered; that as, through my various efforts in Literature and steps in life, you have believed in me, borne with me, and been generous to me, far beyond the common uses of mere relationship or sympathy of mind, so you may kindly accept, in sight of the public, this poor sign of esteem, gratitude, and affection from — Your unforgetting

E.B.B.

39 DEVONSHIRE PLACE: *October 17, 1856.*

AURORA LEIGH

FIRST BOOK

Of writing many books there is no end;
And I who have written much in prose and verse
For others' uses, will write now for mine, —
Will write my story for my better self,
As when you paint your portrait for a friend,
Who keeps it in a drawer and looks at it
Long after he has ceased to love you, just
To hold together what he was and is.

I, writing thus, am still what men call young;
I have not so far left the coasts of life
To travel inland, that I cannot hear
That murmur of the outer Infinite
Which unweaned babies smile at in their sleep
When wondered at for smiling; not so far,
But still I catch my mother at her post
Beside the nursery door, with finger up,
'Hush, hush — here's too much noise!' while her sweet eyes
Leap forward, taking part against her word
In the child's riot. Still I sit and feel
My father's slow hand, when she had left us both,
Stroke out my childish curls across his knee,
And hear Assunta's daily jest (she knew
He liked it better than a better jest)
Inquire how many golden scudi went
To make such ringlets. O my father's hand,
Stroke heavily, heavily the poor hair down,
Draw, press the child's head closer to thy knee!
I'm still too young, too young, to sit alone.
I write. My mother was a Florentine,
Whose rare blue eyes were shut from seeing me

When scarcely I was four years old, my life
A poor spark snatched up from a failing lamp
Which went out therefore. She was weak and frail;
She could not bear the joy of giving life,
The mother's rapture slew her. If her kiss
Had left a longer weight upon my lips
It might have steadied the uneasy breath,
And reconciled and fraternized my soul
With the new order. As it was, indeed,
I felt a mother-want about the world,
And still went seeking, like a bleating lamb
Left out at night in shutting up the fold, —
As restless as a nest-deserted bird
Grown chill through something being away, though what
It knows not. I, Aurora Leigh, was born
To make my father sadder, and myself
Not overjoyous, truly. Women know
The way to rear up children (to be just),
They know a simple, merry, tender knack
Of tying sashes, fitting baby-shoes,
And stringing pretty words that make no sense,
And kissing full sense into empty words,
Which things are corals to cut life upon,
Although such trifles: children learn by such,
Love's holy earnest in a pretty play
And get not over-early solemnized,
But seeing, as in a rose-bush, Love's Divine
Which burns and hurts not, — not a single bloom, —
Become aware and unafraid of Love.
Such good do mothers. Fathers love as well
— Mine did, I know, — but still with heavier brains,
And wills more consciously responsible,
And not as wisely, since less foolishly;
So mothers have God's license to be missed.

My father was an austere Englishman,
Who, after a dry lifetime spent at home
In college-learning, law, and parish talk,
Was flooded with a passion unaware,

His whole provisioned and complacent past
Drowned out from him that moment. As he stood
In Florence, where he had come to spend a month
And note the secret of Da Vinci's drains,
He musing somewhat absently perhaps
Some English question . . . whether men should pay
The unpopular but necessary tax
With left or right hand — in the alien sun
In that great square of the Santissima
There drifted past him (scarcely marked enough
To move his comfortable island scorn)
A train of priestly banners, cross and psalm,
The white-veiled rose-crowned maidens holding up
Tall tapers, weighty for such wrists, aslant
To the blue luminous tremor of the air,
And letting drop the white wax as they went
To eat the bishop's wafer at the church;
From which long trail of chanting priests and girls,
A face flashed like a cymbal on his face
And shook with silent clangor brain and heart,
Transfiguring him to music. Thus, even thus,
He too received his sacramental gift
With eucharistic meanings; for he loved.

And thus beloved, she died. I've heard it said
That but to see him in the first surprise
Of widower and father, nursing me,
Unmothered little child of four years old,
His large man's hands afraid to touch my curls,
As if the gold would tarnish, — his grave lips
Contriving such a miserable smile
As if he knew needs must, or I should die,
And yet 't was hard, — would almost make the stones
Cry out for pity. There's a verse he set
In Santa Croce to her memory, —
'Weep for an infant too young to weep much
When death removed this mother' — stops the mirth
To-day on women's faces when they walk
With rosy children hanging on their gowns

Under the cloister to escape the sun
That scorches in the piazza. After which
He left our Florence and made haste to hide
Himself, his prattling child, and silent grief,
Among the mountains above Pelago;
Because unmothered babes, he thought, had need
Of mother nature more than others use,
And Pan's white goats, with udders warm and full
Of mystic contemplations, come to feed
Poor milkless lips of orphans like his own —
Such scholar-scraps he talked, I've heard from friends,
For even prosaic men who wear grief long
Will get to wear it as a hat aside
With a flower stuck in 't. Father, then, and child,
We lived among the mountains many years,
God's silence on the outside of the house,
And we who did not speak too loud within,
And old Assunta to make up the fire,
Crossing herself whene'er a sudden flame
Which lightened from the firewood, made alive
That picture of my mother on the wall.

The painter drew it after she was dead,
And when the face was finished, throat and hands,
Her cameriera carried him, in hate
Of the English-fashioned shroud, the last brocade
She dressed in at the Pitti; 'he should paint
No sadder thing than that,' she swore, 'to wrong
Her poor signora.' Therefore very strange
The effect was. I, a little child, would crouch
For hours upon the floor with knees drawn up,
And gaze across them, half in terror, half
In adoration, at the picture there, —
That swan-like supernatural white life
Just sailing upward from the red stiff silk
Which seemed to have no part in it nor power
To keep it from quite breaking out of bounds.
For hours I sat and stared. Assunta's awe
And my poor father's melancholy eyes

Still pointed that way. That way went my thoughts
When wandering beyond sight. And as I grew
In years, I mixed, confused, unconsciously,
Whatever I last read or heard or dreamed,
Abhorrent, admirable, beautiful,
Pathetical, or ghastly, or grotesque,
With still that face . . . which did not therefore change,
But kept the mystic level of all forms,
Hates, fears, and admirations, was by turns
Ghost, fiend, and angel, fairy, witch, and sprite,
A dauntless Muse who eyes a dreadful Fate,
A loving Psyche who loses sight of Love,
A still Medusa with mild milky brows
All curdled and all clothed upon with snakes
Whose slime falls fast as sweat will; or anon
Our Lady of the Passion, stabbed with swords
Where the Babe sucked; or Lamia in her first
Moonlighted pallor, ere she shrunk and blinked
And shuddering wriggled down to the unclean;
Or my own mother, leaving her last smile
In her last kiss upon the baby-mouth
My father pushed down on the bed for that, —
Or my dead mother, without smile or kiss,
Buried at Florence. All which images,
Concentred on the picture, glassed themselves
Before my meditative childhood, as
The incoherencies of change and death
Are represented fully, mixed and merged,
In the smooth fair mystery of perpetual Life.
And while I stared away my childish wits
Upon my mother's picture (ah, poor child!),
My father, who through love had suddenly
Thrown off the old conventions, broken loose
From chin-bands of the soul, like Lazarus,
Yet had no time to learn to talk and walk
Or grow anew familiar with the sun, —
Who had reached to freedom, not to action, lived,
But lived as one entranced, with thoughts, not aims, —
Whom love had unmade from a common man,

But not completed to an uncommon man, —
My father taught me what he had learnt the best
Before he died and left me, — grief and love.
And, seeing we had books among the hills,
Strong words of counselling souls confederate
With vocal pines and waters, — out of books
He taught me all the ignorance of men,
And how God laughs in heaven when any man
Says 'Here I'm learned; this I understand;
In that, I am never caught at fault or doubt.'
He sent the schools to school, demonstrating
A fool will pass for such through one mistake,
While a philosopher will pass for such,
Through said mistakes being ventured in the gross
And heaped up to a system.
                                        I am like,
They tell me, my dear father. Broader brows
Howbeit, upon a slenderer undergrowth
Of delicate features, — paler, near as grave;
But then my mother's smile breaks up the whole,
And makes it better sometimes than itself.
So, nine full years, our days were hid with God
Among his mountains: I was just thirteen,
Still growing like the plants from unseen roots
In tongue-tied Springs, — and suddenly awoke
To full life and life's needs and agonies
With an intense, strong, struggling heart beside
A stone-dead father. Life, struck sharp on death,
Makes awful lightning. His last word was 'Love —'
'Love, my child, love, love!' — (then he had done with grief)
'Love, my child.' Ere I answered he was gone,
And none was left to love in all the world.

There, ended childhood. What succeeded next
I recollect as, after fevers, men
Thread back the passage of delirium,
Missing the turn still, baffled by the door;
Smooth endless days, notched here and there with knives,
A weary, wormy darkness, spurred i' the flank

With flame, that it should eat and end itself
Like some tormented scorpion. Then at last
I do remember clearly how there came
A stranger with authority, not right
(I thought not), who commanded, caught me up
From old Assunta's neck; how, with a shriek,
She let me go, — while I, with ears too full
Of my father's silence to shriek back a word,
In all a child's astonishment at grief
Stared at the wharf-edge where she stood and moaned,
My poor Assunta, where she stood and moaned!
The white walls, the blue hills, my Italy,
Drawn backward from the shuddering steamer-deck,
Like one in anger drawing back her skirts
Which suppliants catch at. Then the bitter sea
Inexorably pushed between us both
And, sweeping up the ship with my despair,
Threw us out as a pasture to the stars.

Ten nights and days we voyaged on the deep;
Ten nights and days without the common face
Of any day or night; the moon and sun
Cut off from the green reconciling earth,
To starve into a blind ferocity
And glare unnatural; the very sky
(Dropping its bell-net down upon the sea,
As if no human heart should 'scape alive)
Bedraggled with the desolating salt,
Until it seemed no more that holy heaven
To which my father went. All new and strange;
The universe turned stranger, for a child.

Then land! — then, England! Oh, the frosty cliffs
Looked cold upon me. Could I find a home
Among those mean red houses through the fog?
And when I heard my father's language first
From alien lips which had no kiss for mine
I wept aloud, then laughed, then wept, then wept,
And some one near me said the child was mad

Through much sea-sickness. The train swept us on:
Was this my father's England? the great isle?
The ground seemed cut up from the fellowship
Of verdure, field from field, as man from man;
The skies themselves looked low and positive,
As almost you could touch them with a hand,
And dared to do it they were so far off
From God's celestial crystals; all things blurred
And dull and vague. Did Shakespeare and his mates
Absorb the light here? — not a hill or stone
With heart to strike a radiant color up
Or active outline on the indifferent air.

I think I see my father's sister stand
Upon the hall-step of her country-house
To give me welcome. She stood straight and calm,
Her somewhat narrow forehead braided tight
As if for taming accidental thoughts
From possible pulses; brown hair pricked with gray
By frigid use of life (she was not old,
Although my father's elder by a year),
A nose drawn sharply, yet in delicate lines;
A close mild mouth, a little soured about
The ends, through speaking unrequited loves
Or peradventure niggardly half-truths;
Eyes of no color, — once they might have smiled,
But never, never have forgot themselves
In smiling; cheeks, in which was yet a rose
Of perished summers, like a rose in a book,
Kept more for ruth than pleasure, — if past bloom,
Past fading also.
                        She had lived, we'll say,
A harmless life, she called a virtuous life,
A quiet life, which was not life at all
(But that, she had not lived enough to know),
Between the vicar and the county squires,
The lord-lieutenant looking down sometimes
From the empyrean to assure their souls
Against chance vulgarisms, and, in the abyss,

The apothecary, looked on once a year
To prove their soundness of humility.
The poor-club exercised her Christian gifts
Of knitting stockings, stitching petticoats,
Because we are of one flesh, after all,
And need one flannel (with a proper sense
Of difference in the quality) — and still
The book-club, guarded from your modern trick
Of shaking dangerous questions from the crease,
Preserved her intellectual. She had lived
A sort of cage-bird life, born in a cage,
Accounting that to leap from perch to perch
Was act and joy enough for any bird.
Dear heaven, how silly are the things that live
In thickets, and eat berries!
                       I, alas,
A wild bird scarcely fledged, was brought to her cage,
And she was there to meet me. Very kind.
Bring the clean water, give out the fresh seed.
She stood upon the steps to welcome me,
Calm, in black garb. I clung about her neck, —
Young babes, who catch at every shred of wool
To draw the new light closer, catch and cling
Less blindly. In my ears my father's word
Hummed ignorantly, as the sea in shells,
'Love, love, my child.' She, black there with my grief,
Might feel my love — she was his sister once —
I clung to her. A moment she seemed moved,
Kissed me with cold lips, suffered me to cling,
And drew me feebly through the hall into
The room she sat in.
                   There, with some strange spasm
Of pain and passion, she wrung loose my hands
Imperiously, and held me at arm's length,
And with two gray-steel naked-bladed eyes
Searched through my face, — ay, stabbed it through and through,
Through brows and cheeks and chin, as if to find
A wicked murderer in my innocent face,
If not here, there perhaps. Then, drawing breath,

She struggled for her ordinary calm —
And missed it rather, — told me not to shrink,
As if she had told me not to lie or swear, —
'She loved my father and would love me too
As long as I deserved it.' Very kind.

I understood her meaning afterward;
She thought to find my mother in my face,
And questioned it for that. For she, my aunt,
Had loved my father truly, as she could,
And hated, with the gall of gentle souls,
My Tuscan mother who had fooled away
A wise man from wise courses, a good man
From obvious duties, and, depriving her,
His sister, of the household precedence,
Had wronged his tenants, robbed his native land,
And made him mad, alike by life and death,
In love and sorrow. She had pored for years
What sort of woman could be suitable
To her sort of hate, to entertain it with,
And so, her very curiosity
Became hate too, and all the idealism
She ever used in life was used for hate,
Till hate, so nourished, did exceed at last
The love from which it grew, in strength and heat,
And wrinkled her smooth conscience with a sense
Of disputable virtue (say not, sin)
When Christian doctrine was enforced at church.

And thus my father's sister was to me
My mother's hater. From that day she did
Her duty to me (I appreciate it
In her own word as spoken to herself),
Her duty, in large measure, well pressed out,
But measured always. She was generous, bland,
More courteous than was tender, gave me still
The first place, — as if fearful that God's saints
Would look down suddenly and say 'Herein
You missed a point, I think, through lack of love.'

Alas, a mother never is afraid
Of speaking angrily to any child,
Since love, she knows, is justified of love.

And I, I was a good child on the whole,
A meek and manageable child. Why not?
I did not live, to have the faults of life:
There seemed more true life in my father's grave
Than in all England. Since *that* threw me off
Who fain would cleave (his latest will, they say,
Consigned me to his land), I only thought
Of lying quiet there where I was thrown
Like sea-weed on the rocks, and suffering her
To prick me to a pattern with her pin,
Fibre from fibre, delicate leaf from leaf,
And dry out from my drowned anatomy
The last sea-salt left in me.
                  So it was.
I broke the copious curls upon my head
In braids, because she liked smooth-ordered hair.
I left off saying my sweet Tuscan words
Which still at any stirring of the heart
Came up to float across the English phrase
As lilies (*Bene* or *Che che*), because
She liked my father's child to speak his tongue.
I learnt the collects and the catechism,
The creeds, from Athanasius back to Nice,
The Articles, the Tracts *against* the times
(By no means Buonaventure's 'Prick of Love'),
And various popular synopses of
Inhuman doctrines never taught by John,
Because she liked instructed piety.
I learnt my complement of classic French
(Kept pure of Balzac and neologism)
And German also, since she liked a range
Of liberal education, — tongues, not books.
I learnt a little algebra, a little
Of the mathematics, — brushed with extreme flounce
The circle of the sciences, because

She misliked women who are frivolous.
I learnt the royal genealogies
Of Oviedo, the internal laws
Of the Burmese empire, — by how many feet
Mount Chimborazo outsoars Teneriffe,
What navigable river joins itself
To Lara, and what census of the year five
Was taken at Klagenfurt, — because she liked
A general insight into useful facts.
I learnt much music, — such as would have been
As quite impossible in Johnson's day
As still it might be wished — fine sleights of hand
And unimagined fingering, shuffling off
The hearer's soul through hurricanes of notes
To a noisy Tophet; and I drew . . . . costumes
From French engravings, nereids neatly draped
(With smirks of simmering godship): I washed in
Landscapes from nature (rather say, washed out).
I danced the polka and Cellarius,
Spun glass, stuffed birds, and modelled flowers in wax,
Because she liked accomplishments in girls.
I read a score of books on womanhood
To prove, if women do not think at all,
They may teach thinking (to a maiden aunt
Or else the author), — books that boldly assert
Their right of comprehending husband's talk
When not too deep, and even of answering
With pretty 'may it please you,' or 'so it is,' —
Their rapid insight and fine aptitude,
Particular worth and general missionariness,
As long as they keep quiet by the fire
And never say 'no' when the world says 'ay,'
For that is fatal, — their angelic reach
Of virtue, chiefly used to sit and darn,
And fatten household sinners, — their, in brief,
Potential faculty in everything
Of abdicating power in it: she owned
She liked a woman to be womanly,
And English women, she thanked God and sighed

(Some people always sigh in thanking God),
Were models to the universe. And last
I learnt cross-stitch, because she did not like
To see me wear the night with empty hands
A-doing nothing. So, my shepherdess
Was something after all (the pastoral saints
Be praised for't), leaning lovelorn with pink eyes
To match her shoes, when I mistook the silks;
Her head uncrushed by that round weight of hat
So strangely similar to the tortoise shell
Which slew the tragic poet.
                  By the way,
The works of women are symbolical.
We sew, sew, prick our fingers, dull our sight,
Producing what? A pair of slippers, sir,
To put on when you're weary — or a stool
To stumble over and vex you . . . 'curse that stool!'
Or else at best, a cushion, where you lean
And sleep, and dream of something we are not
But would be for your sake. Alas, alas!
This hurts most, this — that, after all, we are paid
The worth of our work, perhaps.
                    In looking down
Those years of education (to return)
I wonder if Brinvilliers suffered more
In the water-torture . . . flood succeeding flood
To drench the incapable throat and split the veins . . .
Than I did. Certain of your feebler souls
Go out in such a process; many pine
To a sick, inodorous light; my own endured:
I had relations in the Unseen, and drew
The elemental nutriment and heat
From nature, as earth feels the sun at nights,
Or as a babe sucks surely in the dark.
I kept the life thrust on me, on the outside
Of the inner life with all its ample room
For heart and lungs, for will and intellect,
Inviolable by conventions. God,
I thank thee for that grace of thine!

At first
I felt no life which was not patience, — did
The thing she bade me, without heed to a thing
Beyond it, sat in just the chair she placed,
With back against the window, to exclude
The sight of the great lime-tree on the lawn,
Which seemed to have come on purpose from the woods
To bring the house a message, — ay, and walked
Demurely in her carpeted low rooms,
As if I should not, hearkening my own steps,
Misdoubt I was alive. I read her books,
Was civil to her cousin, Romney Leigh,
Gave ear to her vicar, tea to her visitors,
And heard them whisper, when I changed a cup
(I blushed for joy at that), — 'The Italian child,
For all her blue eyes and her quiet ways,
Thrives ill in England: she is paler yet
Than when we came the last time; she will die.'

'Will die.' My cousin, Romney Leigh, blushed too,
With sudden anger, and approaching me
Said low between his teeth, 'You're wicked now?
You wish to die and leave the world a-dusk
For others, with your naughty light blown out?'
I looked into his face defyingly;
He might have known that, being what I was,
'T was natural to like to get away
As far as dead folk can: and then indeed
Some people make no trouble when they die.
He turned and went abruptly, slammed the door,
And shut his dog out.

                    Romney, Romney Leigh.
I have not named my cousin hitherto,
And yet I used him as a sort of friend;
My elder by few years, but cold and shy
And absent . . . tender, when he thought of it,
Which scarcely was imperative, grave betimes,
As well as early master of Leigh Hall,
Whereof the nightmare sat upon his youth,

214

Repressing all its seasonable delights,
And agonizing with a ghastly sense
Of universal hideous want and wrong
To incriminate possession. When he came
From college to the country, very oft
He crossed the hill on visits to my aunt,
With gifts of blue grapes from the hothouses,
A book in one hand, — mere statistics (if
I chanced to lift the cover), count of all
The goats whose beards grow sprouting down toward hell
Against God's separative judgment-hour.
And she, she almost loved him, — even allowed
That sometimes he should seem to sigh my way;
It made him easier to be pitiful,
And sighing was his gift. So, undisturbed,
At whiles she let him shut my music up
And push my needles down, and lead me out
To see in that south angle of the house
The figs grow black as if by a Tuscan rock,
On some light pretext. She would turn her head
At other moments, go to fetch a thing,
And leave me breath enough to speak with him,
For his sake; it was simple.
                     Sometimes too
He would have saved me utterly, it seemed,
He stood and looked so.
                  Once, he stood so near,
He dropped a sudden hand upon my head
Bent down on woman's work, as soft as rain —
But then I rose and shook it off as fire,
The stranger's touch that took my father's place
Yet dared seem soft.
                I used him for a friend
Before I ever knew him for a friend.
'T was better, 't was worse also, afterward:
We came so close, we saw our differences
Too intimately. Always Romney Leigh
Was looking for the worms, I for the gods.
A godlike nature his; the gods look down,

Incurious of themselves; and certainly
'T is well I should remember, how, those days,
I was a worm too, and he looked on me.

A little by his act perhaps, yet more
By something in me, surely not my will,
I did not die. But slowly, as one in swoon,
To whom life creeps back in the form of death,
With a sense of separation, a blind pain
Of blank obstruction, and a roar i' the ears
Of visionary chariots which retreat
As earth grows clearer . . . slowly, by degrees,
I woke, rose up . . . where was I? in the world;
For uses therefore I must count worthwhile.

I had a little chamber in the house,
As green as any privet-hedge a bird
Might choose to build in, though the nest itself
Could show but dead-brown sticks and straws; the walls
Were green, the carpet was pure green, the straight
Small bed was curtained greenly, and the folds
Hung green about the window which let in
The out-door world with all its greenery.
You could not push your head out and escape
A dash of dawn-dew from the honeysuckle,
But so you were baptized into the grace
And privilege of seeing. . . .
                                    First, the lime
(I had enough there, of the lime, be sure, —
My morning-dream was often hummed away
By the bees in it); past the lime, the lawn,
Which, after sweeping broadly round the house,
Went trickling through the shrubberies in a stream
Of tender turf, and wore and lost itself
Among the acacias, over which you saw
The irregular line of elms by the deep lane
Which stopped the grounds and dammed the overflow
Of arbutus and laurel. Out of sight
The lane was; sunk so deep, no foreign tramp

Nor drover of wild ponies out of Wales
Could guess if lady's hall or tenant's lodge
Dispensed such odors, — though his stick well-crooked
Might reach the lowest trail of blossoming briar
Which dipped upon the wall. Behind the elms,
And through their tops, you saw the folded hills
Striped up and down with hedges (burly oaks
Projecting from the line to show themselves),
Through which my cousin Romney's chimneys smoked
As still as when a silent mouth in frost
Breathes, showing where the woodlands hid Leigh Hall;
While, far above, a jut of table-land,
A promontory without water, stretched, —
You could not catch it if the days were thick,
Or took it for a cloud; but, otherwise,
The vigorous sun would catch it up at eve
And use it for an anvil till he had filled
The shelves of heaven with burning thunderbolts,
Protesting against night and darkness: — then,
When all his setting trouble was resolved
To a trance of passive glory, you might see
In apparition on the golden sky
(Alas, my Giotto's background!) the sheep run
Along the fine clear outline, small as mice
That run along a witch's scarlet thread.

Not a grand nature. Not my chestnut-woods
Of Vallombrosa, cleaving by the spurs
To the precipices. Not my headlong leaps
Of waters, that cry out for joy or fear
In leaping through the palpitating pines,
Like a white soul tossed out to eternity
With thrills of time upon it. Not indeed
My multitudinous mountains, sitting in
The magic circle, with the mutual touch
Electric, panting from their full deep hearts
Beneath the influent heavens, and waiting for
Communion and commission. Italy
Is one thing, England one.

On English ground
You understand the letter, — ere the fall
How Adam lived in a garden. All the fields
Are tied up fast with hedges, nosegay like;
The hills are crumpled plains, the plains parterres,
The trees, round, woolly, ready to be clipped,
And if you seek for any wilderness
You find, at best, a park. A nature tamed
And grown domestic like a barn-door fowl,
Which does not awe you with its claws and beak,
Nor tempt you to an eyrie too high up,
But which, in cackling, sets you thinking of
Your eggs to-morrow at breakfast, in the pause
Of finer meditation.
                    Rather say,
A sweet familiar nature, stealing in
As a dog might, or child, to touch your hand
Or pluck your gown, and humbly mind you so
Of presence and affection, excellent
For inner uses, from the things without.

I could not be unthankful, I who was
Entreated thus and holpen. In the room
I speak of, ere the house was well awake,
And also after it was well asleep,
I sat alone, and drew the blessing in
Of all that nature. With a gradual step,
A stir among the leaves, a breath, a ray,
It came in softly, while the angels made
A place for it beside me. The moon came,
And swept my chamber clean of foolish thoughts.
The sun came, saying, 'Shall I lift this light
Against the lime-tree, and you will not look?
I make the birds sing — listen! but, for you,
God never hears your voice, excepting when
You lie upon the bed at nights and weep.'

Then, something moved me. Then, I wakened up
More slowly than I verily write now,

But wholly, at last, I wakened, opened wide
The window and my soul, and let the airs
And out-door sights sweep gradual gospels in,
Regenerating what I was. O Life,
How oft we throw it off and think, — 'Enough,
Enough of life in so much! — here's a cause
For rupture; — herein we must break with Life,
Or be ourselves unworthy; here we are wronged,
Maimed, spoiled for aspiration: farewell, Life!'
And so, as froward babes, we hide our eyes
And think all ended. — Then, Life calls to us
In some transformed, apocalyptic voice,
Above us, or below us, or around:
Perhaps we name it Nature's voice, or Love's,
Tricking ourselves, because we are more ashamed
To own our compensations than our griefs:
Still, Life's voice! — still, we make our peace with Life.

And I, so young then, was not sullen. Soon
I used to get up early, just to sit
And watch the morning quicken in the gray,
And hear the silence open like a flower
Leaf after leaf, — and stroke with listless hand
The woodbine through the window, till at last
I came to do it with a sort of love,
At foolish unaware: whereat I smiled, —
A melancholy smile, to catch myself
Smiling for joy.
              Capacity for joy
Admits temptation. It seemed, next, worth while
To dodge the sharp sword set against my life;
To slip down stairs through all the sleepy house,
As mute as any dream there, and escape
As a soul from the body, out of doors,
Glide through the shrubberies, drop into the lane,
And wander on the hills an hour or two,
Then back again before the house should stir.

Or else I sat on in my chamber green,
And lived my life, and thought my thoughts, and prayed

My prayers without the vicar; read my books,
Without considering whether they were fit
To do me good. Mark, there. We get no good
By being ungenerous, even to a book,
And calculating profits, — so much help
By so much reading. It is rather when
We gloriously forget ourselves and plunge
Soul-forward, headlong, into a book's profound,
Impassioned for its beauty and salt of truth —
'T is then we get the right good from a book.
I read much. What my father taught before
From many a volume, Love re-emphasized
Upon the self-same pages: Theophrast
Grew tender with the memory of his eyes,
And Ælian made mine wet. The trick of Greek
And Latin he had taught me, as he would
Have taught me wrestling or the game of fives
If such he had known, — most like a shipwrecked man
Who heaps his single platter with goats' cheese
And scarlet berries; or like any man
Who loves but one, and so gives all at once,
Because he has it, rather than because
He counts it worthy. Thus, my father gave:
And thus, as did the women formerly
By young Achilles, when they pinned a veil
Across the boy's audacious front, and swept
With tuneful laughs the silver-fretted rocks,
He wrapt his little daughter in his large
Man's doublet, careless did it fit or no.

But, after I had read for memory,
I read for hope. The path my father's foot
Had trod me out (which suddenly broke off
What time he dropped the wallet of the flesh
And passed), alone I carried on, and set
My child-heart 'gainst the thorny underwood
To reach the grassy shelter of the trees.
Ah babe i' the wood, without a brother-babe!
My own self-pity, like the red-breast bird,
Flies back to cover all that past with leaves.

Sublimest danger, over which none weeps,
When any young wayfaring soul goes forth
Alone, unconscious of the perilous road,
The day-sun dazzling in his limpid eyes,
To thrust his own way, he an alien, through
The world of books! Ah, you! — you think it fine,
You clap hands — 'A fair day!' — you cheer him on,
As if the worst, could happen, were to rest
Too long beside a fountain. Yet, behold,
Behold! — the world of books is still the world,
And worldings in it are less merciful
And more puissant. For the wicked there
Are winged like angels; every knife that strikes
Is edged from elemental fire to assail
A spiritual life; the beautiful seems right
By force of beauty, and the feeble wrong
Because of weakness; power is justified
Though armed against Saint Michael; many a crown
Covers bald foreheads. In the book-world, true,
There's no lack, neither, of God's saints and kings,
That shake the ashes of the grave aside
From their calm locks and undiscomfited
Look steadfast truths against Time's changing mask.
True, many a prophet teaches in the roads;
True, many a seer pulls down the flaming heavens
Upon his own head in strong martyrdom
In order to light men a moment's space.
But stay! — who judges? — who distinguishes
'Twixt Saul and Nahash justly, at first sight,
And leaves king Saul precisely at the sin,
To serve king David? who discerns at once
The sound of the trumpets, when the trumpets blow
For Alaric as well as Charlemagne?
Who judges wizards, and can tell true seers
From conjurers? the child, there? Would you leave
That child to wander in a battle-field
And push his innocent smile against the guns;
Or even in a catacomb, — his torch
Grown ragged in the fluttering air, and all
The dark a-mutter round him? not a child.

THE BROWNINGS

I read books bad and good — some bad and good
At once (good aims not always make good books:
Well-tempered spades turn up ill-smelling soils
In digging vineyards even); books that prove
God's being so definitely, that man's doubt
Grows self-defined the other side the line,
Made atheist by suggestion; moral books,
Exasperating to license; genial books,
Discounting from the human dignity;
And merry books, which set you weeping when
The sun shines, — ay, and melancholy books,
Which make you laugh that any one should weep
In this disjointed life for one wrong more.

The world of books is still the world, I write,
And both worlds have God's providence, thank God,
To keep and hearten: with some struggle, indeed,
Among the breakers, some hard swimming through
The deeps — I lost breath in my soul sometimes
And cried 'God save me if there's any God,'
But, even so, God saved me; and, being dashed
From error on to error, every turn
Still brought me nearer to the central truth.

I thought so. All this anguish in the thick
Of men's opinions . . . press and counterpress,
Now up, now down, now underfoot, and now
Emergent . . . all the best of it, perhaps,
But throws you back upon a noble trust
And use of your own instinct, — merely proves
Pure reason stronger than bare inference
At strongest. Try it, — fix against heaven's wall
The scaling-ladders of school logic — mount
Step by step! — sight goes faster; that still ray
Which strikes out from you, how, you cannot tell,
And why, you know not (did you eliminate,
That such as you indeed should analyze?)
Goes straight and fast as light, and high as God.

The cygnet finds the water, but the man

Is born in ignorance of his element
And feels out blind at first, disorganized
By sin i' the blood, — his spirit-insight dulled
And crossed by his sensations. Presently
He feels it quicken in the dark sometimes,
When, mark, be reverent, be obedient,
For such dumb motions of imperfect life
Are oracles of vital Deity
Attesting the Hereafter. Let who says
'The soul's a clean white paper,' rather say,
A palimpsest, a prophet's holograph
Defiled, erased and covered by a monk's; —
The apocalypse, by a Longus! poring on
Which obscene text, we may discern perhaps
Some fair, fine trace of what was written once,
Some upstroke of an alpha and omega
Expressing the old scripture.
                              Books, books, books!
I had found the secret of a garret-room
Piled high with cases in my father's name,
Piled high, packed large, — where, creeping in and out
Among the giant fossils of my past,
Like some small nimble mouse between the ribs
Of a mastodon, I nibbled here and there
At this or that box, pulling through the gap,
In heats of terror, haste, victorious joy,
The first book first. And how I felt it beat
Under my pillow, in the morning's dark,
An hour before the sun would let me read!
My books! At last because the time was ripe,
I chanced upon the poets.
                          As the earth
Plunges in fury, when the internal fires
Have reached and pricked her heart, and, throwing flat
The marts and temples, the triumphal gates
And towers of observation, clears herself
To elemental freedom — thus, my soul,
At poetry's divine first finger-touch,
Let go conventions and sprang up surprised,

THE BROWNINGS

Convicted of the great eternities
Before two worlds.
                          What's this, Aurora Leigh,
You write so of the poets, and not laugh?
Those virtuous liars, dreamers after dark,
Exaggerators of the sun and moon,
And soothsayers in a tea-cup?
                          I write so
Of the only truth-tellers now left to God,
The only speakers of essential truth,
Opposed to relative, comparative,
And temporal truths; the only holders by
His sun-skirts, through conventional gray glooms;
The only teachers who instruct mankind
From just a shadow on a charnel-wall
To find man's veritable stature out
Erect, sublime, — the measure of a man,
And that's the measure of an angel, says
The apostle. Ay, and while your common men
Lay telegraphs, gauge railroads, reign, reap, dine,
And dust the flaunty carpets of the world
For kings to walk on, or our president,
The poet suddenly will catch them up
With his voice like a thunder, — 'This is soul,
This is life, this word is being said in heaven,
Here's God down on us! what are you about?'
How all those workers start amid their work,
Look round, look up, and feel, a moment's space,
That carpet-dusting, though a pretty trade,
Is not the imperative labor after all.

My own best poets, am I one with you,
That thus I love you, — or but one through love?
Does all this smell of thyme about my feet
Conclude my visit to your holy hill
In personal presence, or but testify
The rustling of your vesture through my dreams
With influent odors? When my joy and pain,
My thought and aspiration, like the stops

224

Of pipe or flute, are absolutely dumb
Unless melodious, do you play on me
My pipers, — and if, sooth, you did not blow,
Would no sound come? or is the music mine,
As a man's voice or breath is called his own,
Inbreathed by the Life-breather? There's a doubt
For cloudy seasons!
          But the sun was high
When first I felt my pulses set themselves
For concord; when the rhythmic turbulence
Of blood and brain swept outward upon words,
As wind upon the alders, blanching them
By turning up their under-natures till
They trembled in dilation. O delight
And triumph of the poet, who would say
A man's mere 'yes,' a woman's common 'no,'
A little human hope of that or this,
And says the word so that it burns you through
With a special revelation, shakes the heart
Of all the men and women in the world,
As if one came back from the dead and spoke,
With eyes too happy, a familiar thing
Become divine i' the utterance! while for him
The poet, speaker, he expands with joy;
The palpitating angel in his flesh
Thrills inly with consenting fellowship
To those innumerous spirits who sun themselves
Outside of time.
          O life, O poetry,
— Which means life in life! cognizant of life
Beyond this blood-beat, passionate for truth
Beyond these senses! — poetry, my life,
My eagle, with both grappling feet still hot
From Zeus's thunder, who hast ravished me
Away from all the shepherds, sheep, and dogs,
And set me in the Olympian roar and round
Of luminous faces for a cup-bearer,
To keep the mouths of all the godheads moist
For everlasting laughters, — I myself

Half drunk across the beaker with their eyes!
How those gods look!
                Enough so, Ganymede,
We shall not bear above a round or two.
We drop the golden cup at Herè's foot
And swoon back to the earth, — and find ourselves
Face-down among the pine-cones, cold with dew,
While the dogs bark, and many a shepherd scoffs,
'What's come now to the youth?' Such ups and downs
Have poets.
           Am I such indeed? The name
Is royal, and to sign it like a queen
Is what I dare not, — though some royal blood
Would seem to tingle in me now and then,
With sense of power and ache, — with imposthumes
And manias usual to the race. Howbeit
I dare not: 't is too easy to go mad
And ape a Bourbon in a crown of straws;
The thing's too common.
              Many fervent souls
Strike rhyme on rhyme, who would strike steel on steel
If steel had offered, in a restless heat
Of doing something. Many tender souls
Have strung their losses on a rhyming thread,
As children cowslips: — the more pains they take,
The work more withers. Young men, ay, and maids,
Too often sow their wild oats in tame verse,
Before they sit down under their own vine
And live for use. Alas, near all the birds
Will sing at dawn, — and yet we do not take
The chaffering swallow for the holy lark.
In those days, though, I never analyzed,
Not even myself. Analysis comes late.
You catch a sight of Nature, earliest,
In full front sun-face, and your eyelids wink
And drop before the wonder of 't; you miss
The form, through seeing the light. I lived, those days,
And wrote because I lived — unlicensed else;
My heart beat in my brain. Life's violent flood

226

Abolished bounds, — and, which my neighbor's field,
Which mine, what mattered? it is thus in youth!
We play at leap-frog over the god Term;
The love within us and the love without
Are mixed, confounded; if we are loved or love,
We scarce distinguish: thus, with other power;
Being acted on and acting seem the same:
In that first onrush of life's chariot-wheels,
We know not if the forests move or we.

And so, like most young poets, in a flush
Of individual life I poured myself
Along the veins of others, and achieved
Mere lifeless imitations of live verse,
And made the living answer for the dead,
Profaning nature. 'Touch not, do not taste,
Nor handle,' — we're too legal, who write young:
We beat the phorminx till we hurt our thumbs,
As if still ignorant of counterpoint;
We call the Muse, — 'O Muse, benignant Muse,' —
As if we had seen her purple-braided head,
With the eyes in it, start between the boughs
As often as a stag's. What make-believe,
With so much earnest! what effete results
From virile efforts! what cold wire-drawn odes
From such white heats! — bucolics, where the cows
Would scare the writer if they splashed the mud
In lashing off the flies, — didactics, driven
Against the heels of what the master said;
And counterfeiting epics, shrill with trumps
A babe might blow between two straining cheeks
Of bubbled rose, to make his mother laugh;
And elegiac griefs, and songs of love,
Like cast-off nosegays picked up on the road,
The worse for being warm: all these things, writ
On happy mornings, with a morning heart,
That leaps for love, is active for resolve,
Weak for art only. Oft, the ancient forms
Will thrill, indeed, in carrying the young blood.

The wine-skins, now and then, a little warped,
Will crack even, as the new wine gurgles in.
Spare the old bottles! — spill not the new wine.

By Keats's soul, the man who never stepped
In gradual progress like another man,
But, turning grandly on his central self,
Ensphered himself in twenty perfect years
And died, not young (the life of a long life
Distilled to a mere drop, falling like a tear
Upon the world's cold cheek to make it burn
For ever); by that strong excepted soul,
I count it strange and hard to understand
That nearly all young poets should write old,
That Pope was sexagenary at sixteen,
And beardless Byron academical,
And so with others. It may be perhaps
Such have not settled long and deep enough
In trance, to attain to clairvoyance, — and still
The memory mixes with the vision, spoils,
And works it turbid.

           Or perhaps, again,
In order to discover the Muse-Sphinx,
The melancholy desert must sweep round,
Behind you as before. —

                For me, I wrote
False poems, like the rest, and thought them true
Because myself was true in writing them.
I peradventure have writ true ones since
With less complacence.

              But I could not hide
My quickening inner life from those at watch.
They saw a light at a window, now and then,
They had not set there: who had set it there?
My father's sister started when she caught
My soul agaze in my eyes. She could not say
I had no business with a sort of soul,
But plainly she objected, — and demurred
That souls were dangerous things to carry straight

228

Through all the split saltpetre of the world.
She said sometimes, 'Aurora, have you done
Your task this morning? have you read that book?
And are you ready for the crochet here?' —
As if she said, 'I know there's something wrong;
I know I have not ground you down enough
To flatten and bake you to a wholesome crust
For household uses and proprieties,
Before the rain has got into my barn
And set the grains a-sprouting. What, you're green
With out-door impudence? you almost grow?'
To which I answered, 'Would she hear my task,
And verify my abstract of the book?
Or should I sit down to the crochet work?
Was such her pleasure?' Then I sat and teased
The patient needle till it split the thread,
Which oozed off from it in meandering lace
From hour to hour. I was not, therefore, sad;
My soul was singing at a work apart
Behind the wall of sense, as safe from harm
As sings the lark when sucked up out of sight
In vortices of glory and blue air.

And so, through forced work and spontaneous work,
The inner life informed the outer life,
Reduced the irregular blood to a settled rhythm,
Made cool the forehead with fresh-sprinkling dreams,
And, rounding to the spheric soul the thin,
Pined body, struck a color up the cheeks
Though somewhat faint. I clenched my brows across
My blue eyes greatening in the looking-glass,
And said 'We'll live, Aurora! we'll be strong.
The dogs are on us — but we will not die.'

Whoever lives true life will love true love.
I learnt to love that England. Very oft,
Before the day was born, or otherwise
Through secret windings of the afternoons,
I threw my hunters off and plunged myself

Among the deep hills, as a hunted stag
Will take the waters, shivering with the fear
And passion of the course. And when at last
Escaped, so many a green slope built on slope
Betwixt me and the enemy's house behind,
I dared to rest, or wander, in a rest
Made sweeter for the step upon the grass,
And view the ground's most gentle dimplement
(As if God's finger touched but did not press
In making England), such an up and down
Of verdure, — nothing too much up or down,
A ripple of land; such little hills, the sky
Can stoop to tenderly and the wheatfields climb;
Such nooks of valleys lined with orchises,
Fed full of noises by invisible streams;
And open pastures where you scarcely tell
White daisies from white dew, — at intervals
The mythic oaks and elm-trees standing out
Self-poised upon their prodigy of shade, —
I thought my father's land was worthy too
Of being my Shakespeare's.
                          Very oft alone,
Unlicensed; not unfrequently with leave
To walk the third with Romney and his friend
The rising painter, Vincent Carrington,
Whom men judge hardly as bee-bonneted,
Because he holds that, paint a body well,
You paint a soul by implication, like
The grand first Master. Pleasant walks! for if
He said 'When I was last in Italy,'
It sounded as an instrument that's played
Too far off for the tune — and yet it's fine
To listen.
            Ofter we walked only two
If cousin Romney pleased to walk with me.
We read, or talked, or quarrelled, as it chanced.
We were not lovers, nor even friends well-matched:
Say rather, scholars upon different tracks,
And thinkers disagreed: he, overfull

Of what is, and I, haply, overbold
For what might be.
       But then the thrushes sang,
And shook my pulses and the elms' new leaves:
At which I turned, and held my finger up,
And bade him mark that, howsoe'er the world
Went ill, as he related, certainly
The thrushes still sang in it. At the word
His brow would soften, — and he bore with me
In melancholy patience, not unkind,
While breaking into voluble ecstasy
I flattered all the beauteous country round,
As poets use, the skies, the clouds, the fields,
The happy violets hiding from the roads
The primroses run down to, carrying gold;
The tangled hedgerows, where the cows push out
Impatient horns and tolerant churning mouths
'Twixt dripping ash-boughs, — hedgerows all alive
With birds and gnats and large white butterflies
Which look as if the may-flower had caught life
And palpitated forth upon the wind;
Hills, vales, woods, netted in a silver mist,
Farms, granges, doubled up among the hills;
And cattle grazing in the watered vales,
And cottage-chimneys smoking from the woods,
And cottage-gardens smelling everywhere,
Confused with smell of orchards. 'See,' I said,
'And see! is God not with us on the earth?
And shall we put Him down by aught we do?
Who says there's nothing for the poor and vile
Save poverty and wickedness? behold!'
And ankle-deep in English grass I leaped
And clapped my hands, and called all very fair.
In the beginning when God called all good,
Even then was evil near us, it is writ;
But we indeed who call things good and fair,
The evil is upon us while we speak;
Deliver us from evil, let us pray.

[End of First Book]

THE BROWNINGS

from SECOND BOOK

*[Romney has proposed to Aurora, and
she has written declining.]*

* * * * *

The next week passed in silence, so the next,
And several after: Romney did not come
Nor my aunt chide me. I lived on and on,
As if my heart were kept beneath a glass,
And everybody stood, all eyes and ears,
To see and hear it tick. I could not sit,
Nor walk, nor take a book, nor lay it down,
Nor sew on steadily, nor drop a stitch,
And a sigh with it, but I felt her looks
Still cleaving to me, like the sucking asp
To Cleopatra's breast, persistently
Through the intermittent pantings. Being observed,
When observation is not sympathy,
Is just being tortured. If she said a word,
A 'thank you,' or an 'if it please you, dear,'
She meant a commination, or, at best,
An exorcism against the devildom
Which plainly held me. So with all the house.
Susannah could not stand and twist my hair
Without such glancing at the looking-glass
To see my face there, that she missed the plait.
And John, — I never sent my plate for soup,
Or did not send it, but the foolish John
Resolved the problem, 'twixt his napkined thumbs,
Of what was signified by taking soup
Or choosing mackerel. Neighbors who dropped in
On morning visits, feeling a joint wrong,
Smiled admonition, sat uneasily,
And talked, with measured, emphasized reserve,
Of parish news, like doctors to the sick,

When not called in, — as if, with leave to speak,
They might say something. Nay, the very dog
Would watch me from his sun-patch on the floor,
In alternation with the large black fly
Not yet in reach of snapping. So I lived.

A Roman died so; smeared with honey, teased
By insects, stared to torture by the noon:
And many patient souls 'neath English roofs
Have died like Romans. I, in looking back,
Wish only, now, I had borne the plague of all
With meeker spirits than were rife at Rome.

* * * * *

from THIRD BOOK

[*Aurora reads her letters.*]

* * * * *

Leave the lamp, Susan, and go up to bed.
The room does very well; I have to write
Beyond the stroke of midnight. Get away;
Your steps, for ever buzzing in the room,
Tease me like gnats. Ah, letters! throw them down
At once, as I must have them, to be sure,
Whether I bid you never bring me such
At such an hour, or bid you. No excuse;
You choose to bring them, as I choose perhaps
To throw them in the fire. Now get to bed,
And dream, if possible, I am not cross.

Why what a pettish, petty thing I grow, —
A mere mere woman, a mere flaccid nerve,
A kerchief left out all night in the rain,
Turned soft so, — overtasked and overstrained

And overlived in this close London life!
And yet I should be stronger.
                                   Never burn
Your letters, poor Aurora! for they stare
With red seals from the table, saying each,
'Here's something that you know not.' Out, alas,
'Tis scarcely that the world's more good and wise
Or even straighter and more consequent
Since yesterday at this time — yet, again,
If but one angel spoke from Ararat
I should be very sorry not to hear:
So open all the letters! let me read.
Blanche Ord, the writer in the 'Lady's Fan,'
Requests my judgment on . . . that, afterwards.
Kate Ward desires the model of my cloak,
And signs 'Elisha to you.' Pringle Sharpe
Presents his work on 'Social Conduct,' craves
A little money for his pressing debts . . .
From me, who scarce have money for my needs;
Art's fiery chariot which we journey in
Being apt to singe our singing-robes to holes,
Although you ask me for my cloak, Kate Ward!
Here's Rudgely knows it, — editor and scribe;
He's 'forced to marry where his heart is not,
Because the purse lacks where he lost his heart,'
Ah, — lost it because no one picked it up;
That's really loss, — (and passable impudence).
My critic Hammond flatters prettily,
And wants another volume like the last.
My critic Belfair wants another book
Entirely different, which will sell (and live?),
A striking book, yet not a startling book,
The public blames originalities
(You must not pump spring-water unawares
Upon a gracious public full of nerves):
Good things, not subtle, new yet orthodox,
As easy reading as the dog-eared page
That's fingered by said public fifty years,
Since first taught spelling by its grandmother,

And yet a revelation in some sort:
That's hard, my critic Belfair. So — what next?
My critic Stokes objects to abstract thoughts;
'Call a man John, a woman Joan,' says he,
'And do not prate so of *humanities*:'
Whereat I call my critic simply, Stokes.
My critic Jobson recommends more mirth
Because a cheerful genius suits the times,
And all true poets laugh unquenchably
Like Shakespeare and the gods. That's very hard.
The gods may laugh, and Shakespeare; Dante smiled
With such a needy heart on two pale lips,
We cry 'Weep rather, Dante.' Poems are
Men, if true poems: and who dares exclaim
At any man's door, 'Here, 'tis understood
The thunder fell last week and killed a wife
And scared a sickly husband — what of that?
Get up, be merry, shout and clap your hands,
Because a cheerful genius suits the times — '?
None says so to the man, and why indeed
Should any to the poem? A ninth seal;
The apocalypse is drawing to a close.
Ha, — this from Vincent Carrington, — 'Dear friend,
I want good counsel. Will you lend me wings
To raise me to the subject, in a sketch
I'll bring to-morrow — may I? at eleven?
A poet's only born to turn to use:
So save you! for the world . . . and Carrington.'
'(Writ after.) Have you heard of Romney Leigh,
Beyond what's said of him in newspapers,
His phalansteries there, his speeches here,
His pamphlets, pleas, and statements, everywhere?
He dropped *me* long ago, but no one drops
A golden apple — though indeed one day
You hinted that, but jested. Well, at least
You know Lord Howe who sees him . . . whom he sees
And *you* see and I hate to see, — for Howe
Stands high upon the brink of theories,
Observes the swimmers and cries "Very fine,"

But keeps dry linen equally, — unlike
That gallant breaster, Romney. Strange it is,
Such sudden madness seizing a young man
To make earth over again, — while I'm content
To make the pictures. Let me bring the sketch.
A tiptoe Danae, overbold and hot,
Both arms aflame to meet her wishing Jove
Halfway, and burn him faster down; the face
And breasts upturned and straining, the loose locks
All glowing with the anticipated gold.
Or here's another on the self-same theme.
She lies here — flat upon her prison-floor,
The long hair swathed about her to the heel
Like wet seaweed. You dimly see her through
The glittering haze of that prodigious rain,
Half blotted out of nature by a love
As heavy as fate. I'll bring you either sketch.
I think, myself, the second indicates
More passion.'
             Surely. Self is put away,
And calm with abdication. She is Jove,
And no more Danae — greater thus. Perhaps
The painter symbolizes unaware
Two states of the recipient artist-soul,
One, forward, personal, wanting reverence,
Because aspiring only. We'll be calm,
And know that, when indeed our Joves come down,
We all turn stiller than we have ever been.

Kind Vincent Carrington. I'll let him come.
He talks of Florence, — and may say a word
Of something as it chanced seven years ago,
A hedgehog in the path, or a lame bird,
In those green country walks, in that good time
When certainly I was so miserable . . .
I seem to have missed a blessing ever since.

The music soars within the little lark,
And the lark soars. It is not thus with men.

We do not make our places with our strains, —
Content, while they rise, to remain behind
Alone on earth instead of so in heaven.
No matter; I bear on my broken tale.

When Romney Leigh and I had parted thus,
I took a chamber up three flights of stairs
Not far from being as steep as some larks climb,
And there, in a certain house in Kensington,
Three years I lived and worked. Get leave to work
In this world — 'tis the best you get at all;
For God, in cursing, gives us better gifts
Than men in benediction. God says, 'Sweat
For foreheads,' men say 'crowns,' and so we are crowned,
Ay, gashed by some tormenting circle of steel
Which snaps with a secret spring. Get work, get work;
Be sure 'tis better than what you work to get.

Serene and unafraid of solitude,
I worked the short days out, — and watched the sun
On lurid morns or monstrous afternoons
(Like some Druidic idol's fiery brass
With fixed unflickering outline of dead heat,
From which the blood of wretches pent inside
Seems oozing forth to incarnadine the air)
Push out through fog with his dilated disk,
And startle the slant roofs and chimney-pots
With splashes of fierce color. Or I saw
Fog only, the great tawny weltering fog
Involve the passive city, strangle it
Alive, and draw it off into the void,
Spires, bridges, streets, and squares, as if a sponge
Had wiped out London, — or as noon and night
Had clapped together and utterly struck out
The intermediate time, undoing themselves
In the act. Your city poets see such things
Not despicable. Mountains of the south,
When drunk and mad with elemental wines
They rend the seamless mist and stand up bare,
Make fewer singers, haply. No one sings,

Descending Sinai: on Parnassus mount
You take a mule to climb and not a muse
Except in fable and figure: forests chant
Their anthems to themselves, and leave you dumb.
But sit in London at the day's decline,
And view the city perish in the mist
Like Pharaoh's armaments in the deep Red Sea,
The chariots, horsemen, footmen, all the host,
Sucked down and choked to silence — then, surprised
By a sudden sense of vision and of tune,
You feel as conquerors though you did not fight,
And you and Israel's other singing girls,
Ay, Miriam with them, sing the song you choose.
I worked with patience, which means almost power:
I did some excellent things indifferently,
Some bad things excellently. Both were praised,
The latter loudest. And by such a time
That I myself had set them down as sins
Scarce worth the price of sackcloth, week by week
Arrived some letter through the sedulous post,
Like these I've read, and yet dissimilar,
With pretty maiden seals, — initials twined
Of lilies, or a heart marked *Emily*
(Convicting Emily of being all heart);
Or rarer tokens from young bachelors,
Who wrote from college with the same goose-quill,
Suppose, they had just been plucked of, and a snatch
From Horace, 'Collegisse juvat,' set
Upon the first page. Many a letter, signed
Or unsigned, showing the writers at eighteen
Had lived too long, although a muse should help
Their dawn by holding candles, — compliments
To smile or sigh at. Such could pass with me
No more than coins from Moscow circulate
At Paris: would ten roubles buy a tag
Of ribbon on the boulevard, worth a sou?
I smiled that all this youth should love me, — sighed
That such a love could scarcely raise them up
To love what was more worthy than myself;

Then sighed again, again, less generously,
To think the very love they lavished so
Proved me inferior. The strong loved me not,
And he . . . my cousin Romney . . . did not write.
I felt the silent finger of his scorn
Prick every bubble of my frivolous fame
As my breath blew it, and resolve it back
To the air it came from. Oh, I justified
The measure he had taken of my height:
The thing was plain — he was not wrong a line;
I played at art, made thrusts with a toy-sword,
Amused the lads and maidens.
                              Came a sigh
Deep, hoarse with resolution, — I would work
To better ends, or play in earnest. 'Heavens,
I think I should be almost popular
If this went on!' — I ripped my verses up,
And found no blood upon the rapier's point;
The heart in them was just an embryo's heart
Which never yet had beat, that it should die;
Just gasps of make-believe galvanic life;
Mere tones, inorganized to any tune.

*   *   *   *   *

[Lady Waldemar calls on Aurora.]

A lady called upon me on such a day.
She had the low voice of your English dames,
Unused, it seems, to need rise half a note
To catch attention, — and their quiet mood,
As if they lived too high above the earth
For that to put them out in anything:
So gentle, because verily so proud;
So wary and afraid of hurting you,
By no means that you are not really vile,
But that they would not touch you with their foot
To push you to your place; so self-possessed
Yet gracious and conciliating, it takes

An effort in their presence to speak truth:
You know the sort of woman, — brilliant stuff,
And out of nature. 'Lady Waldemar.'
She said her name quite simply, as if it meant
Not much indeed, but something, — took my hands,
And smiled as if her smile could help my case,
And dropped her eyes on me and let them melt.
'Is this,' she said, 'the Muse'?

                'No sybil even,'
I answered, 'since she fails to guess the cause
Which taxed you with this visit, madam.'

                     'Good,'
She said; 'I value what's sincere at once.
Perhaps if I had found a literal Muse,
The visit might have taxed me. As it is,
You wear your blue so chiefly in your eyes,
My fair Aurora, in a frank good way,
It comforts me entirely for your fame,
As well as for the trouble of ascent
To this Olympus.'

               There, a silver laugh
Ran rippling through her quickened little breaths
The steep stair somewhat justified.

                   'But still
Your ladyship has left me curious why
You dared the risk of finding the said Muse?'

'Ah, — keep me, notwithstanding, to the point,
Like any pedant? Is the blue in eyes
As awful as in stockings after all,
I wonder, that you'd have my business out
Before I breathe — exact the epic plunge
In spite of gasps? Well, naturally you think
I've come here, as the lion-hunters go
To deserts, to secure you with a trap
For exhibition in my drawing-rooms
On zoologic soirées? Not in the least.
Roar softly at me; I am frivolous,
I dare say; I have played at wild-beast shows

Like other women of my class, — but now
I meet my lion simply as Androcles
Met his . . . when at his mercy.'
                                    So, she bent
Her head, as queens may mock, — then lifting up
Her eyelids with a real grave queenly look,
Which ruled and would not spare, not even herself, —
'I think you have a cousin: — Romney Leigh.'
'You bring a word from *him?*' — my eyes leapt up
To the very height of hers, — 'a word from *him?*'
'I bring a word about him, actually.
But first' (she pressed me with her urgent eyes),
'You do not love him, — you?'
                                    'You're frank at least
In putting questions, madam,' I replied;
'I love my cousin cousinly — no more.'
'I guessed as much. I'm ready to be frank
In answering also, if you'll question me,
Or even for something less. You stand outside,
You artist women, of the common sex;
You share not with us, and exceed us so
Perhaps by what you're mulcted in, your hearts
Being starved to make your heads: so run the old
Traditions of you. I can therefore speak
Without the natural shame which creatures feel
When speaking on their level, to their like.
There's many a papist she, would rather die
Than own to her maid she put a ribbon on
To catch the indifferent eye of such a man,
Who yet would count adulteries on her beads
At holy Mary's shrine and never blush;
Because the saints are so far off, we lose
All modesty before them. Thus, to-day.
'Tis I, love Romney Leigh.'
                                    'Forbear,' I cried.
'If here's no Muse, still less is any saint;
Nor even a friend, that Lady Waldemar
Should make confessions' . . .
                                    'That's unkindly said:

If no friend, what forbids to make a friend
To join to our confession ere we have done?
I love your cousin. If it seems unwise
To say so, it's still foolisher (we're frank)
To feel so. My first husband left me young,
And pretty enough, so please you, and rich enough,
To keep my booth in Mayfair with the rest
To happy issues. There are marquises
Would serve seven years to call me wife, I know,
And, after seven, I might consider it,
For there's some comfort in a marquisate
When all's said, — yes, but after the seven years;
I, now, love Romney. You put up your lip,
So like a Leigh! so like him! — Pardon me,
I'm well aware I do not derogate
In loving Romney Leigh. The name is good,
The means are excellent, but the man, the man —
Heaven help us both, — I am near as mad as he,
In loving such an one.'
                    She slowly swung
Her heavy ringlets till they touched her smile,
As reasonably sorry for herself,
And thus continued.
                    'Of a truth, Miss Leigh,
I have not, without struggle, come to this.
I took a master in the German tongue,
I gamed a little, went to Paris twice;
But, after all, this love! . . . you eat of love,
And do as vile a thing as if you ate
Of garlic — which, whatever else you eat,
Tastes uniformly acrid, till your peach
Reminds you of your onion. Am I coarse?
Well, love's coarse, nature's coarse — ah, there's the rub.
We fair fine ladies, who park out our lives
From common sheep-paths, cannot help the crows
From flying over, — we're as natural still
As Blowsalinda. Drape us perfectly
In Lyons velvet, — we are not, for that,
Lay-figures, look you: we have hearts within,

Warm, live, improvident, indecent hearts,
As ready for outrageous ends and acts
As any distressed sempstress of them all
That Romney groans and toils for. We catch love,
And other fevers, in the vulgar way:
Love will not be outwitted by our wit,
Nor outrun by our equipages: — mine
Persisted, spite of efforts. All my cards
Turned up but Romney Leigh; my German stopped
At germane Wertherism; my Paris rounds
Returned me from the Champs Elysées just
A ghost, and sighing like Dido's. I came home
Uncured, — convicted rather to myself
Of being in love . . . in love! That's coarse, you'll say,
I'm talking garlic.'

*   *   *   *

[*Marian Erle, who is in love with Romney, tells Aurora how she ran away from home when her mother tried to hand her over to the Squire.*]

They yelled at her,
As famished hounds at a hare. She heard them yell;
She felt her name hiss after her from the hills,
Like shot from guns. On, on. And now she had cast
The voices off with the uplands. On. Mad fear
Was running in her feet and killing the ground;
The white roads curled as if she burnt them up,
The green fields melted, wayside trees fell back
To make room for her. Then her head grew vexed;
Trees, fields, turned on her and ran after her;
She heard the quick pants of the hills behind,
Their keen air pricked her neck: she had lost her feet,
Could run no more, yet somehow went as fast,
The horizon red 'twixt steeples in the east
So sucked her forward, forward, while her heart
Kept swelling, swelling, till it swelled so big
It seemed to fill her body, — when it burst

And overflowed the world and swamped the light;
'And now I am dead and safe,' thought Marian Erle —
She had dropped, she had fainted.
                                As the sense returned,
The night had passed — not life's night. She was 'ware
Of heavy tumbling motions, creaking wheels,
The driver shouting to the lazy team
That swung their rankling bells against her brain,
While, through the wagon's coverture and chinks,
The cruel yellow morning pecked at her
Alive or dead upon the straw inside, —
At which her soul ached back into the dark
And prayed, 'no more of that.' A wagoner
Had found her in a ditch beneath the moon,
As white as moonshine save for the oozing blood.
At first he thought her dead; but when he had wiped
The mouth and heard it sigh, he raised her up,
And laid her in his wagon in the straw,
And so conveyed her to the distant town
To which his business called himself, and left
That heap of misery at the hospital.

                *   *   *   *   *

from FOURTH BOOK

[Romney is to marry Marian in spite of her social inferiority,
but the congregation in church waits for her arrival in vain. She
has run away.]

                *   *   *   *   *

                                Well,
A month passed so, and then the notice came,
On such a day the marriage at the Church.
I was not backward.
                        Half Saint Giles in frieze

244

Was bidden to meet Saint James in cloth of gold,
And, after contract at the altar, pass
To eat a marriage-feast on Hampstead Heath.
Of course the people came in uncompelled,
Lame, blind, and worse — sick, sorrowful, and worse —
The humors of the peccant social wound
All pressed out, poured down upon Pimlico,
Exasperating the unaccustomed air
With a hideous interfusion. You'd suppose
A finished generation, dead of plague,
Swept outward from their graves into the sun,
The moil of death upon them. What a sight!
A holiday of miserable men
Is sadder than a burial-day of kings.
They clogged the streets, they oozed into the church
In a dark slow stream, like blood. To see that sight,
The noble ladies stood up in their pews,
Some pale for fear, a few as red for hate,
Some simply curious, some just insolent,
And some in wondering scorn, — 'What next? what next?'
These crushed their delicate rose-lips from the smile
That misbecame them in a holy place,
With broidered hems of perfumed handkerchiefs;
Those passed the salts, with confidence of eyes
And simultaneous shiver of moiré silk:
While all the aisles, alive and black with heads,
Crawled slowly toward the altar from the street,
As bruised snakes crawl and hiss out of a hole
With shuddering involution, swaying slow
From right to left, and then from left to right,
In pants and pauses. What an ugly crest
Of faces rose upon you everywhere
From that crammed mass! you did not usually
See faces like them in the open day:
They hide in cellars, not to make you mad
As Romney Leigh is. — Faces! — O my God,
We call those, faces? men's and women's . . . ay,
And children's; — babies, hanging like a rag
Forgotten on their mother's neck, — poor mouths,

Wiped clean of mother's milk by mother's blow
Before they are taught her cursing. Faces? . . . phew,
We'll call them vices, festering to despairs,
Or sorrows, petrifying to vices: not
A finger-touch of God left whole on them,
All ruined, lost — the countenance worn out
As the garment, the will dissolute as the act,
The passions loose and draggling in the dirt
To trip a foot up at the first free step!
Those, faces? 'twas as if you had stirred up hell
To heave its lowest dreg-fiends uppermost
In fiery swirls of slime, — such strangled fronts,
Such obdurate jaws were thrown up constantly
To twit you with your race, corrupt your blood,
And grind to devilish colors all your dreams
Henceforth, — though, haply, you should drop asleep
By clink of silver waters, in a muse
On Raffael's mild Madonna of the Bird.

I've waked and slept through many nights and days
Since then, — but still that day will catch my breath
Like a nightmare. There are fatal days, indeed,
In which the fibrous years have taken root
So deeply, that they quiver to their tops
Whene'er you stir the dust of such a day.

My cousin met me with his eyes and hand,
And then, with just a word, ... that 'Marian Erle
Was coming with her bridesmaids presently,'
Made haste to place me by the altar-stair
Where he and other noble gentlemen
And high-born ladies waited for the bride.

We waited. It was early: there was time
For greeting and the morning's compliment,
And gradually a ripple of women's talk
Arose and fell and tossed about a spray
Of English s's, soft as a silent hush,
And, notwithstanding, quite as audible

As louder phrases thrown out by the men.
— 'Yes, really, if we need to wait in church,
We need to talk there.' — 'She? 'tis Lady Ayr,
In blue — not purple! that's the dowager.'
— 'She looks as young' — 'She flirts as young, you mean.
Why, if you had seen her upon Thursday night,
You'd call Miss Norris modest.' — '*You* again!
I waltzed with you three hours back. Up at six,
Up still at ten; scarce time to change one's shoes:
I feel as white and sulky as a ghost,
So pray don't speak to me, Lord Belcher.' — 'No,
I'll look at you instead, and it's enough
While you have that face.' 'In church, my lord! fie, fie!'
— 'Adair, you stayed for the Division?' — 'Lost
By one.' 'The devil it is! I'm sorry for't.
And if I had not promised Mistress Grove' . . . .
'You might have kept your word to Liverpool.'
— 'Constituents must remember, after all,
We're mortal.' — 'We remind them of it.' — 'Hark,
The bride comes! here she comes, in a stream of milk!'
— 'There? Dear, you are asleep still; don't you know
The five Miss Granvilles? always dressed in white
To show they're ready to be married.' — 'Lower!
The aunt is at your elbow.' — 'Lady Maud,
Did Lady Waldemar tell you she had seen
This girl of Leigh's?' 'No, — wait! 'twas Mistress Brookes,
Who told me Lady Waldemar told her —
No, 'twasn't Mistress Brookes.' — 'She's pretty?' — 'Who?
Mistress Brookes? Lady Waldemar?' — 'How hot!
Pray is't the law to-day we're not to breathe?
You're treading on my shawl — I thank you, sir.'
— 'They say the bride's a mere child, who can't read,
But knows the things she shouldn't, with wide-awake
Great eyes. I'd go through fire to look at her.'
— 'You do, I think.' — 'And Lady Waldemar
(You see her; sitting close to Romney Leigh.
How beautiful she looks, a little flushed!)
Has taken up the girl, and methodized
Leigh's folly. Should I have come here, you suppose,

Except she'd asked me?' — 'She'd have served him more
By marrying him herself.'
　　　　　　'Ah — there she comes,
The bride, at last!'
　　　　　　　'Indeed, no. Past eleven.
She puts off her patched petticoat to-day
And puts on Mayfair manners, so begins
By setting us to wait.' — 'Yes, yes, this Leigh
Was always odd; it's in the blood, I think;
His father's uncle's cousin's second son
Was, was . . . you understand me; and for him,
He's stark, — has turned quite lunatic upon
This modern question of the poor — the poor.
An excellent subject when you're moderate;
You've seen Prince Albert's model lodging-house?
Does honor to his Royal Highness. Good!
But would he stop his carriage in Cheapside
To shake a common fellow by the fist
Whose name was . . . Shakespeare? No. We draw a line,
And if we stand not by our order, we
In England, we fall headlong. Here's a sight, —
A hideous sight, a most indecent sight!
My wife would come, sir, or I had kept her back.
By heaven, sir, when poor Damiens' trunk and limbs
Were torn by horses, women of the court
Stood by and stared, exactly as to-day
On this dismembering of society,
With pretty, troubled faces.'
　　　　　　　　'Now, at last.
She comes now.'
　　　　　　'Where? who sees? you push me, sir,
Beyond the point of what is mannerly.
You're standing, madam, on my second flounce.
I do beseech you . . .'
　　　　　　　'No — it's not the bride.
Half-past eleven. How late. The bridegroom, mark,
Gets anxious and goes out.'
　　　　　　　　'And as I said,
These Leighs! our best blood running in the rut!

It's something awful. We had pardoned him
A simple misalliance got up aside
For a pair of sky-blue eyes; the House of Lords
Has winked at such things, and we've all been young;
But here's an intermarriage reasoned out,
A contract (carried boldly to the light
To challenge observation, pioneer
Good acts by a great example) 'twixt the extremes
Of martyrized society, — on the left
The well-born, on the right the merest mob,
To treat as equals! — 'tis anarchical;
It means more than it says; 'tis damnable.
Why, sir, we can't have even our coffee good,
Unless we strain it.'
                            'Here, Miss Leigh!'
                                          'Lord Howe,
You're Romney's friend. What's all this waiting for?'

'I cannot tell. The bride has lost her head
(And way, perhaps!) to prove her sympathy
With the bridegroom.'
                            'What, — you also, disapprove!'

'Oh, I approve of nothing in the world,'
He answered, 'not of you, still less of me,
Nor even of Romney, though he's worth us both.
We're all gone wrong. The tune in us is lost;
And whistling down back alleys to the moon
Will never catch it.'

                *   *   *   *   *

THE BROWNINGS

from FIFTH BOOK

[*Aurora on poetry and the age.*]

* * * * *

The critics say that epics have died out
With Agamemnon and the goat-nursed gods;
I'll not believe it. I could never deem,
As Payné Knight did (the mythic mountaineer
Who travelled higher than he was born to live,
And showed sometimes the goitre in his throat
Discoursing of an image seen through fog),
That Homer's heroes measured twelve feet high.
They were but men: — his Helen's hair turned gray
Like any plain Miss Smith's who wears a front;
And Hector's infant whimpered at a plume
As yours last Friday at a turkey-cock.
All actual heroes are essential men,
And all men possible heroes: every age,
Heroic in proportions, double-faced,
Looks backward and before, expects a morn
And claims an epos.
          Ay, but every age
Appears to souls who live in't (ask Carlyle)
Most unheroic. Ours, for instance, ours:
The thinkers scout it, and the poets abound
Who scorn to touch it with a finger-tip:
A pewter age, — mixed metal, silver-washed;
An age of scum, spooned off the richer past,
An age of patches for old gaberdines,
An age of mere transition, meaning nought
Except that what succeeds must shame it quite
If God please. That's wrong thinking, to my mind,
And wrong thoughts make poor poems.

Every age,
Through being beheld too close, is ill-discerned
By those who have not lived past it. We'll suppose
Mount Athos carved, as Alexander schemed,
To some colossal statue of a man.
The peasants, gathering brushwood in his ear,
Had guessed as little as the browsing goats
Of form or feature of humanity
Up there, — in fact, had travelled five miles off
Or ere the giant image broke on them,
Full human profile, nose and chin distinct,
Mouth, muttering rhythms of silence up the sky
And fed at evening with the blood of suns;
Grand torso, — hand, that flung perpetually
The largesse of a silver river down
To all the country pastures. 'Tis even thus
With times we live in, — evermore too great
To be apprehended near.
But poets should
Exert a double vision; should have eyes
To see near things as comprehensively
As if afar they took their point of sight,
And distant things as intimately deep
As if they touched them. Let us strive for this.
I do distrust the poet who discerns
No character or glory in his times,
And trundles back his soul five hundred years,
Past moat and drawbridge, into a castle-court,
To sing — oh, not of lizard or of toad
Alive i' the ditch there, — 't were excusable,
But of some black chief, half knight, half sheep-lifter,
Some beauteous dame, half chattel and half queen,
As dead as must be, for the greater part,
The poems made on their chivalric bones;
And that's no wonder: death inherits death.

Nay, if there's room for poets in this world
A little overgrown (I think there is),
Their sole work is to represent the age,

Their age, not Charlemagne's, — this live, throbbing age,
That brawls, cheats, maddens, calculates, aspires,
And spends more passion, more heroic heat,
Betwixt the mirrors of its drawing-rooms,
Than Roland with his knights at Roncesvalles.
To flinch from modern varnish, coat or flounce,
Cry out for togas and the picturesque,
Is fatal, — foolish too. King Arthur's self
Was commonplace to Lady Guenever;
And Camelot to minstrels seemed as flat
As Fleet Street to our poets.

* * * * *

[*Aurora on London social life.*]

It always makes me sad to go abroad,
And now I'm sadder that I went to-night
Among the lights and talkers at Lord Howe's.
His wife is gracious, with her glossy braids,
And even voice, and gorgeous eyeballs, calm
As her other jewels. If she's somewhat cold,
Who wonders, when her blood has stood so long
In the ducal reservoir she calls her line
By no means arrogantly? she's not proud;
Not prouder than the swan is of the lake
He has always swum in; — 'tis her element;
And so she takes it with a natural grace,
Ignoring tadpoles. She just knows perhaps
There *are* who travel without outriders,
Which isn't her fault. Ah, to watch her face,
When good Lord Howe expounds his theories
Of social justice and equality!
'Tis curious, what a tender, tolerant bend
Her neck takes: for she loves him, likes his talk,
'Such clever talk — that dear, odd Algernon!'
She listens on, exactly as if he talked
Some Scandinavian myth of Lemures,
Too pretty to dispute, and too absurd.

She's gracious to me as her husband's friend,
And would be gracious were I not a Leigh,
Being used to smile just so, without her eyes,
On Joseph Strangways the Leeds mesmerist,
And Delia Dobbs the lecturer from 'the States'
Upon the 'Woman's question.' Then, for him,
I like him; he's my friend. And all the rooms
Were full of crinkling silks that swept about
The fine dust of most subtle courtesies.
What then? — why then, we come home to be sad.

*   *   *   *   *

from SIXTH BOOK

[*Aurora has met Marian by chance in Paris.*]

*   *   *   *   *

Then she led
The way, and I, as by a narrow plank
Across devouring waters, followed her,
Stepping by her footsteps, breathing by her breath,
And holding her with eyes that would not slip;
And so, without a word, we walked a mile,
And so, another mile, without a word.

Until the peopled streets being all dismissed,
House-rows and groups all scattered like a flock,
The market-gardens thickened, and the long
White walls beyond, like spiders' outside threads,
Stretched, feeling blindly toward the country-fields,
Through half-built habitations and half-dug
Foundations, — intervals of trenchant chalk
That bit betwixt the grassy uneven turfs
Where goats (vine-tendrils trailing from their mouths)
Stood perched on edges of the cellarage

Which should be, staring as about to leap
To find their coming Bacchus. All the place
Seemed less a cultivation than a waste.
Men work here, only, — scarce begin to live:
All's sad, the country struggling with the town,
Like an untamed hawk upon a strong man's fist,
That beats its wings and tries to get away,
And cannot choose be satisfied so soon
To hop through court-yards with its right foot tied,
The vintage plains and pastoral hills in sight.

We stopped beside a house too high and slim
To stand there by itself, but waiting till
Five others, two on this side, three on that,
Should grow up from the sullen second floor
They pause at now, to build it to a row.
The upper windows partly were unglazed
Meantime, — a meagre, unripe house: a line
Of rigid poplars elbowed it behind,
And, just in front, beyond the lime and bricks
That wronged the grass between it and the road,
A great acacia with its slender trunk
And overpoise of multitudinous leaves
(In which a hundred fields might spill their dew
And intense verdure, yet find room enough)
Stood reconciling all the place with green.
I followed up the stair upon her step.
She hurried upward, shot across a face,
A woman's, on the landing, — 'How now, now!
Is no one to have holidays but you?
You said an hour, and stayed three hours, I think,
And Julie waiting for your betters here?
Why if he had waked he might have waked, for me.'
— Just murmuring an excusing word, she passed
And shut the rest out with the chamber-door,
Myself shut in beside her.
                                    'Twas a room
Scarce larger than a grave, and near as bare;
Two stools, a pallet-bed; I saw the room:

254

A mouse could find no sort of shelter in't,
Much less a greater secret; curtainless, —
The window fixed you with its torturing eye,
Defying you to take a step apart
If peradventure you would hide a thing.
I saw the whole room, I and Marian there
Alone.

*   *   *   *   *

from SEVENTH BOOK

[Aurora and Marian travel to Italy, after hearing that Romney
is to marry Lady Waldemar.]

*   *   *   *   *

The next day we took train to Italy
And fled on southward in the roar of steam.
The marriage-bells of Romney must be loud,
To sound so clear through all: I was not well,
And truly, though the truth is like a jest,
I could not choose but fancy, half the way,
I stood alone i' the belfry, fifty bells
Of naked iron, mad with merriment
(As one who laughs and cannot stop himself),
All clanking at me, in me, over me,
Until I shrieked a shriek I could not hear,
And swooned with noise, — but still, along my swoon,
Was 'ware the baffled changes backward rang
Prepared, at each emerging sense, to beat
And crash it out with clangor. I was weak;
I struggled for the posture of my soul
In upright consciousness of place and time,
But evermore, 'twixt waking and asleep,
Slipped somehow, staggered, caught at Marian's eyes
A moment (it is very good for strength

To know that some one needs you to be strong),
And so recovered what I called myself,
For that time.   I just knew it when we swept
Above the old roofs of Dijon: Lyons dropped
A spark into the night, half trodden out
Unseen. But presently the winding Rhone
Washed out the moonlight large along his banks
Which strained their yielding curves out clear and clean
To hold it, — shadow of town and castle blurred
Upon the hurrying river. Such an air
Blew thence upon the forehead — half an air
And half a water — that I leaned and looked,
Then, turning back on Marian, smiled to mark
That she looked only on her child, who slept,
His face toward the moon too.   So we passed
The liberal open country and the close,
And shot through tunnels, like a lightning-wedge
By great Thor-hammers driven through the rock,
Which, quivering through the intestine blackness, splits,
And lets it in at once: the train swept in
Athrob with effort, trembling with resolve,
The fierce denouncing whistle wailing on
And dying off smothered in the shuddering dark,
While we, self-awed, drew troubled breath, oppressed
As other Titans underneath the pile
And nightmare of the mountains. Out, at last,
To catch the dawn afloat upon the land!
— Hills, slung forth broadly and gauntly everywhere,
Not cramped in their foundations, pushing wide
Rich outspreads of the vineyards and the corn
(As if they entertained i' the name of France),
While down their straining sides streamed manifest
A soil as red as Charlemagne's knightly blood,
To consecrate the verdure. Some one said
'Marseilles!' And lo, the city of Marseilles,
With all her ships behind her, and beyond,

The scimitar of ever-shining sea
For right-hand use, bared blue against the sky!

*   *   *   *   *

The days went by. I took up the old days,
With all their Tuscan pleasures worn and spoiled,
Like some lost book we dropped in the long grass
On such a happy summer afternoon
When last we read it with a loving friend,
And find in autumn when the friend is gone,
The grass cut short, the weather changed, too late,
And stare at, as at something wonderful
For sorrow, — thinking how two hands before
Had held up what is left to only one,
And how we smiled when such a vehement nail
Impressed the tiny dint here which presents
This verse in fire forever. Tenderly
And mournfully I lived. I knew the birds
And insects, — which looked fathered by the flowers
And emulous of their hues: I recognized
The moths, with that great overpoise of wings
Which make a mystery of them how at all
They can stop flying: butterflies, that bear
Upon their blue wings such red embers round,
They seem to scorch the blue air into holes
Each flight they take: and fireflies, that suspire
In short soft lapses of transported flame
Across the tingling Dark, while overhead
The constant and inviolable stars
Outburn those light-of-love: melodious owls
(If music had but one note and was sad,
'Twould sound just so), and all the silent swirl
Of bats that seem to follow in the air
Some grand circumference of a shadowy dome
To which we are blind: and then the nightingales,
Which pluck our heart across a garden-wall
(When walking in the town) and carry it
So high into the bowery almond-trees
We tremble and are afraid, and feel as if

The golden flood of moonlight unaware
Dissolved the pillars of the steady earth
And made it less substantial. And I knew
The harmless opal snakes, the large-mouthed frogs
(Those noisy vaunters of their shallow streams);
And lizards, the green lightnings of the wall,
Which, if you sit down quiet, nor sigh loud,
Will flatter you and take you for a stone,
And flash familiarly about your feet
With such prodigious eyes in such small heads! —
I knew them (though they had somewhat dwindled from
My childish imagery), and kept in mind
How last I sat among them equally,
In fellowship and mateship, as a child
Feels equal still toward insect, beast, and bird,
Before the Adam in him has forgone
All privilege of Eden, — making friends
And talk with such a bird or such a goat,
And buying many a two-inch-wide rush-cage
To let out the caged cricket on a tree,
Saying 'Oh my dear grillino, were you cramped?
And are you happy with the ilex-leaves?
And do you love me who have let you go?
Say *yes* in singing, and I'll understand.'

* * * * *

And many a Tuscan eve I wandered down
The cypress alley like a restless ghost
That tries its feeble ineffectual breath
Upon its own charred funeral-brands put out
Too soon, where black and stiff stood up the trees
Against the broad vermilion of the skies.
Such skies! — all clouds abolished in a sweep
Of God's skirt, with a dazzle to ghosts and men,
As down I went, saluting on the bridge
The hem of such before 'twas caught away
Beyond the peaks of Lucca. Underneath,
The river, just escaping from the weight
Of that intolerable glory, ran

In acquiescent shadow murmurously;
While, up beside it, streamed the festa-folk
With fellow-murmurs from their feet and fans,
And *issimo* and *ino* and sweet poise
Of vowels in their pleasant scandalous talk;
Returning from the grand-duke's dairy-farm
Before the trees grew dangerous at eight
(For 'trust no tree by moonlight,' Tuscans say),
To eat their ice at Donay's tenderly, —
Each lovely lady close to a cavalier
Who holds her dear fan while she feeds her smile
On meditative spoonfuls of vanille
And listens to his hot-breathed vows of love
Enough to thaw her cream and scorch his beard.
'Twas little matter. I could pass them by
Indifferently, not fearing to be known.
No danger of being wrecked upon a friend,
And forced to take an iceberg for an isle!
The very English, here, must wait and learn
To hang the cobweb of their gossip out
To catch a fly. I'm happy. It's sublime,
This perfect solitude of foreign lands!
To be, as if you had not been till then,
And were then, simply that you chose to be:
To spring up, not be brought forth from the ground,
Like grasshoppers at Athens, and skip thrice
Before a woman makes a pounce on you
And plants you in her hair! — possess, yourself,
A new world all alive with creatures new,
New sun, new moon, new flowers, new people — ah,
And be possessed by none of them! no right
In one, to call your name, inquire your where,
Or what you think of Mister Someone's book,
Or Mister Other's marriage or decease,
Or how's the headache which you had last week,
Or why you look so pale still, since it's gone?
— Such most surprising riddance of one's life
Comes next one's death; 'tis disembodiment
Without the pang. I marvel, people choose

To stand stock-still like fakirs, till the moss
Grows on them and they cry out, self-admired,
'How verdant and how virtuous!' Well, I'm glad;
Or should be, if grown foreign to myself
As surely as to others.
                              Musing so,
I walked the narrow unrecognizing streets,
Where many a palace-front peers gloomily
Through stony visors iron-barred (prepared
Alike, should foe or lover pass that way,
For guest or victim), and came wandering out
Upon the churches with mild open doors
And plaintive wail of vespers, where a few,
Those chiefly women, sprinkled round in blots
Upon the dusky pavement, knelt and prayed
Toward the altar's silver glory.

                 *   *   *   *   *

So many Tuscan evenings passed the same.
I could not lose a sunset on the bridge,
And would not miss a vigil in the church,
And liked to mingle with the outdoor crowd
So strange and gay and ignorant of my face,
For men you know not are as good as trees.
And only once, at the Santissima,
I almost chanced upon a man I knew,
Sir Blaise Delorme. He saw me certainly,
And somewhat hurried, as he crossed himself,
The smoothness of the action, — then half bowed,
But only half, and merely to my shade,
I slipped so quick behind the porphyry plinth
And left him dubious if 'twas really I
Or peradventure Satan's usual trick
To keep a mounting saint uncanonized.
But he was safe for that time, and I too;
The argent angels in the altar-flare
Absorbed his soul next moment. The good man!
In England we were scarce acquaintances,
That here in Florence he should keep my thought

Beyond the image on his eye, which came
And went: and yet his thought disturbed my life:
For, after that, I oftener sat at home
On evenings, watching how they fined themselves
With gradual conscience to a perfect night,
Until the moon, diminished to a curve,
Lay out there like a sickle for his hand
Who cometh down at last to reap the earth.
At such times, ended seemed my trade of verse;
I feared to jingle bells upon my robe
Before the four-faced silent cherubim.
With God so near me, could I sing of God?
I did not write, nor read, nor even think,
But sat absorbed amid the quickening glooms,
Most like some passive broken lump of salt
Dropped in by chance to a bowl of œnomel,
To spoil the drink a little and lose itself,
Dissolving slowly, slowly, until lost.

[*End of Seventh Book*]

from EIGHTH BOOK

[*Aurora unexpectedly meets Romney again, in Florence.*]

*   *   *   *   *

The heavens were making room to hold the night,
The sevenfold heavens unfolding all their gates
To let the stars out slowly (prophesied
In close-approaching advent, not discerned),
While still the cue-owls from the cypresses
Of the Poggio called and counted every pulse
Of the skyey palpitation. Gradually
The purple and transparent shadows slow
Had filled up the whole valley to the brim,
And flooded all the city, which you saw

As some drowned city in some enchanted sea,
Cut off from nature, — drawing you who gaze,
With passionate desire, to leap and plunge
And find a sea-king with a voice of waves,
And treacherous soft eyes, and slippery locks
You cannot kiss but you shall bring away
Their salt upon your lips. The duomo bell
Strikes ten, as if it struck ten fathoms down,
So deep; and twenty churches answer it
The same, with twenty various instances.
Some gaslights tremble along squares and streets;
The Pitti's palace-front is drawn in fire;
And, past the quays, Maria Novella Place,
In which the mystic obelisks stand up
Triangular, pyramidal, each based
Upon its four-square brazen tortoises,
To guard that fair church, Buonarroti's Bride,
That stares out from her large blind dial eyes,
(Her quadrant and armillary dials, black
With rhythms of many suns and moons) in vain
Inquiry for so rich a soul as his.
Methinks I have plunged, I see it all so clear . . .
And, O my heart, . . . the sea-king!
                                        In my ears
The sound of waters. There he stood, my king!

*   *   *   *   *

AN AUGUST VOICE

[*Napoleon III is imagined in 1859 urging the Florentines to call back their Grand Duke — see the note to* Casa Guidi Windows, *page 195.*]

'*Una voce augusta.*' — MONITORE TOSCANO

I.

You'll take back your Grand-duke?
    I made the treaty upon it.
Just venture a quiet rebuke;
    Dall' Ongaro write him a sonnet;
Ricasoli gently explain
    Some need of the constitution:
He'll swear to it over again,
    Providing an 'easy solution.'
You'll call back the Grand-duke.

II.

You'll take back your Grand-duke?
    I promised the Emperor Francis
To argue the case by his book,
    And ask you to meet his advances.
The Ducal cause, we know
    (Whether you or he be the wronger),
Has very strong points; — although
    Your bayonets, there, have stronger.
You'll call back the Grand-duke.

III.

You'll take back your Grand-duke?
  He is not pure altogether.
For instance, the oath which he took
  (In the Forty-eight rough weather)
He'd 'nail your flag to his mast,'
  Then softly scuttled the boat you
Hoped to escape in at last,
  And both by a 'Proprio motu.'
You'll call back the Grand-duke.

IV.

You'll take back your Grand-duke?
  The scheme meets nothing to shock it
In this smart letter, look,
  We found in Radetsky's pocket;
Where his Highness in sprightly style
  Of the flower of his Tuscans wrote,
'These heads be the hottest in file;
  Pray shoot them the quickest.' Quote,
And call back the Grand-duke.

V.

You'll take back your Grand-duke?
  There *are* some things to object to.
He cheated, betrayed, and forsook,
  Then called in the foe to protect you.
He taxed you for wines and for meats
  Throughout that eight years' pastime
Of Austria's drum in your streets —
  Of course you remember the last time
You called back your Grand-duke?

VI.

You'll take back the Grand-duke?
  It is not race he is poor in,
Although he never could brook
  The patriot cousin at Turin.
His love of kin you discern,
  By his hate of your flag and me —
So decidedly apt to turn
  All colors at the sight of the Three.
You'll call back the Grand-duke.

VII.

You'll take back your Grand-duke?
  'Twas weak that he fled from the Pitti;
But consider how little he shook
  At thought of bombarding your city!
And, balancing that with this,
  The Christian rule is plain for us;
. . . Or the Holy Father's Swiss
  Have shot his Perugians in vain for us.
You'll call back the Grand-duke.

VIII.

Pray take back your Grand-duke.
  — I, too, have suffered persuasion.
All Europe, raven and rook,
  Screeched at me armed for your nation.
Your cause in my heart struck spurs;
  I swept such warnings aside for you:
My very child's eyes, and Hers,
  Grew like my brother's who died for you.
You'll call back the Grand-duke?

IX.

You'll take back your Grand-duke?
　My French fought nobly with reason, —
Left many a Lombardy nook
　Red as with wine out of season.
Little we grudged what was done there,
　Paid freely your ransom of blood:
Our heroes stark in the sun there
　We would not recall if we could.
You'll call back the Grand-duke?

X.

You'll take back your Grand-duke?
　His son rode fast as he got off
That day on the enemy's hook,
　When *I* had an epaulet shot off.
Though splashed (as I saw him afar — no,
　Near) by those ghastly rains,
The mark, when you've washed him in Arno,
　Will scarcely be larger than Cain's.
You'll call back the Grand-duke?

XI.

You'll take back your Grand-duke?
　'Twill be so simple, quite beautiful:
The shepherd recovers his crook,
　. . . If you should be sheep, and dutiful.
I spoke a word worth chalking
　On Milan's wall — but stay,
Here's Poniatowsky talking, —
　You'll listen to *him* to-day,
And call back the Grand-duke.

266

XII.

You'll take back your Grand-duke?
    Observe, there's no one to force it, —
Unless the Madonna, Saint Luke
    Drew for you, choose to endorse it.
I charge you, by great Saint Martino
    And prodigies quickened by wrong,
Remember your Dead on Ticino;
    Be worthy, be constant, be strong —
Bah! — call back the Grand-duke!!

BIANCA AMONG THE NIGHTINGALES

I.

The cypress stood up like a church
    That night we felt our love would hold,
And saintly moonlight seemed to search
    And wash the whole world clean as gold;
The olives crystallized the vales'
    Broad slopes until the hills grew strong:
The fireflies and the nightingales
    Throbbed each to either, flame and song.
The nightingales, the nightingales!

II.

Upon the angle of its shade
    The cypress stood, self-balanced high;
Half up, half down, as double-made,
    Along the ground, against the sky;
And we, too! from such soul-height went
    Such leaps of blood, so blindly driven,
We scarce knew if our nature meant

267

Most passionate earth or intense heaven.
The nightingales, the nightingales!

III.

We paled with love, we shook with love,
    We kissed so close we could not vow;
Till Giulio whispered 'Sweet, above
    God's Ever guaranties this Now.'
And through his words the nightingales
    Drove straight and full their long clear call,
Like arrows through heroic mails,
    And love was awful in it all.
The nightingales, the nightingales!

IV.

O cold white moonlight of the north,
    Refresh these pulses, quench this hell!
O coverture of death drawn forth
    Across this garden-chamber . . . well!
But what have nightingales to do
    In gloomy England, called the free . . .
(Yes, free to die in! . . .) when we two
    Are sundered, singing still to me?
And still they sing, the nightingales!

V.

I think I hear him, how he cried
    'My own soul's life!' between their notes.
Each man has but one soul supplied,
    And that's immortal. Though his throat's
On fire with passion now, to *her*
    He can't say what to me he said!
And yet he moves her, they aver.
    The nightingales sing through my head, —
The nightingales, the nightingales!

VI.

He says to her what moves her most.
He would not name his soul within
Her hearing, — rather pays her cost
With praises to her lips and chin.
Man has but one soul, 'tis ordained,
And each soul but one love, I add;
Yet souls are damned and love's profaned;
These nightingales will sing me mad!
The nightingales, the nightingales!

VII.

I marvel how the birds can sing.
There's little difference, in their view,
Betwixt our Tuscan trees that spring
As vital flames into the blue,
And dull round blots of foliage meant,
Like saturated sponges here
To suck the fogs up. As content
Is he too in this land, 'tis clear.
And still they sing, the nightingales.

VIII.

My Native Florence! dear, forgone!
I see across the Alpine ridge
How the last feast-day of Saint John
Shot rockets from Carraia bridge.
The luminous city, tall with fire,
Trod deep down in that river of ours,
While many a boat with lamp and choir
Skimmed birdlike over glittering towers.
I will not hear these nightingales.

IX.

I seem to float, *we* seem to float
　　Down Arno's stream in festive guise;
A boat strikes flame into our boat,
　　And up that lady seems to rise
As then she rose. The shock had flashed
　　A vision on us! What a head,
What leaping eyeballs! — beauty dashed
　　To splendor by a sudden dread.
And still they sing, the nightingales.

X.

Too bold to sin, too weak to die;
　　Such women are so. As for me,
I would we had drowned there, he and I,
　　That moment, loving perfectly.
He had not caught her with her loosed
　　Gold ringlets . . . rarer in the south . . .
Nor heard the 'Grazie tanto' bruised
　　To sweetness by her English mouth.
And still they sing, the nightingales.

XI.

She had not reached him at my heart
　　With her fine tongue, as snakes indeed
Kill flies; nor had I, for my part,
　　Yearned after, in my desperate need,
And followed him as he did her
　　To coasts left bitter by the tide,
Whose very nightingales, elsewhere
　　Delighting, torture and deride!
For still they sing, the nightingales.

XII.

A worthless woman; mere cold clay
  As all false things are: but so fair,
She takes the breath of men away
  Who gaze upon her unaware.
I would not play her larcenous tricks
  To have her looks! She lied and stole,
And spat into my love's pure pyx
  The rank saliva of her soul.
And still they sing, the nightingales.

XIII.

I would not for her white and pink,
  Though such he likes — her grace of limb,
Though such he has praised — nor yet, I think,
  For life itself, though spent with him,
Commit such sacrilege, affront
  God's nature which is love, intrude
'Twixt two affianced souls, and hunt
  Like spiders, in the altar's wood.
I cannot bear these nightingales.

XIV.

If she chose sin, some gentler guise
  She might have sinned in, so it seems:
She might have pricked out both my eyes,
  And I still seen him in my dreams!
— Or drugged me in my soup or wine,
  Nor left me angry afterward:
To die here with his hand in mine,
  His breath upon me, were not hard.
(Our Lady hush these nightingales!)

XV.

But set a springe for *him*, 'mio ben,'
  My only good, my first last love! —
Though Christ knows well what sin is, when
  He sees some things done they must move
Himself to wonder. Let her pass.
  I think of her by night and day.
Must *I* too join her . . . out, alas! . . .
  With Giulio, in each word I say?
And evermore the nightingales!

XVI.

Giulio, my Giulio! — sing they so,
  And you be silent? Do I speak,
And you not hear? An arm you throw
  Round some one, and I feel so weak?
— Oh, owl-like birds! They sing for spite,
  They sing for hate, they sing for doom,
They'll sing through death who sing through night,
  They'll sing and stun me in the tomb —
The nightingales, the nightingales!

AMY'S CRUELTY

Fair Amy of the terraced house,
  Assist me to discover
Why you who would not hurt a mouse
  Can torture so your lover.

You give your coffee to the cat,
  You stroke the dog for coming,
And all your face grows kinder at
  The little brown bee's humming.

272

But when *he* haunts your door . . . the town
Marks coming and marks going . . .
You seem to have stitched your eyelids down
To that long piece of sewing!

You never give a look, not you,
Nor drop him a 'Good morning,'
To keep his long day warm and blue,
So fretted by your scorning.

She shook her head — 'The mouse and bee
For crumb or flower will linger:
The dog is happy at my knee,
The cat purrs at my finger.

'But *he* . . . to *him*, the least thing given
Means great things at a distance;
He wants my world, my sun, my heaven,
Soul, body, whole existence.

'They say love gives as well as takes;
But I'm a simple maiden, —
My mother's first smile when she wakes
I still have smiled and prayed in.

'I only know my mother's love
Which gives all and asks nothing;
And this new loving sets the groove
Too much the way of loathing.

'Unless he gives me all in change,
I forfeit all things by him:
The risk is terrible and strange —
I tremble, doubt, . . . deny him.

'He's sweetest friend or hardest foe,
Best angel or worst devil;
I either hate or . . . love him so,
I can't be merely civil!

'You trust a woman who puts forth
   Her blossoms thick as summer's?
You think she dreams what love is worth,
   Who casts it to new-comers?

'Such love's a cowslip-ball to fling,
   A moment's pretty pastime;
I give . . . all me, if anything,
   The first time and the last time.

'Dear neighbor of the trellised house,
   A man should murmur never,
Though treated worse than dog and mouse,
   Till doated on for ever!'

THE BEST THING IN THE WORLD

What's the best thing in the world?
June-rose, by May-dew impearled;
Sweet south-wind, that means no rain;
Truth, not cruel to a friend;
Pleasure, not in haste to end;
Beauty, not self-decked and curled
Till its pride is over-plain;
Light, that never makes you wink;
Memory, that gives no pain;
Love, when, *so*, you're loved again.
What's the best thing in the world?
— Something out of it, I think.

A MUSICAL INSTRUMENT

I.

What was he doing, the great god Pan,
    Down in the reeds by the river?
Spreading ruin and scattering ban,
Splashing and paddling with hoofs of a goat,
And breaking the golden lilies afloat
    With the dragon-fly on the river.

II.

He tore out a reed, the great god Pan,
    From the deep cool bed of the river:
The limpid water turbidly ran,
And the broken lilies a-dying lay,
And the dragon-fly had fled away,
    Ere he brought it out of the river.

III.

High on the shore sat the great god Pan
    While turbidly flowed the river;
And hacked and hewed as a great god can,
With his hard bleak steel at the patient reed,
Till there was not a sign of the leaf indeed
    To prove it fresh from the river.

IV.

He cut it short, did the great god Pan,
    (How tall it stood in the river!)
Then drew the pith, like the heart of a man,
Steadily from the outside ring,
And notched the poor dry empty thing
    In holes, as he sat by the river.

V.

'This is the way,' laughed the great god Pan
  (Laughed while he sat by the river),
'The only way, since gods began
To make sweet music, they could succeed.'
Then, dropping his mouth to a hole in the reed,
  He blew in power by the river.

VI.

Sweet, sweet, sweet, O Pan!
  Piercing sweet by the river!
Blinding sweet, O great god Pan!
The sun on the hill forgot to die,
And the lilies revived, and the dragon-fly
  Came back to dream on the river.

VII.

Yet half a beast is the great god Pan,
  To laugh as he sits by the river,
Making a poet out of a man:
The true gods sigh for the cost and pain, —
For the reed which grows nevermore again
  As a reed with the reeds in the river.

'DIED . . .'

(*The Times* Obituary)

I.

What shall we add now? He is dead.
  And I who praise and you who blame,
  With wash of words across his name,
Find suddenly declared instead —
'On Sunday, third of August, dead.'

II.

Which stops the whole we talked to-day.
  I, quickened to a plausive glance
  At his large general tolerance
By common people's narrow way,
Stopped short in praising. Dead, they say.

III.

And you, who had just put in a sort
  Of cold deduction — 'rather, large
  Through weakness of the continent marge,
Than greatness of the thing contained' —
Broke off. Dead! — there, you stood restrained.

IV.

As if we had talked in following one
  Up some long gallery. 'Would you choose
  An air like that? The gait is loose —
Or noble.' Sudden in the sun
An oubliette winks. Where *is* he? Gone.

V.

Dead. Man's 'I was' by God's 'I am' —
  All hero-worship comes to that.
  High heart, high thought, high fame, as flat
As a gravestone. Bring your *Jacet jam* —
The epitaph's an epigram.

VI.

Dead. There's an answer to arrest
  All carping. Dust's his natural place?
  He'll let the flies buzz round his face
And, though you slander, not protest?
— From such an one, exact the Best?

VII.

Opinions gold or brass are null.
  We chuck our flattery or abuse,
  Called Cæsar's due, as Charon's dues,
I' the teeth of some dead sage or fool,
To mend the grinning of a skull.

VIII.

Be abstinent in praise and blame.
  The man's still mortal, who stands first,
  And mortal only, if last and worst.
Then slowly lift so frail a fame,
Or softly drop so poor a shame.

A VIEW ACROSS THE ROMAN CAMPAGNA

1861

I.

Over the dumb Campagna-sea,
  Out in the offing through mist and rain,
Saint Peter's Church heaves silently
  Like a mighty ship in pain,
  Facing the tempest with struggle and strain.

II.

Motionless waifs of ruined towers,
  Soundless breakers of desolate land:
The sullen surf of the mist devours
  That mountain-range upon either hand,
  Eaten away from its outline grand.

278

III.

And over the dumb Campagna-sea
  Where the ship of the Church heaves on to wreck,
Alone and silent as God must be,
    The Christ walks. Ay, but Peter's neck
    Is stiff to turn on the foundering deck.

IV.

Peter, Peter! if such be thy name,
  Now leave the ship for another to steer,
And proving thy faith evermore the same,
    Come forth, tread out through the dark and drear,
    Since He who walks on the sea is here.

V.

Peter, Peter! He does not speak;
  He is not as rash as in old Galilee:
Safer a ship, though it toss and leak,
    Than a reeling foot on a rolling sea!
    And he's got to be round in the girth, thinks he.

VI.

Peter, Peter! He does not stir;
  His nets are heavy with silver fish;
He reckons his gains, and is keen to infer
    — 'The broil on the shore, if the Lord should wish;
    But the sturgeon goes to the Cæsar's dish.'

VII.

Peter, Peter! thou fisher of men,
  Fisher of fish wouldst thou live instead?
Haggling for pence with the other Ten,
    Cheating the market at so much a head,
    Griping the Bag of the traitor Dead?

VIII.

At the triple crow of the Gallic cock
Thou weep'st not, thou, though thine eyes be dazed:
What bird comes next in the tempest-shock?
— Vultures! see, — as when Romulus gazed, —
To inaugurate Rome for a world amazed!

THE NORTH AND THE SOUTH

ROME, MAY, 1861

[*Hans Christian Andersen visited Rome in 1861.*]

I.

'Now give us lands where the olives grow,'
  Cried the North to the South,
'Where the sun with a golden mouth can blow
Blue bubbles of grapes down a vineyard-row!'
  Cried the North to the South.

'Now give us men from the sunless plain,'
  Cried the South to the North,
'By need of work in the snow and the rain,
Made strong, and brave by familiar pain!'
  Cried the South to the North.

II.

'Give lucider hills and intenser seas,'
  Said the North to the South.
'Since ever by symbols and bright degrees
Art, childlike, climbs to the dear Lord's knees,'
  Said the North to the South.

'Give strenuous souls for belief and prayer,'
    Said the South to the North,
'That stand in the dark on the lowest stair,
While affirming of God, "He is certainly there,"'
    Said the South to the North.

III.

'Yet oh for the skies that are softer and higher!'
    Sighed the North to the South;
For the flowers that blaze, and the trees that aspire,
And the insects made of a song or a fire!'
    Sighed the North to the South.

'And oh for a seer to discern the same!'
    Sighed the South to the North;
'For a poet's tongue of baptismal flame,
To call the tree or the flower by its name!'
    Sighed the South to the North.

IV.

The North sent therefore a man of men
    As a grace to the South;
And thus to Rome came Andersen.
—'Alas, but must you take him again?'
    Said the South to the North.

FROM HEINE

I.

I

Out of my own great woe
I make my little songs,
Which rustle their feathers in throngs
And beat on her heart even so.

II

They found the way, for their part,
Yet come again, and complain:
Complain, and are not fain
To say what they saw in her heart.

II.

I

Art thou indeed so adverse?
Art thou so changed indeed?
Against the woman who wrongs me
I cry to the world in my need.

II

O recreant lips unthankful,
How could ye speak evil, say,
Of the man who so well has kissed you
On many a fortunate day?

III.

I

My child, we were two children,
Small, merry by childhood's law;
We used to crawl to the hen-house
And hide ourselves in the straw.

II

We crowed like cocks, and whenever
The passers near us drew —
Cock-a-doodle! they thought
'Twas a real cock that crew.

III

The boxes about our courtyard
We carpeted to our mind,
And lived there both together —
Kept house in a noble kind.

IV

The neighbor's old cat often
Came to pay us a visit;
We made her a bow and curtsey,
Each with a compliment in it.

V

After her health we asked
Our care and regard to evince —
(We have made the very same speeches
To many an old cat since).

VI

We also sat and wisely
Discoursed, as old folk do,
Complaining how all went better
In those good times we knew, —

VII

How love and truth and believing
Had left the world to itself,
And how so dear was the coffee,
And how so rare was the pelf.

VIII

The children's games are over,
The rest is over with youth —
The world, the good games, the good times,
The belief, and the love, and the truth.

IV.

I

Thou lovest me not, thou lovest me not!
'Tis scarcely worth a sigh:
Let me look in thy face, and no king in his place
Is a gladder man than I.

II

Thou hatest me well, thou hatest me well —
Thy little red mouth has told:
Let it reach me a kiss, and, however it is,
My child, I am well consoled.

V.

I

My own sweet Love, if thou in the grave,
The darksome grave, wilt be,
Then will I go down by the side, and crave
Love-room for thee and me.

II

I kiss and caress and press thee wild,
Thou still, thou cold, thou white!
I wail, I tremble, and weeping mild,
Turn to a corpse at the right.

III

The Dead stand up, the midnight calls,
They dance in airy swarms —
We two keep still where the grave-shade falls,
And I lie on in thine arms.

IV

The Dead stand up, the Judgment-day
    Bids such to weal or woe —
But nought shall trouble us where we stay
    Embraced and embracing below.

VI.

I

The years they come and go,
    The races drop in the grave,
Yet never the love doth so
    Which here in my heart I have.

II

Could I see thee but once, one day,
    And sink down so on my knee,
And die in thy sight while I say,
    'Lady, I love but thee!'

ROBERT BROWNING

1812–1889

from PAULINE

*   *   *   *   *

Night, and one single ridge of narrow path
Between the sullen river and the woods
Waving and muttering, for the moonless night
Has shaped them into images of life,
Like the uprising of the giant-ghosts,
Looking on earth to know how their sons fare:
Thou art so close by me, the roughest swell
Of wind in the tree-tops hides not the panting
Of thy soft breasts. No, we will pass to morning —
Morning, the rocks and valleys and old woods.
How the sun brightens in the mist, and here,
Half in the air, like creatures of the place,
Trusting the element, living on high boughs
That swing in the wind — look at the silver spray
Flung from the foam-sheet of the cataract
Amid the broken rocks! Shall we stay here
With the wild hawks? No, ere the hot noon come,
Dive we down — safe! See this our new retreat
Walled in with a sloped mound of matted shrubs,
Dark, tangled, old and green, still sloping down
To a small pool whose waters lie asleep
Amid the trailing boughs turned water-plants:
And tall trees overarch to keep us in,
Breaking the sunbeams into emerald shafts,
And in the dreamy water one small group
Of two or three strange trees are got together
Wondering at all around, as strange beasts herd
Together far from their own land: all wildness,
No turf nor moss, for boughs and plants pave all,
And tongues of bank go shelving in the lymph,

Where the pale-throated snake reclines his head,
And old grey stones lie making eddies there,
The wild-mice cross them dry-shod. Deeper in!
Shut thy soft eyes — now look — still deeper in!
This is the very heart of the woods all round
Mountain-like heaped above us; yet even here
One pond of water gleams; far off the river
Sweeps like a sea, barred out from land; but one —
One thin clear sheet has overleaped and wound
Into this silent depth, which gained, it lies
Still, as but let by sufferance; the trees bend
O'er it as wild men watch a sleeping girl,
And through their roots long creeping plants out-stretch
Their twined hair, steeped and sparkling; farther on,
Tall rushes and thick flag-knots have combined
To narrow it; so, at length, a silver thread,
It winds, all noiselessly through the deep wood
Till thro' a cleft-way, thro' the moss and stone,
It joins its parent-river with a shout.

Up for the glowing day, leave the old woods!
See, they part like a ruined arch: the sky!
Nothing but sky appears, so close the roots
And grass of the hill-top level with the air —
Blue sunny air, where a great cloud floats laden
With light, like a dead whale that white birds pick,
Floating away in the sun in some north sea.
Air, air, fresh life-blood, thin and searching air,
The clear, dear breath of God that loveth us,
Where small birds reel and winds take their delight!
Water is beautiful, but not like air:
See, where the solid azure waters lie
Made as of thickened air, and down below,
The fern-ranks like a forest spread themselves
As though each pore could feel the element;
Where the quick glancing serpent winds his way,
Float with me there, Pauline! — but not like air.

*   *   *   *   *

ROBERT BROWNING

SORDELLO

from BOOK THE FIRST

* * * * *

In Mantua territory half is slough,
Half pine-tree forest; maples, scarlet oaks
Breed o'er the river-beds; even Mincio chokes
With sand the summer through: but 'tis morass
In winter up to Mantua walls. There was,
Some thirty years before this evening's coil,
One spot reclaimed from the surrounding spoil,
Goito; just a castle built amid
A few low mountains; firs and larches hid
Their main defiles, and rings of vineyard bound
The rest. Some captured creature in a pound,
Whose artless wonder quite precludes distress,
Secure beside in its own loveliness,
So peered with airy head, below, above,
The castle at its toils, the lapwings love
To glean among at grape-time. Pass within.
A maze of corridors contrived for sin,
Dusk winding-stairs, dim galleries got past,
You gain the inmost chambers, gain at last
A maple-panelled room: that haze which seems
Floating about the panel, if there gleams
A sunbeam over it, will turn to gold
And in light-graven characters unfold
The Arab's wisdom everywhere; what shade
Marred them a moment, those slim pillars made,
Cut like a company of palms to prop
The roof, each kissing top entwined with top,
Leaning together; in the carver's mind
Some knot of bacchanals, flushed cheek combined

With straining forehead, shoulders purpled, hair
Diffused between, who in a goat-skin bear
A vintage; graceful sister-palms! But quick
To the main wonder, now. A vault, see; thick
Black shade about the ceiling, though fine slits
Across the buttress suffer light by fits
Upon a marvel in the midst. Nay, stoop —
A dullish grey-streaked cumbrous font, a group
Round it, — each side of it, where'er one sees, —
Upholds it; shrinking Caryatides
Of just-tinged marble like Eve's lilied flesh
Beneath her maker's finger when the fresh
First pulse of life shot brightening the snow.
The font's edge burthens every shoulder, so
They muse upon the ground, eyelids half closed;
Some, with meek arms behind their backs disposed,
Some, crossed above their bosoms, some, to veil
Their eyes, some, propping chin and cheek so pale,
Some, hanging slack an utter helpless length
Dead as a buried vestal whose whole strength
Goes when the grate above shuts heavily.
So dwell these noiseless girls, patient to see,
Like priestesses because of sin impure
Penanced for ever, who resigned endure,
Having that once drunk sweetness to the dregs.
And every eve, Sordello's visit begs
Pardon for them: constant as eve he came
To sit beside each in her turn, the same
As one of them, a certain space: and awe
Made a great indistinctness till he saw
Sunset slant cheerful through the buttress-chinks,
Gold seven times globed; surely our maiden shrinks
And a smile stirs her as if one faint grain
Her load were lightened, one shade less the stain
Obscured her forehead, yet one more bead slipt
From off the rosary whereby the crypt
Keeps count of the contritions of its charge?
Then with a step more light, a heart more large,

He may depart, leave her and every one
To linger out the penance in mute stone.

*   *   *   *   *

from BOOK THE FOURTH

*   *   *   *   *

Let us scale this tall
Huge foursquare line of red brick garden-wall
Bastioned within by trees of every sort
On three sides, slender, spreading, long and short;
Each grew as it contrived, the poplar ramped,
The fig-tree reared itself, — but stark and cramped,
Made fools of, like tamed lions: whence, on the edge,
Running 'twixt trunk and trunk to smooth one ledge
Of shade, were shrubs inserted, warp and woof,
Which smothered up that variance. Scale the roof
Of solid tops, and o'er the slope you slide
Down to a grassy space level and wide,
Here and there dotted with a tree, but trees
Of rarer leaf, each foreigner at ease,
Set by itself: and in the centre spreads,
Borne upon three uneasy leopards' heads,
A laver, broad and shallow, one bright spirt
Of water bubbles in. The walls begirt
With trees leave off on either hand; pursue
Your path along a wondrous avenue
Those walls abut on, heaped of gleamy stone,
With aloes leering everywhere, grey-grown
From many a Moorish summer: how they wind
Out of the fissures! likelier to bind
The building than those rusted cramps which drop
Already in the eating sunshine. Stop,
You fleeting shapes above there! Ah, the pride
Or else despair of the whole country-side!
A range of statues, swarming o'er with wasps,
God, goddess, woman, man, the Greek rough-rasps

In crumbling Naples marble – meant to look
Like those Messina marbles Constance took
Delight in, or Taurello's self conveyed
To Mantua for his mistress, Adelaide, –
A certain font with caryatides
Since cloistered at Goito; only, these
Are up and doing, not abashed, a troop
Able to right themselves – who see you, stoop
Their arms o' the instant after you! Unplucked
By this or that, you pass; for they conduct
To terrace raised on terrace, and, between,
Creatures of brighter mould and braver mien
Than any yet, the choicest of the Isle
No doubt. Here, left a sullen breathing-while,
Up-gathered on himself the Fighter stood
For his last fight, and, wiping treacherous blood
Out of the eyelids just held ope beneath
Those shading fingers in their iron sheath,
Steadied his strengths amid the buzz and stir
Of the dusk hideous amphitheatre
At the announcement of his over-match
To wind the day's diversion up, dispatch
The pertinacious Gaul: while, limbs one heap,
The Slave, no breath in her round mouth, watched leap
Dart after dart forth, as her hero's car
Clove dizzily the solid of the war
– Let coil about his knees for pride in him.
We reach the farthest terrace, and the grim
San Pietro Palace stops us.

* * * * *

from PIPPA PASSES

Day!
Faster and more fast,
O'er night's brim, day boils at last:
Boils, pure gold, o'er the cloud-cup's brim

Where spurting and suppressed it lay,
For not a froth-flake touched the rim
Of yonder gap in the solid gray
Of the eastern cloud, an hour away;
But forth one wavelet, then another, curled,
Till the whole sunrise, not to be suppressed,
Rose, reddened, and its seething breast
Flickered in bounds, grew gold, then overflowed the world.

Oh, Day, if I squander a wavelet of thee,
A mite of my twelve hours' treasure,
The least of thy gazes or glances,
(Be they grants thou art bound to or gifts above measure)
One of thy choices or one of thy chances,
(Be they tasks God imposed thee or freaks at thy pleasure)
— My Day, if I squander such labour or leisure,
Then shame fall on Asolo, mischief on me!

*   *   *   *

All service ranks the same with God:
If now, as formerly he trod
Paradise, his presence fills
Our earth, each only as God wills
Can work — God's puppets, best and worst,
Are we; there is no last nor first.

Say not "a small event!" Why "small"?
Costs it more pain that this, ye call
A "great event," should come to pass,
Than that? Untwine me from the mass
Of deeds which make up life, one deed
Power shall fall short in or exceed!

*   *   *   *

The year's at the spring
And day's at the morn;
Morning's at seven;
The hill-side's dew-pearled;

The lark's on the wing;
The snail's on the thorn:
God's in his heaven —
All's right with the world!

*   *   *   *   *

You'll love me yet! — and I can tarry
    Your love's protracted growing:
June reared that bunch of flowers you carry
    From seeds of April's sowing.

I plant a heartful now: some seed
    At least is sure to strike,
And yield — what you'll not pluck indeed,
    Not love, but, may be, like.

You'll look at least on love's remains,
    A grave's one violet:
Your look? — that pays a thousand pains.
    What's death? You'll love me yet!

*   *   *   *   *

Overhead the tree-tops meet,
Flowers and grass spring 'neath one's feet;
There was nought above me, nought below,
My childhood had not learned to know:
For, what are the voices of birds
— Ay, and of beasts, — but words, our words,
Only so much more sweet?
The knowledge of that with my life begun.
But I had so near made out the sun,
And counted your stars, the seven and one,
Like the fingers of my hand:
Nay, I could all but understand
Wherefore through heaven the white moon ranges;
And just when out of her soft fifty changes
No unfamiliar face might overlook me —
Suddenly God took me.

*   *   *   *   *

MY LAST DUCHESS

FERRARA

That's my last Duchess painted on the wall,
Looking as if she were alive. I call
That piece a wonder, now: Frà Pandolf's hands
Worked busily a day, and there she stands.
Will't please you sit and look at her? I said
"Frà Pandolf" by design, for never read
Strangers like you that pictured countenance,
The depth and passion of its earnest glance,
But to myself they turned (since none puts by
The curtain I have drawn for you, but I)
And seemed as they would ask me, if they durst,
How such a glance came there; so, not the first
Are you to turn and ask thus. Sir, 'twas not
Her husband's presence only, called that spot
Of joy into the Duchess' cheek: perhaps
Frà Pandolf chanced to say "Her mantle laps
"Over my lady's wrist too much," or "Paint
"Must never hope to reproduce the faint
"Half-flush that dies along her throat:" such stuff
Was courtesy, she thought, and cause enough
For calling up that spot of joy. She had
A heart — how shall I say? — too soon made glad,
Too easily impressed; she liked whate'er
She looked on, and her looks went everywhere.
Sir, 'twas all one! My favour at her breast,
The dropping of the daylight in the West,
The bough of cherries some officious fool
Broke in the orchard for her, the white mule
She rode with round the terrace — all and each
Would draw from her alíke the approving speech,

Or blush, at least. She thanked men, — good! but thanked
Somehow — I know not how — as if she ranked
My gift of a nine-hundred-years-old name
With anybody's gift. Who'd stoop to blame
This sort of trifling? Even had you skill
In speech — (which I have not) — to make your will
Quite clear to such an one, and say, "Just this
"Or that in you disgusts me; here you miss,
"Or there exceed the mark" — and if she let
Herself be lessoned so, nor plainly set
Her wits to yours, forsooth, and made excuse,
— E'en then would be some stooping; and I choose
Never to stoop. Oh sir, she smiled, no doubt,
Whene'er I passed her; but who passed without
Much the same smile? This grew; I gave commands;
Then all smiles stopped together. There she stands
As if alive. Will't please you rise? We'll meet
The company below, then. I repeat,
The Count your master's known munificence
Is ample warrant that no just pretence
Of mine for dowry will be disallowed;
Though his fair daughter's self, as I avowed
At starting, is my object. Nay, we'll go
Together down, sir. Notice Neptune, though,
Taming a sea-horse, thought a rarity,
Which Claus of Innsbruck cast in bronze for me!

INCIDENT OF THE FRENCH CAMP

I.

You know, we French stormed Ratisbon:
    A mile or so away,
On a little mound, Napoleon
    Stood on our storming-day;

With neck out-thrust, you fancy how,
　Legs wide, arms locked behind,
As if to balance the prone brow
　Oppressive with its mind.

II.

Just as perhaps he mused "My plans
　"That soar, to earth may fall,
"Let once my army-leader Lannes
　"Waver at yonder wall," —
Out 'twixt the battery-smokes there flew
　A rider, bound on bound
Full-galloping; nor bridle drew
　Until he reached the mound.

III.

Then off there flung in smiling joy,
　And held himself erect
By just his horse's mane, a boy:
　You hardly could suspect —
(So tight he kept his lips compressed,
　Scarce any blood came through)
You looked twice ere you saw his breast
　Was all but shot in two.

IV.

"Well," cried he, "Emperor, by God's grace
　"We've got you Ratisbon!
"The Marshal's in the market-place,
　"And you'll be there anon
"To see your flag-bird flap his vans
　"Where I, to heart's desire,
"Perched him!" The chief's eye flashed; his plans
　Soared up again like fire.

V.

The chief's eye flashed; but presently
Softened itself, as sheathes
A film the mother-eagle's eye
When her bruised eaglet breathes;
"You're wounded!" "Nay," the soldier's pride
Touched to the quick, he said:
"I'm killed, Sire!" And his chief beside
Smiling the boy fell dead.

SOLILOQUY OF THE SPANISH CLOISTER

I.

Gr-r-r — there go, my heart's abhorrence!
    Water your damned flower-pots, do!
If hate killed men, Brother Lawrence,
    God's blood, would not mine kill you!
What? your myrtle-bush wants trimming?
    Oh, that rose has prior claims —
Needs its leaden vase filled brimming?
    Hell dry you up with its flames!

II.

At the meal we sit together:
    Salve tibi! I must hear
Wise talk of the kind of weather,
    Sort of season, time of year:
Not a plenteous cork-crop: scarcely
    Dare we hope oak-galls, I doubt:
What's the Latin name for "parsley"?
    What's the Greek name for Swine's Snout?

III.

Whew! We'll have our platter burnished,
  Laid with care on our own shelf!
With a fire-new spoon we're furnished,
  And a goblet for ourself,
Rinsed like something sacrificial
  Ere 'tis fit to touch our chaps —
Marked with L. for our initial!
  (He-he! There his lily snaps!)

IV.

Saint, forsooth! While brown Dolores
  Squats outside the Convent bank
With Sanchicha, telling stories,
  Steeping tresses in the tank,
Blue-black, lustrous, thick like horsehairs,
  — Can't I see his dead eye glow,
Bright as 'twere a Barbary corsair's?
  (That is, if he'd let it show!)

V.

When he finishes refection,
  Knife and fork he never lays
Cross-wise, to my recollection,
  As do I, in Jesu's praise.
I the Trinity illustrate,
  Drinking watered orange-pulp —
In three sips the Arian frustrate;
  While he drains his at one gulp.

VI.

Oh, those melons? If he's able
  We're to have a feast! so nice!
One goes to the Abbot's table,

All of us get each a slice.
How go on your flowers? None double
Not one fruit-sort can you spy?
Strange! — And I, too, at such trouble,
Keep them close-nipped on the sly!

VII.

There's a great text in Galatians,
Once you trip on it, entails
Twenty-nine distinct damnations,
One sure, if another fails:
If I trip him just a-dying,
Sure of heaven as sure can be,
Spin him round and send him flying
Off to hell, a Manichee?

VIII.

Or, my scrofulous French novel
On grey paper with blunt type!
Simply glance at it, you grovel
Hand and foot in Belial's gripe:
If I double down its pages
At the woeful sixteenth print,
When he gathers his greengages,
Ope a sieve and slip it in't?

IX.

Or, there's Satan! — one might venture
Pledge one's soul to him, yet leave
Such a flaw in the indenture
As he'd miss till, past retrieve,
Blasted lay that rose-acacia
We're so proud of! *Hy, Zy, Hine* . . .
'St, there's Vespers! *Plena gratiâ*
Ave, Virgo! Gr-r-r — you swine!

IN A GONDOLA

He sings.

I send my heart up to thee, all my heart
    In this my singing.
For the stars help me, and the sea bears part;
    The very night is clinging
Closer to Venice' streets to leave one space
    Above me, whence thy face
May light my joyous heart to thee its dwelling-place.

She speaks.

Say after me, and try to say
My very words, as if each word
Came from you of your own accord,
In your own voice, in your own way:
"This woman's heart and soul and brain
"Are mine as much as this gold chain
"She bids me wear; which" (say again)
"I choose to make by cherishing
"A precious thing, or choose to fling
"Over the boat-side, ring by ring."
And yet once more say . . . no word more!
Since words are only words. Give o'er!

Unless you call me, all the same,
Familiarly by my pet name,
Which if the Three should hear you call,
And me reply to, would proclaim
At once our secret to them all.
Ask of me, too, command me, blame —
Do, break down the partition-wall
'Twixt us, the daylight world beholds
Curtained in dusk and splendid folds!

What's left but — all of me to take?
I am the Three's: prevent them, slake
Your thirst! 'Tis said, the Arab sage,
In practising with gems, can loose
Their subtle spirit in his cruce
And leave but ashes: so, sweet mage,
Leave them my ashes when thy use
Sucks out my soul, thy heritage!

He sings.

I.

Past we glide, and past, and past!
  What's that poor Agnese doing
Where they make the shutters fast?
  Grey Zanobi's just a-wooing
To his couch the purchased bride:
  Past we glide!

II.

Past we glide, and past, and past!
  Why's the Pucci Palace flaring
Like a beacon to the blast?
  Guests by hundreds, not one caring
If the dear host's neck were wried:
  Past we glide!

She sings.

I.

The moth's kiss, first!
Kiss me as if you made believe
You were not sure, this eve,
How my face, your flower, had pursed
Its petals up; so, here and there

You brush it, till I grow aware
Who wants me, and wide ope I burst.

II.

The bee's kiss, now!
Kiss me as if you entered gay
My heart at some noonday,
A bud that dares not disallow
The claim, so all is rendered up,
And passively its shattered cup
Over your head to sleep I bow.

He sings.

I.

What are we two?
I am a Jew,
And carry thee, farther than friends can pursue,
To a feast of our tribe;
Where they need thee to bribe
The devil that blasts them unless he imbibe
Thy . . . Scatter the vision for ever! And now,
As of old, I am I, thou art thou!

II.

Say again, what we are?
The sprite of a star,
I lure thee above where the destinies bar
My plumes their full play
Till a ruddier ray
Than my pale one announce there is withering away
Some . . . Scatter the vision for ever! And now,
As of old, I am I, thou art thou!

He muses.

Oh, which were best, to roam or rest?

The land's lap or the water's breast?
To sleep on yellow millet-sheaves,
Or swim in lucid shallows just
Eluding water-lily leaves,
An inch from Death's black fingers, thrust
To lock you, whom release he must;
Which life were best on Summer eves?

He speaks, musing.

Lie back; could thought of mine improve you?
From this shoulder let there spring
A wing; from this, another wing;
Wings, not legs and feet, shall move you!
Snow-white must they spring, to blend
With your flesh, but I intend
They shall deepen to the end,
Broader, into burning gold,
Till both wings crescent-wise enfold
Your perfect self, from 'neath your feet
To o'er your head, where, lo, they meet
As if a million sword-blades hurled
Defiance from you to the world!

Rescue me thou, the only real!
And scare away this mad ideal
That came, nor motions to depart!
Thanks! Now, stay ever as thou art!

Still he muses.

I.

What if the Three should catch at last
Thy serenader? While there's cast
Paul's cloak about my head, and fast
Gian pinions me, Himself has past
His stylet thro' my back; I reel;
And . . . is it thou I feel?

II.

They trail me, these three godless knaves,
Past every church that saints and saves,
Nor stop till, where the cold sea raves
By Lido's wet accursed graves,
They scoop mine, roll me to its brink,
And . . . on thy breast I sink!

She replies, musing.

Dip your arm o'er the boat-side, elbow-deep,
As I do: thus: were death so unlike sleep,
Caught this way? Death's to fear from flame or steel,
Or poison doubtless; but from water — feel!
Go find the bottom! Would you stay me? There!
Now pluck a great blade of that ribbon-grass
To plait in where the foolish jewel was,
I flung away: since you have praised my hair,
'Tis proper to be choice in what I wear.

He speaks.

Row home? must we row home? Too surely
Know I where its front's demurely
Over the Giudecca piled;
Window just with window mating,
Door on door exactly waiting,
All's the set face of a child:
But behind it, where's a trace
Of the staidness and reserve,
And formal lines without a curve,
In the same child's playing-face?
No two windows look one way
O'er the small sea-water thread
Below them. Ah, the autumn day
I, passing, saw you overhead!
First, out a cloud of curtain blew,
Then a sweet cry, and last came you —
To catch your lory that must needs

THE BROWNINGS

Escape just then, of all times then,
To peck a tall plant's fleecy seeds,
And make me happiest of men.
I scarce could breathe to see you reach
So far back o'er the balcony
To catch him ere he climbed too high
Above you in the Smyrna peach
That quick the round smooth cord of gold,
This coiled hair on your head, unrolled,
Fell down you like a gorgeous snake
The Roman girls were wont, of old,
When Rome there was, for coolness' sake
To let lie curling o'er their bosoms.
Dear lory, may his beak retain
Ever its delicate rose stain
As if the wounded lotus-blossoms
Had marked their thief to know again!

Stay longer yet, for others' sake
Than mine! What should your chamber do?
— With all its rarities that ache
In silence while day lasts, but wake
At night-time and their life renew,
Suspended just to pleasure you
Who brought against their will together
These objects, and, while day lasts, weave
Around them such a magic tether
That dumb they look: your harp, believe,
With all the sensitive tight strings
Which dare not speak, now to itself
Breathes slumberously, as if some elf
Went in and out the chords, his wings
Make murmur wheresoe'er they graze,
As an angel may, between the maze
Of midnight palace-pillars, on
And on, to sow God's plagues, have gone
Through guilty glorious Babylon.
And while such murmurs flow, the nymph
Bends o'er the harp-top from her shell

As the dry limpet for the lymph
Come with a tune he knows so well.
And how your statues' hearts must swell!
And how your pictures must descend
To see each other, friend with friend!
Oh, could you take them by surprise,
You'd find Schidone's eager Duke
Doing the quaintest courtesies
To that prim saint by Haste-thee-Luke!
And, deeper into her rock den,
Bold Castelfranco's Magdalen
You'd find retreated from the ken
Of that robed counsel-keeping Ser —
As if the Tizian thinks of her,
And is not, rather, gravely bent
On seeing for himself what toys
Are these, his progeny invent,
What litter now the board employs
Whereon he signed a document
That got him murdered! Each enjoys
Its night so well, you cannot break
The sport up, so, indeed must make
More stay with me, for others' sake.

She speaks.

I.

To-morrow, if a harp-string, say,
Is used to tie the jasmine back
That overfloods my room with sweets,
Contrive your Zorzi somehow meets
My Zanze! If the ribbon's black,
The Three are watching: keep away!

II.

Your gondola — let Zorzi wreathe
A mesh of water-weeds about

Its prow, as if he unaware
Had struck some quay or bridge-foot stair!
That I may throw a paper out
As you and he go underneath.

There's Zanze's vigilant taper; safe are we.
Only one minute more to-night with me?
Resume your past self of a month ago!
Be you the bashful gallant, I will be
The lady with the colder breast than snow.
Now bow you, as becomes, nor touch my hand
More than I touch yours when I step to land,
And say, "All thanks, Siora!" —
        Heart to heart
And lips to lips! Yet once more, ere we part,
Clasp me and make me thine, as mine thou art!
     [*He is surprised, and stabbed.*
It was ordained to be so, sweet! — and best
Comes now, beneath thine eyes, upon thy breast.
Still kiss me! Care not for the cowards! Care
Only to put aside thy beauteous hair
My blood will hurt! The Three, I do not scorn
To death, because they never lived: but I
Have lived indeed, and so — (yet one more kiss) — can die!

WARING

I.

I

What's become of Waring
Since he gave us all the slip,
Chose land-travel or seafaring,
Boots and chest or staff and scrip,
Rather than pace up and down
Any longer London town?

II

Who'd have guessed it from his lip
Or his brow's accustomed bearing,
On the night he thus took ship
Or started landward? — little caring
For us, it seems, who supped together
(Friends of his too, I remember)
And walked home thro' the merry weather,
The snowiest in all December.
I left his arm that night myself
For what's-his-name's, the new prose-poet
Who wrote the book there, on the shelf —
How, forsooth, was I to know it
If Waring meant to glide away
Like a ghost at break of day?
Never looked he half so gay!

III

He was prouder than the devil:
How he must have cursed our revel!
Ay and many other meetings,
Indoor visits, outdoor greetings,
As up and down he paced this London,
With no work done, but great works undone,
Where scarce twenty knew his name.
Why not, then, have earlier spoken,
Written, bustled? Who's to blame
If your silence kept unbroken?
"True, but there were sundry jottings,
"Stray-leaves, fragments, blurrs and blottings,
"Certain first steps were achieved
"Already which" — (is that your meaning?)
"Had well borne out whoe'er believed
"In more to come!" But who goes gleaning
Hedgeside chance-blades, while full-sheaved
Stand cornfields by him? Pride, o'erweening

Pride alone, puts forth such claims
O'er the day's distinguished names.

IV

Meantime, how much I loved him,
I find out now I've lost him.
I who cared not if I moved him,
Who could so carelessly accost him,
Henceforth never shall get free
Of his ghostly company,
His eyes that just a little wink
As deep I go into the merit
Of this and that distinguished spirit —
His cheeks' raised colour, soon to sink,
As long I dwell on some stupendous
And tremendous (Heaven defend us!)
Monstr'-inform'-ingens-horrend-ous
Demoniaco-seraphic
Penman's latest piece of graphic.
Nay, my very wrist grows warm
With his dragging weight of arm.
E'en so, swimmingly appears,
Through one's after-supper musings,
Some lost lady of old years
With her beauteous vain endeavour
And goodness unrepaid as ever;
The face, accustomed to refusings,
We, puppies that we were . . . Oh never
Surely, nice of conscience, scrupled
Being aught like false, forsooth, to?
Telling aught but honest truth to?
What a sin, had we centupled
Its possessor's grace and sweetness!
No! she heard in its completeness
Truth, for truth's a weighty matter,
And truth, at issue, we can't flatter!
Well, 'tis done with; she's exempt
From damning us thro' such a sally;

And so she glides, as down a valley,
Taking up with her contempt,
Past our reach; and in, the flowers
Shut her unregarded hours.

V

Oh, could I have him back once more,
This Waring, but one half-day more!
Back, with the quiet face of yore,
So hungry for acknowledgment
Like mine! I'd fool him to his bent.
Feed, should not he, to heart's content?
I'd say, "to only have conceived,
"Planned your great works, apart from progress,
"Surpasses little works achieved!"
I'd lie so, I should be believed.
I'd make such havoc of the claims
Of the day's distinguished names
To feast him with, as feasts an ogress
Her feverish sharp-toothed gold-crowned child!
Or as one feasts a creature rarely
Captured here, unreconciled
To capture; and completely gives
Its pettish humours license, barely
Requiring that it lives.

VI

Ichabod, Ichabod,
The glory is departed!
Travels Waring East away?
Who, of knowledge, by hearsay,
Reports a man upstarted
Somewhere as a god,
Hordes grown European-hearted,
Millions of the wild made tame
On a sudden at his fame?
In Vishnu-land what Avatar?

Or who in Moscow, toward the Czar,
With the demurest of footfalls
Over the Kremlin's pavement bright
With serpentine and syenite,
Steps, with five other Generals
That simultaneously take snuff,
For each to have pretext enough
And kerchiefwise unfold his sash
Which, softness' self, is yet the stuff
To hold fast where a steel chain snaps,
And leave the grand white neck no gash?
Waring in Moscow, to those rough
Cold northern natures born perhaps,
Like the lambwhite maiden dear
From the circle of mute kings
Unable to repress the tear,
Each as his sceptre down he flings,
To Dian's fane at Taurica,
Where now a captive priestess, she alway
Mingles her tender grave Hellenic speech
With theirs, tuned to the hailstone-beaten beach
As pours some pigeon, from the myrrhy lands
Rapt by the whirlblast to fierce Scythian strands
Where breed the swallows, her melodious cry
Amid their barbarous twitter!
In Russia? Never! Spain were fitter!
Ay, most likely 'tis in Spain
That we and Waring meet again
Now, while he turns down that cool narrow lane
Into the blackness, out of grave Madrid
All fire and shine, abrupt as when there's slid
Its stiff gold blazing pall
From some black coffin-lid.
Or, best of all,
I love to think
The leaving us was just a feint;
Back here to London did he slink,
And now works on without a wink
Of sleep, and we are on the brink

Of something great in fresco-paint:
Some garret's ceiling, walls and floor,
Up and down and o'er and o'er
He splashes, as none splashed before
Since great Caldara Polidore.
Or Music means this land of ours
Some favour yet, to pity won
By Purcell from his Rosy Bowers, —
"Give me my so-long promised son,
"Let Waring end what I begun!"
Then down he creeps and out he steals
Only when the night conceals
His face; in Kent 'tis cherry-time,
Or hops are picking: or at prime
Of March he wanders as, too happy,
Years ago when he was young,
Some mile eve when woods grew sappy
And the early moths had sprung
To life from many a trembling sheath
Woven the warm boughs beneath;
While small birds said to themselves
What should soon be actual song,
And young gnats, by tens and twelves,
Made as if they were the throng
That crowd around and carry aloft
The sound they have nursed, so sweet and pure,
Out of a myriad noises soft,
Into a tone that can endure
Amid the noise of a July noon
When all God's creatures crave their boon,
All at once and all in tune,
And get it, happy as Waring then,
Having first within his ken
What a man might do with men:
And far too glad, in the even-glow,
To mix with the world he meant to take
Into his hand, he told you, so —
And out of it his world to make,
To contract and to expand

As he shut or oped his hand.
Oh Waring, what's to really be?
A clear stage and a crowd to see!
Some Garrick, say, out shall not he
The heart of Hamlet's mystery pluck?
Or, where most unclean beasts are rife,
Some Junius — am I right? — shall tuck
His sleeve, and forth with flaying-knife!
Some Chatterton shall have the luck
Of calling Rowley into life!
Some one shall somehow run a muck
With this old world for want of strife
Sound asleep. Contrive, contrive
To rouse us, Waring! Who's alive?
Our men scarce seem in earnest now.
Distinguished names! — but 'tis, somehow,
As if they played at being names
Still more distinguished, like the games
Of children. Turn our sport to earnest
With a visage of the sternest!
Bring the real times back, confessed
Still better than our very best!

II.

I

"When I last saw Waring . . ."
(How all turned to him who spoke!
You saw Waring? Truth or joke?
In land-travel or sea-faring?)

II

"We were sailing by Triest
"Where a day or two we harboured:
"A sunset was in the West,
"When, looking over the vessel's side,

"One of our company espied
"A sudden speck to larboard.
"And as a sea-duck flies and swims
"At once, so came the light craft up,
"With its sole lateen sail that trims
"And turns (the water round its rims
"Dancing, as round a sinking cup)
"And by us like a fish it curled,
"And drew itself up close beside,
"Its great sail on the instant furled,
"And o'er its thwarts a shrill voice cried,
"(A neck as bronzed as a Lascar's)
" 'Buy wine of us, you English Brig?
" 'Or fruit, tobacco and cigars?
" 'A pilot for you to Triest?
" 'Without one, look you ne'er so big,
" 'They'll never let you up the bay!
" 'We natives should know best.'
"I turned, and 'just those fellows' way,'
"Our captain said, 'The 'long-shore thieves
" 'Are laughing at us in their sleeves.'

III

"In truth, the boy leaned laughing back;
"And one, half-hidden by his side
"Under the furled sail, soon I spied,
"With great grass hat and kerchief black,
"Who looked up with his kingly throat,
"Said somewhat, while the other shook
"His hair back from his eyes to look
"Their longest at us; then the boat,
"I know not how, turned sharply round,
"Laying her whole side on the sea
"As a leaping fish does; from the lee
"Into the weather, cut somehow
"Her sparkling path beneath our bow
"And so went off, as with a bound,
"Into the rosy and golden half

317

"O' the sky, to overtake the sun
"And reach the shore, like the sea-calf
"Its singing cave; yet I caught one
"Glance ere away the boat quite passed,
"And neither time nor toil could mar
"Those features: so I saw the last
"Of Waring!" — You? Oh, never star
Was lost here but it rose afar!
Look East, where whole new thousands are!
In Vishnu-land what Avatar?

CRISTINA

I.

She should never have looked at me
    If she meant I should not love her!
There are plenty . . . men, you call such,
    I suppose . . . she may discover
All her soul to, if she pleases,
    And yet leave much as she found them:
But I'm not so, and she knew it
    When she fixed me, glancing round them.

II.

What? To fix me thus meant nothing?
    But I can't tell (there's my weakness)
What her look said! — no vile cant, sure,
    About "need to strew the bleakness
"Of some lone shore with its pearl-seed.
    "That the sea feels" — no "strange yearning
"That such souls have, most to lavish
    "Where there's chance of least returning."

III.

Oh, we're sunk enough here, God knows!
  But not quite so sunk that moments,
Sure tho' seldom, are denied us,
  When the spirit's true endowments
Stand out plainly from its false ones,
  And apprise it if pursuing
Or the right way or the wrong way,
  To its triumph or undoing.

IV.

There are flashes struck from midnights,
  There are fire-flames noondays kindle,
Whereby piled-up honours perish,
  Whereby swollen ambitions dwindle,
While just this or that poor impulse,
  Which for once had play unstifled,
Seems the sole work of a life-time
  That away the rest have trifled.

V.

Doubt you if, in some such moment,
  As she fixed me, she felt clearly,
Ages past the soul existed,
  Here an age 'tis resting merely,
And hence fleets again for ages,
  While the true end, sole and single,
It stops here for is, this love-way,
  With some other soul to mingle?

VI.

Else it loses what it lived for,
  And eternally must lose it;
Better ends may be in prospect,

Deeper blisses (if you choose it),
But this life's end and this love-bliss
Have been lost here. Doubt you whether
This she felt as, looking at me,
Mine and her souls rushed together?

VII.

Oh, observe! Of course, next moment,
The world's honours, in derision,
Trampled out the light for ever:
Never fear but there's provision
Of the devil's to quench knowledge
Lest we walk the earth in rapture!
— Making those who catch God's secret
Just so much more prize their capture!

VIII.

Such am I: the secret's mine now!
She has lost me, I have gained her;
Her soul's mine: and thus, grown perfect,
I shall pass my life's remainder.
Life will just hold out the proving
Both our powers, alone and blended:
And then, come next life quickly!
This world's use will have been ended.

JOHANNES AGRICOLA IN MEDITATION

There's heaven above, and night by night
I look right through its gorgeous roof;
No suns and moons though e'er so bright
Avail to stop me; splendour-proof
I keep the broods of stars aloof:
For I intend to get to God,

For 'tis to God I speed so fast,
For in God's breast, my own abode,
   Those shoals of dazzling glory, passed,
   I lay my spirit down at last.
I lie where I have always lain,
   God smiles as he has always smiled;
Ere suns and moons could wax and wane,
   Ere stars were thundergirt, or piled
   The heavens, God thought on me his child;
Ordained a life for me, arrayed
   Its circumstances every one
To the minutest; ay, God said
   This head this hand should rest upon
   Thus, ere he fashioned star or sun.
And having thus created me,
   Thus rooted me, he bade me grow,
Guiltless for ever, like a tree
   That buds and blooms, nor seeks to know
   The law by which it prospers so:
But sure that thought and word and deed
   All go to swell his love for me,
Me, made because that love had need
   Of something irreversibly
   Pledged solely its content to be.
Yes, yes, a tree which must ascend,
   No poison-gourd foredoomed to stoop!
I have God's warrant, could I blend
   All hideous sins, as in a cup,
   To drink the mingled venoms up;
Secure my nature will convert
   The draught to blossoming gladness fast:
While sweet dews turn to the gourd's hurt,
   And bloat, and while they bloat it, blast,
   As from the first its lot was cast.
For as I lie, smiled on, full-fed
   By unexhausted power to bless,
I gaze below on hell's fierce bed,
   And those its waves of flame oppress,
   Swarming in ghastly wretchedness;

Whose life on earth aspired to be
One altar-smoke, so pure! — to win
If not love like God's love for me,
At least to keep his anger in;
And all their striving turned to sin.
Priest, doctor, hermit, monk grown white
With prayer, the broken-hearted nun,
The martyr, the wan acolyte,
The incense-swinging child, — undone
Before God fashioned star or sun!
God, whom I praise; how could I praise,
If such as I might understand,
Make out and reckon on his ways,
And bargain for his love, and stand,
Paying a price, at his right hand?

PORPHYRIA'S LOVER

The rain set early in to-night,
The sullen wind was soon awake,
It tore the elm-tops down for spite,
And did its worst to vex the lake:
I listened with heart fit to break.
When glided in Porphyria; straight
She shut the cold out and the storm,
And kneeled and made the cheerless grate
Blaze up, and all the cottage warm;
Which done, she rose, and from her form
Withdrew the dripping cloak and shawl,
And laid her soiled gloves by, untied
Her hat and let the damp hair fall,
And, last, she sat down by my side
And called me. When no voice replied,
She put my arm about her waist,
And made her smooth white shoulder bare,
And all her yellow hair displaced,

And, stooping, made my cheek lie there,
  And spread, o'er all, her yellow hair,
Murmuring how she loved me — she
  Too weak, for all her heart's endeavour,
To set its struggling passion free
  From pride, and vainer ties dissever,
  And give herself to me for ever.
But passion sometimes would prevail,
  Nor could to-night's gay feast restrain
A sudden thought of one so pale
  For love of her, and all in vain:
  So, she was come through wind and rain.
Be sure I looked up at her eyes
  Happy and proud; at last I knew
Porphyria worshipped me; surprise
  Made my heart swell, and still it grew
  While I debated what to do.
That moment she was mine, mine, fair,
  Perfectly pure and good: I found
A thing to do, and all her hair
  In one long yellow string I wound
  Three times her little throat around,
And strangled her. No pain felt she;
  I am quite sure she felt no pain.
As a shut bud that holds a bee,
  I warily oped her lids: again
  Laughed the blue eyes without a stain.
And I untightened next the tress
  About her neck; her cheek once more
Blushed bright beneath my burning kiss:
  I propped her head up as before,
  Only, this time my shoulder bore
Her head, which droops upon it still:
  The smiling rosy little head,
So glad it has its utmost will,
  That all it scorned at once is fled,
  And I, its love, am gained instead!
Porphyria's love: she guessed not how

Her darling one wish would be heard.
And thus we sit together now,
   And all night long we have not stirred,
   And yet God has not said a word!

THE PIED PIPER OF HAMELIN

A CHILD'S STORY

[Written for, and inscribed to, W. M. the Younger.]

I.

Hamelin Town's in Brunswick,
   By famous Hanover city;
The river Weser, deep and wide,
Washes its wall on the southern side;
A pleasanter spot you never spied;
   But, when begins my ditty,
Almost five hundred years ago,
To see the townsfolk suffer so
   From vermin, was a pity.

II.

Rats!
They fought the dogs and killed the cats,
   And bit the babies in the cradles,
And ate the cheeses out of the vats,
   And licked the soup from the cooks' own ladles,
Split open the kegs of salted sprats,
Made nests inside men's Sunday hats,
And even spoiled the women's chats
      By drowning their speaking
      With shrieking and squeaking
In fifty different sharps and flats.

III.

At last the people in a body
    To the Town Hall came flocking:
" 'Tis clear," cried they, "our Mayor's a noddy;
    "And as for our Corporation — shocking
"To think we buy gowns lined with ermine
"For dolts that can't or won't determine
"What's best to rid us of our vermin!
"You hope, because you're old and obese,
"To find in the furry civic robe ease?
"Rouse up, sirs! Give your brains a racking
"To find the remedy we're lacking,
"Or, sure as fate, we'll send you packing!"
At this the Mayor and Corporation
Quaked with a mighty consternation.

IV.

An hour they sat in council,
    At length the Mayor broke silence:
"For a guilder I'd my ermine gown sell,
    "I wish I were a mile hence!
"It's easy to bid one rack one's brain —
"I'm sure my poor head aches again,
"I've scratched it so, and all in vain.
"Oh for a trap, a trap, a trap!"
Just as he said this, what should hap
At the chamber door but a gentle tap?
"Bless us," cried the Mayor, "what's that?"
(With the Corporation as he sat,
Looking little though wondrous fat;
Nor brighter was his eye, nor moister
Than a too-long-opened oyster,
Save when at noon his paunch grew mutinous
For a plate of turtle green and glutinous)
"Only a scraping of shoes on the mat?
"Anything like the sound of a rat
"Makes my heart go pit-a-pat!"

V.

"Come in!" — the Mayor cried, looking bigger:
And in did come the strangest figure!
His queer long coat from heel to head
Was half of yellow and half of red,
And he himself was tall and thin,
With sharp blue eyes, each like a pin,
And light loose hair, yet swarthy skin,
No tuft on cheek nor beard on chin,
But lips where smiles went out and in;
There was no guessing his kith and kin:
And nobody could enough admire
The tall man and his quaint attire.
Quoth one: "It's as my great-grandsire,
"Starting up at the Trump of Doom's tone,
"Had walked this way from his painted tombstone!"

VI.

He advanced to the council-table:
And, "Please your honours," said he, "I'm able,
"By means of a secret charm, to draw
    "All creatures living beneath the sun,
    "That creep or swim or fly or run,
"After me so as you never saw!
"And I chiefly use my charm
"On creatures that do people harm,
"The mole and toad and newt and viper;
"And people call me the Pied Piper."
(And here they noticed round his neck
    A scarf of red and yellow stripe,
To match with his coat of the self-same cheque;
    And at the scarf's end hung a pipe;
And his fingers, they noticed, were ever straying
As if impatient to be playing
Upon this pipe, as low it dangled
Over his vesture so old-fangled.)

"Yet," said he, "poor piper as I am,
"In Tartary I freed the Cham,
  "Last June, from his huge swarms of gnats;
"I eased in Asia the Nizam
  "Of a monstrous brood of vampyre-bats:
"And as for what your brain bewilders,
  "If I can rid your town of rats
"Will you give me a thousand guilders?"
"One? fifty thousand!"—was the exclamation
Of the astonished Mayor and Corporation.

VII.

Into the street the Piper stept,
  Smiling first a little smile,
As if he knew what magic slept
  In his quiet pipe the while;
Then, like a musical adept,
To blow the pipe his lips he wrinkled,
And green and blue his sharp eyes twinkled,
Like a candle-flame where salt is sprinkled;
And ere three shrill notes the pipe uttered,
You heard as if an army muttered;
And the muttering grew to a grumbling;
And the grumbling grew to a mighty rumbling;
And out of the houses the rats came tumbling.
Great rats, small rats, lean rats, brawny rats,
Brown rats, black rats, grey rats, tawny rats,
Grave old plodders, gay young friskers,
  Fathers, mothers, uncles, cousins,
Cocking tails and pricking whiskers,
  Families by tens and dozens,
Brothers, sisters, husbands, wives—
Followed the Piper for their lives.
From street to street he piped advancing,
And step for step they followed dancing,
Until they came to the river Weser,
  Wherein all plunged and perished!
—Save one who, stout as Julius Cæsar,

327

Swam across and lived to carry
  (As he, the manuscript he cherished)
To Rat-land home his commentary:
Which was, "At the first shrill notes of the pipe,
"I heard a sound as of scraping tripe,
"And putting apples, wondrous ripe,
"Into a cider-press's gripe:
"And a moving away of pickle-tub-boards,
"And a leaving ajar of conserve-cupboards,
"And a drawing the corks of train-oil-flasks,
"And a breaking the hoops of butter-casks:
"And it seemed as if a voice
  "(Sweeter far than by harp or by psaltery
"Is breathed) called out, 'Oh rats, rejoice!
  " 'The world is grown to one vast drysaltery!
" 'So munch on, crunch on, take your nuncheon,
" 'Breakfast, supper, dinner, luncheon!'
"And just as a bulky sugar-puncheon,
"All ready staved, like a great sun shone
"Glorious scarce an inch before me,
"Just as methought it said, 'Come, bore me!'
"— I found the Weser rolling o'er me."

VIII.

You should have heard the Hamelin people
Ringing the bells till they rocked the steeple.
"Go," cried the Mayor, "and get long poles,
"Poke out the nests and block up the holes!
"Consult with carpenters and builders,
"And leave in our town not even a trace
"Of the rats!" — when suddenly, up the face
Of the Piper perked in the market-place,
With a, "First, if you please, my thousand guilders!"

IX.

A thousand guilders! The Mayor looked blue;
So did the Corporation too.

328

For council dinners made rare havoc
With Claret, Moselle, Vin-de-Grave, Hock;
And half the money would replenish
Their cellar's biggest butt with Rhenish.
To pay this sum to a wandering fellow
With a gipsy coat of red and yellow!
"Beside," quoth the Mayor with a knowing wink,
"Our business was done at the river's brink;
"We saw with our eyes the vermin sink,
"And what's dead can't come to life, I think.
"So, friend, we're not the folks to shrink
"From the duty of giving you something for drink,
"And a matter of money to put in your poke;
"But as for the guilders, what we spoke
"Of them, as you very well know, was in joke.
"Beside, our losses have made us thrifty.
"A thousand guilders! Come, take fifty!"

X.

The Piper's face fell, and he cried
"No trifling! I can't wait, beside!
"I've promised to visit by dinnertime
"Bagdat, and accept the prime
"Of the Head-Cook's pottage, all he's rich in,
"For having left, in the Caliph's kitchen,
"Of a nest of scorpions no survivor:
"With him I proved no bargain-driver,
"With you, don't think I'll bate a stiver!
"And folks who put me in a passion
"May find me pipe after another fashion."

XI.

"How?" cried the Mayor, "d'ye think I brook
"Being worse treated than a Cook?
"Insulted by a lazy ribald
"With idle pipe and vesture piebald?
"You threaten us, fellow? Do your worst,
"Blow your pipe there till you burst!"

XII.

Once more he stept into the street
  And to his lips again
  Laid his long pipe of smooth straight cane;
And ere he blew three notes (such sweet
Soft notes as yet musician's cunning
  Never gave the enraptured air)
There was a rustling that seemed like a bustling
Of merry crowds justling at pitching and hustling,
Small feet were pattering, wooden shoes clattering,
Little hands clapping and little tongues chattering,
And, like fowls in a farm-yard when barley is scattering,
Out came the children running.
All the little boys and girls,
With rosy cheeks and flaxen curls,
And sparkling eyes and teeth like pearls,
Tripping and skipping, ran merrily after
The wonderful music with shouting and laughter.

XIII.

The Mayor was dumb, and the Council stood
As if they were changed into blocks of wood,
Unable to move a step, or cry
To the children merrily skipping by,
— Could only follow with the eye
That joyous crowd at the Piper's back.
But how the Mayor was on the rack,
And the wretched Council's bosoms beat,
As the Piper turned from the High Street
To where the Weser rolled its waters
Right in the way of their sons and daughters!
However he turned from South to West,
And to Koppelberg Hill his steps addressed,
And after him the children pressed;
Great was the joy in every breast.
"He never can cross that mighty top!

"He's forced to let the piping drop,
"And we shall see our children stop!"
When, lo, as they reached the mountain-side,
A wondrous portal opened wide,
As if a cavern was suddenly hollowed;
And the Piper advanced and the children followed,
And when all were in to the very last,
The door in the mountain-side shut fast.
Did I say, all? No! One was lame,
    And could not dance the whole of the way;
And in after years, if you would blame
    His sadness, he was used to say, —
"It's dull in our town since my playmates left!
"I can't forget that I'm bereft
"Of all the pleasant sights they see,
"Which the Piper also promised me.
"For he led us, he said, to a joyous land,
"Joining the town and just at hand,
"Where waters gushed and fruit-trees grew
"And flowers put forth a fairer hue,
"And everything was strange and new;
"The sparrows were brighter than peacocks here,
"And their dogs outran our fallow deer,
"And honey-bees had lost their stings,
"And horses were born with eagles' wings:
"And just as I became assured
"My lame foot would be speedily cured,
"The music stopped and I stood still,
"And found myself outside the hill,
"Left alone against my will,
"To go now limping as before,
"And never hear of that country more!"

XIV.

Alas, alas for Hamelin!
    There came into many a burgher's pate
    A text which says that heaven's gate
    Opes to the rich at as easy rate

THE BROWNINGS

As the needle's eye takes a camel in!
The mayor sent East, West, North and South,
To offer the Piper, by word of mouth,
    Wherever it was men's lot to find him,
Silver and gold to his heart's content,
If he'd only return the way he went,
    And bring the children behind him.
But when they saw 'twas a lost endeavour,
And Piper and dancers were gone for ever,
They made a decree that lawyers never
    Should think their records dated duly
If, after the day of the month and year,
These words did not as well appear,
"And so long after what happened here
    "On the Twenty-second of July,
"Thirteen hundred and seventy-six:"
And the better in memory to fix
The place of the children's last retreat,
They called it, the Pied Piper's Street —
Where any one playing on pipe or tabor
Was sure for the future to lose his labour.
Nor suffered they hostelry or tavern
    To shock with mirth a street so solemn;
But opposite the place of the cavern
    They wrote the story on a column,
And on the great church-window painted
The same, to make the world acquainted
How their children were stolen away,
And there it stands to this very day.
And I must not omit to say
That in Transylvania there's a tribe
Of alien people who ascribe
The outlandish ways and dress
On which their neighbours lay such stress,
To their fathers and mothers having risen
Out of some subterraneous prison
Into which they were trepanned
Long time ago in a mighty band
Out of Hamelin town in Brunswick land,
But how or why, they don't understand.

XV.

So, Willy, let me and you be wipers
Of scores out with all men — especially pipers!
And, whether they pipe us free fróm rats or fróm mice,
If we've promised them aught, let us keep our promise!

"HOW THEY BROUGHT THE GOOD
NEWS FROM GHENT TO AIX"

[16 — .]

I.

I sprang to the stirrup, and Joris, and he;
I galloped, Dirck galloped, we galloped all three;
"Good speed!" cried the watch, as the gate-bolts undrew;
"Speed!" echoed the wall to us galloping through;
Behind shut the postern, the lights sank to rest,
And into the midnight we galloped abreast.

II.

Not a word to each other; we kept the great pace
Neck by neck, stride by stride, never changing our place;
I turned in my saddle and made its girths tight,
Then shortened each stirrup, and set the pique right,
Rebuckled the cheek-strap, chained slacker the bit,
Nor galloped less steadily Roland a whit.

III.

'Twas moonset at starting; but while we drew near
Lokeren, the cocks crew and twilight dawned clear;
At Boom, a great yellow star came out to see;

At Düffeld, 'twas morning as plain as could be;
And from Mecheln church-steeple we heard the half-chime,
So, Joris broke silence with, "Yet there is time!"

IV.

At Aershot, up leaped of a sudden the sun,
And against him the cattle stood black every one,
To stare thro' the mist at us galloping past,
And I saw my stout galloper Roland at last,
With resolute shoulders, each butting away
The haze, as some bluff river headland its spray:

V.

And his low head and crest, just one sharp ear bent back
For my voice, and the other pricked out on his track;
And one eye's black intelligence, — ever that glance
O'er its white edge at me, his own master, askance!
And the thick heavy spume-flakes which aye and anon
His fierce lips shook upwards in galloping on.

VI.

By Hasselt, Dirck groaned; and cried Joris, "Stay spur!
"Your Roos galloped bravely, the fault's not in her,
"We'll remember at Aix" — for one heard the quick wheeze
Of her chest, saw the stretched neck and staggering knees,
And sunk tail, and horrible heave of the flank,
As down on her haunches she shuddered and sank.

VII.

So, we were left galloping, Joris and I,
Past Looz and past Tongres, no cloud in the sky;
The broad sun above laughed a pitiless laugh,
'Neath our feet broke the brittle bright stubble like chaff;
Till over by Dalhem a dome-spire sprang white,
And "Gallop," gasped Joris, "for Aix is in sight!"

VIII.

"How they'll greet us!" — and all in a moment his roan
Rolled neck and croup over, lay dead as a stone;
And there was my Roland to bear the whole weight
Of the news which alone could save Aix from her fate,
With his nostrils like pits full of blood to the brim,
And with circles of red for his eye-sockets' rim.

IX.

Then I cast loose my buffcoat, each holster let fall,
Shook off both my jack-boots, let go belt and all,
Stood up in the stirrup, leaned, patted his ear,
Called my Roland his pet-name, my horse without peer;
Clapped my hands, laughed and sang, any noise, bad or good,
Till at length into Aix Roland galloped and stood.

X.

And all I remember is — friends flocking round
As I sat with his head 'twixt my knees on the ground;
And no voice but was praising this Roland of mine,
As I poured down his throat our last measure of wine,
Which (the burgesses voted by common consent)
Was no more than his due who brought good news from Ghent.

THE ITALIAN IN ENGLAND

That second time they hunted me
From hill to plain, from shore to sea,
And Austria, hounding far and wide
Her blood-hounds thro' the country-side,
Breathed hot and instant on my trace, —
I made six days a hiding-place

THE BROWNINGS

Of that dry green old aqueduct
Where I and Charles, when boys, have plucked
The fire-flies from the roof above,
Bright creeping thro' the moss they love:
— How long it seems since Charles was lost!
Six days the soldiers crossed and crossed
The country in my very sight;
And when that peril ceased at night,
The sky broke out in red dismay
With signal fires; well, there I lay
Close covered o'er in my recess,
Up to the neck in ferns and cress,
Thinking on Metternich our friend,
And Charles's miserable end,
And much beside, two days; the third,
Hunger o'ercame me when I heard
The peasants from the village go
To work among the maize; you know,
With us in Lombardy, they bring
Provisions packed on mules, a string
With little bells that cheer their task,
And casks, and boughs on every cask
To keep the sun's heat from the wine;
These I let pass in jingling line,
And, close on them, dear noisy crew,
The peasants from the village, too;
For at the very rear would troop
Their wives and sisters in a group
To help, I knew. When these had passed,
I threw my glove to strike the last,
Taking the chance: she did not start,
Much less cry out, but stooped apart,
One instant rapidly glanced round,
And saw me beckon from the ground.
A wild bush grows and hides my crypt;
She picked my glove up while she stripped
A branch off, then rejoined the rest
With that; my glove lay in her breast.
Then I drew breath; they disappeared:
It was for Italy I feared.

An hour, and she returned alone
Exactly where my glove was thrown.
Meanwhile came many thoughts: on me
Rested the hopes of Italy.
I had devised a certain tale
Which, when 'twas told her, could not fail
Persuade a peasant of its truth;
I meant to call a freak of youth
This hiding, and give hopes of pay,
And no temptation to betray.
But when I saw that woman's face,
Its calm simplicity of grace,
Our Italy's own attitude
In which she walked thus far, and stood,
Planting each naked foot so firm,
To crush the snake and spare the worm —
At first sight of her eyes, I said,
"I am that man upon whose head
"They fix the price, because I hate
"The Austrians over us: the State
"Will give you gold — oh, gold so much! —
"If you betray me to their clutch,
"And be your death, for aught I know,
"If once they find you saved their foe.
"Now, you must bring me food and drink,
"And also paper, pen and ink,
"And carry safe what I shall write
"To Padua, which you'll reach at night
"Before the duomo shuts; go in,
"And wait till Tenebræ begin;
"Walk to the third confessional,
"Between the pillar and the wall,
"And kneeling whisper, *Whence comes peace?*
"Say it a second time, then cease;
"And if the voice inside returns,
"From Christ and Freedom; what concerns
"The cause of Peace? — for answer, slip
"My letter where you placed your lip;
"Then come back happy we have done

337

"Our mother service — I, the son,
"As you the daughter of our land!"

Three mornings more, she took her stand
In the same place, with the same eyes:
I was no surer of sun-rise
Than of her coming. We conferred
Of her own prospects, and I heard
She had a lover — stout and tall,
She said — then let her eyelids fall,
"He could do much" — as if some doubt
Entered her heart, — then, passing out,
"She could not speak for others, who
"Had other thoughts; herself she knew:"
And so she brought me drink and food.
After four days, the scouts pursued
Another path; at last arrived
The help my Paduan friends contrived
To furnish me: she brought the news.
For the first time I could not choose
But kiss her hand, and lay my own
Upon her head — "This faith was shown
"To Italy, our mother; she
"Uses my hand and blesses thee."
She followed down to the sea-shore;
I left and never saw her more.

How very long since I have thought
Concerning — much less wished for — aught
Beside the good of Italy,
For which I live and mean to die!
I never was in love; and since
Charles proved false, what shall now convince
My inmost heart I have a friend?
However, if I pleased to spend
Real wishes on myself — say, three —
I know at least what one should be.
I would grasp Metternich until
I felt his red wet throat distil
In blood thro' these two hands. And next,

—Nor much for that am I perplexed—
Charles, perjured traitor, for his part,
Should die slow of a broken heart
Under his new employers. Last
—Ah, there, what should I wish? For fast
Do I grow old and out of strength.
If I resolved to seek at length
My father's house again, how scared
They all would look, and unprepared!
My brothers live in Austria's pay
—Disowned me long ago, men say;
And all my early mates who used
To praise me so—perhaps induced
More than one early step of mine—
Are turning wise: while some opine
"Freedom grows license," some suspect
"Haste breeds delay," and recollect
They always said, such premature
Beginnings never could endure!
So, with a sullen "All's for best,"
The land seems settling to its rest.
I think then, I should wish to stand
This evening in that dear, lost land,
Over the sea the thousand miles,
And know if yet that woman smiles
With the calm smile; some little farm
She lives in there, 1.0 doubt: what harm
If I sat on the door-side bench,
And, while her spindle made a trench
Fantastically in the dust,
Inquired of all her fortunes—just
Her children's ages and their names,
And what may be the husband's aims
For each of them. I'd talk this out,
And sit there, for an hour about,
Then kiss her hand once more, and lay
Mine on her head, and go my way.

So much for idle wishing—how
It steals the time! To business now.

THE ENGLISHMAN IN ITALY

PIANO DI SORRENTO

Fortù, Fortù, my beloved one,
    Sit here by my side,
On my knees put up both little feet!
    I was sure, if I tried,
I could make you laugh spite of Scirocco.
    Now, open your eyes,
Let me keep you amused till he vanish
    In black from the skies,
With telling my memories over
    As you tell your beads;
All the Plain saw me gather, I garland
    — The flowers or the weeds.

Time for rain! for your long hot dry Autumn
    Had net-worked with brown
The white skin of each grape on the bunches,
    Marked like a quail's crown,
Those creatures you make such account of,
    Whose heads, — speckled white
Over brown like a great spider's back,
    As I told you last night, —
Your mother bites off for her supper.
    Red-ripe as could be,
Pomegranates were chapping and splitting
    In halves on the tree:
And betwixt the loose walls of great flintstone,
    Or in the thick dust
On the path, or straight out of the rock-side,
    Wherever could thrust
Some burnt sprig of bold hardy rock-flower
    Its yellow face up,

For the prize were great butterflies fighting,
    Some five for one cup.
So, I guessed, ere I got up this morning,
    What change was in store,
By the quick rustle-down of the quail-nets
    Which woke me before
I could open my shutter, made fast
    With a bough and a stone,
And look thro' the twisted dead vine-twigs,
    Sole lattice that's known.
Quick and sharp rang the rings down the net-poles,
    While, busy beneath,
Your priest and his brother tugged at them,
    The rain in their teeth.
And out upon all the flat house-roofs
    Where split figs lay drying,
The girls took the frails under cover:
    Nor use seemed in trying
To get out the boats and go fishing,
    For, under the cliff,
Fierce the black water frothed o'er the blind-rock.
    No seeing our skiff
Arrive about noon from Amalfi,
    — Our fisher arrive,
And pitch down his basket before us,
    All trembling alive
With pink and grey jellies, your sea-fruit;
    You touch the strange lumps,
And mouths gape there, eyes open, all manner
    Of horns and of humps,
Which only the fisher looks grave at,
    While round him like imps
Cling screaming the children as naked
    And brown as his shrimps;
Himself too as bare to the middle
    — You see round his neck
The string and its brass coin suspended,
    That saves him from wreck.

But to-day not a boat reached Salerno,
    So back, to a man,
Came our friends, with whose help in the vineyards
    Grape-harvest began.
In the vat, halfway up in our house-side,
    Like blood the juice spins,
While your brother all bare-legged is dancing
    Till breathless he grins
Dead-beaten in effort on effort
    To keep the grapes under,
Since still when he seems all but master,
    In pours the fresh plunder
From girls who keep coming and going
    With basket on shoulder,
And eyes shut against the rain's driving;
    Your girls that are older, —
For under the hedges of aloe,
    And where, on its bed
Of the orchard's black mould, the love-apple
    Lies pulpy and red,
All the young ones are kneeling and filling
    Their laps with the snails
Tempted out by this first rainy weather, —
    Your best of regales,
As to-night will be proved to my sorrow,
    When, supping in state,
We shall feast our grape-gleaners (two dozen,
    Three over one plate)
With lasagne so tempting to swallow
    In slippery ropes,
And gourds fried in great purple slices,
    That colour of popes.
Meantime, see the grape bunch they've brought you:
    The rain-water slips
O'er the heavy blue bloom on each globe
    Which the wasp to your lips
Still follows with fretful persistence:
    Nay, taste, while awake,
This half of a curd-white smooth cheese-ball
    That peels, flake by flake,

Like an onion, each smoother and whiter;
    Next, sip this weak wine
From the thin green glass flask, with its stopper,
    A leaf of the vine;
And end with the prickly-pear's red flesh
    That leaves thro' its juice
The stony black seeds on your pearl-teeth.
    Scirocco is loose!
Hark, the quick, whistling pelt of the olives
    Which, thick in one's track,
Tempt the stranger to pick up and bite them,
    Tho' not yet half black!
How the old twisted olive trunks shudder,
    The medlars let fall
Their hard fruit, and the brittle great fig-trees
    Snap off, figs and all,
For here comes the whole of the tempest!
    No refuge, but creep
Back again to my side and my shoulder,
    And listen or sleep.

O how will your country show next week,
    When all the vine-boughs
Have been stripped of their foliage to pasture
    The mules and the cows?
Last eve, I rode over the mountains;
    Your brother, my guide,
Soon left me, to feast on the myrtles
    That offered, each side,
Their fruit-balls, black, glossy and luscious, —
    Or strip from the sorbs
A treasure, or, rosy and wondrous,
    Those hairy gold orbs!
But my mule picked his sure sober path out,
    Just stopping to neigh
When he recognized down in the valley
    His mates on their way
With the faggots and barrels of water;
    And soon we emerged

From the plain, where the woods could scarce follow;
    And still as we urged
Our way, the woods wondered, and left us,
    As up still we trudged
Though the wild path grew wilder each instant,
    And place was e'en grudged
'Mid the rock-chasms and piles of loose stones
    Like the loose broken teeth
Of some monster which climbed there to die
    From the ocean beneath —
Place was grudged to the silver-grey fume-weed
    That clung to the path,
And dark rosemary ever a-dying
    That, 'spite the wind's wrath,
So loves the salt rock's face to seaward,
    And lentisks as staunch
To the stone where they root and bear berries,
    And . . . what shows a branch
Coral-coloured, transparent, with circlets
    Of pale seagreen leaves;
Over all trod my mule with the caution
    Of gleaners o'er sheaves,
Still, foot after foot like a lady,
    Till, round after round,
He climbed to the top of Calvano,
    And God's own profound
Was above me, and round me the mountains,
    And under, the sea,
And within me my heart to bear witness
    What was and shall be.
Oh, heaven and the terrible crystal!
    No rampart excludes
Your eye from the life to be lived
    In the blue solitudes.
Oh, those mountains, their infinite movement!
    Still moving with you;
For, ever some new head and breast of them
    Thrusts into view

To observe the intruder; you see it
　　If quickly you turn
And, before they escape you surprise them.
　　They grudge you should learn
How the soft plains they look on, lean over
　　And love (they pretend)
— Cower beneath them, the flat sea-pine crouches,
　　The wild fruit-trees bend,
E'en the myrtle-leaves curl, shrink and shut:
　　All is silent and grave:
'Tis a sensual and timorous beauty,
　　How fair! but a slave.
So, I turned to the sea; and there slumbered
　　As greenly as ever
Those isles of the siren, your Galli;
　　No ages can sever
The Three, nor enable their sister
　　To join them, — halfway
On the voyage, she looked at Ulysses —
　　No farther to-day,
Tho' the small one, just launched in the wave,
　　Watches breast-high and steady
From under the rock, her bold sister
　　Swum halfway already.
Fortù, shall we sail there together
　　And see from the sides
Quite new rocks show their faces, new haunts
　　Where the siren abides?
Shall we sail round and round them, close over
　　The rocks, tho' unseen,
That ruffle the grey glassy water
　　To glorious green?
Then scramble from splinter to splinter,
　　Reach land and explore,
On the largest, the strange square black turret
　　With never a door,
Just a loop to admit the quick lizards;
　　Then, stand there and hear

345

The birds' quiet singing, that tells us
   What life is, so clear?
— The secret they sang to Ulysses
   When, ages ago,
He heard and he knew this life's secret
   I hear and I know.

Ah, see! The sun breaks o'er Calvano;
   He strikes the great gloom
And flutters it o'er the mount's summit
   In airy gold fume.
All is over. Look out, see the gipsy,
   Our tinker and smith,
Has arrived, set up bellows and forge,
   And down-squatted forthwith
To his hammering, under the wall there;
   One eye keeps aloof
The urchins that itch to be putting
   His jews'-harps to proof,
While the other, thro' locks of curled wire,
   Is watching how sleek
Shines the hog, come to share in the windfall
   — Chew, abbot's own cheek!
All is over. Wake up and come out now,
   And down let us go,
And see the fine things got in order
   At church for the show
Of the Sacrament, set forth this evening.
   To-morrow's the Feast
Of the Rosary's Virgin, by no means
   Of Virgins the least,
As you'll hear in the off-hand discourse
   Which (all nature, no art)
The Dominican brother, these three weeks,
   Was getting by heart.
Not a pillar nor post but is dizened
   With red and blue papers;
All the roof waves with ribbons, each altar
   A-blaze with long tapers;

346

But the great masterpiece is the scaffold
    Rigged glorious to hold
All the fiddlers and fifers and drummers
    And trumpeters bold,
Not afraid of Bellini nor Auber,
    Who, when the priest's hoarse,
Will strike us up something that's brisk
    For the feast's second course.
And then will the flaxen-wigged Image
    Be carried in pomp
Thro' the plain, while in gallant procession
    The priests mean to stomp.
All round the glad church lie old bottles
    With gunpowder stopped,
Which will be, when the Image re-enters,
    Religiously popped;
And at night from the crest of Calvano
    Great bonfires will hang,
On the plain will the trumpets join chorus,
    And more poppers bang.
At all events, come — to the garden
    As far as the wall;
See me tap with a hoe on the plaster
    Till out there shall fall
A scorpion with wide angry nippers!

    — "Such trifles!" you say?
Fortù, in my England at home,
    Men meet gravely to-day
And debate, if abolishing Corn-laws
    Be righteous and wise
— If 'twere proper, Scirocco should vanish
    In black from the skies!

THE LOST LEADER

I.

Just for a handful of silver he left us,
　Just for a riband to stick in his coat —
Found the one gift of which fortune bereft us,
　Lost all the others she lets us devote;
They, with the gold to give, doled him out silver,
　So much was theirs who so little allowed:
How all our copper had gone for his service!
　Rags — were they purple, his heart had been proud!
We that had loved him so, followed him, honoured him,
　Lived in his mild and magnificent eye,
Learned his great language, caught his clear accents,
　Made him our pattern to live and to die!
Shakespeare was of us, Milton was for us,
　Burns, Shelley, were with us, — they watch from their graves!
He alone breaks from the van and the freemen,
　— He alone sinks to the rear and the slaves!

II.

We shall march prospering, — not thro' his presence;
　Songs may inspirit us, — not from his lyre;
Deeds will be done, — while he boasts his quiescence,
　Still bidding crouch whom the rest bade aspire:
Blot out his name, then, record one lost soul more,
　One task more declined, one more footpath untrod,
One more devils'-triumph and sorrow for angels,
　One wrong more to man, one more insult to God!
Life's night begins: let him never come back to us!
　There would be doubt, hesitation and pain,
Forced praise on our part — the glimmer of twilight,
　Never glad confident morning again!

348

Best fight on well, for we taught him — strike gallantly,
　　Menace our heart ere we master his own;
Then let him receive the new knowledge and wait us,
　　Pardoned in heaven, the first by the throne!

THE LOST MISTRESS

I.

All's over, then: does truth sound bitter
　　As one at first believes?
Hark, 'tis the sparrows' good-night twitter
　　About your cottage eaves!

II.

And the leaf-buds on the vine are woolly,
　　I noticed that, to-day;
One day more bursts them open fully
　　— You know the red turns grey.

III.

To-morrow we meet the same then, dearest?
　　May I take your hand in mine?
Mere friends are we, — well, friends the merest
　　Keep much that I resign:

IV.

For each glance of the eye so bright and black,
　　Though I keep with heart's endeavour, —
Your voice, when you wish the snowdrops back,
　　Though it stay in my soul for ever! —

V.

Yet I will but say what mere friends say,
Or only a thought stronger;
I will hold your hand but as long as all may,
Or so very little longer!

HOME-THOUGHTS, FROM ABROAD

I.

Oh, to be in England
Now that April's there,
And whoever wakes in England
Sees, some morning, unaware,
That the lowest boughs and the brushwood sheaf
Round the elm-tree bole are in tiny leaf,
While the chaffinch sings on the orchard bough
In England — now!

II.

And after April, when May follows,
And the whitethroat builds, and all the swallows!
Hark, where my blossomed pear-tree in the hedge
Leans to the field and scatters on the clover
Blossoms and dewdrops — at the bent spray's edge —
That's the wise thrush; he sings each song twice over,
Lest you should think he never could recapture
The first fine careless rapture!
And though the fields look rough with hoary dew,
All will be gay when noontide wakes anew
The buttercups, the little children's dower
— Far brighter than this gaudy melon-flower!

HOME-THOUGHTS, FROM THE SEA

Nobly, nobly Cape Saint Vincent to the North-west died away;
Sunset ran, one glorious blood-red, reeking into Cadiz Bay;
Bluish 'mid the burning water, full in face Trafalgar lay;
In the dimmest North-east distance dawned Gibraltar grand and gray;
"Here and here did England help me: how can I help England?" — say,
Whoso turns as I, this evening, turn to God to praise and pray,
While Jove's planet rises yonder, silent over Africa.

THE BISHOP ORDERS HIS TOMB AT
SAINT PRAXED'S CHURCH

ROME, 15 —.

Vanity, saith the preacher, vanity!
Draw round my bed: is Anselm keeping back?
Nephews — sons mine . . . ah God, I know not! Well —
She, men would have to be your mother once,
Old Gandolf envied me, so fair she was!
What's done is done, and she is dead beside,
Dead long ago, and I am Bishop since,
And as she died so must we die ourselves,
And thence ye may perceive the world's a dream.
Life, how and what is it? As here I lie
In this state-chamber, dying by degrees,
Hours and long hours in the dead night, I ask
"Do I live, am I dead?" Peace, peace seems all.
Saint Praxed's ever was the church for peace;
And so, about this tomb of mine. I fought
With tooth and nail to save my niche, ye know:
— Old Gandolf cozened me, despite my care;
Shrewd was that snatch from out the corner South

351

He graced his carrion with, God curse the same!
Yet still my niche is not so cramped but thence
One sees the pulpit o' the epistle-side,
And somewhat of the choir, those silent seats,
And up into the aery dome where live
The angels, and a sunbeam's sure to lurk:
And I shall fill my slab of basalt there,
And 'neath my tabernacle take my rest,
With those nine columns round me, two and two,
The odd one at my feet where Anselm stands:
Peach-blossom marble all, the rare, the ripe
As fresh-poured red wine of a mighty pulse.
— Old Gandolf with his paltry onion-stone,
Put me where I may look at him! True peach,
Rosy and flawless: how I earned the prize!
Draw close: that conflagration of my church
— What then? So much was saved if aught were missed!
My sons, ye would not be my death? Go dig
The white-grape vineyard where the oil-press stood,
Drop water gently till the surface sink,
And if ye find . . . Ah God, I know not, I! . . .
Bedded in store of rotten fig-leaves soft,
And corded up in a tight olive-frail,
Some lump, ah God, of *lapis lazuli,*
Big as a Jew's head cut off at the nape,
Blue as a vein o'er the Madonna's breast . . .
Sons, all have I bequeathed you, villas, all,
That brave Frascati villa with its bath,
So, let the blue lump poise between my knees,
Like God the Father's globe on both his hands
Ye worship in the Jesu Church so gay,
For Gandolf shall not choose but see and burst!
Swift as a weaver's shuttle fleet our years:
Man goeth to the grave, and where is he?
Did I say basalt for my slab, sons? Black —
'Twas ever antique-black I meant! How else
Shall ye contrast my frieze to come beneath?
The bas-relief in bronze ye promised me,
Those Pans and Nymphs ye wot of, and perchance

Some tripod, thyrsus, with a vase or so,
The Saviour at his sermon on the mount,
Saint Praxed in a glory, and one Pan
Ready to twitch the Nymph's last garment off,
And Moses with the tables . . . but I know
Ye mark me not! What do they whisper thee,
Child of my bowels, Anselm? Ah, ye hope
To revel down my villas while I gasp
Bricked o'er with beggar's mouldy travertine
Which Gandolf from his tomb-top chuckles at!
Nay, boys, ye love me — all of jasper, then!
'Tis jasper ye stand pledged to, lest I grieve.
My bath must needs be left behind, alas!
One block, pure green as a pistachio-nut,
There's plenty jasper somewhere in the world —
And have I not Saint Praxed's ear to pray
Horses for ye, and brown Greek manuscripts,
And mistresses with great smooth marbly limbs?
— That's if ye carve my epitaph aright,
Choice Latin, picked phrase, Tully's every word,
No gaudy ware like Gandolf's second line —
Tully, my masters? Ulpian serves his need!
And then how I shall lie through centuries,
And hear the blessed mutter of the mass,
And see God made and eaten all day long,
And feel the steady candle-flame, and taste
Good strong thick stupefying incense-smoke!
For as I lie here, hours of the dead night,
Dying in state and by such slow degrees,
I fold my arms as if they clasped a crook,
And stretch my feet forth straight as stone can point,
And let the bedclothes, for a mortcloth, drop
Into great laps and folds of sculptor's-work:
And as yon tapers dwindle, and strange thoughts
Grow, with a certain humming in my ears,
About the life before I lived this life,
And this life too, popes, cardinals and priests,
Saint Praxed at his sermon on the mount,
Your tall pale mother with her talking eyes,

And new-found agate urns as fresh as day,
And marble's language, Latin pure, discreet,
— Aha, ELUCESCEBAT quoth our friend?
No Tully, said I, Ulpian at the best!
Evil and brief hath been my pilgrimage.
All *lapis*, all, sons! Else I give the Pope
My villas! Will ye ever eat my heart?
Ever your eyes were as a lizard's quick,
They glitter like your mother's for my soul,
Or ye would heighten my impoverished frieze,
Piece out its starved design, and fill my vase
With grapes, and add a vizor and a Term,
And to the tripod ye would tie a lynx
That in his struggle throws the thyrsus down,
To comfort me on my entablature
Whereon I am to lie till I must ask
"Do I live, am I dead?" There, leave me, there!
For ye have stabbed me with ingratitude
To death — ye wish it — God, ye wish it! Stone —
Gritstone, a-crumble! Clammy squares which sweat
As if the corpse they keep were oozing through —
And no more *lapis* to delight the world!
Well go! I bless ye. Fewer tapers there,
But in a row: and, going, turn your backs
— Ay, like departing altar-ministrants,
And leave me in my church, the church for peace,
That I may watch at leisure if he leers —
Old Gandolf, at me, from his onion-stone,
As still he envied me, so fair she was!

GARDEN FANCIES

I. THE FLOWER'S NAME

Here's the garden she walked across,
   Arm in my arm, such a short while since:

Hark, now I push its wicket, the moss
   Hinders the hinges and makes them wince!
She must have reached this shrub ere she turned,
   As back with that murmur the wicket swung;
For she laid the poor snail, my chance foot spurned,
   To feed and forget it the leaves among.

II.

Down this side of the gravel-walk
   She went while her robe's edge brushed the box:
And here she paused in her gracious talk
   To point me a moth on the milk-white phlox.
Roses, ranged in valiant row,
   I will never think that she passed you by!
She loves you noble roses, I know;
   But yonder, see, where the rock-plants lie!

III.

This flower she stopped at, finger on lip,
   Stooped over, in doubt, as settling its claim;
Till she gave me, with pride to make no slip,
   Its soft meandering Spanish name:
What a name! Was it love or praise?
   Speech half-asleep or song half-awake?
I must learn Spanish, one of these days,
   Only for that slow sweet name's sake.

IV.

Roses, if I live and do well,
   I may bring her, one of these days,
To fix you fast with as fine a spell,
   Fit you each with his Spanish phrase;
But do not detain me now; for she lingers
   There, like sunshine over the ground,
And ever I see her soft white fingers
   Searching after the bud she found.

V.

Flower, you Spaniard, look that you grow not,
  Stay as you are and be loved for ever!
Bud, if I kiss you 'tis that you blow not:
  Mind, the shut pink mouth opens never!
For while it pouts, her fingers wrestle,
  Twinkling the audacious leaves between,
Till round they turn and down they nestle —
  Is not the dear mark still to be seen?

VI.

Where I find her not, beauties vanish;
  Whither I follow her, beauties flee;
Is there no method to tell her in Spanish
  June's twice June since she breathed it with me?
Come, bud, show me the least of her traces,
  Treasure my lady's lightest footfall!
— Ah, you may flout and turn up your faces —
  Roses, you are not so fair after all!

II. SIBRANDUS SCHAFNABURGENSIS

Plague take all your pedants, say I!
  He who wrote what I hold in my hand,
Centuries back was so good as to die,
  Leaving this rubbish to cumber the land;
This, that was a book in its time,
  Printed on paper and bound in leather,
Last month in the white of a matin-prime
  Just when the birds sang all together.

II.

Into the garden I brought it to read,
  And under the arbute and laurustine

356

Read it, so help me grace in my need,
   From title-page to closing line.
Chapter on chapter did I count,
   As a curious traveller counts Stonehenge;
Added up the mortal amount;
   And then proceeded to my revenge.

III.

Yonder's a plum-tree with a crevice
   An owl would build in, were he but sage;
For a lap of moss, like a fine pont-levis
   In a castle of the Middle Age,
Joins to a lip of gum, pure amber;
   When he'd be private, there might he spend
Hours alone in his lady's chamber:
   Into this crevice I dropped our friend.

IV.

Splash, went he, as under he ducked,
   — At the bottom, I knew, rain-drippings stagnate:
Next, a handful of blossoms I plucked
   To bury him with, my bookshelf's magnate;
Then I went in-doors, brought out a loaf,
   Half a cheese, and a bottle of Chablis;
Lay on the grass and forgot the oaf
   Over a jolly chapter of Rabelais.

V.

Now, this morning, betwixt the moss
   And gum that locked our friend in limbo,
A spider had spun his web across,
   And sat in the midst with arms akimbo:
So, I took pity, for learning's sake,
   And, *de profundis, accentibus lætis,*
Cantate! quoth I, as I got a rake;
   And up I fished his delectable treatise.

357

VI.

Here you have it, dry in the sun,
  With all the binding all of a blister,
And great blue spots where the ink has run,
  And reddish streaks that wink and glister
O'er the page so beautifully yellow:
  Oh, well have the droppings played their tricks!
Did he guess how toadstools grow, this fellow?
  Here's one stuck in his chapter six!

VII.

How did he like it when the live creatures
  Tickled and toused and browsed him all over,
And worm, slug, eft, with serious features,
  Came in, each one, for his right of trover?
— When the water-beetle with great blind deaf face
  Made of her eggs the stately deposit,
And the newt borrowed just so much of the preface
  As tiled in the top of his black wife's closet?

VIII.

All that life and fun and romping,
  All that frisking and twisting and coupling,
While slowly our poor friend's leaves were swamping
  And clasps were cracking and covers suppling!
As if you had carried sour John Knox
  To the play-house at Paris, Vienna or Munich,
Fastened him into a front-row box,
  And danced off the ballet with trousers and tunic.

IX.

Come, old martyr! What, torment enough is it?
  Back to my room shall you take your sweet self.
Good-bye, mother-beetle; husband-eft, *sufficit!*
  See the snug niche I have made on my shelf!

A.'s book shall prop you up, B.'s shall cover you,
  Here's C. to be grave with, or D. to be gay,
And with E. on each side, and F. right over you,
  Dry-rot at ease till the Judgment-day!

THE LABORATORY

ANCIEN RÉGIME

I.

Now that I, tying thy glass mask tightly,
May gaze thro' these faint smokes curling whitely,
As thou pliest thy trade in this devil's-smithy —
Which is the poison to poison her, prithee?

II.

He is with her, and they know that I know
Where they are, what they do: they believe my tears flow
While they laugh, laugh at me, at me fled to the drear
Empty church, to pray God in, for them! — I am here.

III.

Grind away, moisten and mash up thy paste,
Pound at thy powder, — I am not in haste!
Better sit thus, and observe thy strange things,
Than go where men wait me and dance at the King's.

IV.

That in the mortar — you call it a gum?
Ah, the brave tree whence such gold oozings come!
And yonder soft phial, the exquisite blue,
Sure to taste sweetly, — is that poison too?

V.

Had I but all of them, thee and thy treasures,
What a wild crowd of invisible pleasures!
To carry pure death in an earring, a casket,
A signet, a fan-mount, a filigree basket!

VI.

Soon, at the King's, a mere lozenge to give,
And Pauline should have just thirty minutes to live!
But to light a pastile, and Elise, with her head
And her breast and her arms and her hands, should drop dead!

VII.

Quick — is it finished? The colour's too grim!
Why not soft like the phial's, enticing and dim?
Let it brighten her drink, let her turn it and stir,
And try it and taste, ere she fix and prefer!

VIII.

What a drop! She's not little, no minion like me!
That's why she ensnared him: this never will free
The soul from those masculine eyes, — say, "no!"
To that pulse's magnificent come-and-go.

IX.

For only last night, as they whispered, I brought
My own eyes to bear on her so, that I thought
Could I keep them one half minute fixed, she would fall
Shrivelled; she fell not; yet this does it all!

X.

Not that I bid you spare her the pain;
Let death be felt and the proof remain:

Brand, burn up, bite into its grace —
He is sure to remember her dying face!

XI.

Is it done? Take my mask off! Nay, be not morose;
It kills her, and this prevents seeing it close:
The delicate droplet, my whole fortune's fee!
If it hurts her, beside, can it ever hurt me?

XII.

Now, take all my jewels, gorge gold to your fill,
You may kiss me, old man, on my mouth if you will!
But brush this dust off me, lest horror it brings
Ere I know it — next moment I dance at the King's!

THE CONFESSIONAL

[SPAIN]

I.

It is a lie — their Priests, their Pope,
Their Saints, their . . . all they fear or hope
Are lies, and lies — there! through my door
And ceiling, there! and walls and floor,
There, lies, they lie — shall still be hurled
Till spite of them I reach the world!

II.

You think Priests just and holy men!
Before they put me in this den
I was a human creature too,
With flesh and blood like one of you,

A girl that laughed in beauty's pride
Like lilies in your world outside.

III.

I had a lover — shame avaunt!
This poor wrenched body, grim and gaunt,
Was kissed all over till it burned,
By lips the truest, love e'er turned
His heart's own tint: one night they kissed
My soul out in a burning mist.

IV.

So, next day when the accustomed train
Of things grew round my sense again,
"That is a sin," I said: and slow
With downcast eyes to church I go,
And pass to the confession-chair,
And tell the old mild father there.

V.

But when I falter Beltran's name,
"Ha?" quoth the father; "much I blame
"The sin; yet wherefore idly grieve?
"Despair not — strenuously retrieve!
"Nay, I will turn this love of thine
"To lawful love, almost divine;

VI.

"For he is young, and led astray,
"This Beltran, and he schemes, men say,
"To change the laws of church and state;
"So, thine shall be an angel's fate,
"Who, ere the thunder breaks, should roll
"Its cloud away and save his soul.

VII.

"For, when he lies upon thy breast,
"Thou mayst demand and be possessed
"Of all his plans, and next day steal
"To me, and all those plans reveal,
"That I and every priest, to purge
"His soul, may fast and use the scourge."

VIII.

That father's beard was long and white,
With love and truth his brow seemed bright;
I went back, all on fire with joy,
And, that same evening, bade the boy
Tell me, as lovers should, heart-free,
Something to prove his love of me.

IX.

He told me what he would not tell
For hope of heaven or fear of hell;
And I lay listening in such pride!
And, soon as he had left my side,
Tripped to the church by morning-light
To save his soul in his despite.

X.

I told the father all his schemes,
Who were his comrades, what their dreams;
"And now make haste," I said, "to pray
"The one spot from his soul away;
"To-night he comes, but not the same
"Will look!" At night he never came.

XI.

Nor next night; on the after-morn,
I went forth with a strength new-born.
The church was empty; something drew
My steps into the street; I knew
It led me to the market-place:
Where, lo, on high, the father's face!

XII.

That horrible black scaffold dressed,
That stapled block . . . God sink the rest!
That head strapped back, that blinding vest,
Those knotted hands and naked breast,
Till near one busy hangman pressed,
And, on the neck these arms caressed . . .

XIII.

No part in aught they hope or fear!
No heaven with them, no hell! — and here,
No earth, not so much space as pens
My body in their worst of dens
But shall bear God and man my cry,
Lies — lies, again — and still, they lie!

from THE FLIGHT OF THE DUCHESS

[Now grown up, the Duke returns home.]

VI.

Well, such as he was, he must marry, we heard:
And out of a convent, at the word,

Came the lady, in time of spring.
— Oh, old thoughts they cling, they cling!
That day, I know, with a dozen oaths
I clad myself in thick hunting-clothes
Fit for the chase of urochs or buffle
In winter-time when you need to muffle.
But the Duke had a mind we should cut a figure,
　　And so we saw the lady arrive:
My friend, I have seen a white crane bigger!
　　She was the smallest lady alive,
Made in a piece of nature's madness,
Too small, almost, for the life and gladness
　　That over-filled her, as some hive
Out of the bears' reach on the high trees
Is crowded with its safe merry bees:
In truth, she was not hard to please!
Up she looked, down she looked, round at the mead,
Straight at the castle, that's best indeed
To look at from outside the walls:
As for us, styled the "serfs and thralls,"
She as much thanked me as if she had said it,
　　(With her eyes, do you understand?)
Because I patted her horse while I led it;
　　And Max, who rode on her other hand,
Said, no bird flew past but she inquired
What its true name was, nor ever seemed tired —
If that was an eagle she saw hover,
And the green and grey bird on the field was the plover.
When suddenly appeared the Duke:
　　And as down she sprung, the small foot pointed
On to my hand, — as with a rebuke,
　　And as if his backbone were not jointed,
The Duke stepped rather aside than forward,
　　And welcomed her with his grandest smile;
　　And, mind you, his mother all the while
Chilled in the rear, like a wind to Nor'ward;
And up, like a weary yawn, with its pullies
Went, in a shriek, the rusty portcullis;
And, like a glad sky the north-wind sullies,

The lady's face stopped its play,
As if her first hair had grown grey;
For such things must begin some one day.

*   *   *   *   *

[*But the Duchess is not permitted to play any real part in the Duke's life.*]

XI.

Now you must know that when the first dizziness
   Of flap-hats and buff-coats and jack-boots subsided,
   The Duke put this question, "The Duke's part provided,
   "Had not the Duchess some share in the business?"
For out of the mouth of two or three witnesses
Did he establish all fit-or-unfitnesses:
And, after much laying of heads together,
Somebody's cap got a notable feather
By the announcement with proper unction
That he had discovered the lady's function;
Since ancient authors gave this tenet,
   "When horns wind a mort and the deer is at siege,
"Let the dame of the castle prick forth on her jennet,
   "And, with water to wash the hands of her liege
"In a clean ewer with a fair toweling,
"Let her preside at the disemboweling."
Now, my friend, if you had so little religion
   As to catch a hawk, some falcon-lanner,
   And thrust her broad wings like a banner
Into a coop for a vulgar pigeon;
And if day by day and week by week
   You cut her claws, and sealed her eyes,
   And clipped her wings, and tied her beak,
   Would it cause you any great surprise
If, when you decided to give her an airing,
You found she needed a little preparing?
— I say, should you be such a curmudgeon,
If she clung to the perch, as to take it in dudgeon?
Yet when the Duke to his lady signified,

Just a day before, as he judged most dignified,
In what a pleasure she was to participate, —
 And, instead of leaping wide in flashes,
 Her eyes just lifted their long lashes,
As if pressed by fatigue even he could not dissipate,
And duly acknowledged the Duke's fore-thought,
But spoke of her health, if her health were worth aught,
Of the weight by day and the watch by night,
And much wrong now that used to be right,
So, thanking him, declined the hunting, —
Was conduct ever more affronting?
With all the ceremony settled —
 With the towel ready, and the sewer
 Polishing up his oldest ewer
 And the jennet pitched upon, a piebald,
 Black-barred, cream-coated and pink eye-balled, —
No wonder if the Duke was nettled!
And when she persisted nevertheless, —
Well, I suppose here's the time to confess
That there ran half round our lady's chamber
A balcony none of the hardest to clamber;
And that Jacynth the tire-woman, ready in waiting,
Stayed in call outside, what need of relating?
And since Jacynth was like a June rose, why, a fervent
Adorer of Jacynth of course was your servant;
And if she had the habit to peep through the casement,
 How could I keep at any vast distance?
 And so, as I say, on the lady's persistence,
The Duke, dumb-stricken with amazement,
Stood for a while in a sultry smother,
 And then, with a smile that partook of the awful,
Turned her over to his yellow mother
 To learn what was held decorous and lawful;
And the mother smelt blood with a cat-like instinct,
As her cheek quick whitened thro' all its quince-tint.
Oh, but the lady heard the whole truth at once!
 What meant she? — Who was she? — Her duty and station,
The wisdom of age and the folly of youth, at once,
 Its decent regard and its fitting relation —

In brief, my friend, set all the devils in hell free
And turn them out to carouse in a belfry
And treat the priests to a fifty-part canon,
And then you may guess how that tongue of hers ran on!
Well, somehow or other it ended at last
And, licking her whiskers, out she passed;
And after her, — making (he hoped) a face
   Like Emperor Nero or Sultan Saladin,
Stalked the Duke's self with the austere grace
   Of ancient hero or modern paladin,
From door to staircase — oh such a solemn
Unbending of the vertebral column!

        *   *   *   *   *

[*The Duchess has run away with the Gipsies, and the Duke is left with his mother, the old Duchess.*]

XVI.

When the liquor's out why clink the cannikin?
I did think to describe you the panic in
The redoubtable breast of our master the mannikin,
And what was the pitch of his mother's yellowness,
   How she turned as a shark to snap the spare-rib
   Clean off, sailors say, from a pearl-diving Carib,
When she heard, what she called the flight of the feloness
— But it seems such child's play,
What they said and did with the lady away!
And to dance on, when we've lost the music,
Always made me — and no doubt makes you — sick.
Nay, to my mind, the world's face looked so stern
As that sweet form disappeared through the postern,
She that kept it in constant good humour,
It ought to have stopped; there seemed nothing to do more.
But the world thought otherwise and went on,
And my head's one that its spite was spent on:
Thirty years are fled since that morning,
And with them all my head's adorning.
Nor did the old Duchess die outright,

As you expect, of suppressed spite,
The natural end of every adder
Not suffered to empty its poison-bladder:
But she and her son agreed, I take it,
That no one should touch on the story to wake it,
For the wound in the Duke's pride rankled fiery,
So, they made no search and small inquiry —
And when fresh Gipsies have paid us a visit, I've
Noticed the couple were never inquisitive,
But told them they're folks the Duke don't want here,
And bade them make haste and cross the frontier.
Brief, the Duchess was gone and the Duke was glad of it,
    And the old one was in the young one's stead,
    And took, in her place, the household's head,
And a blessed time the household had of it!
And were I not, as a man may say, cautious
How I trench, more than needs, on the nauseous,
I could favour you with sundry touches
Of the paint-smutches with which the Duchess
Heightened the mellowness of her cheek's yellowness
(To get on faster) until at last her
Cheek grew to be one master-plaster
Of mucus and fucus from mere use of ceruse:
In short, she grew from scalp to udder
Just the object to make you shudder.

*   *   *   *   *

EARTH'S IMMORTALITIES

FAME

See, as the prettiest graves will do in time,
Our poet's wants the freshness of its prime;
Spite of the sexton's browsing horse, the sods
Have struggled through its binding osier rods;

Headstone and half-sunk footstone lean awry,
Wanting the brick-work promised by-and-by;
How the minute grey lichens, plate o'er plate,
Have softened down the crisp-cut name and date!

LOVE

So, the year's done with!
    (*Love me for ever!*)
All March begun with,
    April's endeavour;
May-wreaths that bound me
    June needs must sever;
Now snows fall round me,
    Quenching June's fever —
    (*Love me for ever!*)

MEETING AT NIGHT

I.

The grey sea and the long black land;
And the yellow half-moon large and low;
And the startled little waves that leap
In fiery ringlets from their sleep,
As I gain the cove with pushing prow,
And quench its speed i' the slushy sand.

II.

Then a mile of warm sea-scented beach;
Three fields to cross till a farm appears;
A tap at the pane, the quick sharp scratch
And blue spurt of a lighted match,
And a voice less loud, thro' its joys and fears,
Than the two hearts beating each to each!

PARTING AT MORNING

Round the cape of a sudden came the sea,
And the sun looked over the mountain's rim:
And straight was a path of gold for him,
And the need of a world of men for me.

TIME'S REVENGES

I've a Friend, over the sea;
I like him, but he loves me.
It all grew out of the books I write;
They find such favour in his sight
That he slaughters you with savage looks
Because you don't admire my books.
He does himself though, — and if some vein
Were to snap to-night in this heavy brain,
To-morrow month, if I lived to try,
Round should I just turn quietly,
Or out of the bedclothes stretch my hand
Till I found him, come from his foreign land
To be my nurse in this poor place,
And make my broth and wash my face
And light my fire and, all the while,
Bear with his old good-humoured smile
That I told him "Better have kept away
"Than come and kill me, night and day,
"With, worse than fever throbs and shoots,
"The creaking of his clumsy boots."
I am as sure that this he would do,
As that Saint Paul's is striking two.
And I think I rather . . . woe is me!

371

—Yes, rather would see him than not see,
If lifting a hand could seat him there
Before me in the empty chair
To-night, when my head aches indeed,
And I can neither think nor read
Nor make these purple fingers hold
The pen; this garret's freezing cold!

And I've a Lady—there he wakes,
The laughing fiend and prince of snakes
Within me, at her name, to pray
Fate send some creature in the way
Of my love for her, to be down-torn,
Upthrust and outward-borne,
So I might prove myself that sea
Of passion which I needs must be!
Call my thoughts false and my fancies quaint
And my style infirm and its figures faint,
All the critics say, and more blame yet,
And not one angry word you get.
But, please you, wonder I would put
My cheek beneath that lady's foot
Rather than trample under mine
The laurels of the Florentine,
And you shall see how the devil spends
A fire God gave for other ends!
I tell you, I stride up and down
This garret, crowned with love's best crown,
And feasted with love's perfect feast,
To think I kill for her, at least,
Body and soul and peace and fame,
Alike youth's end and manhood's aim,
—So is my spirit, as flesh with sin,
Filled full, eaten out and in
With the face of her, the eyes of her,
The lips, the little chin, the stir
Of shadow round her mouth; and she
—I'll tell you,—calmly would decree

That I should roast at a slow fire,
If that would compass her desire
And make her one whom they invite
To the famous ball to-morrow night.

There may be heaven; there must be hell;
Meantime, there is our earth here — well!

LOVE AMONG THE RUINS

I.

Where the quiet-coloured end of evening smiles,
    Miles and miles
On the solitary pastures where our sheep
    Half-asleep
Tinkle homeward thro' the twilight, stray or stop
    As they crop —
Was the site once of a city great and gay,
    (So they say)
Of our country's very capital, its prince
    Ages since
Held his court in, gathered councils, wielding far
    Peace or war.

II.

Now, — the country does not even boast a tree,
    As you see,
To distinguish slopes of verdure, certain rills
    From the hills
Intersect and give a name to, (else they run
    Into one)
Where the domed and daring palace shot its spires
    Up like fires

O'er the hundred-gated circuit of a wall
    Bounding all,
Made of marble, men might march on nor be pressed,
    Twelve abreast.

III.

And such plenty and perfection, see, of grass
    Never was!
Such a carpet as, this summer-time, o'erspreads
    And embeds
Every vestige of the city, guessed alone,
    Stock or stone —
Where a multitude of men breathed joy and woe
    Long ago;
Lust of glory pricked their hearts up, dread of shame
    Struck them tame;
And that glory and that shame alike, the gold
    Bought and sold.

IV.

Now, — the single little turret that remains
    On the plains,
By the caper overrooted, by the gourd
    Overscored,
While the patching houseleek's head of blossom winks
    Through the chinks —
Marks the basement whence a tower in ancient time
    Sprang sublime,
And a burning ring, all round, the chariots traced
    As they raced,
And the monarch and his minions and his dames
    Viewed the games.

V.

And I know, while thus the quiet-coloured eve
    Smiles to leave

To their folding, all our many-tinkling fleece
    In such peace,
And the slopes and rills in undistinguished grey
    Melt away —
That a girl with eager eyes and yellow hair
    Waits me there
In the turret whence the charioteers caught soul
    For the goal,
When the king looked, where she looks now, breathless, dumb
    Till I come.

VI.

But he looked upon the city, every side,
    Far and wide,
All the mountains topped with temples, all the glades'
    Colonnades,
All the causeys, bridges, aqueducts, — and then,
    All the men!
When I do come, she will speak not, she will stand,
    Either hand
On my shoulder, give her eyes the first embrace
    Of my face,
Ere we rush, ere we extinguish sight and speech
    Each on each.

VII.

In one year they sent a million fighters forth
    South and North,
And they built their gods a brazen pillar high
    As the sky,
Yet reserved a thousand chariots in full force —
    Gold, of course.
Oh heart! oh blood that freezes, blood that burns!
    Earth's returns

For whole centuries of folly, noise and sin!
    Shut them in,
With their triumphs and their glories and the rest!
    Love is best.

A LOVERS' QUARREL

I.

Oh, what a dawn of day!
How the March sun feels like May!
    All is blue again
    After last night's rain,
And the South dries the hawthorn-spray.
    Only, my Love's away!
I'd as lief that the blue were grey.

II.

Runnels, which rillets swell,
Must be dancing down the dell,
    With a foaming head
    On the beryl bed
Paven smooth as a hermit's cell;
    Each with a tale to tell,
Could my Love but attend as well.

III.

Dearest, three months ago!
When we lived blocked-up with snow, —
    When the wind would edge
    In and in his wedge,
In, as far as the point could go —
    Not to our ingle, though,
Where we loved each the other so!

IV.

Laughs with so little cause!
We devised games out of straws.
 We would try and trace
 One another's face
In the ash, as an artist draws;
 Free on each other's flaws,
How we chattered like two church daws!

V.

What's in the "Times"? — a scold
At the Emperor deep and cold;
 He has taken a bride
 To his gruesome side,
That's as fair as himself is bold:
 There they sit ermine-stoled,
And she powders her hair with gold.

VI.

Fancy the Pampas' sheen!
Miles and miles of gold and green
 Where the sunflowers blow
 In a solid glow,
And — to break now and then the screen —
 Black neck and eyeballs keen,
Up a wild horse leaps between!

VII.

Try, will our table turn?
Lay your hands there light, and yearn
 Till the yearning slips
 Thro' the finger-tips
In a fire which a few discern,
 And a very few feel burn,
And the rest, they may live and learn!

VIII.

Then we would up and pace,
For a change, about the place,
 Each with arm o'er neck:
 'Tis our quarter-deck,
We are seamen in woeful case.
 Help in the ocean-space!
Or, if no help, we'll embrace.

IX.

See, how she looks now, dressed
In a sledging-cap and vest!
 'Tis a huge fur cloak —
 Like a reindeer's yoke
Falls the lappet along the breast:
 Sleeves for her arms to rest,
Or to hang, as my Love likes best.

X.

Teach me to flirt a fan
As the Spanish ladies can,
 Or I tint your lip
 With a burnt stick's tip
And you turn into such a man!
 Just the two spots that span
Half the bill of the young male swan.

XI.

Dearest, three months ago
When the mesmerizer Snow
 With his hand's first sweep
 Put the earth to sleep:
'Twas a time when the heart could show
 All — how was earth to know,
'Neath the mute hand's to-and-fro?

XII.

Dearest, three months ago
When we loved each other so,
    Lived and loved the same
    Till an evening came
When a shaft from the devil's bow
    Pierced to our ingle-glow,
And the friends were friend and foe!

XIII.

Not from the heart beneath —
'Twas a bubble born of breath,
    Neither sneer nor vaunt,
    Nor reproach nor taunt.
See a word, how it severeth!
    Oh, power of life and death
In the tongue, as the Preacher saith!

XIV.

Woman, and will you cast
For a word, quite off at last
    Me, your own, your You, —
    Since, as truth is true,
I was You all the happy past —
    Me do you leave aghast
With the memories We amassed?

XV.

Love, if you knew the light
That your soul casts in my sight,
    How I look to you
    For the pure and true
And the beauteous and the right, —
    Bear with a moment's spite
When a mere mote threats the white!

XVI.

What of a hasty word?
Is the fleshly heart not stirred
    By a worm's pin-prick
    Where its roots are quick?
See the eye, by a fly's foot blurred —
    Ear, when a straw is heard
Scratch the brain's coat of curd!

XVII.

Foul be the world or fair
More or less, how can I care?
    'Tis the world the same
    For my praise or blame,
And endurance is easy there.
    Wrong in the one thing rare —
Oh, it is hard to bear!

XVIII.

Here's the spring back or close,
When the almond-blossom blows:
    We shall have the word
    In a minor third
There is none but the cuckoo knows:
    Heaps of the guelder-rose!
I must bear with it, I suppose.

XIX.

Could but November come,
Were the noisy birds struck dumb
    At the warning slash
    Of his driver's-lash —
I would laugh like the valiant Thumb
    Facing the castle glum
And the giant's fee-faw-fum!

XX.

Then, were the world well stripped
Of the gear wherein equipped
    We can stand apart,
    Heart dispense with heart
In the sun, with the flowers unnipped, —
    Oh, the world's hangings ripped,
We were both in a bare-walled crypt!

XXI.

Each in the crypt would cry
"But one freezes here! and why?
    "When a heart, as chill,
    "At my own would thrill
"Back to life, and its fires out-fly?
    "Heart, shall we live or die?
"The rest, . . . settle by-and-by!"

XXII.

So, she'd efface the score,
And forgive me as before.
    It is twelve o'clock:
    I shall hear her knock
In the worst of a storm's uproar,
    I shall pull her through the door,
I shall have her for evermore!

EVELYN HOPE

I.

Beautiful Evelyn Hope is dead!
  Sit and watch by her side an hour.
That is her book-shelf, this her bed;
  She plucked that piece of geranium-flower,
Beginning to die too, in the glass;
  Little has yet been changed, I think:
The shutters are shut, no light may pass
  Save two long rays thro' the hinge's chink.

II.

Sixteen years old when she died!
  Perhaps she had scarcely heard my name;
It was not her time to love; beside,
  Her life had many a hope and aim,
Duties enough and little cares,
  And now was quiet, now astir,
Till God's hand beckoned unawares, —
  And the sweet white brow is all of her.

III.

Is it too late then, Evelyn Hope?
  What, your soul was pure and true,
The good stars met in your horoscope,
  Made you of spirit, fire and dew —
And, just because I was thrice as old
  And our paths in the world diverged so wide,
Each was nought to each, must I be told?
  We were fellow mortals, nought beside?

IV.

No, indeed! for God above
    Is great to grant, as mighty to make,
And creates the love to reward the love:
    I claim you still, for my own love's sake!
Delayed it may be for more lives yet,
    Through worlds I shall traverse, not a few:
Much is to learn, much to forget
    Ere the time be come for taking you.

V.

But the time will come, — at last it will,
    When, Evelyn Hope, what meant (I shall say)
In the lower earth, in the years long still,
    That body and soul so pure and gay?
Why your hair was amber, I shall divine,
    And your mouth of your own geranium's red —
And what you would do with me, in fine,
    In the new life come in the old one's stead.

VI.

I have lived (I shall say) so much since then,
    Given up myself so many times,
Gained me the gains of various men,
    Ransacked the ages, spoiled the climes;
Yet one thing, one, in my soul's full scope,
    Either I missed or itself missed me:
And I want and find you, Evelyn Hope!
    What is the issue? let us see!

VII.

I loved you, Evelyn, all the while.
    My heart seemed full as it could hold?
There was place and to spare for the frank young smile,

And the red young mouth, and the hair's young gold.
So, hush, — I will give you this leaf to keep:
See, I shut it inside the sweet cold hand!
There, that is our secret: go to sleep!
You will wake, and remember, and understand.

UP AT A VILLA — DOWN IN THE CITY

(AS DISTINGUISHED BY AN ITALIAN PERSON OF QUALITY)

I.

Had I but plenty of money, money enough and to spare,
The house for me, no doubt, were a house in the city-square;
Ah, such a life, such a life, as one leads at the window there!

II.

Something to see, by Bacchus, something to hear, at least!
There, the whole day long, one's life is a perfect feast;
While up at a villa one lives, I maintain it, no more than a beast.

III.

Well now, look at our villa! stuck like the horn of a bull
Just on a mountain-edge as bare as the creature's skull,
Save a mere shag of a bush with hardly a leaf to pull!
— I scratch my own, sometimes, to see if the hair's turned wool.

IV.

But the city, oh the city — the square with the houses! Why?
They are stone-faced, white as a curd, there's something to take the eye!
Houses in four straight lines, not a single front awry;
You watch who crosses and gossips, who saunters, who hurries by;
Green blinds, as a matter of course, to draw when the sun gets high;
And the shops with fanciful signs which are painted properly.

V.

What of a villa? Though winter be over in March by rights,
'Tis May perhaps ere the snow shall have withered well off the heights:
You've the brown ploughed land before, where the oxen steam and
  wheeze,
And the hills over-smoked behind by the faint grey olive-trees.

VI.

Is it better in May, I ask you? You've summer all at once;
In a day he leaps complete with a few strong April suns.
'Mid the sharp short emerald wheat, scarce risen three fingers well,
The wild tulip, at end of its tube, blows out its great red bell
Like a thin clear bubble of blood, for the children to pick and sell.

VII.

Is it ever hot in the square? There's a fountain to spout and splash!
In the shade it sings and springs; in the shine such foam-bows flash
On the horses with curling fish-tails, that prance and paddle and pash
Round the lady atop in her conch — fifty gazers do not abash,
Though all that she wears is some weeds round her waist in a sort of sash.

VIII.

All the year long at the villa, nothing to see though you linger,
Except yon cypress that points like death's lean lifted forefinger.
Some think fireflies pretty, when they mix i' the corn and mingle,
Or thrid the stinking hemp till the stalks of it seem a-tingle.
Late August or early September, the stunning cicala is shrill,
And the bees keep their tiresome whine round the resinous firs on the
  hill.
Enough of the seasons, — I spare you the months of the fever and chill.

IX.

Ere you open your eyes in the city, the blessed church-bells begin:
No sooner the bells leave off than the diligence rattles in:

You get the pick of the news, and it costs you never a pin.
By-and-by there's the travelling doctor gives pills, lets blood, draws
    teeth;
Or the Pulcinello-trumpet breaks up the market beneath.
At the post-office such a scene-picture — the new play, piping hot!
And a notice how, only this morning, three liberal thieves were shot.
Above it, behold the Archbishop's most fatherly of rebukes,
And beneath, with his crown and his lion, some little new law of the
    Duke's!
Or a sonnet with flowery marge, to the Reverend Don So-and-so
Who is Dante, Boccaccio, Petrarca, Saint Jerome and Cicero,
"And moreover," (the sonnet goes rhyming,) "the skirts of Saint Paul
    has reached,
"Having preached us those six Lent-lectures more unctuous than ever he
    preached."
Noon strikes, — here sweeps the procession! our Lady borne smiling and
    smart
With a pink gauze gown all spangles, and seven swords stuck in her heart!
Bang-whang-whang goes the drum, *tootle-te-tootle* the fife;
No keeping one's haunches still: it's the greatest pleasure in life.

X.

But bless you, it's dear — it's dear! fowls, wine, at double the rate.
They have clapped a new tax upon salt, and what oil pays passing the
    gate
It's a horror to think of. And so, the villa for me, not the city!
Beggars can scarcely be choosers: but still — ah, the pity, the pity!
Look, two and two go the priests, then the monks with cowls and sandals,
And the penitents dressed in white shirts, a-holding the yellow candles;
One, he carries a flag up straight, and another a cross with handles,
And the Duke's guard brings up the rear, for the better prevention of
    scandals:
Bang-whang-whang goes the drum, *tootle-te-tootle* the fife.
Oh, a day in the city-square, there is no such pleasure in life!

FRA LIPPO LIPPI

I am poor brother Lippo, by your leave!
You need not clap your torches to my face.
Zooks, what's to blame? you think you see a monk!
What, 'tis past midnight, and you go the rounds,
And here you catch me at an alley's end
Where sportive ladies leave their doors ajar?
The Carmine's my cloister: hunt it up,
Do, — harry out, if you must show your zeal,
Whatever rat, there, haps on his wrong hole,
And nip each softling of a wee white mouse,
Weke, weke, that's crept to keep him company!
Aha, you know your betters! Then, you'll take
Your hand away that's fiddling on my throat,
And please to know me likewise. Who am I?
Why, one, sir, who is lodging with a friend
Three streets off — he's a certain . . . how d'ye call?
Master — a . . . Cosimo of the Medici,
I' the house that caps the corner. Boh! you were best!
Remember and tell me, the day you're hanged,
How you affected such a gullet's-gripe!
But you, sir, it concerns you that your knaves
Pick up a manner nor discredit you:
Zooks, are we pilchards, that they sweep the streets
And count fair prize what comes into their net?
He's Judas to a tittle, that man is!
Just such a face! Why, sir, you make amends.
Lord, I'm not angry! Bid your hangdogs go
Drink out this quarter-florin to the health
Of the munificent House that harbours me
(And many more beside, lads! more beside!)
And all's come square again. I'd like his face —
His, elbowing on his comrade in the door
With the pike and lantern, — for the slave that holds

John Baptist's head a-dangle by the hair
With one hand ("Look you, now," as who should say)
And his weapon in the other, yet unwiped!
It's not your chance to have a bit of chalk,
A wood-coal or the like? or you should see!
Yes, I'm the painter, since you style me so.
What, brother Lippo's doings, up and down,
You know them and they take you? like enough!
I saw the proper twinkle in your eye —
'Tell you, I liked your looks at very first.
Let's sit and set things straight now, hip to haunch.
Here's spring come, and the nights one makes up bands
To roam the town and sing out carnival,
And I've been three weeks shut within my mew,
A-painting for the great man, saints and saints
And saints again. I could not paint all night —
Ouf! I leaned out of window for fresh air.
There came a hurry of feet and little feet,
A sweep of lute-strings, laughs, and whifts of song, —
Flower o' the broom,
Take away love, and our earth is a tomb!
Flower o' the quince,
I let Lisa go, and what good in life since?
Flower o' the thyme — and so on. Round they went.
Scarce had they turned the corner when a titter
Like the skipping of rabbits by moonlight, — three slim shapes,
And a face that looked up . . . zooks, sir, flesh and blood,
That's all I'm made of! Into shreds it went,
Curtain and counterpane and coverlet,
All the bed-furniture — a dozen knots,
There was a ladder! Down I let myself,
Hands and feet, scrambling somehow, and so dropped,
And after them. I came up with the fun
Hard by Saint Laurence, hail fellow, well met, —
Flower o' the rose,
If I've been merry, what matter who knows?
And so as I was stealing back again
To get to bed and have a bit of sleep
Ere I rise up to-morrow and go work

388

On Jerome knocking at his poor old breast
With his great round stone to subdue the flesh,
You snap me of the sudden. Ah, I see!
Though your eye twinkles still, you shake your head —
Mine's shaved — a monk, you say — the sting's in that!
If Master Cosimo announced himself,
Mum's the word naturally; but a monk!
Come, what am I a beast for? tell us, now!
I was a baby when my mother died
And father died and left me in the street.
I starved there, God knows how, a year or two
On fig-skins, melon-parings, rinds and shucks,
Refuse and rubbish. One fine frosty day,
My stomach being empty as your hat,
The wind doubled me up and down I went.
Old Aunt Lapaccia trussed me with one hand,
(Its fellow was a stinger as I knew)
And so along the wall, over the bridge,
By the straight cut to the convent. Six words there,
While I stood munching my first bread that month:
"So, boy, you're minded," quoth the good fat father
Wiping his own mouth, 'twas refection-time, —
"To quit this very miserable world?
"Will you renounce" . . . "the mouthful of bread?" thought I;
By no means! Brief, they made a monk of me;
I did renounce the world, its pride and greed,
Palace, farm, villa, shop and banking-house,
Trash, such as these poor devils of Medici
Have given their hearts to — all at eight years old.
Well, sir, I found in time, you may be sure,
'Twas not for nothing — the good bellyful,
The warm serge and the rope that goes all round,
And day-long blessed idleness beside!
"Let's see what the urchin's fit for" — that came next.
Not overmuch their way, I must confess.
Such a to-do! They tried me with their books:
Lord, they'd have taught me Latin in pure waste!
Flower o' the clove,
All the Latin I construe is, "amo" I love!

But, mind you, when a boy starves in the streets
Eight years together, as my fortune was,
Watching folk's faces to know who will fling
The bit of half-stripped grape-bunch he desires,
And who will curse or kick him for his pains, —
Which gentleman processional and fine,
Holding a candle to the Sacrament,
Will wink and let him lift a plate and catch
The droppings of the wax to sell again,
Or holla for the Eight and have him whipped, —
How say I? — nay, which dog bites, which lets drop
His bone from the heap of offal in the street, —
Why, soul and sense of him grow sharp alike,
He learns the look of things, and none the less
For admonition from the hunger-pinch.
I had a store of such remarks, be sure,
Which, after I found leisure, turned to use.
I drew men's faces on my copy-books,
Scrawled them within the antiphonary's marge,
Joined legs and arms to the long music-notes,
Found eyes and nose and chin for A's and B's,
And made a string of pictures of the world
Betwixt the ins and outs of verb and noun,
On the wall, the bench, the door. The monks looked black.
"Nay," quoth the Prior, "turn him out, d'ye say?
"In no wise. Lose a crow and catch a lark.
"What if at last we get our man of parts,
"We Carmelites, like those Camaldolese
"And Preaching Friars, to do our church up fine
"And put the front on it that ought to be!"
And hereupon he bade me daub away.
Thank you! my head being crammed, the walls a blank,
Never was such prompt disemburdening.
First, every sort of monk, the black and white,
I drew them, fat and lean: then, folk at church,
From good old gossips waiting to confess
Their cribs of barrel-droppings, candle-ends, —
To the breathless fellow at the altar-foot,
Fresh from his murder, safe and sitting there

With the little children round him in a row
Of admiration, half for his beard and half
For that white anger of his victim's son
Shaking a fist at him with one fierce arm,
Signing himself with the other because of Christ
(Whose sad face on the cross sees only this
After the passion of a thousand years)
Till some poor girl, her apron o'er her head,
(Which the intense eyes looked through) came at eve
On tiptoe, said a word, dropped in a loaf,
Her pair of earrings and a bunch of flowers
(The brute took growling), prayed, and so was gone.
I painted all, then cried " 'Tis ask and have;
"Choose, for more's ready!" — laid the ladder flat,
And showed my covered bit of cloister-wall.
The monks closed in a circle and praised loud
Till checked, taught what to see and not to see,
Being simple bodies, — "That's the very man!
"Look at the boy who stoops to pat the dog!
"That woman's like the Prior's niece who comes
"To care about his asthma: it's the life!"
But there my triumph's straw-fire flared and funked;
Their betters took their turn to see and say:
The Prior and the learned pulled a face
And stopped all that in no time. "How? what's here?
"Quite from the mark of painting, bless us all!
"Faces, arms, legs and bodies like the true
"As much as pea and pea! it's devil's-game!
"Your business is not to catch men with show,
"With homage to the perishable clay,
"But lift them over it, ignore it all,
"Make them forget there's such a thing as flesh.
"Your business is to paint the souls of men —
"Man's soul, and it's a fire, smoke . . . no, it's not . . .
"It's vapour done up like a new-born babe —
"(In that shape when you die it leaves your mouth)
"It's . . . well, what matters talking, it's the soul!
"Give us no more of body than shows soul!
"Here's Giotto, with his Saint a-praising God,

"That sets us praising, — why not stop with him?
"Why put all thoughts of praise out of our head
"With wonder at lines, colours, and what not?
"Paint the soul, never mind the legs and arms!
"Rub all out, try at it a second time.
"Oh, that white smallish female with the breasts,
"She's just my niece . . . Herodias, I would say, —
"Who went and danced and got men's heads cut off!
"Have it all out!" Now, is this sense, I ask?
A fine way to paint soul, by painting body
So ill, the eye can't stop there, must go further
And can't fare worse! Thus, yellow does for white
When what you put for yellow's simply black,
And any sort of meaning looks intense
When all beside itself means and looks nought.
Why can't a painter lift each foot in turn,
Left foot and right foot, go a double step,
Make his flesh liker and his soul more like,
Both in their order? Take the prettiest face,
The Prior's niece . . . patron-saint — is it so pretty
You can't discover if it means hope, fear,
Sorrow or joy? won't beauty go with these?
Suppose I've made her eyes all right and blue,
Can't I take breath and try to add life's flash,
And then add soul and heighten them three-fold?
Or say there's beauty with no soul at all —
(I never saw it — put the case the same —)
If you get simple beauty and nought else,
You get about the best thing God invents:
That's somewhat: and you'll find the soul you have missed,
Within yourself, when you return him thanks.
"Rub all out!" Well, well, there's my life, in short,
And so the thing has gone on ever since.
I'm grown a man no doubt, I've broken bounds:
You should not take a fellow eight years old
And make him swear to never kiss the girls.
I'm my own master, paint now as I please —
Having a friend, you see, in the Corner-house!
Lord, it's fast holding by the rings in front —

392

Those great rings serve more purposes than just
To plant a flag in, or tie up a horse!
And yet the old schooling sticks, the old grave eyes
Are peeping o'er my shoulder as I work,
The heads shake still — "It's art's decline, my son!
"You're not of the true painters, great and old;
"Brother Angelico's the man, you'll find;
"Brother Lorenzo stands his single peer:
"Fag on at flesh, you'll never make the third!"
Flower o' the pine,
You keep your mistr . . . manners, and I'll stick to mine!
I'm not the third, then: bless us, they must know!
Don't you think they're the likeliest to know,
They with their Latin? So, I swallow my rage,
Clench my teeth, suck my lips in tight, and paint
To please them — sometimes do and sometimes don't;
For, doing most, there's pretty sure to come
A turn, some warm eve finds me at my saints —
A laugh, a cry, the business of the world —
(*Flower o' the peach,*
Death for us all, and his own life for each!)
And my whole soul revolves, the cup runs over,
The world and life's too big to pass for a dream,
And I do these wild things in sheer despite,
And play the fooleries you catch me at,
In pure rage! The old mill-horse, out at grass
After hard years, throws up his stiff heels so,
Although the miller does not preach to him
The only good of grass is to make chaff.
What would men have? Do they like grass or no —
May they or mayn't they? all I want's the thing
Settled for ever one way. As it is,
You tell too many lies and hurt yourself:
You don't like what you only like too much,
You do like what, if given you at your word,
You find abundantly detestable.
For me, I think I speak as I was taught;
I always see the garden and God there
A-making man's wife: and, my lesson learned,

The value and significance of flesh,
I can't unlearn ten minutes afterwards.

   You understand me: I'm a beast, I know.
But see, now — why, I see as certainly
As that the morning-star's about to shine,
What will hap some day. We've a youngster here
Comes to our convent, studies what I do,
Slouches and stares and lets no atom drop:
His name is Guidi — he'll not mind the monks —
They call him Hulking Tom, he lets them talk —
He picks my practice up — he'll paint apace,
I hope so — though I never live so long,
I know what's sure to follow. You be judge!
You speak no Latin more than I, belike;
However, you're my man, you've seen the world
— The beauty and the wonder and the power,
The shapes of things, their colours, lights and shades,
Changes, surprises, — and God made it all!
— For what? Do you feel thankful, ay or no,
For this fair town's face, yonder river's line,
The mountain round it and the sky above,
Much more the figures of man, woman, child,
These are the frame to? What's it all about?
To be passed over, despised? or dwelt upon,
Wondered at? oh, this last of course! — you say.
But why not do as well as say, — paint these
Just as they are, careless what comes of it?
God's works — paint anyone, and count it crime
To let a truth slip. Don't object, "His works
"Are here already; nature is complete:
"Suppose you reproduce her — (which you can't)
"There's no advantage! you must beat her, then."
For, don't you mark? we're made so that we love
First when we see them painted, things we have passed
Perhaps a hundred times nor cared to see;
And so they are better, painted — better to us,
Which is the same thing. Art was given for that;
God uses us to help each other so,

Lending our minds out. Have you noticed, now,
Your cullion's hanging face? A bit of chalk,
And trust me but you should, though! How much more,
If I drew higher things with the same truth!
That were to take the Prior's pulpit-place,
Interpret God to all of you! Oh, oh,
It makes me mad to see what men shall do
And we in our graves! This world's no blot for us,
Nor blank; it means intensely, and means good:
To find its meaning is my meat and drink.
"Ay, but you don't so instigate to prayer!"
Strikes in the Prior: "when your meaning's plain
"It does not say to folk — remember matins,
"Or, mind you fast next Friday!" Why, for this
What need of art at all? A skull and bones,
Two bits of stick nailed crosswise, or, what's best,
A bell to chime the hour with, does as well.
I painted a Saint Laurence six months since
At Prato, splashed the fresco in fine style:
"How looks my painting, now the scaffold's down?"
I ask a brother: "Hugely," he returns —
"Already not one phiz of your three slaves
"Who turn the Deacon off his toasted side,
"But's scratched and prodded to our heart's content,
"The pious people have so eased their own
"With coming to say prayers there in a rage:
"We get on fast to see the bricks beneath.
"Expect another job this time next year,
"For pity and religion grow i' the crowd —
"Your painting serves its purpose!" Hang the fools!

— That is — you'll not mistake an idle word
Spoke in a huff by a poor monk, God wot,
Tasting the air this spicy night which turns
The unaccustomed head like Chianti wine!
Oh, the church knows! don't misreport me, now!
It's natural a poor monk out of bounds
Should have his apt word to excuse himself:

And hearken how I plot to make amends.
I have bethought me: I shall paint a piece
. . . There's for you! Give me six months, then go, see
Something in Sant' Ambrogio's! Bless the nuns!
They want a cast o' my office. I shall paint
God in the midst, Madonna and her babe,
Ringed by a bowery flowery angel-brood,
Lilies and vestments and white faces, sweet
As puff on puff of grated orris-root
When ladies crowd to Church at midsummer.
And then i' the front, of course a saint or two —
Saint John, because he saves the Florentines,
Saint Ambrose, who puts down in black and white
The convent's friends and gives them a long day,
And Job, I must have him there past mistake,
The man of Uz (and Us without the z,
Painters who need his patience). Well, all these
Secured at their devotion, up shall come
Out of a corner when you least expect,
As one by a dark stair into a great light,
Music and talking, who but Lippo! I! —
Mazed, motionless and moonstruck — I'm the man!
Back I shrink — what is this I see and hear?
I, caught up with my monk's-things by mistake,
My old serge gown and rope that goes all round,
I, in this presence, this pure company!
Where's a hole, where's a corner for escape?
Then steps a sweet angelic slip of a thing
Forward, puts out a soft palm — "Not so fast!"
— Addresses the celestial presence, "nay —
"He made you and devised you, after all,
"Though he's none of you! Could Saint John there draw —
"His camel-hair make up a painting-brush?
"We come to brother Lippo for all that,
"*Iste perfecit opus!*" So, all smile —
I shuffle sideways with my blushing face
Under the cover of a hundred wings
Thrown like a spread of kirtles when you're gay

And play hot cockles, all the doors being shut,
Till, wholly unexpected, in there pops
The hothead husband! Thus I scuttle off
To some safe bench behind, not letting go
The palm of her, the little lily thing
That spoke the good word for me in the nick,
Like the Prior's niece . . . Saint Lucy, I would say.
And so all's saved for me, and for the church
A pretty picture gained. Go, six months hence!
Your hand, sir, and good-bye: no lights, no lights!
The street's hushed, and I know my own way back,
Don't fear me! There's the grey beginning. Zooks!

A TOCCATA OF GALUPPI'S

I.

Oh Galuppi, Baldassaro, this is very sad to find!
I can hardly misconceive you; it would prove me deaf and blind;
But although I take your meaning, 'tis with such a heavy mind!

II.

Here you come with your old music, and here's all the good it brings.
What, they lived once thus at Venice where the merchants were the
    kings,
Where Saint Mark's is, where the Doges used to wed the sea with rings?

III.

Ay, because the sea's the street there; and 'tis arched by . . . what
    you call
. . . Shylock's bridge with houses on it, where they kept the carnival:
I was never out of England — it's as if I saw it all.

IV.

Did young people take their pleasure when the sea was warm in May?
Balls and masks begun at midnight, burning ever to mid-day,
When they made up fresh adventures for the morrow, do you say?

V.

Was a lady such a lady, cheeks so round and lips so red, —
On her neck the small face buoyant, like a bell-flower on its bed,
O'er the breast's superb abundance where a man might base his head?

VI.

Well, and it was graceful of them — they'd break talk off and afford
— She, to bite her mask's black velvet — he, to finger on his sword,
While you sat and played Toccatas, stately at the clavichord?

VII.

What? Those lesser thirds so plaintive, sixths diminished, sigh on sigh,
Told them something? Those suspensions, those solutions — "Must we
    die?"
Those commiserating sevenths — "Life might last! we can but try!"

VIII.

"Were you happy?" — "Yes." — "And are you still as happy?" — "Yes. And
    you?"
— "Then, more kisses!" — "Did I stop them, when a million seemed so
    few?"
Hark, the dominant's persistence till it must be answered to!

IX.

So, an octave struck the answer. Oh, they praised you, I dare say!
"Brave Galuppi! that was music! good alike at grave and gay!
"I can always leave off talking when I hear a master play!"

X.

Then they left you for their pleasure: till in due time, one by one,
Some with lives that came to nothing, some with deeds as well undone,
Death stepped tacitly and took them where they never see the sun.

XI.

But when I sit down to reason, think to take my stand nor swerve,
While I triumph o'er a secret wrung from nature's close reserve,
In you come with your cold music till I creep thro' every nerve.

XII.

Yes, you, like a ghostly cricket, creaking where a house was burned:
Dust and ashes, dead and done with, Venice spent what Venice earned.
The soul, doubtless, is immortal — where a soul can be discerned.

XIII.

Yours for instance: you know physics, something of geology,
Mathematics are your pastime; souls shall rise in their degree;
Butterflies may dread extinction, — you'll not die, it cannot be!

XIV.

As for Venice and her people, merely born to bloom and drop,
Here on earth they bore their fruitage, mirth and folly were the crop:
What of soul was left, I wonder, when the kissing had to stop?

XV.

Dust and ashes!" So you creak it, and I want the heart to scold.
Dear dead women, with such hair, too — what's become of all the gold
Used to hang and brush their bosoms? I feel chilly and grown old.

BY THE FIRE-SIDE

I.

How well I know what I mean to do
  When the long dark autumn-evenings come:
And where, my soul, is thy pleasant hue?
  With the music of all thy voices, dumb
In life's November too!

II.

I shall be found by the fire, suppose,
  O'er a great wise book as beseemeth age,
While the shutters flap as the cross-wind blows
  And I turn the page, and I turn the page,
Not verse now, only prose!

III.

Till the young ones whisper, finger on lip,
  "There he is at it, deep in Greek:
"Now then, or never, out we slip
  "To cut from the hazels by the creek
"A mainmast for our ship!"

IV.

I shall be at it indeed, my friends:
  Greek puts already on either side
Such a branch-work forth as soon extends
  To a vista opening far and wide,
And I pass out where it ends.

V.

The outside-frame, like your hazel-trees:
    But the inside-archway widens fast,
And a rarer sort succeeds to these,
    And we slope to Italy at last
And youth, by green degrees.

VI.

I follow wherever I am led,
    Knowing so well the leader's hand:
Oh woman-country, wooed not wed,
    Loved all the more by earth's male-lands,
Laid to their hearts instead!

VII.

Look at the ruined chapel again
    Half-way up in the Alpine gorge!
Is that a tower, I point you plain,
    Or is it a mill, or an iron-forge
Breaks solitude in vain?

VIII.

A turn, and we stand in the heart of things;
    The woods are round us, heaped and dim;
From slab to slab how it slips and springs,
    The thread of water single and slim,
Through the ravage some torrent brings!

IX.

Does it feed the little lake below?
    That speck of white just on its marge
Is Pella; see, in the evening-glow,
    How sharp the silver spear-heads charge
When Alp meets heaven in snow!

X.

On our other side is the straight-up rock;
   And a path is kept 'twixt the gorge and it
By boulder-stones where lichens mock
   The marks on a moth, and small ferns fit
Their teeth to the polished block.

XI.

Oh the sense of the yellow mountain-flowers,
   And thorny balls, each three in one,
The chestnuts throw on our path in showers!
   For the drop of the woodland fruit's begun,
These early November hours,

XII.

That crimson the creeper's leaf across
   Like a splash of blood, intense, abrupt,
O'er a shield else gold from rim to boss,
   And lay it for show on the fairy-cupped
Elf-needled mat of moss,

XIII.

By the rose-flesh mushrooms, undivulged
   Last evening — nay, in to-day's first dew
Yon sudden coral nipple bulged,
   Where a freaked fawn-coloured flaky crew
Of toadstools peep indulged.

XIV.

And yonder, at foot of the fronting ridge
   That takes the turn to a range beyond,
Is the chapel reached by the one-arched bridge
   Where the water is stopped in a stagnant pond
Danced over by the midge.

XV.

The chapel and bridge are of stone alike,
    Blackish-grey and mostly wet;
Cut hemp-stalks steep in the narrow dyke.
    See here again, how the lichens fret
And the roots of the ivy strike!

XVI.

Poor little place, where its one priest comes
    On a festa-day, if he comes at all,
To the dozen folk from their scattered homes,
    Gathered within that precinct small
By the dozen ways one roams —

XVII.

To drop from the charcoal-burners' huts,
    Or climb from the hemp-dressers' low shed,
Leave the grange where the woodman stores his nuts,
    Or the wattled cote where the fowlers spread
Their gear on the rock's bare juts.

XVIII.

It has some pretension too, this front,
    With its bit of fresco half-moon-wise
Set over the porch, Art's early wont:
    'Tis John in the Desert, I surmise,
But has borne the weather's brunt —

XIX.

Not from the fault of the builder, though,
    For a pent-house properly projects
Where three carved beams make a certain show,
    Dating — good thought of our architect's —
'Five, six, nine, he lets you know.

XX.

And all day long a bird sings there,
    And a stray sheep drinks at the pond at times;
The place is silent and aware;
    It has had its scenes, its joys and crimes,
But that is its own affair.

XXI.

My perfect wife, my Leonor,
    Oh heart, my own, oh eyes, mine too,
Whom else could I dare look backward for,
    With whom beside should I dare pursue
The path grey heads abhor?

XXII.

For it leads to a crag's sheer edge with them;
    Youth, flowery all the way, there stops —
Not they; age threatens and they contemn,
    Till they reach the gulf wherein youth drops,
One inch from life's safe hem!

XXIII.

With me, youth led . . . I will speak now,
    No longer watch you as you sit
Reading by fire-light, that great brow
    And the spirit-small hand propping it,
Mutely, my heart knows how —

XXIV.

When, if I think but deep enough,
    You are wont to answer, prompt as rhyme;
And you, too, find without rebuff
    Response your soul seeks many a time
Piercing its fine flesh-stuff.

XXV.

My own, confirm me! If I tread
  This path back, is it not in pride
To think how little I dreamed it led
  To an age so blest that, by its side,
Youth seems the waste instead?

XXVI.

My own, see where the years conduct!
  At first, 'twas something our two souls
Should mix as mists do; each is sucked
  In each now: on, the new stream rolls,
Whatever rocks obstruct.

XXVII.

Think, when our one soul understands
  The great Word which makes all things new,
When earth breaks up and heaven expands,
  How will the change strike me and you
In the house not made with hands?

XXVIII.

Oh I must feel your brain prompt mine,
  Your heart anticipate my heart,
You must be just before, in fine,
  See and make me see, for your part,
New depths of the divine!

XXIX.

But who could have expected this
  When we two drew together first
Just for the obvious human bliss,
  To satisfy life's daily thirst
With a thing men seldom miss?

XXX.

Come back with me to the first of all,
  Let us lean and love it over again,
Let us now forget and now recall,
  Break the rosary in a pearly rain,
And gather what we let fall!

XXXI.

What did I say? — that a small bird sings
  All day long, save when a brown pair
Of hawks from the wood float with wide wings
  Strained to a bell: 'gainst noon-day glare
You count the streaks and rings.

XXXII.

But at afternoon or almost eve
  'Tis better; then the silence grows
To that degree, you half believe
  It must get rid of what it knows,
Its bosom does so heave.

XXXIII.

Hither we walked then, side by side,
  Arm in arm and cheek to cheek,
And still I questioned or replied,
  While my heart, convulsed to really speak,
Lay choking in its pride.

XXXIV.

Silent the crumbling bridge we cross,
  And pity and praise the chapel sweet,
And care about the fresco's loss,
  And wish for our souls a like retreat,
And wonder at the moss.

XXXV.

Stoop and kneel on the settle under,
    Look through the window's grated square:
Nothing to see! For fear of plunder,
    The cross is down and the altar bare,
As if thieves don't fear thunder.

XXXVI.

We stoop and look in through the grate,
    See the little porch and rustic door,
Read duly the dead builder's date;
    Then cross the bridge that we crossed before,
Take the path again — but wait!

XXXVII.

Oh moment, one and infinite!
    The water slips o'er stock and stone;
The West is tender, hardly bright:
    How grey at once is the evening grown —
One star, its chrysolite!

XXXVIII.

We two stood there with never a third,
    But each by each, as each knew well:
The sights we saw and the sounds we heard,
    The lights and the shades made up a spell
Till the trouble grew and stirred.

XXXIX.

Oh, the little more, and how much it is!
    And the little less, and what worlds away!
How a sound shall quicken content to bliss,
    Or a breath suspend the blood's best play,
And life be a proof of this!

XL.

Had she willed it, still had stood the screen
  So slight, so sure, 'twixt my love and her:
I could fix her face with a guard between,
  And find her soul as when friends confer,
Friends — lovers that might have been.

XLI.

For my heart had a touch of the woodland-time,
  Wanting to sleep now over its best.
Shake the whole tree in the summer-prime,
  But bring to the last leaf no such test!
"Hold the last fast!" runs the rhyme.

XLII.

For a chance to make your little much,
  To gain a lover and lose a friend,
Venture the tree and a myriad such,
  When nothing you mar but the year can mend:
But a last leaf — fear to touch!

XLIII.

Yet should it unfasten itself and fall
  Eddying down till it find your face
At some slight wind — best chance of all!
  Be your heart henceforth its dwelling-place
You trembled to forestall!

XLIV.

Worth how well, those dark grey eyes,
  That hair so dark and dear, how worth
That a man should strive and agonize,
  And taste a veriest hell on earth
For the hope of such a prize!

XLV.

You might have turned and tried a man,
  Set him a space to weary and wear,
And prove which suited more your plan,
  His best of hope or his worst despair,
Yet end as he began.

XLVI.

But you spared me this, like the heart you are,
  And filled my empty heart at a word.
If two lives join, there is oft a scar,
  They are one and one, with a shadowy third;
One near one is too far.

XLVII.

A moment after, and hands unseen
  Were hanging the night around us fast;
But we knew that a bar was broken between
  Life and life: we were mixed at last
In spite of the mortal screen.

XLVIII.

The forests had done it; there they stood;
  We caught for a moment the powers at play:
They had mingled us so, for once and good,
  Their work was done — we might go or stay,
They relapsed to their ancient mood.

XLIX.

How the world is made for each of us!
  How all we perceive and know in it
Tends to some moment's product thus,
  When a soul declares itself — to wit,
By its fruit, the thing it does!

L.

Be hate that fruit or love that fruit,
    It forwards the general deed of man,
And each of the Many helps to recruit
    The life of the race by a general plan;
Each living his own, to boot.

LI.

I am named and known by that moment's feat;
    There took my station and degree;
So grew my own small life complete,
    As nature obtained her best of me —
One born to love you, sweet!

LII.

And to watch you sink by the fire-side now
    Back again, as you mutely sit
Musing by fire-light, that great brow
    And the spirit-small hand propping it,
Yonder, my heart knows how!

LIII.

So, earth has gained by one man the more,
    And the gain of earth must be heaven's gain too;
And the whole is well worth thinking o'er
    When autumn comes: which I mean to do
    One day, as I said before.

ROBERT BROWNING

AN EPISTLE

CONTAINING THE STRANGE MEDICAL EXPERIENCE
OF KARSHISH, THE ARAB PHYSICIAN

Karshish, the picker-up of learning's crumbs,
The not-incurious in God's handiwork
(This man's-flesh he hath admirably made,
Blown like a bubble, kneaded like a paste,
To coop up and keep down on earth a space
That puff of vapour from his mouth, man's soul)
— To Abib, all-sagacious in our art,
Breeder in me of what poor skill I boast,
Like me inquisitive how pricks and cracks
Befall the flesh through too much stress and strain,
Whereby the wily vapour fain would slip
Back and rejoin its source before the term, —
And aptest in contrivance (under God)
To baffle it by deftly stopping such: —
The vagrant Scholar to his Sage at home
Sends greeting (health and knowledge, fame with peace)
Three samples of true snakestone — rarer still,
One of the other sort, the melon-shaped,
(But fitter, pounded fine, for charms than drugs)
And writeth now the twenty-second time.

My journeyings were brought to Jericho:
Thus I resume. Who studious in our art
Shall count a little labour unrepaid?
I have shed sweat enough, left flesh and bone
On many a flinty furlong of this land.
Also, the country-side is all on fire
With rumours of a marching hitherward:
Some say Vespasian cometh, some, his son.
A black lynx snarled and pricked a tufted ear;

Lust of my blood inflamed his yellow balls:
I cried and threw my staff and he was gone.
Twice have the robbers stripped and beaten me,
And once a town declared me for a spy;
But at the end, I reach Jerusalem,
Since this poor covert where I pass the night,
This Bethany, lies scarce the distance thence
A man with plague-sores at the third degree
Runs till he drops down dead. Thou laughest here!
'Sooth, it elates me, thus reposed and safe,
To void the stuffing of my travel-scrip
And share with thee whatever Jewry yields.
A viscid choler is observable
In tertians, I was nearly bold to say;
And falling-sickness hath a happier cure
Than our school wots of: there's a spider here
Weaves no web, watches on the ledge of tombs,
Sprinkled with mottles on an ash-grey back;
Take five and drop them . . . but who knows his mind,
The Syrian runagate I trust this to?
His service payeth me a sublimate
Blown up his nose to help the ailing eye.
Best wait: I reach Jerusalem at morn,
There set in order my experiences,
Gather what most deserves, and give thee all —
Or I might add, Judæa's gum-tragacanth
Scales off in purer flakes, shines clearer-grained,
Cracks 'twixt the pestle and the porphyry,
In fine exceeds our produce. Scalp-disease
Confounds me, crossing so with leprosy —
Thou hadst admired one sort I gained at Zoar —
But zeal outruns discretion. Here I end.

  Yet stay: my Syrian blinketh gratefully,
Protesteth his devotion is my price —
Suppose I write what harms not, though he steal?
I half resolve to tell thee, yet I blush,
What set me off a-writing first of all.
An itch I had, a sting to write, a tang!

For, be it this town's barrenness — or else
The Man had something in the look of him —
His case has struck me far more than 'tis worth.
So, pardon if — (lest presently I lose
In the great press of novelty at hand
The care and pains this somehow stole from me)
I bid thee take the thing while fresh in mind,
Almost in sight — for, wilt thou have the truth?
The very man is gone from me but now,
Whose ailment is the subject of discourse.
Thus then, and let thy better wit help all!

'Tis but a case of mania — subinduced
By epilepsy, at the turning-point
Of trance prolonged unduly some three days:
When, by the exhibition of some drug
Or spell, exorcization, stroke of art
Unknown to me and which 'twere well to know,
The evil thing out-breaking all at once
Left the man whole and sound of body indeed, —
But, flinging (so to speak) life's gates too wide,
Making a clear house of it too suddenly,
The first conceit that entered might inscribe
Whatever it was minded on the wall
So plainly at that vantage, as it were,
(First come, first served) that nothing subsequent
Attaineth to erase those fancy-scrawls
The just-returned and new-established soul
Hath gotten now so thoroughly by heart
That henceforth she will read or these or none.
And first — the man's own firm conviction rests
That he was dead (in fact they buried him)
— That he was dead and then restored to life
By a Nazarene physician of his tribe:
— 'Sayeth, the same bade "Rise," and he did rise.
"Such cases are diurnal," thou wilt cry.
Not so this figment! — not, that such a fume,
Instead of giving way to time and health,
Should eat itself into the life of life,

413

As saffron tingeth flesh, blood, bones and all!
For see, how he takes up the after-life.
The man – it is one Lazarus a Jew,
Sanguine, proportioned, fifty years of age,
The body's habit wholly laudable,
As much, indeed, beyond the common health
As he were made and put aside to show.
Think, could we penetrate by any drug
And bathe the wearied soul and worried flesh,
And bring it clear and fair, by three days' sleep!
Whence has the man the balm that brightens all?
This grown man eyes the world now like a child.
Some elders of his tribe, I should premise,
Led in their friend, obedient as a sheep,
To bear my inquisition. While they spoke,
Now sharply, now with sorrow, – told the case, –
He listened not except I spoke to him,
But folded his two hands and let them talk,
Watching the flies that buzzed: and yet no fool.
And that's a sample how his years must go.
Look, if a beggar, in fixed middle-life,
Should find a treasure, – can he use the same
With straitened habits and with tastes starved small,
And take at once to his impoverished brain
The sudden element that changes things,
That sets the undreamed-of rapture at his hand
And puts the cheap old joy in the scorned dust?
Is he not such an one as moves to mirth –
Warily parsimonious, when no need,
Wasteful as drunkenness at undue times?
All prudent counsel as to what befits
The golden mean, is lost on such an one:
The man's fantastic will is the man's law.
So here – we call the treasure knowledge, say,
Increased beyond the fleshly faculty –
Heaven opened to a soul while yet on earth,
Earth forced on a soul's use while seeing heaven:
The man is witless of the size, the sum,
The value in proportion of all things,

Or whether it be little or be much.
Discourse to him of prodigious armaments
Assembled to besiege his city now,
And of the passing of a mule with gourds —
'Tis one! Then take it on the other side,
Speak of some trifling fact, — he will gaze rapt
With stupor at its very littleness,
(Far as I see) as if in that indeed
He caught prodigious import, whole results;
And so will turn to us the bystanders
In ever the same stupor (note this point)
That we too see not with his opened eyes.
Wonder and doubt come wrongly into play,
Preposterously, at cross purposes.
Should his child sicken unto death, — why, look
For scarce abatement of his cheerfulness,
Or pretermission of the daily craft!
While a word, gesture, glance from that same child
At play or in the school or laid asleep,
Will startle him to an agony of fear,
Exasperation, just as like. Demand
The reason why — "'tis but a word," object —
"A gesture" — he regards thee as our lord
Who lived there in the pyramid alone,
Looked at us (dost thou mind?) when, being young,
We both would unadvisedly recite
Some charm's beginning, from that book of his,
Able to bid the sun throb wide and burst
All into stars, as suns grown old are wont.
Thou and the child have each a veil alike
Thrown o'er your heads, from under which ye both
Stretch your blind hands and trifle with a match
Over a mine of Greek fire, did ye know!
He holds on firmly to some thread of life —
(It is the life to lead perforcedly)
Which runs across some vast distracting orb
Of glory on either side that meagre thread,
Which, conscious of, he must not enter yet —
The spiritual life around the earthly life:

The law of that is known to him as this,
His heart and brain move there, his feet stay here.
So is the man perplext with impulses
Sudden to start off crosswise, not straight on,
Proclaiming what is right and wrong across,
And not along, this black thread through the blaze—
"It should be" baulked by "here it cannot be."
And oft the man's soul springs into his face
As if he saw again and heard again
His sage that bade him "Rise" and he did rise.
Something, a word, a tick o' the blood within
Admonishes: then back he sinks at once
To ashes, who was very fire before,
In sedulous recurrence to his trade
Whereby he earneth him the daily bread;
And studiously the humbler for that pride,
Professedly the faultier that he knows
God's secret, while he holds the thread of life.
Indeed the especial marking of the man
Is prone submission to the heavenly will—
Seeing it, what it is, and why it is.
'Sayeth, he will wait patient to the last
For that same death which must restore his being
To equilibrium, body loosening soul
Divorced even now by premature full growth:
He will live, nay, it pleaseth him to live
So long as God please, and just how God please.
He even seeketh not to please God more
(Which meaneth, otherwise) than as God please.
Hence, I perceive not he affects to preach
The doctrine of his sect whate'er it be,
Make proselytes as madmen thirst to do:
How can he give his neighbour the real ground,
His own conviction? Ardent as he is—
Call his great truth a lie, why, still the old
"Be it as God please" reassureth him.
I probed the sore as thy disciple should:
"How, beast," said I, "this stolid carelessness
"Sufficeth thee, when Rome is on her march

"To stamp out like a little spark thy town,
"Thy tribe, thy crazy tale and thee at once?"
He merely looked with his large eyes on me.
The man is apathetic, you deduce?
Contrariwise, he loves both old and young,
Able and weak, affects the very brutes
And birds — how say I? flowers of the field —
As a wise workman recognizes tools
In a master's workshop, loving what they make.
Thus is the man as harmless as a lamb:
Only impatient, let him do his best,
At ignorance and carelessness and sin —
An indignation which is promptly curbed:
As when in certain travel I have feigned
To be an ignoramus in our art
According to some preconceived design,
And happed to hear the land's practitioners
Steeped in conceit sublimed by ignorance,
Prattle fantastically on disease,
Its cause and cure — and I must hold my peace!

Thou wilt object — Why have I not ere this
Sought out the sage himself, the Nazarene
Who wrought this cure, inquiring at the source,
Conferring with the frankness that befits?
Alas! it grieveth me, the learned leech
Perished in a tumult many years ago,
Accused, — our learning's fate, — of wizardry,
Rebellion, to the setting up a rule
And creed prodigious as described to me.
His death, which happened when the earthquake fell
(Prefiguring, as soon appeared, the loss
To occult learning in our lord the sage
Who lived there in the pyramid alone)
Was wrought by the mad people — that's their wont!
On vain recourse, as I conjecture it,
To his tried virtue, for miraculous help —
How could he stop the earthquake? That's their way!

417

The other imputations must be lies:
But take one, though I loathe to give it thee,
In mere respect for any good man's fame.
(And after all, our patient Lazarus
Is stark mad; should we count on what he says?
Perhaps not: though in writing to a leech
'Tis well to keep back nothing of a case.)
This man so cured regards the curer, then,
As — God forgive me! who but God himself,
Creator and sustainer of the world,
That came and dwelt in flesh on it awhile!
— 'Sayeth that such an one was born and lived,
Taught, healed the sick, broke bread at his own house,
Then died, with Lazarus by, for aught I know,
And yet was . . . what I said nor choose repeat,
And must have so avouched himself, in fact,
In hearing of this very Lazarus
Who saith — but why all this of what he saith?
Why write of trivial matters, things of price
Calling at every moment for remark?
I noticed on the margin of a pool
Blue-flowering borage, the Aleppo sort,
Aboundeth, very nitrous. It is strange!

Thy pardon for this long and tedious case,
Which, now that I review it, needs must seem
Unduly dwelt on, prolixly set forth!
Nor I myself discern in what is writ
Good cause for the peculiar interest
And awe indeed this man has touched me with.
Perhaps the journey's end, the weariness
Had wrought upon me first. I met him thus:
I crossed a ridge of short sharp broken hills
Like an old lion's cheek teeth. Out there came
A moon made like a face with certain spots
Multiform, manifold and menacing:
Then a wind rose behind me. So we met
In this old sleepy town at unaware,

The man and I. I send thee what is writ.
Regard it as a chance, a matter risked
To this ambiguous Syrian — he may lose,
Or steal, or give it thee with equal good.
Jerusalem's repose shall make amends
For time this letter wastes, thy time and mine;
Till when, once more thy pardon and farewell!

The very God! think, Abib; dost thou think?
So, the All-Great, were the All-Loving too —
So, through the thunder comes a human voice
Saying, "O heart I made, a heart beats here!
"Face, my hands fashioned, see it in myself!
"Thou hast no power nor mayst conceive of mine,
"But love I gave thee, with myself to love,
"And thou must love me who have died for thee!"
The madman saith He said so: it is strange.

MESMERISM

I.

All I believed is true!
    I am able yet
    All I want, to get
By a method as strange as new:
Dare I trust the same to you?

II.

If at night, when doors are shut,
    And the wood-worm picks,
    And the death-watch ticks,
And the bar has a flag of smut,
And a cat's in the water-butt —

III.

And the socket floats and flares,
  And the house-beams groan,
  And a foot unknown
Is surmised on the garret-stairs,
And the locks slip unawares —

IV.

And the spider, to serve his ends,
  By a sudden thread,
  Arms and legs outspread,
On the table's midst descends,
Comes to find, God knows what friends! —

V.

If since eve drew in, I say,
  I have sat and brought
  (So to speak) my thought
To bear on the woman away,
Till I felt my hair turn grey —

VI.

Till I seemed to have and hold,
  In the vacancy
  'Twixt the wall and me,
From the hair-plait's chestnut gold
To the foot in its muslin fold —

VII.

Have and hold, then and there,
  Her, from head to foot,
  Breathing and mute,
Passive and yet aware,
In the grasp of my steady stare —

VIII.

Hold and have, there and then,
    All her body and soul
    That completes my whole,
All that women add to men
In the clutch of my steady ken —

IX.

Having and holding, till
    I imprint her fast
    On the void at last
As the sun does whom he will
By the calotypist's skill —

X.

Then, — if my heart's strength serve,
    And through all and each
    Of the veils I reach
To her soul and never swerve,
Knitting an iron nerve —

XI.

Command her soul to advance
    And inform the shape
    Which has made escape
And before my countenance
Answers me glance for glance —

XII.

I, still with a gesture fit
    Of my hands that best
    Do my soul's behest,
Pointing the power from it,
While myself do steadfast sit —

XIII.

Steadfast and still the same
On my object bent,
While the hands give vent
To my ardour and my aim
And break into very flame —

XIV.

Then I reach, I must believe,
Not her soul in vain,
For to me again
It reaches, and past retrieve
Is wound in the toils I weave;

XV.

And must follow as I require,
As befits a thrall,
Bringing flesh and all,
Essence and earth-attire,
To the source of the tractile fire:

XVI.

Till the house called hers, not mine,
With a growing weight
Seems to suffocate
If she break not its leaden line
And escape from its close confine.

XVII.

Out of doors into the night!
On to the maze
Of the wild wood-ways,
Not turning to left nor right
From the pathway, blind with sight —

XVIII.

Making thro' rain and wind
  O'er the broken shrubs,
  'Twixt the stems and stubs,
With a still, composed, strong mind,
Nor a care for the world behind —

XIX.

Swifter and still more swift,
  As the crowding peace
  Doth to joy increase
In the wide blind eyes uplift
Thro' the darkness and the drift!

XX.

While I — to the shape, I too
  Feel my soul dilate
  Nor a whit abate,
And relax not a gesture due,
As I see my belief come true.

XXI.

For, there! have I drawn or no
  Life to that lip?
  Do my fingers dip
In a flame which again they throw
On the cheek that breaks a-glow?

XXII.

Ha! was the hair so first?
  What, unfilleted,
  Made alive, and spread
Through the void with a rich outburst,
Chestnut gold-interspersed?

XXIII.

Like the doors of a casket-shrine,
    See, on either side,
    Her two arms divide
Till the heart betwixt makes sign,
Take me, for I am thine!

XXIV.

"Now — now" — the door is heard!
    Hark, the stairs! and near —
    Nearer — and here —
"Now!" and at call the third
She enters without a word.

XXV.

On doth she march and on
    To the fancied shape;
    It is, past escape,
Herself, now: the dream is done
And the shadow and she are one.

XXVI.

First I will pray. Do Thou
    That ownest the soul,
    Yet wilt grant control
To another, nor disallow
For a time, restrain me now!

XXVII.

I admonish me while I may,
    Not to squander guilt,
    Since require Thou wilt
At my hand its price one day!
What the price is, who can say?

A SERENADE AT THE VILLA

I.

That was I, you heard last night,
　When there rose no moon at all,
Nor, to pierce the strained and tight
　Tent of heaven, a planet small:
Life was dead and so was light.

II.

Not a twinkle from the fly,
　Not a glimmer from the worm;
When the crickets stopped their cry,
　When the owls forbore a term,
You heard music; that was I.

III.

Earth turned in her sleep with pain,
　Sultrily suspired for proof:
In at heaven and out again,
　Lightning! — where it broke the roof,
Bloodlike, some few drops of rain.

IV.

What they could my words expressed,
　O my love, my all, my one!
Singing helped the verses best,
　And when singing's best was done,
To my lute I left the rest.

V.

So wore night; the East was gray,
   White the broad-faced hemlock-flowers:
There would be another day;
   Ere its first of heavy hours
Found me, I had passed away.

VI.

What became of all the hopes,
   Words and song and lute as well?
Say, this struck you — "When life gropes
   "Feebly for the path where fell
"Light last on the evening slopes,

VII.

"One friend in that path shall be,
   "To secure my step from wrong;
"One to count night day for me,
   "Patient through the watches long,
"Serving most with none to see."

VIII.

Never say — as something bodes —
   "So, the worst has yet a worse!
"When life halts 'neath double loads,
   "Better the taskmaster's curse
"Than such music on the roads!

IX.

"When no moon succeeds the sun,
   "Nor can pierce the midnight's tent
"Any star, the smallest one,
   "While some drops, where lightning rent,
"Show the final storm begun —

X.

"When the fire-fly hides its spot,
    "When the garden-voices fail
"In the darkness thick and hot, —
    "Shall another voice avail,
"That shape be where these are not?

XI.

"Has some plague a longer lease,
    "Proffering its help uncouth?
"Can't one even die in peace?
    "As one shuts one's eyes on youth,
"Is that face the last one sees?"

XII.

Oh how dark your villa was,
    Windows fast and obdurate!
How the garden grudged me grass
    Where I stood — the iron gate
Ground its teeth to let me pass!

MY STAR

All that I know
    Of a certain star
Is, it can throw
    (Like the angled spar)
Now a dart of red,
    Now a dart of blue;
Till my friends have said
    They would fain see, too,
My star that dartles the red and the blue!
Then it stops like a bird; like a flower, hangs furled:

They must solace themselves with the Saturn above it.
What matter to me if their star is a world?
Mine has opened its soul to me; therefore I love it.

INSTANS TYRANNUS

I.

Of the million or two, more or less,
I rule and possess,
One man, for some cause undefined,
Was least to my mind.

II.

I struck him, he grovelled of course —
For, what was his force?
I pinned him to earth with my weight
And persistence of hate:
And he lay, would not moan, would not curse,
As his lot might be worse.

III.

"Were the object less mean, would he stand
"At the swing of my hand!
"For obscurity helps him and blots
"The hole where he squats."
So, I set my five wits on the stretch
To inveigle the wretch.
All in vain! Gold and jewels I threw,
Still he couched there perdue;
I tempted his blood and his flesh,
Hid in roses my mesh,
Choicest cates and the flagon's best spilth:
Still he kept to his filth.

IV.

Had he kith now or kin, were access
To his heart, did I press:
Just a son or a mother to seize!
No such booty as these.
Were it simply a friend to pursue
'Mid my million or two,
Who could pay me in person or pelf
What he owes me himself!
No: I could not but smile through my chafe:
For the fellow lay safe
As his mates do, the midge and the nit,
— Through minuteness, to wit.

V.

Then a humour more great took its place
At the thought of his face,
The droop, the low cares of the mouth,
The trouble uncouth
'Twixt the brows, all that air one is fain
To put out of its pain.
And, "no!" I admonished myself,
"Is one mocked by an elf,
"Is one baffled by toad or by rat?
"The gravamen's in that!
"How the lion, who crouches to suit
"His back to my foot,
"Would admire that I stand in debate!
"But the small turns the great
"If it vexes you, — that is the thing!
"Toad or rat vex the king?
"Though I waste half my realm to unearth
"Toad or rat, 'tis well worth!"

VI.

So, I soberly laid my last plan
To extinguish the man.
Round his creep-hole, with never a break
Ran my fires for his sake;
Over-head, did my thunder combine
With my underground mine:
Till I looked from my labour content
To enjoy the event.

VII.

When sudden . . . how think ye, the end?
Did I say "without friend"?
Say rather, from marge to blue marge
The whole sky grew his targe
With the sun's self for visible boss,
While an Arm ran across
Which the earth heaved beneath like a breast
Where the wretch was safe prest!
Do you see? Just my vengeance complete,
The man sprang to his feet,
Stood erect, caught at God's skirts, and prayed!
— So, I was afraid!

"CHILDE ROLAND TO THE DARK TOWER CAME"

(See Edgar's song in "LEAR.")

I.

My first thought was, he lied in every word,
That hoary cripple, with malicious eye
Askance to watch the working of his lie

On mine, and mouth scarce able to afford
Suppression of the glee, that pursed and scored
  Its edge, at one more victim gained thereby.

II.

What else should he be set for, with his staff?
  What, save to waylay with his lies, ensnare
  All travellers who might find him posted there,
And ask the road? I guessed what skull-like laugh
Would break, what crutch 'gin write my epitaph
  For pastime in the dusty thoroughfare,

III.

If at his counsel I should turn aside
  Into that ominous tract which, all agree,
  Hides the Dark Tower. Yet acquiescingly
I did turn as he pointed: neither pride
Nor hope rekindling at the end descried,
  So much as gladness that some end might be.

IV.

For, what with my whole world-wide wandering,
  What with my search drawn out thro' years, my hope
  Dwindled into a ghost not fit to cope
With that obstreperous joy success would bring,
I hardly tried now to rebuke the spring
  My heart made, finding failure in its scope.

V.

As when a sick man very near to death
  Seems dead indeed, and feels begin and end
  The tears and takes the farewell of each friend,
And hears one bid the other go, draw breath
Freelier outside, ("since all is o'er," he saith,
  "And the blow fallen no grieving can amend;")

VI.

While some discuss if near the other graves
  Be room enough for this, and when a day
  Suits best for carrying the corpse away,
With care about the banners, scarves and staves:
And still the man hears all, and only craves
  He may not shame such tender love and stay.

VII.

Thus, I had so long suffered in this quest,
  Heard failure prophesied so oft, been writ
  So many times among "The Band" — to wit,
The knights who to the Dark Tower's search addressed
Their steps — that just to fail as they, seemed best,
  And all the doubt was now — should I be fit?

VIII.

So, quiet as despair, I turned from him,
  That hateful cripple, out of his highway
  Into the path he pointed. All the day
Had been a dreary one at best, and dim
Was settling to its close, yet shot one grim
  Red leer to see the plain catch its estray.

IX.

For mark! no sooner was I fairly found
  Pledged to the plain, after a pace or two,
  Than, pausing to throw backward a last view
O'er the safe road, 'twas gone; grey plain all round:
Nothing but plain to the horizon's bound.
  I might go on; nought else remained to do.

X.

So, on I went. I think I never saw
  Such starved ignoble nature; nothing throve:
  For flowers — as well expect a cedar grove!
But cockle, spurge, according to their law
Might propagate their kind, with none to awe,
  You'd think; a burr had been a treasure-trove.

XI.

No! penury, inertness and grimace,
  In some strange sort, were the land's portion. "See
  "Or shut your eyes," said Nature peevishly,
"It nothing skills: I cannot help my case:
" 'Tis the Last Judgment's fire must cure this place,
  "Calcine its clods and set my prisoners free."

XII.

If there pushed any ragged thistle-stalk
  Above its mates, the head was chopped; the bents
  Were jealous else. What made those holes and rents
In the dock's harsh swarth leaves, bruised as to baulk
All hope of greenness? 'tis a brute must walk
  Pashing their life out, with a brute's intents.

XIII.

As for the grass, it grew as scant as hair
  In leprosy; thin dry blades pricked the mud
  Which underneath looked kneaded up with blood.
One stiff blind horse, his every bone a-stare,
Stood stupefied, however he came there:
  Thrust out past service from the devil's stud!

XIV.

Alive? he might be dead for aught I know,
  With that red gaunt and colloped neck a-strain,
  And shut eyes underneath the rusty mane;
Seldom went such grotesqueness with such woe;
I never saw a brute I hated so;
  He must be wicked to deserve such pain.

XV.

I shut my eyes and turned them on my heart.
  As a man calls for wine before he fights,
  I asked one draught of earlier, happier sights,
Ere fitly I could hope to play my part.
Think first, fight afterwards — the soldier's art:
  One taste of the old time sets all to rights.

XVI.

Not it! I fancied Cuthbert's reddening face
  Beneath its garniture of curly gold,
  Dear fellow, till I almost felt him fold
An arm in mine to fix me to the place,
That way he used. Alas, one night's disgrace!
  Out went my heart's new fire and left it cold.

XVII.

Giles then, the soul of honour — there he stands
  Frank as ten years ago when knighted first.
  What honest man should dare (he said) he durst.
Good — but the scene shifts — faugh! what hangman hands
Pin to his breast a parchment? His own bands
  Read it. Poor traitor, spit upon and curst!

XVIII.

Better this present than a past like that;
  Back therefore to my darkening path again!
  No sound, no sight as far as eye could strain.
Will the night send a howlet or a bat?
I asked: when something on the dismal flat
  Came to arrest my thoughts and change their train.

XIX.

A sudden little river crossed my path
  As unexpected as a serpent comes.
  No sluggish tide congenial to the glooms;
This, as it frothed by, might have been a bath
For the fiend's glowing hoof — to see the wrath
  Of its black eddy bespate with flakes and spumes.

XX.

So petty yet so spiteful! All along,
  Low scrubby alders kneeled down over it;
  Drenched willows flung them headlong in a fit
Of mute despair, a suicidal throng:
The river which had done them all the wrong,
  Whate'er that was, rolled by, deterred no whit.

XXI.

Which, while I forded, — good saints, how I feared
  To set my foot upon a dead man's cheek,
  Each step, or feel the spear I thrust to seek
For hollows, tangled in his hair or beard!
— It may have been a water-rat I speared,
  But, ugh! it sounded like a baby's shriek.

XXII.

Glad was I when I reached the other bank.
　　Now for a better country. Vain presage!
　　Who were the strugglers, what war did they wage,
Whose savage trample thus could pad the dank
Soil to a plash? Toads in a poisoned tank,
　　Or wild cats in a red-hot iron cage —

XXIII.

The fight must so have seemed in that fell cirque.
　　What penned them there, with all the plain to choose?
　　No foot-print leading to that horrid mews,
None out of it. Mad brewage set to work
Their brains, no doubt, like galley-slaves the Turk
　　Pits for his pastime, Christians against Jews.

XXIV.

And more than that — a furlong on — why, there!
　　What bad use was that engine for, that wheel,
　　Or brake, not wheel — that harrow fit to reel
Men's bodies out like silk? with all the air
Of Tophet's tool, on earth left unaware,
　　Or brought to sharpen its rusty teeth of steel.

XXV.

Then came a bit of stubbed ground, once a wood,
　　Next a marsh, it would seem, and now mere earth
　　Desperate and done with; (so a fool finds mirth,
Makes a thing and then mars it, till his mood
Changes and off he goes!) within a rood —
　　Bog, clay and rubble, sand and stark black dearth.

XXVI.

Now blotches rankling, coloured gay and grim,
  Now patches where some leanness of the soil's
  Broke into moss or substances like boils;
Then came some palsied oak, a cleft in him
Like a distorted mouth that splits its rim
  Gaping at death, and dies while it recoils.

XXVII.

And just as far as ever from the end!
  Nought in the distance but the evening, nought
  To point my footstep further! At the thought,
A great black bird, Apollyon's bosom-friend,
Sailed past, nor beat his wide wing dragon-penned
  That brushed my cap — perchance the guide I sought.

XXVIII.

For, looking up, aware I somehow grew,
  'Spite of the dusk, the plain had given place
  All round to mountains — with such name to grace
Mere ugly heights and heaps now stolen in view.
How thus they had surprised me, — solve it, you!
  How to get from them was no clearer case.

XXIX.

Yet half I seemed to recognize some trick
  Of mischief happened to me, God knows when —
  In a bad dream perhaps. Here ended, then,
Progress this way. When, in the very nick
Of giving up, one time more, came a click
  As when a trap shuts — you're inside the den!

XXX.

Burningly it came on me all at once,
This was the place! those two hills on the right,
Crouched like two bulls locked horn in horn in fight;
While to the left, a tall scalped mountain . . . Dunce,
Dotard, a-dozing at the very nonce,
After a life spent training for the sight!

XXXI.

What in the midst lay but the Tower itself?
The round squat turret, blind as the fool's heart,
Built of brown stone, without a counterpart
In the whole world. The tempest's mocking elf
Points to the shipman thus the unseen shelf
He strikes on, only when the timbers start.

XXXII.

Not see? because of night perhaps? — why, day
Came back again for that! before it left,
The dying sunset kindled through a cleft:
The hills, like giants at a hunting, lay,
Chin upon hand, to see the game at bay, —
"Now stab and end the creature — to the heft!"

XXXIII.

Not hear? when noise was everywhere! it tolled
Increasing like a bell. Names in my ears
Of all the lost adventurers my peers, —
How such a one was strong, and such was bold,
And such was fortunate, yet each of old
Lost, lost! one moment knelled the woe of years.

XXXIV.

There they stood, ranged along the hill-sides, met
    To view the last of me, a living frame
    For one more picture! in a sheet of flame
I saw them and I knew them all. And yet
Dauntless the slug-horn to my lips I set,
    And blew. *"Childe Roland to the Dark Tower came."*

RESPECTABILITY

I.

Dear, had the world in its caprice
    Deigned to proclaim "I know you both,
    "Have recognized your plighted troth,
"Am sponsor for you: live in peace!" —
How many precious months and years
    Of youth had passed, that speed so fast,
    Before we found it out at last,
The world, and what it fears?

II.

How much of priceless life were spent
    With men that every virtue decks,
    And women models of their sex,
Society's true ornament, —
Ere we dared wander, nights like this,
    Thro' wind and rain, and watch the Seine,
    And feel the Boulevard break again
To warmth and light and bliss?

III.

I know! the world proscribes not love;
    Allows my finger to caress
    Your lips' contour and downiness,
Provided it supply a glove.
    The world's good word! — the Institute!
    Guizot receives Montalembert!
    Eh? Down the court three lampions flare:
Put forward your best foot!

A LIGHT WOMAN

I.

So far as our story approaches the end,
    Which do you pity the most of us three? —
My friend, or the mistress of my friend
    With her wanton eyes, or me?

II.

My friend was already too good to lose,
    And seemed in the way of improvement yet,
When she crossed his path with her hunting-noose
    And over him drew her net.

III.

When I saw him tangled in her toils,
    A shame, said I, if she adds just him
To her nine-and-ninety other spoils,
    The hundredth for a whim!

IV.

And before my friend be wholly hers,
  How easy to prove to him, I said,
An eagle's the game her pride prefers,
  Though she snaps at a wren instead!

V.

So, I gave her eyes my own eyes to take,
  My hand sought hers as in earnest need,
And round she turned for my noble sake,
  And gave me herself indeed.

VI.

The eagle am I, with my fame in the world,
  The wren is he, with his maiden face.
— You look away and your lip is curled?
  Patience, a moment's space!

VII.

For see, my friend goes shaking and white;
  He eyes me as the basilisk:
I have turned, it appears, his day to night,
  Eclipsing his sun's disk.

VIII.

And I did it, he thinks, as a very thief:
  "Though I love her — that, he comprehends —
"One should master one's passions, (love, in chief)
  "And be loyal to one's friends!"

441

IX.

And she, — she lies in my hand as tame
    As a pear late basking over a wall;
Just a touch to try and off it came;
    'Tis mine, — can I let it fall?

X.

With no mind to eat it, that's the worst!
    Were it thrown in the road, would the case assist?
'Twas quenching a dozen blue-flies' thirst
    When I gave its stalk a twist.

XI.

And I, — what I seem to my friend, you see:
    What I soon shall seem to his love, you guess:
What I seem to myself, do you ask of me?
    No hero, I confess.

XII.

'Tis an awkward thing to play with souls,
    And matter enough to save one's own:
Yet think of my friend, and the burning coals
    He played with for bits of stone!

XIII.

One likes to show the truth for the truth;
    That the woman was light is very true:
But suppose she says, — Never mind that youth!
    What wrong have I done to you?

XIV.

Well, any how, here the story stays,
    So far at least as I understand;
And, Robert Browning, you writer of plays,
    Here's a subject made to your hand!

from THE STATUE AND THE BUST

[*The Duke was in love with a lady who gazed from her window but could not leave her room. As she grows old, she has a clay bust made, and facing it is the statue of himself which the Duke has had made.*]

*   *   *   *   *

So! While these wait the trump of doom,
How do their spirits pass, I wonder,
Nights and days in the narrow room?

Still, I suppose, they sit and ponder
What a gift life was, ages ago,
Six steps out of the chapel yonder.

Only they see not God, I know,
Nor all that chivalry of his,
The soldier-saints who, row on row,

Burn upward each to his point of bliss —
Since, the end of life being manifest,
He had burned his way thro' the world to this.

I hear you reproach, "But delay was best,
"For their end was a crime." — Oh, a crime will do
As well, I reply, to serve for a test,

As a virtue golden through and through,
Sufficient to vindicate itself
And prove its worth at a moment's view!

Must a game be played for the sake of pelf?
Where a button goes, 'twere an epigram
To offer the stamp of the very Guelph.

The true has no value beyond the sham:
As well the counter as coin, I submit,
When your table's a hat, and your prize a dram.

Stake your counter as boldly every whit,
Venture as warily, use the same skill,
Do your best, whether winning or losing it,

If you choose to play! — is my principle.
Let a man contend to the uttermost
For his life's set prize, be it what it will!

The counter our lovers staked was lost
As surely as if it were lawful coin:
And the sin I impute to each frustrate ghost

Is — the unlit lamp and the ungirt loin,
Though the end in sight was a vice, I say.
You of the virtue (we issue join)
How strive you? *De te, fabula!*

LOVE IN A LIFE

I.

Room after room,
I hunt the house through
We inhabit together.

Heart, fear nothing, for, heart, thou shalt find her —
Next time, herself! — not the trouble behind her
Left in the curtain, the couch's perfume!
As she brushed it, the cornice-wreath blossomed anew:
Yon looking-glass gleamed at the wave of her feather.

II.

Yet the day wears,
And door succeeds door;
I try the fresh fortune —
Range the wide house from the wing to the centre.
Still the same chance! she goes out as I enter.
Spend my whole day in the quest, — who cares?
But 'tis twilight, you see, — with such suites to explore,
Such closets to search, such alcoves to importune!

LIFE IN A LOVE

Escape me?
Never —
Beloved!
While I am I, and you are you,
So long as the world contains us both,
Me the loving and you the loth,
While the one eludes, must the other pursue.
My life is a fault at last, I fear:
It seems too much like a fate, indeed!
Though I do my best I shall scarce succeed.
But what if I fail of my purpose here?
It is but to keep the nerves at strain,
To dry one's eyes and laugh at a fall,
And, baffled, get up and begin again, —
So the chase takes up one's life, that's all.
While, look but once from your farthest bound
At me so deep in the dust and dark,

445

THE BROWNINGS

No sooner the old hope goes to ground
    Than a new one, straight to the self-same mark,
I shape me —
Ever
Removed!

HOW IT STRIKES A CONTEMPORARY

I only knew one poet in my life:
And this, or something like it, was his way.

    You saw go up and down Valladolid,
A man of mark, to know next time you saw.
His very serviceable suit of black
Was courtly once and conscientious still,
And many might have worn it, though none did:
The cloak, that somewhat shone and showed the threads,
Had purpose, and the ruff, significance.
He walked and tapped the pavement with his cane,
Scenting the world, looking it full in face,
An old dog, bald and blindish, at his heels.
They turned up, now, the alley by the church,
That leads nowhither; now, they breathed themselves
On the main promenade just at the wrong time:
You'd come upon his scrutinizing hat,
Making a peaked shade blacker than itself
Against the single window spared some house
Intact yet with its mouldered Moorish work, —
Or else surprise the ferrel of his stick
Trying the mortar's temper 'tween the chinks
Of some new shop a-building, French and fine.
He stood and watched the cobbler at his trade,
The man who slices lemons into drink,
The coffee-roaster's brazier, and the boys
That volunteer to help him turn its winch.
He glanced o'er books on stalls with half an eye,

And fly-leaf ballads on the vendor's string,
And broad-edge bold-print posters by the wall.
He took such cognizance of men and things,
If any beat a horse, you felt he saw;
If any cursed a woman, he took note;
Yet stared at nobody, — you stared at him,
And found, less to your pleasure than surprise,
He seemed to know you and expect as much.
So, next time that a neighbour's tongue was loosed,
It marked the shameful and notorious fact,
We had among us, not so much a spy,
As a recording chief-inquisitor,
The town's true master if the town but knew!
We merely kept a governor for form,
While this man walked about and took account
Of all thought, said and acted, then went home,
And wrote it fully to our Lord the King
Who has an itch to know things, he knows why,
And reads them in his bedroom of a night.
Oh, you might smile! there wanted not a touch,
A tang of . . . well, it was not wholly ease
As back into your mind the man's look came.
Stricken in years a little, — such a brow
His eyes had to live under! — clear as flint
On either side the formidable nose
Curved, cut and coloured like an eagle's claw.
Had he to do with A.'s surprising fate?
When altogether old B. disappeared
And young C. got his mistress, — was't our friend,
His letter to the King, that did it all?
What paid the bloodless man for so much pains?
Our Lord the King has favourites manifold,
And shifts his ministry some once a month;
Our city gets new governors at whiles, —
But never word or sign, that I could hear,
Notified to this man about the streets
The King's approval of those letters conned
The last thing duly at the dead of night.
Did the man love his office? Frowned our Lord,

Exhorting when none heard — "Beseech me not!
"Too far above my people, — beneath me!
"I set the watch, — how should the people know?
"Forget them, keep me all the more in mind!"
Was some such understanding 'twixt the two?

    I found no truth in one report at least —
That if you tracked him to his home, down lanes
Beyond the Jewry, and as clean to pace,
You found he ate his supper in a room
Blazing with lights, four Titians on the wall,
And twenty naked girls to change his plate!
Poor man, he lived another kind of life
In that new stuccoed third house by the bridge,
Fresh-painted, rather smart than otherwise!
The whole street might o'erlook him as he sat,
Leg crossing leg, one foot on the dog's back,
Playing a decent cribbage with his maid
(Jacynth, you're sure her name was) o'er the cheese
And fruit, three red halves of starved winter-pears,
Or treat of radishes in April. Nine,
Ten, struck the church clock, straight to bed went he.

    My father, like the man of sense he was,
Would point him out to me a dozen times;
"'St — 'St," he'd whisper, "the Corregidor!"
I had been used to think that personage
Was one with lacquered breeches, lustrous belt,
And feathers like a forest in his hat,
Who blew a trumpet and proclaimed the news,
Announced the bull-fights, gave each church its turn,
And memorized the miracle in vogue!
He had a great observance from us boys;
We were in error; that was not the man.

    I'd like now, yet had haply been afraid,
To have just looked, when this man came to die,
And seen who lined the clean gay garret-sides
And stood about the neat low truckle-bed,

With the heavenly manner of relieving guard.
Here had been, mark, the general-in-chief,
Thro' a whole campaign of the world's life and death,
Doing the King's work all the dim day long,
In his old coat and up to knees in mud,
Smoked like a herring, dining on a crust, —
And, now the day was won, relieved at once!
No further show or need for that old coat,
You are sure, for one thing! Bless us, all the while
How sprucely we are dressed out, you and I!
A second, and the angels alter that.
Well, I could never write a verse, — could you?
Let's to the Prado and make the most of time.

THE LAST RIDE TOGETHER

I.

I said — Then, dearest, since 'tis so,
Since now at length my fate I know,
Since nothing all my love avails,
Since all, my life seemed meant for, fails,
    Since this was written and needs must be —
My whole heart rises up to bless
Your name in pride and thankfulness!
Take back the hope you gave, — I claim
Only a memory of the same,
— And this beside, if you will not blame,
    Your leave for one more last ride with me.

II.

My mistress bent that brow of hers;
Those deep dark eyes where pride demurs
When pity would be softening through,
Fixed me a breathing-while or two

With life or death in the balance: right!
The blood replenished me again;
My last thought was at least not vain:
I and my mistress, side by side
Shall be together, breathe and ride,
So, one day more am I deified.
  Who knows but the world may end to-night?

III.

Hush! if you saw some western cloud
All billowy-bosomed, over-bowed
By many benedictions — sun's
And moon's and evening-star's at once —
  And so, you, looking and loving best,
Conscious grew, your passion drew
Cloud, sunset, moonrise, star-shine too,
Down on you, near and yet more near,
Till flesh must fade for heaven was here! —
Thus leant she and lingered — joy and fear!
  Thus lay she a moment on my breast.

IV.

Then we began to ride. My soul
Smoothed itself out, a long-cramped scroll
Freshening and fluttering in the wind.
Past hopes already lay behind.
  What need to strive with a life awry?
Had I said that, had I done this,
So might I gain, so might I miss.
Might she have loved me? just as well
She might have hated, who can tell!
Where had I been now if the worst befell?
  And here we are riding, she and I.

V.

Fail I alone, in words and deeds?
Why, all men strive and who succeeds?
We rode; it seemed my spirit flew,
Saw other regions, cities new,
    As the world rushed by on either side.
I thought, — All labour, yet no less
Bear up beneath their unsuccess.
Look at the end of work, contrast
The petty done, the undone vast,
This present of theirs with the hopeful past!
    I hoped she would love me; here we ride.

VI.

What hand and brain went ever paired?
What heart alike conceived and dared?
What act proved all its thought had been?
What will but felt the fleshly screen?
    We ride and I see her bosom heave.
There's many a crown for who can reach.
Ten lines, a statesman's life in each!
The flag stuck on a heap of bones,
A soldier's doing! what atones?
They scratch his name on the Abbey-stones.
    My riding is better, by their leave.

VII.

What does it all mean, poet? Well,
Your brains beat into rhythm, you tell
What we felt only; you expressed
You hold things beautiful the best,
    And pace them in rhyme so, side by side.
'Tis something, nay 'tis much: but then,
Have you yourself what's best for men?
Are you — poor, sick, old ere your time —

Nearer one whit your own sublime
Than we who never have turned a rhyme?
Sing, riding's a joy! For me, I ride.

VIII.

And you, great sculptor — so, you gave
A score of years to Art, her slave,
And that's your Venus, whence we turn
To yonder girl that fords the burn!
You acquiesce, and shall I repine?
What, man of music, you grown grey
With notes and nothing else to say,
Is this your sole praise from a friend,
"Greatly his opera's strains intend,
"But in music we know how fashions end!"
I gave my youth; but we ride, in fine.

IX.

Who knows what's fit for us? Had fate
Proposed bliss here should sublimate
My being — had I signed the bond —
Still one must lead some life beyond,
Have a bliss to die with, dim-descried.
This foot once planted on the goal,
This glory-garland round my soul,
Could I descry such? Try and test!
I sink back shuddering from the quest.
Earth being so good, would heaven seem best?
Now, heaven and she are beyond this ride.

X.

And yet — she has not spoke so long!
What if heaven be that, fair and strong
At life's best, with our eyes upturned
Whither life's flower is first discerned,
We, fixed so, ever should so abide?

What if we still ride on, we two
With life for ever old yet new,
Changed not in kind but in degree,
The instant made eternity, —
And heaven just prove that I and she
  Ride, ride together, for ever ride?

THE PATRIOT

AN OLD STORY

I.

It was roses, roses, all the way,
  With myrtle mixed in my path like mad:
The house-roofs seemed to heave and sway,
  The church-spires flamed, such flags they had,
A year ago on this very day.

II.

The air broke into a mist with bells,
  The old walls rocked with the crowd and cries.
Had I said, "Good folk, mere noise repels —
  "But give me your sun from yonder skies!"
They had answered, "And afterward, what else?"

III.

Alack, it was I who leaped at the sun
  To give it my loving friends to keep!
Nought man could do, have I left undone:
  And you see my harvest, what I reap
This very day, now a year is run.

IV.

There's nobody on the house-tops now —
    Just a palsied few at the windows set;
For the best of the sight is, all allow,
    At the Shambles' Gate — or, better yet,
By the very scaffold's foot, I trow.

V.

I go in the rain, and, more than needs,
    A rope cuts both my wrists behind;
And I think, by the feel, my forehead bleeds,
    For they fling, whoever has a mind,
Stones at me for my year's misdeeds.

VI.

Thus I entered, and thus I go!
    In triumphs, people have dropped down dead.
"Paid by the world, what dost thou owe
    "Me?" — God might question; now instead,
'Tis God shall repay: I am safer so.

MASTER HUGUES OF SAXE-GOTHA

I.

Hist, but a word, fair and soft!
    Forth and be judged, Master Hugues!
Answer the question I've put you so oft:
    What do you mean by your mountainous fugues?
See, we're alone in the loft, —

II.

I, the poor organist here,
  Hugues, the composer of note,
Dead though, and done with, this many a year:
  Let's have a colloquy, something to quote,
Make the world prick up its ear!

III.

See, the church empties apace:
  Fast they extinguish the lights.
Hallo there, sacristan! Five minutes' grace!
  Here's a crank pedal wants setting to rights,
Baulks one of holding the base.

IV.

See, our huge house of the sounds,
  Hushing its hundreds at once,
Bids the last loiterer back to his bounds!
  — O you may challenge them, not a response
Get the church-saints on their rounds!

V.

(Saints go their rounds, who shall doubt?
  — March, with the moon to admire,
Up nave, down chancel, turn transept about,
  Supervise all betwixt pavement and spire,
Put rats and mice to the rout —

VI.

Aloys and Jurien and Just —
  Order things back to their place,
Have a sharp eye lest the candlesticks rust,
  Rub the church-plate, darn the sacrament-lace,
Clear the desk-velvet of dust.)

VII.

Here's your book, younger folks shelve!
   Played I not off-hand and runningly,
Just now, your masterpiece, hard number twelve?
   Here's what should strike, could one handle it cunningly:
Help the axe, give it a helve!

VIII.

Page after page as I played,
   Every bar's rest, where one wipes
Sweat from one's brow, I looked up and surveyed,
   O'er my three claviers, yon forest of pipes
Whence you still peeped in the shade.

IX.

Sure you were wishful to speak?
   You, with brow ruled like a score,
Yes, and eyes buried in pits on each cheek,
   Like two great breves, as they wrote them of yore,
Each side that bar, your straight beak!

X.

Sure you said — "Good, the mere notes!
   "Still, couldst thou take my intent,
"Know what procured me our Company's votes —
   "A master were lauded and sciolists shent,
"Parted the sheep from the goats!"

XI.

Well then, speak up, never flinch!
   Quick, ere my candle's a snuff
— Burnt, do you see? to its uttermost inch —
   I believe in you, but that's not enough:
Give my conviction a clinch!

XII.

First you deliver your phrase
  — Nothing propound, that I see,
Fit in itself for much blame or much praise —
  Answered no less, where no answer needs be:
Off start the Two on their ways.

XIII.

Straight must a Third interpose,
  Volunteer needlessly help;
In strikes a Fourth, a Fifth thrusts in his nose,
  So the cry's open, the kennel's a-yelp,
Argument's hot to the close.

XIV.

One dissertates, he is candid;
  Two must discept, — has distinguished;
Three helps the couple, if ever yet man did;
  Four protests; Five makes a dart at the thing wished:
Back to One, goes the case bandied.

XV.

One says his say with a difference;
  More of expounding, explaining!
All now is wrangle, abuse, and vociferance;
  Now there's a truce, all's subdued, self-restraining:
Five, though, stands out all the stiffer hence.

XVI.

One is incisive, corrosive;
  Two retorts, nettled, curt, crepitant;
Three makes rejoinder, expansive, explosive;
  Four overbears them all, strident and strepitant:
Five . . . O Danaides, O Sieve!

XVII.

Now, they ply axes and crowbars;
  Now, they prick pins at a tissue
Fine as a skein of the casuist Escobar's
  Worked on the bone of a lie. To what issue?
Where is our gain at the Two-bars?

XVIII.

Est fuga, volvitur rota.
  On we drift: where looms the dim port?
One, Two, Three, Four, Five, contribute their quota;
  Something is gained, if one caught but the import —
Show it us, Hugues of Saxe-Gotha!

XIX.

What with affirming, denying,
  Holding, risposting, subjoining,
All's like . . . it's like . . . for an instance I'm trying . . .
  There! See our roof, its gilt moulding and groining
Under those spider-webs lying!

XX.

So your fugue broadens and thickens,
  Greatens and deepens and lengthens,
Till we exclaim — "But where's music, the dickens?
  "Blot ye the gold, while your spider-web strengthens
" — Blacked to the stoutest of tickens?"

XXI.

I for man's effort am zealous:
  Prove me such censure unfounded!
Seems it surprising a lover grows jealous —
  Hopes 'twas for something, his organ-pipes sounded,
Tiring three boys at the bellows?

458

XXII.

Is it your moral of Life?
　Such a web, simple and subtle,
Weave we on earth here in impotent strife,
　Backward and forward each throwing his shuttle,
　Death ending all with a knife?

XXIII.

Over our heads truth and nature —
　Still our life's zigzags and dodges,
Ins and outs, weaving a new legislature —
　God's gold just shining its last where that lodges,
Palled beneath man's usurpature.

XXIV.

So we o'ershroud stars and roses,
　Cherub and trophy and garland;
Nothings grow something which quietly closes
　Heaven's earnest eye: not a glimpse of the far land
Gets through our comments and glozes.

XXV.

Ah but traditions, inventions,
　(Say we and make up a visage)
So many men with such various intentions,
　Down the past ages, must know more than this age!
Leave we the web its dimensions!

XXVI.

Who thinks Hugues wrote for the deaf,
　Proved a mere mountain in labour?
Better submit; try again; what's the clef?
　'Faith, 'tis no trifle for pipe and for tabor —
Four flats, the minor in F.

XXVII.

Friend, your fugue taxes the finger:
  Learning it once, who would lose it?
Yet all the while a misgiving will linger,
  Truth's golden o'er us although we refuse it —
Nature, thro' cobwebs we string her.

XXVIII.

Hugues! I advise *meâ pœnâ*
  (Counterpoint glares like a Gorgon)
Bid One, Two, Three, Four, Five, clear the arena!
  Say the word, straight I unstop the full-organ,
Blare out the *mode Palestrina.*

XXIX.

While in the roof, if I'm right there,
  . . . Lo you, the wick in the socket!
Hallo, you sacristan, show us a light there!
  Down it dips, gone like a rocket.
What, you want, do you, to come unawares,
Sweeping the church up for first morning-prayers,
And find a poor devil has ended his cares
At the foot of your rotten-runged rat-riddled stairs?
  Do I carry the moon in my pocket?

BISHOP BLOUGRAM'S APOLOGY

No more wine? then we'll push back chairs and talk.
A final glass for me, though: cool, i' faith!
We ought to have our Abbey back, you see.
It's different, preaching in basilicas,
And doing duty in some masterpiece

Like this of brother Pugin's, bless his heart!
I doubt if they're half baked, those chalk rosettes,
Ciphers and stucco-twiddlings everywhere;
It's just like breathing in a lime-kiln: eh?
These hot long ceremonies of our church
Cost us a little — oh, they pay the price,
You take me — amply pay it! Now, we'll talk.

So, you despise me, Mr. Gigadibs.
No deprecation, — nay, I beg you, sir!
Beside 'tis our engagement: don't you know,
I promised, if you'd watch a dinner out,
We'd see truth dawn together? — truth that peeps
Over the glasses' edge when dinner's done,
And body gets its sop and holds its noise
And leaves soul free a little. Now's the time:
Truth's break of day! You do despise me then.
And if I say, "despise me," — never fear!
I know you do not in a certain sense —
Not in my arm-chair, for example: here,
I well imagine you respect my place
(*Status, entourage,* worldly circumstance)
Quite to its value — very much indeed:
— Are up to the protesting eyes of you
In pride at being seated here for once —
You'll turn it to such capital account!
When somebody, through years and years to come,
Hints of the bishop, — names me — that's enough:
"Blougram? I knew him" — (into it you slide)
"Dined with him once, a Corpus Christi Day,
"All alone, we two; he's a clever man:
"And after dinner, — why, the wine you know, —
"Oh, there was wine, and good! — what with the wine . . .
" 'Faith, we began upon all sorts of talk!
"He's no bad fellow, Blougram; he had seen
"Something of mine he relished, some review:
"He's quite above their humbug in his heart,
"Half-said as much, indeed — the thing's his trade.
"I warrant, Blougram's sceptical at times:

"How otherwise? I liked him, I confess!"
Che che, my dear sir, as we say at Rome,
Don't you protest now! It's fair give and take;
You have had your turn and spoken your home-truths:
The hand's mine now, and here you follow suit.

Thus much conceded, still the first fact stays —
You do despise me; your ideal of life
Is not the bishop's: you would not be I.
You would like better to be Goethe, now,
Or Buonaparte, or, bless me, lower still,
Count D'Orsay, — so you did what you preferred,
Spoke as you thought, and, as you cannot help,
Believed or disbelieved, no matter what,
So long as on that point, whate'er it was,
You loosed your mind, were whole and sole yourself.
— That, my ideal never can include,
Upon that element of truth and worth
Never be based! for say they make me Pope —
(They can't — suppose it for our argument!)
Why, there I'm at my tether's end, I've reached
My height, and not a height which pleases you:
An unbelieving Pope won't do, you say.
It's like those eerie stories nurses tell,
Of how some actor on a stage played Death,
With pasteboard crown, sham orb and tinselled dart,
And called himself the monarch of the world;
Then, going in the tire-room afterward,
Because the play was done, to shift himself,
God touched upon the sleeve familiarly,
The moment he had shut the closet door,
By Death himself. Thus God might touch a Pope
At unawares, ask what his baubles mean,
And whose part he presumed to play just now.
Best be yourself, imperial, plain and true!

So, drawing comfortable breath again,
You weigh and find, whatever more or less
I boast of my ideal realized

462

Is nothing in the balance when opposed
To your ideal, your grand simple life,
Of which you will not realize one jot.
I am much, you are nothing; you would be all,
I would be merely much: you beat me there.

No, friend, you do not beat me: hearken why!
The common problem, yours, mine, every one's,
Is — not to fancy what were fair in life
Provided it could be, — but, finding first
What may be, then find how to make it fair
Up to our means: a very different thing!
No abstract intellectual plan of life
Quite irrespective of life's plainest laws,
But one, a man, who is man and nothing more,
May lead within a world which (by your leave)
Is Rome or London, not Fool's-paradise.
Embellish Rome, idealize away,
Make paradise of London if you can,
You're welcome, nay, you're wise.

                              A simile!
We mortals cross the ocean of this world
Each in his average cabin of a life;
The best's not big, the worst yields elbow-room.
Now for our six months' voyage — how prepare?
You come on shipboard with a landsman's list
Of things he calls convenient: so they are!
An India screen is pretty furniture,
A piano-forte is a fine resource,
All Balzac's novels occupy one shelf,
The new edition fifty volumes long;
And little Greek books, with the funny type
They get up well at Leipsic, fill the next:
Go on! slabbed marble, what a bath it makes!
And Parma's pride, the Jerome, let us add!
'Twere pleasant could Correggio's fleeting glow
Hang full in face of one where'er one roams,
Since he more than the others brings with him

Italy's self, — the marvellous Modenese! —
Yet was not on your list before, perhaps.
— Alas, friend, here's the agent . . . is't the name?
The captain, or whoever's master here —
You see him screw his face up; what's his cry
Ere you set foot on shipboard? "Six feet square!"
If you won't understand what six feet mean,
Compute and purchase stores accordingly —
And if, in pique because he overhauls
Your Jerome, piano, bath, you come on board
Bare — why, you cut a figure at the first
While sympathetic landsmen see you off;
Not afterward, when long ere half seas over,
You peep up from your utterly naked boards
Into some snug and well-appointed berth,
Like mine for instance (try the cooler jug —
Put back the other, but don't jog the ice!)
And mortified you mutter "Well and good;
"He sits enjoying his sea-furniture;
" 'Tis stout and proper, and there's store of it:
"Though I've the better notion, all agree,
"Of fitting rooms up. Hang the carpenter,
"Neat ship-shape fixings and contrivances —
"I would have brought my Jerome, frame and all!"
And meantime you bring nothing: never mind —
You've proved your artist-nature: what you don't
You might bring, so despise me, as I say.

Now come, let's backward to the starting-place.
See my way: we're two college friends, suppose.
Prepare together for our voyage, then;
Each note and check the other in his work, —
Here's mine, a bishop's outfit; criticize!
What's wrong? why won't you be a bishop too?

Why first, you don't believe, you don't and can't,
(Not statedly, that is, and fixedly
And absolutely and exclusively)
In any revelation called divine.

No dogmas nail your faith; and what remains
But say so, like the honest man you are?
First, therefore, overhaul theology!
Nay, I too, not a fool, you please to think,
Must find believing every whit as hard:
And if I do not frankly say as much,
The ugly consequence is clear enough.

Now wait, my friend: well, I do not believe —
If you'll accept no faith that is not fixed,
Absolute and exclusive, as you say.
You're wrong — I mean to prove it in due time.
Meanwhile, I know where difficulties lie
I could not, cannot solve, nor ever shall,
So give up hope accordingly to solve —
(To you, and over the wine). Our dogmas then
With both of us, though in unlike degree,
Missing full credence — overboard with them!
I mean to meet you on your own premise:
Good, there go mine in company with yours!

And now what are we? unbelievers both,
Calm and complete, determinately fixed
To-day, to-morrow and for ever, pray?
You'll guarantee me that? Not so, I think!
In no wise! all we've gained is, that belief,
As unbelief before, shakes us by fits,
Confounds us like its predecessor. Where's
The gain? how can we guard our unbelief,
Make it bear fruit to us? — the problem here.
Just when we are safest, there's a sunset-touch,
A fancy from a flower-bell, some one's death,
A chorus-ending from Euripides, —
And that's enough for fifty hopes and fears
As old and new at once as nature's self,
To rap and knock and enter in our soul,
Take hands and dance there, a fantastic ring,
Round the ancient idol, on his base again, —
The grand Perhaps! We look on helplessly.

There the old misgivings, crooked questions are —
This good God, — what he could do, if he would,
Would, if he could — then must have done long since:
If so, when, where and how? some way must be, —
Once feel about, and soon or late you hit
Some sense, in which it might be, after all.
Why not, "The Way, the Truth, the Life?"

                      — That way
Over the mountain, which who stands upon
Is apt to doubt if it be meant for a road;
While, if he views it from the waste itself,
Up goes the line there, plain from base to brow,
Not vague, mistakeable! what's a break or two
Seen from the unbroken desert either side?
And then (to bring in fresh philosophy)
What if the breaks themselves should prove at last
The most consummate of contrivances
To train a man's eye, teach him what is faith?
And so we stumble at truth's very test!
All we have gained then by our unbelief
Is a life of doubt diversified by faith,
For one of faith diversified by doubt:
We called the chess-board white, — we call it black.

    "Well," you rejoin, "the end's no worse, at least
"We've reason for both colours on the board:
"Why not confess then, where I drop the faith
"And you the doubt, that I'm as right as you?"

    Because, friend, in the next place, this being so,
And both things even, — faith and unbelief
Left to a man's choice, — we'll proceed a step,
Returning to our image, which I like.

    A man's choice, yes — but a cabin-passenger's —
The man made for the special life o' the world —
Do you forget him? I remember though!
Consult our ship's conditions and you find

One and but one choice suitable to all;
The choice, that you unluckily prefer,
Turning things topsy-turvy — they or it
Going to the ground. Belief or unbelief
Bears upon life, determines its whole course,
Begins at its beginning. See the world
Such as it is, — you made it not, nor I;
I mean to take it as it is, — and you,
Not so you'll take it, — though you get nought else.
I know the special kind of life I like,
What suits the most my idiosyncrasy,
Brings out the best of me and bears me fruit
In power, peace, pleasantness and length of days.
I find that positive belief does this
For me, and unbelief, no whit of this.
— For you, it does, however? — that, we'll try!
'Tis clear, I cannot lead my life, at least,
Induce the world to let me peaceably,
Without declaring at the outset, "Friends,
"I absolutely and peremptorily
"Believe!" — I say, faith is my waking life:
One sleeps, indeed, and dreams at intervals,
We know, but waking's the main point with us,
And my provision's for life's waking part.
Accordingly, I use heart, head and hand
All day, I build, scheme, study, and make friends;
And when night overtakes me, down I lie,
Sleep, dream a little, and get done with it,
The sooner the better, to begin afresh.
What's midnight doubt before the dayspring's faith?
You, the philosopher, that disbelieve,
That recognize the night, give dreams their weight —
To be consistent you should keep your bed,
Abstain from healthy acts that prove you man,
For fear you drowse perhaps at unawares!
And certainly at night you'll sleep and dream,
Live through the day and bustle as you please.
And so you live to sleep as I to wake,
To unbelieve as I to still believe?

Well, and the common sense o' the world calls you
Bed-ridden, — and its good things come to me.
Its estimation, which is half the fight,
That's the first-cabin comfort I secure:
The next . . . but you perceive with half an eye!
Come, come, it's best believing, if we may;
You can't but own that!

Next, concede again,
If once we choose belief, on all accounts
We can't be too decisive in our faith,
Conclusive and exclusive in its terms,
To suit the world which gives us the good things.
In every man's career are certain points
Whereon he dares not be indifferent;
The world detects him clearly, if he dare,
As baffled at the game, and losing life.
He may care little or he may care much
For riches, honour, pleasure, work, repose,
Since various theories of life and life's
Success are extant which might easily
Comport with either estimate of these;
And whoso chooses wealth or poverty,
Labour or quiet, is not judged a fool
Because his fellow would choose otherwise:
We let him choose upon his own account
So long as he's consistent with his choice.
But certain points, left wholly to himself,
When once a man has arbitrated on,
We say he must succeed there or go hang.
Thus, he should wed the woman he loves most
Or needs most, whatsoe'er the love or need —
For he can't wed twice. Then, he must avouch,
Or follow, at the least, sufficiently,
The form of faith his conscience holds the best,
Whate'er the process of conviction was:
For nothing can compensate his mistake
On such a point, the man himself being judge:
He cannot wed twice, nor twice lose his soul.

Well now, there's one great form of Christian faith
I happened to be born in — which to teach
Was given me as I grew up, on all hands,
As best and readiest means of living by;
The same on examination being proved
The most pronounced moreover, fixed, precise
And absolute form of faith in the whole world —
Accordingly, most potent of all forms
For working on the world. Observe, my friend!
Such as you know me, I am free to say,
In these hard latter days which hamper one,
Myself — by no immoderate exercise
Of intellect and learning, but the tact
To let external forces work for me,
— Bid the street's stones be bread and they are bread;
Bid Peter's creed, or rather, Hildebrand's,
Exalt me o'er my fellows in the world
And make my life an ease and joy and pride;
It does so, — which for me's a great point gained,
Who have a soul and body that exact
A comfortable care in many ways.
There's power in me and will to dominate
Which I must exercise, they hurt me else:
In many ways I need mankind's respect,
Obedience, and the love that's born of fear:
While at the same time, there's a taste I have,
A toy of soul, a titillating thing,
Refuses to digest these dainties crude.
The naked life is gross till clothed upon:
I must take what men offer, with a grace
As though I would not, could I help it, take!
An uniform I wear though over-rich —
Something imposed on me, no choice of mine;
No fancy-dress worn for pure fancy's sake
And despicable therefore! now folk kneel
And kiss my hand — of course the Church's hand.
Thus I am made, thus life is best for me,
And thus that it should be I have procured;
And thus it could not be another way,
I venture to imagine.

THE BROWNINGS

You'll reply,
So far my choice, no doubt, is a success;
But were I made of better elements,
With nobler instincts, purer tastes, like you,
I hardly would account the thing success
Though it did all for me I say.

But, friend,
We speak of what is; not of what might be,
And how 'twere better if 'twere otherwise.
I am the man you see here plain enough:
Grant I'm a beast, why, beasts must lead beasts' lives!
Suppose I own at once to tail and claws;
The tailless man exceeds me: but being tailed
I'll lash out lion fashion, and leave apes
To dock their stump and dress their haunches up.
My business is not to remake myself,
But make the absolute best of what God made.
Or — our first simile — though you prove me doomed
To a viler berth still, to the steerage-hole,
The sheep-pen or the pig-stye, I should strive
To make what use of each were possible;
And as this cabin gets upholstery,
That hutch should rustle with sufficient straw.

But, friend, I don't acknowledge quite so fast
I fail of all your manhood's lofty tastes
Enumerated so complacently,
On the mere ground that you forsooth can find
In this particular life I choose to lead
No fit provision for them. Can you not?
Say you, my fault is I address myself
To grosser estimators than should judge?
And that's no way of holding up the soul,
Which, nobler, needs men's praise perhaps, yet knows
One wise man's verdict outweighs all the fools' —
Would like the two, but, forced to choose, takes that.
I pine among my million imbeciles
(You think) aware some dozen men of sense

470

Eye me and know me, whether I believe
In the last winking Virgin, as I vow,
And am a fool, or disbelieve in her
And am a knave, — approve in neither case,
Withhold their voices though I look their way:
Like Verdi when, at his worst opera's end
(The thing they gave at Florence, — what's its name?)
While the mad houseful's plaudits near out-bang
His orchestra of salt-box, tongs and bones,
He looks through all the roaring and the wreaths
Where sits Rossini patient in his stall.

Nay, friend, I meet you with an answer here —
That even your prime men who appraise their kind
Are men still, catch a wheel within a wheel,
See more in a truth than the truth's simple self,
Confuse themselves. You see lads walk the street
Sixty the minute; what's to note in that?
You see one lad o'erstride a chimney-stack;
Him you must watch — he's sure to fall, yet stands!
Our interest's on the dangerous edge of things.
The honest thief, the tender murderer,
The superstitious atheist, demirep
That loves and saves her soul in new French books —
We watch while these in equilibrium keep
The giddy line midway: one step aside,
They're classed and done with. I, then, keep the line
Before your sages, — just the men to shrink
From the gross weights, coarse scales and labels broad
You offer their refinement. Fool or knave?
Why needs a bishop be a fool or knave
When there's a thousand diamond weights between?
So, I enlist them. Your picked twelve, you'll find,
Profess themselves indignant, scandalized
At thus being held unable to explain
How a superior man who disbelieves
May not believe as well: that's Schelling's way!
It's through my coming in the tail of time,
Nicking the minute with a happy tact.

471

Had I been born three hundred years ago
They'd say, "What's strange? Blougram of course believes;"
And, seventy years since, "disbelieves of course."
But now, "He may believe; and yet, and yet
"How can he?" All eyes turn with interest.
Whereas, step off the line on either side —
You, for example, clever to a fault,
The rough and ready man who write apace,
Read somewhat seldomer, think perhaps even less —
You disbelieve! Who wonders and who cares?
Lord So-and-so — his coat bedropped with wax,
All Peter's chains about his waist, his back
Brave with the needlework of Noodledom —
Believes! Again, who wonders and who cares?
But I, the man of sense and learning too,
The able to think yet act, the this, the that,
I, to believe at this late time of day!
Enough; you see, I need not fear contempt.

— Except it's yours! Admire me as these may,
You don't. But whom at least do you admire?
Present your own perfection, your ideal,
Your pattern man for a minute — oh, make haste,
Is it Napoleon you would have us grow?
Concede the means; allow his head and hand,
(A large concession, clever as you are)
Good! In our common primal element
Of unbelief (we can't believe, you know —
We're still at that admission, recollect!)
Where do you find — apart from, towering o'er
The secondary temporary aims
Which satisfy the gross taste you despise —
Where do you find his star? — his crazy trust
God knows through what or in what? it's alive
And shines and leads him, and that's all we want.
Have we aught in our sober night shall point
Such ends as his were, and direct the means
Of working out our purpose straight as his,
Nor bring a moment's trouble on success

With after-care to justify the same?
— Be a Napoleon, and yet disbelieve —
Why, the man's mad, friend, take his light away!
What's the vague good o' the world, for which you dare
With comfort to yourself blow millions up?
We neither of us see it! we do see
The blown-up millions — spatter of their brains
And writhing of their bowels and so forth,
In that bewildering entanglement
Of horrible eventualities
Past calculation to the end of time!
Can I mistake for some clear word of God
(Which were my ample warrant for it all)
His puff of hazy instinct, idle talk,
"The State, that's I," quack-nonsense about crowns,
And (when one beats the man to his last hold)
A vague idea of setting things to rights,
Policing people efficaciously,
More to their profit, most of all to his own;
The whole to end that dismallest of ends
By an Austrian marriage, cant to us the Church,
And resurrection of the old *régime*?
Would I, who hope to live a dozen years,
Fight Austerlitz for reasons such and such?
No: for, concede me but the merest chance
Doubt may be wrong — there's judgment, life to come!
With just that chance, I dare not. Doubt proves right?
This present life is all? — you offer me
Its dozen noisy years, without a chance
That wedding an archduchess, wearing lace,
And getting called by divers new-coined names,
Will drive off ugly thoughts and let me dine,
Sleep, read and chat in quiet as I like!
Therefore I will not.

                Take another case;
Fit up the cabin yet another way.
What say you to the poets? shall we write
Hamlet, Othello — make the world our own,

Without a risk to run of either sort?
I can't! — to put the strongest reason first.
"But try," you urge, "the trying shall suffice;
"The aim, if reached or not, makes great the life:
"Try to be Shakespeare, leave the rest to fate!"
Spare my self-knowledge — there's no fooling me!
If I prefer remaining my poor self,
I say so not in self-dispraise but praise.
If I'm a Shakespeare, let the well alone;
Why should I try to be what now I am?
If I'm no Shakespeare, as too probable, —
His power and consciousness and self-delight
And all we want in common, shall I find —
Trying for ever? while on points of taste
Wherewith, to speak it humbly, he and I
Are dowered alike — I'll ask you, I or he,
Which in our two lives realizes most?
Much, he imagined — somewhat, I possess.
He had the imagination; stick to that!
Let him say, "In the face of my soul's works
"Your world is worthless and I touch it not
"Lest I should wrong them" — I'll withdraw my plea.
But does he say so? look upon his life!
Himself, who only can, gives judgment there.
He leaves his towers and gorgeous palaces
To build the trimmest house in Stratford town;
Saves money, spends it, owns the worth of things,
Giulio Romano's pictures, Dowland's lute;
Enjoys a show, respects the puppets, too,
And none more, had he seen its entry once,
Than "Pandulph, of fair Milan cardinal."
Why then should I who play that personage,
The very Pandulph Shakespeare's fancy made,
Be told that had the poet chanced to start
From where I stand now (some degree like mine
Being just the goal he ran his race to reach)
He would have run the whole race back, forsooth,
And left being Pandulph, to begin write plays?
Ah, the earth's best can be but the earth's best!

Did Shakespeare live, he could but sit at home
And get himself in dreams the Vatican,
Greek busts, Venetian paintings, Roman walls,
And English books, none equal to his own,
Which I read, bound in gold (he never did).
— Terni's fall, Naples' bay and Gothard's top —
Eh, friend? I could not fancy one of these;
But, as I pour this claret, there they are:
I've gained them — crossed St. Gothard last July
With ten mules to the carriage and a bed
Slung inside; is my hap the worse for that?
We want the same things, Shakespeare and myself,
And what I want, I have: he, gifted more,
Could fancy he too had them when he liked,
But not so thoroughly that, if fate allowed,
He would not have them also in my sense.
We play one game; I send the ball aloft
No less adroitly that of fifty strokes
Scarce five go o'er the wall so wide and high
Which sends them back to me: I wish and get.
He struck balls higher and with better skill,
But at a poor fence level with his head,
And hit — his Stratford house, a coat of arms,
Successful dealings in his grain and wool, —
While I receive heaven's incense in my nose
And style myself the cousin of Queen Bess.
Ask him, if this life's all, who wins the game?

   Believe — and our whole argument breaks up.
Enthusiasm's the best thing, I repeat;
Only, we can't command it; fire and life
Are all, dead matter's nothing, we agree:
And be it a mad dream or God's very breath,
The fact's the same, — belief's fire, once in us,
Makes of all else mere stuff to show itself:
We penetrate our life with such a glow
As fire lends wood and iron — this turns steel,
That burns to ash — all's one, fire proves its power
For good or ill, since men call flare success.

But paint a fire, it will not therefore burn.
Light one in me, I'll find it food enough!
Why, to be Luther — that's a life to lead,
Incomparably better than my own.
He comes, reclaims God's earth for God, he says,
Sets up God's rule again by simple means,
Re-opens a shut book, and all is done.
He flared out in the flaring of mankind;
Such Luther's luck was: how shall such be mine?
If he succeeded, nothing's left to do:
And if he did not altogether — well,
Strauss is the next advance. All Strauss should be
I might be also. But to what result?
He looks upon no future: Luther did.
What can I gain on the denying side?
Ice makes no conflagration. State the facts,
Read the text right, emancipate the world—
The emancipated world enjoys itself
With scarce a thank-you: Blougram told it first
It could not owe a farthing, — not to him
More than Saint Paul! 'twould press its pay, you think?
Then add there's still that plaguy hundredth chance
Strauss may be wrong. And so a risk is run —
For what gain? not for Luther's, who secured
A real heaven in his heart throughout his life,
Supposing death a little altered things.

  "Ay, but since really you lack faith," you cry,
"You run the same risk really on all sides,
"In cool indifference as bold unbelief.
"As well be Strauss as swing 'twixt Paul and him.
"It's not worth having, such imperfect faith,
"No more available to do faith's work
"Than unbelief like mine. Whole faith, or none!"

  Softly, my friend! I must dispute that point.
Once own the use of faith, I'll find you faith.
We're back on Christian ground. You call for faith:
I show you doubt, to prove that faith exists.

The more of doubt, the stronger faith, I say,
If faith o'ercomes doubt. How I know it does?
By life and man's free will, God gave for that!
To mould life as we choose it, shows our choice:
That's our one act, the previous work's his own.
You criticize the soul? it reared this tree —
This broad life and whatever fruit it bears!
What matter though I doubt at every pore,
Head-doubts, heart-doubts, doubts at my fingers' ends,
Doubts in the trivial work of every day,
Doubts at the very bases of my soul
In the grand moments when she probes her self —
If finally I have a life to show,
The thing I did, brought out in evidence
Against the thing done to me underground
By hell and all its brood, for aught I know?
I say, whence sprang this? shows it faith or doubt?
All's doubt in me; where's break of faith in this?
It is the idea, the feeling and the love,
God means mankind should strive for and show forth
Whatever be the process to that end, —
And not historic knowledge, logic sound,
And metaphysical acumen, sure!
"What think ye of Christ," friend? when all's done and said,
Like you this Christianity or not?
It may be false, but will you wish it true?
Has it your vote to be so if it can?
Trust you an instinct silenced long ago
That will break silence and enjoin you love
What mortified philosophy is hoarse.
And all in vain, with bidding you despise?
If you desire faith — then you've faith enough:
What else seeks God — nay, what else seek ourselves?
You form a notion of me, we'll suppose,
On hearsay; it's a favourable one:
"But still" (you add), "there was no such good man,
"Because of contradiction in the facts.
"One proves, for instance, he was born in Rome,
"This Blougram; yet throughout the tales of him

"I see he figures as an Englishman."
Well, the two things are reconcileable.
But would I rather you discovered that,
Subjoining — "Still, what matter though they be?
"Blougram concerns me nought, born here or there."

Pure faith indeed — you know not what you ask!
Naked belief in God the Omnipotent,
Omniscient, Omnipresent, sears too much
The sense of conscious creatures to be borne.
It were the seeing him, no flesh shall dare.
Some think, Creation's meant to show him forth:
I say it's meant to hide him all it can,
And that's what all the blessed evil's for.
Its use in Time is to environ us,
Our breath, our drop of dew, with shield enough
Against that sight till we can bear its stress.
Under a vertical sun, the exposed brain
And lidless eye and disemprisoned heart
Less certainly would wither up at once
Than mind, confronted with the truth of him.
But time and earth case-harden us to live;
The feeblest sense is trusted most; the child
Feels God a moment, ichors o'er the place,
Plays on and grows to be a man like us.
With me, faith means perpetual unbelief
Kept quiet like the snake 'neath Michael's foot
Who stands calm just because he feels it writhe.
Or, if that's too ambitious, — here's my box —
I need the excitation of a pinch
Threatening the torpor of the inside-nose
Nigh on the imminent sneeze that never comes.
"Leave it in peace" advise the simple folk:
Make it aware of peace by itching-fits,
Say I — let doubt occasion still more faith!

You'll say, once all believed, man, woman, child,
In that dear middle-age these noodles praise.
How you'd exult if I could put you back

Six hundred years, blot out cosmogony,
Geology, ethnology, what not,
(Greek endings, each the little passing-bell
That signifies some faith's about to die),
And set you square with Genesis again, —
When such a traveller told you his last news,
He saw the ark a-top of Ararat
But did not climb there since 'twas getting dusk
And robber-bands infest the mountain's foot!
How should you feel, I ask, in such an age,
How act? As other people felt and did;
With soul more blank than this decanter's knob,
Believe — and yet lie, kill, rob, fornicate
Full in belief's face, like the beast you'd be!

No, when the fight begins within himself,
A man's worth something. God stoops o'er his head,
Satan looks up between his feet — both tug —
He's left, himself, i' the middle: the soul wakes
And grows. Prolong that battle through his life!
Never leave growing till the life to come!
Here, we've got callous to the Virgin's winks
That used to puzzle people wholesomely:
Men have outgrown the shame of being fools.
What are the laws of nature, not to bend
If the Church bid them? — brother Newman asks.
Up with the Immaculate Conception, then —
On to the rack with faith! — is my advice.
Will not that hurry us upon our knees,
Knocking our breasts, "It can't be — yet it shall!
"Who am I, the worm, to argue with my Pope?
"Low things confound the high things!" and so forth.
That's better than acquitting God with grace
As some folk do. He's tried — no case is proved,
Philosophy is lenient — he may go!

You'll say, the old system's not so obsolete
But men believe still: ay, but who and where?
King Bomba's lazzaroni foster yet

The sacred flame, so Antonelli writes;
But even of these, what ragamuffin-saint
Believes God watches him continually,
As he believes in fire that it will burn,
Or rain that it will drench him? Break fire's law,
Sin against rain, although the penalty
Be just a singe or soaking? "No," he smiles;
"Those laws are laws that can enforce themselves."

    The sum of all is — yes, my doubt is great,
My faith's still greater, then my faith's enough.
I have read much, thought much, experienced much,
Yet would die rather than avow my fear
The Naples' liquefaction may be false,
When set to happen by the palace-clock
According to the clouds or dinner-time.
I hear you recommend, I might at least
Eliminate, decrassify my faith
Since I adopt it; keeping what I must
And leaving what I can — such points as this.
I won't — that is, I can't throw one away.
Supposing there's no truth in what I hold
About the need of trial to man's faith,
Still, when you bid me purify the same,
To such a process I discern no end.
Clearing off one excrescence to see two,
There's ever a next in size, now grown as big,
That meets the knife: I cut and cut again!
First cut the Liquefaction, what comes last
But Fichte's clever cut at God himself?
Experimentalize on sacred things!
I trust nor hand nor eye nor heart nor brain
To stop betimes: they all get drunk alike.
The first step, I am master not to take.

    You'd find the cutting-process to your taste
As much as leaving growths of lies unpruned,
Nor see more danger in it, — you retort.
Your taste's worth mine; but my taste proves more wise

When we consider that the steadfast hold
On the extreme end of the chain of faith
Gives all the advantage, makes the difference
With the rough purblind mass we seek to rule:
We are their lords, or they are free of us,
Just as we tighten or relax our hold.
So, other matters equal, we'll revert
To the first problem — which, if solved my way
And thrown into the balance, turns the scale —
How we may lead a comfortable life,
How suit our luggage to the cabin's size.

Of course you are remarking all this time
How narrowly and grossly I view life,
Respect the creature-comforts, care to rule
The masses, and regard complacently
"The cabin," in our old phrase. Well, I do.
I act for, talk for, live for this world now,
As this world prizes action, life and talk:
No prejudice to what next world may prove,
Whose new laws and requirements, my best pledge
To observe then, is that I observe these now,
Shall do hereafter what I do meanwhile.
Let us concede (gratuitously though)
Next life relieves the soul of body, yields
Pure spiritual enjoyment: well, my friend,
Why lose this life i' the meantime, since its use
May be to make the next life more intense?

Do you know, I have often had a dream
(Work it up in your next month's article)
Of man's poor spirit in its progress, still
Losing true life for ever and a day
Through ever trying to be and ever being —
In the evolution of successive spheres —
Before its actual sphere and place of life,
Halfway into the next, which having reached,
It shoots with corresponding foolery
Halfway into the next still, on and off!

As when a traveller, bound from North to South,
Scouts fur in Russia: what's its use in France?
In France spurns flannel: where's its need in Spain?
In Spain drops cloth, too cumbrous for Algiers!
Linen goes next, and last the skin itself,
A superfluity at Timbuctoo.
When, through his journey, was the fool at ease?
I'm at ease now, friend; worldly in this world,
I take and like its way of life; I think
My brothers, who administer the means,
Live better for my comfort — that's good too;
And God, if he pronounce upon such life,
Approves my service, which is better still.
If he keep silence, — why, for you or me
Or that brute beast pulled-up in to-day's "Times,"
What odds is't, save to ourselves, what life we lead?

You meet me at this issue: you declare, —
All special-pleading done with — truth is truth,
And justifies itself by undreamed ways.
You don't fear but it's better, if we doubt,
To say so, act up to our truth perceived
However feebly. Do then, — act away!
'Tis there I'm on the watch for you. How one acts
Is, both of us agree, our chief concern:
And how you'll act is what I fain would see
If, like the candid person you appear,
You dare to make the most of your life's scheme
As I of mine, live up to its full law
Since there's no higher law that counterchecks.
Put natural religion to the test
You've just demolished the revealed with —quick,
Down to the root of all that checks your will,
All prohibition to lie, kill and thieve,
Or even to be an atheistic priest!
Suppose a pricking to incontinence —
Philosophers deduce you chastity
Or shame, from just the fact that at the first
Whoso embraced a woman in the field,

482

Threw club down and forewent his brains beside,
So, stood a ready victim in the reach
Of any brother savage, club in hand;
Hence saw the use of going out of sight
In wood or cave to prosecute his loves:
I read this in a French book t'other day.
Does law so analysed coerce you much?
Oh, men spin clouds of fuzz where matters end,
But you who reach where the first thread begins,
You'll soon cut that! — which means you can, but won't,
Through certain instincts, blind, unreasoned-out,
You dare not set aside, you can't tell why,
But there they are, and so you let them rule.
Then, friend, you seem as much a slave as I,
A liar, conscious coward and hypocrite,
Without the good the slave expects to get,
In case he has a master after all!
You own your instincts? why, what else do I,
Who want, am made for, and must have a God
Ere I can be aught, do aught? — no mere name
Want, but the true thing with what proves its truth,
To wit, a relation from that thing to me,
Touching from head to foot — which touch I feel,
And with it take the rest, this life of ours!
I live my life here; yours you dare not live.

— Not as I state it, who (you please subjoin)
Disfigure such a life and call it names.
While, to your mind, remains another way
For simple men: knowledge and power have rights,
But ignorance and weakness have rights too.
There needs no crucial effort to find truth
If here or there or anywhere about:
We ought to turn each side, try hard and see,
And if we can't, be glad we've earned at least
The right, by one laborious proof the more,
To graze in peace earth's pleasant pasturage.
Men are not angels, neither are they brutes:
Something we may see, all we cannot see.

What need of lying? I say, I see all,
And swear to each detail the most minute
In what I think a Pan's face — you, mere cloud:
I swear I hear him speak and see him wink,
For fear, if once I drop the emphasis,
Mankind may doubt there's any cloud at all.
You take the simple life — ready to see,
Willing to see (for no cloud's worth a face) —
And leaving quiet what no strength can move,
And which, who bids you move? who has the right?
I bid you; but you are God's sheep, not mine:
"*Pastor est tui Dominus.*" You find
In this the pleasant pasture of our life
Much you may eat without the least offence,
Much you don't eat because your maw objects,
Much you would eat but that your fellow-flock
Open great eyes at you and even butt,
And thereupon you like your mates so well
You cannot please yourself, offending them;
Though when they seem exorbitantly sheep,
You weigh your pleasure with their butts and bleats
And strike the balance. Sometimes certain fears
Restrain you, real checks since you find them so;
Sometimes you please yourself and nothing checks:
And thus you graze through life with not one lie,
And like it best.

        But do you, in truth's name?
If so, you beat — which means you are not I —
Who needs must make earth mine and feed my fill
Not simply unbutted at, unbickered with,
But motioned to the velvet of the sward
By those obsequious wethers' very selves.
Look at me, sir; my age is double yours:
At yours, I knew beforehand, so enjoyed,
What now I should be — as, permit the word,
I pretty well imagine your whole range
And stretch of tether twenty years to come.
We both have minds and bodies much alike:

In truth's name, don't you want my bishopric,
My daily bread, my influence and my state?
You're young. I'm old; you must be old one day;
Will you find then, as I do hour by hour,
Women their lovers kneel to, who cut curls
From your fat lap-dog's ear to grace a brooch —
Dukes, who petition just to kiss your ring —
With much beside you know or may conceive?
Suppose we die to-night: well, here am I,
Such were my gains, life bore this fruit to me,
While writing all the same my articles
On music, poetry, the fictile vase
Found at Albano, chess, Anacreon's Greek.
But you — the highest honour in your life,
The thing you'll crown yourself with, all your days,
Is — dining here and drinking this last glass
I pour you out in sign of amity
Before we part for ever. Of your power
And social influence, worldly worth in short,
Judge what's my estimation by the fact,
I do not condescend to enjoin, beseech,
Hint secrecy on one of all these words!
You're shrewd and know that should you publish one
The world would brand the lie — my enemies first,
Who'd sneer — "the bishop's an arch-hypocrite
"And knave perhaps, but not so frank a fool."
Whereas I should not dare for both my ears
Breathe one such syllable, smile one such smile,
Before the chaplain who reflects myself —
My shade's so much more potent than your flesh.
What's your reward, self-abnegating friend?
Stood you confessed of those exceptional
And privileged great natures that dwarf mine —
A zealot with a mad ideal in reach,
A poet just about to print his ode,
A statesman with a scheme to stop this war,
An artist whose religion is his art —
I should have nothing to object: such men
Carry the fire, all things grow warm to them,

Their drugget's worth my purple, they beat me.
But you, — you're just as little those as I —
You, Gigadibs, who, thirty years of age,
Write statedly for Blackwood's Magazine,
Believe you see two points in Hamlet's soul
Unseized by the Germans yet — which view you'll print —
Meantime the best you have to show being still
That lively lightsome article we took
Almost for the true Dickens, — what's its name?
"The Slum and Cellar, or Whitechapel life
"Limned after dark!" it made me laugh, I know,
And pleased a month, and brought you in ten pounds.
— Success I recognize and compliment,
And therefore give you, if you choose, three words
(The card and pencil-scratch is quite enough)
Which whether here, in Dublin or New York,
Will get you, prompt as at my eyebrow's wink,
Such terms as never you aspired to get
In all our own reviews and some not ours.
Go write your lively sketches! be the first
"Blougram, or The Eccentric Confidence" —
Or better simply say, "The Outward-bound."
Why, men as soon would throw it in my teeth
As copy and quote the infamy chalked broad
About me on the church-door opposite.
You will not wait for that experience though,
I fancy, howsoever you decide,
To discontinue — not detesting, not
Defaming, but at least — despising me!

Over his wine so smiled and talked his hour
Sylvester Blougram, styled in partibus
Episcopus, nec non — (the deuce knows what
It's changed to by our novel hierarchy)
With Gigadibs the literary man,
Who played with spoons, explored his plate's design,
And ranged the olive-stones about its edge,

While the great bishop rolled him out a mind
Long crumpled, till creased consciousness lay smooth.

For Blougram, he believed, say, half he spoke.
The other portion, as he shaped it thus
For argumentatory purposes,
He felt his foe was foolish to dispute.
Some arbitrary accidental thoughts
That crossed his mind, amusing because new,
He chose to represent as fixtures there,
Invariable convictions (such they seemed
Beside his interlocutor's loose cards
Flung daily down, and not the same way twice)
While certain hell-deep instincts, man's weak tongue
Is never bold to utter in their truth
Because styled hell-deep ('tis an old mistake
To place hell at the bottom of the earth)
He ignored these, — not having in readiness
Their nomenclature and philosophy:
He said true things, but called them by wrong names.
"On the whole," he thought, "I justify myself
"On every point where cavillers like this
"Oppugn my life: he tries one kind of fence,
"I close, he's worsted, that's enough for him.
"He's on the ground: if ground should break away
"I take my stand on, there's a firmer yet
"Beneath it, both of us may sink and reach.
"His ground was over mine and broke the first:
"So, let him sit with me this many a year!"

He did not sit five minutes. Just a week
Sufficed his sudden healthy vehemence.
Something had struck him in the "Outward-bound"
Another way than Blougram's purpose was:
And having bought, not cabin-furniture
But settler's-implements (enough for three)
And started for Australia — there, I hope,
By this time he has tested his first plough,
And studied his last chapter of St. John.

MEMORABILIA

I.

Ah, did you once see Shelley plain,
  And did he stop and speak to you
And did you speak to him again?
  How strange it seems and new!

II.

But you were living before that,
  And also you are living after;
And the memory I started at —
  My starting moves your laughter.

III.

I crossed a moor, with a name of its own
  And a certain use in the world no doubt,
Yet a hand's-breadth of it shines alone
  'Mid the blank miles round about:

IV.

For there I picked up on the heather
  And there I put inside my breast
A moulted feather, an eagle-feather!
  Well, I forget the rest.

ANDREA DEL SARTO

(CALLED "THE FAULTLESS PAINTER")

But do not let us quarrel any more,
No, my Lucrezia; bear with me for once:
Sit down and all shall happen as you wish.
You turn your face, but does it bring your heart?
I'll work then for your friend's friend, never fear,
Treat his own subject after his own way,
Fix his own time, accept too his own price,
And shut the money into this small hand
When next it takes mine. Will it? tenderly?
Oh, I'll content him, — but to-morrow, Love!
I often am much wearier than you think,
This evening more than usual, and it seems
As if — forgive now — should you let me sit
Here by the window with your hand in mine
And look a half-hour forth on Fiesole,
Both of one mind, as married people use,
Quietly, quietly the evening through,
I might get up to-morrow to my work
Cheerful and fresh as ever. Let us try.
To-morrow, how you shall be glad for this!
Your soft hand is a woman of itself,
And mine the man's bared breast she curls inside.
Don't count the time lost, neither; you must serve
For each of the five pictures we require:
It saves a model. So! keep looking so —
My serpentining beauty, rounds on rounds!
— How could you ever prick those perfect ears,
Even to put the pearl there! oh, so sweet —
My face, my moon, my everybody's moon,
Which everybody looks on and calls his,
And, I suppose, is looked on by in turn,

While she looks — no one's: very dear, no less.
You smile? why, there's my picture ready made,
There's what we painters call our harmony!
A common greyness silvers everything, —
All in a twilight, you and I alike
— You, at the point of your first pride in me
(That's gone you know), — but I, at every point;
My youth, my hope, my art, being all toned down
To yonder sober pleasant Fiesole.
There's the bell clinking from the chapel-top;
That length of convent-wall across the way
Holds the trees safer, huddled more inside;
The last monk leaves the garden; days decrease,
And autumn grows, autumn in everything.
Eh? the whole seems to fall into a shape
As if I saw alike my work and self
And all that I was born to be and do,
A twilight-piece. Love, we are in God's hand.
How strange now, looks the life he makes us lead;
So free we seem, so fettered fast we are!
I feel he laid the fetter: let it lie!
This chamber for example — turn your head —
All that's behind us! You don't understand
Nor care to understand about my art,
But you can hear at least when people speak:
And that cartoon, the second from the door
— It is the thing, Love! so such things should be —
Behold Madonna! — I am bold to say.
I can do with my pencil what I know,
What I see, what at bottom of my heart
I wish for, if I ever wish so deep —
Do easily, too — when I say, perfectly,
I do not boast, perhaps: yourself are judge,
Who listened to the Legate's talk last week,
And just as much they used to say in France.
At any rate 'tis easy, all of it!
No sketches first, no studies, that's long past:
I do what many dream of, all their lives,
— Dream? strive to do, and agonize to do,

And fail in doing. I could count twenty such
On twice your fingers, and not leave this town,
Who strive — you don't know how the others strive
To paint a little thing like that you smeared
Carelessly passing with your robes afloat, —
Yet do much less, so much less, Someone says,
(I know his name, no matter) — so much less!
Well, less is more, Lucrezia: I am judged.
There burns a truer light of God in them,
In their vexed beating stuffed and stopped-up brain,
Heart, or whate'er else, than goes on to prompt
This low-pulsed forthright craftsman's hand of mine.
Their works drop groundward, but themselves, I know,
Reach many a time a heaven that's shut to me,
Enter and take their place there sure enough,
Though they come back and cannot tell the world.
My works are nearer heaven, but I sit here.
The sudden blood of these men! at a word —
Praise them, it boils, or blame them, it boils too.
I, painting from myself and to myself,
Know what I do, am unmoved by men's blame
Or their praise either. Somebody remarks
Morello's outline there is wrongly traced,
His hue mistaken; what of that? or else,
Rightly traced and well ordered; what of that?
Speak as they please, what does the mountain care?
Ah, but a man's reach should exceed his grasp,
Or what's a heaven for? All is silver-grey
Placid and perfect with my art: the worse!
I know both what I want and what might gain,
And yet how profitless to know, to sigh
"Had I been two, another and myself,
"Our head would have o'erlooked the world!" No doubt.
Yonder's a work now, of that famous youth
The Urbinate who died five years ago.
('Tis copied, George Vasari sent it me.)
Well, I can fancy how he did it all,
Pouring his soul, with kings and popes to see,
Reaching, that heaven might so replenish him,

Above and through his art — for it gives way;
That arm is wrongly put — and there again —
A fault to pardon in the drawing's lines,
Its body, so to speak: its soul is right,
He means right — that, a child may understand.
Still, what an arm! and I could alter it:
But all the play, the insight and the stretch —
Out of me, out of me! And wherefore out?
Had you enjoined them on me, given me soul,
We might have risen to Rafael, I and you!
Nay, Love, you did give all I asked, I think —
More than I merit, yes, by many times.
But had you — oh, with the same perfect brow,
And perfect eyes, and more than perfect mouth,
And the low voice my soul hears, as a bird
The fowler's pipe, and follows to the snare —
Had you, with these the same, but brought a mind!
Some women do so. Had the mouth there urged
"God and the glory! never care for gain.
"The present by the future, what is that?
"Live for fame, side by side with Agnolo!
"Rafael is waiting: up to God, all three!"
I might have done it for you. So it seems:
Perhaps not. All is as God over-rules.
Beside, incentives come from the soul's self;
The rest avail not. Why do I need you?
What wife had Rafael, or has Agnolo?
In this world, who can do a thing, will not;
And who would do it, cannot, I perceive:
Yet the will's somewhat — somewhat, too, the power —
And thus we half-men struggle. At the end,
God, I conclude, compensates, punishes.
'Tis safer for me, if the award be strict,
That I am something underrated here,
Poor this long while, despised, to speak the truth.
I dared not, do you know, leave home all day,
For fear of chancing on the Paris lords.
The best is when they pass and look aside;
But they speak sometimes; I must bear it all.

Well may they speak! That Francis, that first time,
And that long festal year at Fontainebleau!
I surely then could sometimes leave the ground,
Put on the glory, Rafael's daily wear,
In that humane great monarch's golden look, —
One finger in his beard or twisted curl
Over his mouth's good mark that made the smile,
One arm about my shoulder, round my neck,
The jingle of his gold chain in my ear,
I painting proudly with his breath on me,
All his court round him, seeing with his eyes,
Such frank French eyes, and such a fire of souls
Profuse, my hand kept plying by those hearts, —
And, best of all, this, this, this face beyond,
This in the background, waiting on my work,
To crown the issue with a last reward!
A good time, was it not, my kingly days?
And had you not grown restless . . . but I know —
'Tis done and past; 'twas right, my instinct said;
Too live the life grew, golden and not grey,
And I'm the weak-eyed bat no sun should tempt
Out of the grange whose four walls make his world.
How could it end in any other way?
You called me, and I came home to your heart.
The triumph was — to reach and stay there; since
I reached it ere the triumph, what is lost?
Let my hands frame your face in your hair's gold,
You beautiful Lucrezia that are mine!
"Rafael did this, Andrea painted that;
"The Roman's is the better when you pray,
"But still the other's Virgin was his wife —"
Men will excuse me. I am glad to judge
Both pictures in your presence; clearer grows
My better fortune, I resolve to think.
For, do you know, Lucrezia, as God lives,
Said one day Agnolo, his very self,
To Rafael . . . I have known it all these years . . .
(When the young man was flaming out his thoughts
Upon a palace-wall for Rome to see,

Too lifted up in heart because of it)
"Friend, there's a certain sorry little scrub
"Goes up and down our Florence, none cares how,
"Who, were he set to plan and execute
"As you are, pricked on by your popes and kings,
"Would bring the sweat into that brow of yours!"
To Rafael's! — And indeed the arm is wrong.
I hardly dare . . . yet, only you to see,
Give the chalk here — quick, thus the line should go!
Ay, but the soul! he's Rafael! rub it out!
Still, all I care for, if he spoke the truth,
(What he? why, who but Michel Agnolo?
Do you forget already words like those?)
If really there was such a chance, so lost, —
Is, whether you're — not grateful — but more pleased.
Well, let me think so. And you smile indeed!
This hour has been an hour! Another smile?
If you would sit thus by me every night
I should work better, do you comprehend?
I mean that I should earn more, give you more.
See, it is settled dusk now; there's a star;
Morello's gone, the watch-lights show the wall,
The cue-owls speak the name we call them by.
Come from the window, love, — come in, at last,
Inside the melancholy little house
We built to be so gay with. God is just.
King Francis may forgive me: oft at nights
When I look up from painting, eyes tired out,
The walls become illumined, brick from brick
Distinct, instead of mortar, fierce bright gold,
That gold of his I did cement them with!
Let us but love each other. Must you go?
That Cousin here again? he waits outside?
Must see you — you, and not with me? Those loans?
More gaming debts to pay? you smiled for that?
Well, let smiles buy me! have you more to spend?
While hand and eye and something of a heart
Are left me, work's my ware, and what's it worth?
I'll pay my fancy. Only let me sit

The grey remainder of the evening out,
Idle, you call it, and muse perfectly
How I could paint, were I but back in France,
One picture, just one more — the Virgin's face,
Not yours this time! I want you at my side
To hear them — that is, Michel Agnolo —
Judge all I do and tell you of its worth.
Will you? To-morrow, satisfy your friend.
I take the subjects for his corridor,
Finish the portrait out of hand — there, there,
And throw him in another thing or two
If he demurs; the whole should prove enough
To pay for this same Cousin's freak. Beside,
What's better and what's all I care about,
Get you the thirteen scudi for the ruff!
Love, does that please you? Ah, but what does he,
The Cousin! what does he to please you more?

I am grown peaceful as old age to-night.
I regret little, I would change still less.
Since there my past life lies, why alter it?
The very wrong to Francis! — it is true
I took his coin, was tempted and complied,
And built this house and sinned, and all is said.
My father and my mother died of want.
Well, had I riches of my own? you see
How one gets rich! Let each one bear his lot.
They were born poor, lived poor, and poor they died:
And I have laboured somewhat in my time
And not been paid profusely. Some good son
Paint my two hundred pictures — let him try!
No doubt, there's something strikes a balance. Yes,
You loved me quite enough, it seems to-night.
This must suffice me here. What would one have?
In heaven, perhaps, new chances, one more chance —
Four great walls in the New Jerusalem,
Meted on each side by the angel's reed,
For Leonard, Rafael, Agnolo and me
To cover — the three first without a wife,

While I have mine! So — still they overcome
Because there's still Lucrezia, — as I choose.

Again the Cousin's whistle! Go, my Love.

IN THREE DAYS

I.

So, I shall see her in three days
And just one night, but nights are short,
Then two long hours, and that is morn.
See how I come, unchanged, unworn!
Feel, where my life broke off from thine,
How fresh the splinters keep and fine, —
Only a touch and we combine!

II.

Too long, this time of year, the days!
But nights, at least the nights are short.
As night shows where her one moon is,
A hand's-breadth of pure light and bliss,
So life's night gives my lady birth
And my eyes hold her! What is worth
The rest of heaven, the rest of earth?

III.

O loaded curls, release your store
Of warmth and scent, as once before
The tingling hair did, lights and darks
Outbreaking into fairy sparks,
When under curl and curl I pried
After the warmth and scent inside,

496

Thro' lights and darks how manifold —
The dark inspired, the light controlled!
As early Art embrowns the gold.

IV.

What great fear, should one say, "Three days
"That change the world might change as well
"Your fortune; and if joy delays,
"Be happy that no worse befell!"
What small fear, if another says,
"Three days and one short night beside
"May throw no shadow on your ways;
"But years must teem with change untried,
"With chance not easily defied,
"With an end somewhere undescried."
No fear! — or if a fear be born
This minute, it dies out in scorn.
Fear? I shall see her in three days
And one night, now the nights are short,
Then just two hours, and that is morn.

IN A YEAR

I.

Never any more,
    While I live,
Need I hope to see his face
    As before.
Once his love grown chill,
    Mine may strive:
Bitterly we re-embrace,
    Single still.

II.

Was it something said,
  Something done,
Vexed him? was it touch of hand,
  Turn of head?
Strange! that very way
  Love begun:
I as little understand
  Love's decay.

III.

When I sewed or drew,
  I recall
How he looked as if I sung,
  — Sweetly too.
If I spoke a word,
  First of all
Up his cheek the colour sprung,
  Then he heard.

IV.

Sitting by my side,
  At my feet,
So he breathed but air I breathed,
  Satisfied!
I, too, at love's brim
  Touched the sweet:
I would die if death bequeathed
  Sweet to him.

V.

"Speak, I love thee best!"
  He exclaimed:

498

"Let thy love my own foretell!"
    I confessed:
"Clasp my heart on thine
    "Now unblamed,
"Since upon thy soul as well
    "Hangeth mine!"

VI.

Was it wrong to own,
    Being truth?
Why should all the giving prove
    His alone?
I had wealth and ease,
    Beauty, youth:
Since my lover gave me love,
    I gave these.

VII.

That was all I meant,
    — To be just,
And the passion I had raised,
    To content.
Since he chose to change
    Gold for dust,
If I gave him what he praised
    Was it strange?

VIII.

Would he loved me yet,
    On and on,
While I found some way undreamed
    — Paid my debt!
Gave more life and more,
    Till, all gone,
He should smile "She never seemed
    "Mine before.

499

IX.

"What, she felt the while,
    "Must I think?
"Love's so different with us men!"
    He should smile:
"Dying for my sake —
    "White and pink!
"Can't we touch these bubbles then
    "But they break?"

X.

Dear, the pang is brief,
    Do thy part,
Have thy pleasure! How perplexed
    Grows belief!
Well, this cold clay clod
    Was man's heart:
Crumble it, and what comes next?
    Is it God?

OLD PICTURES IN FLORENCE

I.

The morn when first it thunders in March,
    The eel in the pond gives a leap, they say:
As I leaned and looked over the aloed arch
    Of the villa-gate this warm March day,
No flash snapped, no dumb thunder rolled
    In the valley beneath where, white and wide
And washed by the morning water-gold,
    Florence lay out on the mountain-side.

II.

River and bridge and street and square
    Lay mine, as much at my beck and call,
Through the live translucent bath of air,
    As the sights in a magic crystal ball.
And of all I saw and of all I praised,
    The most to praise and the best to see
Was the startling bell-tower Giotto raised:
    But why did it more than startle me?

III.

Giotto, how, with that soul of yours,
    Could you play me false who loved you so?
Some slights if a certain heart endures
    Yet it feels, I would have your fellows know!
I' faith, I perceive not why I should care
    To break a silence that suits them best,
But the thing grows somewhat hard to bear
    When I find a Giotto join the rest.

IV.

On the arch where olives overhead
    Print the blue sky with twig and leaf,
(That sharp curled leaf which they never shed)
    'Twixt the aloes, I used to lean in chief,
And mark through the winter afternoons,
    By a gift God grants me now and then,
In the mild decline of those suns like moons,
    Who walked in Florence, besides her men.

V.

They might chirp and chaffer, come and go
    For pleasure or profit, her men alive —
My business was hardly with them, I trow,

But with empty cells of the human hive;
— With the chapter-room, the cloister-porch,
The church's apsis, aisle or nave,
Its crypt, one fingers along with a torch,
Its face set full for the sun to shave.

VI.

Wherever a fresco peels and drops,
    Wherever an outline weakens and wanes
Till the latest life in the painting stops,
    Stands One whom each fainter pulse-tick pains:
One, wishful each scrap should clutch the brick,
    Each tinge not wholly escape the plaster,
— A lion who dies of an ass's kick,
    The wronged great soul of an ancient Master.

VII.

For oh, this world and the wrong it does!
    They are safe in heaven with their backs to it,
The Michaels and Rafaels, you hum and buzz
    Round the works of, you of the little wit!
Do their eyes contract to the earth's old scope,
    Now that they see God face to face,
And have all attained to be poets, I hope?
    'Tis their holiday now, in any case.

VIII.

Much they reck of your praise and you!
    But the wronged great souls — can they be quit
Of a world where their work is all to do,
    Where you style them, you of the little wit,
Old Master This and Early the Other,
    Not dreaming that Old and New are fellows:
A younger succeeds to an elder brother,
    Da Vincis derive in good time from Dellos.

IX.

And here where your praise might yield returns,
  And a handsome word or two give help,
Here, after your kind, the mastiff girns
  And the puppy pack of poodles yelp.
What, not a word for Stefano there,
  Of brow once prominent and starry,
Called Nature's Ape and the world's despair
  For his peerless painting? (See Vasari.)

X.

There stands the Master. Study, my friends,
  What a man's work comes to! So he plans it,
Performs it, perfects it, makes amends
  For the toiling and moiling, and then, *sic transit!*
Happier the thrifty blind-folk labour,
  With upturned eye while the hand is busy,
Not sidling a glance at the coin of their neighbour!
  'Tis looking downward that makes one dizzy.

XI.

"If you knew their work you would deal your dole."
  May I take upon me to instruct you?
When Greek Art ran and reached the goal,
  Thus much had the world to boast *in fructu* —
The Truth of Man, as by God first spoken,
  Which the actual generations garble,
Was re-uttered, and Soul (which Limbs betoken)
  And Limbs (Soul informs) made new in marble.

XII.

So, you saw yourself as you wished you were,
  As you might have been, as you cannot be;

503

Earth here, rebuked by Olympus there:
  And grew content in your poor degree
With your little power, by those statues' godhead,
  And your little scope, by their eyes' full sway,
And your little grace, by their grace embodied,
  And your little date, by their forms that stay.

XIII.

You would fain be kinglier, say, than I am?
  Even so, you will not sit like Theseus.
You would prove a model? The Son of Priam
  Has yet the advantage in arms' and knees' use.
You're wroth — can you slay your snake like Apollo?
  You're grieved — still Niobe's the grander!
You live — there's the Racers' frieze to follow:
  You die — there's the dying Alexander.

XIV.

So, testing your weakness by their strength,
  Your meagre charms by their rounded beauty,
Measured by Art in your breadth and length,
  You learned — to submit is a mortal's duty.
— When I say "you" 'tis the common soul,
  The collective, I mean: the race of Man
That receives life in parts to live in a whole,
  And grow here according to God's clear plan.

XV.

Growth came when, looking your last on them all,
  You turned your eyes inwardly one fine day
And cried with a start — What if we so small
  Be greater and grander the while than they?
Are they perfect of lineament, perfect of stature?
  In both, of such lower types are we
Precisely because of our wider nature;
  For time, theirs — ours, for eternity.

XVI.

To-day's brief passion limits their range;
    It seethes with the morrow for us and more.
They are perfect — how else? they shall never change:
    We are faulty — why not? we have time in store.
The Artificer's hand is not arrested
    With us; we are rough-hewn, nowise polished:
They stand for our copy, and, once invested
    With all they can teach, we shall see them abolished.

XVII.

'Tis a life-long toil till our lump be leaven —
    The better! What's come to perfection perishes.
Things learned on earth, we shall practise in heaven:
    Works done least rapidly, Art most cherishes.
Thyself shalt afford the example, Giotto!
    Thy one work, not to decrease or diminish,
Done at a stroke, was just (was it not?) "O!"
    Thy great Campanile is still to finish.

XVIII.

Is it true that we are now, and shall be hereafter,
    But what and where depend on life's minute?
Hails heavenly cheer or infernal laughter
    Our first step out of the gulf or in it?
Shall Man, such step within his endeavour,
    Man's face, have no more play and action
Than joy which is crystallized for ever,
    Or grief, an eternal petrifaction?

XIX.

On which I conclude, that the early painters,
    To cries of "Greek Art and what more wish you?" —
Replied, "To become now self-acquainters,

"And paint man man, whatever the issue!
"Make new hopes shine through the flesh they fray,
"New fears aggrandize the rags and tatters:
"To bring the invisible full into play!
"Let the visible go to the dogs — what matters?"

XX.

Give these, I exhort you, their guerdon and glory
    For daring so much, before they well did it.
The first of the new, in our race's story,
    Beats the last of the old; 'tis no idle quiddit.
The worthies began a revolution,
    Which if on earth you intend to acknowledge,
Why, honour them now! (ends my allocution)
    Nor confer your degree when the folk leave college.

XXI.

There's a fancy some lean to and others hate —
    That, when this life is ended, begins
New work for the soul in another state,
    Where it strives and gets weary, loses and wins:
Where the strong and the weak, this world's congeries,
    Repeat in large what they practised in small,
Through life after life in unlimited series;
    Only the scale's to be changed, that's all.

XXII.

Yet I hardly know. When a soul has seen
    By the means of Evil that Good is best,
And, through earth and its noise, what is heaven's serene, —
    When our faith in the same has stood the test —
Why, the child grown man, you burn the rod,
    The uses of labour are surely done;
There remaineth a rest for the people of God:
    And I have had troubles enough, for one.

XXIII.

But at any rate I have loved the season
    Of Art's spring-birth so dim and dewy;
My sculptor is Nicolo the Pisan,
    My painter — who but Cimabue?
Nor ever was man of them all indeed,
    From these to Ghiberti and Ghirlandajo,
Could say that he missed my critic-meed.
    So, now to my special grievance — heigh ho!

XXIV.

Their ghosts still stand, as I said before,
    Watching each fresco flaked and rasped,
Blocked up, knocked out, or whitewashed o'er:
    — No getting again what the church has grasped!
The works on the wall must take their chance;
    "Works never conceded to England's thick clime!"
(I hope they prefer their inheritance
    Of a bucketful of Italian quick-lime.)

XXV.

When they go at length, with such a shaking
    Of heads o'er the old delusion, sadly
Each master his way through the black streets taking
    Where many a lost work breathes though badly —
Why don't they bethink them of who has merited?
    Why not reveal, while their pictures dree
Such doom, how a captive might be out-ferreted?
    Why is it they never remember me?

XXVI.

Not that I expect the great Bigordi,
    Nor Sandro to hear me, chivalric, bellicose;
Nor the wronged Lippino; and not a word I

Say of a scrap of Frà Angelico's:
But are you too fine, Taddeo Gaddi,
    To grant me a taste of your intonaco,
Some Jerome that seeks the heaven with a sad eye?
    Not a churlish saint, Lorenzo Monaco?

XXVII.

Could not the ghost with the close red cap,
    My Pollajolo, the twice a craftsman,
Save me a sample, give me the hap
    Of a muscular Christ that shows the draughtsman?
No Virgin by him the somewhat petty,
    Of finical touch and tempera crumbly —
Could not Alesso Baldovinetti
    Contribute so much, I ask him humbly?

XXVIII.

Margheritone of Arezzo,
    With the grave-clothes garb and swaddling barret
(Why purse up mouth and beak in a pet so,
    You bald old saturnine poll-clawed parrot?)
Not a poor glimmering Crucifixion,
    Where in the foreground kneels the donor?
If such remain, as is my conviction,
    The hoarding it does you but little honour.

XXIX.

They pass; for them the panels may thrill,
    The tempera grow alive and tinglish;
Their pictures are left to the mercies still
    Of dealers and stealers, Jews and the English,
Who, seeing mere money's worth in their prize,
    Will sell it to somebody calm as Zeno
At naked High Art, and in ecstasies
    Before some clay-cold vile Carlino!

XXX.

No matter for these! But Giotto, you,
  Have you allowed, as the town-tongues babble it, —
Oh, never! it shall not be counted true —
  That a certain precious little tablet
Which Buonarroti eyed like a lover, —
  Was buried so long in oblivion's womb
And, left for another than I to discover,
  Turns up at last! and to whom? — to whom?

XXXI.

I, that have haunted the dim San Spirito,
  (Or was it rather the Ognissanti?)
Patient on altar-step planting a weary toe!
  Nay, I shall have it yet! *Detur amanti!*
My Koh-i-noor — or (if that's a platitude)
  Jewel of Giamschid, the Persian Sofi's eye;
So, in anticipative gratitude,
  What if I take up my hope and prophesy?

XXXII.

When the hour grows ripe, and a certain dotard
  Is pitched, no parcel that needs invoicing,
To the worse side of the Mont Saint Gothard,
  We shall begin by way of rejoicing;
None of that shooting the sky (blank cartridge),
  Nor a civic guard, all plumes and lacquer,
Hunting Radetzky's soul like a partridge
  Over Morello with squib and cracker.

XXXIII.

This time we'll shoot better game and bag 'em hot —
  No mere display at the stone of Dante,
But a kind of sober Witanagemot

THE BROWNINGS

(Ex: "Casa Guidi," *quod videas ante*)
Shall ponder, once Freedom restored to Florence,
How Art may return that departed with her.
Go, hated house, go each trace of the Loraine's,
And bring us the days of Orgagna hither!

XXXIV.

How we shall prologize, how we shall perorate,
    Utter fit things upon art and history,
Feel truth at blood-heat and falsehood at zero rate,
    Make of the want of the age no mystery;
Contrast the fructuous and sterile eras,
    Show — monarchy ever its uncouth cub licks
Out of the bear's shape into Chimæra's,
    While Pure Art's birth is still the republic's.

XXXV.

Then one shall propose in a speech (curt Tuscan,
    Expurgate and sober, with scarcely an *"issimo,"*)
To end now our half-told tale of Cambuscan,
    And turn the bell-tower's *alt* to *altissimo:*
And fine as the beak of a young beccaccia
    The Campanile, the Duomo's fit ally,
Shall soar up in gold full fifty braccia,
    Completing Florence, as Florence Italy.

XXXVI.

Shall I be alive that morning the scaffold
    Is broken away, and the long-pent fire,
Like the golden hope of the world, unbaffled
    Springs from its sleep, and up goes the spire
While "God and the People" plain for its motto,
    Thence the new tricolour flaps at the sky?
At least to foresee that glory of Giotto
    And Florence together, the first am I!

"DE GUSTIBUS—"

I.

Your ghost will walk, you lover of trees,
   (If our loves remain)
    In an English lane,
By a cornfield-side a-flutter with poppies.
Hark, those two in the hazel coppice —
A boy and a girl, if the good fates please,
   Making love, say, —
   The happier they!
Draw yourself up from the light of the moon,
And let them pass, as they will too soon,
   With the bean-flowers' boon,
   And the blackbird's tune,
   And May, and June!

II.

What I love best in all the world
Is a castle, precipice-encurled,
In a gash of the wind-grieved Apennine
Or look for me, old fellow of mine,
(If I get my head from out the mouth
O' the grave, and loose my spirit's bands,
And come again to the land of lands) —
In a sea-side house to the farther South,
Where the baked cicala dies of drouth,
And one sharp tree — 'tis a cypress — stands,
By the many hundred years red-rusted,
Rough iron-spiked, ripe fruit-o'ercrusted,
My sentinel to guard the sands
To the water's edge. For, what expands
Before the house, but the great opaque

Blue breadth of sea without a break?
While, in the house, for ever crumbles
Some fragment of the frescoed walls,
From blisters where a scorpion sprawls.
A girl bare-footed brings, and tumbles
Down on the pavement, green-flesh melons,
And says there's news to-day — the king
Was shot at, touched in the liver-wing,
Goes with his Bourbon arm in a sling:
— She hopes they have not caught the felons.
Italy, my Italy!
Queen Mary's saying serves for me —
        (When fortune's malice
        Lost her — Calais) —
Open my heart and you will see
Graved inside of it, "Italy."
Such lovers old are I and she:
So it always was, so shall ever be!

HOLY-CROSS DAY

ON WHICH THE JEWS WERE FORCED TO ATTEND
AN ANNUAL CHRISTIAN SERMON IN ROME

["Now was come about Holy-Cross Day, and now must my lord preach his first sermon to the Jews: as it was of old cared for in the merciful bowels of the Church, that, so to speak, a crumb at least from her conspicuous table here in Rome should be, though but once yearly, cast to the famishing dogs, under-trampled and bespitten-upon beneath the feet of the guests. And a moving sight in truth, this, of so many of the besotted blind restif and ready-to-perish Hebrews! now maternally brought — nay (for He saith, 'Compel them to come in') haled, as it were, by the head and hair, and against their obstinate hearts, to partake of the heavenly grace. What awakening, what striving with tears, what working of a yeasty conscience! Nor was my lord wanting to himself on so apt an occasion; witness the abundance of conversions which did incontinently reward him: though not to my lord be altogether the glory." — *Diary by the Bishop's Secretary, 1600.*]

What the Jews really said, on thus being driven to church, was rather to this effect: —

I.

Fee, faw, fum! bubble and squeak!
Blessedest Thursday's the fat of the week.
Rumble and tumble, sleek and rough,
Stinking and savoury, smug and gruff,
Take the church-road, for the bell's due chime
Gives us the summons — 'tis sermon-time!

II.

Boh, here's Barnabas! Job, that's you?
Up stumps Solomon — bustling too?
Shame, man! greedy beyond your years
To handsel the bishop's shaving-shears?
Fair play's a jewel! Leave friends in the lurch?
Stand on a line ere you start for the church!

III.

Higgledy piggledy, packed we lie,
Rats in a hamper, swine in a stye,
Wasps in a bottle, frogs in a sieve,
Worms in a carcase, fleas in a sleeve.
Hist! square shoulders, settle your thumbs
And buzz for the bishop — here he comes.

IV.

Bow, wow, wow — a bone for the dog!
I liken his Grace to an acorned hog.
What, a boy at his side, with the bloom of a lass,
To help and handle my lord's hour-glass!

Didst ever behold so lithe a chine?
His cheek hath laps like a fresh-singed swine.

V.

Aaron's asleep — shove hip to haunch,
Or somebody deal him a dig in the paunch!
Look at the purse with the tassel and knob,
And the gown with the angel and thingumbob!
What's he at, quotha? reading his text!
Now you've his curtsey — and what comes next?

VI.

See to our converts — you doomed black dozen —
No stealing away — nor cog nor cozen!
You five, that were thieves, deserve it fairly;
You seven, that were beggars, will live less sparely;
You took your turn and dipped in the hat,
Got fortune — and fortune gets you; mind that!

VII.

Give your first groan — compunction's at work;
And soft! from a Jew you mount to a Turk.
Lo, Micah, — the selfsame beard on chin
He was four times already converted in!
Here's a knife, clip quick — it's a sign of grace —
Or he ruins us all with his hanging-face.

VIII.

Whom now is the bishop a-leering at?
I know a point where his text falls pat.
I'll tell him to-morrow, a word just now
Went to my heart and made me vow
I meddle no more with the worst of trades —
Let somebody else pay his serenades.

IX.

Groan all together now, whee — hee — hee!
It's a-work, it's a-work, ah, woe is me!
It began, when a herd of us, picked and placed,
Were spurred through the Corso, stripped to the waist;
Jew brutes, with sweat and blood well spent
To usher in worthily Christian Lent.

X.

It grew, when the hangman entered our bounds,
Yelled, pricked us out to his church like hounds:
It got to a pitch, when the hand indeed
Which gutted my purse would throttle my creed:
And it overflows when, to even the odd,
Men I helped to their sins help me to their God.

XI.

But now, while the scapegoats leave our flock,
And the rest sit silent and count the clock,
Since forced to muse the appointed time
On these precious facts and truths sublime, —
Let us fitly employ it, under our breath,
In saying Ben Ezra's Song of Death.

XII.

For Rabbi Ben Ezra, the night he died,
Called sons and sons' sons to his side,
And spoke, "This world has been harsh and strange;
"Something is wrong: there needeth a change.
"But what, or where? at the last or first?
"In one point only we sinned, at worst.

XIII.

"The Lord will have mercy on Jacob yet,
"And again in his border see Israel set.
"When Judah beholds Jerusalem,
"The stranger-seed shall be joined to them:
"To Jacob's House shall the Gentiles cleave.
"So the Prophet saith and his sons believe.

XIV.

"Ay, the children of the chosen race
"Shall carry and bring them to their place:
"In the land of the Lord shall lead the same,
"Bondsmen and handmaids. Who shall blame,
"When the slaves enslave, the oppressed ones o'er
"The oppressor triumph for evermore?

XV.

"God spoke, and gave us the word to keep,
"Bade never fold the hands nor sleep
" 'Mid a faithless world, — at watch and ward,
"Till Christ at the end relieve our guard.
"By His servant Moses the watch was set:
"Though near upon cock-crow, we keep it yet.

XVI.

"Thou! if thou wast He, who at mid-watch came,
"By the starlight, naming a dubious name!
"And if, too heavy with sleep — too rash
"With fear — O Thou, if that martyr-gash
"Fell on Thee coming to take thine own,
"And we gave the Cross, when we owed the Throne —

XVII.

"Thou art the Judge. We are bruised thus.
"But, the Judgment over, join sides with us!
"Thine too is the cause! and not more thine
"Than ours, is the work of these dogs and swine,
"Whose life laughs through and spits at their creed!
"Who maintain Thee in word, and defy Thee in deed!

XVIII.

"We withstood Christ then? Be mindful how
"At least we withstand Barabbas now!
"Was our outrage sore? But the worst we spared,
"To have called these — Christians, had we dared!
"Let defiance to them pay mistrust of Thee,
"And Rome make amends for Calvary!

XIX.

"By the torture, prolonged from age to age,
"By the infamy, Israel's heritage,
"By the Ghetto's plague, by the garb's disgrace,
"By the badge of shame, by the felon's place,
"By the branding-tool, the bloody whip,
"And the summons to Christian fellowship, —

XX.

"We boast our proof that at least the Jew
"Would wrest Christ's name from the Devil's crew.
"Thy face took never so deep a shade
"But we fought them in it, God our aid!
"A trophy to bear, as we march, thy band,
"South, East, and on to the Pleasant Land!"

                    [*Pope Gregory XVI. abolished this bad
                        business of the Sermon.* — R.B.]

POPULARITY

I.

Stand still, true poet that you are!
    I know you; let me try and draw you.
Some night you'll fail us: when afar
    You rise, remember one man saw you,
    Knew you, and named a star!

II.

My star, God's glow-worm! Why extend
    That loving hand of his which leads you
Yet locks you safe from end to end
    Of this dark world, unless he needs you,
    Just saves your light to spend?

III.

His clenched hand shall unclose at last,
    I know, and let out all the beauty:
My poet holds the future fast,
    Accepts the coming ages' duty,
    Their present for this past.

IV.

That day, the earth's feast-master's brow
    Shall clear, to God the chalice raising;
"Others give best at first, but thou
    "Forever set'st our table praising,
    "Keep'st the good wine till now!"

518

V.

Meantime, I'll draw you as you stand,
　With few or none to watch and wonder:
I'll say — a fisher, on the sand
　By Tyre the old, with ocean-plunder,
A netful, brought to land.

VI.

Who has not heard how Tyrian shells
　Enclosed the blue, that dye of dyes
Whereof one drop worked miracles,
　And coloured like Astarte's eyes
Raw silk the merchant sells?

VII.

And each bystander of them all
　Could criticize, and quote tradition
How depths of blue sublimed some pall
　— To get which, pricked a king's ambition;
Worth sceptre, crown and ball.

VIII.

Yet there's the dye, in that rough mesh,
　The sea has only just o'erwhispered!
Live whelks, each lip's beard dripping fresh,
　As if they still the water's lisp heard
Through foam the rock-weeds thresh.

IX.

Enough to furnish Solomon
　Such hangings for his cedar-house,
That, when gold-robed he took the throne
　In that abyss of blue, the Spouse
Might swear his presence shone

X.

Most like the centre-spike of gold
  Which burns deep in the blue-bell's womb,
What time, with ardours manifold,
  The bee goes singing to her groom,
Drunken and overbold.

XI.

Mere conchs! not fit for warp or woof!
  Till cunning come to pound and squeeze
And clarify, — refine to proof
  The liquor filtered by degrees,
While the world stands aloof.

XII.

And there's the extract, flasked and fine,
  And priced and saleable at last!
And Hobbs, Nobbs, Stokes and Nokes combine
  To paint the future from the past,
Put blue into their line.

XIII.

Hobbs hints blue, — straight he turtle eats:
  Nobbs prints blue, — claret crowns his cup:
Nokes outdares Stokes in azure feats, —
  Both gorge. Who fished the murex up?
What porridge had John Keats?

ROBERT BROWNING

THE HERETIC'S TRAGEDY

A MIDDLE-AGE INTERLUDE

ROSA MUNDI; SEU, FULCITE ME FLORIBUS. A CONCEIT OF
MASTER GYSBRECHT, CANON-REGULAR OF SAINT JODOCUS-BY-
THE-BAR, YPRES CITY. CANTUQUE, *Virgilius*. AND HATH OFTEN
BEEN SUNG AT HOCK-TIDE AND FESTIVALS. GAVISUS ERAM,
Jessides.

(*It would seem to be a glimpse from the burning of
Jacques du Bourg-Molay, at Paris, A.D. 1314; as distorted
by the refraction from Flemish brain to brain, during the
course of a couple of centuries. R.B.*)

I.

PREADMONISHETH THE ABBOT DEODAET.

The Lord, we look to once for all,
    Is the Lord we should look at, all at once:
He knows not to vary, saith Saint Paul,
    Nor the shadow of turning, for the nonce.
See him no other than as he is!
    Give both the infinitudes their due —
Infinite mercy, but, I wis,
    As infinite a justice too.
                [*Organ: plagal-cadence.*
    As infinite a justice too.

521

II.

ONE SINGETH.

John, Master of the Temple of God,
  Falling to sin the Unknown Sin,
What he bought of Emperor Aldabrod,
  He sold it to Sultan Saladin:
Till, caught by Pope Clement, a-buzzing there,
  Hornet-prince of the mad wasps' hive,
And clipt of his wings in Paris square,
  They bring him now to be burned alive.
    [*And wanteth there grace of lute or
      clavicithern, ye shall say to con-
      firm him who singeth* —
We bring John now to be burned alive.

III.

In the midst is a goodly gallows built;
  'Twixt fork and fork, a stake is stuck;
But first they set divers tumbrils a-tilt,
  Make a trench all round with the city muck;
Inside they pile log upon log, good store;
  Faggots no few, blocks great and small,
Reach a man's mid-thigh, no less, no more, —
  For they mean he should roast in the sight of all.

CHORUS.

We mean he should roast in the sight of all.

IV.

Good sappy bavins that kindle forthwith;
  Billets that blaze substantial and slow;

Pine-stump split deftly, dry as pith;
   Larch-heart that chars to a chalk-white glow:
Then up they hoist me John in a chafe,
   Sling him fast like a hog to scorch,
Spit in his face, then leap back safe,
   Sing "Laudes" and bid clap-to the torch.

CHORUS.

Laus Deo — who bids clap-to the torch.

V.

John of the Temple, whose fame so bragged,
   Is burning alive in Paris square!
How can he curse, if his mouth is gagged?
   Or wriggle his neck, with a collar there?
Or heave his chest, which a band goes round?
   Or threat with his fist, since his arms are spliced?
Or kick with his feet, now his legs are bound?
   — Thinks John, I will call upon Jesus Christ.
        [Here one crosseth himself.

VI.

Jesus Christ — John had bought and sold,
   Jesus Christ — John had eaten and drunk;
To him, the Flesh meant silver and gold.
   (*Salvâ reverentiâ.*)
Now it was, "Saviour, bountiful lamb,
   "I have roasted thee Turks, though men roast me!
"See thy servant, the plight wherein I am!
   "Art thou a saviour? Save thou me!"

CHORUS.

'Tis John the mocker cries, "Save thou me!"

523

VII.

Who maketh God's menace an idle word?
—Saith, it no more means what it proclaims,
Than a damsel's threat to her wanton bird? —
    For she too prattles of ugly names.
— Saith, he knoweth but one thing, — what he knows?
    That God is good and the rest is breath;
Why else is the same styled Sharon's rose?
    Once a rose, ever a rose, he saith.

CHORUS.

O, John shall yet find a rose, he saith!

VIII.

Alack, there be roses and roses, John!
    Some, honied of taste like your leman's tongue:
Some, bitter; for why? (roast gaily on!)
    Their tree struck root in devil's-dung.
When Paul once reasoned of righteousness
    And of temperance and of judgment to come,
Good Felix trembled, he could no less:
    John, snickering, crook'd his wicked thumb.

CHORUS.

What cometh to John of the wicked thumb?

IX.

Ha ha, John plucketh now at his rose
    To rid himself of a sorrow at heart!
Lo, — petal on petal, fierce rays unclose;
    Anther on anther, sharp spikes outstart;
And with blood for dew, the bosom boils;
    And a gust of sulphur is all its smell;

And lo, he is horribly in the toils
Of a coal-black giant flower of hell!

CHORUS.

What maketh heaven, That maketh hell.

X.

So, as John called now, through the fire amain,
 On the Name, he had cursed with, all his life —
To the Person, he bought and sold again —
 For the Face, with his daily buffets rife —
Feature by feature It took its place:
 And his voice, like a mad dog's choking bark,
At the steady whole of the Judge's face —
 Died. Forth John's soul flared into the dark.

SUBJOINETH THE ABBOT DEODAET.

God help all poor souls lost in the dark!

TWO IN THE CAMPAGNA

I.

I wonder do you feel to-day
 As I have felt since, hand in hand,
We sat down on the grass, to stray
 In spirit better through the land,
This morn of Rome and May?

II.

For me, I touched a thought, I know,
 Has tantalized me many times,

THE BROWNINGS

(Like turns of thread the spiders throw
  Mocking across our path) for rhymes
To catch at and let go.

III.

Help me to hold it! First it left
  The yellowing fennel, run to seed
There, branching from the brickwork's cleft,
  Some old tomb's ruin: yonder weed
Took up the floating weft,

IV.

Where one small orange cup amassed
  Five beetles, — blind and green they grope
Among the honey-meal: and last,
  Everywhere on the grassy slope
I traced it. Hold it fast!

V.

The champaign with its endless fleece
  Of feathery grasses everywhere!
Silence and passion, joy and peace,
  An everlasting wash of air —
Rome's ghost since her decease.

VI.

Such life here, through such lengths of hours,
  Such miracles performed in play,
Such primal naked forms of flowers,
  Such letting nature have her way
While heaven looks from its towers!

VII.

How say you? Let us, O my dove,
  Let us be unashamed of soul,
As earth lies bare to heaven above!
  How is it under our control
To love or not to love?

VIII.

I would that you were all to me,
  You that are just so much, no more.
Nor yours nor mine, nor slave nor free!
  Where does the fault lie? What the core
O' the wound, since wound must be?

IX.

I would I could adopt your will,
  See with your eyes, and set my heart
Beating by yours, and drink my fill
  At your soul's springs, — your part my part
In life, for good and ill.

X.

No. I yearn upward, touch you close,
  Then stand away. I kiss your cheek,
Catch your soul's warmth, — I pluck the rose
  And love it more than tongue can speak —
Then the good minute goes.

XI.

Already how am I so far
  Out of that minute? Must I go
Still like the thistle-ball, no bar,
  Onward, whenever light winds blow,
Fixed by no friendly star?

527

XII.

Just when I seemed about to learn!
    Where is the thread now? Off again!
The old trick! Only I discern —
    Infinite passion, and the pain
Of finite hearts that yearn.

A GRAMMARIAN'S FUNERAL

SHORTLY AFTER THE REVIVAL OF LEARNING IN EUROPE

Let us begin and carry up this corpse,
        Singing together.
Leave we the common crofts, the vulgar thorpes
        Each in its tether
Sleeping safe on the bosom of the plain,
        Cared-for till cock-crow:
Look out if yonder be not day again
        Rimming the rock-row!
That's the appropriate country; there, man's thought,
        Rarer, intenser,
Self-gathered for an outbreak, as it ought,
        Chafes in the censer.
Leave we the unlettered plain its herd and crop;
        Seek we sepulture
On a tall mountain, citied to the top,
        Crowded with culture!
All the peaks soar, but one the rest excels;
        Clouds overcome it;
No! yonder sparkle is the citadel's
        Circling its summit.
Thither our path lies; wind we up the heights:
        Wait ye the warning?

Our low life was the level's and the night's;
    He's for the morning.
Step to a tune, square chests, erect each head,
    'Ware the beholders!
This is our master, famous calm and dead,
    Borne on our shoulders.

Sleep, crop and herd! sleep, darkling thorpe and croft,
    Safe from the weather!
He, whom we convoy to his grave aloft,
    Singing together,
He was a man born with thy face and throat,
    Lyric Apollo!
Long he lived nameless: how should spring take note
    Winter would follow?
Till lo, the little touch, and youth was gone!
    Cramped and diminished,
Moaned he, "New measures, other feet anon!
    "My dance is finished?"
No, that's the world's way: (keep the mountain-side,
    Make for the city!)
He knew the signal, and stepped on with pride
    Over men's pity;
Left play for work, and grappled with the world
    Bent on escaping:
"What's in the scroll," quoth he, "thou keepest furled?
    "Show me their shaping,
"Theirs who most studied man, the bard and sage, —
    "Give!" — So, he gowned him,
Straight got by heart that book to its last page:
    Learned, we found him.
Yea, but we found him bald too, eyes like lead,
    Accents uncertain:
"Time to taste life," another would have said,
    "Up with the curtain!"
This man said rather, "Actual life comes next?
    "Patience a moment!
"Grant I have mastered learning's crabbed text,
    "Still there's the comment.

"Let me know all! Prate not of most or least,
   "Painful or easy!
"Even to the crumbs I'd fain eat up the feast,
   "Ay, nor feel queasy."
Oh, such a life as he resolved to live,
   When he had learned it,
When he had gathered all books had to give!
   Sooner, he spurned it.
Image the whole, then execute the parts —
   Fancy the fabric
Quite, ere you build, ere steel strike fire from quartz,
   Ere mortar dab brick!

(Here's the town-gate reached: there's the market-place
   Gaping before us.)
Yea, this in him was the peculiar grace
   (Hearten our chorus!)
That before living he'd learn how to live —
   No end to learning:
Earn the means first — God surely will contrive
   Use for our earning.
Others mistrust and say, "But time escapes:
   "Live now or never!"
He said, "What's time? Leave Now for dogs and apes!
   "Man has Forever."
Back to his book then: deeper drooped his head:
   Calculus racked him:
Leaden before, his eyes grew dross of lead:
   Tussis attacked him.
"Now, master, take a little rest!" — not he!
   (Caution redoubled,
Step two abreast, the way winds narrowly!)
   Not a whit troubled
Back to his studies, fresher than at first,
   Fierce as a dragon
He (soul-hydroptic with a sacred thirst)
   Sucked at the flagon.

Oh, if we draw a circle premature,
    Heedless of far gain,
Greedy for quick returns of profit, sure
    Bad is our bargain!
Was it not great? did not he throw on God,
    (He loves the burthen) —
God's task to make the heavenly period
    Perfect the earthen?
Did not he magnify the mind, show clear
    Just what it all meant?
He would not discount life, as fools do here,
    Paid by instalment.
He ventured neck or nothing — heaven's success
    Found, or earth's failure:
"Wilt thou trust death or not?" He answered "Yes:
    "Hence with life's pale lure!"
That low man seeks a little thing to do,
    Sees it and does it:
This high man, with a great thing to pursue,
    Dies ere he knows it.
That low man goes on adding one to one,
    His hundred's soon hit:
This high man, aiming at a million,
    Misses an unit.
That, has the world here — should he need the next,
    Let the world mind him!
This, throws himself on God, and unperplexed
    Seeking shall find him.
So, with the throttling hands of death at strife,
    Ground he at grammar;
Still, thro' the rattle, parts of speech were rife:
    While he could stammer
He settled *Hoti's* business — let it be! —
    Properly based *Oun* —
Gave us the doctrine of the enclitic *De*,
    Dead from the waist down.
Well, here's the platform, here's the proper place:
    Hail to your purlieus,

All ye highfliers of the feathered race,
    Swallows and curlews!
Here's the top-peak; the multitude below
    Live, for they can, there:
This man decided not to Live but Know —
    Bury this man there?
Here — here's his place, where meteors shoot, clouds form,
    Lightnings are loosened,
Stars come and go! Let joy break with the storm,
    Peace let the dew send!
Lofty designs must close in like effects:
    Loftily lying,
Leave him — still loftier than the world suspects,
    Living and dying.

ONE WAY OF LOVE

I.

All June I bound the rose in sheaves.
Now, rose by rose, I strip the leaves
And strew them where Pauline may pass.
She will not turn aside? Alas!
Let them lie. Suppose they die?
The chance was they might take her eye.

II.

How many a month I strove to suit
These stubborn fingers to the lute!
To-day I venture all I know.
She will not hear my music? So!
Break the string; fold music's wing:
Suppose Pauline had bade me sing!

III.

My whole life long I learned to love.
This hour my utmost art I prove
And speak my passion — heaven or hell?
She will not give me heaven? 'Tis well!
Lose who may — I still can say,
Those who win heaven, blest are they!

ANOTHER WAY OF LOVE

I.

June was not over
    Though past the full,
And the best of her roses
    Had yet to blow,
    When a man I know
(But shall not discover,
    Since ears are dull,
And time discloses)
Turned him and said with a man's true air,
Half sighing a smile in a yawn, as 'twere, —
"If I tire of your June, will she greatly care?"

II.

Well, dear, in-doors with you!
    True! serene deadness
Tries a man's temper.
    What's in the blossom
    June wears on her bosom?
Can it clear scores with you?
    Sweetness and redness.
    Eadem semper!

Go, let me care for it greatly or slightly!
If June mend her bower now, your hand left unsightly
By plucking the roses, — my June will do rightly.

III.

And after, for pastime,
   If June be refulgent
With flowers in completeness,
   All petals, no prickles,
   Delicious as trickles
Of wine poured at mass-time, —
   And choose One indulgent
   To redness and sweetness:
Or if, with experience of man and of spider,
June use my June-lightning, the strong insect-ridder,
And stop the fresh film-work, — why, June will consider.

MISCONCEPTIONS

I.

This is a spray the Bird clung to,
   Making it blossom with pleasure,
Ere the high tree-top she sprung to,
   Fit for her nest and her treasure.
   Oh, what a hope beyond measure
Was the poor spray's, which the flying feet hung to, —
So to be singled out, built in, and sung to!

II.

This is a heart the Queen leant on,
   Thrilled in a minute erratic,
Ere the true bosom she bent on,
   Meet for love's regal dalmatic.

Oh, what a fancy ecstatic
Was the poor heart's, ere the wanderer went on —
Love to be saved for it, proffered to, spent on!

ONE WORD MORE

TO E.B.B.

1855

I.

There they are, my fifty men and women
Naming me the fifty poems finished!
Take them, Love, the book and me together:
Where the heart lies, let the brain lie also.

II.

Rafael made a century of sonnets,
Made and wrote them in a certain volume
Dinted with the silver-pointed pencil
Else he only used to draw Madonnas:
These, the world might view — but one, the volume.
Who that one, you ask? Your heart instructs you.
Did she live and love it all her life-time?
Did she drop, his lady of the sonnets,
Die, and let it drop beside her pillow
Where it lay in place of Rafael's glory,
Rafael's cheek so duteous and so loving —
Cheek, the world was wont to hail a painter's,
Rafael's cheek, her love had turned a poet's?

III.

You and I would rather read that volume,
(Taken to his beating bosom by it)

535

Lean and list the bosom-beats of Rafael,
Would we not? than wonder at Madonnas —
Her, San Sisto names, and Her, Foligno,
Her, that visits Florence in a vision,
Her, that's left with lilies in the Louvre —
Seen by us and all the world in circle.

IV.

You and I will never read that volume.
Guido Reni, like his own eye's apple
Guarded long the treasure-book and loved it.
Guido Reni dying, all Bologna
Cried, and the world cried too, "Ours, the treasure!"
Suddenly, as rare things will, it vanished.

V.

Dante once prepared to paint an angel:
Whom to please? You whisper "Beatrice."
While he mused and traced it and retraced it,
(Peradventure with a pen corroded
Still by drops of that hot ink he dipped for,
When, his left-hand i' the hair o' the wicked,
Back he held the brow and pricked its stigma,
Bit into the live man's flesh for parchment,
Loosed him, laughed to see the writing rankle,
Let the wretch go festering through Florence) —
Dante, who loved well because he hated,
Hated wickedness that hinders loving,
Dante standing, studying his angel, —
In there broke the folk of his Inferno.
Says he — "Certain people of importance"
(Such he gave his daily dreadful line to)
"Entered and would seize, forsooth, the poet."
Says the poet — "Then I stopped my painting."

VI.

You and I would rather see that angel,
Painted by the tenderness of Dante,
Would we not? — than read a fresh Inferno.

VII.

You and I will never see that picture.
While he mused on love and Beatrice,
While he softened o'er his outlined angel,
In they broke, those "people of importance:"
We and Bice bear the loss for ever.

VIII.

What of Rafael's sonnets, Dante's picture?
This: no artist lives and loves, that longs not
Once, and only once, and for one only,
(Ah, the prize!) to find his love a language
Fit and fair and simple and sufficient —
Using nature that's an art to others,
Not, this one time, art that's turned his nature.
Ay, of all the artists living, loving,
None but would forego his proper dowry, —
Does he paint? he fain would write a poem, —
Does he write? he fain would paint a picture,
Put to proof art alien to the artist's,
Once, and only once, and for one only,
So to be the man and leave the artist,
Gain the man's joy, miss the artist's sorrow.

IX.

Wherefore? Heaven's gift takes earth's abatement!
He who smites the rock and spreads the water,
Bidding drink and live a crowd beneath him,

Even he, the minute makes immortal,
Proves, perchance, but mortal in the minute,
Desecrates, belike, the deed in doing.
While he smites, how can he but remember,
So he smote before, in such a peril,
When they stood and mocked — "Shall smiting help us?"
When they drank and sneered — "A stroke is easy!"
When they wiped their mouths and went their journey,
Throwing him for thanks — "But drought was pleasant."
Thus old memories mar the actual triumph;
Thus the doing savours of disrelish;
Thus achievement lacks a gracious somewhat;
O'er-importuned brows becloud the mandate,
Carelessness or consciousness — the gesture.
For he bears an ancient wrong about him,
Sees and knows again those phalanxed faces,
Hears, yet one time more, the 'customed prelude —
"How shouldst thou, of all men, smite, and save us?"
Guesses what is like to prove the sequel —
"Egypt's flesh-pots — nay, the drought was better."

X.

Oh, the crowd must have emphatic warrant!
Theirs, the Sinai-forehead's cloven brilliance,
Right-arm's rod-sweep, tongue's imperial fiat.
Never dares the man put off the prophet.

XI.

Did he love one face from out the thousands,
(Were she Jethro's daughter, white and wifely,
Were she but the Æthiopian bondslave,)
He would envy yon dumb patient camel,
Keeping a reserve of scanty water
Meant to save his own life in the desert;
Ready in the desert to deliver
(Kneeling down to let his breast be opened)
Hoard and life together for his mistress.

538

XII.

I shall never, in the years remaining,
Paint you pictures, no, nor carve you statues,
Make you music that should all-express me;
So it seems: I stand on my attainment.
This of verse alone, one life allows me;
Verse and nothing else have I to give you.
Other heights in other lives, God willing:
All the gifts from all the heights, your own, Love!

XIII.

Yet a semblance of resource avails us —
Shade so finely touched, love's sense must seize it.
Take these lines, look lovingly and nearly,
Lines I write the first time and the last time.
He who works in fresco, steals a hair-brush,
Curbs the liberal hand, subservient proudly,
Cramps his spirit, crowds its all in little,
Makes a strange art of an art familiar,
Fills his lady's missal-marge with flowerets.
He who blows thro' bronze, may breathe thro' silver,
Fitly serenade a slumbrous princess.
He who writes, may write for once as I do.

XIV.

Love, you saw me gather men and women,
Live or dead or fashioned by my fancy,
Enter each and all, and use their service,
Speak from every mouth, — the speech, a poem.
Hardly shall I tell my joys and sorrows,
Hopes and fears, belief and disbelieving:
I am mine and yours — the rest be all men's,
Karshish, Cleon, Norbert and the fifty.
Let me speak this once in my true person,
Not as Lippo, Roland or Andrea,

539

Though the fruit of speech be just this sentence:
Pray you, look on these my men and women,
Take and keep my fifty poems finished;
Where my heart lies, let my brain lie also!
Poor the speech; be how I speak, for all things.

XV.

Not but that you know me! Lo, the moon's self!
Here in London, yonder late in Florence,
Still we find her face, the thrice-transfigured.
Curving on a sky imbrued with colour,
Drifted over Fiesole by twilight,
Came she, our new crescent of a hair's-breadth.
Full she flared it, lamping Samminiato,
Rounder 'twixt the cypresses and rounder,
Perfect till the nightingales applauded.
Now, a piece of her old self, impoverished,
Hard to greet, she traverses the houseroofs,
Hurries with unhandsome thrift of silver,
Goes dispiritedly, glad to finish.

XVI.

What, there's nothing in the moon note-worthy?
Nay: for if that moon could love a mortal,
Use, to charm him (so to fit a fancy),
All her magic ('tis the old sweet mythos),
She would turn a new side to her mortal,
Side unseen of herdsman, huntsman, steersman —
Blank to Zoroaster on his terrace,
Blind to Galileo on his turret,
Dumb to Homer, dumb to Keats — him, even!
Think, the wonder of the moonstruck mortal —
When she turns round, comes again in heaven,
Opens out anew for worse or better!
Proves she like some portent of an iceberg
Swimming full upon the ship it founders,
Hungry with huge teeth of splintered crystals?
Proves she as the paved work of a sapphire

Seen by Moses when he climbed the mountain?
Moses, Aaron, Nadab and Abihu
Climbed and saw the very God, the Highest,
Stand upon the paved work of a sapphire.
Like the bodied heaven in his clearness
Shone the stone, the sapphire of that paved work,
When they ate and drank and saw God also!

XVII.

What were seen? None knows, none ever shall know.
Only this is sure — the sight were other,
Not the moon's same side, born late in Florence,
Dying now impoverished here in London.
God be thanked, the meanest of his creatures
Boasts two soul-sides, one to face the world with,
One to show a woman when he loves her!

XVIII.

This I say of me, but think of you, Love!
This to you — yourself my moon of poets!
Ah, but that's the world's side, there's the wonder,
Thus they see you, praise you, think they know you!
There, in turn I stand with them and praise you —
Out of my own self, I dare to phrase it.
But the best is when I glide from out them,
Cross a step or two of dubious twilight,
Come out on the other side, the novel
Silent silver lights and darks undreamed of,
Where I hush and bless myself with silence.

XIX.

Oh, their Rafael of the dear Madonnas,
Oh, their Dante of the dread Inferno,
Wrote one song — and in my brain I sing it,
Drew one angel — borne, see, on my bosom!

R. B.

from JAMES LEE'S WIFE

IN THE DOORWAY

I.

The swallow has set her six young on the rail,
    And looks sea-ward:
The water's in stripes like a snake, olive-pale
    To the leeward, —
On the weather-side, black, spotted white with the wind.
"Good fortune departs, and disaster's behind," —
Hark, the wind with its wants and its infinite wail!

II.

Our fig-tree, that leaned for the saltness, has furled
    Her five fingers,
Each leaf like a hand opened wide to the world
    Where there lingers
No glint of the gold, Summer sent for her sake:
How the vines writhe in rows, each impaled on its stake!
My heart shrivels up and my spirit shrinks curled.

III.

Yet here are we two; we have love, house enough,
    With the field there,
This house of four rooms, that field red and rough,
    Though it yield there,
For the rabbit that robs, scarce a blade or a bent;
If a magpie alight now, it seems an event;
And they both will be gone at November's rebuff.

IV.

But why must cold spread? but wherefore bring change
    To the spirit,
God meant should mate his with an infinite range,
    And inherit
His power to put life in the darkness and cold?
Oh, live and love worthily, bear and be bold!
Whom Summer made friends of, let Winter estrange!

DÎS ALITER VISUM; OR, LE BYRON
DE NOS JOURS

I.

Stop, let me have the truth of that!
    Is that all true? I say, the day
Ten years ago when both of us
    Met on a morning, friends — as thus
We meet this evening, friends or what? —

II.

Did you — because I took your arm
    And sillily smiled, "A mass of brass
"That sea looks, blazing underneath!"
    While up the cliff-road edged with heath,
We took the turns nor came to harm —

III.

Did you consider "Now makes twice
    "That I have seen her, walked and talked
"With this poor pretty thoughtful thing,

543

"Whose worth I weigh: she tries to sing;
"Draws, hopes in time the eye grows nice;

IV.

"Reads verse and thinks she understands;
"Loves all, at any rate, that's great,
"Good, beautiful; but much as we
"Down at the bath-house love the sea,
"Who breathe its salt and bruise its sands:

V.

"While . . . do but follow the fishing-gull
"That flaps and floats from wave to cave!
"There's the sea-lover, fair my friend!
"What then? Be patient, mark and mend!
"Had you the making of your scull?"

VI.

And did you, when we faced the church
   With spire and sad slate roof, aloof
From human fellowship so far,
   Where a few graveyard crosses are,
And garlands for the swallows' perch, —

VII.

Did you determine, as we stepped
   O'er the lone stone fence, "Let me get
"Her for myself, and what's the earth
   "With all its art, verse, music, worth —
"Compared with love, found, gained, and kept?

VIII.

"Schumann's our music-maker now;
   "Has his march-movement youth and mouth?

544

"Ingres's the modern man that paints;
   "Which will lean on me, of his saints?
"Heine for songs; for kisses, how?"

IX.

And did you, when we entered, reached
   The votive frigate, soft aloft
Riding on air this hundred years,
   Safe-smiling at old hopes and fears, —
Did you draw profit while she preached?

X.

Resolving, "Fools we wise men grow!
   "Yes, I could easily blurt out curt
"Some question that might find reply
   "As prompt in her stopped lips, dropped eye,
"And rush of red to cheek and brow:

XI.

"Thus were a match made, sure and fast,
   " 'Mid the blue weed-flowers round the mound
"Where, issuing, we shall stand and stay
   "For one more look at baths and bay,
"Sands, sea-gulls, and the old church last —

XII.

"A match 'twixt me, bent, wigged and lamed,
   "Famous, however, for verse and worse,
"Sure of the Fortieth spare Arm-chair
   "When gout and glory seat me there,
"So, one whose love-freaks pass unblamed, —

XIII.

"And this young beauty, round and sound
   "As a mountain-apple, youth and truth

"With loves and doves, at all events
  "With money in the Three per Cents;
"Whose choice of me would seem profound: —

XIV.

"She might take me as I take her.
  "Perfect the hour would pass, alas!
"Climb high, love high, what matter? Still,
  "Feet, feelings, must descend the hill:
"An hour's perfection can't recur.

XV.

"Then follows Paris and full time
  "For both to reason: 'Thus with us!'
"She'll sigh, 'Thus girls give body and soul
  " 'At first word, think they gain the goal,
" 'When 'tis the starting-place they climb!

XVI.

" 'My friend makes verse and gets renown;
  " 'Have they all fifty years, his peers?
" 'He knows the world, firm, quiet and gay;
  " 'Boys will become as much one day:
" 'They're fools; he cheats, with beard less brown.

XVII.

" 'For boys say, *Love me or I die!*
  " 'He did not say, *The truth is, youth*
" '*I want, who am old and know too much;*
  " '*I'd catch youth: lend me sight and touch!*
" '*Drop heart's blood where life's wheels grate dry!*'

XVIII.

"While I should make rejoinder" — (then
  It was, no doubt, you ceased that least

Light pressure of my arm in yours)
   " 'I can conceive of cheaper cures
" 'For a yawning-fit o'er books and men.

XIX.

" 'What? All I am, was, and might be,
   " 'All, books taught, art brought, life's whole strife,
" 'Painful results since precious, just
   " 'Were fitly exchanged, in wise disgust,
" 'For two cheeks freshened by youth and sea?

XX.

" 'All for a nosegay! — what came first;
   " 'With fields on flower, untried each side;
" 'I rally, need my books and men,
   " 'And find a nosegay': drop it, then,
"No match yet made for best or worst!"

XXI.

That ended me. You judged the porch
   We left by, Norman; took our look
At sea and sky; wondered so few
   Find out the place for air and view;
Remarked the sun began to scorch;

XXII.

Descended, soon regained the baths,
   And then, good-bye! Years ten since then:
Ten years! We meet: you tell me, now,
   By a window-seat for that cliff-brow,
On carpet-stripes for those sand-paths.

XXIII.

Now I may speak: you fool, for all
   Your lore! *Who* made things plain in vain?

What was the sea for? What, the grey
    Sad church, that solitary day,
Crosses and graves and swallows' call?

XXIV.

Was there nought better than to enjoy?
    No feat which, done, would make time break,
And let us pent-up creatures through
    Into eternity, our due?
No forcing earth teach heaven's employ?

XXV.

No wise beginning, here and now,
    What cannot grow complete (earth's feat)
And heaven must finish, there and then?
    No tasting earth's true food for men,
Its sweet in sad, its sad in sweet?

XXVI.

No grasping at love, gaining a share
    O' the sole spark from God's life at strife
With death, so, sure of range above
    The limits here? For us and love,
Failure; but, when God fails, despair.

XXVII.

This you call wisdom? Thus you add
    Good unto good again, in vain?
You loved, with body worn and weak;
    I loved, with faculties to seek:
Were both loves worthless since ill-clad?

XXVIII.

Let the mere star-fish in his vault
    Crawl in a wash of weed, indeed,

Rose-jacynth to the finger-tips:
  He, whole in body and soul, outstrips
Man, found with either in default.

XXIX.

But what's whole, can increase no more,
  Is dwarfed and dies, since here's its sphere.
The devil laughed at you in his sleeve!
  You knew not? That I well believe;
Or you had saved two souls: nay, four.

XXX.

For Stephanie sprained last night her wrist,
  Ankle or something. "Pooh," cry you?
At any rate she danced, all say,
  Vilely; her vogue has had its day.
Here comes my husband from his whist.

CALIBAN UPON SETEBOS; OR,
NATURAL THEOLOGY IN THE ISLAND

"Thou thoughtest that I was altogether such a one as thyself."

['Will sprawl, now that the heat of day is best,
Flat on his belly in the pit's much mire,
With elbows wide, fists clenched to prop his chin.
And, while he kicks both feet in the cool slush,
And feels about his spine small eft-things course,
Run in and out each arm, and make him laugh:
And while above his head a pompion-plant,
Coating the cave-top as a brow its eye,
Creeps down to touch and tickle hair and beard,
And now a flower drops with a bee inside,
And now a fruit to snap at, catch and crunch, —

He looks out o'er yon sea which sunbeams cross
And recross till they weave a spider-web
(Meshes of fire, some great fish breaks at times)
And talks to his own self, howe'er he please,
Touching that other, whom his dam called God.
Because to talk about Him, vexes — ha,
Could He but know! and time to vex is now,
When talk is safer than in winter-time.
Moreover Prosper and Miranda sleep
In confidence he drudges at their task,
And it is good to cheat the pair, and gibe,
Letting the rank tongue blossom into speech.]

Setebos, Setebos, and Setebos!
'Thinketh, He dwelleth i' the cold o' the moon.

'Thinketh He made it, with the sun to match,
But not the stars; the stars came otherwise;
Only made clouds, winds, meteors, such as that:
Also this isle, what lives and grows thereon,
And snaky sea which rounds and ends the same.

'Thinketh, it came of being ill at ease:
He hated that He cannot change His cold,
Nor cure its ache. 'Hath spied an icy fish
That longed to 'scape the rock-stream where she lived,
And thaw herself within the lukewarm brine
O' the lazy sea her stream thrusts far amid,
A crystal spike 'twixt two warm walls of wave;
Only, she ever sickened, found repulse
At the other kind of water, not her life,
(Green-dense and dim-delicious, bred o' the sun)
Flounced back from bliss she was not born to breathe,
And in her old bounds buried her despair,
Hating and loving warmth alike: so He.

'Thinketh, He made thereat the sun, this isle,
Trees and the fowls here, beast and creeping thing.
Yon otter, sleek-wet, black, lithe as a leech;

Yon auk, one fire-eye in a ball of foam,
That floats and feeds; a certain badger brown
He hath watched hunt with that slant white-wedge eye
By moonlight; and the pie with the long tongue
That pricks deep into oakwarts for a worm,
And says a plain word when she finds her prize,
But will not eat the ants; the ants themselves
That build a wall of seeds and settled stalks
About their hole — He made all these and more,
Made all we see, and us, in spite: how else?
He could not, Himself, make a second self
To be His mate; as well have made Himself:
He would not make what he mislikes or slights,
An eyesore to Him, or not worth His pains:
But did, in envy, listlessness or sport,
Make what Himself would fain, in a manner, be —
Weaker in most points, stronger in a few,
Worthy, and yet mere playthings all the while,
Things He admires and mocks too, — that is it.
Because, so brave, so better though they be,
It nothing skills if He begin to plague.
Look now, I melt a gourd-fruit into mash,
Add honeycomb and pods, I have perceived,
Which bite like finches when they bill and kiss, —
Then, when froth rises bladdery, drink up all,
Quick, quick, till maggots scamper through my brain;
Last, throw me on my back i' the seeded thyme,
And wanton, wishing I were born a bird.
Put case, unable to be what I wish,
I yet could make a live bird out of clay:
Would not I take clay, pinch my Caliban
Able to fly? — for, there, see, he hath wings,
And great comb like the hoopoe's to admire,
And there, a sting to do his foes offence,
There, and I will that he begin to live,
Fly to yon rock-top, nip me off the horns
Of grigs high up that make the merry din,
Saucy through their veined wings, and mind me not.
In which feat, if his leg snapped, brittle clay,

And he lay stupid-like, — why, I should laugh;
And if he, spying me, should fall to weep,
Beseech me to be good, repair his wrong,
Bid his poor leg smart less or grow again, —
Well, as the chance were, this might take or else
Not take my fancy: I might hear his cry,
And give the mankin three sound legs for one,
Or pluck the other off, leave him like an egg,
And lessoned he was mine and merely clay.
Were this no pleasure, lying in the thyme,
Drinking the mash, with brain become alive,
Making and marring clay at will? So He.

'Thinketh, such shows nor right nor wrong in Him,
Nor kind, nor cruel: He is strong and Lord.
'Am strong myself compared to yonder crabs
That march now from the mountain to the sea;
'Let twenty pass, and stone the twenty-first,
Loving not, hating not, just choosing so.
'Say, the first straggler that boasts purple spots
Shall join the file, one pincer twisted off;
'Say, this bruised fellow shall receive a worm,
And two worms he whose nippers end in red;
As it likes me each time, I do: so He.

Well then, 'supposeth He is good i' the main,
Placable if His mind and ways were guessed,
But rougher than His handiwork, be sure!
Oh, He hath made things worthier than Himself,
And envieth that, so helped, such things do more
Than He who made them! What consoles but this?
That they, unless through Him, do nought at all,
And must submit: what other use in things?
'Hath cut a pipe of pithless elder-joint
That, blown through, gives exact the scream o' the jay
When from her wing you twitch the feathers blue:
Sound this, and little birds that hate the jay
Flock within stone's throw, glad their foe is hurt:
Put case such pipe could prattle and boast forsooth

"I catch the birds, I am the crafty thing,
"I make the cry my maker cannot make
"With his great round mouth; he must blow through mine!"
Would not I smash it with my foot? So He.

But wherefore rough, why cold and ill at ease?
Aha, that is a question! Ask, for that,
What knows, — the something over Setebos
That made Him, or He, may be, found and fought,
Worsted, drove off and did to nothing, perchance.
There may be something quiet o'er His head,
Out of His reach, that feels nor joy nor grief,
Since both derive from weakness in some way.
I joy because the quails come; would not joy
Could I bring quails here when I have a mind:
This Quiet, all it hath a mind to, doth.
'Esteemeth stars the outposts of its couch,
But never spends much thought nor care that way.
It may look up, work up, — the worse for those
It works on! 'Careth but for Setebos
The many-handed as a cuttle-fish,
Who, making Himself feared through what He does,
Looks up, first, and perceives he cannot soar
To what is quiet and hath happy life;
Next looks down here, and out of very spite
Makes this a bauble-world to ape yon real,
These good things to match those as hips do grapes.
'Tis solace making baubles, ay, and sport.
Himself peeped late, eyed Prosper at his books
Careless and lofty, lord now of the isle:
Vexed, 'stitched a book of broad leaves, arrow-shaped,
Wrote thereon, he knows what, prodigious words;
Has peeled a wand and called it by a name;
Weareth at whiles for an enchanter's robe
The eyed skin of a supple oncelot;
And hath an ounce sleeker than youngling mole,
A four-legged serpent he makes cower and couch,
Now snarl, now hold its breath and mind his eye,
And saith she is Miranda and my wife:

'Keeps for his Ariel a tall pouch-bill crane
He bids go wade for fish and straight disgorge;
Also a sea-beast, lumpish, which he snared,
Blinded the eyes of, and brought somewhat tame,
And split its toe-webs, and now pens the drudge
In a hole o' the rock and calls him Caliban;
A bitter heart that bides its time and bites.
'Plays thus at being Prosper in a way,
Taketh his mirth with make-believes: so He.

His dam held that the Quiet made all things
Which Setebos vexed only: 'holds not so.
Who made them weak, meant weakness He might vex.
Had He meant other, while His hand was in,
Why not make horny eyes no thorn could prick,
Or plate my scalp with bone against the snow,
Or overscale my flesh 'neath joint and joint,
Like an orc's armour? Ay, — so spoil His sport!
He is the One now: only He doth all.
"Saith, He may like, perchance, what profits Him.
Ay, himself loves what does him good; but why?
'Gets good no otherwise. This blinded beast
Loves whoso places flesh-meat on his nose,
But, had he eyes, would want no help, but hate
Or love, just as it liked him: He hath eyes.
Also it pleaseth Setebos to work,
Use all His hands, and exercise much craft,
By no means for the love of what is worked.
'Tasteth, himself, no finer good i' the world
When all goes right, in this safe summer-time,
And he wants little, hungers, aches not much,
Than trying what to do with wit and strength.
'Falls to make something: 'piled yon pile of turfs,
And squared and stuck there squares of soft white chalk,
And, with a fish-tooth, scratched a moon on each,
And set up endwise certain spikes of tree,
And crowned the whole with a sloth's skull a-top,
Found dead i' the woods, too hard for one to kill.

No use at all i' the work, for work's sole sake;
'Shall some day knock it down again: so He.

'Saith He is terrible: watch His feats in proof!
One hurricane will spoil six good months' hope.
He hath a spite against me, that I know,
Just as He favours Prosper, who knows why?
So it is, all the same, as well I find.
'Wove wattles half the winter, fenced them firm
With stone and stake to stop she-tortoises
Crawling to lay their eggs here: well, one wave,
Feeling the foot of Him upon its neck,
Gaped as a snake does, lolled out its large tongue,
And licked the whole labour flat: so much for spite.
'Saw a ball flame down late (yonder it lies)
Where, half an hour before, I slept i' the shade:
Often they scatter sparkles: there is force!
'Dug up a newt He may have envied once
And turned to stone, shut up inside a stone.
Please Him and hinder this? — What Prosper does?
Aha, if He would tell me how! Not He!
There is the sport: discover how or die!
All need not die, for of the things o' the isle
Some flee afar, some dive, some run up trees;
Those at His mercy, — why, they please Him most
When . . . when . . . . well, never try the same way twice!
Repeat what act has pleased, He may grow wroth.
You must not know His ways, and play Him off,
Sure of the issue. 'Doth the like himself:
'Spareth a squirrel that it nothing fears
But steals the nut from underneath my thumb,
And when I threat, bites stoutly in defence:
'Spareth an urchin that contrariwise,
Curls up into a ball, pretending death
For fright at my approach: the two ways please.
But what would move my choler more than this,
That either creature counted on its life
To-morrow and next day and all days to come,
Saying, forsooth, in the inmost of its heart,

"Because he did so yesterday with me,
"And otherwise with such another brute,
"So must he do henceforth and always." — Ay?
Would teach the reasoning couple what "must" means!
'Doth as he likes, or wherefore Lord? So He.

'Conceiveth all things will continue thus,
And we shall have to live in fear of Him
So long as He lives, keeps His strength: no change,
If He have done His best, make no new world
To please Him more, so leave off watching this, —
If He surprise not even the Quiet's self
Some strange day, — or, suppose, grow into it
As grubs grow butterflies: else, here are we,
And there is He, and nowhere help at all.

'Believeth with the life, the pain shall stop.
His dam held different, that after death
He both plagued enemies and feasted friends:
Idly! He doth His worst in this our life,
Giving just respite lest we die through pain,
Saving last pain for worst, — with which, an end.
Meanwhile, the best way to escape His ire
Is, not to seem too happy. 'Sees, himself,
Yonder two flies, with purple films and pink,
Bask on the pompion-bell above: kills both.
'Sees two black painful beetles roll their ball
On head and tail as if to save their lives:
Moves them the stick away they strive to clear.

Even so, 'would have Him misconceive, suppose
This Caliban strives hard and ails no less,
And always, above all else, envies Him;
Wherefore he mainly dances on dark nights,
Moans in the sun, gets under holes to laugh,
And never speaks his mind save housed as now:
Outside, 'groans, curses. If He caught me here,
O'erheard this speech, and asked "What chucklest at?"
'Would, to appease Him, cut a finger off,

Or of my three kid yearlings burn the best,
Or let the toothsome apples rot on tree,
Or push my tame beast for the orc to taste:
While myself lit a fire, and made a song
And sung it, *"What I hate, be consecrate*
"To celebrate Thee and Thy state, no mate
"For Thee; what see for envy in poor me?"
Hoping the while, since evils sometimes mend,
Warts rub away and sores are cured with slime,
That some strange day, will either the Quiet catch
And conquer Setebos, or likelier He
Decrepit may doze, doze, as good as die.

———————————

[What, what? A curtain o'er the world at once!
Crickets stop hissing; not a bird — or, yes,
There scuds His raven that has told Him all!
It was fool's play, this prattling! Ha! The wind
Shoulders the pillared dust, death's house o' the move,
And fast invading fires begin! White blaze —
A tree's head snaps — and there, there, there, there, there,
His thunder follows! Fool to gibe at Him!
Lo! 'Lieth flat and loveth Setebos!
'Maketh his teeth meet through his upper lip,
Will let those quails fly, will not eat this month
One little mess of whelks, so he may 'scape!]

CONFESSIONS

I.

What is he buzzing in my ears?
  "Now that I come to die,
"Do I view the world as a vale of tears?"
  Ah, reverend sir, not I!

II.

What I viewed there once, what I view again
    Where the physic bottles stand
On the table's edge, — is a suburb lane,
    With a wall to my bedside hand.

III.

That lane sloped, much as the bottles do,
    From a house you could descry
O'er the garden-wall: is the curtain blue
    Or green to a healthy eye?

IV.

To mine, it serves for the old June weather
    Blue above lane and wall;
And that farthest bottle labelled "Ether"
    Is the house o'ertopping all.

V.

At a terrace, somewhere near the stopper,
    There watched for me, one June,
A girl: I know, sir, it's improper,
    My poor mind's out of tune.

VI.

Only, there was a way . . . you crept
    Close by the side, to dodge
Eyes in the house, two eyes except:
    They styled their house "The Lodge."

558

VII.

What right had a lounger up their lane?
   But, by creeping very close,
With the good wall's help, — their eyes might strain
   And stretch themselves to Oes,

VIII.

Yet never catch her and me together,
   As she left the attic, there,
By the rim of the bottle labelled "Ether,"
   And stole from stair to stair,

IX.

And stood by the rose-wreathed gate. Alas,
   We loved, sir — used to meet:
How sad and bad and mad it was —
   But then, how it was sweet!

MAY AND DEATH

I.

I wish that when you died last May,
   Charles, there had died along with you
Three parts of spring's delightful things;
   Ay, and, for me, the fourth part too.

II.

A foolish thought, and worse, perhaps!
   There must be many a pair of friends
Who, arm in arm, deserve the warm
   Moon-births and the long evening-ends.

III.

So, for their sake, be May still May!
 Let their new time, as mine of old,
Do all it did for me: I bid
 Sweet sights and sounds throng manifold.

IV.

Only, one little sight, one plant,
 Woods have in May, that starts up green
Save a sole streak which, so to speak,
 Is spring's blood, spilt its leaves between, —

V.

That, they might spare; a certain wood
 Might miss the plant; their loss were small:
But I, — whene'er the leaf grows there,
 Its drop comes from my heart, that's all.

PROSPICE

Fear death? — to feel the fog in my throat,
 The mist in my face,
When the snows begin, and the blasts denote
 I am nearing the place,
The power of the night, the press of the storm,
 The post of the foe;
Where he stands, the Arch Fear in a visible form,
 Yet the strong man must go:
For the journey is done and the summit attained,
 And the barriers fall,
Though a battle's to fight ere the guerdon be gained,
 The reward of it all.

ROBERT BROWNING

I was ever a fighter, so — one fight more,
  The best and the last!
I would hate that death bandaged my eyes and forbore,
  And bade me creep past.
No! let me taste the whole of it, fare like my peers
  The heroes of old,
Bear the brunt, in a minute pay glad life's arrears
  Of pain, darkness and cold.
For sudden the worst turns the best to the brave,
  The black minute's at end,
And the elements' rage, the fiend-voices that rave,
  Shall dwindle, shall blend,
Shall change, shall become first a peace out of pain,
  Then a light, then thy breast,
O thou soul of my soul! I shall clasp thee again,
  And with God be the rest!

YOUTH AND ART

I.

It once might have been, once only:
  We lodged in a street together,
You, a sparrow on the housetop lonely,
  I, a lone she-bird of his feather.

II.

Your trade was with sticks and clay,
  You thumbed, thrust, patted and polished,
Then laughed "They will see some day
  "Smith made, and Gibson demolished."

561

III.

My business was song, song, song;
  I chirped, cheeped, trilled and twittered,
"Kate Brown's on the boards ere long,
  "And Grisi's existence embittered!"

IV.

I earned no more by a warble
  Than you by a sketch in plaster;
You wanted a piece of marble,
  I needed a music-master.

V.

We studied hard in our styles,
  Chipped each at a crust like Hindoos,
For air looked out on the tiles,
  For fun watched each other's windows.

VI.

You lounged, like a boy of the South,
  Cap and blouse — nay, a bit of beard too;
Or you got it, rubbing your mouth
  With fingers the clay adhered to.

VII.

And I — soon managed to find
  Weak points in the flower-fence facing,
Was forced to put up a blind
  And be safe in my corset-lacing.

VIII.

No harm! It was not my fault
  If you never turned your eye's tail up
As I shook upon E *in alt*,
  Or ran the chromatic scale up:

IX.

For spring bade the sparrows pair,
  And the boys and girls gave guesses,
And stalls in our street looked rare
  With bulrush and watercresses.

X.

Why did not you pinch a flower
  In a pellet of clay and fling it
Why did not I put a power
  Of thanks in a look, or sing it?

XI.

I did look, sharp as a lynx,
  (And yet the memory rankles)
When models arrived, some minx
  Tripped up-stairs, she and her ankles.

XII.

But I think I gave you as good!
  "That foreign fellow, — who can know
"How she pays, in a playful mood,
  "For his tuning her that piano?"

XIII.

Could you say so, and never say
  "Suppose we join hands and fortunes,
"And I fetch her from over the way,
  "Her, piano, and long tunes and short tunes?"

XIV.

No, no: you would not be rash,
  Nor I rasher and something over:
You've to settle yet Gibson's hash,
  And Grisi yet lives in clover.

XV.

But you meet the Prince at the Board,
  I'm queen myself at *bals-paré,*
I've married a rich old lord,
  And you're dubbed knight and an R.A.

XVI.

Each life unfulfilled, you see;
  It hangs still, patchy and scrappy:
We have not sighed deep, laughed free,
  Starved, feasted, despaired, — been happy.

XVII.

And nobody calls you a dunce,
  And people suppose me clever:
This could but have happened once,
  And we missed it, lost it for ever.

A FACE

If one could have that little head of hers
   Painted upon a background of pale gold,
Such as the Tuscan's early art prefers!
   No shade encroaching on the matchless mould
Of those two lips, which should be opening soft
   In the pure profile; not as when she laughs,
For that spoils all: but rather as if aloft
   Yon hyacinth, she loves so, leaned its staff's
Burthen of honey-coloured buds to kiss
And capture 'twixt the lips apart for this.
Then her lithe neck, three fingers might surround,
   How it should waver on the pale gold ground
Up to the fruit-shaped, perfect chin it lifts!
   I know, Correggio loves to mass, in rifts
Of heaven, his angel faces, orb on orb
Breaking its outline, burning shades absorb:
But these are only massed there, I should think,
   Waiting to see some wonder momently
Grow out, stand full, fade slow against the sky
   (That's the pale ground you'd see this sweet face by),
All heaven, meanwhile, condensed into one eye
Which fears to lose the wonder, should it wink.

MR. SLUDGE, "THE MEDIUM"

Now, don't, sir! Don't expose me! Just this once!
This was the first and only time, I'll swear, —
Look at me, — see, I kneel, — the only time,
I swear, I ever cheated, — yes, by the soul
Of Her who hears — (your sainted mother, sir!)

All, except this last accident, was truth —
This little kind of slip! — and even this,
It was your own wine, sir, the good champagne,
(I took it for Catawba, you're so kind)
Which put the folly in my head!

     "Get up?"
You still inflict on me that terrible face?
You show no mercy? — Not for Her dear sake,
The sainted spirit's, whose soft breath even now
Blows on my cheek — (don't you feel something, sir?)
You'll tell?

   Go tell, then! Who the devil cares
What such a rowdy chooses to . . .

       Aie — aie — aie!
Please, sir! your thumbs are through my windpipe, sir!
Ch — ch!

   Well, sir, I hope you've done it now!
Oh Lord! I little thought, sir, yesterday,
When your departed mother spoke those words
Of peace through me, and moved you, sir, so much,
You gave me — (very kind it was of you)
These shirt-studs — (better take them back again,
Please, sir) — yes, little did I think so soon
A trifle of trick, all through a glass too much
Of his own champagne, would change my best of friends
Into an angry gentleman!

      Though, 'twas wrong.
I don't contest the point; your anger's just:
Whatever put such folly in my head,
I know 'twas wicked of me. There's a thick
Dusk undeveloped spirit (I've observed)
Owes me a grudge — a negro's, I should say,
Or else an Irish emigrant's; yourself
Explained the case so well last Sunday, sir,
When we had summoned Franklin to clear up

A point about those shares i' the telegraph:
Ay, and he swore . . . or might it be Tom Paine? . . .
Thumping the table close by where I crouched,
He'd do me soon a mischief: that's come true!
Why, now your face clears! I was sure it would!
Then, this one time . . . don't take your hand away,
Through yours I surely kiss your mother's hand . . .
You'll promise to forgive me? — or, at least,
Tell nobody of this? Consider, sir!
What harm can mercy do? Would but the shade
Of the venerable dead-one just vouchsafe
A rap or tip! What bit of paper's here?
Suppose we take a pencil, let her write,
Make the least sign, she urges on her child
Forgiveness? There now! Eh? Oh! 'Twas your foot
And not a natural creak, sir?

                          Answer, then!
Once, twice, thrice . . . see, I'm waiting to say "thrice!"
All to no use? No sort of hope for me?
It's all to post to Greeley's newspaper?

What? If I told you all about the tricks?
Upon my soul! — the whole truth, and nought else,
And how there's been some falsehood — for your part,
Will you engage to pay my passage out,
And hold your tongue until I'm safe on board?
England's the place, not Boston — no offence!
I see what makes you hesitate: don't fear!
I mean to change my trade and cheat no more,
Yes, this time really it's upon my soul!
Be my salvation! — under Heaven, of course.
I'll tell some queer things. Sixty Vs must do.
A trifle, though, to start with! We'll refer
The question to this table?

                        How you're changed!
Then split the difference; thirty more, we'll say.
Ay, but you leave my presents! Else I'll swear

'Twas all through those: you wanted yours again,
So, picked a quarrel with me, to get them back!
Tread on a worm, it turns, sir! If I turn,
Your fault! 'Tis you'll have forced me! Who's obliged
To give up life yet try no self-defence?
At all events, I'll run the risk. Eh?

                           Done!
May I sit, sir? This dear old table, now!
Please, sir, a parting egg-nogg and cigar!
I've been so happy with you! Nice stuffed chairs,
And sympathetic sideboards; what an end
To all the instructive evenings! (It's alight.)
Well, nothing lasts, as Bacon came and said.
Here goes, — but keep your temper, or I'll scream!

Fol-lol-the-rido-liddle-iddle-ol!
You see, sir, it's your own fault more than mine;
It's all your fault, you curious gentlefolk!
You're prigs, — excuse me, — like to look so spry,
So clever, while you cling by half a claw
To the perch whereon you puff yourselves at roost,
Such piece of self-conceit as serves for perch
Because you chose it, so it must be safe.
Oh, otherwise you're sharp enough! You spy
Who slips, who slides, who holds by help of wing,
Wanting real foothold, — who can't keep upright
On the other perch, your neighbour chose, not you:
There's no outwitting you respecting him!
For instance, men love money — that, you know
And what men do to gain it: well, suppose
A poor lad, say a help's son in your house,
Listening at keyholes, hears the company
Talk grand of dollars, V-notes, and so forth,
How hard they are to get, how good to hold,
How much they buy, — if, suddenly, in pops he —
"I've got a V-note!" — what do you say to him?
What's your first word which follows your last kick?
"Where did you steal it, rascal?" That's because

He finds you, fain would fool you, off your perch,
Not on the special piece of nonsense, sir,
Elected your parade-ground: let him try
Lies to the end of the list, — "He picked it up,
"His cousin died and left it him by will,
"The President flung it to him, riding by,
"An actress trucked it for a curl of his hair,
"He dreamed of luck and found his shoe enriched,
"He dug up clay, and out of clay made gold" —
How would you treat such possibilities?
Would not you, prompt, investigate the case
With cow-hide? "Lies, lies, lies," you'd shout: and why?
Which of the stories might not prove mere truth?
This last, perhaps, that clay was turned to coin!
Let's see, now, give him me to speak for him!
How many of your rare philosophers,
In plaguy books I've had to dip into,
Believed gold could be made thus, saw it made
And made it? Oh, with such philosophers
You're on your best behaviour! While the lad —
With him, in a trice, you settle likelihoods,
Nor doubt a moment how he got his prize:
In his case, you hear, judge and execute,
All in a breath: so would most men of sense.

But let the same lad hear you talk as grand
At the same keyhole, you and company,
Of signs and wonders, the invisible world;
How wisdom scouts our vulgar unbelief
More than our vulgarest credulity;
How good men have desired to see a ghost,
What Johnson used to say, what Wesley did,
Mother Goose thought, and fiddle-diddle-dee: —
If he break in with, "Sir, I saw a ghost!"
Ah, the ways change! He finds you perched and prim;
It's a conceit of yours that ghosts may be:
There's no talk now of cow-hide. "Tell it out!
"Don't fear us! Take your time and recollect!
"Sit down first: try a glass of wine, my boy!

"And, David, (is not that your Christian name?)
"Of all things, should this happen twice — it may —
"Be sure, while fresh in mind, you let us know!"
Does the boy blunder, blurt out this, blab that,
Break down in the other, as beginners will?
All's candour, all's considerateness — "No haste!
"Pause and collect yourself! We understand!
"That's the bad memory, or the natural shock,
"Or the unexplained *phenomena!*"

          Egad,
The boy takes heart of grace; finds, never fear,
The readiest way to ope your own heart wide,
Show — what I call your peacock-perch, pet post
To strut, and spread the tail, and squawk upon!
"Just as you thought, much as you might expect!
"There be more things in heaven and earth, Horatio," . . .
And so on. Shall not David take the hint,
Grow bolder, stroke you down at quickened rate?
If he ruffle a feather, it's "Gently, patiently!
"Manifestations are so weak at first!
"Doubting, moreover, kills them, cuts all short,
"Cures with a vengeance!"

        There, sir, that's your style!
You and your boy — such pains bestowed on him,
Or any headpiece of the average worth,
To teach, say, Greek, would perfect him apace,
Make him a Person ("Porson?" thank you, sir!)
Much more, proficient in the art of lies.
You never leave the lesson! Fire alight,
Catch you permitting it to die! You've friends;
There's no withholding knowledge, — least from those
Apt to look elsewhere for their souls' supply:
Why should not you parade your lawful prize?
Who finds a picture, digs a medal up,
Hits on a first edition, — he henceforth
Gives it his name, grows notable: how much more,
Who ferrets out a "medium"? "David's yours,

"You highly-favoured man? Then, pity souls
"Less privileged! Allow us share your luck!"
So, David holds the circle, rules the roast,
Narrates the vision, peeps in the glass ball,
Sets-to the spirit-writing, hears the raps,
As the case may be.

        Now mark! To be precise —
Though I say, "lies" all these, at this first stage,
'Tis just for science' sake: I call such grubs
By the name of what they'll turn to, dragonflies.
Strictly, it's what good people style untruth;
But yet, so far, not quite the full-grown thing:
It's fancying, fable-making, nonsense-work —
What never meant to be so very bad —
The knack of story-telling, brightening up
Each dull old bit of fact that drops its shine.
One does see somewhat when one shuts one's eyes,
If only spots and streaks; tables do tip
In the oddest way of themselves: and pens, good Lord,
Who knows if you drive them or they drive you?
'Tis but a foot in the water and out again;
Not that duck-under which decides your dive.
Note this, for it's important: listen why.

I'll prove, you push on David till he dives
And ends the shivering. Here's your circle, now:
Two-thirds of them, with heads like you their host,
Turn up their eyes, and cry, as you expect,
"Lord, who'd have thought it!" But there's always one
Looks wise, compassionately smiles, submits
"Of your veracity no kind of doubt,
"But — do you feel so certain of that boy's?
"Really, I wonder! I confess myself
"More chary of my faith!" That's galling, sir!
What, he the investigator, he the sage,
When all's done? Then, you just have shut your eyes,
Opened your mouth, and gulped down David whole,
You! Terrible were such catastrophe!

So, evidence is redoubled, doubled again,
And doubled besides; once more, "He heard, we heard,
"You and they heard, your mother and your wife,
"Your children and the stranger in your gates:
"Did they or did they not?" So much for him,
The black sheep, guest without the wedding-garb,
The doubting Thomas! Now's your turn to crow:
"He's kind to think you such a fool: Sludge cheats?
"Leave you alone to take precautions!"

         Straight
The rest join chorus. Thomas stands abashed,
Sips silent some such beverage as this,
Considers if it be harder, shutting eyes
And gulping David in good fellowship,
Than going elsewhere, getting, in exchange,
With no egg-nogg to lubricate the food,
Some just as tough a morsel. Over the way,
Holds Captain Sparks his court: is it better there?
Have not you hunting-stories, scalping-scenes,
And Mexican War exploits to swallow plump
If you'd be free o' the stove-side, rocking-chair,
And trio of affable daughters?

        Doubt succumbs!
Victory! All your circle's yours again!
Out of the clubbing of submissive wits,
David's performance rounds, each chink gets patched,
Every protrusion of a point's filed fine,
All's fit to set a-rolling round the world,
And then return to David finally,
Lies seven-feet thick about his first half-inch.
Here's a choice birth o' the supernatural,
Poor David's pledged to! You've employed no tool
The laws exclaim at, save the devil's own,
Yet screwed him into henceforth gulling you
To the top o' your bent, — all out of one half-lie!

You hold, if there's one half or a hundredth part
Of a lie, that's his fault, — his be the penalty!

I dare say! You'd prove firmer in his place?
You'd find the courage, — that first flurry over,
That mild bit of romancing-work at end, —
To interpose with "It gets serious, this;
"Must stop here. Sir, I saw no ghost at all.
"Inform your friends I made . . . well, fools of them,
"And found you ready-made. I've lived in clover
"These three weeks: take it out in kicks of me!"
I doubt it. Ask your conscience! Let me know,
Twelve months hence, with how few embellishments
You've told almighty Boston of this passage
Of arms between us, your first taste o' the foil
From Sludge who could not fence, sir! Sludge, your boy!
I lied, sir, — there! I got up from my gorge
On offal in the gutter, and preferred
Your canvas-backs: I took their carver's size,
Measured his modicum of intelligence,
Tickled him on the cockles of his heart
With a raven feather, and next week found myself
Sweet and clean, dining daintily, dizened smart,
Set on a stool buttressed by ladies' knees,
Every soft smiler calling me her pet,
Encouraging my story to uncoil
And creep out from its hole, inch after inch,
"How last night, I no sooner snug in bed,
"Tucked up, just as they left me, — than came raps!
"While a light whisked" . . . "Shaped somewhat like a star?"
"Well, like some sort of stars, ma'am." — "So we thought!
"And any voice? Not yet? Try hard, next time,
"If you can't hear a voice; we think you may:
"At least, the Pennsylvanian 'mediums' did."
Oh, next time comes the voice! "Just as we hoped!"
Are not the hopers proud now, pleased, profuse
O' the natural acknowledgment?

Of course!
So, off we push, illy-oh-yo, trim the boat,
On we sweep with a cataract ahead,
We're midway to the Horseshoe: stop, who can,

The dance of bubbles gay about our prow!
Experiences become worth waiting for,
Spirits now speak up, tell their inmost mind,
And compliment the "medium" properly,
Concern themselves about his Sunday coat,
See rings on his hand with pleasure. Ask yourself
How you'd receive a course of treats like these!
Why, take the quietest hack and stall him up,
Cram him with corn a month, then out with him
Among his mates on a bright April morn,
With the turf to tread; see if you find or no
A caper in him, if he bucks or bolts!
Much more a youth whose fancies sprout as rank
As toadstool-clump from melon-bed. 'Tis soon,
"Sirrah, you spirit, come, go, fetch and carry,
"Read, write, rap, rub-a-dub, and hang yourself!"
I'm spared all further trouble; all's arranged;
Your circle does my business; I may rave
Like an epileptic dervish in the books,
Foam, fling myself flat, rend my clothes to shreds;
No matter: lovers, friends and countrymen
Will lay down spiritual laws, read wrong things right
By the rule o' reverse. If Francis Verulam
Styles himself Bacon, spells the name beside
With a y and a k, says he drew breath in York,
Gave up the ghost in Wales when Cromwell reigned,
(As, sir, we somewhat fear he was apt to say,
Before I found the useful book that knows)
Why, what harm's done? The circle smiles apace,
"It was not Bacon, after all, you see!
"We understand; the trick's but natural:
"Such spirits' individuality
"Is hard to put in evidence: they incline
"To gibe and jeer, these undeveloped sorts.
"You see, their world's much like a jail broke loose,
"While this of ours remains shut, bolted, barred,
"With a single window to it. Sludge, our friend,
"Serves as this window, whether thin or thick,
"Or stained or stainless; he's the medium-pane

"Through which, to see us and be seen, they peep:
"They crowd each other, hustle for a chance,
"Tread on their neighbour's kibes, play tricks enough!
"Does Bacon, tired of waiting, swerve aside?
"Up in his place jumps Barnum — 'I'm your man,
" 'I'll answer you for Bacon!' Try once more!"

Or else it's — "What's a 'medium'? He's a means,
"Good, bad, indifferent, still the only means
"Spirits can speak by; he may misconceive,
"Stutter and stammer, — he's their Sludge and drudge,
"Take him or leave him; they must hold their peace,
"Or else, put up with having knowledge strained
"To half-expression through his ignorance.
"Suppose, the spirit Beethoven wants to shed
"New music he's brimful of; why, he turns
"The handle of this organ, grinds with Sludge,
"And what he poured in at the mouth o' the mill
"As a Thirty-third Sonata, (fancy now!)
"Comes from the hopper as bran-new Sludge, nought else,
"The Shakers' Hymn in G, with a natural F,
"Or the 'Stars and Stripes' set to consecutive fourths."

Sir, where's the scrape you did not help me through,
You that are wise? And for the fools, the folk
Who came to see, — the guests, (observe that word!)
Pray do you find guests criticize your wine,
Your furniture, your grammar, or your nose?
Then, why your "medium"? What's the difference?
Prove your madeira red-ink and gamboge, —
Your Sludge, a cheat — then, somebody's a goose
For vaunting both as genuine. "Guests!" Don't fear!
They'll make a wry face, nor too much of that,
And leave you in your glory.

                              "No, sometimes
"They doubt and say as much!" Ay, doubt they do!
And what's the consequence? "Of course they doubt" —
(You triumph) "that explains the hitch at once!

"Doubt posed our 'medium,' puddled his pure mind;
"He gave them back their rubbish: pitch chaff in,
"Could flour come out o' the honest mill?" So, prompt
Applaud the faithful: cases flock in point,
"How, when a mocker willed a 'medium' once
"Should name a spirit James whose name was George,
" 'James' cried the 'medium,' — 'twas the test of truth!"
In short, a hit proves much, a miss proves more.
Does this convince? The better: does it fail?
Time for the double-shotted broadside, then —
The grand means, last resource. Look black and big!
"You style us idiots, therefore — why stop short?
"Accomplices in rascality: this we hear
"In our own house, from our invited guest
"Found brave enough to outrage a poor boy
"Exposed by our good faith! Have you been heard?
"Now, then, hear us; one man's not quite worth twelve.
"You see a cheat? Here's some twelve see an ass:
"Excuse me if I calculate: good day!"
Out slinks the sceptic, all the laughs explode.
Sludge waves his hat in triumph!

                                    Or — he don't.
There's something in real truth (explain who can!)
One casts a wistful eye at, like the horse
Who mopes beneath stuffed hay-racks and won't munch
Because he spies a corn-bag: hang that truth,
It spoils all dainties proffered in its place!
I've felt at times when, cockered, cosseted
And coddled by the aforesaid company,
Bidden enjoy their bullying, — never fear,
But o'er their shoulders spit at the flying man, —
I've felt a child; only, a fractious child
That, dandled soft by nurse, aunt, grandmother,
Who keep him from the kennel, sun and wind,
Good fun and wholesome mud, — enjoined be sweet,
And comely and superior, — eyes askance
The ragged sons o' the gutter at their game,
Fain would be down with them i' the thick o' the filth,

Making dirt-pies, laughing free, speaking plain,
And calling granny the grey old cat she is.
I've felt a spite, I say, at you, at them,
Huggings and humbug — gnashed my teeth to mark
A decent dog pass! It's too bad, I say,
Ruining a soul so!

        But what's "so," what's fixed,
Where may one stop? Nowhere! The cheating's nursed
Out of the lying, softly and surely spun
To just your length, sir! I'd stop soon enough:
But you're for progress. "All old, nothing new?
"Only the usual talking through the mouth,
"Or writing by the hand? I own, I thought
"This would develop, grow demonstrable,
"Make doubt absurd, give figures we might see,
"Flowers we might touch. There's no one doubts you, Sludge!
"You dream the dreams, you see the spiritual sights,
"The speeches come in your head, beyond dispute.
"Still, for the sceptics' sake, to stop all mouths,
"We want some outward manifestation! — well,
"The Pennsylvanians gained such; why not Sludge?
"He may improve with time!"

        Ay, that he may!
He sees his lot: there's no avoiding fate.
'Tis a trifle at first. "Eh, David? Did you hear?
"You jogged the table, your foot caused the squeak,
"This time you're . . . joking, are you not, my boy?"
"N-n-no!" — and I'm done for, bought and sold henceforth.
The old good easy jog-trot way, the . . . eh?
The . . . not so very false, as falsehood goes,
The spinning out and drawing fine, you know, —
Really mere novel-writing of a sort,
Acting, or improvising, make-believe,
Surely not downright cheatery, — any how,
'Tis done with and my lot cast; Cheat's my name:
The fatal dash of brandy in your tea
Has settled what you'll have the souchong's smack:
The caddy gives way to the dram-bottle.

Then, it's so cruel easy! Oh, those tricks
That can't be tricks, those feats by sleight of hand,
Clearly no common conjuror's! — no indeed!
A conjuror? Choose me any craft i' the world
A man puts hand to; and with six months' pains
I'll play you twenty tricks miraculous
To people untaught the trade: have you seen glass blown,
Pipes pierced? Why, just this biscuit that I chip,
Did you ever watch a baker toss one flat
To the oven? Try and do it! Take my word,
Practise but half as much, while limbs are lithe,
To turn, shove, tilt a table, crack your joints,
Manage your feet, dispose your hands aright,
Work wires that twitch the curtains, play the glove
At end o' your slipper, — then put out the lights
And . . . there, there, all you want you'll get, I hope!
I found it slip, easy as an old shoe.

Now, lights on table again! I've done my part,
You take my place while I give thanks and rest.
"Well, Judge Humgruffin, what's your verdict, sir?
"You, hardest head in the United States, —
"Did you detect a cheat here? Wait! Let's see!
"Just an experiment first, for candour's sake!
"I'll try and cheat you, Judge! The table tilts:
"Is it I that move it? Write! I'll press your hand:
"Cry when I push, or guide your pencil, Judge!"
Sludge still triumphant! "That a rap, indeed?
"That, the real writing? Very like a whale!
"Then, if, sir, you — a most distinguished man,
"And, were the Judge not here, I'd say, . . . no matter!
"Well, sir, if you fail, you can't take us in, —
"There's little fear that Sludge will!"

                              Won't he, ma'am?
But what if our distinguished host, like Sludge,
Bade God bear witness that he played no trick,
While you believed that what produced the raps
Was just a certain child who died, you know,

And whose last breath you thought your lips had felt?
Eh? That's a capital point, ma'am: Sludge begins
At your entreaty with your dearest dead,
The little voice set lisping once again,
The tiny hand made feel for yours once more,
The poor lost image brought back, plain as dreams,
Which image, if a word had chanced recall,
The customary cloud would cross your eyes,
Your heart return the old tick, pay its pang!
A right mood for investigation, this!
One's at one's ease with Saul and Jonathan,
Pompey and Cæsar: but one's own lost child . . .
I wonder, when you heard the first clod drop
From the spadeful at the grave-side, felt you free
To investigate who twitched your funeral scarf
Or brushed your flounces? Then, it came of course
You should be stunned and stupid; then, (how else?)
Your breath stopped with your blood, your brain struck work.
But now, such causes fail of such effects,
All's changed, — the little voice begins afresh,
Yet you, calm, consequent, can test and try
And touch the truth. "Tests? Didn't the creature tell
"Its nurse's name, and say it lived six years,
"And rode a rocking-horse? Enough of tests!
"Sludge never could learn that!"

                             He could not, eh?
You compliment him. "Could not?" Speak for yourself!
I'd like to know the man I ever saw
Once, — never mind where, how, why, when, — once saw,
Of whom I do not keep some matter in mind
He'd swear I "could not" know, sagacious soul!
What? Do you live in this world's blow of blacks,
Palaver, gossipry, a single hour
Nor find one smut has settled on your nose,
Of a smut's worth, no more, no less? — one fact
Out of the drift of facts, whereby you learn
What someone was, somewhere, somewhen, somewhy?
You don't tell folk — "See what has stuck to me!

"Judge Humgruffin, our most distinguished man,
"Your uncle was a tailor, and your wife
"Thought to have married Miggs, missed him, hit you!" —
Do you, sir, though you see him twice a-week?
"No," you reply, "what use retailing it?
"Why should I?" But, you see, one day you *should*,
Because one day there's much use, — when this fact
Brings you the Judge upon both gouty knees
Before the supernatural; proves that Sludge
Knows, as you say, a thing he "could not" know:
Will not Sludge thenceforth keep an outstretched face
The way the wind drives?

                "Could not!" Look you now,
I'll tell you a story! There's a whiskered chap,
A foreigner, that teaches music here
And gets his bread, — knowing no better way:
He says, the fellow who informed of him
And made him fly his country and fall West
Was a hunchback cobbler, sat, stitched soles and sang,
In some outlandish place, the city Rome,
In a cellar by their Broadway, all day long;
Never asked questions, stopped to listen or look,
Nor lifted nose from lapstone; let the world
Roll round his three-legged stool, and news run in
The ears he hardly seemed to keep pricked up.
Well, that man went on Sundays, touched his pay,
And took his praise from government, you see;
For something like two dollars every week,
He'd engage tell you some one little thing
Of some one man, which led to many more,
(Because one truth leads right to the world's end)
And make you that man's master — when he dined
And on what dish, where walked to keep his health
And to what street. His trade was, throwing thus
His sense out, like an ant-eater's long tongue,
Soft, innocent, warm, moist, impassible,
And when 'twas crusted o'er with creatures — slick,
Their juice enriched his palate. "Could not Sludge!"

I'll go yet a step further, and maintain,
Once the imposture plunged its proper depth
I' the rotten of your natures, all of you, —
(If one's not mad nor drunk, and hardly then)
It's impossible to cheat — that's, be found out!
Go tell your brotherhood this first slip of mine,
All to-day's tale, how you detected Sludge,
Behaved unpleasantly, till he was fain confess,
And so has come to grief! You'll find, I think,
Why Sludge still snaps his fingers in your face.
There now, you've told them! What's their prompt reply?
"Sir, did that youth confess he had cheated me,
"I'd disbelieve him. He may cheat at times;
"That's in the 'medium'-nature, thus they're made,
"Vain and vindictive, cowards, prone to scratch.
"And so all cats are; still, a cat's the beast
"You coax the strange electric sparks from out,
"By rubbing back its fur; not so a dog,
"Nor lion, nor lamb: 'tis the cat's nature, sir!
"Why not the dog's? Ask God, who made them beasts!
"D'ye think the sound, the nicely-balanced man
"(Like me" — aside) — "like you yourself," — (aloud)
" — He's stuff to make a 'medium'? Bless your soul,
" 'Tis these hysteric, hybrid half-and-halfs,
"Equivocal, worthless vermin yield the fire!
"We take such as we find them, 'ware their tricks,
"Wanting their service. Sir, Sludge took in you —
"How, I can't say, not being there to watch:
"He was tried, was tempted by your easiness, —
"He did not take in me!"

          Thank you for Sludge!
I'm to be grateful to such patrons, eh,
When what you hear's my best word? 'Tis a challenge
"Snap at all strangers, half-tamed prairie-dog,
"So you cower duly at your keeper's beck!
"Cat, show what claws were made for, muffling them
"Only to me! Cheat others if you can,
"Me, if you dare!" And, my wise sir, I dared —

Did cheat you first, made you cheat others next,
And had the help o' your vaunted manliness
To bully the incredulous. You used me?
Have not I used you, taken full revenge,
Persuaded folk they knew not their own name,
And straight they'd own the error! Who was the fool
When, to an awe-struck wide-eyed open-mouthed
Circle of sages, Sludge would introduce
Milton composing baby-rhymes, and Locke
Reasoning in gibberish, Homer writing Greek
In noughts and crosses, Asaph setting psalms
To crotchet and quaver? I've made a spirit squeak
In sham voice for a minute, then outbroke
Bold in my own, defying the imbeciles —
Have copied some ghost's pothooks, half a page,
Then ended with my own scrawl undisguised.
"All right! The ghost was merely using Sludge,
"Suiting itself from his imperfect stock!"
Don't talk of gratitude to me! For what?
For being treated as a showman's ape,
Encouraged to be wicked and make sport,
Fret or sulk, grin or whimper, any mood
So long as the ape be in it and no man —
Because a nut pays every mood alike.
Curse your superior, superintending sort,
Who, since you hate smoke, send up boys that climb
To cure your chimney, bid a "medium" lie
To sweep your truth down! Curse your women too,
Your insolent wives and daughters, that fire up
Or faint away if a male hand squeeze theirs
Yet, to encourage Sludge, may play with Sludge
As only a "medium," only the kind of thing
They must humour, fondle . . . oh, to misconceive
Were too preposterous! But I've paid them out!
They've had their wish — called for the naked truth,
And in she tripped, sat down and bade them stare:
They had to blush a little and forgive!
"The fact is, children talk so; in next world
"All our conventions are reversed, — perhaps

"Made light of: something like old prints, my dear!
"The Judge has one, he brought from Italy,
"A metropolis in the background, — o'er a bridge,
"A team of trotting roadsters, — cheerful groups
"Of wayside travellers, peasants at their work,
"And, full in front, quite unconcerned, why not?
"Three nymphs conversing with a cavalier,
"And never a rag among them: 'fine,' folk cry —
"And heavenly manners seem not much unlike!
"Let Sludge go on; we'll fancy it's in print!"
If such as came for wool, sir, went home shorn,
Where is the wrong I did them? 'Twas their choice;
They tried the adventure, ran the risk, tossed up
And lost, as some one's sure to do in games;
They fancied I was made to lose, — smoked glass
Useful to spy the sun through, spare their eyes:
And had I proved a red-hot iron plate
They thought to pierce, and, for their pains, grew blind,
Whose were the fault but theirs? While, as things go,
Their loss amounts to gain, the more's the shame!
They've had their peep into the spirit-world,
And all this world may know it! They've fed fat
Their self-conceit which else had starved: what chance
Save this, of cackling o'er a golden egg
And compassing distinction from the flock,
Friends of a feather? Well, they paid for it,
And not prodigiously; the price o' the play,
Not counting certain pleasant interludes,
Was scarce a vulgar play's worth. When you buy
The actor's talent, do you dare propose
For his soul beside? Whereas my soul you buy!
Sludge acts Macbeth, obliged to be Macbeth,
Or you'll not hear his first word! Just go through
That slight formality, swear himself's the Thane,
And thenceforth he may strut and fret his hour,
Spout, spawl, or spin his target, no one cares!
Why hadn't I leave to play tricks, Sludge as Sludge?
Enough of it all! I've wiped out scores with you —
Vented your fustian, let myself be streaked

Like tom-fool with your ochre and carmine,
Worn patchwork your respectable fingers sewed
To metamorphose somebody, — yes, I've earned
My wages, swallowed down my bread of shame,
And shake the crumbs off — where but in your face?

As for religion — why, I served it sir!
I'll stick to that! With my *phenomena*
I laid the atheist sprawling on his back,
Propped up Saint Paul, or, at least, Swedenborg!
In fact, it's just the proper way to baulk
These troublesome fellows — liars, one and all,
Are not these sceptics? Well, to baffle them,
No use in being squeamish: lie yourself!
Erect your buttress just as wide o' the line,
Your side, as they build up the wall on theirs;
Where both meet, midway in a point, is truth
High overhead: so, take your room, pile bricks,
Lie! Oh, there's titillation in all shame!
What snow may lose in white, snow gains in rose!
Miss Stokes turns — Rahab, — nor a bad exchange!
Glory be on her, for the good she wrought,
Breeding belief anew 'neath ribs of death,
Browbeating now the unabashed before,
Ridding us of their whole life's gathered straws
By a live coal from the altar! Why, of old,
Great men spent years and years in writing books
To prove we've souls, and hardly proved it then:
Miss Stokes with her live coal, for you and me!
Surely, to this good issue, all was fair —
Not only fondling Sludge, but, even suppose
He let escape some spice of knavery, — well,
In wisely being blind to it! Don't you praise
Nelson for setting spy-glass to blind eye
And saying . . . what was it — that he could not see
The signal he was bothered with? Ay, indeed!

I'll go beyond: there's a real love of a lie,
Liars find ready-made for lies they make,

584

As hand for glove, or tongue for sugar-plum.
At best, 'tis never pure and full belief;
Those furthest in the quagmire, — don't suppose
They strayed there with no warning, got no chance
Of a filth-speck in their face, which they clenched teeth,
Bent brow against! Be sure they had their doubts,
And fears, and fairest challenges to try
The floor o' the seeming solid sand! But no!
Their faith was pledged, acquaintance too apprised,
All but the last step ventured, kerchiefs waved,
And Sludge called "pet": 'twas easier marching on
To the promised land; join those who, Thursday next,
Meant to meet Shakespeare; better follow Sludge —
Prudent, oh sure! —on the alert, how else? —
But making for the mid-bog, all the same!
To hear your outcries, one would think I caught
Miss Stokes by the scruff o' the neck, and pitched her flat,
Foolish-face-foremost! Hear these simpletons,
That's all I beg, before my work's begun,
Before I've touched them with my finger-tip!
Thus they await me (do but listen, now!
It's reasoning, this is, — I can't imitate
The baby voice, though) "In so many tales
"Must be some truth, truth though a pinpoint big,
"Yet, some: a single man's deceived, perhaps —
"Hardly, a thousand: to suppose one cheat
"Can gull all these, were more miraculous far
"Than aught we should confess a miracle" —
And so on. Then the Judge sums up — (it's rare)
Bids you respect the authorities that leap
To the judgment-seat at once, — why don't you note
The limpid nature, the unblemished life,
The spotless honour, indisputable sense
Of the first upstart with his story? What —
Outrage a boy on whom you ne'er till now
Set eyes, because he finds raps trouble him?

Fools, these are: ay, and how of their opposites
Who never did, at bottom of their hearts,

585

Believe for a moment? — Men emasculate,
Blank of belief, who played, as eunuchs use,
With superstition safely, — cold of blood,
Who saw what made for them i' the mystery,
Took their occasion, and supported Sludge
— As proselytes? No, thank you, far too shrewd!
— But promisers of fair play, encouragers
O' the claimant; who in candour needs must hoist
Sludge up on Mars' Hill, get speech out of Sludge
To carry off, criticize, and cant about!
Didn't Athens treat Saint Paul so? — at any rate,
It's "a new thing" philosophy fumbles at.
Then there's the other picker-out of pearl
From dung-heaps, — ay, your literary man,
Who draws on his kid gloves to deal with Sludge
Daintily and discreetly, — shakes a dust
O' the doctrine, flavours thence, he well knows how,
The narrative or the novel, — half-believes,
All for the book's sake, and the public's stare,
And the cash that's God's sole solid in this world!
Look at him! Try to be too bold, too gross
For the master! Not you! He's the man for muck;
Shovel it forth, full-splash, he'll smooth your brown
Into artistic richness, never fear!
Find him the crude stuff; when you recognize
Your lie again, you'll doff your hat to it,
Dressed out for company! "For company,"
I say, since there's the relish of success:
Let all pay due respect, call the lie truth,
Save the soft silent smirking gentleman
Who ushered in the stranger: you must sigh
"How melancholy, he, the only one
"Fails to perceive the bearing of the truth
"Himself gave birth to!" — There's the triumph's smack!
That man would choose to see the whole world roll
I' the slime o' the slough, so he might touch the tip
Of his brush with what I call the best of browns —
Tint ghost-tales, spirit-stories, past the power
Of the outworn umber and bistre!

586

Yet I think

There's a more hateful form of foolery —
The social sage's, Solomon of saloons
And philosophic diner-out, the fribble
Who wants a doctrine for a chopping-block
To try the edge of his faculty upon,
Prove how much common sense he'll hack and hew
I' the critical minute 'twixt the soup and fish!
These were my patrons: these, and the like of them
Who, rising in my soul now, sicken it, —
These I have injured! Gratitude to these?
The gratitude, forsooth, of a prostitute
To the greenhorn and the bully — friends of hers,
From the wag that wants the queer jokes for his club,
To the snuff-box-decorator, honest man,
Who just was at his wits' end where to find
So genial a Pasiphae! All and each
Pay, compliment, protect from the police:
And how she hates them for their pains, like me!
So much for my remorse at thanklessness
Toward a deserving public!

But, for God?

Ay, that's a question! Well, sir, since you press —
(How you do tease the whole thing out of me!
I don't mean you, you know, when I say "them":
Hate you, indeed! But that Miss Stokes, that Judge!
Enough, enough — with sugar: thank you, sir!)
Now for it, then! Will you believe me, though?
You've heard what I confess; I don't unsay
A single word: I cheated when I could,
Rapped with my toe-joints, set sham hands at work,
Wrote down names weak in sympathetic ink,
Rubbed odic lights with ends of phosphor-match,
And all the rest; believe that: believe this,
By the same token, though it seem to set
The crooked straight again, unsay the said,
Stick up what I've knocked down; I can't help that
It's truth! I somehow vomit truth to-day.

587

This trade of mine — I don't know, can't be sure
But there was something in it, tricks and all!
Really, I want to light up my own mind.
They were tricks, — true, but what I mean to add
Is also true. First, — don't it strike you, sir?
Go back to the beginning, — the first fact
We're taught is, there's a world beside this world,
With spirits, not mankind, for tenantry;
That much within that world once sojourned here,
That all upon this world will visit there,
And therefore that we, bodily here below,
Must have exactly such an interest
In learning what may be the ways o' the world
Above us, as the disembodied folk
Have (by all analogic likelihood)
In watching how things go in the old home
With us, their sons, successors, and what not.
Oh yes, with added powers probably,
Fit for the novel state, — old loves grown pure,
Old interests understood aright, — they watch!
Eyes to see, ears to hear, and hands to help,
Proportionate to advancement: they're ahead,
That's all — do what we do, but noblier done —
Use plate, whereas we eat our meals off delf,
(To use a figure).

                    Concede that, and I ask
Next what may be the mode of intercourse
Between us men here, and those once-men there?
First comes the Bible's speech; then, history
With the supernatural element, — you know —
All that we sucked in with our mothers' milk,
Grew up with, got inside of us at last,
Till it's found bone of bone and flesh of flesh.
See now, we start with the miraculous,
And know it used to be, at all events:
What's the first step we take, and can't but take,
In arguing from the known to the obscure?
Why this: "What was before, may be to-day.

"Since Samuel's ghost appeared to Saul, of course
"My brother's spirit may appear to me."
Go tell your teacher that! What's his reply?
What brings a shade of doubt for the first time
O'er his brow late so luminous with faith?
"Such things have been," says he, "and there's no doubt
"Such things may be: but I advise mistrust
"Of eyes, ears, stomach, and, more than all, your brain,
"Unless it be of your great-grandmother,
"Whenever they propose a ghost to you!"
The end is, there's a composition struck;
'Tis settled, we've some way of intercourse
Just as in Saul's time; only, different:
How, when and where, precisely, — find it out!
I want to know, then, what's so natural
As that a person born into this world
And seized on by such teaching, should begin
With firm expectancy and a frank look-out
For his own allotment, his especial share
I' the secret, — his particular ghost, in fine?
I mean, a person born to look that way,
Since natures differ: take the painter-sort.
One man lives fifty years in ignorance
Whether grass be green or red, — "No kind of eye
"For colour," say you; while another picks
And puts away even pebbles, when a child,
Because of bluish spots and pinky veins —
"Give him forthwith a paint-box!" Just the same
Was I born . . . "medium," you won't let me say, —
Well, seer of the supernatural
Everywhen, everyhow and everywhere, —
Will that do?

        I and all such boys of course
Started with the same stock of Bible-truth;
Only, — what in the rest you style their sense,
Instinct, blind reasoning but imperative,
This, betimes, taught them the old world had one law
And ours another: "New world, new laws," cried they:

"None but old laws, seen everywhere at work,"
Cried I, and by their help explained my life
The Jews' way, still a working way to me.
Ghosts made the noises, fairies waved the lights,
Or Santa Claus slid down on New Year's Eve
And stuffed with cakes the stocking at my bed,
Changed the worn shoes, rubbed clean the fingered slate
O' the sum that came to grief the day before.

This could not last long: soon enough I found
Who had worked wonders thus, and to what end:
But did I find all easy, like my mates?
Henceforth no supernatural any more?
Not a whit: what projects the billiard-balls?
"A cue," you answer: "Yes, a cue," said I;
"But what hand, off the cushion, moved the cue?
"What unseen agency, outside the world,
"Prompted its puppets to do this and that,
"Put cakes and shoes and slates into their mind,
"These mothers and aunts, nay even schoolmasters?"
Thus high I sprang, and there have settled since.
Just so I reason, in sober earnest still,
About the greater godsends, what you call
The serious gains and losses of my life.
What do I know or care about your world
Which either is or seems to be? This snap
O' my fingers, sir! My care is for myself;
Myself am whole and sole reality
Inside a raree-show and a market-mob
Gathered about it: that's the use of things.
'Tis easy saying they serve vast purposes,
Advantage their grand selves: be it true or false,
Each thing may have two uses. What's a star?
A world, or a world's sun: doesn't it serve
As taper also, time-piece, weather-glass,
And almanac? Are stars not set for signs
When we should shear our sheep, sow corn, prune trees?
The Bible says so.

Well, I add one use
To all the acknowledged uses, and declare
If I spy Charles's Wain at twelve to-night,
It warns me, "Go, nor lose another day,
"And have your hair cut, Sludge!" You laugh: and why?
Were such a sign too hard for God to give?
No: but Sludge seems too little for such grace:
Thank you, sir! So you think, so does not Sludge!
When you and good men gape at Providence,
Go into history and bid us mark
Not merely powder-plots prevented, crowns
Kept on kings' heads by miracle enough,
But private mercies — oh, you've told me, sir,
Of such interpositions! How yourself
Once, missing on a memorable day
Your handkerchief — just setting out, you know, —
You must return to fetch it, lost the train,
And saved your precious self from what befell
The thirty-three whom Providence forgot.
You tell, and ask me what I think of this?
Well, sir, I think then, since you needs must know,
What matter had you and Boston city to boot
Sailed skyward, like burnt onion-peelings? Much
To you, no doubt: for me — undoubtedly
The cutting of my hair concerns me more,
Because, however sad the truth may seem,
Sludge is of all-importance to himself.
You set apart that day in every year
For special thanksgiving, were a heathen else:
Well, I who cannot boast the like escape,
Suppose I said "I don't thank Providence
"For my part, owing it no gratitude"?
"Nay, but you owe as much" — you'd tutor me,
"You, every man alive, for blessings gained
"In every hour o' the day, could you but know!
"I saw my crowning mercy: all have such,
"Could they but see!" Well, sir, why don't they see?
"Because they won't look, — or perhaps, they can't."
Then, sir, suppose I can, and will, and do

Look, microscopically as is right,
Into each hour with its infinitude
Of influences at work to profit Sludge?
For that's the case: I've sharpened up my sight
To spy a providence in the fire's going out,
The kettle's boiling, the dime's sticking fast
Despite the hole i' the pocket. Call such facts
Fancies, too petty a work for Providence,
And those same thanks which you exact from me
Prove too prodigious payment: thanks for what,
If nothing guards and guides us little men?
No, no, sir! You must put away your pride,
Resolve to let Sludge into partnership!
I live by signs and omens: looked at the roof
Where the pigeons settle — "If the further bird,
"The white, takes wing first, I'll confess when thrashed;
"Not, if the blue does" — so I said to myself
Last week, lest you should take me by surprise:
Off flapped the white, — and I'm confessing, sir!
Perhaps 'tis Providence's whim and way
With only me, i' the world: how can you tell?
"Because unlikely!" Was it likelier, now,
That this our one out of all worlds beside,
The what-d'you-call-'em millions, should be just
Precisely chosen to make Adam for,
And the rest o' the tale? Yet the tale's true, you know:
Such undeserving clod was graced so once;
Why not graced likewise undeserving Sludge?
Are we merit-mongers, flaunt we filthy rags?
All you can bring against my privilege
Is, that another way was taken with you, —
Which I don't question. It's pure grace, my luck:
I'm broken to the way of nods and winks,
And need no formal summoning. You've a help;
Holloa his name or whistle, clap your hands,
Stamp with your foot or pull the bell: all's one,
He understands you want him, here he comes.
Just so, I come at the knocking: you, sir, wait
The tongue o' the bell, nor stir before you catch

Reason's clear tingle, nature's clapper brisk,
Or that traditional peal was wont to cheer
Your mother's face turned heavenward: short of these
There's no authentic intimation, eh?
Well, when you hear, you'll answer them, start up
And stride into the presence, top of toe,
And there find Sludge beforehand, Sludge that sprang
At noise o' the knuckle on the partition-wall!
I think myself the more religious man.
Religion's all or nothing; it's no mere smile
O' contentment, sigh of aspiration, sir —
No quality o' the finelier-tempered clay
Like its whiteness or its lightness; rather, stuff
O' the very stuff, life of life, and self of self.
I tell you, men won't notice; when they do,
They'll understand. I notice nothing else:
I'm eyes, ears, mouth of me, one gaze and gape,
Nothing eludes me, everything's a hint,
Handle and help. It's all absurd, and yet
There's something in it all, I know: how much?
No answer! What does that prove? Man's still man,
Still meant for a poor blundering piece of work
When all's done; but, if somewhat's done, like this,
Or not done, is the case the same? Suppose
I blunder in my guess at the true sense
O' the knuckle-summons, nine times out of ten, —
What if the tenth guess happen to be right?
If the tenth shovel-load of powdered quartz
Yield me the nugget? I gather, crush, sift all,
Pass o'er the failure, pounce on the success.
To give you a notion, now — (let who wins, laugh!)
When first I see a man, what do I first?
Why, count the letters which make up his name,
And as their number chances, even or odd,
Arrive at my conclusion, trim my course:
Hiram H. Horsefall is your honoured name,
And haven't I found a patron, sir, in you?
"Shall I cheat this stranger?" I take apple-pips,
Stick one in either canthus of my eye,

And if the left drops first — (your left, sir, stuck)
I'm warned, I let the trick alone this time.
You, sir, who smile, superior to such trash,
You judge of character by other rules:
Don't your rules sometimes fail you? Pray, what rule
Have you judged Sludge by hitherto?

                                    Oh, be sure,
You, everybody blunders, just as I,
In simpler things than these by far! For see:
I knew two farmers, — one, a wiseacre
Who studied seasons, rummaged almanacs,
Quoted the dew-point, registered the frost,
And then declared, for outcome of his pains,
Next summer must be dampish: 'twas a drought.
His neighbour prophesied such drought would fall,
Saved hay and corn, made cent. per cent. thereby,
And proved a sage indeed: how came his lore?
Because one brindled heifer, late in March,
Stiffened her tail of evenings, and somehow
He got into his head that drought was meant!
I don't expect all men can do as much:
Such kissing goes by favour. You must take
A certain turn of mind for this, — a twist
I' the flesh, as well. Be lazily alive,
Open-mouthed, like my friend the ant-eater,
Letting all nature's loosely-guarded motes
Settle and, slick, be swallowed! Think yourself
The one i' the world, the one for whom the world
Was made, expect it tickling at your mouth!
Then will the swarm of busy buzzing flies,
Clouds of coincidence, break egg-shell, thrive,
Breed, multiply, and bring you food enough.

I can't pretend to mind your smiling, sir!
Oh, what you mean is this! Such intimate way,
Close converse, frank exchange of offices,
Strict sympathy of the immeasurably great
With the infinitely small, betokened here

By a course of signs and omens, raps and sparks, —
How does it suit the dread traditional text
O' the "Great and Terrible Name"? Shall the Heaven of Heavens
Stoop to such child's play?

                      Please, sir, go with me
A moment, and I'll try to answer you.
The "*Magnum et terribile*" (is that right?)
Well, folk began with this in the early day;
And all the acts they recognized in proof
Were thunders, lightnings, earthquakes, whirlwinds, dealt
Indisputably on men whose death they caused.
There, and there only, folk saw Providence
At work, — and seeing it, 'twas right enough
All heads should tremble, hands wring hands amain,
And knees knock hard together at the breath
O' the Name's first letter; why, the Jews, I'm told,
Won't write it down, no, to this very hour,
Nor speak aloud: you know best if't be so.
Each ague-fit of fear at end, they crept
(Because somehow people once born must live)
Out of the sound, sight, swing and sway o' the Name,
Into a corner, the dark rest of the world,
And safe space where as yet no fear had reached;
'Twas there they looked about them, breathed again,
And felt indeed at home, as we might say.
The current o' common things, the daily life,
This had their due contempt; no Name pursued
Man from the mountain-top where fires abide,
To his particular mouse-hole at its foot
Where he ate, drank, digested, lived in short:
Such was man's vulgar business, far too small
To be worth thunder: "small," folk kept on, "small,"
With much complacency in those great days!
A mote of sand, you know, a blade of grass —
What was so despicable as mere grass,
Except perhaps the life o' the worm or fly
Which fed there? These were "small" and men were great.
Well, sir, the old way's altered somewhat since,

And the world wears another aspect now:
Somebody turns our spyglass round, or else
Puts a new lens in it: grass, worm, fly grow big:
We find great things are made of little things,
And little things go lessening till at last
Comes God behind them. Talk of mountains now?
We talk of mould that heaps the mountain, mites
That throng the mould, and God that makes the mites.
The Name comes close behind a stomach-cyst,
The simplest of creations, just a sac
That's mouth, heart, legs and belly at once, yet lives
And feels, and could do neither, we conclude,
If simplified still further one degree:
The small becomes the dreadful and immense!
Lightning, forsooth? No word more upon that!
A tin-foil bottle, a strip of greasy silk,
With a bit of wire and knob of brass, and there's
Your dollar's-worth of lightning! But the cyst —
The life of the least of the little things?

                                        No, no!
Preachers and teachers try another tack,
Come near the truth this time: they put aside
Thunder and lightning: "That's mistake," they cry,
"Thunderbolts fall for neither fright nor sport,
"But do appreciable good, like tides,
"Changes o' the wind, and other natural facts —
" 'Good' meaning good to man, his body or soul.
"Mediate, immediate, all things minister
"To man, — that's settled: be our future text
" 'We are His children!' " So, they now harangue
About the intention, the contrivance, all
That keeps up an incessant play of love, —
See the Bridgewater book.

                              Amen to it!
Well, sir, I put this question: I'm a child?
I lose no time, but take you at your word:
How shall I act a child's part properly?

Your sainted mother, sir, — used you to live
With such a thought as this a-worrying you?
"She has it in her power to throttle me,
"Or stab or poison: she may turn me out,
"Or lock me in, — nor stop at this to-day,
"But cut me off to-morrow from the estate
"I look for" — (long may you enjoy it, sir!)
"In brief, she may unchild the child I am.'
You never had such crotchets? Nor have I!
Who, frank confessing childship from the first,
Cannot both fear and take my ease at once,
So, don't fear, — know what might be, well enough,
But know too, child-like, that it will not be,
At least in my case, mine, the son and heir
O' the kingdom, as yourself proclaim my style.
But do you fancy I stop short at this?
Wonder if suit and service, son and heir
Needs must expect, I dare pretend to find?
If, looking for signs proper to such an one,
I straight perceive them irresistible?
Concede that homage is a son's plain right,
And, never mind the nods and raps and winks,
'Tis the pure obvious supernatural
Steps forward, does its duty: why, of course!
I have presentiments; my dreams come true:
I fancy a friend stands whistling all in white
Blithe as a boblink, and he's dead I learn.
I take dislike to a dog my favourite long,
And sell him; he goes mad next week and snaps.
I guess that stranger will turn up to-day
I have not seen these three years; there's his knock.
I wager "sixty peaches on that tree!" —
That I pick up a dollar in my walk,
That your wife's brother's cousin's name was George —
And win on all points. Oh, you wince at this?
You'd fain distinguish between gift and gift,
Washington's oracle and Sludge's itch
O' the elbow when at whist he ought to trump?
With Sludge it's too absurd? Fine, *draw the line
Somewhere, but, sir, your somewhere is not mine!*

597

Bless us, I'm turning poet! It's time to end.
How you have drawn me out, sir! All I ask
Is — am I heir or not heir? If I'm he,
Then, sir, remember, that same personage
(To judge by what we read i' the newspaper)
Requires, beside one nobleman in gold
To carry up and down his coronet,
Another servant, probably a duke,
To hold egg-nogg in readiness: why want
Attendance, sir, when helps in his father's house
Abound, I'd like to know?

                       Enough of talk!
My fault is that I tell too plain a truth.
Why, which of those who say they disbelieve,
Your clever people, but has dreamed his dream,
Caught his coincidence, stumbled on his fact
He can't explain, (he'll tell you smilingly)
Which he's too much of a philosopher
To count as supernatural, indeed,
So calls a puzzle and problem, proud of it:
Bidding you still be on your guard, you know,
Because one fact don't make a system stand,
Nor prove this an occasional escape
Of spirit beneath the matter: that's the way!
Just so wild Indians picked up, piece by piece,
The fact in California, the fine gold
That underlay the gravel – hoarded these,
But never made a system stand, nor dug!
So wise men hold out in each hollowed palm
A handful of experience, sparkling fact
They can't explain; and since their rest of life
Is all explainable, what proof in this?
Whereas I take the fact, the grain of gold,
And fling away the dirty rest of life,
And add this grain to the grain each fool has found
O' the million other such philosophers, –
Till I see gold, all gold and only gold,
Truth questionless though unexplainable,

And the miraculous proved the commonplace!
The other fools believed in mud, no doubt —
Failed to know gold they saw: was that so strange?
Are all men born to play Bach's fiddle-fugues,
"Time" with the foil in carte, jump their own height,
Cut the mutton with the broadsword, skate a five,
Make the red hazard with the cue, clip nails
While swimming, in five minutes row a mile,
Pull themselves three feet up with the left arm,
Do sums of fifty figures in their head,
And so on, by the scores of instances?
The Sludge with luck, who sees the spiritual facts
His fellows strive and fail to see, may rank
With these, and share the advantage.

                             Ay, but share
The drawback! Think it over by yourself;
I have not heart, sir, and the fire's gone grey.
Defect somewhere compensates for success,
Everyone knows that. Oh, we're equals, sir!
The big-legged fellow has a little arm
And a less brain, though big legs win the race:
Do you suppose I 'scape the common lot?
Say, I was born with flesh so sensitive,
Soul so alert, that, practice helping both,
I guess what's going on outside the veil,
Just as a prisoned crane feels pairing-time
In the islands where his kind are, so must fall
To capering by himself some shiny night,
As if your back-yard were a plot of spice —
Thus am I 'ware o' the spirit-world: while you,
Blind as a beetle that way, — for amends,
Why, you can double fist and floor me, sir!
Ride that hot hardmouthed horrid horse of yours,
Laugh while it lightens, play with the great dog,
Speak your mind though it vex some friend to hear,
Never brag, never bluster, never blush, —
In short, you've pluck, when I'm a coward — there!
I know it, I can't help it, — folly or no,

THE BROWNINGS

I'm paralyzed, my hand's no more a hand,
Nor my head a head, in danger: you can smile
And change the pipe in your cheek. Your gift's not mine.
Would you swap for mine? No! but you'd add my gift
To yours: I dare say! I too sigh at times,
Wish I were stouter, could tell truth nor flinch,
Kept cool when threatened, did not mind so much
Being dressed gaily, making strangers stare,
Eating nice things; when I'd amuse myself,
I shut my eyes and fancy in my brain
I'm — now the President, now Jenny Lind,
Now Emerson, now the Benicia Boy —
With all the civilized world a-wondering
And worshipping. I know it's folly and worse;
I feel such tricks sap, honeycomb the soul,
But I can't cure myself: despond, despair,
And then, hey, presto, there's a turn o' the wheel,
Under comes uppermost, fate makes full amends;
Sludge knows and sees and hears a hundred things
You all are blind to, — I've my taste of truth,
Likewise my touch of falsehood, — vice no doubt,
But you've your vices also: I'm content.
What, sir? You won't shake hands? "Because I cheat!"
"You've found me out in cheating!" That's enough
To make an apostle swear! Why, when I cheat,
*Mean to cheat, do cheat, and am caught in the act,
Are you, or, rather, am I sure o' the fact?*
(There's verse again, but I'm inspired somehow.)
Well then I'm not sure! I may be, perhaps,
Free as a babe from cheating: how it began,
My gift, — no matter; what 'tis got to be
In the end now, that's the question; answer that!
Had I seen, perhaps, what hand was holding mine,
Leading me whither, I had died of fright:
So, I was made believe I led myself.
If I should lay a six-inch plank from roof
To roof, you would not cross the street, one step,
Even at your mother's summons: but, being shrewd,
If I paste paper on each side the plank

And swear 'tis solid pavement, why, you'll cross
Humming a tune the while, in ignorance
Beacon Street stretches a hundred feet below:
I walked thus, took the paper-cheat for stone.
Some impulse made me set a thing o' the move
Which, started once, ran really by itself;
Beer flows thus, suck the siphon; toss the kite,
It takes the wind and floats of its own force.
Don't let truth's lump rot stagnant for the lack
Of a timely helpful lie to leaven it!
Put a chalk-egg beneath the clucking hen,
She'll lay a real one, laudably deceived,
Daily for weeks to come. I've told my lie,
And seen truth follow, marvels none of mine;
All was not cheating, sir, I'm positive!
I don't know if I move your hand sometimes
When the spontaneous writing spreads so far,
If my knee lifts the table all that height,
Why the inkstand don't fall off the desk a-tilt,
Why the accordion plays a prettier waltz
Than I can pick out on the piano-forte,
Why I speak so much more than I intend,
Describe so many things I never saw.
I tell you, sir, in one sense, I believe
Nothing at all, — that everybody can,
Will, and does cheat: but in another sense
I'm ready to believe my very self —
That every cheat's inspired, and every lie
Quick with a germ of truth.

                              You ask perhaps
Why I should condescend to trick at all
If I know a way without it? This is why!
There's a strange secret sweet self-sacrifice
In any desecration of one's soul
To a worthy end, — isn't it Herodotus
(I wish I could read Latin!) who describes
The single gift o' the land's virginity,
Demanded in those old Egyptian rites,

601

THE BROWNINGS

(I've but a hazy notion — help me, sir!)
For one purpose in the world, one day in a life,
One hour in a day — thereafter, purity,
And a veil thrown o'er the past for evermore!
Well, now, they understood a many things
Down by Nile city, or wherever it was!
I've always vowed, after the minute's lie,
And the end's gain, — truth should be mine henceforth.
This goes to the root o' the matter, sir, — this plain
Plump fact: accept it and unlock with it
The wards of many a puzzle!

                Or, finally,
Why should I set so fine a gloss on things?
What need I care? I cheat in self-defence,
And there's my answer to a world of cheats!
Cheat? To be sure, sir! What's the world worth else?
Who takes it as he finds, and thanks his stars?
Don't it want trimming, turning, furbishing up
And polishing over? Your so-styled great men,
Do they accept one truth as truth is found,
Or try their skill at tinkering? What's your world?
Here are you born, who are, I'll say at once,
Of the luckiest kind, whether in head and heart,
Body and soul, or all that helps them both.
Well, now, look back: what faculty of yours
Came to its full, had ample justice done
By growing when rain fell, biding its time,
Solidifying growth when earth was dead,
Spiring up, broadening wide, in seasons due?
Never! You shot up and frost nipped you off,
Settled to sleep when sunshine bade you sprout;
One faculty thwarted its fellow: at the end,
All you boast is "I had proved a topping tree
"In other climes" — yet this was the right clime
Had you foreknown the seasons. Young, you've force
Wasted like well-streams: old, — oh, then indeed,
Behold a labyrinth of hydraulic pipes
Through which you'd play off wondrous waterwork;

Only, no water's left to feed their play.
Young, — you've a hope, an aim, a love: it's tossed
And crossed and lost: you struggle on, some spark
Shut in your heart against the puffs around,
Through cold and pain; these in due time subside,
Now then for age's triumph, the hoarded light
You mean to loose on the altered face of things, —
Up with it on the tripod! It's extinct.
Spend your life's remnant asking, which was best,
Light smothered up that never peeped forth once,
Or the cold cresset with full leave to shine?
Well, accept this too, — seek the fruit of it
Not in enjoyment, proved a dream on earth,
But knowledge, useful for a second chance,
Another life, — you've lost this world — you've gained
Its knowledge for the next. What knowledge, sir,
Except that you know nothing? Nay, you doubt
Whether 'twere better have made you man or brute,
If aught be true, if good and evil clash.
No foul, no fair, no inside, no outside,
There's your world!

       Give it me! I slap it brisk
With harlequin's pasteboard sceptre: what's it now?
Changed like a rock-flat, rough with rusty weed,
At first wash-over o' the returning wave!
All the dry dead impracticable stuff
Starts into life and light again; this world
Pervaded by the influx from the next.
I cheat, and what's the happy consequence?
You find full justice straightway dealt you out,
Each want supplied, each ignorance set at ease,
Each folly fooled. No life-long labour now
As the price of worse than nothing! No mere film
Holding you chained in iron, as it seems,
Against the outstretch of your very arms
And legs i' the sunshine moralists forbid!
What would you have? Just speak and, there, you see!
You're supplemented, made a whole at last,

Bacon advises, Shakespeare writes you songs,
And Mary Queen of Scots embraces you.
Thus it goes on, not quite like life perhaps,
But so near, that the very difference piques,
Shows that e'en better than this best will be —
This passing entertainment in a hut
Whose bare walls take your taste since, one stage more,
And you arrive at the palace: all half real,
And you, to suit it, less than real beside,
In a dream, lethargic kind of death in life,
That helps the interchange of natures, flesh
Transfused by souls, and such souls! Oh, 'tis choice!
And if at whiles the bubble, blown too thin,
Seem nigh on bursting, — if you nearly see
The real world through the false, — what *do* you see?
Is the old so ruined? You find you're in a flock
O' the youthful, earnest, passionate — genius, beauty,
Rank and wealth also, if you care for these:
And all depose their natural rights, hail you,
(That's me, sir) as their mate and yoke-fellow,
Participate in Sludgehood — nay, grow mine,
I veritably possess them — banish doubt,
And reticence and modesty alike!
Why, here's the Golden Age, old Paradise
Or new Eutopia! Here's true life indeed,
And the world well won now, mine for the first time!

And all this might be, may be, and with good help
Of a little lying shall be: so, Sludge lies!
Why, he's at worst your poet who sings how Greeks
That never were, in Troy which never was,
Did this or the other impossible great thing!
He's Lowell — it's a world (you smile applause),
Of his own invention — wondrous Longfellow,
Surprising Hawthorne! Sludge does more than they,
And acts the books they write: the more his praise!

But why do I mount to poets? Take plain prose —
Dealers in common sense, set these at work,

What can they do without their helpful lies?
Each states the law and fact and face o' the thing
Just as he'd have them, finds what he thinks fit,
Is blind to what missuits him, just records
What makes his case out, quite ignores the rest.
It's a History of the World, the Lizard Age,
The Early Indians, the Old Country War,
Jerome Napoleon, whatsoever you please,
All as the author wants it. Such a scribe
You pay and praise for putting life in stones,
Fire into fog, making the past your world.
There's plenty of "How did you contrive to grasp
"The thread which led you through this labyrinth?
"How build such solid fabric out of air?
"How on so slight foundation found this tale,
"Biography, narrative?" or, in other words,
"How many lies did it require to make
"The portly truth you here present us with?"
"Oh," quoth the penman, purring at your praise,
" 'Tis fancy all; no particle of fact:
"I was poor and threadbare when I wrote that book
" 'Bliss in the Golden City.' I, at Thebes?
"We writers paint out of our heads, you see!"
" — Ah, the more wonderful the gift in you,
"The more creativeness and godlike craft!"
But I, do I present you with my piece,
It's "What, Sludge? When my sainted mother spoke
"The verses Lady Jane Grey last composed
"About the rosy bower in the seventh heaven
"Where she and Queen Elizabeth keep house, —
"You made the raps? 'Twas your invention that?
"Cur, slave and devil!" — eight fingers and two thumbs
Stuck in my throat!

            Well, if the marks seem gone,
'Tis because stiffish cock-tail, taken in time,
Is better for a bruise than arnica.
There, sir! I bear no malice: 'tisn't in me.
I know I acted wrongly: still, I've tried

What I could say in my excuse, — to show
The devil's not all devil . . . I don't pretend,
He's angel, must less such a gentleman
As you, sir! And I've lost you, lost myself,
Lost all-l-l-l- . . .

        No — are you in earnest, sir?
O yours, sir, is an angel's part! I know
What prejudice prompts, and what's the common course
Men take to soothe their ruffled self-conceit:
Only you rise superior to it all!
No, sir, it don't hurt much; it's speaking long
That makes me choke a little: the marks will go!
What? Twenty V-notes more, and outfit too,
And not a word to Greeley? One — one kiss
O' the hand that saves me! You'll not let me speak,
I well know, and I've lost the right, too true!
But I must say, sir, if She hears (she does)
Your sainted . . . Well, sir, — be it so! That's, I think,
My bed-room candle. Good-night! Bl-l-less you, sir!

R-r-r, you brute-beast and blackguard! Cowardly scamp!
I only wish I dared burn down the house
And spoil your sniggering! Oh what, you're the man?
You're satisfied at last? You've found out Sludge?
We'll see that presently: my turn, sir, next!
I too can tell my story: brute, — do you hear? —
You throttled your sainted mother, that old hag,
In just such a fit of passion: no, it was . . .
To get this house of hers, and many a note
Like these . . . I'll pocket them, however . . . five,
Ten, fifteen . . . ay, you gave her throat the twist,
Or else you poisoned her! Confound the cuss!
Where was my head? I ought to have prophesied
He'll die in a year and join her: that's the way.

I don't know where my head is: what had I done?
How did it all go? I said he poisoned her,

606

And hoped he'd have grace given him to repent,
Whereon he picked this quarrel, bullied me
And called me cheat: I thrashed him, — who could help?
He howled for mercy, prayed me on his knees
To cut and run and save him from disgrace:
I do so, and once off, he slanders me.
An end of him! Begin elsewhere anew!
Boston's a hole, the herring-pond is wide,
V-notes are something, liberty still more.
Beside, is he the only fool in the world?

APPARENT FAILURE

"We shall soon lose a celebrated building."
Paris Newspaper

I.

No, for I'll save it! Seven years since,
   I passed through Paris, stopped a day
To see the baptism of your Prince;
   Saw, made my bow, and went my way:
Walking the heat and headache off,
   I took the Seine-side, you surmise,
Thought of the Congress, Gortschakoff,
   Cavour's appeal and Buol's replies,
So sauntered till — what met my eyes?

II.

Only the Doric little Morgue!
   The dead-house where you show your drowned:
Petrarch's Vaucluse makes proud the Sorgue,
   Your Morgue has made the Seine renowned.
One pays one's debt in such a case;

I plucked up heart and entered, — stalked,
Keeping a tolerable face
Compared with some whose cheeks were chalked:
Let them! No Briton's to be baulked!

III.

First came the silent gazers; next,
    A screen of glass, we're thankful for;
Last, the sight's self, the sermon's text,
    The three men who did most abhor
Their life in Paris yesterday,
    So killed themselves: and now, enthroned
Each on his copper couch, they lay
    Fronting me, waiting to be owned.
I thought, and think, their sin's atoned.

IV.

Poor men, God made, and all for that!
    The reverence struck me; o'er each head
Religiously was hung its hat,
    Each coat dripped by the owner's bed,
Sacred from touch: each had his berth,
    His bounds, his proper place of rest,
Who last night tenanted on earth
    Some arch, where twelve such slept abreast, —
Unless the plain asphalte seemed best.

V.

How did it happen, my poor boy?
    You wanted to be Buonaparte
And have the Tuileries for toy,
    And could not, so it broke your heart?
You, old one by his side, I judge,
    Were, red as blood, a socialist,
A leveller! Does the Empire grudge
    You've gained what no Republic missed?
Be quiet, and unclench your fist!

VI.

And this — why, he was red in vain,
    Or black, — poor fellow that is blue!
What fancy was it turned your brain?
    Oh, women were the prize for you!
Money gets women, cards and dice
    Get money, and ill-luck gets just
The copper couch and one clear nice
    Cool squirt of water o'er your bust,
The right thing to extinguish lust!

VII.

It's wiser being good than bad;
    It's safer being meek than fierce:
It's fitter being sane than mad.
    My own hope is, a sun will pierce
The thickest cloud earth ever stretched;
    That, after Last, returns the First,
Though a wide compass round be fetched;
    That what began best, can't end worst,
Nor what God blessed once, prove accurst.

from THE RING AND THE BOOK

[BOOK I — *here given in full — tells how* The Ring and the
Book *came to be written, and outlines the story of how Count
Guido Franceschini wounded his wife Pompilia* (fatally, in
the outcome) *and killed her foster parents.* BOOK II, Half-
Rome, *presents a speaker not unsympathetic to Guido.* BOOK
III, The Other Half-Rome, *a speaker sympathetic to Pom-
pilia.* BOOK IV, Tertium Quid, *presents one who weighs the
pros and cons.* BOOK V, Count Guido Franceschini, *is
Guido's speech to the judges.* BOOK VI, Giuseppe Capon-

sacchi, *has as its speaker the young priest who tried to protect Pompilia. In* BOOK VII, Pompilia, *we hear Pompilia on the point of death.* BOOK VIII, Dominus Hyacinthus de Archangelis, *presents the lawyer who defends Guido;* BOOK IX, Juris Doctor Johannes Baptista Bottinius, *the prosecutor.* BOOK X, The Pope, *presents the Pope's judgement on Guido.* BOOK XI, Guido, *allows the condemned Guido to speak again.* BOOK XII, The Book and the Ring, *balances* BOOK I *and pulls together the threads of this 'Roman murder story'.*]

I. — THE RING AND THE BOOK

Do you see this Ring?
     'Tis Rome-work, made to match
(By Castellani's imitative craft)
Etrurian circlets found, some happy morn,
After a dropping April; found alive
Spark-like 'mid unearthed slope-side figtree-roots
That roof old tombs at Chiusi: soft, you see,
Yet crisp as jewel-cutting. There's one trick,
(Craftsmen instruct me) one approved device
And but one, fits such slivers of pure gold
As this was, — such mere oozings from the mine,
Virgin as oval tawny pendent tear
At beehive-edge when ripened combs o'erflow, —
To bear the file's tooth and the hammer's tap:
Since hammer needs must widen out the round,
And file emboss it fine with lily-flowers,
Ere the stuff grow a ring-thing right to wear.
That trick is, the artificer melts up wax
With honey, so to speak; he mingles gold
With gold's alloy, and, duly tempering both,
Effects a manageable mass, then works:
But his work ended, once the thing a ring,
Oh, there's repristination! Just a spirt
O' the proper fiery acid o'er its face,
And forth the alloy unfastened flies in fume;
While, self-sufficient now, the shape remains,

ROBERT BROWNING

The rondure brave, the lilied loveliness,
Gold as it was, is, shall be evermore:
Prime nature with an added artistry —
No carat lost, and you have gained a ring.
What of it? 'Tis a figure, a symbol, say;
A thing's sign: now for the thing signified.

Do you see this square old yellow Book, I toss
I' the air, and catch again, and twirl about
By the crumpled vellum covers, — pure crude fact
Secreted from man's life when hearts beat hard,
And brains, high-blooded, ticked two centuries since?
Examine it yourselves! I found this book,
Gave a *lira* for it, eightpence English just,
(Mark the predestination!) when a Hand,
Always above my shoulder, pushed me once,
One day still fierce 'mid many a day struck calm,
Across a Square in Florence, crammed with booths,
Buzzing and blaze, noontide and market-time,
Toward Baccio's marble, — ay, the basement-ledge
O' the pedestal where sits and menaces
John of the Black Bands with the upright spear,
'Twixt palace and church, — Riccardi where they lived,
His race, and San Lorenzo where they lie.
This book, — precisely on that palace-step
Which, meant for lounging knaves o' the Medici,
Now serves re-venders to display their ware, —
'Mongst odds and ends of ravage, picture-frames
White through the worn gilt, mirror-sconces chipped,
Bronze angel-heads once knobs attached to chests,
(Handled when ancient dames chose forth brocade)
Modern chalk drawings, studies from the nude,
Samples of stone, jet, breccia, porphyry
Polished and rough, sundry amazing busts
In baked earth, (broken, Providence be praised!)
A wreck of tapestry, proudly-purposed web
When reds and blues were indeed red and blue,
Now offered as a mat to save bare feet
(Since carpets constitute a cruel cost)

611

Treading the chill scagliola bedward: then
A pile of brown-etched prints, two *crazie* each,
Stopped by a conch a-top from fluttering forth
— Sowing the Square with works of one and the same
Master, the imaginative Sienese
Great in the scenic backgrounds — (name and fame
None of you know, nor does he fare the worse:)
From these . . . Oh, with a Lionard going cheap
If it should prove, as promised, that Joconde
Whereof a copy contents the Louvre! — these
I picked this book from. Five compeers in flank
Stood left and right of it as tempting more —
A dogseared Spicilegium, the fond tale
O' the Frail One of the Flower, by young Dumas,
Vulgarized Horace for the use of schools,
The Life, Death, Miracles of Saint Somebody,
Saint Somebody Else, his Miracles, Death and Life, —
With this, one glance at the lettered back of which,
And "Stall!" cried I: a *lira* made it mine.

Here it is, this I toss and take again;
Small-quarto size, part print part manuscript:
A book in shape but, really, pure crude fact
Secreted from man's life when hearts beat hard,
And brains, high-blooded, ticked two centuries since.
Give it me back! The thing's restorative
I' the touch and sight.

                    That memorable day,
(June was the month, Lorenzo named the Square)
I leaned a little and overlooked my prize
By the low railing round the fountain-source
Close to the statue, where a step descends:
While clinked the cans of copper, as stooped and rose
Thick-ankled girls who brimmed them, and made place
For marketmen glad to pitch basket down,
Dip a broad melon-leaf that holds the wet,
And whisk their faded fresh. And on I read
Presently, though my path grew perilous

Between the outspread straw-work, piles of plait
Soon to be flapping, each o'er two black eyes
And swathe of Tuscan hair, on festas fine:
Through fire-irons, tribes of tongs, shovels in sheaves,
Skeleton bedsteads, wardrobe-drawers agape,
Rows of tall slim brass lamps with dangling gear, —
And worse, cast clothes a-sweetening in the sun:
None of them took my eye from off my prize.
Still read I on, from written title-page
To written index, on, through street and street,
At the Strozzi, at the Pillar, at the Bridge;
Till, by the time I stood at home again
In Casa Guidi by Felice Church,
Under the doorway where the black begins
With the first stone-slab of the staircase cold,
I had mastered the contents, knew the whole truth
Gathered together, bound up in this book,
Print three-fifths, written supplement the rest.
"*Romana Homicidiorum*" — nay,
Better translate — "A Roman murder-case:
"Position of the entire criminal cause
"Of Guido Franceschini, nobleman,
"With certain Four the cutthroats in his pay,
"Tried, all five, and found guilty and put to death
"By heading or hanging as befitted ranks,
"At Rome on February Twenty Two,
"Since our salvation Sixteen Ninety Eight:
"Wherein it is disputed if, and when,
"Husbands may kill adulterous wives, yet 'scape
"The customary forfeit."

                    Word for word,
So ran the title-page: murder, or else
Legitimate punishment of the other crime,
Accounted murder by mistake, — just that
And no more, in a Latin cramp enough
When the law had her eloquence to launch,
But interfilleted with Italian streaks
When testimony stooped to mother-tongue, —
That, was this old square yellow book about.

Now, as the ingot, ere the ring was forged,
Lay gold, (beseech you, hold that figure fast!)
So, in this book lay absolutely truth,
Fanciless fact, the documents indeed,
Primary lawyer-pleadings for, against,
The aforesaid Five; real summed-up circumstance
Adduced in proof of these on either side,
Put forth and printed, as the practice was,
At Rome, in the Apostolic Chamber's type,
And so submitted to the eye o' the Court
Presided over by His Reverence
Rome's Governor and Criminal Judge, — the trial
Itself, to all intents, being then as now
Here in the book and nowise out of it;
Seeing, there properly was no judgment-bar,
No bringing of accuser and accused,
And whoso judged both parties, face to face
Before some court, as we conceive of courts.
There was a Hall of Justice; that came last:
For Justice had a chamber by the hall
Where she took evidence first, summed up the same,
Then sent accuser and accused alike,
In person of the advocate of each,
To weigh its worth, thereby arrange, array
The battle. 'Twas the so-styled Fisc began,
Pleaded (and since he only spoke in print
The printed voice of him lives now as then)
The public Prosecutor — "Murder's proved;
"With five . . . what we call qualities of bad,
"Worse, worst, and yet worse still, and still worse yet;
"Crest over crest crowning the cockatrice,
"That beggar hell's regalia to enrich
"Count Guido Franceschini: punish him!"
Thus was the paper put before the court
In the next stage, (no noisy work at all,)
To study at ease. In due time like reply
Came from the so-styled Patron of the Poor,
Official mouthpiece of the five accused
Too poor to fee a better, — Guido's luck

Or else his fellows', — which, I hardly know, —
An outbreak as of wonder at the world,
A fury-fit of outraged innocence,
A passion of betrayed simplicity:
"Punish Count Guido? For what crime, what hint
"O' the colour of a crime, inform us first!
"Reward him rather! Recognize, we say,
"In the deed done, a righteous judgment dealt!
"All conscience and all courage, — there's our Count
"Charactered in a word; and, what's more strange,
"He had companionship in privilege,
"Found four courageous conscientious friends:
"Absolve, applaud all five, as props of law,
"Sustainers of society! — perchance
"A trifle over-hasty with the hand
"To hold her tottering ark, had tumbled else;
"But that's a splendid fault whereat we wink,
"Wishing your cold correctness sparkled so!"
Thus paper second followed paper first,
Thus did the two join issue — nay, the four,
Each pleader having an adjunct. "True, he killed
" — So to speak — in a certain sort — his wife,
"But laudably, since thus it happed!" quoth one:
Whereat, more witness and the case postponed.
"Thus it happed not, since thus he did the deed,
"And proved himself thereby portentousest
"Of cutthroats and a prodigy of crime,
"As the woman that he slaughtered was a saint,
"Martyr and miracle!" quoth the other to match:
Again, more witness, and the case postponed.
"A miracle, ay — of lust and impudence;
"Hear my new reasons!" interposed the first:
" — Coupled with more of mine!" pursued his peer.
"Beside, the precedents, the authorities!"
From both at once a cry with an echo, that!
That was a firebrand at each fox's tail
Unleashed in a cornfield: soon spread flare enough,
As hurtled thither and there heaped themselves
From earth's four corners, all authority

And precedent for putting wives to death,
Or letting wives live, sinful as they seem.
How legislated, now, in this respect,
Solon and his Athenians? Quote the code
Of Romulus and Rome! Justinian speak!
Nor modern Baldo, Bartolo be dumb!
The Roman voice was potent, plentiful;
Cornelia de Sicariis hurried to help
Pompeia de Parricidiis; Julia de
Something-or-other jostled *Lex* this-and-that;
King Solomon confirmed Apostle Paul:
That nice decision of Dolabella, eh?
That pregnant instance of Theodoric, oh!
Down to that choice example Ælian gives
(An instance I find much insisted on)
Of the elephant who, brute-beast though he were,
Yet understood and punished on the spot
His master's naughty spouse and faithless friend;
A true tale which has edified each child,
Much more shall flourish favoured by our court!
Pages of proof this way, and that way proof,
And always — once again the case postponed.

Thus wrangled, brangled, jangled they a month,
— Only on paper, pleadings all in print,
Nor ever was, except i' the brains of men,
More noise by word of mouth than you hear now —
Till the court cut all short with "Judged, your cause.
"Receive our sentence! Praise God! We pronounce
"Count Guido devilish and damnable:
"His wife Pompilia in thought, word and deed,
"Was perfect pure, he murdered her for that:
"As for the Four who helped the One, all Five —
"Why, let employer and hirelings share alike
"In guilt and guilt's reward, the death their due!"

So was the trial at end, do you suppose?
"Guilty you find him, death you doom him to?
"Ay, were not Guido, more than needs, a priest,

"Priest and to spare!" — this was a shot reserved;
I learn this from epistles which begin
Here where the print ends, — see the pen and ink
Of the advocate, the ready at a pinch! —
"My client boasts the clerkly privilege,
"Has taken minor orders many enough,
"Shows still sufficient chrism upon his pate
"To neutralize a blood-stain: *presbyter*,
"*Primæ tonsuræ, subdiaconus*,
"*Sacerdos*, so he slips from underneath
"Your power, the temporal, slides inside the robe
"Of mother Church: to her we make appeal
"By the Pope, the Church's head!"

                     A parlous plea,
Put in with noticeable effect, it seems;
"Since straight," — resumes the zealous orator,
Making a friend acquainted with the facts, —
"Once the word 'clericality' let fall,
"Procedure stopped and freer breath was drawn
"By all considerate and responsible Rome."
Quality took the decent part, of course;
Held by the husband, who was noble too:
Or, for the matter of that, a churl would side
With too-refined susceptibility,
And honour which, tender in the extreme,
Stung to the quick, must roughly right itself
At all risks, not sit still and whine for law
As a Jew would, if you squeezed him to the wall,
Brisk-trotting through the Ghetto. Nay, it seems,
Even the Emperor's Envoy had his say
To say on the subject; might not see, unmoved,
Civility menaced throughout Christendom
By too harsh measure dealt her champion here.
Lastly, what made all safe, the Pope was kind,
From his youth up, reluctant to take life,
If mercy might be just and yet show grace;
Much more unlikely then, in extreme age,
To take a life the general sense bade spare.
'Twas plain that Guido would go scatheless yet.

617

But human promise, oh, how short of shine!
How topple down the piles of hope we rear!
How history proves . . . nay, read Herodotus!
Suddenly starting from a nap, as it were,
A dog-sleep with one shut, one open orb,
Cried the Pope's great self, — Innocent by name
And nature too, and eighty-six years old,
Antonio Pignatelli of Naples, Pope
Who had trod many lands, known many deeds,
Probed many hearts, beginning with his own,
And now was far in readiness for God, —
'Twas he who first bade leave those souls in peace,
Those Jansenists, re-nicknamed Molinists,
('Gainst whom the cry went, like a frowsy tune,
Tickling men's ears — the sect for a quarter of an hour
I' the teeth of the world which, clown-like, loves to chew
Be it but a straw 'twixt work and whistling-while,
Taste some vituperation, bite away,
Whether at marjoram-sprig or garlic-clove,
Aught it may sport with, spoil, and then spit forth)
"Leave them alone," bade he, "those Molinists!
"Who may have other light than we perceive,
"Or why is it the whole world hates them thus?"
Also he peeled off that last scandal-rag
Of Nepotism; and so observed the poor
That men would merrily say, "Halt, deaf and blind,
"Who feed on fat things, leave the master's self
"To gather up the fragments of his feast,
"These be the nephews of Pope Innocent! —
"His own meal costs but five carlines a day,
"Poor-priest's allowance, for he claims no more."
— He cried of a sudden, this great good old Pope,
When they appealed in last resort to him,
"I have mastered the whole matter: I nothing doubt.
"Though Guido stood forth priest from head to heel,
"Instead of, as alleged, a piece of one, —
"And further, were he, from the tonsured scalp
"To the sandaled sole of him, my son and Christ's,
"Instead of touching us by finger-tip

"As you assert, and pressing up so close
"Only to set a blood-smutch on our robe, —
"I and Christ would renounce all right in him.
"Am I not Pope, and presently to die,
"And busied how to render my account,
"And shall I wait a day ere I decide
"On doing or not doing justice here?
"Cut off his head to-morrow by this time,
"Hang up his four mates, two on either hand,
"And end one business more!"

                So said, so done —
Rather so writ, for the old Pope bade this,
I find, with his particular chirograph,
His own no such infirm hand, Friday night;
And next day, February Twenty Two,
Since our salvation Sixteen Ninety Eight,
— Not at the proper head-and-hanging-place
On bridge-foot close by Castle Angelo,
Where custom somewhat staled the spectacle,
('Twas not so well i' the way of Rome, beside,
The noble Rome, the Rome of Guido's rank)
But at the city's newer gayer end, —
The cavalcading promenading place
Beside the gate and opposite the church
Under the Pincian gardens green with Spring,
'Neath the obelisk 'twixt the fountains in the Square,
Did Guido and his fellows find their fate,
All Rome for witness, and — my writer adds —
Remonstrant in its universal grief,
Since Guido had the suffrage of all Rome.
This is the bookful; thus far take the truth,
The untempered gold, the fact untampered with,
The mere ring-metal ere the ring be made!
And what has hitherto come of it? Who preserves
The memory of this Guido, and his wife
Pompilia, more than Ademollo's name,
The etcher of those prints, two *crazie* each,
Saved by a stone from snowing broad the Square

With scenic backgrounds? Was this truth of force?
Able to take its own part as truth should,
Sufficient, self-sustaining? Why, if so —
Yonder's a fire, into it goes my book,
As who shall say me nay, and what the loss?
You know the tale already: I may ask,
Rather than think to tell you, more thereof, —
Ask you not merely who were he and she,
Husband and wife, what manner of mankind,
But how you hold concerning this and that
Other yet-unnamed actor in the piece.
The young frank handsome courtly Canon, now,
The priest, declared the lover of the wife,
He who, no question, did elope with her,
For certain bring the tragedy about,
Giuseppe Caponsacchi; — his strange course
I' the matter, was it right or wrong or both?
Then the old couple, slaughtered with the wife
By the husband as accomplices in crime,
Those Comparini, Pietro and his spouse, —
What say you to the right or wrong of that,
When, at a known name whispered through the door
Of a lone villa on a Christmas night,
It opened that the joyous hearts inside
Might welcome as it were an angel-guest
Come in Christ's name to knock and enter, sup
And satisfy the loving ones he saved;
And so did welcome devils and their death?
I have been silent on that circumstance
Although the couple passed for close of kin
To wife and husband, were by some accounts
Pompilia's very parents: you know best.
Also that infant the great joy was for,
That Gaetano, the wife's two-weeks' babe,
The husband's first-born child, his son and heir,
Whose birth and being turned his night to day —
Why must the father kill the mother thus
Because she bore his son and saved himself?

Well, British Public, ye who like me not,
(God love you!) and will have your proper laugh
At the dark question, laugh it! I laugh first.
Truth must prevail, the proverb vows; and truth
— Here is it all i' the book at last, as first
There it was all i' the heads and hearts of Rome
Gentle and simple, never to fall nor fade
Nor be forgotten. Yet, a little while,
The passage of a century or so,
Decads thrice five, and here's time paid his tax,
Oblivion gone home with her harvesting,
And all left smooth again as scythe could shave.
Far from beginning with you London folk,
I took my book to Rome first, tried truth's power
On likely people. "Have you met such names?
"Is a tradition extant of such facts?
"Your law-courts stand, your records frown a-row:
"What if I rove and rummage?" " — Why, you'll waste
"Your pains and end as wise as you began!"
Everyone snickered: "names and facts thus old
"Are newer much than Europe news we find
"Down in to-day's *Diario*. Records, quotha?
"Why, the French burned them, what else do the French?
"The rap-and-rending nation! And it tells
"Against the Church, no doubt, — another gird
"At the Temporality, your Trial, of course?"
" — Quite otherwise this time," submitted I;
"Clean for the Church and dead against the world,
"The flesh and the devil, does it tell for once."
" — The rarer and the happier! All the same,
"Content you with your treasure of a book,
"And waive what's wanting! Take a friend's advice!
"It's not the custom of the country. Mend
"Your ways indeed and we may stretch a point:
"Go get you manned by Manning and new-manned
"By Newman and, mayhap, wise-manned to boot
"By Wiseman, and we'll see or else we won't!
"Thanks meantime for the story, long and strong,
"A pretty piece of narrative enough,

"Which scarce ought so to drop out, one would think,
"From the more curious annals of our kind.
"Do you tell the story, now, in off-hand style,
"Straight from the book? Or simply here and there,
"(The while you vault it through the loose and large)
"Hang to a hint? Or is there book at all,
"And don't you deal in poetry, make-believe,
"And the white lies it sounds like?"

                                    Yes and no!
From the book, yes; thence bit by bit I dug
The lingot truth, that memorable day,
Assayed and knew my piecemeal gain was gold, —
Yes; but from something else surpassing that,
Something of mine which, mixed up with the mass,
Made it bear hammer and be firm to file.
Fancy with fact is just one fact the more;
To-wit, that fancy has informed, transpierced,
Thridded and so thrown fast the facts else free,
As right through ring and ring runs the djereed
And binds the loose, one bar without a break.
I fused my live soul and that inert stuff,
Before attempting smithcraft, on the night
After the day when, — truth thus grasped and gained, —
The book was shut and done with and laid by
On the cream-coloured massive agate, broad
'Neath the twin cherubs in the tarnished frame
O' the mirror, tall thence to the ceiling-top.
And from the reading, and that slab I leant
My elbow on, the while I read and read,
I turned, to free myself and find the world,
And stepped out on the narrow terrace, built
Over the street and opposite the church,
And paced its lozenge-brickwork sprinkled cool;
Because Felice-church-side stretched, a-glow
Through each square window fringed for festival,
Whence came the clear voice of the cloistered ones
Chanting a chant made for midsummer nights —
I know not what particular praise of God,

It always came and went with June. Beneath
I' the street, quick shown by openings of the sky
When flame fell silently from cloud to cloud,
Richer than that gold snow Jove rained on Rhodes,
The townsmen walked by twos and threes, and talked,
Drinking the blackness in default of air —
A busy human sense beneath my feet:
While in and out the terrace-plants, and round
One branch of tall datura, waxed and waned
The lamp-fly lured there, wanting the white flower.
Over the roof o' the lighted church I looked
A bowshot to the street's end, north away
Out of the Roman gate to the Roman road
By the river, till I felt the Apennine.
And there would lie Arezzo, the man's town,
The woman's trap and cage and torture-place,
Also the stage where the priest played his part,
A spectacle for angels, — ay, indeed,
There lay Arezzo! Farther then I fared,
Feeling my way on through the hot and dense,
Romeward, until I found the wayside inn
By Castelnuovo's few mean hut-like homes
Huddled together on the hill-foot bleak,
Bare, broken only by that tree or two
Against the sudden bloody splendour poured
Cursewise in day's departure by the sun
O'er the low house-roof of that squalid inn
Where they three, for the first time and the last,
Husband and wife and priest, met face to face.
Whence I went on again, the end was near,
Step by step, missing none and marking all,
Till Rome itself, the ghastly goal, I reached.
Why, all the while, — how could it otherwise? —
The life in me abolished the death of things,
Deep calling unto deep: as then and there
Acted itself over again once more
The tragic piece. I saw with my own eyes
In Florence as I trod the terrace, breathed
The beauty and the fearfulness of night,

How it had run, this round from Rome to Rome —
Because, you are to know, they lived at Rome,
Pompilia's parents, as they thought themselves,
Two poor ignoble hearts who did their best
Part God's way, part the other way than God's,
To somehow make a shift and scramble through
The world's mud, careless if it splashed and spoiled,
Provided they might so hold high, keep clean
Their child's soul, one soul white enough for three,
And lift it to whatever star should stoop,
What possible sphere of purer life than theirs
Should come in aid of whiteness hard to save.
I saw the star stoop, that they strained to touch,
And did touch and depose their treasure on,
As Guido Franceschini took away
Pompilia to be his for evermore,
While they sang "Now let us depart in peace,
"Having beheld thy glory, Guido's wife!"
I saw the star supposed, but fog o' the fen,
Gilded star-fashion by a glint from hell;
Having been heaved up, haled on its gross way,
By hands unguessed before, invisible help
From a dark brotherhood, and specially
Two obscure goblin creatures, fox-faced this,
Cat-clawed the other, called his next of kin
By Guido the main monster, — cloaked and caped,
Making as they were priests, to mock God more, —
Abate Paul, Canon Girolamo.
These who had rolled the starlike pest to Rome
And stationed it to suck up and absorb
The sweetness of Pompilia, rolled again
That bloated bubble, with her soul inside,
Back to Arezzo and a palace there —
Or say, a fissure in the honest earth
Whence long ago had curled the vapour first,
Blown big by nether fires to appal day:
It touched home, broke, and blasted far and wide.
I saw the cheated couple find the cheat
And guess what foul rite they were captured for, —

Too fain to follow over hill and dale
That child of theirs caught up thus in the cloud
And carried by the Prince o' the Power of the Air
Whither he would, to wilderness or sea.
I saw them, in the potency of fear,
Break somehow through the satyr-family
(For a grey mother with a monkey-mien,
Mopping and mowing, was apparent too,
As, confident of capture, all took hands
And danced about the captives in a ring)
— Saw them break through, breathe safe, at Rome again,
Saved by the selfish instinct, losing so
Their loved one left with haters. These I saw,
In recrudescency of baffled hate,
Prepare to wring the uttermost revenge
From body and soul thus left them: all was sure,
Fire laid and cauldron set, the obscene ring traced,
The victim stripped and prostrate: what of God?
The cleaving of a cloud, a cry, a crash,
Quenched lay their cauldron, cowered i' the dust the crew,
As, in a glory of armour like Saint George,
Out again sprang the young good beauteous priest
Bearing away the lady in his arms,
Saved for a splendid minute and no more.
For, whom i' the path did that priest come upon,
He and the poor lost lady borne so brave,
— Checking the song of praise in me, had else
Swelled to the full for God's will done on earth —
Whom but a dusk misfeatured messenger,
No other than the angel of this life,
Whose care is lest men see too much at once.
He made the sign, such God-glimpse must suffice,
Nor prejudice the Prince o' the Power of the Air,
Whose ministration piles us overhead
What we call, first, earth's roof and, last, heaven's floor,
Now grate o' the trap, then outlet of the cage:
So took the lady, left the priest alone,
And once more canopied the world with black.
But through the blackness I saw Rome again,

And where a solitary villa stood
In a lone garden-quarter: it was eve,
The second of the year, and oh so cold!
Ever and anon there flittered through the air
A snow-flake, and a scanty couch of snow
Crusted the grass-walk and the garden-mould.
All was grave, silent, sinister, — when, ha?
Glimmeringly did a pack of were-wolves pad
The snow, those flames were Guido's eyes in front,
And all five found and footed it, the track,
To where a threshold-streak of warmth and light
Betrayed the villa-door with life inside,
While an inch outside were those blood-bright eyes,
And black lips wrinkling o'er the flash of teeth,
And tongues that lolled — Oh God that madest man!
They parleyed in their language. Then one whined —
That was the policy and master-stroke —
Deep in his throat whispered what seemed a name —
"Open to Caponsacchi!" Guido cried:
"Gabriel!" cried Lucifer at Eden-gate.
Wide as a heart, opened the door at once,
Showing the joyous couple, and their child
The two-weeks' mother, to the wolves, the wolves
To them. Close eyes! And when the corpses lay
Stark-stretched, and those the wolves, their wolf-work done,
Were safe-embosomed by the night again,
I knew a necessary change in things;
As when the worst watch of the night gives way,
And there comes duly, to take cognizance,
The scrutinizing eye-point of some star —
And who despairs of a new daybreak now?
Lo, the first ray protruded on those five!
It reached them, and each felon writhed transfixed
Awhile they palpitated on the spear
Motionless over Tophet: stand or fall?
"I say, the spear should fall — should stand, I say!"
Cried the world come to judgment, granting grace
Or dealing doom according to world's wont,
Those world's-bystanders grouped on Rome's cross-road

At prick and summons of the primal curse
Which bids man love as well as make a lie.
There prattled they, discoursed the right and wrong,
Turned wrong to right, proved wolves sheep and sheep wolves,
So that you scarce distinguished fell from fleece;
Till out spoke a great guardian of the fold,
Stood up, put forth his hand that held the crook,
And motioned that the arrested point decline:
Horribly off, the wriggling dead-weight reeled,
Rushed to the bottom and lay ruined there.
Though still at the pit's mouth, despite the smoke
O' the burning, tarriers turned again to talk
And trim the balance, and detect at least
A touch of wolf in what showed whitest sheep,
A cross of sheep redeeming the whole wolf, —
Vex truth a little longer: — less and less,
Because years came and went, and more and more
Brought new lies with them to be loved in turn.
Till all at once the memory of the thing, —
The fact that, wolves or sheep, such creatures were, —
Which hitherto, however men supposed,
Had somehow plain and pillar-like prevailed
I' the midst of them, indisputably fact,
Granite, time's tooth should grate against, not graze, —
Why, this proved sandstone, friable, fast to fly
And give its grain away at wish o' the wind.
Ever and ever more diminutive,
Base gone, shaft lost, only entablature,
Dwindled into no bigger than a book,
Lay of the column; and that little, left
By the roadside 'mid the ordure, shards and weeds.
Until I haply, wandering that lone way,
Kicked it up, turned it over, and recognized,
For all the crumblement, this abacus,
This square old yellow book, — could calculate
By this the lost proportions of the style.

This was it from, my fancy with those facts,
I used to tell the tale, turned gay to grave,

But lacked a listener seldom; such alloy,
Such substance of me interfused the gold
Which, wrought into a shapely ring therewith,
Hammered and filed, fingered and favoured, last
Lay ready for the renovating wash
O' the water. "How much of the tale was true?"
I disappeared; the book grew all in all;
The lawyers' pleadings swelled back to their size, —
Doubled in two, the crease upon them yet,
For more commodity of carriage, see! —
And these are letters, veritable sheets
That brought posthaste the news to Florence, writ
At Rome the day Count Guido died, we find,
To stay the craving of a client there,
Who bound the same and so produced my book.
Lovers of dead truth, did ye fare the worse?
Lovers of live truth, found ye false my tale?

Well, now; there's nothing in nor out o' the world
Good except truth: yet this, the something else,
What's this then, which proves good yet seems untrue?
This that I mixed with truth, motions of mine
That quickened, made the inertness malleolable
O' the gold was not mine, — what's your name for this?
Are means to the end, themselves in part the end?
Is fiction which makes fact alive, fact too?
The somehow may be thishow.
                                    I find first
Writ down for every A B C of fact,
"In the beginning God made heaven and earth;"
From which, no matter with what lisp, I spell
And speak you out a consequence — that man,
Man, — as befits the made, the inferior thing, —
Purposed, since made, to grow, not make in turn,
Yet forced to try and make, else fail to grow, —
Formed to rise, reach at, if not grasp and gain
The good beyond him, — which attempt is growth, —
Repeats God's process in man's due degree,
Attaining man's proportionate result, —

Creates, no, but resuscitates, perhaps.
Inalienable, the arch-prerogative
Which turns thought, act — conceives, expresses too!
No less, man, bounded, yearning to be free,
May so project his surplusage of soul
In search of body, so add self to self
By owning what lay ownerless before, —
So find, so fill full, so appropriate forms —
That, although nothing which had never life
Shall get life from him, be, not having been,
Yet, something dead may get to live again,
Something with too much life or not enough,
Which, either way imperfect, ended once:
An end whereat man's impulse intervenes,
Makes new beginning, starts the dead alive,
Completes the incomplete and saves the thing.
Man's breath were vain to light a virgin wick, —
Half-burned-out, all but quite-quenched wicks o' the lamp
Stationed for temple-service on this earth,
These indeed let him breathe on and relume!
For such man's feat is, in the due degree,
— Mimic creation, galvanism for life,
But still a glory portioned in the scale.
Why did the mage say, — feeling as we are wont
For truth, and stopping midway short of truth,
And resting on a lie, — "I raise a ghost"?
"Because," he taught adepts, "man makes not man.
"Yet by a special gift, an art of arts,
"More insight and more outsight and much more
"Will to use both of these than boast my mates,
"I can detach from me, commission forth
"Half of my soul; which in its pilgrimage
"O'er old unwandered waste ways of the world,
"May chance upon some fragment of a whole,
"Rag of flesh, scrap of bone in dim disuse,
"Smoking flax that fed fire once: prompt therein
"I enter, spark-like, put old powers to play,
"Push lines out to the limit, lead forth last
"(By a moonrise through a ruin of a crypt)

"What shall be mistily seen, murmuringly heard,
"Mistakenly felt: then write my name with Faust's!"
Oh, Faust, why Faust? Was not Elisha once? —
Who bade them lay his staff on a corpse-face.
There was no voice, no hearing: he went in
Therefore, and shut the door upon them twain,
And prayed unto the Lord: and he went up
And lay upon the corpse, dead on the couch,
And put his mouth upon its mouth, his eyes
Upon its eyes, his hands upon its hands,
And stretched him on the flesh; the flesh waxed warm:
And he returned, walked to and fro the house,
And went up, stretched him on the flesh again,
And the eyes opened. 'Tis a credible feat
With the right man and way.
                              Enough of me!
The Book! I turn its medicinable leaves
In London now till, as in Florence erst,
A spirit laughs and leaps through every limb,
And lights my eye, and lifts me by the hair,
Letting me have my will again with these
— How title I the dead alive once more?

Count Guido Franceschini the Aretine,
Descended of an ancient house, though poor,
A beak-nosed bushy-bearded black-haired lord,
Lean, pallid, low of stature yet robust,
Fifty years old, — having four years ago
Married Pompilia Comparini, young,
Good, beautiful, at Rome, where she was born,
And brought her to Arezzo, where they lived
Unhappy lives, whatever curse the cause, —
This husband, taking four accomplices,
Followed this wife to Rome, where she was fled
From their Arezzo to find peace again,
In convoy, eight months earlier, of a priest,
Aretine also, of still nobler birth,
Giuseppe Caponsacchi, — caught her there
Quiet in a villa on a Christmas night,

With only Pietro and Violante by,
Both her putative parents; killed the three,
Aged, they, seventy each, and she, seventeen,
And, two weeks since, the mother of his babe
First-born and heir to what the style was worth
O' the Guido who determined, dared and did
This deed just as he purposed point by point.
Then, bent upon escape, but hotly pressed,
And captured with his co-mates that same night,
He, brought to trial, stood on this defence —
Injury to his honour caused the act;
And since his wife was false, (as manifest
By flight from home in such companionship,)
Death, punishment deserved of the false wife
And faithless parents who abetted her
I' the flight aforesaid, wronged nor God nor man.
"Nor false she, nor yet faithless they," replied
The accuser; "cloaked and masked this murder glooms;
"True was Pompilia, loyal too the pair;
"Out of the man's own heart a monster curled
"Which — crime coiled with connivancy at crime —
"His victim's breast, he tells you, hatched and reared;
"Uncoil we and stretch stark the worm of hell!"
A month the trial swayed this way and that
Ere judgment settled down on Guido's guilt;
Then was the Pope, that good Twelfth Innocent,
Appealed to: who well weighed what went before,
Affirmed the guilt and gave the guilty doom.

Let this old woe step on the stage again!
Act itself o'er anew for men to judge,
Not by the very sense and sight indeed —
(Which take at best imperfect cognizance,
Since, how heart moves brain, and how both move hand,
What mortal ever in entirety saw?)
— No dose of purer truth than man digests,
But truth with falsehood, milk that feeds him now,
Not strong meat he may get to bear some day —
To-wit, by voices we call evidence,

Uproar in the echo, live fact deadened down,
Talked over, bruited abroad, whispered away,
Yet helping us to all we seem to hear:
For how else know we save by worth of word?

Here are the voices presently shall sound
In due succession. First, the world's outcry
Around the rush and ripple of any fact
Fallen stonewise, plumb on the smooth face of things;
The world's guess, as it crowds the bank o' the pool,
At what were figure and substance, by their splash:
Then, by vibrations in the general mind,
At depth of deed already out of reach.
This threefold murder of the day before, —
Say, Half-Rome's feel after the vanished truth;
Honest enough, as the way is: all the same,
Harbouring in the centre of its sense
A hidden germ of failure, shy but sure,
To neutralize that honesty and leave
That feel for truth at fault, as the way is too.
Some prepossession such as starts amiss,
By but a hair's breadth at the shoulder-blade,
The arm o' the feeler, dip he ne'er so bold;
So leads arm waveringly, lets fall wide
O' the mark its finger, sent to find and fix
Truth at the bottom, that deceptive speck.
With this Half-Rome, — the source of swerving, call
Over-belief in Guido's right and wrong
Rather than in Pompilia's wrong and right:
Who shall say how, who shall say why? 'Tis there —
The instinctive theorizing whence a fact
Looks to the eye as the eye likes the look.
Gossip in a public place, a sample-speech.
Some worthy, with his previous hint to find
A husband's side the safer, and no whit
Aware he is not Æacus the while, —
How such an one supposes and states fact
To whosoever of a multitude
Will listen, and perhaps prolong thereby

632

The not-unpleasant flutter at the breast,
Born of a certain spectacle shut in
By the church Lorenzo opposite. So, they lounge
Midway the mouth o' the street, on Corso side,
'Twixt palace Fiano and palace Ruspoli,
Linger and listen; keeping clear o' the crowd,
Yet wishful one could lend that crowd one's eyes,
(So universal is its plague of squint)
And make hearts beat our time that flutter false:
— All for the truth's sake, mere truth, nothing else!
How Half-Rome found for Guido much excuse.

Next, from Rome's other half, the opposite feel
For truth with a like swerve, like unsuccess, —
Or if success, by no skill but more luck
This time, through siding rather with the wife,
Because a fancy-fit inclined that way,
Than with the husband. One wears drab, one pink;
Who wears pink, ask him "Which shall win the race,
"Of coupled runners like as egg and egg?"
" — Why, if I must choose, he with the pink scarf."
Doubtless for some such reason choice fell here.
A piece of public talk to correspond
At the next stage of the story; just a day
Let pass and new day brings the proper change.
Another sample-speech i' the market-place
O' the Barberini by the Capucins;
Where the old Triton, at his fountain-sport,
Bernini's creature plated to the paps,
Puffs up steel sleet which breaks to diamond dust,
A spray of sparkles snorted from his conch,
High over the caritellas, out o' the way
O' the motley merchandizing multitude.
Our murder has been done three days ago,
The frost is over and gone, the south wind laughs,
And, to the very tiles of each red roof
A-smoke i' the sunshine, Rome lies gold and glad:
So, listen how, to the other half of Rome,
Pompilia seemed a saint and martyr both!

Then, yet another day let come and go,
With pause prelusive still of novelty,
Hear a fresh speaker! — neither this nor that
Half-Rome aforesaid; something bred of both:
One and one breed the inevitable three.
Such is the personage harangues you next;
The elaborated product, *tertium quid*:
Rome's first commotion in subsidence gives
The curd o' the cream, flower o' the wheat, as it were,
And finer sense o' the city. Is this plain?
You get a reasoned statement of the case,
Eventual verdict of the curious few
Who care to sift a business to the bran
Nor coarsely bolt it like the simpler sort.
Here, after ignorance, instruction speaks;
Here, clarity of candour, history's soul,
The critical mind, in short: no gossip-guess.
What the superior social section thinks,
In person of some man of quality
Who, — breathing musk from lace-work and brocade,
His solitaire amid the flow of frill,
Powdered peruke on nose, and bag at back,
And cane dependent from the ruffled wrist, —
Harangues in silvery and selectest phrase
'Neath waxlight in a glorified saloon
Where mirrors multiply the girandole:
Courting the approbation of no mob,
But Eminence This and All-Illustrious That
Who take snuff softly, range in well-bred ring,
Card-table-quitters for observance' sake,
Around the argument, the rational word —
Still, spite its weight and worth, a sample-speech.
How Quality dissertated on the case.

So much for Rome and rumour; smoke comes first:
Once let smoke rise untroubled, we descry
Clearlier what tongues of flame may spire and spit
To eye and ear, each with appropriate tinge
According to its food, or pure or foul.

The actors, no mere rumours of the act,
Intervene. First you hear Count Guido's voice,
In a small chamber that adjoins the court,
Where Governor and Judges, summoned thence,
Tommati, Venturini and the rest,
Find the accused ripe for declaring truth.
Soft-cushioned sits he; yet shifts seat, shirks touch,
As, with a twitchy brow and wincing lip
And cheek that changes to all kinds of white,
He proffers his defence, in tones subdued
Near to mock-mildness now, so mournful seems
The obtuser sense truth fails to satisfy;
Now, moved, from pathos at the wrong endured,
To passion; for the natural man is roused
At fools who first do wrong then pour the blame
Of their wrong-doing, Satan-like, on Job.
Also his tongue at times is hard to curb;
Incisive, nigh satiric bites the phrase,
Rough-raw, yet somehow claiming privilege
— It is so hard for shrewdness to admit
Folly means no harm when she calls black white!
— Eruption momentary at the most,
Modified forthwith by a fall o' the fire,
Sage acquiescence; for the world's the world,
And, what it errs in, Judges rectify:
He feels he has a fist, then folds his arms
Crosswise and makes his mind up to be meek.
And never once does he detach his eye
From those ranged there to slay him or to save,
But does his best man's-service for himself,
Despite, — what twitches brow and makes lip wince, —
His limbs' late taste of what was called the Cord,
Or Vigil-torture more facetiously.
Even so; they were wont to tease the truth
Out of loth witness (toying, trifling time)
By torture: 'twas a trick, a vice of the age,
Here, there and everywhere, what would you have?
Religion used to tell Humanity
She gave him warrant or denied him course.

And since the course was much to his own mind,
Of pinching flesh and pulling bone from bone
To unhusk truth a-hiding in its hulls,
Nor whisper of a warning stopped the way,
He, in their joint behalf, the burly slave,
Bestirred him, mauled and maimed all recusants,
While, prim in place, Religion overlooked;
And so had done till doomsday, never a sign
Nor sound of interference from her mouth,
But that at last the burly slave wiped brow,
Let eye give notice as if soul were there,
Muttered " 'Tis a vile trick, foolish more than vile,
"Should have been counted sin; I make it so:
"At any rate no more of it for me —
"Nay, for I break the torture-engine thus!"
Then did Religion start up, stare amain,
Look round for help and see none, smile and say
"What, broken is the rack? Well done of thee!
"Did I forget to abrogate its use?
"Be the mistake in common with us both!
" — One more fault our blind age shall answer for,
"Down in my book denounced though it must be
"Somewhere. Henceforth find truth by milder means!"
Ah but, Religion, did we wait for thee
To ope the book, that serves to sit upon,
And pick such place out, we should wait indeed!
That is all history: and what is not now,
Was then, defendants found it to their cost.
How Guido, after being tortured, spoke.

Also hear Caponsacchi who comes next,
Man and priest — could you comprehend the coil! —
In days when that was rife which now is rare.
How, mingling each its multifarious wires,
Now heaven, now earth, now heaven and earth at once,
Had plucked at and perplexed their puppet here,
Played off the young frank personable priest;
Sworn fast and tonsured plain heaven's celibate,
And yet earth's clear-accepted servitor,

A courtly spiritual Cupid, squire of dames
By law of love and mandate of the mode.
The Church's own, or why parade her seal,
Wherefore that chrism and consecrative work?
Yet verily the world's, or why go badged
A prince of sonneteers and lutanists,
Show colour of cach vanity in vogue
Borne with decorum due on blameless breast?
All that is changed now, as he tells the court
How he had played the part excepted at;
Tells it, moreover, now the second time:
Since, for his cause of scandal, his own share
I' the flight from home and husband of the wife,
He has been censured, punished in a sort
By relegation, — exile, we should say,
To a short distance for a little time, —
Whence he is summoned on a sudden now,
Informed that she, he thought to save, is lost,
And, in a breath, bidden re-tell his tale,
Since the first telling somehow missed effect,
And then advise in the matter. There stands he,
While the same grim black-panelled chamber blinks
As though rubbed shiny with the sins of Rome
Told the same oak for ages — wave-washed wall
Against which sets a sea of wickedness.
There, where you yesterday heard Guido speak,
Speaks Caponsacchi; and there face him too
Tommati, Venturini and the rest
Who, eight months earlier, scarce repressed the smile,
Forewent the wink; waived recognition so
Of peccadillos incident to youth,
Especially youth high-born; for youth means love,
Vows can't change nature, priests are only men,
And love likes stratagem and subterfuge
Which age, that once was youth, should recognize,
May blame, but needs not press too hard upon.
Here sit the old Judges then, but with no grace
Of reverend carriage, magisterial port:
For why? The accused of eight months since, — the same

637

Who cut the conscious figure of a fool,
Changed countenance, dropped bashful gaze to ground,
While hesitating for an answer then, —
Now is grown judge himself, terrifies now
This, now the other culprit called a judge,
Whose turn it is to stammer and look strange,
As he speaks rapidly, angrily, speech that smites:
And they keep silence, bear blow after blow,
Because the seeming-solitary man,
Speaking for God, may have an audience too,
Invisible, no discreet judge provokes.
How the priest Caponsacchi said his say.

Then a soul sighs its lowest and its last
After the loud ones, — so much breath remains
Unused by the four-days'-dying; for she lived
Thus long, miraculously long, 'twas thought,
Just that Pompilia might defend herself.
How, while the hireling and the alien stoop,
Comfort, yet question, — since the time is brief,
And folk, allowably inquisitive,
Encircle the low pallet where she lies
In the good house that helps the poor to die, —
Pompilia tells the story of her life.
For friend and lover, — leech and man of law
Do service; busy helpful ministrants
As varied in their calling as their mind,
Temper and age: and yet from all of these,
About the white bed under the arched roof,
Is somehow, as it were, evolved a one, —
Small separate sympathies combined and large,
Nothings that were, grown something very much:
As if the bystanders gave each his straw,
All he had, though a trifle in itself,
Which, plaited all together, made a Cross
Fit to die looking on and praying with,
Just as well as if ivory or gold.
So, to the common kindliness she speaks,
There being scarce more privacy at the last

For mind than body: but she is used to bear,
And only unused to the brotherly look.
How she endeavoured to explain her life.

Then, since a Trial ensued, a touch o' the same
To sober us, flustered with frothy talk,
And teach our common sense its helplessness.
For why deal simply with divining-rod,
Scrape where we fancy secret sources flow,
And ignore law, the recognized machine,
Elaborate display of pipe and wheel
Framed to unchoke, pump up and pour apace
Truth till a flowery foam shall wash the world?
The patent truth-extracting process, — ha?
Let us make that grave mystery turn one wheel,
Give you a single grind of law at least!
One orator, of two on either side,
Shall teach us the puissance of the tongue
— That is, o' the pen which simulated tongue
On paper and saved all except the sound
Which never was. Law's speech beside law's thought?
That were too stunning, too immense an odds:
That point of vantage law lets nobly pass.
One lawyer shall admit us to behold
The manner of the making out a case,
First fashion of a speech; the chick in egg,
The masterpiece law's bosom incubates.
How Don Giacinto of the Arcangeli,
Called Procurator of the Poor at Rome,
Now advocate for Guido and his mates, —
The jolly learned man of middle age,
Cheek and jowl all in laps with fat and law,
Mirthful as mighty, yet, as great hearts use,
Despite the name and fame that tempt our flesh,
Constant to that devotion of the hearth,
Still captive in those dear domestic ties! —
How he, — having a cause to triumph with,
All kind of interests to keep intact,
More than one efficacious personage

To tranquillize, conciliate and secure,
And above all, public anxiety
To quiet, show its Guido in good hands, —
Also, as if such burdens were too light,
A certain family-feast to claim his care,
The birthday-banquet for the only son —
Paternity at smiling strife with law —
How he brings both to buckle in one bond;
And, thick at throat, with waterish under-eye,
Turns to his task and settles in his seat
And puts his utmost means in practice now:
Wheezes out law-phrase, whiffles Latin forth,
And, just as though roast lamb would never be,
Makes logic levigate the big crime small:
Rubs palm on palm, rakes foot with itchy foot,
Conceives and inchoates the argument,
Sprinkling each flower appropriate to the time,
— Ovidian quip or Ciceronian crank,
A-bubble in the larynx while he laughs,
As he had fritters deep down frying there.
How he turns, twists, and tries the oily thing
Shall be — first speech for Guido 'gainst the Fisc.

Then with a skip as it were from heel to head,
Leaving yourselves fill up the middle bulk
O' the Trial, reconstruct its shape august,
From such exordium clap we to the close;
Give you, if we dare wing to such a height,
The absolute glory in some full-grown speech
On the other side, some finished butterfly,
Some breathing diamond-flake with leaf-gold fans,
That takes the air, no trace of worm it was,
Or cabbage-bed it had production from.
Giovambattista o' the Bottini, Fisc,
Pompilia's patron by the chance of the hour,
To-morrow her persecutor, — composite, he,
As becomes who must meet such various calls —
Odds of age joined in him with ends of youth.
A man of ready smile and facile tear,

Improvised hopes, despairs at nod and beck,
And language — ah, the gift of eloquence!
Language that goes, goes, easy as a glove,
O'er good and evil, smoothens both to one.
Rashness helps caution with him, fires the straw,
In free enthusiastic careless fit,
On the first proper pinnacle of rock
Which offers, as reward for all that zeal,
To lure some bark to founder and bring gain:
While calm sits Caution, rapt with heavenward eye,
A true confessor's gaze, amid the glare
Beaconing to the breaker, death and hell.
"Well done, thou good and faithful!" she approves:
"Hadst thou let slip a faggot to the beach,
"The crew might surely spy thy precipice
"And save their boat; the simple and the slow
"Might so, forsooth, forestall the wrecker's feet
"Let the next crew be wise and hail in time!"
Just so compounded is the outside man,
Blue juvenile pure eye and pippin cheek,
And brow all prematurely soiled and seamed
With sudden age, bright devastated hair.
Ah, but you miss the very tones o' the voice,
The scrannel pipe that screams in heights of head,
As, in his modest studio, all alone,
The tall wight stands a-tiptoe, strives and strains,
Both eyes shut, like the cockerel that would crow,
Tries to his own self amorously o'er
What never will be uttered else than so —
Since to the four walls, Forum and Mars' Hill,
Speaks out the poesy which, penned, turns prose.
Clavecinist debarred his instrument,
He yet thrums — shirking neither turn nor trill,
With desperate finger on dumb table-edge —
The sovereign rondo, shall conclude his *Suite*,
Charm an imaginary audience there,
From old Corelli to young Haendel, both
I' the flesh at Rome, ere he perforce go print
The cold black score, mere music for the mind —

The last speech against Guido and his gang,
With special end to prove Pompilia pure.
How the Fisc vindicates Pompilia's fame.

Then comes the all but end, the ultimate
Judgment save yours. Pope Innocent the Twelfth,
Simple, sagacious, mild yet resolute,
With prudence, probity and — what beside
From the other world he feels impress at times,
Having attained to fourscore years and six, —
How, when the court found Guido and the rest
Guilty, but law supplied a subterfuge
And passed the final sentence to the Pope,
He, bringing his intelligence to bear
This last time on what ball behoves him drop
In the urn, or white or black, does drop a black,
Send five souls more to just precede his own,
Stand him in stead and witness, if need were,
How he is wont to do God's work on earth.
The manner of his sitting out the dim
Droop of a sombre February day
In the plain closet where he does such work,
With, from all Peter's treasury, one stool,
One table and one lathen crucifix.
There sits the Pope, his thoughts for company;
Grave but not sad, — nay, something like a cheer
Leaves the lips free to be benevolent,
Which, all day long, did duty firm and fast.
A cherishing there is of foot and knee,
A chafing loose-skinned large-veined hand with hand, —
What steward but knows when stewardship earns its wage,
May levy praise, anticipate the lord?
He reads, notes, lays the papers down at last,
Muses, then takes a turn about the room;
Unclasps a huge tome in an antique guise,
Primitive print and tongue half obsolete,
That stands him in diurnal stead; opes page,
Finds place where falls the passage to be conned
According to an order long in use:

And, as he comes upon the evening's chance,
Starts somewhat, solemnizes straight his smile,
Then reads aloud that portion first to last,
And at the end lets flow his own thoughts forth
Likewise aloud, for respite and relief,
Till by the dreary relics of the west
Wan through the half-moon window, all his light,
He bows the head while the lips move in prayer,
Writes some three brief lines, signs and seals the same,
Tinkles a hand-bell, bids the obsequious Sir
Who puts foot presently o' the closet-sill
He watched outside of, bear as superscribed
That mandate to the Governor forthwith:
Then heaves abroad his cares in one good sigh,
Traverses corridor with no arm's help,
And so to sup as a clear conscience should.
The manner of the judgment of the Pope.

Then must speak Guido yet a second time,
Satan's old saw being apt here — skin for skin,
All a man hath that will he give for life.
While life was graspable and gainable,
And bird-like buzzed her wings round Guido's brow,
Not much truth stiffened out the web of words
He wove to catch her: when away she flew
And death came, death's breath rivelled up the lies,
Left bare the metal thread, the fibre fine
Of truth i' the spinning: the true words shone last.
How Guido, to another purpose quite,
Speaks and despairs, the last night of his life,
In that New Prison by Castle Angelo
At the bridge foot: the same man, another voice.
On a stone bench in a close fetid cell,
Where the hot vapour of an agony,
Struck into drops on the cold wall, runs down —
Horrible worms made out of sweat and tears —
There crouch, well nigh to the knees in dungeon-straw,
Lit by the sole lamp suffered for their sake,
Two awe-struck figures, this a Cardinal,

That an Abate, both of old styled friends
O' the thing part man part monster in the midst,
So changed is Franceschini's gentle blood.
The tiger-cat screams now, that whined before,
That pried and tried and trod so gingerly,
Till in its silkiness the trap-teeth joined;
Then you know how the bristling fury foams.
They listen, this wrapped in his folds of red,
While his feet fumble for the filth below;
The other, as beseems a stouter heart,
Working his best with beads and cross to ban
The enemy that comes in like a flood
Spite of the standard set up, verily
And in no trope at all, against him there:
For at the prison-gate, just a few steps
Outside, already, in the doubtful dawn,
Thither, from this side and from that, slow sweep
And settle down in silence solidly,
Crow-wise, the frightful Brotherhood of Death.
Black-hatted and black-hooded huddle they,
Black rosaries a-dangling from each waist;
So take they their grim station at the door,
Torches lit, skull-and-cross-bones-banner spread,
And that gigantic Christ with open arms,
Grounded. Nor lacks there aught but that the group
Break forth, intone the lamentable psalm,
"Out of the deeps, Lord, have I cried to thee!" —
When inside, from the true profound, a sign
Shall bear intelligence that the foe is foiled,
Count Guido Franceschini has confessed,
And is absolved and reconciled with God.
Then they, intoning, may begin their march,
Make by the longest way for the People's Square,
Carry the criminal to his crime's award:
A mob to cleave, a scaffolding to reach,
Two gallows and Mannaia crowning all.
How Guido made defence a second time.

Finally, even as thus by step and step
I led you from the level of to-day

Up to the summit of so long ago,
Here, whence I point you the wide prospect round —
Let me, by like steps, slope you back to smooth,
Land you on mother-earth, no whit the worse,
To feed o' the fat o' the furrow: free to dwell,
Taste our time's better things profusely spread
For all who love the level, corn and wine,
Much cattle and the many-folded fleece.
Shall not my friends go feast again on sward,
Though cognizant of country in the clouds
Higher than wistful eagle's horny eye
Ever unclosed for, 'mid ancestral crags,
When morning broke and Spring was back once more,
And he died, heaven, save by his heart, unreached?
Yet heaven my fancy lifts to, ladder-like, —
As Jack reached, holpen of his beanstalk-rungs!

A novel country: I might make it mine
By choosing which one aspect of the year
Suited mood best, and putting solely that
On panel somewhere in the House of Fame,
Landscaping what I saved, not what I saw:
— Might fix you, whether frost in goblin-time
Startled the moon with his abrupt bright laugh,
Or, August's hair afloat in filmy fire,
She fell, arms wide, face foremost on the world,
Swooned there and so singed out the strength of things.
Thus were abolished Spring and Autumn both,
The land dwarfed to one likeness of the land,
Life cramped corpse-fashion. Rather learn and love
Each facet-flash of the revolving year! —
Red, green and blue that whirl into a white,
The variance now, the eventual unity,
Which make the miracle. See it for yourselves,
This man's act, changeable because alive!
Action now shrouds, nor shows the informing thought;
Man, like a glass ball with a spark a-top,
Out of the magic fire that lurks inside,
Shows one tint at a time to take the eye:

Which, let a finger touch the silent sleep,
Shifted a hair's-breadth shoots you dark for bright,
Suffuses bright with dark, and baffles so
Your sentence absolute for shine or shade.
Once set such orbs, — white styled, black stigmatized, —
A-rolling, see them once on the other side
Your good men and your bad men every one
From Guido Franceschini to Guy Faux,
Oft would you rub your eyes and change your names.
Such, British Public, ye who like me not,
(God love you!) — whom I yet have laboured for,
Perchance more careful whoso runs may read
Than erst when all, it seemed, could read who ran, —
Perchance more careless whoso reads may praise
Than late when he who praised and read and wrote
Was apt to find himself the self-same me, —
Such labour had such issue, so I wrought
This arc, by furtherance of such alloy,
And so, by one spirt, take away its trace
Till, justifiably golden, rounds my ring.

A ring without a posy, and that ring mine?

O lyric Love, half angel and half bird
And all a wonder and a wild desire, —
Boldest of hearts that ever braved the sun,
Took sanctuary within the holier blue,
And sang a kindred soul out to his face, —
Yet human at the red-ripe of the heart —
When the first summons from the darkling earth
Reached thee amid thy chambers, blanched their blue,
And bared them of the glory — to drop down,
To toil for man, to suffer or to die, —
This is the same voice: can thy soul know change?
Hail then, and hearken from the realms of help!
Never may I commence my song, my due
To God who best taught song by gift of thee,
Except with bent head and beseeching hand —

That still, despite the distance and the dark,
What was, again may be; some interchange
Of grace, some splendour once thy very thought,
Some benediction anciently thy smile:
— Never conclude, but raising hand and head
Thither where eyes, that cannot reach, yet yearn
For all hope, all sustainment, all reward,
Their utmost up and on, — so blessing back
In those thy realms of help, that heaven thy home,
Some whiteness which, I judge, thy face makes proud,
Some wanness where, I think, thy foot may fall!

[End of Book I]

from V. — COUNT GUIDO FRANCESCHINI

Thanks, Sir, but, should it please the reverend Court,
I feel I can stand somchow, half sit down
Without help, make shift to even speak, you see,
Fortified by the sip of . . . why, 'tis wine,
Velletri, — and not vinegar and gall,
So changed and good the times grow! Thanks, kind Sir!
Oh, but one sip's enough! I want my head
To save my neck, there's work awaits me still.
How cautious and considerate . . aie, aie, aie,
Nor your fault, sweet Sir! Come, you take to heart
An ordinary matter. Law is law.
Noblemen were exempt, the vulgar thought,
From racking; but, since law thinks otherwise,
I have been put to the rack: all's over now,
And neither wrist — what men style, out of joint:
If any harm be, 'tis the shoulder-blade,
The left one, that seems wrong i' the socket, — Sirs,
Much could not happen, I was quick to faint,
Being past my prime of life, and out of health.
In short, I thank you, — yes, and mean the word.

Needs must the Court be slow to understand
How this quite novel form of taking pain,
This getting tortured merely in the flesh,
Amounts to almost an agreeable change
In my case, me fastidious, plied too much
With opposite treatment, used (forgive the joke)
To the rasp-tooth toying with this brain of mine,
And, in and out my heart, the play o' the probe.
Four years have I been operated on
I' the soul, do you see — its tense or tremulous part —
My self-respect, my care for a good name,
Pride in an old one, love of kindred — just
A mother, brothers, sisters, and the like,
That looked up to my face when days were dim,
And fancied they found light there — no one spot,
Foppishly sensitive, but has paid its pang.
That, and not this you now oblige me with,
That was the Vigil-torment, if you please!
The poor old noble House that drew the rags
O' the Franceschini's once superb array
Close round her, hoped to slink unchallenged by, —
Pluck off these! Turn the drapery inside out
And teach the tittering town how scarlet wears!
Show men the lucklessness, the improvidence
Of the easy-natured Count before this Count,
The father I have some slight feeling for,
Who let the world slide, nor foresaw that friends
Then proud to cap and kiss their patron's shoe,
Would, when the purse he left held spiderwebs,
Properly push his child to wall one day!
Mimic the tetchy humour, furtive glance,
And brow where half was furious, half fatigued,
O' the same son got to be of middle age,
Sour, saturnine, — your humble servant here, —
When things go cross and the young wife, he finds
Take to the window at a whistle's bid,
And yet demurs thereon, preposterous fool! —
Whereat the worthies judge he wants advice
And beg to civilly ask what's evil here,

Perhaps remonstrate on the habit they deem
He's given unduly to, of beating her:
. . . Oh, sure he beats her — why says John so else,
Who is cousin to George who is sib to Tecla's self
Who cooks the meal and combs the lady's hair?
What! 'Tis my wrist you merely dislocate
For the future when you mean me martyrdom?
— Let the old mother's economy alone,
How the brocade-strips saved o' the seamy side
O' the wedding-gown buy raiment for a year?
— How she can dress and dish up — lordly dish
Fit for a duke, lamb's head and purtenance —
With her proud hands, feast household so a week?
No word o' the wine rejoicing God and man
The less when three-parts water? Then, I say,
A trifle of torture to the flesh, like yours,
While soul is spared such foretaste of hell-fire,
Is naught. But I curtail the catalogue
Through policy, — a rhetorician's trick, —
Because I would reserve some choicer points
O' the practice, more exactly parallel
(Having an eye to climax) with what gift,
Eventual grace the Court may have in store
I' the way of plague — what crown of punishments.
When I am hanged or headed, time enough
To prove the tenderness of only that,
Mere heading, hanging, — not their counterpart,
Not demonstration public and precise
That I, having married the mongrel of a drab,
Am bound to grant that mongrel-brat, my wife,
Her mother's birthright-license as is just, —
Let her sleep undisturbed, i' the family style,
Her sleep out in the embraces of a priest,
Nor disallow their bastard as my heir!
Your sole mistake, — dare I submit so much
To the reverend Court? — has been in all this pains
To make a stone roll down hill, — rack and wrench
And rend a man to pieces, all for what?
Why — make him ope mouth in his own defence,

Show cause for what he has done, the irregular deed,
(Since that he did it, scarce dispute can be)
And clear his fame a little, beside the luck
Of stopping even yet, if possible,
Discomfort to his flesh from noose or axe —
For that, out come the implements of law!
May it content my lords the gracious Court
To listen only half so patient-long
As I will in that sense profusely speak,
And — fie, they shall not call in screws to help!
I killed Pompilia Franceschini, Sirs;
Killed too the Comparini, husband, wife,
Who called themselves, by a notorious lie,
Her father and her mother to ruin me.
There's the irregular deed: you want no more
Than right interpretation of the same,
And truth so far — am I to understand?
To that then, with convenient speed, — because
Now I consider, — yes, despite my boast,
There is an ailing in this omoplat
May clip my speech all too abruptly short,
Whatever the good-will in me. Now for truth!

* * * * *

Such was the pact: Pompilia from the first
Broke it, refused from the beginning day
Either in body or soul to cleave to mine,
And published it forthwith to all the world.
No rupture, — you must join ere you can break, —
Before we had cohabited a month
She found I was a devil and no man, —
Made common cause with those who found as much,
Her parents, Pietro and Violante, — moved
Heaven and earth to the rescue of all three.
In four months' time, the time o' the parents' stay,
Arezzo was a-ringing, bells in a blaze,
With the unimaginable story rife
I' the mouth of man, woman and child — to-wit
My misdemeanour. First the lighter side,

Ludicrous face of things, — how very poor
The Franceschini had become at last,
The meanness and the misery of each shift
To save a soldo, stretch and make ends meet.
Next, the more hateful aspect, — how myself
With cruelty beyond Caligula's
Had stripped and beaten, robbed and murdered them,
The good old couple, I decoyed, abused,
Plundered and then cast out, and happily so,
Since, — in due course the abominable comes, —
Woe worth the poor young wife left lonely here!
Repugnant in my person as my mind,
I sought, — was ever heard of such revenge?
— To lure and bind her to so cursed a couch,
Such co-embrace with sulphur, snake and toad,
That she was fain to rush forth, call the stones
O' the common street to save her, not from hate
Of mine merely, but . . . must I burn my lips
With the blister of the lie? . . . the satyr-love
Of who but my own brother, the young priest,
Too long enforced to lenten fare belike,
Now tempted by the morsel tossed him full
I' the trencher where lay bread and herbs at best.
Mark, this yourselves say! — this, none disallows,
Was charged to me by the universal voice
At the instigation of my four-months' wife! —
And then you ask "Such charges so preferred,
"(Truly or falsely, here concerns us not)
"Pricked you to punish now if not before? —
"Did not the harshness double itself, the hate
"Harden?" I answer "Have it your way and will!"
Say my resentment grew apace: what then?
Do you cry out on the marvel? When I find
That pure smooth egg which, laid within my nest,
Could not but hatch a comfort to us all,
Issues a cockatrice for me and mine,
Do you stare to see me stamp on it? Swans are soft:
Is it not clear that she you call my wife,
That any wife of any husband, caught

Whetting a sting like this against his breast, —
Speckled with fragments of the fresh-broke shell,
Married a month and making outcry thus, —
Proves a plague-prodigy to God and man?
She married: what was it she married for,
Counted upon and meant to meet thereby?
"Love" suggests some one, "love, a little word
"Whereof we have not heard one syllable."
So, the Pompilia, child, girl, wife, in one,
Wanted the beating pulse, the rolling eye,
The frantic gesture, the devotion due
From Thyrsis to Neæra! Guido's love —
Why not Provençal roses in his shoe,
Plume to his cap, and trio of guitars
At casement, with a bravo close beside?
Good things all these are, clearly claimable
When the fit price is paid the proper way.
Had it been some friend's wife, now, threw her fan
At my foot, with just this pretty scrap attached,
"Shame, death, damnation — fall these as they may,
"So I find you, for a minute! Come this eve!"
— Why, at such sweet self-sacrifice, — who knows?
I might have fired up, found me at my post,
Ardent from head to heel, nor feared catch cough.
Nay, had some other friend's . . . say, daughter, tripped
Upstairs and tumbled flat and frank on me,
Bareheaded and barefooted, with loose hair
And garments all at large, — cried "Take me thus!
"Duke So-and-So, the greatest man in Rome —
"To escape his hand and heart have I broke bounds,
"Traversed the town and reached you!" — then, indeed,
The lady had not reached a man of ice!
I would have rummaged, ransacked at the word
Those old odd corners of an empty heart
For remnants of dim love the long disused,
And dusty crumblings of romance! But here,
We talk of just a marriage, if you please —
The every-day conditions and no more;
Where do these bind me to bestow one drop

Of blood shall dye my wife's true-love-knot pink?
Pompilia was no pigeon, Venus' pet,
That shuffled from between her pressing paps
To sit on my rough shoulder, — but a hawk,
I bought at a hawk's price and carried home
To do hawk's service — at the Rotunda, say,
Where, six o' the callow nestlings in a row,
You pick and choose and pay the price for such.
I have paid my pound, await my penny's worth,
So, hoodwink, starve and properly train my bird,
And, should she prove a haggard, — twist her neck!
Did I not pay my name and style, my hope
And trust, my all? Through spending these amiss
I am here! 'Tis scarce the gravity of the Court
Will blame me that I never piped a tune,
Treated my falcon-gentle like my finch.

*　*　*　*　*

Tell me: if on that day when I found first
That Caponsacchi thought the nearest way
To his church was some half-mile round by my door,
And that he so admired, shall I suppose,
The manner of the swallows' come-and-go
Between the props o' the window overhead, —
That window happening to be my wife's, —
As to stand gazing by the hour on high,
Of May-eves, while she sat and let him smile, —
If I, — instead of threatening, talking big,
Showing hair-powder, a prodigious pinch,
For poison in a bottle, — making believe
At desperate doings with a bauble-sword,
And other bugaboo-and-baby-work, —
Had, with the vulgarest household implement,
Calmly and quietly cut off, clean thro' bone
But one joint of one finger of my wife,
Saying "For listening to the serenade,
"Here's your ring-finger shorter a full third:
"Be certain I will slice away next joint,
"Next time that anybody underneath

653

"Seems somehow to be sauntering as he hoped
"A flower would eddy out of your hand to his
"While you please fidget with the branch above
"O' the rose-tree in the terrace!" — had I done so,
Why, there had followed a quick sharp scream, some pain,
Much calling for plaister, damage to the dress,
A somewhat sulky countenance next day,
Perhaps reproaches, — but reflections too!
I don't hear much of harm that Malchus did
After the incident of the ear, my lords!
Saint Peter took the efficacious way;
Malchus was sore but silenced for his life:
He did not hang himself i' the Potter's Field
Like Judas, who was trusted with the bag
And treated to sops after he proved a thief.
So, by this time, my true and obedient wife
Might have been telling beads with a gloved hand;
Awkward a little at pricking hearts and darts
On sampler possibly, but well otherwise:
Not where Rome shudders now to see her lie.
I give that for the course a wise man takes;
I took the other however, tried the fool's,
The lighter remedy, brandished rapier dread
With cork-ball at the tip, boxed Malchus' ear
Instead of severing the cartilage,
Called her a terrible nickname, and the like,
And there an end: and what was the end of that?
What was the good effect o' the gentle course?
Why, one night I went drowsily to bed,
Dropped asleep suddenly, not suddenly woke,
But did wake with rough rousing and loud cry,
To find noon in my face, a crowd in my room,
Fumes in my brain, fire in my throat, my wife
Gone God knows whither, — rifled vesture-chest,
And ransacked money-coffer. "What does it mean?"
The servants had been drugged too, stared and yawned
"It must be that our lady has eloped!"
— "Whither and with whom?" — "With whom but the Canon's self?
"One recognizes Caponsacchi there!" —

*　　*　　*　　*　　*

The case was soon decided: both weights, cast
I' the balance, vibrate, neither kicks the beam,
Here away, there away, this now and now that.
To every one o' my grievances law gave
Redress, could purblind eye but see the point.
The wife stood a convicted runagate
From house and husband, — driven to such a course
By what she somehow took for cruelty,
Oppression and imperilment of life —
Not that such things were, but that so they seemed:
Therefore, the end conceded lawful, (since
To save life there's no risk should stay our leap)
It follows that all means to the lawful end
Are lawful likewise, — poison, theft and flight.
As for the priest's part, did he meddle or make,
Enough that he too thought life jeopardized;
Concede him then the colour charity
Casts on a doubtful course, — if blackish white
Or whitish black, will charity hesitate?
What did he else but act the precept out,
Leave, like a provident shepherd, his safe flock
To follow the single lamb and strayaway?
Best hope so and think so, — that the ticklish time
I' the carriage, the tempting privacy, the last
Somewhat ambiguous accident at the inn,
— All may bear explanation: may? then, must!
The letters, — do they so incriminate?
But what if the whole prove a prank o' the pen,
Flight of the fancy, none of theirs at all,
Bred of the vapours of my brain belike,
Or at worst mere exercise of scholar's-wit
In the courtly Caponsacchi: verse, convict?
Did not Catullus write less seemly once?
Yet *doctus* and unblemished he abides.
Wherefore so ready to infer the worst?
Still, I did righteously in bringing doubts
For the law to solve, — take the solution now!

"Seeing that the said associates, wife and priest,
"Bear themselves not without some touch of blame
" — Else why the pother, scandal and outcry
"Which trouble our peace and require chastisement?
"We, for complicity in Pompilia's flight
"And deviation, and carnal intercourse
"With the same, do set aside and relegate
"The Canon Caponsacchi for three years
"At Civita in the neighbourhood of Rome:
"And we consign Pompilia to the care
"Of a certain Sisterhood of penitents
"I' the city's self, expert to deal with such."
Word for word, there's your judgment! Read it, lords,
Re-utter your deliberate penalty
For the crime yourselves establish! Your award —
Who chop a man's right-hand off at the wrist
For tracing with forefinger words in wine
O' the table of a drinking-booth that bear
Interpretation as they mocked the Church!

* * * * *

And so, all yet uncertain save the will
To do right, and the daring aught save leave
Right undone, I did find myself at last
I' the dark before the villa with my friends,
And made the experiment, the final test,
Ultimate chance that ever was to be
For the wretchedness inside. I knocked, pronounced
The name, the predetermined touch for truth,
"What welcome for the wanderer? Open straight —"
To the friend, physician, friar upon his rounds,
Traveller belated, beggar lame and blind?
No, but — "to Caponsacchi!" And the door
Opened.
          And then, — why, even then, I think,
I' the minute that confirmed my worst of fears,
Surely, — I pray God that I think aright! —
Had but Pompilia's self, the tender thing
Who once was good and pure, was once my lamb

And lay in my bosom, had the well-known shape
Fronted me in the door-way, — stood there faint
With the recent pang perhaps of giving birth
To what might, though by miracle, seem my child, —
Nay more, I will say, had even the aged fool
Pietro, the dotard, in whom folly and age
Wrought, more than enmity or malevolence,
To practise and conspire against my peace, —
Had either of these but opened, I had paused.
But it was she the hag, she that brought hell
For a dowry with her to her husband's house,
She the mock-mother, she that made the match
And married me to perdition, spring and source
O' the fire inside me that boiled up from heart
To brain and hailed the Fury gave it birth, —
Violante Comparini, she it was,
With the old grin amid the wrinkles yet,
Opened: as if in turning from the Cross,
With trust to keep the sight and save my soul,
I had stumbled, first thing, on the serpent's head
Coiled with a leer at foot of it.
                              There was the end!
Then was I rapt away by the impulse, one
Immeasurable everlasting wave of a need
To abolish that detested life. 'Twas done:
You know the rest and how the folds o' the thing,
Twisting for help, involved the other two
More or less serpent-like: how I was mad,
Blind, stamped on all, the earth-worms with the asp,
And ended so.
                    You came on me that night,
Your officers of justice, — caught the crime
In the first natural frenzy of remorse?
Twenty miles off, sound sleeping as a child
On a cloak i' the straw which promised shelter first,
With the bloody arms beside me, — was it not so?
Wherefore not? Why, how else should I be found?
I was my own self, had my sense again,
My soul safe from the serpents. I could sleep:

Indeed and, dear my lords, I shall sleep now,
Spite of my shoulder, in five minutes' space,
When you dismiss me, having truth enough!
It is but a few days are passed, I find,
Since this adventure. Do you tell me, four?
Then the dead are scarce quiet where they lie,
Old Pietro, old Violante, side by side
At the church Lorenzo, — oh, they know it well!
So do I. But my wife is still alive,
Has breath enough to tell her story yet,
Her way, which is not mine, no doubt at all.
And Caponsacchi, you have summoned him, —
Was he so far to send for? Not at hand?
I thought some few o' the stabs were in his heart,
Or had not been so lavish: less had served.
Well, he too tells his story, — florid prose
As smooth as mine is rough. You see, my lords,
There will be a lying intoxicating smoke
Born of the blood, — confusion probably, —
For lies breed lies — but all that rests with you!
The trial is no concern of mine; with me
The main of the care is over: I at least
Recognize who took that huge burthen off,
Let me begin to live again. I did
God's bidding and man's duty, so, breathe free;
Look you to the rest! I heard Himself prescribe,
That great Physician, and dared lance the core
Of the bad ulcer; and the rage abates,
I am myself and whole now: I prove cured
By the eyes that see, the ears that hear again,
The limbs that have relearned their youthful play,
The healthy taste of food and feel of clothes
And taking to our common life once more,
All that now urges my defence from death.
The willingness to live, what means it else?

*   *   *   *   *

from VI. — GIUSEPPE CAPONSACCHI

*   *   *   *   *

Come,
Instruct me in procedure! I conceive —
In all due self-abasement might I speak —
How you will deal with Guido: oh, not death!
Death, if it let her life be: otherwise
Not death, — your lights will teach you clearer! I
Certainly have an instinct of my own
I' the matter: bear with me and weigh its worth!
Let us go away — leave Guido all alone
Back on the world again that knows him now!
I think he will be found (indulge so far!)
Not to die so much as slide out of life,
Pushed by the general horror and common hate
Low, lower, — left o' the very ledge of things,
I seem to see him catch convulsively
One by one at all honest forms of life,
At reason, order, decency and use —
To cramp him and get foothold by at least;
And still they disengage them from his clutch.
"What, you are he, then, had Pompilia once
"And so forwent her? Take not up with us!"
And thus I see him slowly and surely edged
Off all the table-land whence life upsprings
Aspiring to be immortality,
As the snake, hatched on hill-top by mischance,
Despite his wriggling, slips, slides, slidders down
Hill-side, lies low and prostrate on the smooth
Level of the outer place, lapsed in the vale:
So I lose Guido in the loneliness,
Silence and dusk, till at the doleful end,
At the horizontal line, creation's verge,

From what just is to absolute nothingness —
Whom is it, straining onward still, he meets?
What other man deep further in the fate,
Who, turning at the prize of a footfall
To flatter him and promise fellowship,
Discovers in the act a frightful face —
Judas, made monstrous by much solitude!
The two are at one now! Let them love their love
That bites and claws like hate, or hate their hate
That mops and mows and makes as it were love!
There, let them each tear each in devil's-fun,
Or fondle this the other while malice aches —
Both teach, both learn detestability!
Kiss him the kiss, Iscariot! Pay that back,
That smatch o' the slaver blistering on your lip,
By the better trick, the insult he spared Christ —
Lure him the lure o' the letters, Aretine!
Lick him o'er slimy-smooth with jelly-filth
O' the verse-and-prose pollution in love's guise!
The cockatrice is with the basilisk!
There let them grapple, denizens o' the dark,
Foes or friends, but indissolubly bound,
In their one spot out of the ken of God
Or care of man, for ever and ever more!

* * * * *

from VII.—POMPILIA

I am just seventeen years and five months old,
And, if I lived one day more, three full weeks;
'Tis writ so in the church's register,
Lorenzo in Lucina, all my names
At length, so many names for one poor child,
— Francesca Camilla Vittoria Angela
Pompilia Comparini, — laughable!

Also 'tis writ that I was married there
Four years ago: and they will add, I hope,
When they insert my death, a word or two, —
Omitting all about the mode of death, —
This, in its place, this which one cares to know,
That I had been a mother of a son
Exactly two weeks. It will be through grace
O' the Curate, not through any claim I have;
Because the boy was born at, so baptized
Close to, the Villa, in the proper church:
A pretty church, I say no word against,
Yet stranger-like, — while this Lorenzo seems
My own particular place, I always say.
I used to wonder, when I stood scarce high
As the bed here, what the marble lion meant,
With half his body rushing from the wall,
Eating the figure of a prostrate man —
(To the right, it is, of entry by the door)
An ominous sign to one baptized like me,
Married, and to be buried there, I hope.
And they should add, to have my life complete,
He is a boy and Gaetan by name —
Gaetano, for a reason, — if the friar
Don Celestine will ask this grace for me
Of Curate Ottoboni: he it was
Baptized me: he remembers my whole life
As I do his grey hair.

                    All these few things
I know are true, — will you remember them?
Because time flies. The surgeon cared for me,
To count my wounds, — twenty-two dagger-wounds,
Five deadly, but I do not suffer much —
Or too much pain, — and am to die to-night.

*   *   *   *   *

Beside, up to my marriage, thirteen years
Were, each day, happy as the day was long:
This may have made the change too terrible.
I know that when Violante told me first

661

The cavalier — she meant to bring next morn,
Whom I must also let take, kiss my hand —
Would be at San Lorenzo the same eve
And marry me, — which over, we should go
Home both of us without him as before,
And, till she bade speak, I must hold my tongue,
Such being the correct way with girl-brides,
From whom one word would make a father blush, —
I know, I say, that when she told me this,
— Well, I no more saw sense in what she said
Than a lamb does in people clipping wool;
Only lay down and let myself be clipped.
And when next day the cavalier who came —
(Tisbe had told me that the slim young man
With wings at head, and wings at feet, and sword
Threatening a monster, in our tapestry,
Would eat a girl else, — was a cavalier)
When he proved Guido Franceschini, — old
And nothing like so tall as I myself,
Hook-nosed and yellow in a bush of beard,
Much like a thing I saw on a boy's wrist,
He called an owl and used for catching birds, —
And when he took my hand and made a smile —
Why, the uncomfortableness of it all
Seemed hardly more important in the case
Than, — when one gives you, say, a coin to spend, —
Its newness or its oldness; if the piece
Weigh properly and buy you what you wish,
No matter whether you get grime or glare!
Men take the coin, return you grapes and figs.
Here, marriage was the coin, a dirty piece
Would purchase me the praise of those I loved:
About what else should I concern myself?

So, hardly knowing what a husband meant,
I supposed this or any man would serve,
No whit the worse for being so uncouth:
For I was ill once and a doctor came
With a great ugly hat, no plume thereto,

Black jerkin and black buckles and black sword,
And white sharp beard over the ruff in front,
And oh so lean, so sour-faced and austere! —
Who felt my pulse, made me put out my tongue,
Then oped a phial, dripped a drop or two
Of a black bitter something, — I was cured!
What mattered the fierce beard or the grim face?
It was the physic beautified the man,
Master Malpichi, — never met his match
In Rome, they said, — so ugly all the same!

*   *   *   *   *

from X. — THE POPE

*   *   *   *   *

And I am bound, the solitary judge,
To weigh the worth, decide upon the plea,
And either hold a hand out, or withdraw
A foot and let the wretch drift to the fall.
Ay, and while thus I dally, dare perchance
Put fancies for a comfort 'twixt this calm
And yonder passion that I have to bear, —
As if reprieve were possible for both
Prisoner and Pope, — how easy were reprieve!
A touch o' the hand-bell here, a hasty word
To those who wait, and wonder they wait long,
I' the passage there, and I should gain the life! —
Yea, though I flatter me with fancy thus,
I know it is but nature's craven-trick.
The case is over, judgment at an end,
And all things done now and irrevocable:
A mere dead man is Franceschini here,
Even as Formosus centuries ago.
I have worn through this sombre wintry day,
With winter in my soul beyond the world's,

Over these dismalest of documents
Which drew night down on me ere eve befell, —
Pleadings and counter-pleadings, figure of fact
Beside fact's self, these summaries to-wit, —
How certain three were slain by certain five:
I read here why it was, and how it went,
And how the chief o' the five preferred excuse,
And how law rather chose defence should lie, —
What argument he urged by wary word
When free to play off wile, start subterfuge,
And what the unguarded groan told, torture's feat
When law grew brutal, outbroke, overbore
And glutted hunger on the truth, at last, —
No matter for the flesh and blood between.
All's a clear rede and no more riddle now.
Truth, nowhere, lies yet everywhere in these —
Not absolutely in a portion, yet
Evolvible from the whole: evolved at last
Painfully, held tenaciously by me.
Therefore there is not any doubt to clear
When I shall write the brief word presently
And chink the hand-bell, which I pause to do.

   * * * * *

I find him bound, then, to begin life well;
Fortified by propitious circumstance,
Great birth, good breeding, with the Church for guide,
How lives he? Cased thus in a coat of proof,
Mailed like a man-at-arms, though all the while
A puny starveling, — does the breast pant big,
The limb swell to the limit, emptiness
Strive to become solidity indeed?
Rather, he shrinks up like the ambiguous fish,
Detaches flesh from shell and outside show,
And steals by moonlight (I have seen the thing)
In and out, now to prey and now to skulk.
Armour he boasts when a wave breaks on beach,
Or bird stoops for the prize: with peril nigh, —
The man of rank, the much-befriended-man,

The man almost affiliate to the Church,
Such is to deal with, let the world beware!
Does the world recognize, pass prudently?
Do tides abate and sea-fowl hunt i' the deep?
Already is the slug from out its mew,
Ignobly faring with all loose and free,
Sand-fly and slush-worm at their garbage-feast,
A naked blotch no better than they all:
Guido has dropped nobility, slipped the Church,
Plays trickster if not cut-purse, body and soul
Prostrate among the filthy feeders — faugh!
And when Law takes him by surprise at last,
Catches the foul thing on its carrion-prey,
Behold, he points to shell left high and dry,
Pleads "But the case out yonder is myself!"
Nay, it is thou, Law prongs amid thy peers,
Congenial vermin; that was none of thee,
Thine outside, — give it to the soldier-crab!

       *   *   *   *   *

                       "Quis pro Domino?
"Who is upon the Lord's side?" asked the Count.
I, who write —
             "On receipt of this command,
"Acquaint Count Guido and his fellows four
"They die to-morrow: could it be to-night,
"The better, but the work to do, takes time.
"Set with all diligence a scaffold up,
"Not in the customary place, by Bridge
"Saint Angelo, where die the common sort;
"But since the man is noble, and his peers
"By predilection haunt the People's Square,
"There let him be beheaded in the midst,
"And his companions hanged on either side:
"So shall the quality see, fear and learn.
"All which work takes time: till to-morrow, then,
"Let there be prayer incessant for the five!"

For the main criminal I have no hope
Except in such a suddenness of fate.

I stood at Naples once, a night so dark
I could have scarce conjectured there was earth
Anywhere, sky or sea or world at all:
But the night's black was burst through by a blaze —
Thunder struck blow on blow, earth groaned and bore,
Through her whole length of mountain visible:
There lay the city thick and plain with spires,
And, like a ghost disshrouded, white the sea.
So may the truth be flashed out by one blow,
And Guido see, one instant, and be saved.
Else I avert my face, nor follow him
Into that sad obscure sequestered state
Where God unmakes but to remake the soul
He else made first in vain; which must not be.
Enough, for I may die this very night:
And how should I dare die, this man let live?

Carry this forthwith to the Governor!

[End of Book X]

from XI. — GUIDO

*   *   *   *   *

Life!
How I could spill this overplus of mine
Among those hoar-haired, shrunk-shanked odds and ends
Of body and soul old age is chewing dry!
Those windlestraws that stare while purblind death
Mows here, mows there, makes hay of juicy me,
And misses just the bunch of withered weed
Would brighten hell and streak its smoke with flame!
How the life I could shed yet never shrink,
Would drench their stalks with sap like grass in May!
Is it not terrible, I entreat you, Sirs? —
With manifold and plenitudinous life,

Prompt at death's menace to give blow for threat,
Answer his "Be thou not!" by "Thus I am!" —
Terrible so to be alive yet die?

How I live, how I see! so, — how I speak!
Lucidity of soul unlocks the lips:
I never had the words at will before.
How I see all my folly at a glance!
"A man requires a woman and a wife:"
There was my folly; I believed the saw.
I knew that just myself concerned myself,
Yet needs must look for what I seemed to lack,
In a woman, — why, the woman's in the man!
Fools we are, how we learn things when too late!
Overmuch life turns round my woman-side:
The male and female in me, mixed before,
Settle of a sudden: I'm my wife outright
In this unmanly appetite for truth,
This careless courage as to consequence,
This instantaneous sight through things and through,
This voluble rhetoric, if you please, — 'tis she!
Here you have that Pompilia whom I slew,
Also the folly for which I slew her!

Fool!

And, fool-like, what is it I wander from?
What did I say of your sharp iron tooth?
Ah, — that I know the hateful thing! this way.
I chanced to stroll forth, many a good year gone,
One warm Spring eve in Rome, and unaware
Looking, mayhap, to count what stars were out,
Came on your fine axe in a frame, that falls
And so cuts off a man's head underneath,
Mannaia, — thus we made acquaintance first:
Out of the way, in a by-part o' the town,
At the Mouth-of-Truth o' the river-side, you know:
One goes by the Capitol: and wherefore coy,
Retiring out of crowded noisy Rome?
Because a very little time ago
It had done service, chopped off head from trunk

Belonging to a fellow whose poor house
The thing must make a point to stand before —
Felice Whatsoever-was-the-name
Who stabled buffaloes and so gained bread,
(Our clowns unyoke them in the ground hard by)
And, after use of much improper speech,
Had struck at Duke Some-title-or-other's face,
Because he kidnapped, carried away and kept
Felice's sister who would sit and sing
I' the filthy doorway while she plaited fringe
To deck the brutes with, — on their gear it goes, —
The good girl with the velvet in her voice.
So did the Duke, so did Felice, so
Did Justice, intervening with her axe.
There the man-mutilating engine stood
At ease, both gay and grim, like a Swiss guard
Off duty, — purified itself as well,
Getting dry, sweet and proper for next week, —
And doing incidental good, 'twas hoped,
To the rough lesson-lacking populace
Who now and then, forsooth, must right their wrongs!
There stood the twelve-foot-square of scaffold, railed
Considerately round to elbow-height,
For fear an officer should tumble thence
And sprain his ankle and be lame a month
Through starting when the axe fell and head too!
Railed likewise were the steps whereby 'twas reached.
All of it painted red: red, in the midst,
Ran up two narrow tall beams barred across,
Since from the summit, some twelve feet to reach,
The iron plate with the sharp shearing edge
Had slammed, jerked, shot, slid, — I shall soon find which! —
And so lay quiet, fast in its fit place,
The wooden half-moon collar, now eclipsed
By the blade which blocked its curvature: apart,
The other half, — the under half-moon board
Which, helped by this, completes a neck's embrace, —
Joined to a sort of desk that wheels aside
Out of the way when done with, — down you kneel,

In you're pushed, over you the other drops,
Tight you're clipped, whiz, there's the blade cleaves its best,
Out trundles body, down flops head on floor,
And where's your soul gone? That, too, I shall find!
This kneeling-place was red, red, never fear!
But only slimy-like with paint, not blood,
For why? a decent pitcher stood at hand,
A broad dish to hold sawdust, and a broom
By some unnamed utensil, — scraper-rake, —
Each with a conscious air of duty done.
Underneath, loungers, — boys and some few men, —
Discoursed this platter, named the other tool,
Just as, when grooms tie up and dress a steed,
Boys lounge and look on, and elucubrate
What the round brush is used for, what the square, —
So was explained — to me the skill-less then —
The manner of the grooming for next world
Undergone by Felice What's-his-name.
There's no such lovely month in Rome as May —
May's crescent is no half-moon of red plank,
And came now tilting o'er the wave i' the west,
One greenish-golden sea, right 'twixt those bars
Of the engine — I began acquaintance with,
Understood, hated, hurried from before,
To have it out of sight and cleanse my soul!
Here it is all again, conserved for use:
Twelve hours hence, I may know more, not hate worse.

＊　　＊　　＊　　＊　　＊

Yes, presently . . . what hour is fleeting now?
When you cut earth away from under me,
I shall be left alone with, pushed beneath
Some such an apparitional dread orb
As the eye of God, since such an eye there glares:
I fancy it go filling up the void
Above my mote-self it devours, or what
Proves — wrath, immensity wreaks on nothingness.
Just how I felt once, couching through the dark,
Hard by Vittiano; young I was, and gay,

And wanting to trap fieldfares: first a spark
Tipped a bent, as a mere dew-globule might
Any stiff grass-stalk on the meadow, — this
Grew fiercer, flamed out full, and proved the sun.
What do I want with proverbs, precepts here?
Away with man! What shall I say to God?
This, if I find the tongue and keep the mind —
"Do Thou wipe out the being of me, and smear
"This soul from off Thy white of things, I blot!
"I am one huge and sheer mistake, — whose fault?
"Not mine at least, who did not make myself!"
Someone declares my wife excused me so!
Perhaps she knew what argument to use.
Grind your teeth, Cardinal: Abate, writhe!
What else am I to cry out in my rage,
Unable to repent one particle
O' the past? Oh, how I wish some cold wise man
Would dig beneath the surface which you scrape,
Deal with the depths, pronounce on my desert
Groundedly! I want simple sober sense,
That asks, before it finishes with a dog,
Who taught the dog that trick you hang him for?
You both persist to call that act a crime,
Which sense would call . . . yes, I maintain it, Sirs, . . .
A blunder! At the worst, I stood in doubt
On cross-road, took one path of many paths:
It leads to the red thing, we all see now,
But nobody saw at first: one primrose-patch
In bank, one singing-bird in bush, the less,
Had warned me from such wayfare: let me prove!
Put me back to the cross-road, start afresh!
Advise me when I take the first false step!
Give me my wife: how should I use my wife,
Love her or hate her? Prompt my action now!
There she is, there she stands alive and pale,
The thirteen-years'-old child, with milk for blood,
Pompilia Comparini, as at first,
Which first is only four brief years ago!
I stand too in the little ground-floor room

O' the father's house at Via Vittoria: see!
Her so-called mother, — one arm round the waist
O' the child to keep her from the toys, let fall
At wonder I can live yet look so grim, —
Ushers her in, with deprecating wave
Of the other, — and she fronts me loose at last,
Held only by the mother's finger-tip.
Struck dumb, — for she was white enough before! —
She eyes me with those frightened balls of black,
As heifer — the old simile comes pat —
Eyes tremblingly the altar and the priest.
The amazed look, all one insuppressive prayer, —
Might she but breathe, set free as heretofore,
Have this cup leave her lips unblistered, bear
Any cross anywhither anyhow,
So but alone, so but apart from me!
You are touched? So am I, quite otherwise,
If 'tis with pity. I resent my wrong,
Being a man: I only show man's soul
Through man's flesh: she sees mine, it strikes her thus!
Is that attractive? To a youth perhaps —
Calf-creature, one-part boy to three-parts girl,
To whom it is a flattering novelty
That he, men use to motion from their path,
Can thus impose, thus terrify in turn
A chit whose terror shall be changed apace
To bliss unbearable when grace and glow,
Prowess and pride descend the throne and touch
Esther in all that pretty tremble, cured
By the dove o' the sceptre! But myself am old,
O' the wane at least, in all things: what do you say
To her who frankly thus confirms my doubt?
I am past the prime, I scare the woman-world,
Done-with that way: you like this piece of news?

*   *   *   *   *

Gaze at her, where I place her, to begin,
Confound me with her gentleness and worth!
The horrible pair have fled and left her now,

671

THE BROWNINGS

She has her husband for her sole concern:
His wife, the woman fashioned for his help,
Flesh of his flesh, bone of his bone, the bride
To groom as is the Church and Spouse to Christ:
There she stands in his presence: "Thy desire
"Shall be to the husband, o'er thee shall he rule!"
— "Pompilia, who declare that you love God,
"You know who said that: then, desire my love,
"Yield me contentment and be ruled aright!"
She sits up, she lies down, she comes and goes,
Kneels at the couch-side, overleans the sill
O' the window, cold and pale and mute as stone,
Strong as stone also. "Well, are they not fled?
"Am I not left, am I not one for all?
"Speak a word, drop a tear, detach a glance,
"Bless me or curse me of your own accord!
"Is it the ceiling only wants your soul,
"Is worth your eyes?" And then the eyes descend,
And do look at me. Is it at the meal?
"Speak!" she obeys, "Be silent!" she obeys,
Counting the minutes till I cry "Depart,"
As brood-bird when you saunter past her eggs.
Departs she? just the same through door and wall
I see the same stone strength of white despair.
And all this will be never otherwise!
Before, the parents' presence lent her life:
She could play off her sex's armoury,
Entreat, reproach, be female to my male,
Try all the shrieking doubles of the hare,
Go clamour to the Commissary, bid
The Archbishop hold my hands and stop my tongue,
And yield fair sport so: but the tactics change,
The hare stands stock-still to enrage the hound!
Since that day when she learned she was no child
Of those she thought her parents, — that their trick
Had tricked me whom she thought sole trickster late, —
Why, I suppose she said within herself
"Then, no more struggle for my parents' sake!
"And, for my own sake, why needs struggle be?"

But is there no third party to the pact?
What of her husband's relish or dislike
For this new game of giving up the game,
This worst offence of not offending more?
I'll not believe but instinct wrought in this,
Set her on to conceive and execute
The preferable plague: how sure they probe —
These jades, the sensitivest soft of man!
The long black hair was wound now in a wisp,
Crowned sorrow better than the wild web late:
No more soiled dress, 'tis trimness triumphs now,
For how should malice go with negligence?
The frayed silk looked the fresher for her spite!
There was an end to springing out of bed,
Praying me, with face buried on my feet,
Be hindered of my pastime, — so an end
To my rejoinder, "What, on the ground at last?
"Vanquished in fight, a supplicant for life?
"What if I raise you? 'Ware the casting down
"When next you fight me!" Then, she lay there, mine:
Now, mine she is if I please wring her neck, —
A moment of disquiet, working eyes,
Protruding tongue, a long sigh, then no more, —
As if one killed the horse one could not ride!
Had I enjoined "Cut off the hair!" — why, snap
The scissors, and at once a yard or so
Had fluttered in black serpents to the floor:
But till I did enjoin it, how she combs,
Uncurls and draws out to the complete length,
Plaits, places the insulting rope on head
To be an eyesore past dishevelment!
Is all done? Then sit still again and stare!
I advise — no one think to bear that look
Of steady wrong, endured as steadily
— Through what sustainment of deluding hope?
Who is the friend i' the background that notes all?
Who may come presently and close accounts?
This self-possession to the uttermost,

How does it differ in aught, save degree,
From the terrible patience of God?

* * * * *

So, let death atone!
So ends mistake, so end mistakers! — end
Perhaps to recommence, — how should I know?
Only, be sure, no punishment, no pain
Childish, preposterous, impossible,
But some such fate as Ovid could foresee, —
Byblis in fluvium, let the weak soul end
In water, *sed Lycaon in lupum*, but
The strong become a wolf for evermore!
Change that Pompilia to a puny stream
Fit to reflect the daisies on its bank!
Let me turn wolf, be whole, and sate, for once, —
Wallow in what is now a wolfishness
Coerced too much by the humanity
That's half of me as well! Grow out of man,
Glut the wolf-nature, — what remains but grow
Into the man again, be man indeed
And all man? Do I ring the changes right?
Deformed, transformed, reformed, informed, conformed!
The honest instinct, pent and crossed through life,
Let surge by death into a visible flow
Of rapture: as the strangled thread of flame
Painfully winds, annoying and annoyed,
Malignant and maligned, thro' stone and ore,
Till earth exclude the stranger: vented once,
It finds full play, is recognized a-top
Some mountain as no such abnormal birth,
Fire for the mount, not streamlet for the vale!
Ay, of the water was that wife of mine —
Be it for good, be it for ill, no run
O' the red thread through that insignificance!
Again, how she is at me with those eyes!
Away with the empty stare! Be holy still,
And stupid ever! Occupy your patch
Of private snow that's somewhere in what world

May now be growing icy round your head,
And aguish at your foot-print, — freeze not me,
Dare follow not another step I take,
Not with so much as those detested eyes,
No, though they follow but to pray me pause
On the incline, earth's edge that's next to hell!
None of your abnegation of revenge!
Fly at me frank, tug while I tear again!
There's God, go tell Him, testify your worst!
Not she! There was no touch in her of hate:
And it would prove her hell, if I reached mine!
To know I suffered, would still sadden her,
Do what the angels might to make amends!
Therefore there's either no such place as hell,
Or thence shall I be thrust forth, for her sake,
And thereby undergo three hells, not one —
I who, with outlet for escape to heaven,
Would tarry if such flight allowed my foe
To raise his head, relieved of that firm foot
Had pinned him to the fiery pavement else!
So am I made, "who did not make myself:"
(How dared she rob my own lip of the word?)
Beware me in what other world may be! —
Pompilia, who have brought me to this pass!
All I know here, will I say there, and go
Beyond the saying with the deed. Some use
There cannot but be for a mood like mine,
Implacable, persistent in revenge.
She maundered "All is over and at end:
"I go my own road, go you where God will!
"Forgive you? I forget you!" There's the saint
That takes your taste, you other kind of men!
How you had loved her! Guido wanted skill
To value such a woman at her worth!
Properly the instructed criticize
"What's here, you simpleton have tossed to take
"Its chance i' the gutter? This a daub, indeed?
"Why, 'tis a Rafael that you kicked to rags!"
Perhaps so: some prefer the pure design:

THE BROWNINGS

Give me my gorge of colour, glut of gold
In a glory round the Virgin made for me!
Titian's the man, not Monk Angelico
Who traces you some timid chalky ghost
That turns the church into a charnel: ay,
Just such a pencil might depict my wife!
She, — since she, also, would not change herself, —
Why could not she come in some heart-shaped cloud,
Rainbowed about with riches, royalty
Rimming her round, as round the tintless lawn
Guardingly runs the selvage cloth of gold?
I would have left the faint fine gauze untouched,
Needle-worked over with its lily and rose,
Let her bleach unmolested in the midst,
Chill that selected solitary spot
Of quietude she pleased to think was life.
Purity, pallor grace the lawn no doubt
When there's the costly bordure to unthread
And make again an ingot: but what's grace
When you want meat and drink and clothes and fire?

* * * * *

You too are petrifactions of a kind:
Move not a muscle that shows mercy. Rave
Another twelve hours, every word were waste!
I thought you would not slay impenitence,
But teased, from men you slew, contrition first, —
I thought you had a conscience. Cardinal,
You know I am wronged! — wronged, say, and wronged, maintain.
Was this strict inquisition made for blood
When first you showed us scarlet on your back,
Called to the College? Your straightforward way
To your legitimate end, — I think it passed
Over a scantling of heads brained, hearts broke,
Lives trodden into dust! How otherwise?
Such was the way o' the world, and so you walked.
Does memory haunt your pillow? Not a whit.
God wills you never pace your garden-path,
One appetizing hour ere dinner-time,

676

But your intrusion there treads out of life
A universe of happy innocent things:
Feel you remorse about that damsel-fly
Which buzzed so near your mouth and flapped your face?
You blotted it from being at a blow:
It was a fly, you were a man, and more,
Lord of created things, so took your course.
Manliness, mind, — these are things fit to save,
Fit to brush fly from: why, because I take
My course, must needs the Pope kill me? — kill you!
You! for this instrument, he throws away,
Is strong to serve a master, and were yours
To have and hold and get much good from out!
The Pope who dooms me needs must die next year;
I'll tell you how the chances are supposed
For his successor: first the Chamberlain,
Old San Cesario, — Colloredo, next, —
Then, one, two, three, four, I refuse to name;
After these, comes Altieri; then come you —
Seventh on the list you come, unless . . . ha, ha,
How can a dead hand give a friend a lift?
Are you the person to despise the help
O' the head shall drop in pannier presently?
So a child seesaws on or kicks away
The fulcrum-stone that's all the sage requires
To fit his lever to and move the world.
Cardinal, I adjure you in God's name,
Save my life, fall at the Pope's feet, set forth
Things your own fashion, not in words like these
Made for a sense like yours who apprehend!
Translate into the Court-conventional
"Count Guido must not die, is innocent!
"Fair, be assured! But what an he were foul,
"Blood-drenched and murder-crusted head to foot?
"Spare one whose death insults the Emperor,
"Nay, outrages the Louis you so love!
"He has friends who will avenge him; enemies
"Who will hate God now with impunity,
"Missing the old coercive: would you send

677

"A soul straight to perdition, dying frank
"An atheist?" Go and say this, for God's sake!
— Why, you don't think I hope you'll say one word?
Neither shall I persuade you from your stand
Nor you persuade me from my station: take
Your crucifix away, I tell you twice!

Come, I am tired of silence! Pause enough!
You have prayed: I have gone inside my soul
And shut its door behind me: 'tis your torch
Makes the place dark: the darkness let alone
Grows tolerable twilight: one may grope
And get to guess at length and breadth and depth.
What is this fact I feel persuaded of —
This something like a foothold in the sea,
Although Saint Peter's bark scuds, billow-borne,
Leaves me to founder where it flung me first?
Spite of your splashing, I am high and dry!
God takes his own part in each thing He made;
Made for a reason, He conserves his work,
Gives each its proper instinct of defence.
My lamblike wife could neither bark nor bite,
She bleated, bleated, till for pity pure
The village roused up, ran with pole and prong
To the rescue, and behold the wolf's at bay!
Shall he try bleating? — or take turn or two,
Since the wolf owns some kinship with the fox,
And, failing to escape the foe by craft,
Give up attempt, die fighting quietly?
The last bad blow that strikes fire in at eye
And on to brain, and so out, life and all,
How can it but be cheated of a pang
If, fighting quietly, the jaws enjoy
One re-embrace in mid back-bone they break,
After their weary work thro' the foe's flesh?
That's the wolf-nature. Don't mistake my trope!
A Cardinal so qualmish? Eminence,
My fight is figurative, blows i' the air,
Brain-war with powers and principalities,

678

Spirit-bravado, no real fisticuffs!
I shall not presently, when the knock comes,
Cling to this bench nor claw the hangman's face,
No, trust me! I conceive worse lots than mine.
Whether it be, the old contagious fit
And plague o' the prison have surprised me too,
The appropriate drunkenness of the death-hour
Crept on my sense, kind work o' the wine and myrrh, —
I know not, — I begin to taste my strength,
Careless, gay even. What's the worth of life?
The Pope's dead now, my murderous old man,
For Tozzi told me so: and you, forsooth —
Why, you don't think, Abate, do your best,
You'll live a year more with that hacking cough
And blotch of crimson where the cheek's a pit?
Tozzi has got you also down in book!
Cardinal, only seventh of seventy near,
Is not one called Albano in the lot?
Go eat your heart, you'll never be a Pope!
Inform me, is it true you left your love,
A Pucci, for promotion in the church?
She's more than in the church, — in the churchyard!
Plautilla Pucci, your affianced bride,
Has dust now in the eyes that held the love, —
And Martinez, suppose they make you Pope,
Stops that with veto, — so, enjoy yourself!
I see you all reel to the rock, you waves —
Some forthright, some describe a sinuous track,
Some, crested brilliantly, with heads above,
Some in a strangled swirl sunk who knows how,
But all bound whither the main-current sets,
Rockward, an end in foam for all of you!
What if I be o'ertaken, pushed to the front
By all you crowding smoother souls behind,
And reach, a minute sooner than was meant,
The boundary whereon I break to mist?
Go to! the smoothest safest of you all,
Most perfect and compact wave in my train,
Spite of the blue tranquillity above,

Spite of the breadth before of lapsing peace,
Where broods the halcyon and the fish leaps free,
Will presently begin to feel the prick
At lazy heart, the push at torpid brain,
Will rock vertiginously in turn, and reel,
And, emulative, rush to death like me.
Later or sooner by a minute then,
So much for the untimeliness of death!
And, as regards the manner that offends,
The rude and rough, I count the same for gain.
Be the act harsh and quick! Undoubtedly
The soul's condensed and, twice itself, expands
To burst thro' life, by alternation due,
Into the other state whate'er it prove.
You never know what life means till you die:
Even throughout life, 'tis death that makes life live,
Gives it whatever the significance.
For see, on your own ground and argument,
Suppose life had no death to fear, how find
A possibility of nobleness
In man, prevented daring any more?
What's love, what's faith without a worst to dread?
Lack-lustre jewelry! but faith and love
With death behind them bidding do or die —
Put such a foil at back, the sparkle's born!
From out myself how the strange colours come!
Is there a new rule in another world?
Be sure I shall resign myself: as here
I recognized no law I could not see,
There, what I see, I shall acknowledge too:
On earth I never took the Pope for God,
In heaven I shall scarce take God for the Pope.
Unmanned, remanned: I hold it probable —
With something changeless at the heart of me
To know me by, some nucleus that's myself:
Accretions did it wrong? Away with them —
You soon shall see the use of fire!
                                    Till when,
All that was, is; and must forever be.

Nor is it in me to unhate my hates, —
I use up my last strength to strike once more
Old Pietro in the wine-house-gossip-face,
To trample underfoot the whine and wile
Of beast Violante, — and I grow one gorge
To loathingly reject Pompilia's pale
Poison my hasty hunger took for food.
A strong tree wants no wreaths about its trunk,
No cloying cups, no sickly sweet of scent,
But sustenance at root, a bucketful.
How else lived that Athenian who died so,
Drinking hot bull's blood, fit for men like me?
I lived and died a man, and take man's chance,
Honest and bold: right will be done to such.

Who are these you have let descend my stair?
Ha, their accursed psalm! Lights at the sill!
Is it "Open" they dare bid you? Treachery!
Sirs, have I spoken one word all this while
Out of the world of words I had to say?
Not one word! All was folly — I laughed and mocked!
Sirs, my first true word, all truth and no lie,
Is — save me notwithstanding! Life is all!
I was just stark mad, — let the madman live
Pressed by as many chains as you please pile!
Don't open! Hold me from them! I am yours,
I am the Granduke's — no, I am the Pope's!
Abate, — Cardinal, — Christ, — Maria, — God, . . .
Pompilia, will you let them murder me?

[End of Book XI]

681

from FIFINE AT THE FAIR

Prologue

AMPHIBIAN

I.

The fancy I had to-day,
    Fancy which turned a fear!
I swam far out in the bay,
    Since waves laughed warm and clear.

II.

I lay and looked at the sun,
    The noon-sun looked at me:
Between us two, no one
    Live creature, that I could see.

III.

Yes! There came floating by
    Me, who lay floating too.
Such a strange butterfly!
    Creature as dear as new:

IV.

Because the membraned wings
    So wonderful, so wide,
So sun-suffused, were things
    Like soul and nought beside.

V.

A handbreadth over head!
    All of the sea my own,
It owned the sky instead;
    Both of us were alone.

VI.

I never shall join its flight,
    For, nought buoys flesh in air.
If it touch the sea — good night!
    Death sure and swift waits there.

VII.

Can the insect feel the better
    For watching the uncouth play
Of limbs that slip the fetter,
    Pretend as they were not clay?

VIII.

Undoubtedly I rejoice
    That the air comports so well
With a creature which had the choice
    Of the land once. Who can tell?

IX.

What if a certain soul
    Which early slipped its sheath,
And has for its home the whole
    Of heaven, thus look beneath,

X.

Thus watch one who, in the world,
    Both lives and likes life's way,
Nor wishes the wings unfurled
    That sleep in the worm, they say?

XI.

But sometimes when the weather
    Is blue, and warm waves tempt
To free oneself of tether,
    And try a life exempt

XII.

From worldly noise and dust,
    In the sphere which overbrims
With passion and thought, — why, just
    Unable to fly, one swims!

XIII.

By passion and thought upborne,
    One smiles to oneself — "They fare
Scarce better, they need not scorn
    Our sea, who live in the air!"

XIV.

Emancipate through passion
    And thought, with sea for sky,
We substitute, in a fashion,
    For heaven — poetry:

XV.

Which sea, to all intent,
    Gives flesh such noon-disport
As a finer element
    Affords the spirit-sort.

XVI.

Whatever they are, we seem:
    Imagine the thing they know;
All deeds they do, we dream;
    Can heaven be else but so?

XVII.

And meantime, yonder streak
    Meets the horizon's verge;
That is the land, to seek
    If we tire or dread the surge:

XVIII.

Land the solid and safe —
    To welcome again (confess!)
When, high and dry, we chafe
    The body, and don the dress.

XIX.

Does she look, pity, wonder
    At one who mimics flight,
Swims — heaven above, sea under,
    Yet always earth in sight?

*   *   *   *   *

XXX.

Witness her, kept waiting all this time!
What happy angle makes Fifine reverberate
Sunshine, least sand-grain, she, of shadiest social state?
No adamantine shield, polished like Helen there,
Fit to absorb the sun, regorge him till the glare,
Dazing the universe, draw Troy-ward those blind beaks
Of equal-sided ships rowed by the well-greaved Greeks!
No Asian mirror, like yon Ptolemaic witch
Able to fix sun fast and tame sun down, enrich,
Not burn the world with beams thus flatteringly rolled
About her, head to foot, turned slavish snakes of gold!
And oh, no tinted pane of oriel sanctity,
Does our Fifine afford, such as permits supply
Of lustrous heaven, revealed, far more than mundane sight
Could master, to thy cell, pure Saint! where, else too bright,
So suits thy sense the orb, that, what outside was noon,
Pales, through thy lozenged blue, to meek benefic moon!
What then? does that prevent each dunghill, we may pass
Daily, from boasting too its bit of looking-glass,
Its sherd which, sun-smit, shines, shoots arrowy fire beyond
That satin-muffled mope, your sulky diamond?

*   *   *   *   *

XCV.

And what I gazed upon was a prodigious Fair,
Concourse immense of men and women, crowned or casqued,
Turbaned or tiar'd, wreathed, plumed, hatted or wigged, but masked —
Always masked, — only, how? No faceshape, beast or bird,
Nay, fish and reptile even, but someone had preferred,
From out its frontispiece, feathered or scaled or curled,
To make the vizard whence himself should view the world,
And where the world believed himself was manifest.
Yet when you came to look, mixed up among the rest
More funnily by far, were masks to imitate

Humanity's mishap: the wrinkled brow, bald pate
And rheumy eyes of Age, peak'd chin and parchment chap,
Were signs of day-work done, and wage-time near, — mishap
Merely; but, Age reduced to simple greed and guile,
Worn apathetic else as some smooth slab, erewhile
A clear-cut man-at-arms i' the pavement, till foot's tread
Effaced the sculpture, left the stone you saw instead, —
Was not that terrible beyond the mere uncouth?
Well, and perhaps the next revolting you was Youth,
Stark ignorance and crude conceit, half smirk, half stare
On that frank fool-face, gay beneath its head of hair
Which covers nothing.

*   *   *   *   *

from ARISTOPHANES' APOLOGY

*   *   *   *   *

Thamuris marching, — lyre and song of Thrace —
(Perpend the first, the worst of woes that were
Allotted lyre and song, ye poet-race!)

Thamuris from Oichalia, feasted there
By kingly Eurutos of late, now bound
For Dorion at the uprise broad and bare

Of Mount Pangaios (ore with earth enwound
Glittered beneath his footstep) — marching gay
And glad, Thessalia through, came, robed and crowned,

From triumph on to triumph, mid a ray
Of early morn, — came, saw and knew the spot
Assigned him for his worst of woes, that day.

Balura — happier while its name was not —
Met him, but nowise menaced; slipt aside,
Obsequious river to pursue its lot

687

Of solacing the valley — say, some wide
Thick busy human cluster, house and home,
Embanked for peace, or thrift that thanks the tide.

Thamuris, marching, laughed "Each flake of foam"
(As sparklingly the ripple raced him by)
"Mocks slower clouds adrift in the blue dome!"

For Autumn was the season; red the sky
Held morn's conclusive signet of the sun
To break the mists up, bid them blaze and die.

Morn had the mastery as, one by one
All pomps produced themselves along the tract
From earth's far ending to near heaven begun.

Was there a ravaged tree? it laughed compact
With gold, a leaf-ball crisp, high-brandished now,
Tempting to onset frost which late attacked.

Was there a wizened shrub, a starveling bough,
A fleecy thistle filched from by the wind,
A weed, Pan's trampling hoof would disallow?

Each, with a glory and a rapture twined
About it, joined the rush of air and light
And force: the world was of one joyous mind.

Say not the birds flew! they forebore their right —
Swam, revelling onward in the roll of things.
Say not the beasts' mirth bounded! that was flight —

How could the creatures leap, no lift of wings?
Such earth's community of purpose, such
The ease of earth's fulfilled imaginings, —

So did the near and far appear to touch
I' the moment's transport, — that an interchange
Of function, far with near, seemed scarce too much;

688

And had the rooted plant aspired to range
With the snake's license, while the insect yearned
To glow fixed as the flower, it were not strange —

No more than if the fluttery tree-top turned
To actual music, sang itself aloft;
Or if the wind, impassioned chantress, earned

The right to soar embodied in some soft
Fine form all fit for cloud-companionship,
And, blissful, once touch beauty chased so oft.

Thamuris, marching, let no fancy slip
Born of the fiery transport; lyre and song
Were his, to smite with hand and launch from lip —

Peerless recorded, since the list grew long
Of poets (saith Homeros) free to stand
Pedestalled mid the Muses' temple-throng,

A statued service, laurelled, lyre in hand,
(Ay, for we see them) — Thamuris of Thrace
Predominating foremost of the band.

Therefore the morn-ray that enriched his face,
If it gave lambent chill, took flame again
From flush of pride; he saw, he knew the place.

What wind arrived with all the rhythms from plain,
Hill, dale, and that rough wildwood interspersed?
Compounding these to one consummate strain,

It reached him, music; but his own outburst
Of victory concluded the account,
And that grew song which was mere music erst.

"Be my Parnassos, thou Pangaian mount!
And turn thee, river, nameless hitherto!
Famed shalt thou vie with famed Pieria's fount!

"Here I await the end of this ado:
Which wins — Earth's poet or the Heavenly Muse." . . .

HOUSE

I.

Shall I sonnet-sing you about myself?
   Do I live in a house you would like to see?
Is it scant of gear, has it store of pelf?
   "Unlock my heart with a sonnet-key?"

II.

Invite the world, as my betters have done?
   "Take notice: this building remains on view,
Its suites of reception every one,
   Its private apartment and bedroom too;

III.

"For a ticket, apply to the Publisher."
   No: thanking the public, I must decline.
A peep through my window, if folk prefer;
   But, please you, no foot over threshold of mine!

IV.

I have mixed with a crowd and heard free talk
   In a foreign land where an earthquake chanced:
And a house stood gaping, nought to baulk
   Man's eye wherever he gazed or glanced.

690

V.

The whole of the frontage shaven sheer,
  The inside gaped: exposed to day,
Right and wrong and common and queer,
  Bare, as the palm of your hand, it lay.

VI.

The owner? Oh, he had been crushed, no doubt!
"Odd tables and chairs for a man of wealth!
What a parcel of musty old books about!
He smoked, — no wonder he lost his health!

VII.

"I doubt if he bathed before he dressed.
  A brasier? — the pagan, he burned perfumes!
You see it is proved, what the neighbours guessed:
  His wife and himself had separate rooms."

VIII.

Friends, the goodman of the house at least
  Kept house to himself till an earthquake came:
'Tis the fall of its frontage permits you feast
  On the inside arrangement you praise or blame.

IX.

Outside should suffice for evidence:
  And whoso desires to penetrate
Deeper, must dive by the spirit-sense —
  No optics like yours, at any rate!

X.

"Hoity toity! A street to explore,
  Your house the exception! 'With this same key
Shakespeare unlocked his heart,' once more!"
  Did Shakespeare? If so, the less Shakespeare he!

NATURAL MAGIC

I.

All I can say is — I saw it!
The room was as bare as your hand.
I locked in the swarth little lady, — I swear,
From the head to the foot of her — well, quite as bare!
"No Nautch shall cheat me," said I, "taking my stand
At this bolt which I draw!" And this bolt — I withdraw it,
And there laughs the lady, not bare, but embowered
With — who knows what verdure, o'erfruited, o'erflowered?
  Impossible! Only — I saw it!

II.

  All I can sing is — I feel it!
This life was as blank as that room;
I let you pass in here. Precaution, indeed?
Walls, ceiling and floor, — not a chance for a weed!
Wide opens the entrance: where's cold now, where's gloom?
No May to sow seed here, no June to reveal it,
Behold you enshrined in these blooms of your bringing,
These fruits of your bearing — nay, birds of your winging!
  A fairy-tale! Only — I feel it!

692

MAGICAL NATURE

I.

Flower — I never fancied, jewel — I profess you!
Bright I see and soft I feel the outside of a flower.
Save but glow inside and — jewel, I should guess you,
Dim to sight and rough to touch: the glory is the dower.

II.

You, forsooth, a flower? Nay, my love, a jewel —
Jewel at no mercy of a moment in your prime!
Time may fray the flower-face: kind be time or cruel,
Jewel, from each facet, flash your laugh at time!

APPEARANCES

I.

And so you found that poor room dull,
Dark, hardly to your taste, my dear?
Its features seemed unbeautiful:
But this I know — 'twas there, not here,
You plighted troth to me, the word
Which — ask that poor room how it heard.

II.

And this rich room obtains your praise
Unqualified, — so bright, so fair,
So all whereat perfection stays?

Ay, but remember — here, not there,
The other word was spoken! Ask
This rich room how you dropped the mask!

PAN AND LUNA

Si credere dignum est. — *Georgic.* iii. 390.

O worthy of belief I hold it was,
Virgil, your legend in those strange three lines!
No question, that adventure came to pass
One black night in Arcadia: yes, the pines,
Mountains and valleys mingling made one mass
Of black with void black heaven: the earth's confines,
The sky's embrace, — below, above, around,
All hardened into black without a bound.

Fill up a swart stone chalice to the brim
With fresh-squeezed yet fast-thickening poppy-juice:
See how the sluggish jelly, late a-swim,
Turns marble to the touch of who would loose
The solid smooth, grown jet from rim to rim,
By turning round the bowl! So night can fuse
Earth with her all-comprising sky. No less,
Light, the least spark, shows air and emptiness.

And thus it proved when — diving into space,
Stript of all vapour, from each web of mist
Utterly film-free — entered on her race
The naked Moon, full-orbed antagonist
Of night and dark, night's dowry: peak to base,
Upstarted mountains, and each valley, kissed
To sudden life, lay silver-bright: in air
Flew she revealed, Maid-Moon with limbs all bare.

Still as she fled, each depth — where refuge seemed —
Opening a lone pale chamber, left distinct

Those limbs: mid still-retreating blue, she teemed
Herself with whiteness, — virginal, uncinct
By any halo save what finely gleamed
To outline not disguise her: heaven was linked
In one accord with earth to quaff the joy,
Drain beauty to the dregs without alloy.

Whereof she grew aware. What help? When, lo,
A succourable cloud with sleep lay dense:
Some pine-tree-top had caught it sailing slow,
And tethered for a prize: in evidence
Captive lay fleece on fleece of piled-up snow
Drowsily patient: flake-heaped how or whence,
The structure of that succourable cloud,
What matter? Shamed she plunged into its shroud.

Orbed — so the woman-figure poets call
Because of rounds on rounds — that apple-shaped
Head which its hair binds close into a ball
Each side the curving ears — that pure undraped
Pout of the sister paps — that . . . Once for all,
Say — her consummate circle thus escaped
With its innumerous circlets, sank absorbed,
Safe in the cloud — O naked Moon full-orbed!

But what means this? The downy swathes combine,
Conglobe, the smothery coy-caressing stuff
Curdles about her! Vain each twist and twine
Those lithe limbs try, encroached on by a fluff
Fitting as close as fits the dented spine
Its flexile ivory outside-flesh: enough!
The plumy drifts contract, condense, constringe,
Till she is swallowed by the feathery springe.

As when a pearl slips lost in the thin foam
Churned on a sea-shore, and, o'er-frothed, conceits
Herself safe-housed in Amphitrite's dome, —
If, through the bladdery wave-worked yeast, she meets
What most she loathes and leaps from, — elf from gnome
No gladlier, — finds that safest of retreats

THE BROWNINGS

Bubble about a treacherous hand wide ope
To grasp her — (divers who pick pearls so grope) —

So lay this Maid-Moon clasped around and caught
By rough red Pan, the god of all that tract:
He it was schemed the snare thus subtly wrought
With simulated earth-breath, — wool-tufts packed
Into a billowy wrappage. Sheep far-sought
For spotless shearings yield such: take the fact
As learned Virgil gives it, — how the breed
Whitens itself for ever: yes, indeed!

If one forefather ram, though pure as chalk
From tinge on fleece, should still display a tongue
Black 'neath the beast's moist palate, prompt men baulk
The propagating plague: he gets no young:
They rather slay him, — sell his hide to caulk
Ships with, first steeped in pitch, — nor hands are wrung
In sorrow for his fate: protected thus,
The purity we love is gained for us.

So did Girl-moon, by just her attribute
Of unmatched modesty betrayed, lie trapped,
Bruised to the breast of Pan, half-god half-brute,
Raked by his bristly boar-sward while he lapped
— Never say, kissed her! that were to pollute
Love's language — which moreover proves unapt
To tell how she recoiled — as who finds thorns
Where she sought flowers — when, feeling, she touched — horns!

Then — does the legend say? — first moon-eclipse
Happened, first swooning-fit which puzzled sore
The early sages? Is that why she dips
Into the dark, a minute and no more,
Only so long as serves her while she rips
The cloud's womb through and, faultless as before,
Pursues her way? No lesson for a maid
Left she, a maid herself thus trapped, betrayed?

696

Ha, Virgil? Tell the rest, you! "To the deep
Of his domain the wildwood, Pan forthwith
Called her, and so she followed" — in her sleep,
Surely? — "by no means spurning him." The myth
Explain who may! Let all else go, I keep
— As of a ruin just a monolith —
Thus much, one verse of five words, each a boon:
Arcadia, night, a cloud, Pan, and the moon.

NEVER THE TIME AND THE PLACE

    Never the time and the place
      And the loved one all together!
    This path — how soft to pace!
      This May — what magic weather!
    Where is the loved one's face?
In a dream that loved one's face meets mine,
    But the house is narrow, the place is bleak
Where, outside, rain and wind combine
    With a furtive ear, if I strive to speak,
    With a hostile eye at my flushing cheek,
    With a malice that marks each word, each sign!
O enemy sly and serpentine,
    Uncoil thee from the waking man!
      Do I hold the Past
      Thus firm and fast
    Yet doubt if the Future hold I can?
This path so soft to pace shall lead
Thro' the magic of May to herself indeed!
Or narrow if needs the house must be,
Outside are the storms and strangers: we —
Oh, close, safe, warm sleep I and she,
— I and she!

from FERISHTAH'S FANCIES

* * * * *

You groped your way across my room i' the dear dark dead of night;
At each fresh step a stumble was: but, once your lamp alight,
Easy and plain you walked again: so soon all wrong grew right!

What lay on floor to trip your foot? Each object, late awry,
Looked fitly placed, nor proved offence to footing free — for why?
The lamp showed all, discordant late, grown simple symmetry.

Be love your light and trust your guide, with these explore my heart!
No obstacle to trip you then, strike hands and souls apart!
Since rooms and hearts are furnished so, — light shows you, — needs
love start?

* * * * *

Verse-making was least of my virtues: I viewed with despair
Wealth that never yet was but might be — all that verse-making were
If the life would but lengthen to wish, let the mind be laid bare.
So I said "To do little is bad, to do nothing is worse" — And made
verse.

Love-making, — how simple a matter! No depths to explore,
No heights in a life to ascend! No disheartening Before.
No affrighting Hereafter, — love now will be love evermore.
So I felt "To keep silence were folly:" — all language above, I made
love.

* * * * *

ROBERT BROWNING

from PARLEYINGS WITH CERTAIN PEOPLE
OF IMPORTANCE IN THEIR DAY

WITH CHRISTOPHER SMART

I.

It seems as if . . . or did the actual chance
Startle me and perplex? Let truth be said!
How might this happen? Dreaming, blindfold led
By visionary hand, did soul's advance
Precede my body's, gain inheritance
Of fact by fancy — so that when I read
At length with waking eyes your Song, instead
Of mere bewilderment, with me first glance
Was but full recognition that in trance
Or merely thought's adventure some old day
Of dim and done-with boyishness, or — well,
Why might it not have been, the miracle
Broke on me as I took my sober way
Through veritable regions of our earth
And made discovery, many a wondrous one?

II.

Anyhow, fact or fancy, such its birth:
I was exploring some huge house, had gone
Through room and room complacently, no dearth
Anywhere of the signs of decent taste,
Adequate culture: wealth had run to waste
Nowise, nor penury was proved by stint:
All showed the Golden Mean without a hint
Of brave extravagance that breaks the rule.
The master of the mansion was no fool
Assuredly, no genius just as sure!

Safe mediocrity had scorned the lure
Of now too much and now too little cost,
And satisfied me sight was never lost
Of moderate design's accomplishment
In calm completeness. On and on I went,
With no more hope than fear of what came next,
Till lo, I push a door, sudden uplift
A hanging, enter, chance upon a shift
Indeed of scene! So — thus it is thou deck'st,
High heaven, our low earth's brick-and-mortar work?

III.

It was the Chapel. That a star, from murk
Which hid, should flashingly emerge at last,
Were small surprise: but from broad day I passed
Into a presence that turned shine to shade.
There fronted me the Rafael Mother-Maid,
Never to whom knelt votarist in shrine
By Nature's bounty helped, by Art's divine
More varied — beauty with magnificence —
Than this: from floor to roof one evidence
Of how far earth may rival heaven. No niche
Where glory was not prisoned to enrich
Man's gaze with gold and gems, no space but glowed
With colour, gleamed with carving — hues which owed
Their outburst to a brush the painter fed
With rainbow-substance — rare shapes never wed
To actual flesh and blood, which, brain-born once,
Became the sculptor's dowry, Art's response
To earth's despair. And all seemed old yet new:
Youth, — in the marble's curve, the canvas' hue,
Apparent, — wanted not the crowning thrill
Of age the consecrator. Hands long still
Had worked here — could it be, what lent them skill
Retained a power to supervise, protect,
Enforce new lessons with the old, connect
Our life with theirs? No merely modern touch
Told me that here the artist, doing much,

Elsewhere did more, perchance does better, lives —
So needs must learn.

IV.

                    Well, these provocatives
Having fulfilled their office, forth I went
Big with anticipation — well-nigh fear —
Of what next room and next for startled eyes
Might have in store, surprise beyond surprise.
Next room and next and next — what followed here?
Why, nothing! not one object to arrest
My passage — everywhere too manifest
The previous decent null and void of best
And worst, mere ordinary right and fit,
Calm commonplace which neither missed, nor hit
Inch-high, inch-low, the placid mark proposed.

V.

Armed with this instance, have I diagnosed
Your case, my Christopher? The man was sound
And sane at starting: all at once the ground
Gave way beneath his step, a certain smoke
Curled up and caught him, or perhaps down broke
A fireball wrapping flesh and spirit both
In conflagration. Then — as heaven were loth
To linger — let earth understand too well
How heaven at need can operate — off fell
The flame-robe, and the untransfigured man
Resumed sobriety, — as he began,
So did he end nor alter pace, not he!

VI.

Now, what I fain would know is — could it be
That he — whoe'er he was that furnished forth
The Chapel, making thus, from South to North,
Rafael touch Leighton, Michelagnolo

Join Watts, was found but once combining so
The elder and the younger, taking stand
On Art's supreme, — or that yourself who sang
A Song where flute-breath silvers trumpet-clang,
And stations you for once on either hand
With Milton and with Keats, empowered to claim
Affinity on just one point — (or blame
Or praise my judgment, thus it fronts you full) —
How came it you resume the void and null,
Subside to insignificance, — live, die
— Proved plainly two mere mortals who drew nigh
One moment — that, to Art's best hierarchy,
This, to the superhuman poet-pair?
What if, in one point only, then and there
The otherwise all-unapproachable
Allowed impingement? Does the sphere pretend
To span the cube's breadth, cover end to end
The plane with its embrace? No, surely! Still,
Contact is contact, sphere's touch no whit less
Than cube's superimposure. Such success
Befell Smart only out of throngs between
Milton and Keats that donned the singing-dress —
Smart, solely of such songmen, pierced the screen
'Twixt thing and word, lit language straight from soul, —
Left no fine film-flake on the naked coal
Live from the censer — shapely or uncouth,
Fire-suffused through and through, one blaze of truth
Undeadened by a lie, — (you have my mind) —
For, think! this blaze outleapt with black behind
And blank before, when Hayley and the rest . . .
But let the dead successors worst and best
Bury their dead: with life be my concern —
Yours with the fire-flame: what I fain would learn
Is just — (suppose me haply ignorant
Down to the common knowledge, doctors vaunt)
Just this — why only once the fire-flame was:
No matter if the marvel came to pass
The way folk judged — if power too long suppressed
Broke loose and maddened, as the vulgar guessed,

Or simply brain-disorder (doctors said),
A turmoil of the particles disturbed
Brain's workaday performance in your head,
Spurred spirit to wild action health had curbed:
And so verse issued in a cataract
Whence prose, before and after, unperturbed
Was wont to wend its way. Concede the fact
That here a poet was who always could —
Never before did — never after would —
Achieve the feat: how were such fact explained?

VII.

Was it that when, by rarest chance, there fell
Disguise from Nature, so that Truth remained
Naked, and whoso saw for once could tell
Us others of her majesty and might
In large, her lovelinesses infinite
In little, — straight you used the power wherewith
Sense, penetrating as through rind to pith
Each object, thoroughly revealed might view
And comprehend the old things thus made new,
So that while eye saw, soul to tongue could trust
Thing which struck word out, and once more adjust
Real vision to right language, till heaven's vault
Pompous with sunset, storm-stirred sea's assault
On the swilled rock-ridge, earth's embosomed brood
Of tree and flower and weed, with all the life
That flies or swims or crawls. in peace or strife,
Above, below, — each had its note and name
For Man to know by, — Man who, now — the same
As erst in Eden, needs that all he sees
Be named him ere he note by what degrees
Of strength and beauty to its end Design
Ever thus operates — (your thought and mine,
No matter for the many dissident) —
So did you sing your Song, so truth found vent
In words for once with you?

VIII.

Then — back was furled
The robe thus thrown aside, and straight the world
Darkened into the old oft-catalogued
Repository of things that sky, wave, land,
Or show or hide, clear late, accretion-clogged
Now, just as long ago, by tellings and
Re-tellings to satiety, which strike
Muffled upon the ear's drum. Very like
None was so startled as yourself when friends
Came, hailed your fast-returning wits: "Health mends
Importantly, for — to be plain with you —
This scribble on the wall was done — in lieu
Of pen and paper — with — ha, ha! — your key
Denting it on the wainscot! Do you see
How wise our caution was? Thus much we stopped
Of babble that had else grown print: and lopped
From your trim bay-tree this unsightly bough —
Smart's who translated Horace! Write us now" . . .
Why, what Smart did write — never afterward
One line to show that he, who paced the sward,
Had reached the zenith from his madhouse cell.

IX.

Was it because you judged (I know full well
You never had the fancy) — judged — as some —
That who makes poetry must reproduce
Thus ever and thus only, as they come,
Each strength, each beauty, everywhere diffuse
Throughout creation, so that eye and ear,
Seeing and hearing, straight shall recognize,
At touch of just a trait, the strength appear, —
Suggested by a line's lapse see arise
All evident the beauty, — fresh surprise
Startling at fresh achievement? "So, indeed,
Wallows the whale's bulk in the waste of brine,

Nor otherwise its feather-tufts make fine
Wild Virgin's Bower when stars faint off to seed!"
(My prose — your poetry I dare not give,
Purpling too much my mere grey argument.)
— Was it because you judged — when fugitive
Was glory found, and wholly gone and spent
Such power of startling up deaf ear, blind eye,
At truth's appearance, — that you humbly bent
The head and, bidding vivid work good-bye,
Doffed lyric dress and trod the world once more
A drab-clothed decent proseman as before?
Strengths, beauties, by one word's flash thus laid bare
— That was effectual service: made aware
Of strengths and beauties, Man but hears the text,
Awaits your teaching. Nature? What comes next?
Why all the strength and beauty? — to be shown
Thus in one word's flash, thenceforth let alone
By Man who needs must deal with aught that's known
Never so lately and so little? Friend,
First give us knowledge, then appoint its use!
Strength, beauty are the means: ignore their end?
As well you stopped at proving how profuse
Stones, sticks, nay stubble lie to left and right
Ready to help the builder, — careless quite
If he should take, or leave the same to strew
Earth idly, — as by word's flash bring in view
Strength, beauty, then bid who beholds the same
Go on beholding. Why gains unemployed?
Nature was made to be by Man enjoyed
First; followed duly by enjoyment's fruit,
Instruction — haply leaving joy behind:
And you, the instructor, would you slack pursuit
Of the main prize, as poet help mankind
Just to enjoy, there leave them? Play the fool,
Abjuring a superior privilege?
Please simply when your function is to rule —
By thought incite to deed? From edge to edge
Of earth's round, strength and beauty everywhere
Pullulate — and must you particularize

All, each and every apparition? Spare
Yourself and us the trouble! Ears and eyes
Want so much strength and beauty, and no less
Nor more, to learn life's lesson by. Oh, yes —
The other method's favoured in our day!
The end ere the beginning: as you may,
Master the heavens before you study earth,
Make you familiar with the meteor's birth
Ere you descend to scrutinize the rose!
I say, o'erstep no least one of the rows
That lead man from the bottom where he plants
Foot first of all, to life's last ladder-top:
Arrived there, vain enough will seem the vaunts
Of those who say — "We scale the skies, then drop
To earth — to find, how all things there are loth
To answer heavenly law: we understand
The meteor's course, and lo, the rose's growth —
How other than should be by law's command!"
Would not you tell such — "Friends, beware lest fume
Offuscate sense: learn earth first ere presume
To teach heaven legislation. Law must be
Active in earth or nowhere: earth you see, —
Or there or not at all, Will, Power and Love
Admit discovery, — as below, above
Seek next law's confirmation! But reverse
The order, where's the wonder things grow worse
Than, by the law your fancy formulates,
They should be? Cease from anger at the fates
Which thwart themselves so madly. Live and learn,
Not first learn and then live, is our concern.

DUBIETY

I will be happy if but for once:
    Only help me, Autumn weather,
Me and my cares to screen, ensconce
    In luxury's sofa-lap of leather!

Sleep? Nay, comfort — with just a cloud
   Suffusing day too clear and bright:
Eve's essence, the single drop allowed
   To sully, like milk, Noon's water-white.

Let gauziness shade. not shroud, — adjust,
   Dim and not deaden, — somehow sheathe
Aught sharp in the rough world's busy thrust,
   If it reach me through dreaming's vapour-wreath.

Be life so, all things ever the same!
   For, what has disarmed the world? Outside,
Quiet and peace: inside, nor blame
   Nor want, nor wish whate'er betide.

What is it like that has happened before?
   A dream? No dream, more real by much.
A vision? But fanciful days of yore
   Brought many: mere musing seems not such.

Perhaps but a memory, after all!
   — Of what came once when a woman leant
To feel for my brow where her kiss might fall.
   Truth ever, truth only the excellent!

NOW

Out of your whole life give but a moment!
All of your life that has gone before,
All to come after it, — so you ignore,
So you make perfect the present, — condense,
In a rapture of rage, for perfection's endowment,
Thought and feeling and soul and sense —
Merged in a moment which gives me at last
You around me for once, you beneath me, above me —
Me — sure that despite of time future, time past, —
This tick of our life-time's one moment you love me!

How long such suspension may linger? Ah, Sweet —
The moment eternal — just that and no more —
When ecstasy's utmost we clutch at the core
While cheeks burn, arms open, eyes shut and lips meet!

HUMILITY

What girl but, having gathered flowers,
Stript the beds and spoilt the bowers,
From the lapful light she carries
Drops a careless bud? — nor tarries
To regain the waif and stray:
"Store enough for home" — she'll say.

So say I too: give your lover
Heaps of loving — under, over,
Whelm him — make the one the wealthy!
Am I all so poor who — stealthy
Work it was! — picked up what fell:
Not the worst bud — who can tell?

SUMMUM BONUM

All the breath and the bloom of the year in
     the bag of one bee:
All the wonder and wealth of the mine in
     the heart of one gem:
In the core of one pearl all the shade and the
     shine of the sea:
Breath and bloom, shade and shine, — won-
     der, wealth, and — how far above them —
     Truth, that's brighter than gem,
     Trust, that's purer than pearl, —

Brightest truth, purest trust in the universe —
all were for me
In the kiss of one girl.

SPECULATIVE

Others may need new life in Heaven —
Man, Nature, Art — made new, assume!
Man with new mind old sense to leaven,
Nature — new light to clear old gloom,
Art that breaks bounds, gets soaring-room.

I shall pray: "Fugitive as precious —
Minutes which passed, — return, remain!
Let earth's old life once more enmesh us,
You with old pleasure, me — old pain,
So we but meet nor part again!"

WHITE WITCHCRAFT

If you and I could change to beasts, what
beast should either be?
Shall you and I play Jove for once? Turn
fox then, I decree!
Shy wild sweet stealer of the grapes! Now
do your worst on me!

And thus you think to spite your friend —
turned loathsome? What, a toad?
So, all men shrink and shun me! Dear men,
pursue your road!
Leave but my crevice in the stone, a reptile's
fit abode!

Now say your worst, Canidia! "He's
loathsome, I allow:
There may or may not lurk a pearl beneath
his puckered brow:
But see his eyes that follow mine — love lasts
there anyhow."

BAD DREAMS I

Last night I saw you in my sleep:
And how your charm of face was changed!
I asked "Some love, some faith you keep?"
You answered "Faith gone, love estranged."

Whereat I woke — a twofold bliss:
Waking was one, but next there came
This other: "Though I felt, for this,
My heart break, I loved on the same."

BAD DREAMS II

You in the flesh and here —
Your very self! Now, wait!
One word! May I hope or fear?
Must I speak in love or hate?
Stay while I ruminate!

The fact and each circumstance
Dare you disown? Not you!
That vast dome, that huge dance,
And the gloom which overgrew
A — possibly festive crew!

For why should men dance at all —
　Why women — a crowd of both —
Unless they are gay? Strange ball —
　Hands and feet plighting troth,
Yet partners enforced and loth!

Of who danced there, no shape
　Did I recognize: thwart, perverse,
Each grasped each, past escape
　In a whirl or weary or worse:
Man's sneer met woman's curse,

While he and she toiled as if
　Their guardian set galley-slaves
To supple chained limbs grown stiff:
　Unmanacled trulls and knaves —
The lash for who misbehaves!

And a gloom was, all the while,
　Deeper and deeper yet
O'ergrowing the rank and file
　Of that army of haters — set
To mimic love's fever-fret.

By the wall-side close I crept,
　Avoiding the livid maze,
And, safely so far, outstepped
　On a chamber — a chapel, says
My memory or betrays —

Closet-like, kept aloof
　From unseemly witnessing
What sport made floor and roof
　Of the Devil's palace ring
While his Damned amused their king.

Ay, for a low lamp burned,
　And a silence lay about
What I, in the midst, discerned

711

Though dimly till, past doubt,
'Twas a sort of throne stood out —

High seat with steps, at least:
And the topmost step was filled
By — whom? What vestured priest?
A stranger to me, — his guild,
His cult, unreconciled

To my knowledge how guild and cult
Are clothed in this world of ours:
I pondered, but no result
Came to — unless that Giaours
So worship the Lower Powers.

When suddenly who entered?
Who knelt — did you guess I saw?
Who — raising that face where centred
Allegiance to love and law
So lately — off-casting awe,

Down-treading reserve, away
Thrusting respect . . . but mine
Stands firm — firm still shall stay!
Ask Satan! for I decline
To tell — what I saw, in fine!

Yet here in the flesh you come —
Your same self, form and face, —
In the eyes, mirth still at home!
On the lips, that commonplace
Perfection of honest grace!

Yet your errand is — needs must be
To palliate — well, explain,
Expurgate in some degree
Your soul of its ugly stain.
Oh, you — the good in grain —

How was it your white took tinge?
    "A mere dream" — never object!
Sleep leaves a door on hinge
    Whence soul, ere our flesh suspect,
Is off and away: detect

Her vagaries when loose, who can!
    Be she pranksome, be she prude,
Disguise with the day began:
    With the night — ah, what ensued
From draughts of a drink hell-brewed?

Then She: "What a queer wild dream!
    And perhaps the best fun is —
Myself had its fellow — I seem
    Scarce awake from yet. 'Twas this —
Shall I tell you? First, a kiss!

"For the fault was just your own, —
    'Tis myself expect apology:
You warned me to let alone
    (Since our studies were mere philology)
That ticklish (you said) Anthology.

"So, I dreamed that I passed *exam*
    Till a question posed me sore:
'Who translated this epigram
    By — an author we best ignore?'
And I answered 'Hannah More'!"

BAD DREAMS III

This was my dream: I saw a Forest
    Old as the earth, no track nor trace
Of unmade man. Thou, Soul, explorest —
    Though in a trembling rapture — space

713

Immeasurable! Shrubs, turned trees,
Trees that touch heaven, support its frieze
Studded with sun and moon and star:
While — oh, the enormous growths that bar
Mine eye from penetrating past
    Their tangled twine where lurks — nay, lives
Royally lone, some brute-type cast
    I' the rough, time cancels, man forgives.

On, Soul! I saw a lucid City
    Of architectural device
Every way perfect. Pause for pity,
    Lightning! nor leave a cicatrice
On those bright marbles, dome and spire,
Structures palatial, — streets which mire
Dares not defile, paved all too fine
For human footstep's smirch, not thine —
Proud solitary traverser,
    My Soul, of silent lengths of way —
With what ecstatic dread, aver,
    Lest life start sanctioned by thy stay!

Ah, but the last sight was the hideous!
    A City, yes, — a Forest, true, —
But each devouring each. Perfidious
    Snake-plants had strangled what I knew
Was a pavilion once: each oak
Held on his horns some spoil he broke
By surreptitiously beneath
Upthrusting: pavements, as with teeth,
Griped huge weed widening crack and split
    In squares and circles stone-work erst.
Oh, Nature — good! Oh, Art — no whit
    Less worthy! Both in one — accurst!

BAD DREAMS IV

It happened thus: my slab, though new,
    Was getting weather-stained, — beside,
Herbage, balm, peppermint o'ergrew
    Letter and letter: till you tried
Somewhat, the Name was scarce descried.

That strong stern man my lover came:
    — Was he my lover? Call him, pray,
My life's cold critic bent on blame
    Of all poor I could do or say
To make me worth his love one day —

One far day when, by diligent
    And dutiful amending faults,
Foibles, all weaknesses which went
    To challenge and excuse assaults
Of culture wronged by taste that halts —

Discrepancies should mar no plan
    Symmetric of the qualities
Claiming respect from — say — a man
    That's strong and stern. "Once more he pries
Into me with those critic eyes!"

No question! so — "Conclude, condemn
    Each failure my poor self avows!
Leave to its fate all you contemn!
    There's Solomon's selected spouse:
Earth needs must hold such maids — choose them!"

Why, he was weeping! Surely gone
    Sternness and strength: with eyes to ground
And voice a broken monotone —

"Only be as you were! Abound
In foibles, faults, — laugh, robed and crowned

"As Folly's veriest queen, — care I
    One feather-fluff? Look pity, Love,
On prostrate me — your foot shall try
    This forehead's use — mount thence above,
And reach what Heaven you dignify!"

Now, what could bring such change about?
    The thought perplexed: till, following
His gaze upon the ground, — why, out
    Came all the secret! So, a thing
Thus simple has deposed my king!

For, spite of weeds that strove to spoil
    Plain reading on the lettered slab,
My name was clear enough — no soil
    Effaced the date when one chance stab
Of scorn . . . if only ghosts might blab!

INAPPREHENSIVENESS

We two stood simply friend-like side by side,
Viewing a twilight country far and wide,
Till she at length broke silence. "How it towers
Yonder, the ruin o'er this vale of ours!
The West's faint flare behind it so relieves
Its rugged outline — sight perhaps deceives,
Or I could almost fancy that I see
A branch wave plain — belike some wind-sown tree
Chance-rooted where a missing turret was.
What would I give for the perspective glass
At home, to make out if 'tis really so!
Has Ruskin noticed here at Asolo
That certain weed-growths on the ravaged wall

716

Seem" . . . something that I could not say at all,
My thought being rather — as absorbed she sent
Look onward after look from eyes distent
With longing to reach Heaven's gate left ajar —
"Oh, fancies that might be, oh, facts that are!
What of a wilding? By you stands, and may
So stand unnoticed till the Judgment Day,
One who, if once aware that your regard
Claimed what his heart holds, — woke, as from its sward
The flower, the dormant passion, so to speak —
Then what a rush of life would startling wreak
Revenge on your inapprehensive stare
While, from the ruin and the West's faint flare,
You let your eyes meet mine, touch what you term
Quietude — that's an universe in germ —
The dormant passion needing but a look
To burst into immense life!"
                              "No, the book
Which noticed how the wall-growths wave" said she
"Was not by Ruskin."
                    I said "Vernon Lee?"

EPILOGUE

At the midnight in the silence of the sleep-time,
    When you set your fancies free,
Will they pass to where — by death, fools think, imprisoned —
Low he lies who once so loved you, whom you loved so,
        —Pity me?

Oh to love so, be so loved, yet so mistaken!
    What had I on earth to do
With the slothful, with the mawkish, the unmanly?
Like the aimless, helpless, hopeless, did I drivel
        — Being — who?

THE BROWNINGS

One who never turned his back but marched breast forward,
  Never doubted clouds would break,
Never dreamed, though right were worsted, wrong would triumph,
Held we fall to rise, are baffled to fight better,
  Sleep to wake.

No, at noonday in the bustle of man's work-time
  Greet the unseen with a cheer!
Bid him forward, breast and back as either should be,
"Strive and thrive!" cry "Speed, — fight on, fare ever
  There as here!"

INDEX OF TITLES

(Asterisk denotes an abridged poem.)

INDEX OF FIRST LINES

(Asterisk denotes first line of excerpt in abridged poems.)

INDEX

My dream is of an island-place, 127
My first thought was, he lied in every word, 430

Never any more,/While I live, 497
Never the time and the place, 697
Night, and one single ridge of narrow path,* 289
Nine years old! The first of any, 157
Nobly, nobly Cape Saint Vincent to the North-west died away, 351
No, for I'll save it! Seven years since, 607
No more wine? then we'll push back chairs and talk, 460
Now, don't, sir! Don't expose me! Just this once! 565
'Now give us lands where the olives grow', 280
Now that I, tying thy glass mask tightly, 359

'O dreary life,' we cry, 'O dreary life!' 138
Of the million or two, more or less, 428
Of writing many books there is no end,* 201
Oh Galuppi, Baldassaro, this is very sad to find! 397
Oh, to be in England, 350
Oh, what a dawn of day! 376
O Rose, who dares to name thee? 167
Others may need new life in Heaven—, 709
Out of my own great woe, 281
Out of your whole life give but a moment! 707
Over the dumb Campagna-sea, 278
O worthy of belief I hold it was, 694

Plague take all your pedants, say I! 356

Room after room, 444
Round the cape of a sudden came the sea, 371

See, as the prettiest graves will do in time, 369
Shall I sonnet-sing you about myself? 690
She ceased: her palfrey's paces sent,* 139
She has laughed as softly as if she sighed, 169
She should never have looked at me, 318
So far as our story approaches the end, 440

You groped your way across my room i' the dear dark dead of night,* 698
You in the flesh and here — , 710
You know, we French stormed Ratisbon, 298
You'll take back your Grand-duke? 263
Your ghost will walk, you lover of trees, 511